THE
EVIDENCE

REFERRAL

TO THE

UNITED STATES HOUSE OF REPRESENTATIVES

PURSUANT TO

TITLE 28, UNITED STATES CODE, § 595(C)

APPENDIX

SUBMITTED BY

THE OFFICE OF THE INDEPENDENT COUNSEL

SEPTEMBER 9, 1998

THE STARR REPORT

THE
EVIDENCE

- The Full Text of President Clinton's Videotaped Grand Jury Testimony
- Monica Lewinsky's Complete Testimony and Interview Statements
- Linda Tripp's Handwritten Notes
- Detailed Chronology of Monica Lewinsky's Contacts with President Clinton
- Monica Lewinsky's Letters to President Clinton and E-mails with Friends
- Analysis Raising Questions about Linda Tripp's Tapes
- Photographs

EDITED AND WITH AN INTRODUCTION BY PHIL KUNTZ

POCKET BOOKS
New York   London   Toronto   Sydney   Tokyo   Singapore

An *Original* Publication of POCKET BOOKS

POCKET BOOKS, a division of Simon & Schuster Inc.
1230 Avenue of the Americas, New York, NY 10020

Introduction and compilation copyright © 1998 by Phil Kuntz

ISBN: 0-671-03499-5

First Pocket Books trade paperback printing September 1998

10   9   8   7   6   5   4   3   2   1

POCKET and colophon are registered trademarks of
Simon & Schuster Inc.

Book design by C. Linda Dingler
Cover design by Brigid Pearson

Printed in the U.S.A.

CONTENTS

INTRODUCTION

by Phil Kuntz

"Mr. President, were you physically intimate with Monica Lewinsky?"

Thus began Deputy Independent Counsel Robert Bittman's extraordinary grand jury interrogation of Bill Clinton. The president's answers to that question and to every conceivable variation of it would help determine whether or not he should be impeached, for his responses could be weighed against the biggest mountain of evidence ever compiled on a single consensual relationship.

By the time Independent Counsel Kenneth Starr was done, his investigators had questioned Ms. Lewinsky more than twenty times. They plumbed the deepest recesses of her computer hard drives to reconstruct every deleted file they could find. They interviewed every significant friend, relative, and co-worker in her life and seemed to have subpoenaed just about every document bearing her name.

Meticulously following the sort of paper trail people always unwittingly leave behind, investigators compiled intricately detailed chronologies, noting every time she had entered the White House during an eighteen-month period and every time she had visited or otherwise communicated with President Clinton. They engaged in legal confrontations with the White House that will have historic consequences.

They drew the president's blood.

At issue was whether the president committed perjury when he denied having sexual relations with Ms. Lewinsky during a deposition in the Paula Jones sexual harassment case or whether he otherwise obstructed justice. It is the evidence that Mr. Starr deemed most important that is excerpted here. When the independent counsel delivered his report on possibly impeachable offenses to the House of Representatives on September 9, 1998, he also dropped off seventeen boxes of evidence, including grand jury transcripts and endless reams of subpoenaed documents. Key evidence was compiled into a six-volume appendix totaling 3,183 pages.

The House Judiciary Committee, which was overseeing the inquiry, engaged in a heated partisan debate over how much the public really needed to know. Republicans argued that the president's insistence that he was "legally accurate" when he denied having had sexual relations with Ms. Lewinsky in the Paula Jones case necessitated the fullest possible disclosure. Democrats argued that the Republicans were merely trying to humiliate the president.

The Republicans controlled Congress, so they won the debate, and the entire six-volume appendix, save 186 discrete redactions, was bound by the Government Printing Office and released as a two-part tome. The GPO began selling copies at 9:30 A.M. on September 21, 1998, for $68.00. Simultaneously, the House released a copy of the videotape of the president's grand jury testimony, which was promptly televised by every major broadcast and cable news outlet.

This volume attempts to take the most compelling of those documents and put them in a reader-friendly order. Excluded were records that merely detailed the president's movements and telephone calls, scores of news media accounts that Mr. Starr deemed important for context, and numerous other extraneous materials. To the extent possible, each part of this book puts documents in chronological order, allowing readers to follow the narrative as the drama unfolded.

The story begins with Ms. Lewinsky's testimony, starting with her affidavit in the Paula Jones case that denied a sexual relationship with President Clinton and following her account through two grand jury appearances and nearly twenty interviews. Her version can be compared to President Clinton's grand jury testimony in part 2. Part 3 includes contemporaneous letters and e-mails that Mr. Starr used to bolster Ms. Lewinsky's testimony. This section also includes her tape-recording friend Linda Tripp's scrawled notes about her talks with Ms. Lewinsky.

Part 4 allows a behind-the-scenes peak at the landmark conflict between the prosecutors and President Clinton's lawyers, as the two sides battled over the traditional power of presidents to speak confidentially with their closest advisors. There is little here or anywhere in Mr. Starr's files about the most crucial piece of physical evidence in the case, Ms. Lewinsky's semen-stained dress. Still, the description of prosecutors obtaining a sample of the president's blood in part 5 is dry yet chilling. For the literary minded, part 6 includes a list of books in the president's now-famous study.

Did the president commit perjury or obstruct justice? The answer lies, if anywhere, in the pages that follow.

—Phil Kuntz
September 22, 1998

Mr. Kuntz is a staff reporter for The Wall Street Journal's *Washington Bureau.*

THE
EVIDENCE

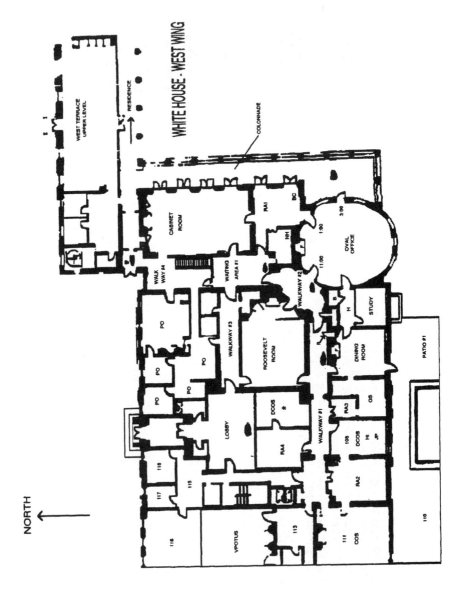

WHITE HOUSE - WEST WING

KEY TO THE WHITE HOUSE MAP

B	President's bathroom	VPOTUS	Vice-President Al Gore
BC	Betty Currie	*	Erskine Bowles then Evelyn Lieberman then Sylvia Mathews
DCOS	Deputy Chief of Staff	1:00	Oval Office door at 1:00 (to Reception Area 1)
		3:00	Oval Office door at 3:00 (to Colonnade)
		11:00	Oval Office door at 11:00 (to Walkway 3)
		108	Deputy Chief of Staff (Harold Ickes then John Podesta)
F	Fireplace	111	Chief of Staff
GS	George Stephanopoulos	113	Vice-President's assistants/secretaries
H	Hallway 1	115	National Security Advisor and staff
HI	Harold Ickes	116	National Security Advisor and staff
JP	John Podesta	117	National Security Advisor and staff
NH	Nancy Hernreich	118	National Security Advisor and staff
P	Pantry		
PO	Press Office		
RA1	Reception Area 1 (assistants to the President)		
RA2	Reception Area 2 (assistants to Chief of Staff and Deputy Chief of Staff)		
RA3	Reception Area 3 (assistants to George Stephanopoulos)		
RA4	Reception Area 4 (assistants to Nancy Hernreich and others)		

Throughout this book, black rules (█████) indicate material deleted by the House Judiciary Committee.

PART ONE

MONICA
LEWINSKY'S
VERSION

Monica's Lewinsky's
Affidavit in the Paula Jones Case

AFFIDAVIT OF JANE DOE 6

1. My name is Jane Doe 6. I am 24 years old and I currently reside at ■
2. On December 19, 1997, I was served with a subpoena from the plaintiff to give a deposition and to produce documents in the lawsuit filed by Paula Corbin Jones against President William Jefferson Clinton and Danny Ferguson.
3. I can not fathom any reason that the plaintiff would seek information from me for her case.
4. I have never met Ms. Jones, nor do I have any information regarding the events she alleges occurred at the Excelsior Hotel on May 8, 1991 or any other information concerning any of the allegations in her case.
5. I worked at the White House in the summer of 1995 as a White House intern. Beginning in December, 1995, I worked in the Office of Legislative Affairs as a staff assistant for correspondence. In April, 1996, I accepted a job as assistant to the Assistant Secretary for Public Affairs at the U.S. Department of Defense. I maintained that job until December 26, 1997. I am currently unemployed but seeking a new job.
6. In the course of my employment at the White House I met President Clinton several times. I also saw the President at a number of social functions held at the White House. When I worked as an intern, he appeared at occasional functions attended by me and several other interns. The correspondence I drafted while I worked at the Office of Legislative Affairs was seen and edited by supervisors who either had the President's signature affixed by mechanism or, I believe, had the President sign the correspondence itself.
7. I have the utmost respect for the President who has always behaved appropriately in my presence.
8. I have never had a sexual relationship with the President, he did not propose that we have a sexual relationship, he did not offer me employment or other benefits in exchange for a sexual relationship, he did not deny me employment or other benefits for rejecting a sexual relationship. I do not know of any other person who had a sexual relationship with the President, was offered employment or ̦other benefits in exchange for a sexual relationship, or was denied employment or other benefits for rejecting a sexual relationship. The occasions that I saw the President after I left my employment at the White House in April, 1996, were official receptions, formal functions or events related to the U.S. Department of Defense, where I was working at the time. There were other people present on those occasions.
9. Since I do not possess any information that could possibly be relevant to the allegations made by Paula Jones or lead to admissible evidence in this case, I asked my attorney to provide this affidavit to plaintiff's counsel. Requiring my deposition in this matter would cause disruption to my life, especially since I am looking for employment, unwar-

ranted attorney's fees and costs, and constitute an invasion of my right to privacy.

I declare under the penalty of perjury that the foregoing is true and correct.

Monica S. Lewinsky
<u>MONICA S. LEWINSKY</u>

849-DC-00000635

DISTRICT OF COLUMBIA, ss:

MONICA S. LEWINSKY, being first duly sworn on oath according to law, deposes and says that she has read the foregoing AFFIDAVIT OF JANE DOE 6 by her subscribed, that the matters stated herein are true to the best of her information, knowledge and belief.

Investigators' Initial Confrontation
with Monica Lewinsky at Pentagon City

1

OFFICE OF THE INDEPENDENT COUNSEL

1/16/98

On January 16, 1998, SSA ███████ and SA ███████ approached MONICA LEWINSKY in the food court area of the Pentagon City, Mall Arlington, Virginia. SSA ███████ immediately identified himself and SA ███████ as agents of the Federal Bureau of Investigation (FBI), detailed to the Office of the Independent Counsel (OIC) for "Whitewater" and requested her presence in a room of the Ritz Carlton Hotel to discuss her status as a person suspected of committing a federal crime. LEWINSKY was advised OIC attorneys were waiting in the room, and that the agents and the attorneys wished to discuss her culpability in criminal activity related to the PAULA JONES civil lawsuit. LEWINSKY was advised she was not under arrest and the agents would not force her to accompany them to the hotel room. LEWINSKY told SSA ███████ he could speak to her attorney. SSA ███████ advised the offer to discuss her legal status was not being offered to her attorney, but to LEWINSKY alone. SSA ███████ explained to LEWINSKY she was being offered an opportunity to meet with the OIC attorneys and agents and hear them explain why they felt she was in trouble without being required to make any statement. SSA ███████ further explained LEWINSKY would then have an opportunity to ask clarifying questions of the attorneys and be better informed as to whether she wanted legal counsel before making any statements, or whether she thought it better to cooperate with the OIC. LEWINSKY voluntarily accompanied the agents to room number 1012 of the Ritz Carlton hotel, under the conditions set forth above.

Also present in room 1016, the adjoining room, were Associate Independent Counsel (AIC) BRUCE UDOLF, AIC MICHAEL EMMICK, AIC STEVEN D. BINHAK, Deputy Independent Counsel JACKIE M. BENNETT, JR., AIC STEPHEN BATES and Contract Investigator COY A. COPELAND, all members of the Office of the Independent Counsel staff. At various times during the day, OIC attorneys entered and departed room 1012. Their movement is not recorded herein. The chronology of the meeting, with all times approximate, is as follows:

1:05 p.m.   LEWINSKY arrived in Room 1012. AIC EMMICK entered Room 1012 and began talking to LEWINSKY.

1:10 p.m.   LEWINSKY given bottled water.

1:33 p.m.   SSA ███████ began reading LEWINSKY her rights as found on the form FD-395, "Interrogation; Advice of Rights." SSA ███████ was unable to finish reading the FD-395.

1:40 p.m.   LEWINSKY was offered a towel.

1:47 p.m.	LEWINSKY was offered water.
2:02 p.m.	The air conditioning in room 1012 was turned on at LEWINSKY's request.
2:13 p.m.	LEWINSKY was offered water. LEWINSKY said, "if I don't cooperate, I can talk to whomever I want".
2:15 p.m.	SA ▮▮▮▮▮ arrived in room 1012.
2:29 p.m.	LEWINSKY stated, "if I leave now, you will charge me now."
2:30 p.m.	LEWINSKY said, "I don't know much about the law."
2:33 p.m.	LEWINSKY asked and was allowed to go to the restroom.
2:36 p.m.	LEWINSKY requested and was given her second bottle of water. LEWINSKY said she is not diabetic and no medication was necessary.
2:50 p.m.	LEWINSKY suggested she take a taxi to her attorney's office. LEWINSKY advised she understands our risks.
3:10 p.m.	LEWINSKY asked if she could be escorted to New York to see her mother, MARCIA LEWIS.
3:20 p.m.	LEWINSKY called her mother, MARCIA LEWIS, in New York.
3:36 p.m.	LEWINSKY requested and was allowed to go to the restroom.
3:45 p.m.	LEWINSKY departed room 1012 unescorted.
3:54 p.m.	LEWINSKY called room 1012 and advised that she was in the lobby, using a pay phone. LEWINSKY advised she changed phones she was using because some people came too close to the phone she had been using. LEWINSKY advised she called to let the Agents know, in case she was being watched.
4:08 p.m.	LEWINSKY voluntarily returned to room 1012. LEWINSKY offered and accepted coffee.
4:12 p.m.	LEWINSKY called MARCIA LEWIS. LEWIS requested to speak with an OIC attorney. AIC EMMICK and SA ▮▮▮▮▮ got on the phone and identified themselves to LEWIS. LEWIS advised she would travel to Washington, DC via AMTRAK Metroliner.
4:20 p.m.	LEWINSKY left room 1012 with AIC BINHAK and SA ▮▮▮▮▮ to use a pay phone in the lobby of the Ritz Carlton Hotel.
4:31 p.m.	LEWINSKY, AIC BINHAK and SA ▮▮▮▮▮ returned to room 1012.
5:00 p.m.	LEWINSKY called her answering machine to retrieve messages.
5:21 p.m.	LEWINSKY requested and received aspirin.
5:40 p.m.	LEWINSKY, AIC EMMICK and SA ▮▮▮▮▮ departed room 1012, en route to the Pentagon City Mall. LEWINSKY, AIC EMMICK and SA ▮▮▮▮▮ walked in the mall.
6:03 p.m.	LEWINSKY requested and was permitted to visit the restroom on the third level of the MACY's department store in the mall.
6:30 p.m.	LEWINSKY, AIC EMMICK and SA ▮▮▮▮▮ dined at MOZZARELLA'S American Grill, within the Pentagon City Mall. LEWINSKY paid for her portion of the dinner.

7:35 p.m.	LEWINSKY, AIC EMMICK and SA ▇▇▇ returned to room 1012.
8:00 p.m.	LEWINSKY payed $2 to SA ▇▇▇ for the cost of her coffee.
8:19 p.m.	MARCIA LEWIS telephoned room 1012, and advised she was on the "163 Northeast Direct", and was experiencing travel delays.
9:05 p.m.	LEWINSKY, SSA ▇▇▇, and SA ▇▇▇ departed room 1012 and LEWINSKY withdrew money from the automatic teller machine on the first floor at the Pentagon City Mall.
9:30 p.m.	Coffee was ordered and brought to room 1012 by room service.
10:16 p.m.	MARCIA LEWIS arrived and all members of the OIC staff left LEWIS and LEWINSKY alone.
10:20 p.m.	A meeting was held in room 1018 between LEWIS, AIC EMMICK, SSA ▇▇▇ and SA ▇▇▇.

LEWIS advised that this was an emotional experience for LEWINSKY. LEWIS advised LEWINSKY was younger than her chronological age. LEWIS asked if tapes were admissible in court. LEWIS advised she wanted to protect LEWINSKY. LEWIS asked how she would know LEWINSKY would not be charged if she cooperated. LEWIS asked about LEWINSKY's safety if LEWINSKY cooperated. LEWIS advised that LEWINSKY talked about suicide six years ago. After LEWINSKY's parents divorced, LEWINSKY saw a therapist, but she is not currently seeing one. LEWIS advised she alone could not take responsibility for convincing LEWINSKY to cooperate with the OIC.

11:02 p.m.	LEWIS requested and was permitted a trip to the restroom.
11:06 p.m.	LEWIS telephonically contacted BERNARD LEWINSKY, her ex-husband, at ▇▇▇.
11:20 p.m.	BERNARD LEWINSKY telephoned room 1018.
11:22 p.m.	AIC EMMICK talked to BERNARD LEWINSKY. Cooperation, an interview, telephone calls, body wires and testimony were mentioned. AIC EMMICK advised BERNARD LEWINSKY that MONICA LEWINSKY was free to leave anytime she wished. 11:30 p.m. MONICA LEWINSKY entered room 1018.
11:32 p.m.	MARCIA LEWIS got back on the phone with BERNARD LEWINSKY. BERNARD LEWINSKY advised he would go to a pay phone and would call back.
11:35 p.m.	BERNARD LEWINSKY telephoned room 1014. BERNARD LEWINSKY advised AIC EMMICK that MONICA LEWINSKY was represented by counsel.
11:36 p.m.	MONICA LEWINSKY talked to BERNARD LEWINSKY on the telephone.
11:37 p.m.	AIC EMMICK spoke with BERNARD LEWINSKY. AIC EMMICK asked MONICA LEWINSKY if she had an attorney and LEWINSKY advised it was GINSBURG. AIC EMMICK advised MONICA LEWINSKY she did not have to accept an attorney she did not select.

MONICA LEWINSKY asked if there was still a chance she would go to jail if she cooperated. MONICA LEWINSKY suggested she may have not told the truth in previous conversations. MONICA LEWINSKY asked, "what if I partially cooperate?"

MARCIA LEWIS asked what would happen if MONICA LEWINSKY gave everything but did not tape anything. MONICA LEWINSKY asked if the PAULA JONES case went away would "this" go away and was advised by AIC EMMICK "no."

MONICA LEWINSKY asked how the OIC would resolve the chance that MONICA LEWINSKY said something to LINDA TRIP that was not true.

MARCIA LEWIS advised that she appreciated the OIC members waiting until she arrived to proceed. MONICA LEWINSKY advised she appreciated having her mother present.

11:55 p.m.	BILL GINSBURG telephoned room 1018 and spoke to AIC EMMICK, who advised GINSBURG he was uncomfortable with the relationship between GINSBURG and MONICA LEWINSKY. MONICA LEWINSKY advised she was not 100% sure it was the right thing to do because GINSBURG was a medical lawyer.
11:59 p.m.	MONICA LEWINSKY advised she was represented by GINSBURG.
12:08 a.m.	GINSBURG was advised by AIC EMMICK that MONICA LEWINSKY always had the right to leave at any time.
12:17 a.m.	MONICA LEWINSKY spoke with GINSBURG, outside the presence of the OIC staff.
12:23 a.m.	AIC EMMICK ended the phone call with GINSBURG and advised MONICA LEWINSKY and MARCIA LEWIS they were free to leave.
12:30 a.m.	MARCIA LEWIS and MONICA LEWINSKY thanked the Agents and the staff of the OIC for being so kind and considerate.
12:45 a.m.	SA ▇▇▇ and SA ▇▇▇ escorted MARCIA LEWIS and MONICA LEWINSKY to LEWINSKY's vehicle, which was parked in the parking garage adjacent to the Pentagon City Mall.

Monica Lewinsky's Proffer

[Editor's Note: This is the statement Monica Lewinsky penned for Independent Counsel Kenneth Starr on February 1, 1998, shortly after the scandal became public. Known in legal circles as a "proffer," this document represents what Ms. Lewinsky intended to tell prosecutors under oath if they granted her immunity.]

1. Ms. Lewinsky had an intimate and emotional relationship with President Clinton beginning in 1995. At various times between 1995 and 1997, Ms. Lewinsky and the President had physically intimate contact. This included oral sex, but excluded intercourse.

2. When asked what should be said if anyone questioned Ms. Lewinsky about her being with the President, he said she should say she was bringing him letters (when she worked in Legislative Affairs) or visiting Betty Currie (after she left the WH). There is truth to both of these statements.

3. After Ms. Lewinsky was informed she was being transferred to the Pentagon, Mr. Clinton told her that a) he promised to bring her back to the WH after the election and (in a subsequent conversation) b) Evelyn Lieberman spearheaded the transfer because she felt the President paid too much attention to me and vice versa. Ms. Lieberman told the Pres. that she didn't care who worked there after the election, but they needed to be careful until then.

After the election, Ms. Lewinsky asked the Pres. to bring her back to the WH. In the following months, Mr. Clinton told Ms. Lewinsky that Bob Nash was handling it and then Marsha Scott became the contact person. Ms. L met with Ms. Scott twice. In the second meeting, Ms. Scott told Ms. L she would detail her from the Pentagon to her (Ms. Scott's) office, so people could see Ms. L's good work and stop referring to her as "The Stalker." Ms. Scott told Ms. L they had to be careful and protect the Pres. Ms. Scott later rescinded her offer to detail Ms. Lewinsky to her office.

Ms. Betty Currie asked Mr. John Podesta to take over placing me in the WH. Three weeks after that, Ms. Linda Tripp informed Ms. L that a friend of Ms. Tripp's in the NSC, Kate, had heard rumors about Ms. L; Ms. L would never work at the WH with a blue pass; and suggested to Ms. Tripp that Ms. L leave Washington, DC.

Following this conversation, Ms. Lewinsky requested of the Pres. that he ask Vernon Jordan to help secure her a non-government position in NY. He agreed to ask Mr. Jordan.

In an effort to help Ms. L, Ms. Currie asked Mr. Podesta to assist, as well. Ms. L believes that the Pres. ~~asked~~ spoke with Mr. Erskine Bowles regarding Ms. L's employment in NY. Mr. Podesta arranged for Ms. L to interview with Amb. Richardson who later offered Ms. L a position in Communications/ Public Affairs at the USUN.

In the beginning of November 1997, Ms. L met with Mr. Jordan. He asked Ms. L why she was there to see him. Ms. L explained to him (in more detail) that she and the Pres. were friends and people got the wrong idea, resulting in Ms. L's 'banishment' to the Pentagon. Ms. L said she was seeking Mr. Jordan's help to begin a new life; he agreed to help.

Ms. L met again with Mr. Jordan in the beginning of December '97, at which time he provided Ms. L with a list of three people to contact and suggested language to use in her letters to them. At some point, Mr. Jordan remarked something about Ms. L being a friend of the Pres. of the United States. Ms. L responded that she never really saw him as "the President"; she spoke to him like a normal man and even got angry with him like a normal man. Mr. Jordan asked what Ms. L got angry about. Ms. L replied that the Pres. doesn't see or call her enough. Mr. Jordan said

Ms. L should take her frustrations out on ~~the~~
him -- not the President.

The following week Ms. L had two interviews in
NY ~~as a result~~ in response to of her letters.

4. After Ms. Lewinsky was informed, by the Pres., that
she was identified as a possible witness in
the Jones case, the Pres. and Ms. L discussed
what she should do. The Pres. told her he
was not sure she would be subpoenaed, but
in the event that she was, she should contact
Ms. Currie. When asked what to do if she
was subpoenaed, the Pres. suggested she
could sign an affidavit to try to satisfy their
inquiry and not be deposed. In general, Ms. L
should say she visited the WH to see Ms. Currie
and, on occasion when working at the WH,
she brought him letters when no one else
was around. Neither of those statements
untrue. To the best of Ms. L's memory, she
does not believe they discussed the content of
any deposition that Ms. L might be involved in
at a later date.

5. After receiving a subpoena two days later, Ms. L contacted Mr. Jordan (because Ms. Currie's brother had been killed in a car accident). Mr. Jordan told Ms. L to come see him ~~that~~ ● at 5 pm because he couldn't understand Ms. L ~~through her tears~~ on the phone, through her tears. Upon Ms. L's request, Mr. Jordan arranged an appointment for her with an attorney, Mr. Frank Carter.

Ms. L expressed ~~any~~ anxiety ● with respect to her subpoena requesting the production of any gifts from the Pres., specifically citing hat pins which the Pres. had in fact given her. Mr. Jordan allayed her concerns by telling her it was standard language. Mr. Jordan asked Ms. Lewinsky two questions: Did you have sex with the Pres. and/or did he ask you for sex? ~~The~~ Ms. L responded to both questions with "no."

Possibly later in that meeting but more probably the next meeting, Ms. L ~~said~~ tried to make it clear to Mr. Jordan that she, in fact, did have a physically intimate relationship with the Pres. ~~On more than one occasion she has expressed concern about signing an affidavit~~

Ms. L made it clear she intended to deny the sexual relationship with the Pres.

On the day Mr. Jordan drove Ms. L to Mr. Carter's office, she showed Mr. Jordan the items she was producing in response to the subpoena. Ms. L believes she made it clear this was not everything she had that could respond to the subpoena, but she thought it was enough to satisfy. ~~and still~~ ~~request~~. Mr. Jordan made no comment about whether or not ~~this~~ what Ms. L brought was right or wrong. Mr. J drove Ms. L to Mr. Carter's office; introduced them; and left.

6. The Pres., through Ms. Currie, invited Ms. L to come see him to get her Christmas presents. They played with Buddy, he gave her the presents, they ~~spoke~~ talked casually and spoke for a few minutes about the case. Ms. L asked him how he thought the ~~Pa~~ attorneys for Paula Jones found out about her. He thought it was probably "that woman from the summer... wit Kathleen Willey" (Linda Tripp) who lead them to Ms. L or possibly the uniformed agents. He shared Ms. L's concern about the hat pin. He asked Ms. L if she had told anyone that he had given it to her and she replied, "no."

14

Ms. L then asked if she should put away (outside her home) the gifts he had given her or, maybe, give them to someone else. ~~Batty~~ [Ms. Currie called Ms. L later that afternoon as said that the Pres. had told her ~~to~~ Ms. L wanted her to hold onto something for ~~her~~. ~~to~~ Ms. L boxed up most of the gifts ~~she~~ had received and gave them to Ms. Currie. It is unknown if Ms. Currie knew the contents of the box.]

Ms. L told the Pres. she was planning to sign an affidavit. When Ms. L and the Pres. discussed when Ms. L was moving to NY, the Pres. thought it might be possible that they would not seek her deposition if she was in NY.

7. Ms. Lewinsky called Mr. Jordan several times concerning her employment in NY. When she called one day especially concerned about the case, Mr. Jordan suggested they meet for breakfast.

At breakfast, Ms. L expressed concern about Ms. Tripp saying she (Ms. L) had trusted her before, but was now suspicious of her.

15

Ms. L said Ms. Tripp may have seen notes
when she was in Ms. L's home. Mr. Jordan
asked if the notes were from the Pres. Ms. L
said that they were notes to the Pres. Mr.
Jordan suggested t Ms. L she check to
make sure they are not there (something
to that effect). Ms. L interpreted that to
mean she should get rid of whatever
is there.

On the
In the car on the way to his office, Ms. L
asked Mr. Jordan if he thought the Pres.
would always be married to Mrs. Clinton.
Mr. Jordan replied that he thought they
would always be married, as they should
be. as Ms. L expressed disappointment and
then Mr. Jordan said, "well, maybe you two
will have an affair when he's out of office.
Ms. L replied that she and the Pres. had alread
had an affair minus having sex - but it
included everything else. Ms. L believes they
did not get into any more detail

After Ms. L received the draft of the affidavit, she called Mr. Jordan to ask that he look it over before she signs it. He instructed her to drop off a copy at his office. They spoke later by phone about the affidavit agreeing to make some changes.

That evening, Ms. L placed a phone call to Ms. Currie asking her to tell the Pres. that she wanted to speak with him before she signed something the next day. He returned Ms. L's call a few hours later. Ms. L told him Mr. Carter had asked her some sample questions that might be asked of her in the deposition and she didn't know how to answer them. Furthermore, she was concerned that if the answers involved naming people in the WH who didn't like her they would try to screw her over. Ms. L asked him how she should respond to the question, "How did you get your job at the Pentagon?" He replied "The people in Legislative Affairs helped you." This is, in fact, part of the truth -- but not the whole truth. The Pres. told Ms. L not to worry about the affidavit as he had seen 15 others.

9. Ms. L started to become wary of Ms. Tripp in the beginning of Dec. 1997, when Ms. Tripp told Ms. L she had received a subpoena in the Jones case and if asked about Ms. L or others, she would divulge all she knew.

10. Ms. L had a physically intimate relationship with the President. Neither the Pres. nor Mr. Jordan (or anyone on their behalf) asked or encouraged ~~Ms L~~ to lie. Ms L was comfortable signing the affidavit with regard to the "sexual relationship" because she could justify to herself that ~~they~~ she and the Pres. did not have sexual intercourse.

11. At some point in the relationship between Ms. L and the President, the President told Ms. L to deny a relationship, if ever asked about it. He also said something to the effect of if ~~two~~ the two people who are involved say it didn't happen — it didn't happen. Ms. L knows this was said some time prior to the subpoena in the Paula Jones case.

2. Item #2 above also occurred prior to the subpoena in the Paula Jones case.

Monica Lewinsky's Fingerprinting Session

1

OFFICE OF THE INDEPENDENT COUNSEL

5/28/98

On May 28, 1998, at approximately 8:30 a.m., MONICA S. LEWINSKY (hereinafter referred to as LEWINSKY) arrived at the Federal Building, 11000 Wilshire Boulevard, Los Angeles, California, for purposes of providing her fingerprints and handwriting exemplars to the Federal Bureau of Investigation, as agreed upon by Deputy Independent Counsel (DIC) ROBERT BITTMAN of the Office of the Independent Counsel (OIC) and WILLIAM GINSBURG, LEWINSKY's attorney. Present were GINSBURG, TODD C. THEODORA, an associate with the law firm of GINSBURG, STEPHAN, ORINGHER & RICHMAN, representing LEWINSKY, BERNARD LEWINSKY, MONICA LEWINSKY's father, Associate Independent Counsel (AIC) EDWARD J. PAGE and writer.

LEWINSKY and her party were escorted from their car to the Federal Building in Los Angeles by Special Agents of the Los Angeles office of the FBI and by officers of the Federal Protective Service.

After being processed for fingerprints by the FBI's ██████, LEWINSKY and her party were accompanied to the 17th floor office of Los Angeles FBI ████████ for the purpose of LEWINSKY providing handwriting exemplars.

The pens used for this examination were as follows: one Bic, round stic, medium, black ink pen; one paper mate pen with black ink; and one paper mate, gel writer, with black ink. At various times during the examination, LEWINSKY was asked to use one of the three different pens. LEWINSKY's attorneys interrupted the examination on numerous occasions so LEWINSKY could consult privately with her attorneys.

MONICA LEWINSKY was first asked to write the alphabet in its entirety, with three different pens, on an 8 1/2 x 11 sheet of paper (unless specified otherwise, each sheet of paper used was 8 1/2 x 11) attached to a pad. On the same sheet of paper, LEWINSKY was asked to write the number one thru ten, three times, using a different pen each time.

LEWINSKY was then asked to perform the same task, this time using a sheet of paper resting only on the desk where she was sitting.

LEWINSKY was then asked to print her name three times on a sheet of paper attached to a pad, each time using a different pen. LEWINSKY was then asked to sign her name on a sheet of paper attached to a pad, each time using a different pen. LEWINSKY was then asked to perform the same task, with the sheet of paper used resting directly on the desk.

LEWINSKY was then asked to sign her name to a photocopy of a blank check. At that time, GINSBURG objected and advised his client not to sign the form. GINSBURG advised that the OIC would need to get a Court Order before his client would sign anything that resembled a check. GINSBURG advised that he had no idea what the OIC had in the way of evidence and he was not going to create an exhibit. GINSBURG asked if he could use the telephone to call his co-counsel. GINSBURG advised he would use his AT&T card when calling. GINSBURG was permitted to use the telephone in ████████ office.

After much discussion and delay, the meeting resumed and GINSBURG was asked if a compromise could be worked out where LEWINSKY would sign the documents and GINSBURG, THEODORA and SA ████████ would initial the front so as to limit any question about the source of the document.

At this time, LEWINSKY asked GINSBURG to have BERNARD LEWINSKY leave because if he stayed, "[the OIC] would subpoena him." Several minutes later, BERNARD LEWINSKY departed, citing the need to see patients.

The meeting resumed several minutes later. GINSBURG replied that he had just received a letter from Deputy Independent Counsel (DIC) ROBERT BITTMAN wherein BITTMAN advised that LEWINSKY had no immunity and anything she did or said could be used against her. GINSBURG advised by allowing his client to write the checks, he would be allowing the OIC to violate her 5th Amendment rights. In addition, BITTMAN's letter stated that SA ████████ and AIC PAGE had no authority to work out any compromise on behalf of the OIC. GINSBURG continued that in fact, BITTMAN had no authority to work out any deals on behalf of the OIC and the only person who did so would be KEN STARR.

GINSBURG advised he would accept only compromises signed by STARR and GINSBURG would accept them as long as GINSBURG was permitted to get handwriting exemplars from STARR. GINSBURG continued that the only compromise he would accept would be from STARR and the OIC should send STARR to Los Angeles to work out the compromise. While refusing to explain his reasoning, GINSBURG paused and explained to AIC PAGE that none of this was personal and, in fact, PAGE and GINSBURG could go out and have a few beers together. However, GINSBURG continued, BITTMAN had drawn a "razor-fine line" in his letter and GINSBURG was going to draw a similarly fine line in representing his client.

AIC PAGE asked GINSBURG if he would permit LEWINSKY to sign checks if PAGE showed GINSBURG a case which held that the request by the OIC was permitted to obtain the exemplars in this manner on the blank check forms. GINSBURG advised he would. PAGE showed GINSBURG such a case, but GINSBURG refused to permit LEWINSKY to fill out the checks.

AIC PAGE asked GINSBURG if GINSBURG understood that the OIC could use LEWINSKY's refusal to provide the requested handwriting exemplars against her at a trial or a proceeding. GINSBURG stated he was aware of that fact.

At approximately 9:30 a.m., GINSBURG was asked if LEWINSKY had consumed any medication during the morning. GINSBURG replied that, to his knowledge, LEWINSKY had not. Upon hearing this, LEWINSKY indicated to GINSBURG that she needed to speak with him, and PAGE and ███████ departed the room. After a break, GINSBURG advised that LEWINSKY had taken "no narcotic, benzodiazepine, or other medication which in [GINSBURG]'s opinion would affect [LEWINSKY]'s coordination or alertness." GINSBURG refused to advise what medication LEWINSKY had taken.

The handwriting examination continued until approximately 10:06 a.m., when LEWINSKY took a break to visit the restroom.

The examination resumed approximately fifteen minutes later. LEWINSKY was asked to write various words and phrases. After LEWINSKY was asked to write "I have only read excerpts from Leaves of Grass before," GINSBURG requested SA ███████ and AIC PAGE to leave the room. Upon resuming the examination, GINSBURG advised that there were several exemplars which appeared to be from the same letter, so GINSBURG would permit no more exemplars from that letter.

LEWINSKY was then asked to write "The Pres., through Ms. Currie." GINSBURG objected and advised that the "proffer was off limits." LEWINSKY was asked to write certain words and phrases and to sign her name on 5 x 7 note paper. Some of the samples taken were done so with the paper attached to the pad and some were taken with the paper resting directly on the desk.

The examination continued and GINSBURG agreed, although he objected earlier, to allow LEWINSKY to sign her name to strips of paper that, though not photocopies of or the same size as checks, more closely resembled a check than an 8 1/2 x 11 piece of paper. GINSBURG would not permit LEWINSKY to write amounts or dates on the pages that were close in size to a check.

At approximately 11:00 a.m., the examination ended, at which time GINSBURG was served grand jury subpoena number D-1319 for LEWINSKY's appearance on June 4, 1998 in Washington, DC to provide handwriting exemplars. GINSBURG advised he thought that a handwriting examination was just completed. GINSBURG was advised that all requested exemplars were not provided, therefore, LEWINSKY would have to come to Washington, DC to do so.

GINSBURG, LEWINSKY and THEODORA were escorted to their car by Special Agents of the FBI's Los Angeles Office and officers of the Federal Protective Service.

Monica Lewinsky's
First Interview with Investigators

1

OFFICE OF THE INDEPENDENT COUNSEL

07/27/98

MONICA S. LEWINSKY was interviewed in Apartment 33B, 300 East 56th Street, New York, New York. Representatives of the Office of Independent Counsel (OIC) included ROBERT J. BITTMAN, Deputy Independent Counsel (DIC), SOLOMON L. WISENBERG, DIC, MARY ANNE WIRTH, Associate Independent Counsel (AIC), and Professor SAM DASH, Consultant. Attorneys present for LEWINSKY included PLATO CACHERIS, Law Offices of PLATO CACHERIS, 1100 Connecticut Avenue NW, Washington, D.C. 20036, telephone 202-775-8700; SYDNEY HOFFMAN of the CACHERIS Law Office; and JACOB STEIN, Law Offices of STEIN, MITCHELL, & MEZINES, 1100 Connecticut Avenue NW, Washington, D.C. 20036, telephone 202-737-7777.

After each of the participants identified themselves, a proffer agreement was executed by LEWINSKY. The agreement had previously been signed on July 24, 1998 by STEIN, CACHERIS, and KENNETH W. STARR, Independent Counsel. A copy of the agreement is attached and marked "Attachment A". LEWINSKY stated that she wished to answer all questions truthfully and completely. LEWINSKY then provided the following information:

LEWINSKY is a 25 year old female with a Bachelor of Science degree in Psychology from Lewis & Clark College in Portland, Oregon. LEWINSKY has been taking two prescription anti-depressants since early February 1995. This medication, at times, causes some memory to be suppressed and this usually expresses itself as the inability to think of certain words during conversation. The drugs are Effexor and Serzone. LEWINSKY stated that she wished to proceed with the above caveat.

LEWINSKY first met the President of the United States, WILLIAM J. CLINTON, in July 1995, soon after beginning her job as an intern in LEON PANETTA's Office in the White House. The occasion was the departure of the President from the South Lawn of the White House. LEWINSKY had obtained her job through a friend of her mother's, WALTER KAYE, and through JAY FOOTLIK, who formerly worked there.

LEWINSKY began her personal relationship with the President on November 15, 1995. This was during the furlough of federal employees when LEWINSKY was in the unique position of having been hired as a paid employee in Legislative Affairs, but before her paper work had been processed. LEWINSKY, who was still an intern working for LEON PANETTA in the West Wing of the White House, saw the President when he came to the West Wing to see PANETTA and HAROLD ICKES. LEWINSKY and the President had flirted previously and they made eye contact on this visit. Later that day there was a cake party for JENNIFER PALMIERI, which the President and LEWINSKY attended. Later the same day, LEWINSKY was walking past the office of GEORGE STEPHANOPOLOUS and noticed that the President was inside the office and a U.S. Secret Service (USSS) Agent was outside. The President motioned for LEWINSKY to come in. LEWINSKY felt that this was her big chance and she advised the President that she "had a crush on him." The President then invited LEWINSKY to the back study behind the Oval Office, where he kissed her.

The relationship then blossomed and eventually included 14 sexual encounters. Sexual encounters included one or more of the following: kissing, hugging, touching, and oral sex on the person of the President, but not intercourse. On one occasion there was unclothed genital contact. Although LEWINSKY and the President had talked about the President performing oral sex on LEWINSKY, this never occurred because many times their encounters occurred during her menstrual cycles. The relationship included about 50 telephone calls, with the majority of them being between 10:00 p.m. and 6:00 a.m. About 15 of these calls were sexually explicit telephone calls, which LEWINSKY refers to as "phone sex" with the President. The President made most of the calls from his residence, but called LEWINSKY from out of town several times, including a call from Florida at the beginning of September 1996, when he was on the campaign trail.

At least seven of the sexual acts occurred in the hallway between the Oval Office and the private study of the President. The President usually left the door between the Oval Office and the Back Office slightly ajar so there would be no suspicion of improper activity and to hear if anyone was trying to contact him. LEWINSKY explained that the Back Office includes the private study, the hallway, the dining room, and the bathroom. The President liked to stand with his back against the door frame to ease his back muscles. When the President wanted to spend time with LEWINSKY, he would call her and either arrange to meet her in the hall, or LEWINSKY would carry some papers into the Oval Office. There were about nine or ten sexual contacts prior to Easter 1996, and about four after LEWINSKY was transferred to the Pentagon. About four of the sexual events occurred on workdays between 9:00 a.m. and 5:00 p.m., with the remainder on weekends. LEWINSKY recounted a few of the sexual contacts as follows:

A. On February 27 or 28 when the President gave LEWINSKY a hatpin and a book. This included kissing, touching, and oral sex to completion.
B. On March 29 or 30 after the knee surgery. This consisted of kissing, touching, oral sex to completion and brief genital contact without clothing but not intercourse.
C. On August 16, 1997, a birthday kiss.
D. On December 28, 1997, a Christmas kiss.

BETTY CURRIE, the President's Secretary, may have seen the President and LEWINSKY hugging on occasion and possibly a kiss on the forehead. During a visit to the private study on July 4th, LEWINSKY was at times crying and fighting with the President, and hugging him, when she saw a gardener, name unknown, who was working outside a window of the back study. The President and LEWINSKY then moved out of sight into the hallway where intimate things sometimes occurred during their relationship. LEWINSKY is unsure whether the gardener observed any arguing or hugging between the President and LEWINSKY. LEWINSKY is unaware of anyone else who could have observed any sexual activity. The President was suspicious of the USSS uniformed people and of LINDA TRIPP. In April 1997, the President asked, during a telephone call to LEWINSKY, whether LEWINSKY had told her mother about their sexual relationship. This was after MARSHA SCOTT had a conversation with WALTER KAYE. LEWINSKY denied that she had. However, this was untrue, inasmuch as LEWINSKY had told her mother of the emotional details of her involvement with the President, and told her that LEWINSKY and the President had "fooled around". On Monday, July 14, 1997, the President asked LEWINSKY if LEWINSKY had told LINDA TRIPP about their relationship. LEWINSKY replied "no." On December 28, 1997, the President asked LEWINSKY if she had revealed the hat pin to anyone and LEWINSKY denied that she had. The President did not believe LEWINSKY.

BAYANI NELVIS knew that LEWINSKY had been alone with the President on December 31, 1995, between 12:00 p.m. and 1:00 p.m., because LEWINSKY had a conversation with NELVIS in the pantry/kitchen area. LEWINSKY and NELVIS were discussing the smoking of cigars. NELVIS offered to get LEWINSKY one of the President's cigars and they entered the pantry door so that NELVIS could get one. At that point, the President came in from the Oval Office to get something for PANETTA and saw LEWINSKY. NELVIS then obtained the item for PANETTA and left LEWINSKY and the President alone in the back rooms. This resulted in LEWINSKY performing oral sex with the President.

NELVIS advised LEWINSKY on one other occasion that a uniformed officer had asked NELVIS the identity of LEWINSKY, after the officer had observed her go into the Oval Office. NELVIS told the officer that LEWINSKY was the daughter of one of the Cabinet Secretaries.

BETTY CURRIE facilitated LEWINSKY's visits with the President so that EVELYN LIEBERMAN, STEPHEN GOODIN, and NANCY HERNREICH, who did not like LEWINSKY, would not find out. CURRIE advised that HERNREICH would be gone on Monday or Tuesday evenings to attend yoga classes and that LIEBERMAN and GOODIN were gone on weekends.

On Good Friday of 1996, LEWINSKY was advised that she was being transferred out of the White House to the Pentagon.

The President called LEWINSKY on Easter Sunday 1996, about 5:00 p.m. or 6:00 p.m., and asked about the RON BROWN incident. LEWINSKY cried about being transferred out and the President asked her to visit him. LEWINSKY carried some papers to the Oval Office and Officer JOHN MUSKETT was there. MUSKETT said he would ask LIEBERMAN if LEWINSKY could see the President, but LEWINSKY skirted the issue by saying that she would only be there for a minute to drop off the papers. The President was sitting at his desk in the Oval Office talking on the telephone, presumably to Mrs. CLINTON, as the President ended the call by saying, "I love you." The President and LEWINSKY went into the back office and the President tried to soothe LEWINSKY by saying, "I promise you if I win in November I'll get you back and you can do what you want." The President said that LIEBERMAN had spearheaded LEWINSKY's transfer because LEWINSKY was paying too much attention to the President and they could not have this prior to the election. LEWINSKY soon began performing oral sex on the President, then the President took a telephone call from a political person, whom LEWINSKY later speculated to be DICK MORRIS. The telephone may have rung in the back office, or the President may have been interrupted by someone from the Oval Office to take the call. LEWINSKY felt cheap performing oral sex while the President was on the telephone. At some later date, after reading about DICK MORRIS in the newspaper, LEWINSKY wondered whether DICK MORRIS was doing the same thing with a prostitute. The President completed the call and hung up. The oral sex was discontinued when the President answered, "Just a minute" as a result of HAROLD ICKES calling out, "Mr. President" from the door of the Oval Office. LEWINSKY had her top off. The President left the room and LEWINSKY departed through the back door after putting her top back on.

After the President won the election, LEWINSKY renewed her efforts to get back to the White House. The President advised LEWINSKY that he would talk to BOB NASH and told her at other times that both MARSHA SCOTT and NASH were working on it. LEWINSKY had given her resume to the President in March 1997. LEWINSKY applied for a job in the White House Press Office and LINDA TRIPP arranged an NSC (National Security Council) interview. LEWINSKY advised MARSHA SCOTT of her applications, but she did not get either job. When LEWINSKY told the President that she had applied for these jobs, the President retorted that he needed to know in advance so that he could do something.

By October 1997, LEWINSKY told the President that she had made up her mind to leave the Pentagon job and move to New York. LEWINSKY mentioned a job at the United Nations (UN). The President said that he would help, and he apparently spoke to JOHN PODESTA, who spoke to BILL RICHARDSON on a trip to Mexico. Ambassador RICHARDSON called LEWINSKY and set up an interview at the Watergate Hotel. Subsequently, RICHARDSON called LEWINSKY at the Pentagon and offered her the job at the UN. LEWINSKY, who had changed her mind about working at the UN, but did not know how to back out, called one of RICHARDSON's assistants and advised that she was more interested in working in the private sector.

LINDA TRIPP suggested to LEWINSKY that the President should be asked to ask VERNON JORDAN for assistance. In early October 1997, while talking to the President on the telephone from 2:30 a.m. to 4:00 a.m., LEWINSKY asked the President to call JORDAN and the President did. This long conversation included an argument about why the President was not bringing LEWINSKY back to the White House.

LEWINSKY was a willing participant in all of the sexual encounters. LEWINSKY and the President had discussed a number of times that they would never tell anyone about their sexual activities. However, in violation of this agreement, LEWINSKY did provide different levels of detail about the sexual relationship to the following persons: ANDY BLEILER, NATALIE UNGVARI, NEYSA ERBLAND, ASHLEY RAINES, CATHRYN ALDAY DAVIS, LINDA TRIPP, DALE YOUNG, Dr. CATHY ESTEP, and Dr. IRENE KASSORLA. LEWINSKY did not tell KATHY BLEILER, and did not tell DENNIS LYTTON of Los Angeles, who is unknown to her.

No sexual incidents occurred from May 1996 or earlier until after the election.

In May 1997, the President said that he did not feel right about his sexual relationship with LEWINSKY and that he just wanted to be friends. LEWINSKY referred to this as "dump day."

The President, at one time or another, made comments to LEWINSKY such as, "You are bright, attractive, and make me feel young;" he liked talking to her; "people like us" (meaning, we are the same), LEWINSKY was "emotive and full of fire"; LEWINSKY was "full of piss and vinegar;" he wished to spend more time with LEWINSKY; he might "have time in three years;" and "What if I'm 75 and have to go to the bathroom fifteen times a day?". The President sometimes called LEWINSKY "sweetie" or "baby." LEWINSKY occasionally called the President "handsome."

On December 17, 1997, during a telephone conversation between 2:00 a.m. and 3:00 a.m., the President advised LEWINSKY that she was on the PAULA JONES witness list. This was the first indication LEWINSKY had that she was to be subpoenaed. LEWINSKY believes that the President had just found out, but if the President found out about the potential witnesses on December 5th or 6th he never gave any indication of this to LEWINSKY. During this call the President advised that LEWINSKY might sign an affidavit to avoid being deposed in the JONES case; that LEWINSKY could say that she was coming to the White House to visit BETTY CURRIE; or that LEWINSKY was carrying papers to the President; and that LEWINSKY should contact BETTY CURRIE if subpoenaed. The President also advised that BETTY CURRIE's brother had been killed, and that the President had a Christmas present for LEWINSKY.

On December 19, 1997, LEWINSKY was served with a subpoena in the PAULA JONES lawsuit, between 4:00 p.m. and 4:30 p.m., at the Pentagon where LEWINSKY was then working. This was very upsetting to LEWINSKY, who then called VERNON JORDAN from a payphone in the Pentagon. JORDAN had been helping LEWINSKY seek employment in New York for the previous month and a half. LEWINSKY went to see JORDAN at his office that afternoon, showed JORDAN the subpoena, and pointed out that it included the production of a hat pin that the President had given LEWINSKY. LEWINSKY asked JORDAN about getting an attorney. JORDAN received a telephone call and asked LEWINSKY to leave the room. After about ten minutes JORDAN came back, but did not identify the caller. JORDAN called an attorney named FRANK CARTER and set up an appointment for LEWINSKY at 10:30 a.m. on the following Monday. JORDAN said there were only two important questions: 1. Did you have sex with the President? 2. Did the President ask you for sex? JORDAN said that he would see the President that evening and would tell him about LEWINSKY's subpoena. In a subsequent meeting, JORDAN assured LEWINSKY that he had advised the President of the subpoena.

LEWINSKY did not visit the President at the White House between December 6th and December 28th, 1997.

On December 28, 1997, LEWINSKY visited the President at the White House. The visit was arranged by BETTY CURRIE. When LEWINSKY arrived she talked to BETTY and played with BUDDY on the carpet with some "people bones" for about ten minutes while the President was on the telephone. The President and LEWINSKY then went into the back study and spent from 45 minutes to an hour together. The President gave LEWINSKY her Christmas gifts at this time. There was no sex on this occasion, but there may have been a kiss and a hug, as the President said that Christmas kisses were an exception to his earlier statement that there would be no more sexual contact between them. LEWINSKY expressed her concern about the gifts that the President had given LEWINSKY and specifically the hat pin that had been subpoenaed by PAULA JONES. The President seemed to know what the JONES subpoena called for in advance and did not seem surprised about the hat pin. The President asked LEWINSKY if she had told anyone about the hat pin and LEWINSKY denied that she had, but may have said that she gave some of the gifts to FRANK CARTER. LEWINSKY was concerned because this was a personal item. LEWINSKY mentioned that DEBBIE SCHIFF may have given her name to the lawyers for PAULA JONES. The President opined that it may have been "that woman from the summer that was involved in the KATHLEEN WILLEY thing." LEWINSKY asked the President if she should give the gifts to someone and the President replied, "I don't know." LEWINSKY and the President discussed her move to New York and the President said that if LEWINSKY was in New York the JONES lawyers might not call; that the sooner LEWINSKY moved the better; and that maybe the lawyers would ignore her. Sometime prior to December 28th the President had suggested that LEWINSKY submit an affidavit in lieu of testifying.

Several hours after leaving the White House LEWINSKY received a telephone call at her apartment from BETTY CURRIE who made the statement, "You have some things to give me?" This call was not a coincidence, but a result of LEWINSKY's earlier conversation with the President. The call may have been on CURRIE's cell phone. LEWINSKY put a GAP box on her bed and placed in it a number of gifts that she had received from the President, except for some innocuous items that would not appear too personal if found in her apartment. The reason for getting some of the gifts out of the apartment was because LEWINSKY suspected that the lawyers for JONES would break into her apartment. LEWINSKY also suspected that the JONES people might tap her telephone. Besides keeping the innocuous gift items, LEWINSKY also kept some of the sentimental items from the President such as the following: a canvas bag from the BLACK DOG store, maybe some BLACK DOG T-shirts, a lithographic book, a big Rockette blanket, a pair of sunglasses, and a wooden box that had contained an earlier present. LEWINSKY kept the sentimental items because she was afraid that she would not get them back. Pursuant to the agreement that LEWINSKY and CURRIE had made during the earlier telephone call, LEWINSKY met CURRIE on 28th street outside LEWINSKY's apartment at about 2:00 p.m.

and gave CURRIE the box of gifts. The box contained a hat pin, some BLACK DOG items, a broach, two signed photographs of The President, and a signed State of the Union address. However, there was no discussion of the contents. LEWINSKY had written "do not throw away" on the box. CURRIE was on her way to visit a relative in the hospital when she stopped by. CURRIE was to keep the box in a closet in CURRIE's home.

In addition to the December 19, 1997 meeting with VERNON JORDAN, LEWINSKY had met JORDAN on several previous occasions. LEWINSKY may have met with JORDAN in late November or the first week in December 1997. LEWINSKY initially met JORDAN in early November 1997, when she spent about 20 minutes in his office. The purpose of this meeting was to ask JORDAN's assistance in obtaining a job in New York. LEWINSKY knew that JORDAN and the President were good friends and JORDAN knew that LEWINSKY and the President were friends. JORDAN indicated that he had spoken with the President and LEWINSKY interpreted this to mean that the President had asked JORDAN for assistance in getting LEWINSKY a job. JORDAN said, "You've come highly recommended." LEWINSKY understood that this meant that the President had spoken to JORDAN. LEWINSKY was somewhat intimidated during this meeting. JORDAN said that he would make some telephone calls on LEWINSKY's behalf before he left Washington for the holidays.

On December 11, 1997, LEWINSKY had lunch with JORDAN at the AKIN, GUMP office, at which time JORDAN recommended that LEWINSKY write letters with certain language to three companies. JORDAN provided the language. LEWINSKY typed the letters and sent copies to JORDAN. During the meeting JORDAN indicated that he knew LEWINSKY's mother's fiance, PETER STRAUS.

At one of the December meetings, JORDAN said to LEWINSKY that LEWINSKY was a friend of the President but, "Your problem is that you're in love—don't deny it." LEWINSKY just laughed in reply. At another of the December meetings with JORDAN, they had breakfast at the HYATT first.

On December 22, 1997, LEWINSKY met with JORDAN for about 15 minutes in his office. LEWINSKY showed JORDAN the gifts that she was taking to CARTER's office. LEWINSKY believes that JORDAN knew that she was not turning over all of the gifts to CARTER. JORDAN did not tell LEWINSKY to hold back any of the items. LEWINSKY told JORDAN that she had phone sex with the President and JORDAN replied that it was alright if the President talked to people. JORDAN asked what phone sex was, but LEWINSKY did not explain. JORDAN grunted and nodded a lot during his meetings with LEWINSKY and this sometimes made it difficult to fully understand him. LEWINSKY and JORDAN had a wink and nod understanding that LEWINSKY was having sex with the President. LEWINSKY does not recall whether JORDAN explained the difference between civil and criminal perjury.

On December 22, 1997 LEWINSKY was driven to FRANK CARTER's office by VERNON JORDAN, where she discussed the JONES subpoena with CARTER. The President had previously suggested an affidavit to avoid testifying and LEWINSKY talked to CARTER about it. The President assumed that the affidavit would be to deny something, although she did not discuss specifics with the President. The pattern was to conceal and deny and there was no reason for the President to think that anything had changed. LEWINSKY had always told the President that she would protect him.

At some point in January 1996, CARTER paged LEWINSKY and advised her that the JONES lawyers had subpoenaed the courier records for the gifts that LEWINSKY sent to the White House. LEWINSKY called for the President but he was out of town. LEWINSKY suggested to BETTY CURRIE that the gifts were for CURRIE and in some cases this would be true. The same night, LEWINSKY asked LINDA TRIPP if ISIKOFF had called her, since ISIKOFF had called LEWINSKY earlier. There had been no earlier contacts by ISIKOFF with BETTY CURRIE.

On January 7, 1998, LEWINSKY signed the JONES affidavit which CARTER had prepared. LEWINSKY took the following gifts to CARTER's office: "The Hope and History" book, all Christmas cards, two signed photos, including the LEWINSKY family photo, and signed letters. There was no agreement with the President, JORDAN, or anyone else that LEWINSKY had to sign the JONES affidavit before getting a job in New York. LEWINSKY never demanded a job from JORDAN in return for a favorable affidavit. Neither the President nor JORDAN ever told LEWINSKY that she had to lie. However, LEWINSKY repeated that there had always been an understanding with the President that they would both deny a sexual relationship.

In January 1998, LEWINSKY met with JORDAN, shortly after she signed the JONES affidavit on January 7, 1998. LEWINSKY gave JORDAN a tie and pocket square, and thanked him for his assistance in getting her a job in New York. JORDAN had helped LEWINSKY get the interviews in New York with MCANDREWS AND FORBES, BURSTON MARSTELLER, and REVLON. JORDAN began helping LEWINSKY after she requested his assistance in a meeting at JORDAN's office in early November 1997. JORDAN helped LEWINSKY because LEWINSKY was a friend of the President. JORDAN was the only one in recent times who had delivered what he promised.

When LEWINSKY was subpoenaed on December 19, 1997, she telephonically discussed it in a cryptic manner with LINDA TRIPP, who had already been subpoenaed. LEWINSKY was concerned that TRIPP would testify about LEWINSKY's sexual relationship with the President, inasmuch as LEWINSKY had advised TRIPP of many details in confidence on different occasions. During previous discussions, TRIPP advised LEWINSKY that she would reveal what LEWINSKY had told her if TRIPP had to testify. LEWINSKY and TRIPP had talked about TRIPP's testimony several times.

At some point LEWINSKY typed on her home computer the talking points about how TRIPP should testify. The contents and ideas for the talking points were a summary of things that LEWINSKY and TRIPP had discussed off and on since March 1997. There was no lawyer involved in preparing the talking points, nor did LEWINSKY receive any instructions from the President, JORDAN, CARTER, or anyone from the White House. LEWINSKY gave the talking points to TRIPP at the Pentagon. TRIPP read the points and made positive statements about them by saying, "That's true," and "This is good." TRIPP had indicated that TRIPP wanted to file an affidavit to avoid testifying in the JONES matter.

LEWINSKY did not always tell TRIPP the truth, i.e. LEWINSKY promised that she would not sign the JONES affidavit until she had the New York job lined up. However, when this promise was made to TRIPP the affidavit had already been signed.

LEWINSKY was not aware that TRIPP was taping her telephone calls, but did suspect that TRIPP may have been recording her during their conversation at the RITZ CARLTON HOTEL on January 13, 1998.

LEWINSKY gave a copy of the affidavit to JORDAN. JORDAN made changes to the first draft of the affidavit, but did not retain a copy. These were minor changes proposed by LEWINSKY and agreed to by JORDAN. CARTER prepared three or four drafts of the affidavit until LEWINSKY and CARTER agreed upon one. Minor changes were made. JORDAN never told LEWINSKY to file the affidavit but did discuss her concerns when LEWINSKY called him.

LEWINSKY prepared a written proffer in her own handwriting at the end of January, 1998. Attached is a copy of the proffer marked "Attachment B". The writing took from six to ten hours and was completed in one sitting. LEWINSKY asked her attorneys, BILL GINSBERG and NATE SPEIGHTS, a few questions. The attorneys were in the hallway outside of the conference room at the COSMOS CLUB when she drafted the proffer. LEWINSKY was not on medication. The proffer is generally accurate and LEWINSKY would disavow nothing in it. NATE SPEIGHTS has a copy of the first draft, which is not significantly different from the second draft. LEWINSKY made the following comments concerning specific statements in the proffer:

A. At the end of paragraph two on page two of the proffer LEWINSKY's recollection is that the words "leave Washington, DC" should read "get out of town."
B. In paragraph marked four on page four the following statement appears "In general, Ms. L should say she visited the WH to see Ms. CURRIE and, on occasion when working at the WH, she brought him letters when no one else was around." LEWINSKY commented that these statements were not untrue, but were misleading in that some facts were omitted from this statement. This was the cover story that the President had suggested that she use.
C. At the bottom of page five the wording of the two lines scratched out is "on more than one occasion Ms. L was concerned about signing an affidavit." LEWINSKY's memory is unclear on this point, but LEWINSKY may or may not have said this to JORDAN.
D. In regard to the bottom paragraph on page five, LEWINSKY said that she cannot now remember whether she told JORDAN about her sexual relationship with the President.
E. In regard to the first sentence on page six, "Ms. L made it clear she intended to deny the sexual relationship with the Pres.", LEWINSKY now is not sure of that statement.

F. In paragraph two of page eight the proffer states "Ms. L replied that she and the Pres. had already had an affair minus having sex,—but it included everything else." LEWINSKY said that this statement meant that she never had intercourse with The President.

G. In regard to paragraph ten on page ten, LEWINSKY discussed signing the affidavit denying a sexual relationship with the President. LEWINSKY said that she had never even thought about giving an affidavit wherein she would admit to having sex with the President. Based on the pattern of LEWINSKY's relationship with the President it was assumed that LEWINSKY would not admit any sexual activity. Neither the President nor anyone ever directed LEWINSKY to say anything or to lie, but neither did the President nor anyone else ever tell LEWINSKY not to lie. No one ever used the term "deny, deny" to her. LEWINSKY now has some guilt about getting JORDAN into trouble. LEWINSKY likes JORDAN. LEWINSKY said that her memory when she wrote the proffer in January would have been better than it is today.

LEWINSKY gave the following gifts to the President:

1. A poem written by LEWINSKY on behalf of the White House interns and presented to the President by KARIN ABRAMSON.
2. In November, 1995 a tie delivered to the President by BETTY CURRIE and worn in the Oval Office the day that MADELINE ALBRIGHT was appointed Secretary of State.
3. End of March, 1996 on the day RON BROWN was killed, a tie from BLOOMINGDALE'S.
4. August, 1996 a tie worn by the President in September, 1996 while signing the Defense Bill. LEWINSKY has a signed photo.
5. Fall, 1997 a CALVIN KLEIN tie worn on California trip.
6. March, 1997 a tie worn to a Governor's race rally in Virginia.
7. December 6, 1997 a tie from London.
8. Antique book on PETER THE GREAT from 1802.
9. LEWINSKY's personal copy of "Vox" (no inscription). LEWINSKY replaced her copy of the book at KRAMER BOOKS. Observed in back study of the President on November 13, 1997.
10. A copy of "The Note Book" by NICHOLAS SPARKS.
11. A copy of "Oy Vey," a book of Jewish jokes. Observed in back study of the President on November 13, 1997.
12. A book on golf.
13. An old school book entitled "Disease and Mispresentation" which was about race relations.
14. A BANANA REPUBLIC casual shirt.
15. A wooden letter opener with a frog on the handle. Observed in back study of the President.
16. A plastic pocket frog.
17. A puzzle on golf mysteries.
18. A card game.
19. A copy of "SHERLOCK HOLMES".
20. An antique standing cigar holder on December 28, 1997.
21. A tie on December 28, 1997.
22. A HARROD's mug on December 28, 1997.

23. A hugs and kisses box on December 28, 1997.
24. A penny medallion with a heart cut out.
25. An antique paperweight with a painting of the White House on November 13th, the day HERNREICH testified. Purchased at flea market at 6th and 7th. President ZEDILLO of Mexico at White House. In political collection in cabinet in back dining room.
26. A STARBUCKS mug from Santa Monica. NELVIS observed the President using the mug.
27. A book about THEODORE ROOSEVELT.
28. A pair of sunglasses in Fall, worn by the President in Africa, photo in U.S. News in January, 1998.
29. A pumpkin pin that the President wore in his lapel on Halloween.
30. A care package in March, 1996 when the President injured his leg.

LEWINSKY received the following gifts from the President, some of which have been previously mentioned:

1. A lithograph on February 27 or 28, 1997 (placed in her purse unwrapped)
2. A hatpin on February 27 or 28, 1997 (placed in purse unwrapped).
3. A large BLACK DOG canvas bag from Martha's Vineyard.
4. A large Rockettes blanket from New York.
5. An ugly but sweet pin of the New York skyline.
6. A small box of cherry chocolates.
7. A pair of joke sunglasses.
8. A stuffed animal from BLACK DOG.
9. A marble bear's head from Vancouver.
10. A London pin wrapped in a Casual Corner box.
11. A Shamrock pin.
12. A compact disk of ANNIE LENNOX.
13. Some "Davidoff" cigars.

On December 6, 1997, LEWINSKY spent about 20 or 25 minutes with the President and had gotten into a big fight with him. LEWINSKY had found out that ELEANOR MONDALE was in with the President while she waited at the northwest gate. LEWINSKY had earlier sent a note to the President that she needed to talk with him. Part of LEWINSKY's anger was caused by BETTY CURRIE, who had told LEWINSKY that the President was meeting with lawyers. LEWINSKY left the northwest gate in a very agitated state and called CURRIE from the Corcoran Gallery. LEWINSKY was very "pissed off" and called CURRIE again from her apartment. CURRIE may have paged her before this call. LEWINSKY called the White House again and talked to the President about MONDALE. During the White House argument LEWINSKY went ballistic and the President said that he never had anyone talk to him like LEWINSKY. LEWINSKY also told the President that things were not moving fast enough with VERNON JORDAN. This meant that she had not found a job in New York yet.

LEWINSKY's affidavit in the JONES case was not accurate in the following respects:

A. That LEWINSKY never had a sexual relationship with the President.

B. That LEWINSKY never was alone with the President after she left the White House.

C. That LEWINSKY only saw the President at public functions.

LEWINSKY said that she had heard rumors from The Hill that CHRIS WALKER may have set her up with TIM KEATING. The word was that she was too sexy to work in the White House. JODIE TORKELSON had wanted to fire LEWINSKY. MARSHA SCOTT said that LEWINSKY was called "the Stalker" at the White House.

In regard to the deposition of the President in the JONES case, LEWINSKY said that she had always assumed that the President would deny any sexual relationships, but the President never said it to LEWINSKY. LEWINSKY asked the President if the ten other women on the witness list were from the White House and the President said that they were all women from the old days in Arkansas.

Monica Lewinsky's
Immunity Deal

AGREEMENT

This is an agreement ("Agreement") between Monica S. Lewinsky and the United States, represented by the Office of the Independent Counsel ("OIC"). The terms of the Agreement are as follows:

1. Ms. Lewinsky agrees to cooperate fully with the OIC, including special agents of the Federal Bureau of Investigation ("FBI") and any other law enforcement agencies that the OIC may require. This cooperation will include the following:

A. Ms. Lewinsky will provide truthful, complete and accurate information to the OIC. She will provide, upon request, any documents, records, or other tangible evidence within her custody or control relating to the matters within the OIC's jurisdiction. She will assist the OIC in gaining access to such materials that are not within her custody and control, and she will assist in locating and gaining the cooperation of other individuals who possess relevant information. Ms. Lewinsky will not attempt to protect any person or entity through false information or omission, and she will not attempt falsely to implicate any person or entity.

B. Ms. Lewinsky will testify truthfully before grand juries in this district and elsewhere, at any trials in this district and elsewhere, and in any other executive, military, judicial or congressional proceedings. Pending a final resolution of this matter, neither Ms. Lewinsky nor her agents will make any statements about this matter to witnesses, subjects, or targets of the OIC's investigation, or their agents, or to representatives of the news media, without first obtaining the OIC's approval.

C. Ms. Lewinsky will be fully debriefed concerning her knowledge of and participation in any activities within the OIC's jurisdiction. This debriefing will be conducted by the OIC, including attorneys, law enforcement agents, and representatives of any other institutions as the OIC may require. Ms. Lewinsky will make herself available for any interviews upon reasonable request.

D. Ms. Lewinsky acknowledges that she has orally proffered information to the OIC on July 27, 1998, pursuant to a proffer agreement. Ms. Lewinsky further represents that the statements she made during that proffer session were truthful and accurate to the best of her knowledge. She agrees that during her cooperation, she will truthfully elaborate with respect to these and other subjects.

E. Ms. Lewinsky agrees that, upon the OIC's request, she will waive any evidentiary privileges she may have, except for the attorney-client privilege.

2. If Ms. Lewinsky fully complies with the terms and understandings set forth in this Agreement, the OIC: 1) will not prosecute her for any crimes committed prior to the date of this Agreement arising out of the investigations within the jurisdiction of the OIC: 2) will grant her derivative use immunity within the meaning and subject to the limitations of 18 United States Code, Section 6002, and will not use, in any criminal prosecution against Ms. Lewinsky, testimony or other information provided by her during the course of her debriefing, testimony, or other cooperation pursuant to this agreement, or any information

derived directly or indirectly from such debriefing, testimony, informa- tion, or other cooperation; and 3) will not prosecute her mother, Marsha Lewis, or her father, Bernard Lewinsky, for any offenses which may have been committed by them prior to this Agreement arising out of the facts summarized above, provided that Ms. Lewis and Mr. Lewinsky cooperate with the OIC's investigation and provide complete and truthful information regarding those facts.

3. If the OIC determines that Ms. Lewinsky has intentionally given false, incomplete, or misleading information or testimony, or has otherwise violated any provision of this Agreement, the OIC may move the United States District Court for the District of Columbia which supervised the grand jury investigating this matter for a finding that Ms. Lewinsky has breached this Agreement, and, upon such a finding by the Court, Ms. Lewinsky shall be subject to prosecution for any federal criminal violation of which the OIC has knowledge, including but not limited to perjury, obstruction of justice, and making false statements to govern- ment agencies. In such a prosecution, the OIC may use information provided by Ms. Lewinsky during the course of her cooperation, and such information, including her statements, will be admissible against her in any grand jury, court, or other official proceedings.

4. Pending a final resolution of this matter, the OIC will not make any statements about this Agreement to representatives of the news media.

5. This is the entire agreement between the parties. There are no other agreements, promises or inducements.

If the foregoing terms are acceptable, please sign, and have your client sign, in the spaces indicated below.

Date: _July 28, 1998_

KENNETH W. STARR
Independent Counsel

I have read this entire Agreement and I have discussed it with my attorneys. I freely and voluntarily enter into this Agreement. I understand that if I violate any provisions of this Agreement, the Agreement will be null and void, and I will be subject to federal prosecution as outlined in the Agreement.

Date: _July 28, 1998_

Monica S. Lewinsky

Counsel for Ms. Lewinsky:

Jacob A. Stein

Plato Cacheris

Monica Lewinsky's
Second Interview

1

OFFICE OF THE INDEPENDENT COUNSEL

07/29/98

MONICA S. LEWINSKY was interviewed under the terms of an immunity agreement, a copy of which is attached hereto, in room 616 of the Watergate Hotel, 2650 Virginia Avenue, Northwest, Washington, D.C. Present for the interview were Associate Independent Counsel (AIC) MICHAEL EMMICK, AIC KARIN IMMERGUT, AIC JULIE MYERS, and LEWINSKY's attorney, PRESTON BURTON. Present for portions of the interview was Deputy Independent Counsel (DIC) ROBERT BITTMAN. After being apprised of the official identities of the interviewers, LEWINSKY provided the following information, beginning at approximately 4:35 p.m.

LEWINSKY was shown a copy of two pages from her day-timer calendars from 1996 and 1997. The original, which is a two-sided document, was provided by LEWINSKY to the Office of the Independent Counsel (OIC) earlier in the day. Those two pages contained all the calendar dates in 1996 and 1997. LEWINSKY advised she made notations in the calendar within a week or two of the event, but not as they happened. LEWINSKY advised the notations were made on the calendar prior to the "scandal" becoming news. LEWINSKY advised there were some dates when an event took place that she did not circle for one reason or another.

LEWINSKY explained that the dates circled on the calendar represent days LEWINSKY either saw President WILLIAM JEFFERSON CLINTON or days he called LEWINSKY. LEWINSKY explained that if CLINTON called her at 2 a.m., she may have circled the day before he actually called, because she associated that time of night with the previous day. LEWINSKY advised she may have a similar document from 1995, but she doubts it since her relationship with CLINTON began in late 1995.

The small, handwritten numbers to the side of the calendar for 1997 represent the number of weeks since LEWINSKY last had physical sex with CLINTON. LEWINSKY explained that from April 7, 1996 until February 28, 1997, she had no physical sex with CLINTON. LEWINSKY distinguished physical sex from phone sex. LEWINSKY explained she and CLINTON engaged in phone sex during this period.

LEWINSKY advised she separately kept track of the days prior to the 1996 election and the days since she worked at the White House, but the small numbers on the 1997 day-timer calendar represented days since her last physical sexual contact with CLINTON.

LEWINSKY advised that the other set of numbers below the months represented the number of times LEWINSKY saw CLINTON in a particular month. LEWINSKY advised that LINDA TRIPP suggested LEWINSKY document her contacts with CLINTON because it helped TRIPP understand LEWINSKY's situation.

LEWINSKY advised that she includes kissing when she uses the term "sexual contact." For the purposes of this interview, LEWINSKY differentiated between the kissing and the other sexual contact, without going into the details of the sexual contact.

[For the purposes of this FD-302, unless otherwise noted, physical sexual contact means more than kissing.]

LEWINSKY advised that on January 7, 1996, CLINTON called LEWINSKY for the first time at home and at her office. LEWINSKY added that on January 7, 1996, she had physical sexual contact with CLINTON. On January 15, 1996, CLINTON called LEWINSKY at her office and at her home. LEWINSKY advised on January 21, 1996 she received a phone call from CLINTON and later had physical sexual contact with him. On January 28, 1996, LEWINSKY was in San Francisco, California. When she returned to her office at the White House, she checked her caller identification feature and saw that CLINTON had called her from the Oval Office.

[LEWINSKY advised that calls from CLINTON when he was in the Oval Office would show up on the caller identification feature as "POTUS." Calls from the White House residence were indicated by a "*."]

On January 30, 1996, there was a going away party for PAT GRIFFIN. LEWINSKY advised this was the first time CLINTON called LEWINSKY at her office during working hours. CLINTON asked LEWINSKY to come see him after the party, but LEWINSKY told him she did not think that would be a good idea. LEWINSKY advised she and CLINTON agreed they would not speak to each other at the party so that others did not get any "wrong" ideas. LEWINSKY explained that in a photograph taken at the going away party, she stood as far away from CLINTON as possible for the same reason. LEWINSKY advised she and CLINTON did not get together on this date.

On February 4, 1996, CLINTON and LEWINSKY engaged in physical sexual contact. On February 7 or 8, 1996, while signing the Telecommunications Bill, CLINTON wore one of the ties LEWINSKY had given him for the first time. LEWINSKY advised CLINTON called her that evening and they engaged in phone sex.

On February 19, 1996, LEWINSKY advised CLINTON broke off their relationship for the first time. LEWINSKY advised she saw CLINTON in person and he said he was feeling guilty about continuing their relationship, so he wanted to break it off.

On March 26, 1996, CLINTON called LEWINSKY in her office at the White House from the White House Residence. LEWINSKY advised CLINTON called from the Residence for the first time, to her knowledge. CLINTON asked LEWINSKY if the caller identification showed anything and she told him it was a star.

On March 29, 1996, CLINTON called LEWINSKY at her office in the White House.

On March 31, 1996, CLINTON and LEWINSKY engaged in physical sexual contact.

On April 7, 1996, CLINTON and LEWINSKY engaged in physical sexual contact. On April 12, 1996, CLINTON called LEWINSKY twice, once during the day and once at night. LEWINSKY advised that during one of these telephone calls, CLINTON told LEWINSKY he would have her back at the White House after the election.

On April 22, 1996, CLINTON called LEWINSKY, but they did not engage in phone sex. LEWINSKY advised she was upset because she hated her job. On April 29, 1996, CLINTON called LEWINSKY at approximately 3 a.m. LEWINSKY advised this call may have actually taken place on April 30th. LEWINSKY advised this was the first time CLINTON left a message on LEWINSKY's answering machine. LEWINSKY recalled that on the message, CLINTON said "aw shucks."

On May 2, 1996, LEWINSKY attended a Saxophone Club event and saw CLINTON. LEWINSKY explained she was very upset because CLINTON had promised to call her that weekend, but did not. CLINTON called LEWINSKY that evening and said he could tell LEWINSKY was upset. CLINTON apologized for not calling LEWINSKY and said that he was sick that weekend. CLINTON also said that if LEWINSKY did not like her job at the Pentagon, he would try to get LEWINSKY a job on the campaign.

LEWINSKY advised CLINTON may have called her on May 6, 1996. LEWINSKY advised that on May 16, 1996, the night Admiral BOORDA committed suicide, CLINTON called LEWINSKY. LEWINSKY tried to initiate phone sex, but CLINTON was not in the mood. The next week, on the day of ▆▆▆▆ funeral, CLINTON came to the Pentagon. Later that night, CLINTON called LEWINSKY and they engaged in phone sex. LEWINSKY advised she thinks the date of the funeral was May 21, 1996.

LEWINSKY advised that, because of a pattern that had developed, LEWINSKY would expect CLINTON to call her when HILLARY RODHAM CLINTON was out of town.

On May 31, 1996, LEWINSKY was out of town and CLINTON left a message on her home telephone answering machine. LEWINSKY thinks CLINTON may have been calling about LEWINSKY coming to a radio address. On June 5, 1996, CLINTON called LEWINSKY in the early evening, inquiring about LEWINSKY and her family attending a radio address, as had been discussed on previous occasions. CLINTON told LEWINSKY he would say something to BETTY CURRIE about arranging the attendance of LEWINSKY's family at the radio address.

The following morning, CURRIE called LEWINSKY and said there was no radio address that week, but a tour would be arranged for LEWINSKY's family.

On June 13, 1996, LEWINSKY and her family attended the arrival ceremony of the President of Ireland, which was held at Ft. Myer, Virginia. CLINTON made a comment about LEWINSKY's hat. On June 14, 1996, LEWINSKY attended a radio address with her family.

On June 23, 1996, CLINTON called LEWINSKY and the two engaged in phone sex. On July 5, 1996, CLINTON called LEWINSKY and the two engaged in phone sex. On July 19, 1996, CLINTON called LEWINSKY at 6:30 a.m. and the two engaged in phone sex. CLINTON exclaimed "good morning!" to the best of LEWINSKY's knowledge after having an orgasm.

LEWINSKY then went down a list of other dates where there was either physical and/or phone contact with CLINTON. LEWINSKY distinguished those contacts that include sex and those that did not. LEWINSKY advised that all telephone calls included some conversation that was not of a sexual nature. The remaining dates in 1996 where LEWINSKY had contact with CLINTON were as follows:

July 28	phone call
August 4	phone sex
August 24	phone call
September 5	phone call, maybe phone sex
September 10	Clinton left a message on LEWINSKY's answering machine.
September 30	phone call
October 22	phone sex
October 23	phone call; earlier that evening, LEWINSKY saw CLINTON at an event related to the Senate.

LEWINSKY advised that there was no contact between her and CLINTON between October 23, 1996 and December 2, 1996.

December 2	phone sex
December 17	LEWINSKY saw CLINTON at some sort of official function.
December 18	phone call
December 30	CLINTON left a message on LEWINSKY's answering machine.

1997

January 12	phone call
February 8	phone sex
February 28	physical contact, including more than just kissing.
March 12	CLINTON calls LEWINSKY for approximately three minutes at work.
March 29	physical contact including more than just kissing.
April 26	phone call; LEWINSKY does not think the two engaged in phone sex.

39

May 17	phone call
May 18	phone call
May 24	LEWINSKY visits and CLINTON breaks up with her. LEWINSKY describes this day as "D-Day."
July 4	physical contact; CLINTON kissed LEWINSKY on the neck.
July 8	LEWINSKY was in Madrid, Spain at the same time CLINTON was. LEWINSKY saw CLINTON at the Ambassador's house. LEWINSKY and CLINTON make eye contact at the embassy.
July 14	LEWINSKY visits CLINTON at the White House. No sexual contact.
July 15	phone call
July 24	LEWINSKY visits, but no sexual contact
August 1	phone call
August 16	LEWINSKY and CLINTON kissed.
September 30	phone call, maybe phone sex
October 9	very long phone call, no sex
October 11	visit; no sexual contact
October 23	phone call
October 30	phone call
November 12	phone call, maybe phone sex
November 13	very brief visit with CLINTON. Mexican President ZEDILLO at the White House.
December 5	LEWINSKY saw CLINTON at an official function.
December 6	LEWINSKY visited with CLINTON.
December 28	In person visit, only kissed.

KATHLEEN WILLEY

Prior to MICHAEL ISIKOFF interviewing LINDA TRIPP in the spring of 1997, TRIPP mentioned KATHLEEN WILLEY's story to LEWINSKY. LEWINSKY advised TRIPP did not mention WILLEY by name at first. LEWINSKY advised TRIPP's story seemed to change over time. TRIPP may have told LEWINSKY about WILLEY's name prior to ISIKOFF interviewing TRIPP. TRIPP told LEWINSKY about ISIKOFF's visit to TRIPP at TRIPP's office.

TRIPP told LEWINSKY that WILLEY was certainly not sexually harassed. TRIPP told LEWINSKY about the ISIKOFF visit the same day of the visit or the next one. At that point, TRIPP said that WILLEY called TRIPP that night.

LEWINSKY urged TRIPP to let someone in the White House know about the ISIKOFF visit. TRIPP said that she would only be comfortable speaking with NANCY HERNREICH or BRUCE LINDSEY. TRIPP said that, during the Whitewater hearings, she was told by her attorney not to talk to LINDSEY. LEWINSKY urged TRIPP to page LINDSEY. TRIPP advised that LINDSEY did not return the pages or telephone messages. LEWINSKY advised that she thinks TRIPP's ego was deflated and she seemed insulted.

In early summer, ISIKOFF contacted TRIPP again. ISIKOFF called TRIPP to ask her to go on the record with her version of the WILLEY matter.

LEWINSKY advised she considered saying something to CLINTON about TRIPP on May 24, 1997, but decided not to. On July 4, 1997, LEWINSKY mentioned to CLINTON that she had a friend who knew something about WILLEY.

LEWINSKY explained that July 4, 1997 was her most emotional visit with CLINTON. LEWINSKY advised the visit lasted more than one hour. The majority of the visit was spent with LEWINSKY and CLINTON being emotionally intimate. Looking back, LEWINSKY is not sure if CLINTON was sincere during this visit. LEWINSKY questions a lot of things since the "scandal" broke. LEWINSKY does not think CLINTON was acting on July 4th, because if he was, he would be the greatest actor in the world. LEWINSKY does not think CLINTON would have fought with her at the beginning of the visit if he was acting. The fight was about a letter LEWINSKY had sent CLINTON the day before, indicating she would tell her parents about their relationship if CLINTON did not help her with a job.

At the end of the visit, LEWINSKY asked CLINTON if he knew KATH-LEEN WILLEY. CLINTON advised he did. LEWINSKY said she had a friend at the Pentagon who had talked to ISIKOFF, who was looking into allegations that CLINTON had sexually harassed a woman who once worked at the White House. CLINTON advised the story was ludicrous. CLINTON seemed surprised about LEWINSKY's friend at the Pentagon.

CLINTON said that WILLEY called HERNREICH earlier that week and was asking about ISIKOFF and WILLEY wanted to know how to get out of it. LEWINSKY told CLINTON that WILLEY may have been covering her tracks. LEWINSKY did not use TRIPP's name. LEWINSKY advised she brought this subject up because she thought CLINTON should know about it. LEWINSKY thought maybe CLINTON could get WILLEY a job to make her happy.

LEWINSKY told CLINTON that her friend once worked at the White House. CLINTON did not ask for TRIPP's name. LEWINSKY was not offended by the WILLEY story because she did not believe it. LEWINSKY said her friend had tried to get in touch with BRUCE LINDSEY, but he did not return her pages to him.

LEWINSKY advised that WILLEY may have sent CLINTON a "mixed signal." LEWINSKY does not believe the PAULA JONES story either. LEWINSKY advised CLINTON and JONES may have had a consensual relationship. LEWINSKY advised she did not get jealous of CLINTON's relationships with other women, so long as they pre-dated her relationship with CLINTON.

LEWINSKY explained how the July 4, 1997 meeting was arranged. LEWINSKY was "pissed" that CLINTON had not responded to her issues related to her job. When LEWINSKY met with MARSHA SCOTT and SCOTT did not know who LEWINSKY was, LEWINSKY was annoyed. LEWINSKY was very frustrated so she sent CLINTON a note.

LEWINSKY advised she wrote the letter on July 3 and delivered it to

41

CURRIE the same day. LEWINSKY advised that the letter had a cold tone. For instance, the letter began "Dear Sir." LEWINSKY advised she did not think the letter was threatening, but when she saw CLINTON on July 4, he indicated he felt it was. CLINTON asked LEWINSKY if she knew that it was against the law to threaten the President of the United States.

LEWINSKY advised that the first time she mentioned the possibility of moving to New York was in this July 3rd letter to CLINTON. LEWINSKY advised she gave the letter to CURRIE at the Northwest gate. LEWINSKY advised the letter was handwritten and mentioned LEWINSKY's mother. LEWINSKY advised TRIPP had no input as to the contents of this letter. LEWINSKY advised that at the end of this letter, she expressed more emotions and even mentioned that she would give CLINTON one more chance.

LEWINSKY advised this letter was the meanest one she had ever sent to CLINTON. LEWINSKY advised the purpose of the letter was to show CLINTON how lucky he was that she was the way she was and that some people in her position, who had had an affair with him, would have played "hard ball" with him. LEWINSKY advised the letter was approximately two to three lined pages.

LEWINSKY advised that on most occasions she handwrote her notes, but she did type some. LEWINSKY advised that she sometimes prepared rough drafts of letters she eventually sent to CLINTON. LEWINSKY advised she often times bought two cards and used one to prepare a draft so that, in the event she made a mistake, she would have a duplicate card available to send.

CURRIE called LEWINSKY on the evening of July 3rd. LEWINSKY asked if CURRIE had given the package to CLINTON. CURRIE said she had and told LEWINSKY to be at the White House at 9 a.m. on July 4th.

LEWINSKY advised that CLINTON said he read the first line of the letter because CURRIE looked upset when she delivered it. CLINTON told LEWINSKY he threw the letter away after reading the first line. LEWINSKY thinks CLINTON read the whole letter. LEWINSKY believes CLINTON is the type of person who would lie about reading the letter. LEWINSKY believes CURRIE is not the type to read it.

LEWINSKY does not believe that CURRIE opened the letters LEWINSKY sent to CLINTON through CURRIE. LEWINSKY advised she typically would send things to CLINTON through CURRIE. LEWINSKY would place the item intended for CLINTON in an envelope marked either "BC" or "Mr. P." LEWINSKY said she would send that item in a larger envelope, which was addressed to CURRIE. LEWINSKY usually sent some sort of gift or card to CURRIE in the larger envelope.

When LEWINSKY first arrived at the Oval Office on July 4th at 9 a.m., LEWINSKY told CLINTON someone was outside the Oval Office, so he suggested they move to the study. While in the study, she saw a White House gardener standing outside. LEWINSKY advised the gardener was standing sideways, so she is not sure if he saw LEWINSKY.

LEWINSKY advised she then left for Madrid soon after July 4. While in Madrid, LEWINSKY went to the United States embassy or the ambassador's house for an official function. LEWINSKY saw CLINTON when she first entered the function. CLINTON was standing in a hall speaking with some of his aides, including MIKE McCURRY. When CLINTON saw LEWINSKY, they made eye contact and all the people CLINTON was speaking with turned and saw LEWINSKY.

LEWINSKY believes this is the only time she was in the same room with BRUCE LINDSEY.

On July 14, 1997, LEWINSKY returned from Bulgaria, the last leg of her European trip. LEWINSKY was awakened at 7:30 p.m. by a telephone call from CURRIE. CURRIE advised that CLINTON was out golfing, but he wanted to see or call LEWINSKY later. LEWINSKY thinks CLINTON assumed she was back from Europe because he was. LEWINSKY advised she travelled with Secretary of Defense WILLIAM COHEN's group, but does not think CLINTON kept track of those types of details.

At approximately 8:30 p.m., CURRIE called LEWINSKY again and asked if LEWINSKY could come to the White House at approximately 9:30 p.m. so CLINTON could see LEWINSKY. CURRIE cleared LEWINSKY into the White House and the two spoke for a few minutes.

CLINTON then came out of the Oval Office and took LEWINSKY into NANCY HERNREICH's office. LEWINSKY advised CLINTON was very cold and distant at this meeting. CLINTON sat on a chair in HERNREICH's office while LEWINSKY sat on a sofa.

CLINTON asked LEWINSKY if the woman she mentioned on July 4th was LINDA TRIPP. LEWINSKY responded that it was. CLINTON said that there was a paper called the "Sludge Report" that mentioned KATHLEEN WILLEY. CLINTON asked LEWINSKY if LEWINSKY had told TRIPP that WILLEY had called HERNREICH.

LEWINSKY advised that at this point, she was not sure how to answer. LEWINSKY advised she had to watch her lie because she was not sure what CLINTON's reaction would be to the truth. LEWINSKY advised that the problem was that WILLEY called HERNREICH and was upset that ISIKOFF knew about WILLEY's previous call to HERNREICH. CLINTON said the only people who knew about WILLEY's first call to HERNREICH were WILLEY, HERNREICH, CLINTON and LEWINSKY. LEWINSKY told CLINTON she (LEWINSKY) must have told TRIPP.

LEWINSKY did not want to think that TRIPP told ISIKOFF about the WILLEY telephone call. LEWINSKY told CLINTON that TRIPP was a big supporter of his and that she had big pictures of CLINTON in her office. CLINTON asked LEWINSKY if she trusted TRIPP. LEWINSKY said she did. CLINTON also asked LEWINSKY if LEWINSKY confided in TRIPP about CLINTON's relationship with LEWINSKY. LEWINSKY said she had not.

CLINTON told LEWINSKY to tell TRIPP to try to get in touch with

LINDSEY again. LEWINSKY would not characterize CLINTON as "emphatic" in this request. LEWINSKY advised the interviewers if LINDSEY made the initial contact with TRIPP, there might be records reflecting that contact. CLINTON told LEWINSKY to call CURRIE the next day to see whether or not LEWINSKY was successful in getting TRIPP to contact LINDSEY. LEWINSKY did not consider TRIPP's knowledge about the WILLEY incident to be that significant because TRIPP had no first hand knowledge about what occured between CLINTON and WILLEY. LEWINSKY advised that CLINTON left her in HERNREICH's office so he could take a conference call with his attorneys. CLINTON returned from his conference call. LEWINSKY advised she spent approximately twenty-five minutes total with CLINTON during this visit. LEWINSKY advised she did not leave the White House until approximately 11:30 p.m. LEWINSKY and CLINTON spent approximately 25 minutes together on this occasion.

LEWINSKY thought it was safe for TRIPP to call LINDSEY. LEWINSKY felt it would look more sinister for LINDSEY to call TRIPP. LEWINSKY was under the impression that WILLEY was not part of the PAULA JONES suit.

LEWINSKY felt bad that she had told TRIPP about the WILLEY call. LEWINSKY felt responsible and felt she wanted to please the President so she was willing to contact TRIPP. CLINTON did not mention TRIPP getting in touch with BOB BENNETT during this call.

The following day, on July 15th, LEWINSKY tried to get information from TRIPP, including the names of the different people at the White House whom TRIPP had spoken to. LEWINSKY knew TRIPP spoke to an IRENE Last Name Unknown (LNU) and a KATE LNU, both of whom worked at the White House. LEWINSKY telephoned CURRIE later that day to let CURRIE know that LEWINSKY had information for CLINTON.

CLINTON called LEWINSKY later that night. LEWINSKY advised CLINTON was in a "shitty" mood. LEWINSKY went through the information she had for CLINTON regarding WILLEY and TRIPP. LEWINSKY advised she and CLINTON did not speak for long as CLINTON was in a bad mood.

LEWINSKY advised that at some point which LEWINSKY believes was after July 24th, she convinced TRIPP to call LINDSEY. In a Thursday evening telephone conversation, TRIPP told LEWINSKY that TRIPP was ready to meet with BOB BENNETT, as suggested to TRIPP by BRUCE LINDSEY. TRIPP said she made the arrangements for noon the following day. TRIPP told LEWINSKY she was nervous.

TRIPP was concerned that her hair did not look right, so she tried to make an appointment at ILEO. This not being successful, TRIPP made one at a salon named "3300 M Street." LEWINSKY paid for TRIPP's haircut. TRIPP was afraid BENNETT was going to say something mean to her, so she moved the appointment with BENNETT back to 3:30 p.m.

TRIPP told LEWINSKY that, before seeing BENNETT, TRIPP thought she should see TRIPP's attorney, KIRBY BEHRE. TRIPP advised that BEHRE forbade her to see BENNETT, so she did not.

LEWINSKY thinks she called CURRIE to tell her about TRIPP, but LEWINSKY did not contact CLINTON directly.

LEWINSKY advised that she thought TRIPP was naive to talk to ISIKOFF and that it could be bad for her career. LEWINSKY thought LINDSEY would curb what TRIPP said to ISIKOFF, after LINDSEY spoke to TRIPP. LEWINSKY advised that when TRIPP first mentioned ISIKOFF, TRIPP was upset. TRIPP was friendly with WILLEY and even helped her draft letters to the President. TRIPP said there was always a possibility WILLEY made her story up. LEWINSKY thought TRIPP was on the "right" team.

When the Newsweek article was released, TRIPP was on vacation. LEWINSKY advised that the quote from TRIPP in the Newsweek article was more than TRIPP had told LEWINSKY.

After the Newsweek article that included BENNETT "slamming" TRIPP, TRIPP said she would write a "tell-all" book if she was fired. LEWINSKY said it was silly. LEWINSKY did not think BENNETT's comments were too bad. LEWINSKY advised TRIPP "scared the shit" out of LEWINSKY when TRIPP mentioned writing a book.

Prior to August 11th, LEWINSKY anonymously called BEHRE and said that TRIPP had been misquoted. LEWINSKY asked if BEHRE was going to release a statement on TRIPP's behalf, responding to the BENNETT quote. LEWINSKY suggested BEHRE call the White House. LEWINSKY thought this would help TRIPP keep her job.

On August 14th, the Washington Times had an article about BEHRE's statement on TRIPP's behalf. Throughout 1997, TRIPP mentioned being deposed in the JONES case. TRIPP said that BEHRE said she would not have to be deposed.

Sometime after August of 1997, TRIPP mentioned something about her attorney being in touch with JONES's attorneys. LEWINSKY advised she does not have a vivid memory, but TRIPP would bring up the JONES case from time to time.

LEWINSKY spoke about her friendship with TRIPP to NEYSA ERBLAND and KATHRYN ALLDAY DAVIS. LEWINSKY's mother did not know much about LEWINSKY's relationship with TRIPP. LEWINSKY tried to stay away from the WILLEY/JONES issue when speaking with CLINTON.

LEWINSKY advised that she did not have much contact with TRIPP in mid- to late November since LEWINSKY and TRIPP were fighting and LEWINSKY had been out of the country during part of this time.

Sometime in the second or third week of December, TRIPP mentioned that she was subpoenaed in the JONES case. TRIPP did not mention when she received the subpoena. This was the first time TRIPP said she would "rat" on LEWINSKY. From this point on, LEWINSKY became more circumspect when dealing with TRIPP.

LEWINSKY advised that, during a conversation with TRIPP in December, TRIPP said that one of the reasons for TRIPP telling the truth about LEWINSKY was that BEHRE would know TRIPP was lying. LEWINSKY asked TRIPP how BEHRE would know she was lying. TRIPP advised that she had written the whole story about LEWINSKY and WILLEY and given it to BEHRE in a sealed envelope, and told BEHRE not to read it unless something happened to TRIPP. LEWINSKY advised LEWINSKY went "ape shit" when she heard this.

LEWINSKY advised she tried to protect TRIPP from getting deposed to protect LEWINSKY, which, in turn, protected CLINTON.

TRIPP's deposition was scheduled for December 18th, but was postponed because WILLEY was having back surgery.

LEWINSKY advised that CLINTON told LEWINSKY she was on the JONES witness list in a telephone conversation on December 17th. LEWINSKY advised she was in New York the previous day for job interviews. LEWINSKY was subpoenaed on December 19, 1997.

"TALKING POINTS"

LEWINSKY advised that, in late December 1997, she was trying to figure things out regarding TRIPP's deposition. LEWINSKY did not return TRIPP's calls. On January 1, 1998, LEWINSKY left a message on TRIPP's answering machine. LEWINSKY advised she was at an impasse as to what to do. LEWINSKY was shocked that TRIPP would reveal LEWINSKY.

LEWINSKY advised it made no sense to her for anyone to make the leap from PAULA JONES to LEWINSKY. LEWINSKY thinks TRIPP was jealous about LEWINSKY's job opportunities in New York. TRIPP wanted LEWINSKY to get a good job, but she was also jealous of LEWINSKY.

LEWINSKY advised that the main reason she looked for a job in New York was because TRIPP said that "KATE at NSC" said LEWINSKY would never get a job in the White House, and if she did, she certainly would not have a blue pass. LEWINSKY advised she separately told CLINTON and KEN BACON she wanted to move to New York because of her mother moving there. LEWINSKY advised that "KATE at NSC" told TRIPP that jobs were created at the White House six days a week. LEWINSKY mentioned STEVEN GOODIN's girlfriend got a job at the White House. LEWINSKY advised TRIPP told LEWINSKY this in an October 6, 1997 telephone call.

On January 9, 1998, LEWINSKY called TRIPP from New York. LEWINSKY was wary of TRIPP, so she said she was calling from a pay phone, but she was actually calling from her mother's apartment. TRIPP said that NORMA ASNES said TRIPP should get a job in public relations in New York. TRIPP told LEWINSKY that TRIPP's Indian friend goes to a psychic and asked the psychic about her friends. The psychic said a friend of her's, whom TRIPP interpreted to be TRIPP, was in imminent danger about what she would say.

During this conversation, TRIPP asked LEWINSKY if LEWINSKY had spoken to CURRIE, JORDAN or CLINTON. LEWINSKY told TRIPP she had not spoken with them from mid-December forward. LEWINSKY told TRIPP she did not care about not speaking with them. TRIPP asked what LEWINSKY was going to do about her deposition. LEWINSKY mentioned her affidavit. TRIPP told LEWINSKY to get a job before LEWINSKY signed it. LEWINSKY did not let TRIPP know that she had already signed the affidavit.

LEWINSKY explained that TRIPP did not like LEWINSKY to exhibit independence. LEWINSKY advised that on November 22, 1997, LEWINSKY wanted to phone CURRIE to apologize, but TRIPP did not want her to. TRIPP and LEWINSKY got into fight over this issue.

LEWINSKY did not want TRIPP to know about all the help LEWINSKY got from VERNON JORDAN. On January 13th or 14th, LEWINSKY called TRIPP at work. During this conversation, TRIPP said that BEHRE did not want TRIPP to sign an affidavit and would not let her commit perjury. LEWINSKY told TRIPP to call ASNES, who could recommend a good "Democratic" attorney.

LEWINSKY told TRIPP that the purpose of the affidavit was to avoid being deposed. LEWINSKY advised that one does this by giving a portion of the whole story, so the attorneys do not think you have anything of relevance to their case. LEWINSKY advised she and TRIPP went through the different things to say in an affidavit. LEWINSKY went through the WILLEY story with TRIPP, including who saw it, that the story could be false, and that WILLEY could have smeared her own lipstick and untucked her own blouse.

LEWINSKY agreed to meet TRIPP on January 13, 1998, because she felt TRIPP had changed her mind about disclosing LEWINSKY's relationship.

On January 14, 1998, LEWINSKY was supposed to take TRIPP to see BEHRE, but the plans changed and LEWINSKY drove TRIPP to TRIPP's car, which was parked at a Metro station. Prior to meeting TRIPP, LEWINSKY sat down at her computer on January 14th and typed out the "Talking Points" in one sitting. LEWINSKY typed the "Talking Points" the same day she gave them to TRIPP.

LEWINSKY advised page one of the "Talking Points" begins with "you are not sure. . . ." LEWINSKY advised these were to be TRIPP's talking points for her meeting with BEHRE. The last part of page one was in reference to TRIPP providing BEHRE a written account of the WILLEY and LEWINSKY matters.

Page two of the "Talking Points" was written out because LEWINSKY thought she would only have a few minutes with TRIPP, so she wanted to have an outline of points for TRIPP to make in an affidavit.

LEWINSKY advised the "Talking Points" were a combination of things TRIPP said to LEWINSKY and TRIPP's public statements. Page two of the "Talking Points" was based on what was in LEWINSKY's affidavit.

Page three of the "Talking Points" was what TRIPP could give to BEHRE for BEHRE to draft an affidavit. LEWINSKY advised she printed the "Talking Points" on her printer in her apartment. LEWINSKY advised she did not save the "Talking Points." LEWINSKY advised she did not save them on her computer for a reason. LEWINSKY was trying to be circumspect about JONES related matters at that point. LEWINSKY thought the JONES' attorneys had tapped her phones. LEWINSKY thought at one point that DEBBIE SCHIFF had given JONES' attorneys LEWINSKY's name so SCHIFF would not have to testify.

LEWINSKY advised the goal of an affidavit is to be as benign as possible, so as to avoid being deposed.

LEWINSKY advised that, looking back, one can see how TRIPP's various public statements about the WILLEY incident are used throughout the "Talking Points." LEWINSKY advised she did not refer to TRIPP's public statements to draft the "Talking Points."

LEWINSKY advised that TRIPP read the "Talking Points" when LEWINSKY gave them to her. TRIPP was thankful to LEWINSKY for them. LEWINSKY advised the "Talking Points" were not a collaborative effort with TRIPP. LEWINSKY typed them up on her own, with no assistance from anyone.

EVIDENCE

LEWINSKY was shown a copy of the Federal Bureau of Investigation's (FBI's) inventory of items taken from her apartment during a consensual search on January 22, 1998. LEWINSKY advised that a note found in her apartment referring to LEWINSKY going to the White House was written on October 11, 1997. LEWINSKY explained to her aunt that LEWINSKY was to meet LEWINSKY's brother in New York, and LEWINSKY would be taking a plane there after going to the White House in the morning.

TIPPER GORE's book has a photograph of CLINTON wearing a tie LEWINSKY gave him. LEWINSKY's father may have purchased the book for her.

LEWINSKY has never been on Air Force One.

The "Saxophone Club" is an offshoot of the Democratic National Committee. LEWINSKY advised that people who donate less than $200 can belong. LEWINSKY was a member.

LEWINSKY advised she attended a cocktail party which was held in New York prior to CLINTON's fiftieth birthday celebration. LEWINSKY purchased a $250 ticket, but when LEWINSKY got to the door, she did not have a reservation. LEWINSKY got assistance from JENNIFER SCULLY, whom LEWINSKY met through WALTER KAYE. LEWINSKY, who was wearing a red dress, saw CLINTON on the rope line and he hugged her and said he liked her dress.

CLINTON gave LEWINSKY the "BLACK DOG" coffee mug.

CLINTON gave LEWINSKY an ANNIE LENNOX compact disc.

LEWINSKY bought the book "Presidential Sex" because of her relationship with CLINTON.

LEWINSKY sent a letter to CLINTON, similar to the one referencing the "New Deal" found in her apartment on January 22, 1998.

The American Express bill of WILLIAM ARBAUGH was sent to LEWINSKY by mistake.

The $10,000 credit card payment LEWINSKY's mother made had nothing to do with LEWINSKY.

LEWINSKY had a spiral notebook in which she documented the early part of her relationship with CLINTON. LEWINSKY advised the notebook was there on January 22, 1998, but not taken during the search. LEWINSKY saw the notebook after the search, but is not sure where it is now.

The notebook is not dated. The first ten pages relate to her relationship with CLINTON. LEWINSKY advised she did not keep a diary.

The blue dress LEWINSKY presented to the OIC was the same one she wore during her "Birthday" picture with CLINTON. LEWINSKY also wore the dress on February 28, 1997, the first time her sexual contact with CLINTON resulted in him ejaculating in her presence. After engaging in sexual contact with CLINTON, LEWINSKY went to MCCORMICK & SCHMICK'S restaurant and then took the dress off when she got home.

The next time LEWINSKY went to wear the dress, she noticed some faint tiny dots, which could be stains of CLINTON's semen, which could have gotten on the dress while LEWINSKY and CLINTON were hugging. LEWINSKY thought it was funny, so she put it back in the closet.

LEWINSKY showed the dress to TRIPP, who advised LEWINSKY to place the dress in a zip-lock bag and put it in a safe deposit box. LEWINSKY did not save the dress as a "trophy." LEWINSKY said she planned to get the dress cleaned before she wore it again.

That Thanksgiving, LEWINSKY told TRIPP she was going to wear the dress. TRIPP told her not to. TRIPP said LEWINSKY looked fat in the dress.

Sometime after LEWINSKY was subpoenaed on December 19th, she moved the dress to her mother's apartment in New York, with the audio cassette tapes containing CLINTON's answering machine messages to LEWINSKY.

CLINTON gave LEWINSKY the "Vancouver bear" on December 28, 1997. CLINTON told LEWINSKY the bear represented strength, and LEWINSKY would have to be strong. LEWINSKY associated that comment with her July 4th conversation with CLINTON. LEWINSKY advised there was never a question she was going to deny her relationship with CLINTON, so she did not associate the bear with that.

The interview ended at 7:41 p.m.

Monica Lewinsky's
Third Interview

1

OFFICE OF THE INDEPENDENT COUNSEL

07/30/98

MONICA S. LEWINSKY was interviewed pursuant to an immunity agreement between the Office of the Independent Counsel (OIC), LEWINSKY, and her attorneys. Present for the interview were Associate Independent Counsel (AIC) MICHAEL EMMICK, AIC KARIN IMMERGUT, AIC MARY ANNE WIRTH, and AIC JULIE MYERS. Representing LEWINSKY were attorneys SYDNEY HOFFMAN and PRESTON BURTON of the law offices of PLATO CACHERIS. AIC WIRTH was not present for the late morning and early afternoon portions of the interview. The interview was conducted in Room 616 of the WATERGATE HOTEL, commencing at 9:40 a.m. and ending at 6:15 p.m. LEWINSKY, a white female, born July 23, 1973, provided the following information:

After the scandal broke and the "talking points" were discussed in the media, LEWINSKY realized that the quotes made by LINDA TRIPP in the Newsweek article on August 11, 1997, and in the article in the Washington Times on August 14, 1997, included concepts that LEWINSKY and TRIPP had discussed. These concepts helped influence the contents of the talking points, which were written by LEWINSKY. LEWINSKY recognized that the above mentioned public statements by LINDA TRIPP closely resembled the talking points. These ideas of TRIPP, that were publicly espoused, pointed to the likelihood that KATHLEEN WILLEY's story was more untrue than factual. TRIPP made varying statements in these articles.

During the meeting between LEWINSKY and the President on December 28, 1997, the President said something to the effect of, "That woman from the summer got you into this." By this, LEWINSKY understood that the President meant LINDA TRIPP, who had been quoted in the above articles. On this occasion, a member of the U.S. Secret Service (USSS) could have observed the President hugging LEWINSKY through the glass, but LEWINSKY is not sure.

LEWINSKY has not heard any of the tapes that TRIPP made of their conversations.

LEWINSKY provided a copy of a two-sided set of calendars for the years 1993, 1994 and 1995 entitled, "1994 Diary, FiloFax." Certain dates are circled on each calendar. On the 1995 portion of the calendar, LEWINSKY circled the dates relating to encounters with ANDY BLEILER.

LEWINSKY said that in March 1998, the ████ matter had arisen, and since she was very sensitive about it, LEWINSKY did not wish to discuss ████████ at this time.

LEWINSKY had created a matrix by spreadsheet in the Fall of 1997 on the Excel program of her computer at the Pentagon, at the request of LINDA TRIPP. This was created on her work computer when her boss, KEN BACON, was out of town. The matrix consisted of the dates of events, telephone calls, and personal meetings with the President. No names or identifying data were typed on the matrix. LEWINSKY made one, or possibly two copies, but did not save the matrix on her computer. LEWINSKY showed or read one copy to TRIPP and believes that she destroyed any other copy. LEWINSKY had first begun confiding in TRIPP in November 1996, at which time TRIPP urged LEWINSKY to go back to the White House to work. TRIPP advised LEWINSKY that she was the kind of woman the President would like and an affair with the President would be a neat thing to tell her grandkids. TRIPP kept hounding LEWINSKY until LEWINSKY finally said, "Look, I've already had an affair with him and it's over."

The President called LEWINSKY between 12:00 p.m. and 2:00 p.m. on January 7, 1996, which was during the snowstorm. He asked LEWINSKY to go to her office in the White House, where he again called her. While chatting, LEWINSKY asked if the President wanted some company, and the President replied that he did. Plans were made that LEWINSKY would go to the Oval Office and the door would be left open.

Upon arriving between 3:00 p.m. and 5:00 p.m., LEWINSKY, who was carrying some papers, saw uniformed USSS Officer LEWIS FOX standing in front of the Oval Office. FOX was probably standing with a USSS plain clothes agent. FOX was not there when LEWINSKY departed. At some point LEWINSKY gave a box of LADY GODIVA chocolates to FOX.

An unidentified USSS plain clothes agent, who usually worked on Sunday afternoons, was present on two different occasions when LEWINSKY was with the President. LEWINSKY met the President by the elevators once and was escorted to the Oval Office. On another occasion the plain clothes agent was present when the President was joking about LEWINSKY's footwear that she had worn because of the snow. The President said, "Chelsea has some like that." This plain clothes agent, whose name LEWINSKY did not know, was a tall, hefty, attractive, white male with light hair. One of these occasions was either January 21, 1996 or February 4, 1996.

A USSS officer named SANDY observed LEWINSKY with the President on December 31, 1995, when they were discussing cigars. SANDY was standing to the left of LEWINSKY, facing the door in the hallway. This was a visit with the President lasting about 20 or 25 minutes. LEWINSKY may have sent a birthday card to SANDY on a later date. SANDY was not further identified.

LEWINSKY was never refused entrance into the President's movie theater by a USSS officer. BAYANI NELVIS had once asked LEWINSKY if she had ever watched a movie with the President, and LEWINSKY responded that she had not, and as a matter of fact had never been in the theater.

On February 19, 1996, LEWINSKY went to the Oval Office without actually being invited; however, this was after talking to the President on the telephone. At this time there was a very tall, thin, plain clothes agent, with a mustache and an olive complexion, on duty. This plain clothes agent let LEWINSKY into the Oval Office between 12:00 p.m. and 2:00 p.m. This was the only time that LEWINSKY ever went to the Oval Office without the President expecting her.

The only time that LEWINSKY ever waited in the ROOSEVELT room was on July 24, 1997, and that was because BETTY CURRIE had her wait there. There were two ladies rooms in the West Wing, one being near LEON PANETTA's office and one past the Oval Office. LEWINSKY used the one near the Oval Office during the furlough. Subsequently, an E-mail came out from ANNE CATALINI that the employees of Legislative Affairs could not go by the Oval Office. There were three ways to go to the other remote offices of Legislative Affairs; one was down the stairs; one was through the West Wing lobby; and the third was past the Oval Office. EVELYN LIEBERMAN advised LEWINSKY to go through the lobby and not by the Oval Office.

Although LEWINSKY does recall a USSS plain clothes agent named GARY, Last Name Unknown (LNU), she does not recall that he ever asked LEWINSKY to leave the pantry or any other location. GARY may have said something like, "What are you up to?," but he never asked her to leave.

LEWINSKY knew a USSS plain clothes supervisor named BRYANT, who was friendly toward her, but LEWINSKY never discussed her relationship with the President with BRYANT. BRYANT could have escorted LEWINSKY to parties, but she has no memory of this.

LEWINSKY saw a USSS plain clothes agent named LOU MERLETTI several times, but had more of an acquaintance than a friendship with him. MERLETTI gave LEWINSKY his business card. LEWINSKY teased MERLETTI about being in so many photos with the President and sometimes joked with him in the hallways. LEWINSKY saw MERLETTI at the "Nutcracker" in December, 1996. MERLETTI was very friendly with LEWINSKY and she sent him a letter once. MERLETTI never saw LEWINSKY with the President to her knowledge. LEWINSKY also sent a gift to MERLETTI after she left the White House.

LEWINSKY has only a vague recollection of USSS plain clothes agent LARRY COCKELL, possibly having seen him on December 28, 1997.

On December 6, 1997, LEWINSKY went to the southwest gate and paged BETTY CURRIE to get in. While waiting, MARSHA SCOTT pulled up in her car, causing LEWINSKY to go to the northwest gate, which was under construction. When LEWINSKY arrived there, she called CURRIE, but there was no answer on CURRIE's phone. Two uniformed USSS officers, names unknown, were on duty. LEWINSKY had Christmas gifts for CURRIE and the President. Since CURRIE's telephone was not answered, LEWINSKY asked the guards to find out where CURRIE was and whether the President was in his office. One of the guards told LEWINSKY that CURRIE was giving a tour to ELEANOR MONDALE and confirmed that the President was in the Oval Office.

While at the northwest gate, LEWINSKY mistook LANNIE DAVIS for JOHN PODESTA, and after this misidentification was clarified, DAVIS was advised that LEWINSKY was waiting for BETTY CURRIE. CURRIE had told LEWINSKY earlier in the day that the President would be meeting with his lawyers on December 6th and that the President probably would not be able to meet with LEWINSKY. After finding out about MONDALE, LEWINSKY did not feel that CURRIE was truthful with her that day. LEWINSKY left the gate crying and very angry.

LEWINSKY called CURRIE from the CORCORAN GALLERY and confronted her about MONDALE visiting. CURRIE became angry also and apparently shouted at the guards for divulging that MONDALE was visiting the President. LEWINSKY assumed this, because CURRIE told LEWINSKY that LEWINSKY had gotten the guards in trouble. Later, when LEWINSKY talked to the President about this, the President asked LEWINSKY, "Do you think I'm stupid enough to go running with someone I'm messing around with?" The President also said that it was none of LEWINSKY's business what MONDALE was doing there; and that LEWINSKY should not be angry with CURRIE. LEWINSKY does not recall a discussion with the President about the guards at the northwest gate.

Later in the day, LEWINSKY bought an airline ticket and traveled to New York.

AIC WIRTH departed at this time and Deputy Independent Counsel (DIC) WISENBERG arrived.

LEWINSKY said that she had seen SARAH FARNSWORTH at the Watergate Apartments recently, but that she did not speak to FARNSWORTH, as they did not like each other.

LEWINSKY stated that she did not wish to discuss the description of anyone's genitalia, but that she disagrees with the description given by PAULA JONES.

LEWINSKY had her first sexual contact with the President on November 15, 1995. After earlier seeing the President at JENNIFER PALMIERI's party, LEWINSKY was walking to the ladies room near the Oval Office about 8:00 p.m. Upon passing the office of GEORGE STEPHANOPOLOUS, LEWINSKY saw a USSS plain clothes agent outside the door and the President inside the office. The President motioned her into STEPHANOPOLOUS's office. There had been flirtation and eye contact between the President and LEWINSKY on other occasions. LEWINSKY wore G-string panties to the earlier party and pulled her jacket up so that the President could see them at the party. No one else observed this.

LEWINSKY, after entering STEPHANOPOLOUS's office, told the President that she had a crush on him. The President asked if LEWINSKY would like to see his back office and she responded affirmatively. Upon arriving there, the President and LEWINSKY began hugging and the President asked if he could kiss LEWINSKY. With her consent the President kissed her with open mouth in a very romantic way. LEWINSKY gave the President a piece of paper with her name and telephone number on it. The President asked if LEWINSKY wanted to meet him back in his office in about ten minutes and LEWINSKY agreed. LEWINSKY returned to PANETTA's outer office, where she had been working. MARTHA FOLEY may have been working and FOLEY may have given LEWINSKY a ride home that night.

LEWINSKY recalled that she was wearing navy blue pants and a dark navy jacket that night. Sometime after 8:00 p.m., and before 10:00 p.m., LEWINSKY returned to the Oval Office and the President took her to the hallway by the back study behind the Oval Office. The lights were off. The President began kissing LEWINSKY and she unbuttoned her jacket. The President pulled her bra up (he only unhooked her bra once in subsequent sexual contacts) and put his hand down into her pants. The President received a telephone call from a Congressman or Senator. While talking on the telephone, the President kept his hand in LEWINSKY's pants to stimulate her, thereby causing her to have an orgasm or two. LEWINSKY then performed oral sex on the President, but he told LEWINSKY to stop before he reached completion. The President said that it was too soon for him to do that, inasmuch as he did not know or trust LEWINSKY well enough. The President tugged on her pink intern pass and said that "this" was going to be a problem.

The President did not know that LEWINSKY had already accepted a paying position that would entitle her to an employee pass. LEWINSKY told the President that she had had an affair with a married man before and that she knew the rules. By this statement LEWINSKY was trying to make the President feel more comfortable. She was sending a signal that she could keep quiet and lie if necessary. LEWINSKY was on "cloud nine." No further plans were made at that time and the President went upstairs to have dinner with Mrs. CLINTON. LEWINSKY speculated that the President's regular girlfriend had been furloughed.

On this or some other occasion the President said that he did not want to get addicted to having sex with LEWINSKY or he would want her all of the time. LEWINSKY and the President had incredible chemistry and were sexually compatible.

On Friday November 17, 1995 pizza was ordered. LEWINSKY picked up the pizza and delivered it to PANETTA's office. LEWINSKY went to CURRIE'S office to announce that the pizza had arrived. GENE SPERLING, GEORGE STEPHANOPOLOUS, and perhaps others were there. LEWINSKY returned to her office. A short time later, the President, CURRIE, and HERNREICH came to PANETTA's outer office. BARRY TOIV bumped into LEWINSKY and got pizza on her outfit. LEWINSKY went to the restroom to clean it off.

The President was standing outside of CURRIE's office when LEWINSKY came out of the restroom. The President invited LEWINSKY over to the Oval Office and they went to the rear study. The door to the Oval Office was left ajar. LEWINSKY asked the President if he remembered her name. LEWIN-SKY advised the President that she had gotten a permanent job in Legislative Affairs. This would allow her to get a blue pass. The President was pleased. The President and LEWINSKY were talking about Jewish things near the bathroom when the President said, "Shut up and kiss me." LEWINSKY said that she had better get back to work before people began to wonder where she was. The President asked LEWINSKY to bring him some pizza. LEWIN-SKY returned to PANETTA's office.

LEWINSKY returned to BETTY CURRIE's office after a little while and BETTY announced, "Girl here with the pizza." BETTY sent LEWINSKY into the Oval Office. The President took the pizza and the two of them went to the bathroom area off the Oval Office.

The President was wearing a light blue shirt and a red tie. The President loosened his tie. They began kissing and the President attempted to unbutton LEWINSKY's jacket. He could not, so she did it. The President kissed LEWINSKY's breasts. When LEWINSKY unbuttoned the President's blue shirt, the President sucked in his stomach, and LEWINSKY kissed his chest. LEWINSKY assured the President that she thought his physical shape was cute.

At some point, BETTY CURRIE came near the Oval Office door and said, "Sir, phone call." The President took the call in the bathroom from a Congressman, who the President called by some "funny," unrecalled nickname. While the President was on the telephone, LEWINSKY performed oral sex on him. The President did not ask LEWINSKY to quit during the phone call, but did not ejaculate. The President never told LEWINSKY that there was no sex between them if he did not ejaculate, but she believed that not reaching completion somehow made the President feel less guilty.

The President said, "I'm usually around on weekends when no one else is around, and you can come and see me." The President complimented LEWINSKY's smile, prettiness, and energy. The President did not tell LEWINSKY how to get access to the Oval Office.

LEWINSKY returned to her office, and a short time later the President returned with his pizza and ate it in front of everyone. The President's tie was back up and he was wearing a distinct cologne.

On December 5, 1995, which was the day of the congressional Christmas Ball, the President signed the photograph of himself wearing the tie that LEWINSKY had given to him. He asked LEWINSKY if she wanted a diet Coke. LEWINSKY usually carried one out of the office for cover.

On December 31, 1995, at about noon, LEWINSKY was in the dining room talking to BAYANI NELVIS, a White House steward, about LEWINSKY recently having smoked her first cigar. NELVIS offered to get LEWINSKY a Presidential cigar and they headed to the President's back study. The President met NELVIS and LEWINSKY in the back hallway and said that he needed to get something to LEON PANETTA. The President gave the item to NELVIS to take to PANETTA. The President said that he had been looking for LEWINSKY, to which LEWINSKY replied that she had given him her number. LEWINSKY thought it was obvious that the President had forgotten her name because he saw LEWINSKY one time in the hallway and said, "Hey kiddo." The President asked why LEWINSKY was there in the back office and LEWINSKY replied that NELVIS was going to get her a Presidential cigar. The President said that he would give LEWINSKY a cigar and they went back into the study. They hugged and kissed. LEWINSKY rubbed his back. The President lifted her top and kissed her chest. LEWINSKY performed oral sex on the President, but he stopped her before completion. LEWINSKY went to leave. The President apparently thought that LEWINSKY had already left and went into the bathroom, where LEWINSKY could hear water running. LEWINSKY was putting her lipstick back on and getting herself together when she observed the President in the bathroom, ■ The President was leaving for the Renaissance weekend in a helicopter soon thereafter.

LEWINSKY believes that KATHLEEN WILLEY is not telling the truth, because the President would not have let her leave without getting herself together.

On January 7, 1996, the President called LEWINSKY for the first time at her apartment. It was the first day of a blizzard. LEWINSKY was surprised when she answered the phone and realized that she was speaking to the President. The President asked LEWINSKY if she was going to the office. LEWINSKY asked the President if he wanted some company and the President replied that he did. The President said he was going to the office in about 45 minutes and LEWINSKY said she would be there in about an hour. LEWINSKY went to her office and the President called her there. LEWINSKY went to the Oval Office and they sat on the sofa and talked. After about ten minutes they went to the bathroom area in the back office. The President had wanted to perform oral sex on LEWINSKY, but she did not want him to because she was having her menstrual period. The President and LEWINSKY had foreplay, but the President stayed above her waist. LEWINSKY performed oral sex on the President, but he did not reach completion. The President and LEWINSKY usually kept their clothing on so that they could recover quickly if interrupted. They went to the Oval Office, where the President sat at his desk and LEWINSKY sat on the sofa. They both knew what the coverup would be to conceal their relationship. They talked and joked around for about 15 minutes before LEWINSKY left. LEWINSKY told the President that he could call her; could listen while she did the talking; and could engage in phone sex. The President said "I'll be around on weekends."

On January 16, 1996, at about 12:30 a.m., the President called LEWINSKY, after having been in Atlanta for MARTIN LUTHER KING day. The President said, "You said that I could call and listen." They had phone sex, with LEWINSKY doing all of the talking. LEWINSKY spoke all of the words. The President ended the call by saying that maybe he would call LEWINSKY tomorrow. The President did not call, which made LEWINSKY feel insecure. LEWINSKY was worried that the President did not like the way she performed phone sex. In thinking about their relationship, LEWINSKY observed that initially she was volunteering all of the information about their personal lives and that the President did not provide any details unless LEWINSKY asked. The President sometimes told personal things, but usually spoke about general things. LEWINSKY wanted to know whether they were going to fall in love or whether it would just be a sexual relationship.

On Sunday, January 21, 1996, which was the first day that a soldier had been killed in Bosnia, LEWINSKY saw the President in the hallway near the elevator. The President was accompanied by a USSS plain clothes agent. While talking in the Oval Office, the President said it was very sad to have someone die as a result of one of his Executive Orders. LEWINSKY was feeling like she had been taken for granted. LEWINSKY wound up in the rear hallway with the President. LEWINSKY was having a "bad hair day" and was wearing her beret. This was the first time that the President had seen her with the beret and told LEWINSKY that she was cute in her hat. LEWINSKY dropped her coat on the floor. The President was wearing olive pants and a green sweater that did not match. As they were heading to the back hallway, LEWINSKY stopped the President and asked him if he was interested in anything more than sex. The President replied that he "cherished his time" with LEWINSKY and that she was a "gift" to him. LEWINSKY treated the President as a regular person and did not stand on ceremony when LEWIN-SKY was with him. The President said he liked that. They kissed and the President kissed her chest. LEWINSKY performed oral sex on the President in the hallway and possibly in the bathroom. The BLAIRs from Arkansas were in town visiting with the President. LEWINSKY went out to BETTY CURRIE's office with the President and he kissed her goodbye in NANCY HERNREICH's office. LEWINSKY started to leave through the other door, found it locked, and turned around to exit through the door of HERNREICH's office where they had entered. LEWINSKY passed the President, ■ The President grinned and kissed LEWINSKY goodbye again. LEWINSKY departed through BETTY CURRIE's office and the garden door. LEWINSKY purposely departed by a different door than the one she had entered, so that the USSS staff would not know when LEWINSKY came and left. The BLAIRs were going out with the CLINTONs to see the VERMEER exhibit.

LEWINSKY spent the weekend ending January 28th in San Francisco. Upon LEWINSKY's return she saw on her caller identification feature that the President had called her office phone while she was in California. On Tuesday, January 30, 1996, the President called LEWINSKY on her office telephone. The display reflected "POTUS." The President said he had seen LEWINSKY getting yogurt and she looked really pretty. The President suggested that they get together after the party for PAT GRIFFIN. LEWIN-SKY responded that they should ignore each other at the party so that people would not get suspicious. The President asked if he could meet LEWINSKY later and LEWINSKY declined, because they had to be careful. EVELYN LIEBERMAN had already taken notice of LEWINSKY.

On Saturday, February 4, 1996, the President called LEWINSKY and they agreed that she would carry some papers and meet in the hallway. This occurred and they went to the back office. LEWINSKY was wearing a black dress with little flowers and combat boots. The President commented on the combat boots. The President unbuttoned LEWINSKY's dress and it hung down. The President pulled up LEWINSKY's bra. The President lifted LEWINSKY's dress up. At that point, LEWINSKY stated that she could not continue with the details while male staff members were present. After a short consultation with her attorney, LEWINSKY continued that she had performed oral sex on the President, but that it was not reciprocal oral sex. The President commented on LEWINSKY's state of arousal. When they were finished in the hallway, after about 45 minutes, the President and LEWINSKY went to the Oval Office, where they talked for another 45 minutes. LEWINSKY characterized the talking as "pillow talk." Upon leaving, the President told LEWINSKY to complete her tasks in another part of the West Wing before returning to her office, so that LEWINSKY would not draw attention by going directly from the Oval Office to her office.

On February 7, 1996, a party was held for STEVE FRISCHETTI. That night the President called LEWINSKY at home. Mrs. CLINTON was out of town. The President signed the telecommunications bill while wearing one of LEWINSKY's ties that day.

On Thursday, February 8, 1996, the President called LEWINSKY and at some point during the conversation they engaged in phone sex. On this occasion both the President and LEWINSKY participated verbally in a portion of the phone sex. LEWINSKY said that most of the time she initiated phone sex, but sometimes the President did. During this call, or in a previous call, the President told LEWINSKY that she reminded him of a character, but LEWINSKY could not recall any further description, other than the character had something to do with London.

On Sunday, February 19, 1996, the President called LEWINSKY from his office. The President sounded weird and LEWINSKY did not know what to make of it. LEWINSKY went to the Oval Office uninvited and observed the tall, thin, Hispanic plain clothes agent that she had described earlier in the interview. LEWINSKY advised that this was the only time she went to the Oval Office uninvited. LEWINSKY had previously told the President about ANDY BLEILER in Portland. The President said, "I don't want to be like that schmuck in Oregon." The President would only hug LEWINSKY that day, and he explained that he did not feel right about their sexual relationship; that he felt guilty; that LEWINSKY could still come by and visit; but that they would only be friends and not fool around.

LEWINSKY advised that during this visit with the President, he received a telephone call from a person whose last name began with an "F". This person and his brother had a sugar growing business in Florida. The President took some notes, hung up, and told LEWINSKY that he had to cut their meeting short so that he could talk to this gentleman. The President said that he was going to sign some legislation that was going to have a detrimental effect on the sugar business, and when he does something that is going to "screw" someone, he likes to tell them first.

On a day at the end of February or early March 1996, the President left a message on LEWINSKY's caller identification feature which indicated that "POTUS" had called. This predicated a discussion about the discovery of their relationship. It was decided that a different telephone would be used by the President when calling LEWINSKY's office, so that the readout would not give them away. This day can be established as the day that a bombing occurred and lives were lost in Israel. The President went to the Israeli Embassy to express his regrets. LEWINSKY observed the President and EVELYN LIEBERMAN in the hallway. The President called LEWINSKY at home at about 10:00 p.m. from upstairs in the residence. The President and LEWINSKY talked for about 20 minutes. LEWINSKY offered to visit, but the President declined, advising that CHELSEA CLINTON was sick.

On Friday, March 29, 1996, the President called LEWINSKY in her office. LEWINSKY had cut her hand and bruised herself. The President observed the wounds when LEWINSKY was passing the Map Room in the hallway that evening. The President was wearing the first tie LEWINSKY had given him. The President spoke to LEWINSKY and said that he was sorry that she had hurt her hand. This occurred in the presence of HAROLD ICKES and BRUCE LINDSEY. During the telephone call, the President offered to invite LEWINSKY to a movie that night if LEWINSKY would hang around in the hall just before the movie started so they could pretend to accidentally run into each other. LEWINSKY declined because staff members such as HERNREICH and STEPHANOPOLOUS would be present in the movie and might question her presence. LEWINSKY did not want people to think that she was hanging around uninvited. JENNIE CRUZANO had previously passed BAYANI NELVIS in the hallway and asked NELVIS why NELVIS was talking to LEWINSKY. LEWINSKY had also heard that EVELYN LIEBERMAN was suspicious of her. LEWINSKY concluded the call by asking whether she could see the President on Sunday.

On Sunday, March 31, 1996, LEWINSKY brought some papers to the Oval Office and entered with a USSS plain clothes agent who poked his head in the back hallway. LEWINSKY and the agent heard the toilet flush and were a bit embarrassed. The President was ill. The President was wearing blue jeans and a T-shirt. After the plain clothes agent departed, the President and LEWINSKY fooled around. They touched and kissed in the hallway. They talked about cigars while the President was chewing on one and then the President looked at LEWINSKY sheepishly and she understood what the President was thinking. LEWINSKY allowed the President to insert the cigar into her vagina. The President placed the cigar into his mouth after withdrawing it from LEWINSKY and said, "It tastes good." The President did not smoke the cigar because smoking is forbidden in the White House. There was no oral sex on this visit. LEWINSKY had brought the President a blue HUGO BOSS tie, concealed among the papers that she carried into the Oval Office. LEWINSKY asked the President if he would wear the tie the following Wednesday for the Office of Legislative Affairs' photograph. The President did wear the tie, but the photograph was not taken due to the death of RON BROWN. This visit was in the late afternoon and lasted from 30 to 45 minutes. LEWINSKY exited via the Rose Garden.

On Easter Sunday, April 7, 1996, LEWINSKY visited the President to discuss her transfer to the Pentagon. This was a result of the President calling LEWINSKY between 5:00 p.m. and 6:00 p.m. During this call LEWINSKY cried and told the President that she had been fired. When LEWINSKY arrived uniformed USSS officer JOHN MUSKETT was there, but LEWINSKY did not recall a plain clothes agent. When LEWINSKY advised MUSKETT that she had some papers for the President, MUSKETT said that he would check with LIEBERMAN about the visit. LEWINSKY quickly said that the President had asked for the papers and that she would only be a minute. LIEBERMAN was not advised to LEWINSKY's knowledge. LEWINSKY went into the back hallway with the President and he said, "I'm sorry they're taking you away—I trust you." The President said, "After the election I'll have you back like this" and snapped his fingers.

LEWINSKY had started performing oral sex on the President when someone from the Oval Office advised the President that he had a telephone call. The President went out to the Oval Office and then took the telephone call in the back office. LEWINSKY put her bra back on at this point. The call was apparently from DICK MORRIS, although LEWINSKY did not know it then. The call concerned campaign strategy. The President wanted LEWINSKY to continue the oral sex while he was on the phone with MORRIS. LEWINSKY complied, but felt cheap doing this. HAROLD ICKES came to the door of the Oval Office and called, "Mr. President," at which time the President bolted out of the back study. LEWINSKY departed the back way and not through the Oval Office. The President called LEWINSKY later and asked why LEWINSKY had left. LEWINSKY replied that ICKES might have walked in. The President asked LEWINSKY to come back the next day to see NANCY HERNREICH about getting a job in the White House.

LEWINSKY advised that the phone sex calls continued after she left her White House job. The President usually called from his residence, or from out of town, and almost always awakened LEWINSKY during the early morning hours. Generally, the President preferred that LEWINSKY do most of the talking during phone sex.

On May 16, 1996, the President called LEWINSKY, but did not want to participate in phone sex. The President felt very badly about Admiral BOORDA committing suicide.

On July 5, 1996, the President called for phone sex when LEWINSKY came back from Bosnia. while LEWINSKY was still talking about her trip and not talking in a sexually explicit manner. LEWINSKY asked, "Aren't you going to wait for me?"

On July 19, 1996, the President telephoned LEWINSKY at 6:30 a.m. and had phone sex. Near the end of the call the President said "good morning" in such a way that LEWINSKY was convinced that he had climaxed. The President then said something like, "What a way to start a day."

On September 5, 1996, the President called from out of town and LEWINSKY tried to convince him that they should have sex. The President said that he could not have intercourse with LEWINSKY and that there were consequences when you became older. This resulted in a fight on the telephone and the President asked if he should stop calling LEWINSKY. LEWINSKY responded that he should not.

On September 10, 1996, the President called from out of town and left a message on LEWINSKY's recorder, inasmuch as she was not home.

On October 21, 1996, the President called and they had phone sex.

On October 22, 1996, the President called and he and LEWINSKY had phone sex. The President seemed to take more control, as he talked more during the sexual portion of the call. The President liked it when LEWINSKY lead the sex talk from the start and began with such questions as, "Where are you?" and "What are you wearing?" Sometimes the President initiated the phone sex and sometimes LEWINSKY did.

On December 2, 1996, the President called LEWINSKY about 10:30 p.m., but after a short time the President hung up to take another call. The President called back a few minutes later and they began having phone sex. The President fell asleep during the call. LEWINSKY had to awaken him. LEWINSKY thought that this was "sweet" that the President would call her when he was so tired.

On February 8, 1997, the President called LEWINSKY and they had phone sex. The President said he wanted LEWINSKY to come by and pick up her hatpin. However, it was snowing that day and the President remarked that he felt bad asking BETTY CURRIE to come in (to facilitate a LEWINSKY visit). LEWINSKY and the President had phone sex.

On February 28, 1997, BETTY CURRIE called LEWINSKY at work at approximately 4:00 p.m. to invite LEWINSKY to the President's radio address. LEWINSKY hurried home to change into a new dress. LEWINSKY attended and took a photograph with the President after the address. STEVE GOODIN, RAHM EMMANUEL, and an unrecalled person were in the Oval Office. CURRIE later related that GOODIN had told her privately that she could not let the President and LEWINSKY be alone. LEWINSKY was nervous about the other visitors seeing her at the address. After the address, LEWINSKY walked to the back office with CURRIE and the President and CURRIE excused herself by going to the dining room and saying, "I'll be right back." The President and LEWINSKY went to the study, where he kissed LEWINSKY, unbuttoned her dress, pulled off her bra, and kissed her on the chest. Someone came into the Oval Office, causing the President and LEWINSKY to go into the bathroom, where the President "undid" his pants LEWINSKY then performed oral sex on the President, but he tried to stop her before completion. They had a discussion about the President not ejaculating. I They continued the oral sex until the President ejaculated and then they hugged.

LEWINSKY returned to the dining room area and CURRIE, who had been talking to BAYANI NELVIS, walked her out. CURRIE was supposed to have acted as a chaperone after GOODIN counseled her. On this visit LEWINSKY was wearing the dress that she later noticed to be stained. LEWINSKY believes the dress may have been stained by the President's semen that day after he ejaculated, but she is not sure. The President gave LEWINSKY a hat pin and a book that day.

On Wednesday, March 12, 1997, the President called LEWINSKY at work and asked LEWINSKY to visit him the next day.

On March 13, 1997, the visit was canceled because the President's schedule was too hectic.

On March 14, 1997, the President called LEWINSKY about the HUGO BOSS tie that LEWINSKY had bought in Georgetown. The President stated that the tie had a big cut in it and that he asked if LEWINSKY could exchange it. LEWINSKY picked up the tie, and after looking at the damage, was of the opinion that it had been deliberately cut. KATHRYN DAVIS's sister, KELLY DAVIS, was in town that day. KELLY DAVIS knows nothing of the relationship between LEWINSKY and the President.

On March 29, 1997, the President's brother, ROGER CLINTON, was in town. A meeting was set up between the President and LEWINSKY. LEWINSKY was supposed to bring back the HUGO BOSS tie that day. LEWINSKY went to the White House and waited in the back study. The President hobbled into the room on crutches as a result of injuring his knee in Florida several weeks earlier. This was one of the few days that the President and LEWINSKY fooled around the entire time in the study. The President was uncomfortable and could not bend over. The President unbuttoned LEWINSKY's blouse, but she did not remove the blouse. The President spent a lot of time concentrating on LEWINSKY. LEWINSKY had four to six orgasms that day. A ray of sunshine was shining directly on LEWINSKY's face while she performed oral sex to completion on the President. The President remarked about LEWINSKY's beauty. The President spent a lot of time talking with LEWINSKY that day.

The President said that he believed that an unnamed foreign Embassy was listening in on the President's official telephones so they would have to be careful in their phone conversations. The President came up with the ruse that if LEWINSKY was ever questioned to just say that they were friends, and they were just doing it to give people a run for their money. After their private meeting the President and LEWINSKY went into BETTY CURRIE's office, where they sang "Try A Little Tenderness." CURRIE then walked LEWINSKY to the door. This was the last real sexual contact that LEWINSKY had with the President, other than kissing, hugging, and brief fondling.

On July 4, 1997, the President kissed LEWINSKY on the neck.

On August 16, 1997, LEWINSKY was with the President near the bathroom in the back office and he gave LEWINSKY an open mouth kiss. It was the President's birthday.

On October 10, 1997 the President called in the early morning hours, but got into a big fight with LEWINSKY. There was no phone sex. This was the longest telephone call from the President.

63

On November 12, 1997, the President was visited by some friend from Arkansas who had a terminal illness. That night, or early the next morning, the President called LEWINSKY and they had phone sex.

On December 28, 1997, LEWINSKY visited the President in the back office. While standing near the doorway to the study, the President gave LEWINSKY an open mouth Christmas kiss. During the kiss the President was looking out the window to make sure they were not being observed.

LEWINSKY and the President touched tongues while kissing on the day of ZEDILLO's visit. As an example of flirtation between LEWINSKY and the President, during the celebration of the President's 49th birthday, the President's elbow had grazed the breast of LEWINSKY. On the occasion of the President's 50th birthday, LEWINSKY was wearing a strapless dress and was in front of a rope line where the President was greeting guests. As the President reached over LEWINSKY to make contact with a well wisher, LEWINSKY reached back and touched the President's crotch. No one else was in a position to observe this.

LEWINSKY sent a few raunchy greeting cards and possibly a few raunchy notes/letters to the President. Although the President liked them, he cautioned her to be careful putting things in writing. LEWINSKY assumes that the President tore the cards and letters up and flushed them down the toilet.

Sometimes when the President and LEWINSKY were fooling around, LEWINSKY would wipe off her lipstick before kissing the President. LEWINSKY did not dress inappropriately while working at the White House, but did wear some low-cut clothing while working at the Pentagon.

LEWINSKY dressed well when seeing the President, but did not wear the same outfit every time. LEWINSKY wore her "lucky" green suit twice and the flower dress twice. The President wore boxer shorts on one occasion, blue briefs on another, and grey shorts when the President hurt his leg. During LEWINSKY's later visits in the back study, the President usually sat in his rocking chair and LEWINSKY sat on the floor below the rocking chair and in between his legs. This arrangement was very intimate and allowed them to touch each other.

LEWINSKY said that she did not make up the sexual activities detailed above, nor did she embellish them. Most of these incidents can be verified through her "personal diary," LINDA TRIPP. LEWINSKY confided in TRIPP on almost a daily basis for a long time, but she never suggested that TRIPP keep records or charts of her activities with the President. In February, 1997, TRIPP asked LEWINSKY to go back over the activities so that TRIPP could figure out a pattern to the sexual encounters. TRIPP was a strategist, and wanted to know if the President only called when he was upset. SCOTT told LEWINSKY that SCOTT would detail LEWINSKY back over to the White House; however, this never happened.

In July, August, or September 1997, LEWINSKY invited BETTY CURRIE to have a drink with her at the HAY ADAMS bar to discuss LEWINSKY's job situation. However, CURRIE and LEWINSKY had coffee, not alcoholic drinks. LEWINSKY had set up the meeting to discuss her job situation. During the conversation, which lasted less than an hour, LEWINSKY reminded CURRIE that REBECCA CAMERON was still dragging her feet in giving LEWINSKY the photograph taken at the President's radio address; that MARSHA SCOTT really had not taken any action to get LEWINSKY back to the White House; and that the President did not seem to be helping either. LEWINSKY's approach was, "Hey, I've been a good girl, I went to the Pentagon, and why won't the President bring me back?" LEWINSKY opined that there was a "turf war" between some of the women at the White House. CURRIE explained that the President had trouble getting people jobs, because that was done at a lower level and that she would talk to MARSHA SCOTT. CURRIE drove her car to the hotel on this occasion.

In discussing BETTY CURRIE, LEWINSKY remarked that CURRIE sometimes acted naive about what was going on, even though CURRIE had observed LEWINSKY show a lot of emotion about the President. LEWINSKY was very angry with CURRIE on December 6, 1997, when LEWINSKY called her from a pay phone. CURRIE had previously told LEWINSKY that the President would be busy all day with his lawyers. LEWINSKY periodically talked to CURRIE about their mutual friend, WALTER KAYE, who knew that the President was fond of LEWINSKY. CURRIE never complained about coming in on weekends to facilitate LEWINSKY's visits to the President. LEWINSKY cultivated CURRIE as a friend, because CURRIE was in a good position to help LEWINSKY. LEWINSKY did not tell CURRIE of her exact relationship with the President, and she and the President attempted to be discreet in front of CURRIE.

On March 29, 1997, CURRIE called from her home to clear LEWINSKY at the White House gate and called from the hospital on October 11, 1997 to do the same. Sometimes, CURRIE conducted private tours on weekends for the President. LEWINSKY knew of no one else at her level that had the degree of access to the President that LEWINSKY did. On "dump day," May 24, 1997, LEWINSKY called CURRIE and advised that LEWINSKY was waiting to see the President. CURRIE said that she had to check Mrs. CLINTON's schedule and said Mrs. CLINTON was going to use the pool that day. This was the only time that LEWINSKY actually knew that CURRIE had factored in the whereabouts of Mrs. CLINTON with LEWINSKY's visits to the President. Mrs. CLINTON never saw LEWINSKY in the Oval Office.

Fourteen photographs of gifts and momentos were displayed to LEWINSKY, who made the following remarks:

1. Ticket to August Ball.
2. Book entitled, "Our Patriotic President," given to the President by LEWINSKY on December 6, 1997. Purchased at New York flea market for $40.00.
3. Antique book entitled "Presidents of the United States of America;" given to the President by dropping off at BETTY CURRIE's home on a weekend in early January 1998, which was the day the President and the First Lady were photographed dancing on the beach in Florida, purchased for $40.00 at Georgetown bookstore off M Street next to the Christian Scientist book store sometime after December 28, 1997.

LEWINSKY included a mushy note in the book. The President acknowledged receipt of the book and note and remarked that LEWINSKY should not have written the note because it was not good to have those things in writing. LEWINSKY's note made reference to the movie "Titanic," which she had seen that weekend.

4. Silver cigar holder purchased at flea market in New York in October/November 1997, for $180.00 in cash. Handed to President in his rocking chair on December 6, 1997, and he said, "It is beautiful." Seen by LINDA TRIPP at work and brother MICHAEL in apartment. LEWINSKY tried to buy DAVIDOFF cigars for holder but unsuccessful. LEWINSKY observed on President's desk in Oval Office on December 28, 1997.

5. STARBUCKS Santa Monica coffee cup purchased at the Los Angeles International Airport and given to President on December 6, 1997; President remarked, "I like big mugs" and LEWINSKY responded, "No, you like big jugs."

6. Gold and blue tie designed by Feraud and purchased in London for 25 pounds in early December, 1997. Presented to President on December 6, 1997.

7. A pin depicting the New York skyline given to LEWINSKY by the President on December 28, 1997.

8. Flower pin for birthday gift handed to LEWINSKY by BETTY CURRIE on behalf of the President in July 1997; may have been CURRIE's personal pin commandeered as last minute gift.

9. Hat pin purchased by the President in Albuquerque on February 28, 1997; LEWINSKY loved it and wore it with her straw hat; told NEYSA about the gift.

10. Green dress from the BLACK DOG shop given to LEWINSKY by the President; LEWINSKY considered it an important personal gift.

11. White T-shirt from BLACK DOG presented by President.

12. Green T-shirt from BLACK DOG presented by President.

13. Ball cap from BLACK DOG presented by President.

14. State Of The Union invitiation signed by President and presented to LEWINSKY in 1996.

15. State Of The Union invitation in envelope (duplicate).

Photographs displayed are further described by the following Bates Stamp number:

1. MSL-DC-00000474
2. V002-DC-00000003
3. V002-DC-00000471
4. V000-DC-00000474
5. V002-DC-00000473
6. V002-DC-00000472
7. 824-DC-00000018
8. 824-DC-00000019
9. 824-DC-00000019
10. 824-DC-00000006
11. 824-DC-00000008
12. 824-DC-00000007
13. 824-DC-00000009

14. 824-DC-00000003
15. 824-DC-00000004

LEWINSKY added that she noticed that BAYANI NELVIS wore the first tie that she had given to the President to one of his grand jury appearances.

The interview was terminated at 6:15 p.m.

Monica Lewinsky's
Fourth Interview

1

OFFICE OF THE INDEPENDENT COUNSEL

07/31/98

MONICA S. LEWINSKY was interviewed under the terms of an immunity agreement between the Office of the Independent Counsel (OIC) and her. Present for the interview were Associate Independent Counsel (AIC) MICHAEL EMMICK, AIC KARIN IMMERGUT, AIC MARY ANNE WIRTH, and AIC CRAIG LERNER. Representing LEWINSKY were attorney PRESTON BURTON and law clerk MATTHEW UMHOFER. Present for parts of the interview was Deputy Independent Counsel (DIC) ROBERT J. BITTMAN. The interview, conducted in Room 616 of the Watergate Hotel, commenced at approximately 10:08 a.m. LEWINSKY provided the following information:

LEWINSKY was shown a photograph of President WILLIAM JEFFERSON CLINTON on the next to last page of the April 13, 1998 issue of THE WEEKLY STANDARD. LEWINSKY advised she purchased and gave CLINTON the sunglasses CLINTON is wearing in the photograph.

December 5, 1997

LEWINSKY advised that on December 5, 1997, she was mad at CLINTON because he would not see her the following day. On November 30, 1997, the Sunday night before leaving for BRUSSELS, LEWINSKY mailed BETTY CURRIE a letter to give to CLINTON. LEWINSKY advised she wrote CLINTON to tell him LEWINSKY needed to see him. LEWINSKY advised she called CURRIE from Europe to see if CLINTON would be available to meet LEWINSKY anytime soon. LEWINSKY advised CURRIE later said CURRIE did not give the letter to CLINTON until December 5, 1997 at 6 p.m.

LEWINSKY advised she attended a Christmas party at the White House the evening of December 5, 1997. LEWINSKY saw CLINTON at the party, which LEWINSKY attended with BOB TYRER, the Chief of Staff to Secretary of Defense WILLIAM COHEN. LEWINSKY advised she saw CLINTON in the greeting line and, before she shook hands with him, she noticed he saw her and began fixing his hair.

LEWINSKY advised she engaged in small talk with CLINTON. LEWINSKY told HILLARY RODHAM CLINTON that she was friends with WALTER KAYE.

DRAFT LETTERS

LEWINSKY provided 12 pages of documents she had in her apartment which related to CLINTON.

LEWINSKY advised that on the evening of December 5, 1997, she typed, on her home computer, a letter to CLINTON she planned to give CURRIE the following day when LEWINSKY delivered CURRIE and CLINTON's Christmas presents. LEWINSKY advised she often printed out drafts of letters so she could proofread them. LEWINSKY provided copies of drafts of the letter, but she ended up seeing CLINTON the next day, so she did not give him the letter.

LEWINSKY advised the purpose of this letter was to make CLINTON feel guilty. LEWINSKY advised that when she was in England the first week of December 1997, she telephoned CURRIE once or twice. LEWINSKY advised she stayed at the GROSVENOR HOUSE and billed her telephone calls to her AMERICAN EXPRESS CARD.

LEWINSKY provided a draft of a two page letter, dated June 26, 1997, to CURRIE in which LEWINSKY provided suggestions for transcription jobs for CURRIE's mother. LEWINSKY eventually sent CURRIE a version of this letter.

LEWINSKY provided two other drafts of letters she eventually sent CLINTON. One is a November 12, 1997 letter to CLINTON in which LEWINSKY expressed her frustration at not being with CLINTON. The second letter was written sometime after LEWINSKY's November 13, 1997 visit to the White House that coincided with Mexican President ZEDILLO's visit, which LEWINSKY refers to simply as "ZEDILLO day."

LEWINSKY provided a copy of a bookmark/penny, a duplicate of which she had given CLINTON on March 29, 1997. LEWINSKY advised she purchased two of the items, gave one to CLINTON and saved one. LEWINSKY advised NATE SPEIGHTS has the other original of this item.

LEWINSKY provided another draft of a letter she wrote after her "ZEDILLO visit."

LEWINSKY provided a copy of a November 6, 1997 letter to VERNON JORDAN. LEWINSKY advised she sent a similar letter to JORDAN on November 6, 1997. LEWINSKY sent the letter to JORDAN via courier, because JORDAN was going out of town the next day. LEWINSKY advised she had taken her resume to JORDAN the previous day when she met with him.

LEWINSKY provided a copy of a list she sent to CLINTON after her meeting with him on October 11, 1997. LEWINSKY advised CLINTON told her to prepare a list of jobs she would be interested in.

LEWINSKY provided a copy of a draft letter related to her career opportunities. LEWINSKY advised the handwriting on the draft is hers, but she cannot remember specifically what she was referring to. LEWINSKY advised she reviewed the letter with LINDA TRIPP.

69

LEWINSKY advised she was focused on public relations firms when she dealt with VERNON JORDAN.

FOLLOW-UP TO PREVIOUS DAY'S INTERVIEW

LEWINSKY advised she did not recall CURRIE ever being in the Oval Office bathroom while LEWINSKY and CLINTON engaged in oral sex. LEWINSKY does recall one instance when CURRIE was in the Executive dining room while LEWINSKY and CLINTON engaged in oral sex in the Oval Office hall and bathroom. CLINTON advised LEWINSKY to keep quiet during this encounter.

LEWINSKY advised that she recalls another occasion CLINTON made a comment to her about being quiet while they engaged in sexual activities.

LEWINSKY advised she recalled that on March 29, 1997, CLINTON put his hand over LEWINSKY's mouth so as to keep her quiet during one of their sexual encounters.

LEWINSKY recalls one occasion in which she had to bite her own hand during sexual activities to keep from making any noise.

LEWINSKY advised CURRIE would always knock and announce herself prior to opening the doors in the Oval Office complex. LEWINSKY advised she and CLINTON were generally not concerned about being overheard during their sexual encounters. LEWINSKY advised they were more concerned with being seen in the Oval Office because of the windows there.

LEWINSKY advised the Oval Office study has windows, but no one is usually stationed there. LEWINSKY is aware of peepholes that allow someone to look into the Oval Office from various points around the Oval Office. LEWINSKY does not recall discussing the peepholes with CLINTON or CURRIE.

CLINTON sometimes expressed concern about people looking into the Oval Office and the study. LEWINSKY recalls that when CLINTON gave her her Christmas kiss on December 28, 1997, he had his eyes wide open, looking out the window.

LEWINSKY advised she most often visited CLINTON during the day. LEWINSKY advised the hallway outside the Oval study was more comfortable because it had no windows. LEWINSKY advised that during the "ZEDILLO visit," CLINTON turned the lights to the study out while she was in there.

LEWINSKY advised that she thinks HILLARY CLINTON called when LEWINSKY was with the President on November 15, 1995. LEWINSKY advised she thinks CURRIE hollered back to CLINTON that HILLARY CLINTON was on the phone.

LEWINSKY advised most of her sexual encounters with CLINTON occurred in the hallway outside the Oval Office study, except for the second visit on November 15, 1995 and the visits on March 29, 1997 and April 7, 1996. LEWINSKY and CLINTON occasionally engaged in sexual activity in the bathroom near the study.

LEWINSKY advised she felt as if she was alone with CLINTON when the two were engaged in intimate contact, but they both were still conscious of the possibility of having to disengage on a moment's notice, so they did not disrobe entirely.

LEWINSKY advised she was never concerned about video cameras around the Oval Office, until the news about the fundraising videos, which occurred in the Fall of 1996. LEWINSKY spoke to LINDA TRIPP about the video tapes, but later learned the videos were not secretly recorded so LEWINSKY's concerns were allayed.

LEWINSKY advised she was concerned about records of telephone calls CLINTON made to LEWINSKY. LEWINSKY's concern was sparked when she read news of the White House turning over phone records to the campaign fund-raising investigators. LEWINSKY expressed concern to CUR-RIE, who told LEWINSKY not to worry since CLINTON used a different phone when he called LEWINSKY. LEWINSKY may have expressed her concern to CLINTON, but she does not recall and she has no recollection of his response.

LEWINSKY advised she recalls one late October 1997 telephone call from CLINTON where CLINTON had to end the call because HILLARY CLINTON had returned home.

LEWINSKY does not recall either of her two telephone calls with CLIN-TON, when CLINTON was on the road, ending abruptly. LEWINSKY does not recall hearing a clicking sound when she spoke with CLINTON on the telephone.

LEWINSKY advised she was discreet about her sexual relationship with CLINTON when dealing with CURRIE. CURRIE was "in the loop" when it came to keeping LEWINSKY's relationship with CLINTON discreet.

LEWINSKY assumes RAHM EMMANUAL was present in the Oval Office on February 28, 1997, and is sure STEVE GOODIN was there. LEWINSKY was told by CURRIE that GOODIN said LEWINSKY could not be alone with CLINTON. LEWINSKY assumes CLINTON was in the Oval Office with GOODIN and CURRIE when GOODIN told CURRIE this. LEWINSKY advised that when she eventually went into the Oval Office with CURRIE shortly thereafter, CLINTON did not seem surprised to see CURRIE with LEWINSKY.

LEWINSKY advised a lot of people tried to protect CLINTON by putting reins on his life, but CURRIE does what CLINTON wants done. LEWINSKY advised CURRIE was more like family to CLINTON than a subordinate. LEWINSKY advised CURRIE had a special relationship with CLINTON. LEWINSKY advised CLINTON found it comforting to have CURRIE in the Oval Office area.

LEWINSKY did not seduce CLINTON, nor did she stalk him. LEWINSKY advised their relationship was mutual, particularly with regard to initiating intimate contact.

LEWINSKY advised that, in her December 17, 1997 telephone conversation with CLINTON, CLINTON advised that if anyone asked LEWINSKY about her visits to the White House after her transfer to the Pentagon, LEWINSKY could always say she was visiting CURRIE. LEWINSKY advised this was not the first time CLINTON mentioned this scenario.

LEWINSKY advised this scenario was familiar to her, but it was not brought up on a regular basis. LEWINSKY advised that until December 17, 1997, no one had ever asked LEWINSKY about her visits to the Oval Office. LEWINSKY advised that when she visited the White House after her transfer to the Pentagon, the primary purpose of the visit was to see CLINTON, but she did see CURRIE, as well.

LEWINSKY advised that CURRIE sometimes drove LEWINSKY out of the White House complex after one of LEWINSKY's visits. On December 28, 1997, LEWINSKY left her visitor's pass in the Oval Office, so CURRIE had to call down to the gate to allow LEWINSKY to leave.

"MEANIES"

LEWINSKY proceeded to provide a description of some of the White House employees who did not like LEWINSKY. LEWINSKY described these people as "meanies."

LEWINSKY's first encounter with EVELYN LIEBERMAN was shortly after LEWINSKY started her job in the Office of Legislative Affairs (OLA). LEWINSKY was taking papers to the West Wing when LIEBERMAN stopped her and asked where she worked. LIEBERMAN also said that LEWINSKY was always trafficking in the West Wing area. LIEBERMAN told LEWINSKY interns were not allowed in front of the Oval Office.

LEWINSKY went to the bathroom and cried and then went to LIEBERMAN's office to clarify that she was no longer an intern and had been hired as a staffer. LIEBERMAN responded derisively by saying "they hired you?" LIEBERMAN then said that she must have mistaken LEWINSKY for someone else. From that moment on, LEWINSKY was wary of LIEBERMAN. LEWINSKY advised she thinks LIEBERMAN was furloughed during the government shutdown, as LEWINSKY does not recall seeing her during that time.

LEWINSKY did not mention her encounter with LIEBERMAN to CLINTON. LEWINSKY believes her encounter with LIEBERMAN occurred in December of 1995 as LEWINSKY did not interact with CLINTON that much during December of 1995.

LEWINSKY advised that she was never reprimanded for dressing inappropriately while employed at the White House. LEWINSKY attributes those stories to a "White House smear campaign."

LEWINSKY cannot recall any other direct encounters with LIEBERMAN. LEWINSKY advised that she had a near encounter on April 7, 1996, because United States Secret Service Uniformed Officer JOHN MUSKETT asked LEWINSKY if he should check with LIEBERMAN to see if he should allow LEWINSKY into the Oval Office. LEWINSKY told MUSKETT that this would not be necessary, since she was just dropping off papers.

CLINTON told LEWINSKY that LIEBERMAN had LEWINSKY transferred to the Pentagon because 1996 was an election year. LEWINSKY advised a lot of people at the White House were wary of LIEBERMAN. LEWINSKY was especially wary of LIEBERMAN because LEWINSKY was having a relationship with CLINTON.

CLINTON telephoned LEWINSKY from Florida on October 22, 1996.

LEWINSKY advised that CURRIE was wary of LIEBERMAN, as well. LEWINSKY advised that on either October 23 or October 24, 1996, LEWINSKY saw and spoke to CLINTON at a fund-raiser for Senate Democrats. That evening, CLINTON called LEWINSKY. During the conversation, LEWINSKY said that she was going to see White House photographer BILLIE SHADDIX at the White House the following day. CLINTON told LEWINSKY to stop by the West Wing.

LEWINSKY told CLINTON to have CURRIE come down to the photo office to escort LEWINSKY to the West Wing. LEWINSKY was unable to see CLINTON and his departure ceremony that day because CURRIE said that LIEBERMAN was in the area and CURRIE had to wait until LIEBERMAN was gone before bringing LEWINSKY to the Oval Office area. CURRIE told LEWINSKY that LIEBERMAN did not like LEWINSKY.

LEWINSKY advised that her mother, MARCIA LEWIS, and step-father, PETER STRAUSS, saw LIEBERMAN at a VOICE OF AMERICA event. LIEBERMAN told MARCIA LEWIS that LEWINSKY was transferred from the White HOUSE due to political expediency. LIEBERMAN added that LEWINSKY was cursed because she was beautiful.

LEWINSKY advised that SUSAN BROPHY and others in the Office of Legislative Affairs called LEWINSKY a "stalker."

LEWINSKY did not express her frustrations with CLINTON that LEWINSKY ended up having to make most of the arrangements to meet with CLINTON.

LEWINSKY advised that STEVE GOODIN initially treated LEWINSKY kindly. LEWINSKY recalled one time when LEWINSKY and JAY FOOTLIK went to the Oval Office so LEWINSKY could deliver a tie to CLINTON. LEWINSKY and FOOTLIK bumped into GOODIN outside BETTY CURRIE's office and the three sang a parody of the song "You don't bring me flowers."

LEWINSKY recalled that on MARTIN LUTHER KING DAY, 1996, PAT GRIFFIN asked LEWINSKY to call LEON PANETTA, who was traveling with the President. LEWINSKY called GOODIN, who half-jokingly said to

LEWINSKY that he only spoke to "principals." Others present laughed at LEWINSKY's expense.

LEWINSKY advised that on May 24, 1997, LEWINSKY was with CLINTON in the study. LEWINSKY had left her LOUIS VUITTON purse on the dining room table in the Executive Dining room. CLINTON had to leave the study at one point and LEWINSKY heard him speaking to GOODIN.

LEWINSKY advised that she was "paranoid" about what people were thinking about her. LEWINSKY advised CLINTON paid a lot of attention to her, sometimes in front of others. LEWINSKY felt that people in the White House did not want to acknowledge that the President might actually like LEWINSKY.

LEWINSKY advised that initially she felt HERNREICH was friendly with her. LEWINSKY saw HERNREICH on April 7, 1996 when LEWINSKY was transferred. HERNREICH told LEWINSKY to come in and see her on April 8, 1996. HERNREICH was very kind to her and consoled her. HERNREICH told LEWINSKY she would see what she could do for LEWINSKY.

After LEWINSKY was transferred, CURRIE specifically mentioned to LEWINSKY when HERNREICH was not around. CURRIE's concern with whether or not HERNREICH was around indicated to LEWINSKY that HERNREICH may have disliked LEWINSKY.

LEWINSKY advised that in early 1997, during telephone conversations on January 12 and February 8, CLINTON told her that BOB NASH was in charge of finding her a job at the White House. LEWINSKY later learned that NASH, head of Presidential Personnel, was in charge of finding jobs outside the White House. LEWINSKY then learned the "ball was passed" to MARSHA SCOTT by the end of April of 1997.

LEWINSKY advised that she spoke to SCOTT's assistant, but got the impression that SCOTT was not aware of who she was and SCOTT never returned the call. LEWINSKY then sent a nasty note to CLINTON, referencing her dealings with SCOTT. LEWINSKY thinks she either sent by courier or hand-delivered the note to CURRIE to give to CLINTON.

Several weeks later, SCOTT called LEWINSKY and said that SCOTT had been out due to back surgery and did not have a chance to call LEWINSKY. LEWINSKY thinks SCOTT either read LEWINSKY's note to CLINTON, or CLINTON conveyed the contents of it to her. SCOTT arranged an appointment for LEWINSKY to meet with her.

LEWINSKY does not recall the length of the meeting, but she does recall SCOTT asking SCOTT's assistant to leave the office during the meeting. LEWINSKY described SCOTT's tone as pleasant. LEWINSKY advised SCOTT had a picture of SCOTT and CLINTON on the wall in her office. In the photograph, CLINTON is wearing a tie LEWINSKY had given him.

SCOTT asked a lot of questions during the meeting, some of which LEWINSKY felt were intrusive. SCOTT said that JODIE TORKELSON and

EVELYN LIEBERMAN did not like LEWINSKY. LEWINSKY felt an unspoken tension with SCOTT, as LEWINSKY was a current lover of CLINTON's,
■ LEWINSKY advised she had two meetings with SCOTT, and is not sure about at which meeting certain things were said. At one meeting, SCOTT indicated she would "detail" LEWINSKY at the White House. In a "detail," the employee works at the White House, but is paid by another agency, like the Defense Department. LEWINSKY advised "detailees" work at the White House for a limited time, prior to going back to their agency or finding a permanent position at the White House.

LEWINSKY advised that LIZ BAILEY told LEWINSKY that SCOTT lost her "detail" post and would be unable to find a position for LEWINSKY. SCOTT told LEWINSKY the reason she was unable to find LEWINSKY a position was because KEN BACON and CLIFF BERNATH at the Pentagon said they did not want to "lose" LEWINSKY.

LEWINSKY got into an argument with SCOTT as SCOTT told LEWINSKY that she would have to wait until December, after certain people left the White House, including LIEBERMAN, before returning to the White House. LEWINSKY said that was not fair and SCOTT said life was not fair. SCOTT said it was not fair that she had incurred $400,000 in attorney's fees simply for working at the White House.

Looking back at the situation, LEWINSKY thinks SCOTT may have been trying to protect CLINTON because of LEWINSKY's association with the KATHLEEN WILLEY/LINDA TRIPP matter.

JOBS

Between September 12 and 26, 1997, CURRIE advised she was going to talk to JOHN PODESTA. On October 7, 1997, LEWINSKY talked to LINDA TRIPP, who had stayed home from work. TRIPP told LEWINSKY that TRIPP's friend, KATE, who worked at the NATIONAL SECURITY COUNCIL, said she had heard that LEWINSKY would not get back at the White House, and if she did, LEWINSKY would not get a job requiring a blue, West Wing pass. TRIPP said that KATE's advice was for LEWINSKY to "get out of town."

This conversation with TRIPP made LEWINSKY so angry she left work early that day. LEWINSKY advised she then decided to move to New York. LEWINSKY advised she had previously considered the idea of moving to New York, but the call from TRIPP was the "straw that broke the camel's back." KATE's comments confirmed LEWINSKY's hunch that she was never going to be brought back to the White House.

LEWINSKY advised that moving to New York was a possibility beginning in July of 1997. LEWINSKY advised a job at the United Nations seemed logical at the time because it was a government agency.

LEWINSKY had been suspicious of not getting a job back at the White House. LEWINSKY advised that, in an October 11, 1997 telephone conversation with CLINTON, she mentioned to him her frustration of not getting a job at the White House. CLINTON said the problem was that lower-level people knew more about the specific job openings than he did.

LEWINSKY advised that on October 9 or 10, 1997, CLINTON called her between 2:00 and 2:30 in the morning. LEWINSKY advised she was asleep when CLINTON called. The call lasted for approximately one and one half hours. LEWINSKY and CLINTON had their biggest fight ever in this telephone conversation. LEWINSKY said both she and CLINTON yelled a lot during the call.

CLINTON said that if he had known how difficult it would be to bring LEWINSKY back to the White House, he would have never let her be transferred in the first place. CLINTON said he was obsessed with her career and wanted to help her. CLINTON said his life was empty except for work. During the fight, CLINTON also said that, if he had known what type of person LEWINSKY was, he would have never become involved with her in the first place. LEWINSKY advised she was very hurt by this comment and started crying.

LEWINSKY advised that CLINTON was in the White House Residence when he made the telephone call to her. LEWINSKY advised that her caller identification feature indicated "unavailable" when CLINTON called her from the Residence. LEWINSKY advised she did not go into detail about what TRIPP said KATE had said. LEWINSKY advised she was vague with CLINTON when discussing why she wanted to move to New York.

LEWINSKY told CLINTON she had to be out of her apartment by the end of October. LEWINSKY advised that the discussion of her job situation was part of her relationship with CLINTON. CLINTON said he would get working on a job in New York for LEWINSKY.

LEWINSKY advised she stayed home from work on October 10, 1997 and had lunch with TRIPP at the CALIFORNIA PIZZA KITCHEN on Connecticut Avenue. LEWINSKY talked about her early morning telephone conversation with CLINTON. LEWINSKY advised she was emotionally exhausted as a result of the content of the phone conversation with CLINTON the night before. LEWINSKY was also disappointed she would not be going back to work at the White House.

The following morning, October 11, 1997, at approximately 8:30 a.m., CURRIE called LEWINSKY from the hospital and said CLINTON wanted to see LEWINSKY at approximately 9:00 a.m., at the White House. CURRIE told LEWINSKY that CLINTON had paged CURRIE to tell her to get in touch with LEWINSKY.

LEWINSKY advised it was CLINTON's wedding anniversary that day, and CLINTON had tasked CURRIE with finding a HALCYON box for HILLARY CLINTON. The White House Garden tours were taking place that day and CURRIE had two friends there on the tour. LEWINSKY chatted with CURRIE's friends as she waited for CLINTON. CLINTON was on the telephone with CAPRICIA MARSHALL, who had attended the wedding of LAURA HARTIGAN in Chicago.

LEWINSKY advised that she saw ANNE McCOY coming toward the Oval Office, so LEWINSKY darted to the back room of the Oval complex to avoid McCOY.

LEWINSKY met alone with CLINTON in the Dining Room. LEWINSKY gave CLINTON a list of jobs in New York she was interested in. LEWINSKY advised she mentioned First Name Unknown (FNU) KAPLAN from CNN. LEWINSKY may have also mentioned VERNON JORDAN during this conversation. LEWINSKY thinks she may have mentioned JORDAN in the previous telephone conversation in which she and CLINTON had a fight. CLINTON was receptive to the idea of JORDAN helping LEWINSKY.

LEWINSKY mentioned JORDAN because TRIPP had said JORDAN was CLINTON's best friend and JORDAN was on the board of directors of many companies. LEWINSKY looked JORDAN up on the Internet and also saw a lot of references to him in stories about CLINTON's trip to Martha's Vineyard.

LEWINSKY advised she did not want a job in the government.

LEWINSKY advised that, at some point, she knew JOHN PODESTA had a role in LEWINSKY getting a job offer at the United Nations. CLINTON said that he did or would talk to PODESTA.

In mid-October, CLINTON was in Latin America and LEWINSKY worked on her letter to CLINTON regarding jobs. LEWINSKY bought a book at BARNES & NOBLE regarding jobs in New York.

LEWINSKY advised she sent her letter, her GS rating, the section of the PLUM Book regarding other Confidential Assistants at the Pentagon being GS-11's, (while LEWINSKY was a GS-9) to CLINTON on October 16, 1997. LEWINSKY believes she mentioned a salary of approximately $60,000.

On October 21, 1997, Ambassador WILLIAM RICHARDSON telephoned LEWINSKY at home. RICHARDSON said he understood from JOHN PODESTA that LEWINSKY was interested in working at the United Nations.

On October 23, 1997, LEWINSKY spoke with CLINTON on the telephone. During the conversation, LEWINSKY and CLINTON spoke about the sunglasses LEWINSKY recently sent CLINTON. (LEWINSKY also sent CLINTON a CALVIN KLEIN tie, the fifth tie she had given him.) During this conversation, LEWINSKY mentioned RICHARDSON's call to her. LEWINSKY tried to steer CLINTON to think of a job other than the United Nations, but CLINTON said he just wanted LEWINSKY to have options.

[LEWINSKY does not recall when she regularly started using the courier service to deliver things to CLINTON. Mid-March of 1997 was the first time LEWINSKY used the service, but she may have not used it regularly until the fall of 1997. TRIPP had said the FEDERAL EXPRESS system was unsafe. LEWINSKY advised that on March 1, 1997, she sent CLINTON a get-well package, which included a magnet of the Seal of the President of the United States for CLINTON's metal crutches; a little license plate that said "BILL" for CLINTON's wheel-chair; and knee-pads with the seal of the President of the United States stitched on them (by LEWINSKY). LEWINSKY purchased the knee-pads at a sporting goods store on the third floor of the Pentagon City mall.]

[LEWINSKY advised her mode of delivering items to the White House depended on the sensitivity of the items. LEWINSKY advised the most secure mode was to give the item directly to CURRIE. LEWINSKY advised the cost of the delivery also played a role in her choosing a specific method. LEWINSKY advised the courier service was the most expensive of the delivery methods. LEWINSKY advised she dropped things off at the New Executive Office Building (NEOB) approximately 3 times and handed the items directly to CURRIE at one of the White House gates approximately five times. LEWINSKY advised she thought of using the Department of Defense courier to the White House, but could not do it.]

LEWINSKY did not feel it was odd for CLINTON to be helping her find a job because she "had a relationship with him."

Sometime before October 30, 1997, LEWINSKY asked CURRIE to tell CLINTON to call LEWINSKY. In the early evening, around 8 p.m., on October 30th, CLINTON called LEWINSKY at home. LEWINSKY said she was anxious about meeting RICHARDSON. CLINTON told LEWINSKY to call CURRIE after the interview to let CLINTON know how the interview went.

LEWINSKY had given CURRIE CLINTON's Halloween presents, including a lapel pin, sometime during the week before Halloween. LEWINSKY advised she saw a photograph of CLINTON wearing the pin and she read that CLINTON mentioned the pin in a speech.

On October 31, 1997, LEWINSKY met with RICHARDSON at the Watergate Hotel. MONA SUTPHEN, RICHARDSON's assistant, met LEWINSKY in the lobby and escorted LEWINSKY to RICHARDSON's room. LEWINSKY advised the setting was very casual as RICHARDSON was eating breakfast when LEWINSKY arrived. RICHARDSON asked LEWINSKY if CURRIE was her mother.

LEWINSKY mentioned working on the United States Consulate to the United Nations' web-site and suggested implementing town hall meetings, similar to the ones the Department of Defense used. LEWINSKY advised the meeting lasted approximately one-half hour.

LEWINSKY did not think the interview was perfunctory or "cake." LEWINSKY advised that REBECCA LNU and SUTPHEN were there, and at times it may have just been RICHARDSON and REBECCA Last Name Unknown (LNU) with LEWINSKY, as SUTPHEN came in and left intermittently.

LEWINSKY does not recall PODESTA's name coming up during the interview.

After LEWINSKY's interview, LEWINSKY's mother and aunt went to the

United Nations in New York. LEWINSKY advised some of the reasons LEWINSKY did not want to work at the United Nations were because LEWINSKY's mother mentioned her concern that a lot of Arabs worked at the United Nations and because the United Nations was somewhat isolated from the business district in New York.

The interview with RICHARDSON ended with LEWINSKY being told that RICHARDSON or his staff would be in touch with her. LEWINSKY spoke to CURRIE after the interview and LEWINSKY was a lot more optimistic about her job opportunities than she was before the interview. CLINTON was out of town at the time.

On November 3, 1997, or later, LEWINSKY received a telephone call from RICHARDSON and was offered a job at the United Nations.

VERNON JORDAN

On either October 23 or 30, 1997, LEWINSKY and CLINTON discussed VERNON JORDAN helping LEWINSKY in her job search.

On November 3 or 4, 1997, CURRIE called LEWINSKY and told her to call JORDAN's secretary GAYLE LNU. CURRIE told LEWINSKY to say she was CURRIE's friend. LEWINSKY advised that CURRIE had called JORDAN to arrange the meeting, so that gave LEWINSKY some indication that CLIN-TON was involved.

In the late morning of November 5, 1997, LEWINSKY had an appointment to see JORDAN. LEWINSKY was nervous as she waited in the lobby for twenty minutes before meeting with JORDAN. LEWINSKY brought the same package she had sent CLINTON earlier, sans the cover sheet and the GS scale.

LEWINSKY sat in JORDAN's office before he came in. JORDAN made LEWINSKY feel nervous. JORDAN was not very effusive in this meeting. The meeting lasted approximately twenty minutes. After introducing each other, JORDAN asked LEWINSKY why she was there. LEWINSKY told JORDAN she was hoping to move to New York. JORDAN asked her why she wanted to leave Washington, D.C. LEWINSKY said that she wanted to get a fresh start.

LEWINSKY mentioned her employment at the White House. JORDAN inquired as to why he never saw LEWINSKY during one of his visits to the White House. LEWINSKY gave JORDAN the "vanilla" story about why she left employment at the White House. LEWINSKY said that LIEBERMAN did not like her. JORDAN said LIEBERMAN disliked him as well. JORDAN said he had spoken to CLINTON about LEWINSKY.

LEWINSKY and JORDAN went over her list of possible employers. LEWINSKY felt awkward in the meeting as JORDAN did not respond to her often. JORDAN mentioned one his daughters worked at one of the companies on LEWINSKY's list. At the end of the meeting, JORDAN said he and LEWINSKY were "in business."

JORDAN said that LEWINSKY came "highly recommended." LEWINSKY is not sure if JORDAN meant that CLINTON said nice things about her, or if he meant CLINTON had mentioned his relationship with LEWINSKY. In their November 12, 1997 telephone conversation, CLINTON said he had spoken to JORDAN.

JORDAN was going out of town the day after LEWINSKY met with him. LEWINSKY called CURRIE and left a couple of messages with JORDAN's secretary, but JORDAN did not return LEWINSKY's call. LEWINSKY called CURRIE to see what she should do, since she had not heard from JORDAN in almost two weeks.

On November 26, 1997, CURRIE paged LEWINSKY while LEWINSKY was in Los Angeles. LEWINSKY called CURRIE from a pay phone at the WILSHIRE COURTYARD MARRIOTT. LEWINSKY was told to call JOR-DAN and she did. JORDAN told LEWINSKY he was leaving for China and he told LEWINSKY to call him around the first week of December. JORDAN told LEWINSKY he was working on her job search.

LEWINSKY was anxious as she had given notice at the Pentagon that she was going to leave, though she did not give a specific date.

On December 8, 1997, LEWINSKY sent, by courier, a package to JORDAN, which included a note, a hat and some chocolate, to remind him she still existed.

During LEWINSKY's December 6, 1997 meeting with CLINTON, she thinks he said he would contact JORDAN. LEWINSKY advised CLINTON was the type of person who would say he was going to do something and not really mean it.

LEWINSKY advised that she had breakfast with VERNON JORDAN on December 31, 1997 at the HYATT. LEWINSKY advised JORDAN paid for the breakfast; LEWINSKY had an egg-white omelette, and JORDAN had cereal or yogurt.

CLINTON's Testimony

LEWINSKY is surprised CLINTON has agreed to testify before the Grand Jury. LEWINSKY thinks CLINTON is walking into a "perjury trap." LEWIN-SKY advised that, with the existence of the dress being leaked, CLINTON may do a "mea culpa." LEWINSKY advised she guessed what CLINTON would say about her when he testified in the JONES case, and she was correct. LEWINSKY advised, though they did not discuss the issue in specific relation to the JONES matter, she and CLINTON had discussed what to say when asked about LEWINSKY's visits to the White House.

LEWINSKY advised she still has feelings towards CLINTON and she finds it hard to provide the OIC questions that may end up hurting CLINTON.

LEWINSKY would ask CLINTON why he wore the same tie twice in once week. (LEWINSKY advised she gave CLINTON the tie.)

LEWINSKY would ask CLINTON why he would give NELVIS the first tie LEWINSKY gave CLINTON. NELVIS then wore it to one of his grand jury appearances. LEWINSKY would ask CLINTON if he was trying to send LEWINSKY a message.

LEWINSKY does not think CLINTON is concerned about BRUCE LINDSEY testifying, as she is unaware of LINDSEY's knowledge of her relationship with CLINTON.

CLINTON advised he made a concerted effort not to have sex with other women. CLINTON seemed to feel guilty about cheating on his wife.

When CLINTON was in Mexico, he became ill. When he returned, he asked LEWINSKY if she could tell he was sick.

During their second telephone conversation of December 2, 1996, CLINTON told LEWINSKY about a jazz musician who had been killed on a boat. CLINTON seemed shocked about the musician's death.

LEWINSKY advised, if she were questioning CLINTON, she would show CLINTON pictures of items she had given him which he had not turned over, to refresh his memory.

LEWINSKY advised she never met CLINTON outside the White House for a private meeting.

The interview ended at approximately 4:40 p.m.

Monica Lewinsky's
Fifth Interview

1

OFFICE OF THE INDEPENDENT COUNSEL

08/01/98

MONICA S. LEWINSKY was interviewed pursuant to an immunity agreement between the Office of the Independent Counsel (OIC), LEWINSKY, and her attorneys. Present for the interview were Associate Independent Counsel (AIC) MICHAEL EMMICK, AIC KARIN IMMERGUT, AIC MARY ANNE WIRTH, AIC CRAIG LERNER, and Deputy Independent Counsel SOLOMON WISENBERG. Representing LEWINSKY were attorneys PRESTON BURTON of the law offices of PLATO CACHERIS, and ROBERT BREDHOFF ot STEIN, MITCHELL & MEZINES. The interview was conducted at the Watergate Hotel in Washington, D.C. beginning at 10:06 a.m. LEWINSKY provided the following information:

LEWINSKY began taking a new prescription medication this morning, which consisted of 10 milligrams of Prozac. LEWINSKY is still taking Serzone; other prescriptions have been discontinued.

When LEWINSKY learned that the President would testify in the PAULA JONES case, she assumed that the President would deny their relationship. There was no explicit agreement that the President would testify in a specific way, but there had been a pattern of denial in their relationship.

Calendars for December 1997 and January 1998 were shown to LEWINSKY. She briefly reviewed and confirmed a number of events occurring during those months. However, LEWINSKY did not remember speaking to BAYANI NELVIS on January 15, 1998.

On her second visit to the White House on December 6, 1997, LEWINSKY was supposed to meet BETTY CURRIE in the basement of the West Wing of the White House, per CURRIE's instructions. LEWINSKY saw MARSHA SCOTT walk by and left the basement to avoid SCOTT. LEWINSKY had earlier avoided SCOTT at the southwest gate. LEWINSKY called CURRIE and then met CURRIE in the West Wing lobby. CURRIE usually directed LEWINSKY away from United States Secret Service (USSS) uniformed guards who were friendly to DEBBIE SCHIFF. CURRIE told LEWINSKY not to come to the northwest gate as, "Those guys are mad at you." CURRIE was referring to the incident earlier in the day. LEWINSKY waited in the President's back study, which she entered through the dining room. The President said that it was very difficult for him to see LEWINSKY that day because "of all of this shit going on" and that he only had one day to see the lawyers about the JONES case. LEWINSKY was surprised that she got into the White House and had thought that she would only be able to talk to the President on the telephone that day. The President said that he had a gift from Vancouver for LEWINSKY. The President then received a call from ERSKINE BOWLES, apparently made an appointment to see BOWLES, and told LEWINSKY to come back another day to get her gift. The President said, "Don't worry, you'll get your gift." The President did not discuss the JONES witness list with LEWINSKY. The President said that he would talk to VERNON JORDAN on LEWINSKY's behalf about jobs. The President also said, "I promise, I won't abandon you." Nothing the President said left LEWINSKY with the impression that their relationship was any different than it was before. The visit lasted about 20 or 25 minutes. CURRIE helped LEWINSKY exit out the back way before BOWLES arrived.

On the evening of December 6, 1997, LEWINSKY went to New York and stayed with her mother. She told her about the Christmas Party on Friday, that LEWINSKY had been very upset on Saturday, and that she had gotten in to see the President on Saturday.

On December 7, 1997, LEWINSKY returned to Washington by airplane. Enroute, LEWINSKY wrote the "whipped cream" card, which she sent in the next day or so. The card said something to the effect of, "Nothing would make me happier than to see you, except to see you naked with a winning lottery ticket in one hand and a can of whipped cream in the other."

On December 8, 1997, LEWINSKY sent a package to VERNON JORDAN containing a white "NATO" ballcap, some chocolate, a note, and possibly a copy of her resume. LEWINSKY did this as a friendly reminder to JORDAN to keep helping her.

Sometime during this week GAIL from JORDAN's office called LEWIN-SKY to set up a meeting.

LEWINSKY does not recall whether she called BETTY CURRIE to ascertain whether the card for the President had arrived, nor does she recall whether she called LINDA TRIPP that day.

In regard to BAYANI NELVIS, LEWINSKY described him as a nice person, but not everyone at the White House treated him right. NELVIS is very loyal to the President. LEWINSKY first met NELVIS during the furlough in November 1995. NELVIS is Filipino, has an accent, and is friendly. NELVIS knew that LEWINSKY had feelings for the President and that she enjoyed a special relationship with the President. When LEWINSKY would have drinks with NELVIS, he would provide personal details about the President. LEWINSKY asked NELVIS about the details of the President's schedule and the President's routine when he was out of town. On one of the Presidential trips, NELVIS called LEWINSKY from Martha's Vineyard and asked her if she wanted to come up there and stay in the house with several other staff members. LEWINSKY had wanted to set up a rendezvous with the President on one of his trips, but declined NELVIS's offer. LEWINSKY met NELVIS once for dinner at the CALIFORNIA PIZZA KITCHEN in Pentagon City. LEWINSKY gave NELVIS one or two ties. NELVIS bought LEWINSKY perfume for her birthday and gave her glasses, golf balls, and cards from Air Force One. NELVIS did not want the President to know that he was friends with LEWINSKY. NELVIS never noticed which ties the President wore from day to day. LEWINSKY did not see NELVIS in Madrid, Spain, but may have seen GLEN MAES. NELVIS told LEWINSKY to be careful around the USSS officers. This conversation may have occurred in the Roosevelt Room on the day that they discussed cigars. NELVIS told LEWINSKY that CATHY CORNELIUS had gone with the advance party on the trip to Russia and that NELVIS took CORNELIUS downtown to shop, since she was afraid to go alone.

In regard to DEBBIE SCHIFF, LEWINSKY observed SCHIFF clomp around the office in the President's shoes on February 28, 1997, at the radio address. This appeared to LEWINSKY to show SCHIFF's familiarity with the President.

On December 11, 1997, LEWINSKY went to the office of VERNON JORDAN for a meeting, which had been arranged by GAIL of his office about December 8th or 9th. LEWINSKY waited in JORDAN's lobby for about 20 minutes. LEWINSKY was very nervous at the meeting and could not decide whether to wear a red headband that she brought to his office. LEWINSKY told JORDAN, "I'm more nervous with you than when I'm with the President." JORDAN tried to be less formal on this visit and to make LEWINSKY feel more at ease. In this visit, which included a turkey sandwich lunch, JORDAN told LEWINSKY the names of people that he had called. JORDAN suggested that LEWINSKY write letters to them with detailed wording that he provided, and asked that he receive copies of the letters. JORDAN explained his assistance by saying, "You're a friend of the President of the United States."

JORDAN asked what the occasions were when LEWINSKY got mad at the President and said, "Don't get mad at the President when he's talking to TONY BLAIR on the telephone; call me and get mad at me." LEWINSKY explained that this was absurd, since she did not know JORDAN's home telephone and why would she talk to him. With a smile JORDAN said, "Don't deny it, your problem is you're in love." LEWINSKY most likely blushed, but did not respond. JORDAN probably knew of LEWINSKY's sexual relationship, but made no explicit statement that he knew.

LEWINSKY advised JORDAN that her mom was engaged to PETER STRAUS and JORDAN said that he knew STRAUS, and tried to call him with LEWINSKY present. JORDAN did not reach STRAUS or LEWINSKY's mother, but he left a message. JORDAN asked why LEWINSKY's mother owned a separate apartment in New York.

LEWINSKY knew that BETTY CURRIE knew VERNON JORDAN. LEWINSKY called JORDAN's office to advise him of the death of CURRIE's brother. LEWINSKY did not have any recollection of JORDAN asking her how LEWINSKY got in to see the President. JORDAN ended the visit of 40 minutes by saying that he would check out other leads, in addition to the three companies that LEWINSKY was to write. LEWINSKY's overall impression upon leaving was that she was going to get a job with JORDAN's help.

On December 11, 1997, LEWINSKY went to the Pentagon from JORDAN's office, typed the letters they had discussed, and talked to LINDA TRIPP.

LEWINSKY still held out hope that the President would get her a job in Communications at the White House.

On December 12, 1997, or sometime during this week, LINDA TRIPP met with her attorney, KIRBY BEHRE. TRIPP wanted LEWINSKY to help TRIPP buy a Christmas gift for BEHRE in the concourse at the Pentagon. TRIPP advised LEWINSKY that she had written out the details of the relationship between LEWINSKY and the President, put them in a sealed envelope, and gave them to BEHRE, to be opened in the event of TRIPP's death. LEWINSKY was aghast. TRIPP also said that if she was asked about LEWINSKY she, TRIPP, was going to tell the truth.

LEWINSKY discussed the TRIPP problem in general terms with her mother.

On December 12 or 13, 1997, there was a going away party for the boyfriend of ASHLEY RAINES, JOEY Last Name Unknown (LNU), who was going to Israel.

On about December 15, 1997, LEWINSKY attended the swearing in of KATHY HAYCOCK in the Vice-President's ceremonial room. Vice-President GORE did the swearing in. The President did not attend. LEWINSKY tried to call BETTY CURRIE, but does not recall talking to her.

On December 17, 1997, at about 2:30 a.m., LEWINSKY received a telephone call from the President. He was not in a jovial mood and had concern in his voice. After about four seconds the President said he would call right back and hung up. About two minutes later, the President called back and said that he had two important things to tell LEWINSKY. First, BETTY CURRIE's brother had been killed in a car accident. They discussed whether LEWINSKY should call her. Then the President said that he had seen the PAULA JONES witness list and that LEWINSKY was on it. The President said, "It broke my heart when I saw your name on the list." The President said not to worry about it and that it did not necessarily mean LEWINSKY would get a subpoena. The President said that it was possible that LEWINSKY would be subpoenaed in a month or so. The President said that LEWINSKY could always say that she was coming to see BETTY, or that LEWINSKY was bringing papers from Legislative Affairs to the President. The President said that if LEWINSKY did get subpoenaed, call BETTY CURRIE and they would work something out. LEWINSKY assumed that this meant that they would help LEWINSKY figure out what to do. The President said, "Maybe you could sign an affidavit." LEWINSKY's impression was that she would sign an affidavit and get out of a deposition.

LEWINSKY told the President that she had some job interviews scheduled in New York. LEWINSKY also said that maybe she would be gone and the lawyers could not find her. The President said that was a possible solution.

LEWINSKY expressed her opinion to the President on how to settle the PAULA JONES case. LEWINSKY had read an article in the Times that people were sending in money to help the President with his legal problems. LEWINSKY advised the President that since PAULA JONES was only asking

85

for $500,000, that the President should pay up to save his family and the country. The President expressed surprise that JONES was only asking for $500,000, as he thought the asking price was $1 million. The President said that he would ask his lawyers. LEWINSKY later cut out the Times article about the contributions and mailed it to MITCH ETTINGER.

The President said that maybe BETTY CURRIE could come in on the weekend and he could give LEWINSKY her Christmas presents. LEWINSKY told the President not to dare bothering CURRIE now just when her brother had died. No discussion of other evidence occurred. Being on the witness list was a relief to LEWINSKY in one way, that is, if both LEWINSKY and TRIPP were subpoenaed, and they both denied the relationship, then the JONES' people would not know about it. This telephone call lasted between 20 and 40 minutes. After hanging up, LEWINSKY cried.

At about 4:00 a.m., on December 17, 1997, LEWINSKY called LINDA TRIPP, awakened her, and spoke with her for about 15 or 20 minutes. By this time, LEWINSKY was suspicious of TRIPP, but not to the point of accusing her of anything. The reason for the call was to discuss the fact that LEWINSKY was on the JONES witness list. LEWINSKY does not recall this discussion in any detail.

Also on December 17, 1997, LEWINSKY visited with BETTY CURRIE in her home and took her some bagels.

On the night of December 17, 1997, LEWINSKY took a plane to New York, where her mother met her at the airport with a car. LEWINSKY was nearly hysterical and told her mother that LINDA TRIPP was going to tell. MARCIA LEWIS was visibly upset. The problems were not discussed with PETER STRAUS.

On December 18, 1997, LEWINSKY had a job interview that went well at McANDREWS and FORBES. An interview at BURSON MARSTELLER the same day did not go well at all and LEWINSKY cried when she left. BURSON did not make a good appearance as a company with LEWINSKY, because they had too many people talking to her and did not seem to be well organized.

On the evening of December 18, 1997, LEWINSKY called LINDA TRIPP from a pay phone at the airport in New York.

On December 19, 1997, LEWINSKY called VERNON JORDAN to discuss her New York interviews. LEWINSKY believes that she probably called TRIPP from the Pentagon but TRIPP may not have been at work that day.

On December 19, 1997, LEWINSKY was at work at the Pentagon. A little before 4:00 p.m., LEWINSKY received a call from a process server, whom she agreed to meet at the Metro entrance, and received the subpoena for the PAULA JONES case. LEWINSKY cried. LEWINSKY went straight to a pay phone and called VERNON JORDAN. JORDAN could not understand LEW-INSKY, because of the crying, and asked her to come to JORDAN's office. LEWINSKY went back to her office, excused herself, went home and changed clothes. LEWINSKY called JORDAN, because the President had previously told her to call BETTY CURRIE, but LEWINSKY felt that she could not call CURRIE so soon after the death of CURRIE's brother.

After arriving at JORDAN's office, LEWINSKY waited in the lobby for awhile and then advised JORDAN that the President had warned her that she was on the JONES witness list and that she had been subpoenaed that afternoon. JORDAN then received a telephone call from an unknown caller, and asked LEWINSKY to step out of his office. LEWINSKY waited in the conference room for about 15 or 20 minutes before JORDAN invited her back to his office. LEWINSKY did not know what to do about the subpoena. JORDAN told LEWINSKY to calm down, that it was a standard subpoena. LEWINSKY told JORDAN that the subpoena also requested a hat pin the President had given her. JORDAN then called FRANK CARTER in LEWINSKY's presence and scheduled an appointment for Monday morning. JORDAN said that there were only two important questions:

1. "Did you have sex with the President?"
2. "Did he ask you for sex?"

LEWINSKY answered "no" to both questions. LEWINSKY believed that JORDAN knew of her sexual relationship with the President, and her impression was that JORDAN wanted to know how LEWINSKY was going to answer these questions when testifying. JORDAN instructed LEWINSKY to come to his office at 10:30 a.m. Monday. LEWINSKY asked JORDAN more than once to make sure to tell the President that she had been subpoenaed, because LEWINSKY could not call CURRIE, who was supposed to tell the President. LEWINSKY also said, "Give him a hug for me." JORDAN responded, "I don't hug guys." JORDAN slapped LEWINSKY on the backside as if to say "get out of here kid." JORDAN said that he would see the President that night and tell him about the subpoena.

LEWINSKY went home, called LINDA TRIPP, and made cryptic statements such as, "The flowers were delivered today," but TRIPP did not understand that LEWINSKY was trying to tell her that she had been subpoenaed that day. LEWINSKY was afraid to come out and tell TRIPP that she had been subpoenaed because LEWINSKY believed that the JONES people had tapped her telephone. LEWINSKY offered to go early to TRIPP's Christmas party the next day to help set up, primarily so that LEWINSKY could talk to TRIPP.

On December 20, 1997, when LEWINSKY arrived at 5:00 p.m. to help set up the party, TRIPP said that she could not understand what LEWINSKY was trying to say the night before. LEWINSKY and TRIPP's Indian friend helped prepare the party food. LEWINSKY did not get a chance to talk to TRIPP until she was leaving and TRIPP came out to the car. LEWINSKY said that she was very worried about the hatpin. LEWINSKY told TRIPP that TRIPP could now feel safe in denying the relationship. This was the first time that LEWINSKY recalls vocalizing that she intended to deny her affair with the President. LEWINSKY received the impression that TRIPP might feel more encouraged to deny knowledge of LEWINSKY's affair. LEWINSKY met TRIPP's friend, KATE LNU, at the party.

The same night, December 20, 1997, LEWINSKY went to a party hosted by a friend of ASHLEY RAINES. LEWINSKY was drinking some by then and started telling RAINES about being in a bit of trouble. RAINES said that she did not want to know. Therefore, few details were provided by LEWINSKY.

On Sunday, December 21, 1997, LEWINSKY had a hangover; probably talked to TRIPP, and figured out which items to take to FRANK CARTER in response to the subpoena.

On Monday, December 22, 1997, LEWINSKY was nervous about going to see her attorney, FRANK CARTER. LEWINSKY called VERNON JORDAN to see if she could come over earlier than 10:30 a.m., because she was scared. There was no discussion about who was going to pay the legal bill, except JORDAN said not to worry about it. LEWINSKY hoped that JORDAN would pay the bill, because he was the President's friend and had a lot of money. At a later date, LEWINSKY had another discussion with JORDAN about CARTER's fee.

LEWINSKY asked JORDAN what if someone called the President on the telephone, and JORDAN responded that the President can talk to people. LEWINSKY advised that she and the President had phone sex together. JORDAN asked what phone sex was. LEWINSKY did not want to explain, but JORDAN again asked. LEWINSKY said, "We're taking care of business on each end while we're talking." The meeting in JORDAN's office lasted about 10 or 15 minutes. LEWINSKY bugged JORDAN to let her know if JORDAN had told the President about the subpoena. JORDAN responded that LEWINSKY had to learn to trust people, and that he had told the President.

Before leaving for CARTER's office on December 22, 1997, LEWINSKY showed JORDAN the items that she was taking to CARTER in response to the subpoena, but artfully indicated to JORDAN that it did not include everything. LEWINSKY had told JORDAN about the hat pin on Friday, and it was not included in the items that she was taking to CARTER. LEWINSKY said to JORDAN, "This is what I'm taking to CARTER, this should do." LEWINSKY agreed that her statement in the first proffer, to the effect that she had made it clear to JORDAN that not all gifts were included, was a true statement. LEWINSKY said that she did not intend to tell CARTER everything, because O. J. SIMPSON told his first lawyer that he did it and had to change lawyers. LEWINSKY informed JORDAN of how the President could settle the PAULA JONES matter, but JORDAN did not warm to the proposal. LEWINSKY assumed that JORDAN knew that she had a physically intimate relationship with the President.

Since there was a driver in the car with JORDAN and LEWINSKY enroute to CARTER's office, their five minute conversation was guarded. HOWARD PASTOR's name was mentioned as someone who could possibly help in the job search. They also discussed the purchase of Christmas presents.

At CARTER's office on December 22, 1997, JORDAN introduced LEWINSKY to CARTER and said that he was a good lawyer. This gave LEWINSKY the impression that this was JORDAN's personal lawyer, but she found out later that this was not true. LEWINSKY and JORDAN sat on the sofa for a few minutes and LEWINSKY told CARTER that the subpoena was ludicrous. JORDAN departed. LEWINSKY suggested an affidavit to CARTER, but he questioned whether there was any reason that LEWINSKY was pulled into this case. LEWINSKY responded that it was because she knew WALTER KAYE and BETTY CURRIE. CARTER asked if LEWINSKY had ever been alone with the President and LEWINSKY responded that she had delivered papers to the President on the weekend and that they had chatted about general topics. CARTER asked LEWINSKY if she had sex with the President and LEWINSKY denied that she had.

LEWINSKY asked CARTER if she could sue JONES's attorneys for invasion of privacy, and asked him if she had to cash the check that they sent with the subpoena. CARTER asked LEWINSKY to look for additional things, such as the photograph of the President wearing one of her ties, and to look for the photograph of LEWINSKY's family with the President. LEWINSKY said that she could not find these items and CARTER said that she had to produce whatever was in her control. CARTER said that this was a standard subpoena and may have just been a fishing expedition. LEWINSKY explained that she did not want to get involved in the JONES case and that she was going to a new job in New York. CARTER suggested that prior to preparing an affidavit for LEWINSKY, he would call the JONES people and maybe have LEWINSKY give them an interview. LEWINSKY urged CARTER to call the BENNETT people, and he agreed to do so. LEWINSKY wanted the President to know that she was a team player. CARTER may have called BENNETT's office in her presence. CARTER said that he would send a retainer agreement in the mail.

LEWINSKY went back to work on December 22, 1997, and may have called VERNON JORDAN from a pay phone. LEWINSKY spoke with LINDA TRIPP at least once in person that afternoon. This conversation consisted of TRIPP telling LEWINSKY not to ask her to lie, and LEWINSKY reminding TRIPP that she had promised not to tell anyone about LEWINSKY's relationship with the President. TRIPP countered with the statement that her promise not to tell was not binding if she was under oath. LEWINSKY replied, "I wasn't thinking about under oath," which meant that she wanted TRIPP to lie no matter what the circumstances. TRIPP kept reminding LEWINSKY that VERNON JORDAN had gotten LEWINSKY a big name lawyer, but suggested that LEWINSKY might want to get an independent lawyer. LEWINSKY thought that perhaps TRIPP was jealous of LEWINSKY. LEWINSKY told TRIPP that she wanted to be in the CLINTON/BENNETT camp. LEWINSKY did not want to acknowledge that TRIPP was "doing her in," and was not always telling TRIPP the truth by this time. LEWINSKY did not think that it was so wrong to lie on the affidavit, because this concerned a personal matter and was none of PAULA JONES's business.

In regard to the E-mail sent and received on LEWINSKY's computer at the Pentagon, at some point during the week after LEWINSKY was subpoenaed, the computer person, FLOYD LNU, said that the E-mail was automatically destroyed every four weeks. FLOYD also told LEWINSKY how to permanently delete E-mail and LEWINSKY then made some deletions of her E-mail, specifically those sent to KATHRYN ALLDAY DAVIS, and a few to TRIPP. Sometime in December 1997, LEWINSKY asked TRIPP to delete the

E-mail that TRIPP had received from LEWINSKY. LEWINSKY did this because E-mail would leave a trail. The President was unaware that LEWINSKY had mentioned him in E-mail and never told LEWINSKY to delete any of her messages.

On December 23, 1997, LEWINSKY was interviewed for a job by an AMERICAN EXPRESS official in Washington. The interviewer advised LEWINSKY that LEWINSKY really did not have the experience necessary for the position. DARCY BACON, wife of KEN BACON, took LEWINSKY to lunch. LEWINSKY may have called TRIPP that night. If so, this was the last time LEWINSKY talked to TRIPP until January, 1998.

December 24, 1997, was LEWINSKY's last day at the Pentagon.

From December 25 to 27, LEWINSKY was in town, LINDA TRIPP did not return her calls. The situation was depressing. LEWINSKY's mother, MARCIA LEWIS, came down from New York on December 26 or 27, as PETER STRAUS had gone skiing. At some point, LEWIS suggested to LEWINSKY that she get in touch with a Christian Scientist woman in New York for counseling.

On December 27, 1997, LEWINSKY called BETTY CURRIE about the Christmas presents the President had for her. CURRIE was giving a White House tour to her church group the next morning so she told LEWINSKY to come in then.

On December 28, 1997, LEWINSKY went to BETTY CURRIE's office at about 8:30 a.m. CURRIE and LEWINSKY played with BUDDY in the Oval Office while the President was on the telephone. LEWINSKY went to the back rooms with the President so that he could get some coffee. LEWINSKY asked the President how her name had gotten on the PAULA JONES witness list. The President responded that it may have been "that woman from last summer" who was involved in the KATHLEEN WILLEY thing, and that maybe she just wants to cause trouble. The President asked LEWINSKY if she had told that woman or anyone else about the hatpin, and LEWINSKY denied that she had. The President suggested that maybe one of the USSS uniform guards or someone else had seen LEWINSKY with the hatpin when she was leaving. LEWINSKY said this could not have happened.
LEWINSKY said that she was concerned about the gifts that the President had given her and suggested to the President that BETTY CURRIE hold the gifts. The President said something like, "I don't know," or "I'll think about it." The President did not tell LEWINSKY what to do with the gifts at that time. LEWINSKY told the President that she was going to sign an affidavit, and that she was moving to New York, to which the President responded, "Good." LEWINSKY probably did not tell CURRIE about receiving the JONES subpoena. CURRIE walked LEWINSKY by the Palm Room, and may have taken that route to avoid a particular guard. LEWINSKY had left her pass in the office and CURRIE asked the guards at the southwest gate to let LEWINSKY out without the pass.

BETTY CURRIE called LEWINSKY at home later in the day, and said, "I understand that you have something for me." LEWINSKY was not surprised that CURRIE called since LEWINSKY had talked to the President about the gifts earlier that day. When CURRIE called, there was no question in LEWINSKY's mind that CURRIE knew what she was calling for. LEWINSKY then took the hat pin, and other selected items that would cause suspicion, and placed them in a box. LEWINSKY kind of compromised in deciding what to give to CURRIE to hold for her; for instance, the books that the President had given her were too sentimental to give back just in case LEWINSKY never got the box back. LEWINSKY put the Leaves of Grass book in her closet in a plastic bag. LEWINSKY gave the box to BETTY CURRIE when CURRIE came by the Watergate about 2:00 p.m. LEWINSKY had sealed the box so that CURRIE would not look at the items, and marked "do not throw away" in hopes that neither CURRIE nor the President would destroy the gifts. By giving the box of gifts to CURRIE, LEWINSKY was, in her mind, placing these items in the President's control. LEWINSKY said that the cassette tapes of the President's messages and the blue dress she wore on February 28, 1997 had already been taken to New York earlier in December. LEWINSKY told CURRIE not to throw the box away. CURRIE did not comment. LEWINSKY also gave CURRIE a small plant and a balloon to take to CURRIE's mother, who was in the hospital.

On December 28 or 29, 1997, LEWINSKY's brother MICHAEL was in town and LEWINSKY traveled to New York.

On December 29 or 30, 1997, LEWINSKY took a test at BURSON, MARSTELLER.

On December 30, 1997, LEWINSKY called VERNON JORDAN to discuss the job situation and was invited by either JORDAN or GAIL, his secretary, to have breakfast with JORDAN the next day. LEWINSKY traveled to Washington by train. LEWINSKY intended to surface the fact to JORDAN that LINDA TRIPP may have been the source of information resulting in LEWINSKY's subpoena by the JONES lawyers since, she had not acknowledged that to the President. LEWINSKY expected JORDAN to advise the President of this information.

On December 31, 1997, LEWINSKY arrived at the PARK HYATT MELROSE RESTAURANT on M Street by taxi, about 8:00 a.m. or 8:30 a.m., and the hostess advised LEWINSKY that Mr. JORDAN was running late. Upon JORDAN's arrival, they sat at JORDAN's usual table. LEWINSKY inquired whether JORDAN was going to the "Renaissance" weekend and he replied that he was not. LEWINSKY advised that she had seen the President. JORDAN and LEWINSKY talked about jobs.

LEWINSKY felt she could not fake the story about TRIPP to the President, but assumed that he would get the message if LEWINSKY told JORDAN; therefore, LEWINSKY said to JORDAN that perhaps the leak to the JONES attorneys had been from one of her friends who spent the night at her house, and who could have seen her notes. JORDAN asked, "The President wrote you notes?" LEWINSKY said the notes were not from the President, but were notes that she had written about him. JORDAN said, "Make sure they're not there." LEWINSKY took this to mean that JORDAN wanted her to destroy the notes. LEWINSKY did go home and throw out the notes, drafts of letters and notes to the President, and a card "Starry, Starry Night." This occurred when LEWINSKY was packing to move to New York and she was eliminating things. LEWINSKY disposed of perhaps 50 pages.

After breakfast on December 31, 1997, JORDAN drove LEWINSKY back to his office. LEWINSKY asked whether the President would always be married to Mrs. CLINTON and JORDAN responded in the affirmative and quoted an unrecalled bible verse to LEWINSKY. JORDAN said, "Maybe you two can have an affair in three years." LEWINSKY responded that they had already had an affair with everything but sex. JORDAN responded with one of his grunts of acknowledgment, but did not appear to want to know any further details.

LEWINSKY then read the transcript from LINDA TRIPP tape number six, pages 12 to 22, concerning her first meeting with JORDAN. In regard to the statement, "The other one also asked you—you didn't tell anyone did you?" LEWINSKY said that she could not recall saying that, but her recollection might improve if she could hear the actual tape.

On January 3 or 4, 1998, LEWINSKY dropped off a book to BETTY CURRIE for the President. The book was entitled Presidents of the United States and contained a romantic note that LEWINSKY had written to the President after she saw the movie "Titanic."

On January 9, 1998, at about 4:00 p.m., a woman from REVLON called, indicated that LEWINSKY's prospects for a job at REVLON were good, and said that a woman from the Human Resources Department would call LEWINSKY on Monday to extend a formal offer.

On January 9, 1998, LEWINSKY probably had a 30 minute call to LINDA TRIPP.

On January 12, 1998, LEWINSKY received an informal job offer from the Human Resources person and informally accepted the job.

On January 13, 1998, LEWINSKY had a five minute conversation with VERNON JORDAN.

LEWINSKY did not recall if she received a telephone call from FRANK CARTER on January 15, 1998, but she did recall that at some point she was paged by FRANK CARTER while shopping at SAFEWAY on Wisconsin Avenue. LEWINSKY called CARTER, at which time CARTER asked if LEWINSKY had ever received packages from the White House, or sent things to the White House by courier. LEWINSKY responded that she had sent packages by courier to BETTY CURRIE at the White House. LEWINSKY called SPEED COURIER SERVICE and found out that their policy was not to reveal any information about deliveries unless subpoenaed. LEWINSKY therefore concluded that the records had already been subpoenaed. LEWINSKY began wondering how the JONES attorneys could have known about the courier service. After thinking about it later, LEWINSKY was suspicious of MARK HUFFMAN, BETTY CURRIE, and LINDA TRIPP.

Later that day, LEWINSKY gave a ride to BETTY CURRIE and asked her about the call that CURRIE had received from MIKE ISIKOFF, in which ISIKOFF asked CURRIE about the package deliveries at the White House. LEWINSKY called LINDA TRIPP to tell TRIPP that if ISIKOFF called, to tell him that TRIPP did not know anything about her relationship with the President.

Between January 13 and January 15, 1998, LEWINSKY had a conversation with BETTY CURRIE about contacting JOHN PODESTA, because LEWINSKY was worried that her former supervisor at the White House, JOHN HILLEY, would not recommend her. LEWINSKY needed a favorable reference for the job at Revlon.

The interviewed terminated at 5:03 p.m.

Monica Lewinsky's
Sixth Interview

1

OFFICE OF THE INDEPENDENT COUNSEL

08/02/98

MONICA S. LEWINSKY was interviewed under the terms of an immunity agreement between the Office of the Independent Counsel (OIC) and her. LEWINSKY was interviewed at the Office of the Independent Counsel, 1001 Pennsylvania Avenue, Washington, DC 20004. Present for the interview were Associate Independent Counsel (AIC) MICHAEL EMMICK, AIC MARY ANNE WIRTH, AIC KARIN IMMERGUT, AIC CRAIG LERNER, AIC JULIE MYERS and Deputy Independent Counsel (DIC) ROBERT BITTMAN. Present representing LEWINSKY were PRESTON BURTON and ROBERT BREDHOFF. LEWINSKY provided the following information, beginning at approximately 10:25 a.m.

On January 4, 1998, LEWINSKY called BETTY CURRIE in the late afternoon to arrange a meeting with CURRIE. LEWINSKY went to CURRIE's home to give CURRIE a package to give to President WILLIAM JEFFERSON CLINTON. LEWINSKY advised this was the first time she went to CURRIE's home to give CURRIE a package to give to CLINTON.

In the package was a book about the Presidents of the United States and a note. LEWINSKY cannot recall exactly when she purchased the book, but it occurred sometime after December 28, 1997. LEWINSKY advised she thinks she purchased the book on January 2 or January 3, 1998. LEWINSKY advised she withdrew $40 from the RIGGS NATIONAL BANK automatic teller machine on Wisconsin Avenue in Georgetown to buy the book.

LEWINSKY advised she purchased the book at a book store next to the Christian Scientist book store on Wisconsin Avenue. LEWINSKY advised she and ASHLEY RAINES saw the movie "Titanic," which prompted her to write the note she enclosed with the book. LEWINSKY advised she was feeling very down when she wrote the note. LEWINSKY described the note as very romantic.

When LEWINSKY saw CURRIE, LEWINSKY asked CURRIE to give the package to CLINTON. LEWINSKY and CURRIE also spoke about LEWINSKY's New Year's Eve encounter with STEVE NEUWIRTH.

LEWINSKY advised she was at CURRIE's residence for approximately twenty minutes.

LEWINSKY advised that giving CURRIE, on December 28, 1997, the box with some of the gifts CLINTON had given LEWINSKY, on December 28th made LEWINSKY feel she was assuring CLINTON that she was on the same team. LEWINSKY does not recall talking about the PAULA JONES case with CURRIE. LEWINSKY may have mentioned LEWINSKY's idea about settling the JONES case with CLINTON on December 17, 1997.

On January 5, 1998, LEWINSKY met with FRANK CARTER, though she can not recall the exact time. LEWINSKY advised CARTER asked her a few difficult questions about sex. LEWINSKY told CARTER she did not have sex with CLINTON. LEWINSKY advised the two went into detail about how a deposition is conducted. LEWINSKY asked if her parents could be present during the deposition. LEWINSKY did not consider the meeting a full preparation session for the deposition.

LEWINSKY advised CARTER told her the types of questions that would be asked during the deposition, including how LEWINSKY got her job at the Pentagon. LEWINSKY advised this worried her as she did not know how to answer questions related to her transfer to the Pentagon without the answers leading to her relationship with CLINTON. LEWINSKY was concerned that the attorneys for JONES would go to people at the White House to verify LEWINSKY's answers and, because some of those people did not like LEWINSKY, they would contradict what LEWINSKY said under oath.

LEWINSKY could not recall taking any items to CARTER's office on January 5, 1998, although she could have, but she definitely recalls doing so on another occasion.

CARTER told LEWINSKY that, in civil cases, a lot of things were done at the last minute, so she probably would not hear about her subpoena being quashed until later.

During one of her meetings with CARTER, LEWINSKY mentioned telling LINDA TRIPP about LEWINSKY's subpoena. CARTER got a copy of the Newsweek article regarding TRIPP and KATHLEEN WILLEY.

LEWINSKY left the meeting with the understanding CARTER was to draft an affidavit and LEWINSKY would pick it up later that day.

LEWINSKY received a copy of the affidavit on January 5 or 6, 1998. LEWINSKY was nervous about signing the affidavit and wanted VERNON JORDAN to review a copy of the affidavit and approve it. LEWINSKY thought that, by having JORDAN approve the affidavit, it was the same as having CLINTON's approval.

On January 5 or 6, 1998 LEWINSKY called CURRIE to tell her LEWIN-SKY needed to talk to CLINTON. (LEWINSKY advised that on her December 28, 1997 meeting with CLINTON, CLINTON told LEWINSKY to call CUR-RIE if LEWINSKY had any questions about anything related to the JONES matter.) LEWINSKY was very cryptic with CURRIE when they talked. LEWINSKY said she was going to sign something the next day and she needed to speak with CLINTON before doing so. LEWINSKY advised she wanted to make CLINTON nervous.

LEWINSKY advised CURRIE called at approximately 7 or 8 p.m. LEWIN-SKY was at the apartment of her aunt, DEBRA FINERMAN, when CURRIE called. LEWINSKY had told CURRIE that is where she would be. CURRIE transferred the call to CLINTON.

LEWINSKY told CLINTON she had spoken to CARTER and went over possible questions that would be asked in her deposition. CLINTON asked LEWINSKY what she was concerned about. LEWINSKY told CLINTON she was worried about giving "vanilla" answers to questions about how LEWIN-SKY got her job at the Pentagon. LEWINSKY was concerned that people at the White House, who did not like LEWINSKY, would "screw" her.

CLINTON told LEWINSKY to say that people in the Office of Legislative Affairs (OLA) found the position and the people in the OLA recommended her for it. LEWINSKY said that she could answer that way. (LEWINSKY advised that explanation was true, but it was not the entire truth.)

LEWINSKY was reassured by what CLINTON said about her transfer to the Pentagon. LEWINSKY and CLINTON spoke about the affidavit. LEWIN-SKY advised she did not want to sign anything until she was reassured by the White House that she would not be "screwed." LEWINSKY asked CLINTON if he wanted to see the affidavit and CLINTON said no, he had seen about fifteen of them.

CLINTON advised he liked the book she had given him. LEWINSKY told CLINTON it cost $40 and CLINTON asked why she paid so much for it. LEWINSKY brought up the subject of the note she gave him with the book. CLINTON said that LEWINSKY should not write things like that on paper. LEWINSKY advised CLINTON was referring to romantic items LEWINSKY had placed in the note. LEWINSKY assumed CLINTON threw away the notes she gave him. LEWINSKY advised the notes would be more incriminating than the gifts.

The telephone call lasted about ten minutes.

LEWINSKY advised that on "ZEDILLO Day," she saw a cutout of the Valentine's Day personal advertisement she had placed in the "Washington Post." LEWINSKY saw CLINTON's copy of the advertisement on the desk in the Oval Office study.

LEWINSKY advised she was annoyed with CLINTON that day because of a photograph in the newspaper that showed CLINTON and HILLARY ROD-HAM CLINTON dancing together on a beach.

LEWINSKY advised that she has January 5 and 6, 1998 confused at this time.

LEWINSKY advised that on January 6, 1998, she received a call from CARTER saying the draft affidavit was ready. Later that day, LEWINSKY called JORDAN's office and was told by JORDAN's secretary GAYLE Last Name Unknown (LNU) that JORDAN was out of town. LEWINSKY stopped by CARTER's office in the afternoon and picked up the draft affidavit, which CARTER had left in an envelope on the first floor of his office.

LEWINSKY took the affidavit home, read it and underlined the areas she was concerned about. LEWINSKY was concerned about the last sentence in paragraph six which read "this would have lasted only a matter of minutes and would not have been a 'private' meeting, that is not behind closed doors." LEWINSKY was also concerned about paragraph eight regarding seeing the President "with crowds of other people present."

LEWINSKY advised she had previously planned on signing the affidavit on January 6, 1998, but decided JORDAN needed to see the affidavit first. LEWINSKY copied the affidavit and dropped it off at JORDAN's office that afternoon. LEWINSKY did not tell CARTER she was showing the affidavit to JORDAN. LEWINSKY advised that having JORDAN's approval was the same as CLINTON's.

LEWINSKY advised that most of the changes made to the draft affidavit she showed JORDAN were LEWINSKY's ideas. LEWINSKY is sure JORDAN commented on the affidavit, but she is not sure if he suggested any changes. LEWINSKY advised she may have crossed out the items she had previously underlined during the course of her discussion with JORDAN. LEWINSKY advised she did not discuss the sexual relationship aspect of the affidavit with JORDAN and only spoke with him for about six minutes.

LEWINSKY told JORDAN she would talk to CARTER the following day to sign the affidavit. LEWINSKY expected JORDAN to let CLINTON know when the affidavit was signed. LEWINSKY asked JORDAN if she should give a signed copy of the affidavit to CLINTON and JORDAN said no. LEWINSKY advised JORDAN never said JORDAN did not want to see the affidavit.

LEWINSKY advised she was unaware of JORDAN's telephone calls that same day to NANCY HERNREICH and CLINTON. After looking at all the telephone contact that was made between JORDAN and CLINTON as reflected on a chart of phone records presented to her by the OIC, LEWIN-SKY advised that it seems suspicious.

LEWINSKY advised she does not recall what she did during the evening of January 6, 1998, but she did feel relieved to be signing the affidavit. LEWINSKY felt that her involvement in the JONES matter would be over.

On January 7, 1998, LEWINSKY met with CARTER at 10:00 a.m. LEWIN-SKY does not recall bringing any items with her. LEWINSKY did bring a copy of the draft affidavit with her. LEWINSKY advised she and CARTER met in CARTER's office. On previous occasions, she and CARTER met in a conference room.

LEWINSKY advised CARTER had three versions of the affidavit to show her. There was not much difference between the three drafts. LEWINSKY advised none of the affidavits mentioned her having a sexual relationship with CLINTON.

LEWINSKY advised that it was her idea not to put anything in the affidavit about being alone with CLINTON. LEWINSKY advised CARTER suggested the language used when describing the procedure of getting CLINTON's signature on official documents.

LEWINSKY thought the statement in her affidavit that she could not fathom any reason why she was subpoenaed was not completely false. LEWINSKY felt the JONES case was about sexual harassment and LEWINSKY was not sexually harassed. LEWINSKY advised LEWINSKY lost her job at the White House because of her sexual relationship with CLINTON. LEWINSKY advised she was involved in a consensual sexual relationship with CLINTON.

LEWINSKY advised she met with CARTER for one hour to an hour and one half. LEWINSKY advised she recalled walking down the hall to have the affidavit notarized. LEWINSKY recalls walking down the hall rationalizing to herself that she did not have a sexual relationship with CLINTON, when, in fact, she had. LEWINSKY rationalized lying about having a "sexual relationship" with CLINTON because they never had sexual intercourse.

LEWINSKY advised she does not have a direct memory of JORDAN's involvement with CARTER after LEWINSKY hired CARTER. LEWINSKY advised that after she looked at the chart of phone records presented to her by the OIC, she believes JORDAN's involvement may have been more substantial than she previously believed.

CARTER told LEWINSKY that he would send a copy of the affidavit to PAULA JONES' attorney, DAVID PYKE. LEWINSKY thought it was obvious that CARTER would apprise BOB BENNETT of her affidavit. LEWINSKY just wanted to do what CLINTON and BENNETT wanted her to do. LEWINSKY may have called JORDAN to let him know the affidavit was signed.

LEWINSKY's goal with the affidavit was not to give the JONES people a "little snag of yarn so they could pull the whole sweater apart."

LEWINSKY advised she was relieved since her conversation with CLINTON, on December 17, 1997, that he was assured she was comfortable with the situation.

LEWINSKY advised she left CARTER's office and soon left for New York to be with her mother. LEWINSKY advised she told her mother about the affidavit, but does not recall her mother's reaction. LEWINSKY took a signed copy of the affidavit with her to New York so she could have it in her possession.

On January 8th, LEWINSKY advised she had an interview at McAN-DREWS & FORBES (M&F) that did not go well at all. LEWINSKY advised she had previously met with RICHARD HALPERIN and someone else from M&F, so she was not sure why this meeting was necessary. LEWINSKY was very concerned after this interview, because, in addition to the interview going poorly, LEWINSKY had not yet heard from BURSON & MAR-STELLER (B&M). LEWINSKY was also concerned that her poor showing at the interview would be a bad reflection on JORDAN.

LEWINSKY called JORDAN several times after the interview to advise him how the interview went. Initially, LEWINSKY left JORDAN messages, but she eventually spoke to him. LEWINSKY sensed that JORDAN was annoyed that nothing had come up yet in the form of a job for LEWINSKY. JORDAN called LEWINSKY back and said that he had spoken to the chairman of M&F, and JORDAN told LEWINSKY not to worry. JORDAN told LEWINSKY someone from M&F would be calling her back to arrange for another interview.

Later that day, JAYMIE DURNAN, or DURNAN's secretary, called LEWINSKY to arrange a meeting for the following day. LEWINSKY advised she may have called JORDAN later that evening, but she did not fax anything to JORDAN's office from her mother's apartment.

On January 9, 1998, sometime in the morning, LEWINSKY called LINDA TRIPP. LEWINSKY told TRIPP she was calling from a pay phone because LEWINSKY was concerned about calling TRIPP from home. LEWINSKY thought JONES' attorneys might be tapping her phones.

LEWINSKY advised TRIPP's tone was different than her most recent calls. TRIPP told LEWINSKY about TRIPP's visit with NORMA ASNES. According to TRIPP, a friend of ASNES's told TRIPP to get a job in New York in the public relations field. TRIPP also told LEWINSKY that TRIPP now thought it was good to be vague on the truth when it came to the deposition.

LEWINSKY told TRIPP that LEWINSKY had had no contact with JOR-DAN, CURRIE or CLINTON since December, even though that was false. LEWINSKY told TRIPP that LEWINSKY had not heard anything about job offers. Neither of these things was true, but LEWINSKY told TRIPP this because LEWINSKY was wary of TRIPP ever since TRIPP said she was going to tell the truth about LEWINSKY's relationship with CLINTON. LEWINSKY did not tell TRIPP that LEWINSKY had signed the affidavit. TRIPP told LEWINSKY not to sign the affidavit until LEWINSKY had a job.

LEWINSKY advised this call with TRIPP put LEWINSKY at ease, so LEWINSKY agreed to meet TRIPP when LEWINSKY returned to Washington, D.C.

On January 9, 1998, between 11:00 a.m. and 11:30 a.m., LEWINSKY met with ALLAIN SEIDMAN and two other people from REVLON. LEWINSKY was very excited to work in the area of public relations that they discussed with her. LEWINSKY may have referenced her previous interview at M&F, and she may have referred to JORDAN. LEWINSKY also interviewed with the Human Resources manager at REVLON.

LEWINSKY advised she called JORDAN after the interview to let him know it went well. LEWINSKY advised she received a telephone call from SEIDMAN, in which LEWINSKY was offered a position at REVLON as a floater in the public relations department. LEWINSKY was advised her salary would be approximately $40,000.

LEWINSKY recalled being annoyed at the salary and she complained to JORDAN about it. JORDAN told LEWINSKY to quit whining.

LEWINSKY does not recall calling CARTER on January 9, 1998. LEWINSKY did call CURRIE from a pay phone at the PIERRE HOTEL, to tell her about the job offer. LEWINSKY thinks CLINTON may have been out of town. LEWINSKY may have asked CURRIE to tell CLINTON about the job offer.

LEWINSKY advised that, in all the times she tried to reach JORDAN, she only got through to him half the time.

LEWINSKY does not recall what she did on January 10, 1998, except for the afternoon, which she spent looking for a tie to give JORDAN. LEWINSKY recalls that on January 11, 1998, STEVE NEUWIRTH called and said he did not want to see LEWINSKY that night or ever again.

LEWINSKY advised that on January 12, 1998, LEWINSKY sat by the phone awaiting a call. CARTER paged LEWINSKY and when she returned the page, CARTER advised her that he had submitted her affidavit to PYKE.

LEWINSKY called CURRIE on January 12, trying to get a recommendation from the OLA. LEWINSKY was also trying to find out if CURRIE had told CLINTON about LEWINSKY's offer.

LEWINSKY traveled on a 6:00 a.m. train from New York to Washington, D.C. LEWINSKY met JORDAN at 9:30 a.m. in JORDAN's new 4th floor office. LEWINSKY met with JORDAN for five minutes and gave him a tie and a pocket square as a sign of her appreciation.

JORDAN was not as warm with LEWINSKY as he had previously been. JORDAN quoted the Bible in referring to helping others. LEWINSKY perceived this to be the end of her working relationship with JORDAN.

LEWINSKY advised she and CURRIE started using the code name "KAY" when they paged each other because someone once saw CURRIE's pager, which contained a message from LEWINSKY. The code name "KAY" was LEWINSKY's idea, because both she and CURRIE knew WALTER KAYE. The code name "MARY" was used for LINDA TRIPP.

LEWINSKY may have received a page from CURRIE on January 13, 1998. LEWINSKY faxed a letter on January 13 or 14, 1998 regarding references at the White House. LEWINSKY mentioned JOHN HILLEY as a person who should write her recommendation. LEWINSKY thinks JOHN PODESTA's name may have come up during a conversation with CURRIE as the person who would arrange for LEWINSKY's reference.

LEWINSKY advised that she told TRIPP several lies during her meeting with TRIPP on January 13, 1998. LEWINSKY told TRIPP she had not signed the affidavit when, in fact she had; LEWINSKY told TRIPP she had not heard about a job, when in fact she had; and LEWINSKY told TRIPP she was taking PAXIL, when she was not. LEWINSKY advised she tried to shift things so that TRIPP thought the situation was everyone against TRIPP and LEWINSKY.

LEWINSKY advised she does not know what she would have done if TRIPP had accepted her offer of the condominium in Australia. LEWINSKY thought the offer could be compared to someone saying they would give someone their first-born. LEWINSKY advised she would have spoken to CURRIE and CLINTON to ensure TRIPP did not lose her job.

On January 14, 1998, LEWINSKY called TRIPP from a pay phone at the WATERGATE Apartments and told TRIPP to have NORMA ASNES get TRIPP a Democratic attorney. TRIPP was scheduled to see KIRBY BEHRE that day to sign an affidavit. TRIPP had told LEWINSKY to get TRIPP pulled out of meetings if LEWINSKY called TRIPP at work.

LEWINSKY prepared the "talking points" at her home computer on January 14, 1998. TRIPP told LEWINSKY she had fired KIRBY BEHRE as her attorney and hired a new one. TRIPP told LEWINSKY she did not want it to look like she was not a "team" player. TRIPP had previously told LEWINSKY that she gave BEHRE a sealed envelope, containing the written summary of the information LEWINSKY had told TRIPP about LEWINSKY's affair with CLINTON, in case anything happened to TRIPP.

LEWINSKY felt pressure to hold TRIPP's hand during TRIPP's affidavit. LEWINSKY drove TRIPP home that evening and gave her the talking points. TRIPP seemed glad to have some guidance for the affidavit.

On January 15, 1998, LEWINSKY returned a page from CARTER. CARTER asked LEWINSKY if she ever received courier packages from the White House. LEWINSKY said she had not received any packages from the White House via courier, but had sent some there using a courier. CARTER said that someone from BENNETT's office had called and mentioned the existence of courier records of items sent to the White House, referencing LEWINSKY.

LEWINSKY went home and called SPEEDY COURIER service and, without identifying herself, asked if they would ever turn over records. The respondent said they would not turn over records unless they had been subpoenaed. This made LEWINSKY think the courier service had been subpoenaed.

LEWINSKY returned CURRIE's page. CURRIE said that MIKE ISIKOFF had called asking about CURRIE's intern. LEWINSKY advised CURRIE must have known about LEWINSKY'S involvement in the JONES case, but cannot remember specifically speaking about it with her. CURRIE said ISIKOFF started asking about courier records.

CURRIE was nervous. LEWINSKY then "freaked out." At that time, LEWINSKY thought it made more sense that CARTER had asked about the records. LEWINSKY thinks CLINTON was out of town because she recalls CURRIE saying she would tell CLINTON when he returned. CURRIE later paged LEWINSKY and LEWINSKY called her. CURRIE asked LEWINSKY to drive her to JORDAN's office. CURRIE's husband had her automobile for the day.

LEWINSKY then called TRIPP and suggested that MARK HOFFMAN from the Pentagon must have been the source of the courier records leak to Newsweek. LEWINSKY advised TRIPP not to talk to Newsweek, if contacted.

LEWINSKY thinks CURRIE went to see JORDAN because JORDAN acted as "damage control." CURRIE may have been concerned about CURRIE's involvement with the LEWINSKY matter. LEWINSKY waited at the "FRONT PAGE" restaurant and had onion soup while CURRIE met with JORDAN. LEWINSKY advised it was raining that day and there was an O.J. SIMPSON interview on the television while she ate.

CURRIE met with JORDAN for approximately twenty minutes. When CURRIE returned to LEWINSKY, CURRIE explained that she had had a drink with JORDAN in his office. CURRIE said she would wait to see CLINTON before deciding what to do. CURRIE said she would call CLINTON in the Residence, first thing in the morning, to let him know CURRIE needed to speak with him.

LEWINSKY considered the discovery of the courier receipts a "big deal" and advised she could sense a lot of tension from CURRIE. LEWINSKY sensed the situation getting out of control.

On January 16th, LEWINSKY went to a gym on Connecticut Avenue and called CURRIE from a pay phone there. CURRIE said she had spoken to CLINTON, who said not to respond to the inquiries from Newsweek.

LEWINSKY advised she felt very low and depressed on January 16, 1998.

LEWINSKY advised she can not easily discuss any further details of January 16, 1998 at this time, as she feels guilty about getting everyone involved.

On January 18, 1998, LEWINSKY was paged by CURRIE. LEWINSKY was told by her attorney, BILL GINSBURG, not to return the pages. LEWINSKY was paged numerous times by CURRIE during that time frame. LEWINSKY returned a couple of the pages by calling CURRIE from a pay phone and leaving cryptic messages, hoping CURRIE would be able to figure out what was happening. LEWINSKY advised on one occasion, she said something about "HOOVER," hoping CURRIE would make the connection to the Federal Bureau of Investigation. LEWINSKY felt responsible for the crisis they were in.

The interview ended at approximately 2 p.m.

Monica Lewinsky's Seventh Interview

1

OFFICE OF THE INDEPENDENT COUNSEL

08/03/98

MONICA S. LEWINSKY was interviewed pursuant to an immunity agreement between the Office of Independent Counsel (OIC), LEWINSKY, and her attorneys. Present for the interview were Associate Independent Counsel (AIC) MICHAEL EMMICK, AIC KARIN IMMERGUT, AIC MARY ANNE WIRTH, and AIC JULIE MYERS. Representing LEWINSKY was Attorney PRESTON BURTON and Law Clerk MATTHEW UMHOFER of the law offices of PLATO CACHERIS. The interview was conducted in Suite 490, 1001 Pennsylvania Avenue NW, Washington, D.C. beginning at 12:07 p.m. LEWINSKY provided the following information:

LEWINSKY first saw the President in person in July 1995, when she attended a function with WALTER KAYE and her mother. At that time LEWINSKY was impressed with how handsome the president appeared.

On August 10, 1995, LEWINSKY attended the birthday party of the President on the grounds of the White House. At that time, LEWINSKY made eye contact with the President and began flirting with him. LEWINSKY does not believe that she would have been hired if anyone knew that they were flirting.

On or about August 13, 1995, LEWINSKY introduced herself to the President at a departure ceremony.

In September, 1995, LEWINSKY reintroduced herself to the President in the basement of the White House as he was passing. The occasion was the visit of LEWINSKY's friend, NATALIE UNGVARI, who was on a tour. LEWINSKY was waiting with U.S. Secret Service (USSS) uniformed officer LEWIS FOX for UNGVARI's return. LEWINSKY had her photograph taken with the President on this occasion.

In October 1995, the President waved at LEWINSKY once in passing.

During the first week in November 1995, LEWINSKY was in New York for the investiture of WALTER KAYE as a civilian aide of the U.S. Army. At this point, LEWINSKY was a second term intern who wanted to get a permanent job in the White House. While there, LEWINSKY received a call from JENNIFER PALMIERI, who advised LEWINSKY of a job opening in the Office of Legislative Affairs (OLA). On the following Monday, LEWINSKY submitted a resume to her supervisor, TRACY BOBOWITZ, or to TIM KEATING. On Wednesday or Thursday, LEWINSKY brought writing samples and was interviewed by KEATING. The interview went well and

LEWINSKY was called soon thereafter to meet SUSAN BROPHY and PAT GRIFFIN. LEWINSKY sent letters to each of them.

On November 10, 1996, KEATING advised LEWINSKY that she had gotten the job, but that the furlough was imminent and the paperwork had not cleared yet. LEWINSKY worked through the furlough as an intern without pay. LEWINSKY took a drug test and met JOCELYN JOLLEY. LEON PANTETTA's office was staffed during the furlough by LEWINSKY and two male interns. During the furlough, the President came to the office of PANETTA as often as five times a day. One of these interns remarked that the President was coming to visit quite frequently and that he, the President, must have had a crush on LEWINSKY.

LEWINSKY was hired in OLA because of her good work as an intern in PANETTA's office. The President's name was never mentioned by KEATING, GRIFFIN, BROPHY, or LEWINSKY during the hiring process. LEWINSKY had not applied for any other jobs. LEWINSKY applied for the OLA job because it met her requirement that she would have a blue badge. This would permit LEWINSKY to go the West Wing and not be relegated to the Old Executive Office Building.

On November 17, 1995, BARRY TOIV commented that LEWINSKY was getting a lot of "face time" with the President for being an intern in PANETTA's office.

On the Friday after Thanksgiving 1995, LEWINSKY was trained briefly by JOCELYN JOLLEY. LEWINSKY began her new job in OLA the first week in December 1995. JOLLEY was out sick at least one day that week and left LEWINSKY to complete a large mailing. LEWINSKY basically fended on her own as there were no interns. JOLLEY had advised that she would handle all Office of Management and Budget (OMB) material related to the furlough. There was a large backlog of letters due to the furlough.

TIM KEATING was pleased with LEWINSKY's work. At around the time of the State of the Union Address, JOLLEY was again absent due to sickness and LEWINSKY was left to complete a lot of work pertaining to the address; LEWINSKY stayed late and got the work done. However, LEWINSKY was very disappointed that neither she, JOLLEY, nor any of the interns were permitted to go to Capitol Hill for the address. LEWINSKY did not wish to be lumped in with JOLLEY when the OLA work was being evaluated, because JOLLEY was frequently absent and came in late many times due to her diabetic condition. JOLLEY advised LEWINSKY that the turn around time on acknowledging congressional inquiries was too long. MAUREEN LEWIS had been doing letters to congressmen after they had traveled with the President. LEWINSKY had started doing these political letters. KEATING found out about it and chewed out LEWINSKY for getting involved in someone else's area of responsibility; told LEWINSKY that she did not know what she was doing; and brought up a few other undisclosed problems. JAMIE RUBIN, BOB RUBIN's son, came on board to be the OLA liaison with the West Wing about this time.

In March 1996, LEWINSKY was visited a second time by her friend,

NATALIE UNGVARI, from San Francisco. LEWINSKY was escorting UNGVARI around the White House on a Sunday and was in the vicinity of the Senate Office. They observed a guy in denim with a baseball cap and LEWINSKY called to him before he went into the men's room in the hall. This person was the President, who had popcorn on his shirt, apparently having just watched a movie. LEWINSKY introduced UNGVARI to the President. LEWINSKY had already told UNGVARI about her relationship with the President by this time. This caused some consternation on the part of LEWINSKY.

About two weeks before LEWINSKY's transfer in early April 1996, KEATING advised LEWINSKY to get her resume to the lady in Administration that sits next to ASHLEY RAINES. This was to complete LEWINSKY's personnel file. On the Friday before Easter, which was two days after RON BROWN was killed, LEWINSKY and JOLLEY were called to KEATING's office separately. KEATING advised that there had been problems in the Correspondence Unit and that JODIE TORKELSON wanted LEWINSKY and JOLLEY fired. Instead, both JOLLEY and LEWINSKY were being transferred to other agencies. JOLLEY was actually demoted.

KEATING advised LEWINSKY that she was too "sexy" to work in the White House, by which KEATING meant that LEWINSKY "could shine more" and could get a better job in the Pentagon. LEWINSKY's work at the White House was not criticized to her knowledge. LEWINSKY never saw it coming and was totally surprised; she wept. LEWINSKY's first reaction was that she would never get to see the President again; her second reaction was that people thought she was spending too much time away from her desk and too much time near the Oval Office. KEATING advised that there were no other openings in the White House at that time, but that perhaps LEWINSKY could come back after the election. KEATING said that LEWINSKY had a job in the Press Office at the Pentagon; that she would probably make more money; and that LEWINSKY should see PATSY THOMASSON about the transition. KEATING also counseled that LEWINSKY could take her vacation to Florida as planned. KEATING requested that LEWINSKY turn her pass in and that he would place LEWINSKY on the access list until the time she departed. KEATING did not ban LEWINSKY from the White House.

At this point, LEWINSKY did not know how BETTY CURRIE felt about her and LEWINSKY actually felt closer to NANCY HERNREICH. On the Monday after being transferred, LEWINSKY went to HERNREICH's office, at which time HERNREICH tried to console LEWINSKY, but told LEWINSKY that she had to interview for the Pentagon job. This was not what KEATING had told her. While leaving, LEWINSKY was stopped by CURRIE. CURRIE observed LEWINSKY crying and tried to console her by saying that sometimes things work out for the best. LEWINSKY believed that EVELYN LIEBERMAN, who had a connection with the First Lady, was the force behind the transfer. LEWINSKY also called ASHLEY RAINES and BAYANI NELVIS to advise them of the transfer.

On Thursday of that week, MARK HUFFMAN from the Pentagon called and advised that LEWINSKY would interview for the job of Confidential Assistant, which included many administrative duties. LEWINSKY interviewed successfully for the job. LEWINSKY objected to the heavy burden of administrative duties and was advised that they would split the job and relieve LEWINSKY of some of those duties. CHARLIE DUNCAN's assistant at the Pentagon said there were no other jobs available there.

LEWINSKY was in touch with WALTER KAYE, who was instrumental in getting LEWINSKY the White House internship. LEWINSKY's parents had known KAYE many years ago in California and KAYE's grandson had been an intern. KAYE became involved politically when he contributed to the Democratic Party after selling his insurance company. ANN MCCOY, another White House employee, gave herself a birthday party in September 1995, which KAYE funded. There was some friction between MCCOY and her friends, and LEWINSKY's mother and aunt, at KAYE's investiture. In addition, MARSHA SCOTT, also a friend of KAYE, apparently felt that LEWINSKY's mother and aunt were somehow a threat to SCOTT. KAYE told DEBRA FINERMAN, LEWINSKY's aunt, that LEWINSKY had been transferred because there were rumors of LEWINSKY's relationship with the President. FINERMAN was angered because KAYE had not tried to defend LEWINSKY. Because of this, LEWINSKY did not attend a scheduled luncheon with KAYE on August 19, 1996.

On April 12, 1996, the President called LEWINSKY to explain why she had been transferred. The President did not know any of the details about the Pentagon job, and when LEWINSKY complained about it, the President advised her that if she did not like it he would get LEWINSKY a job on the campaign. LEWINSKY told the President that the job was boring and that she had complained to PATSY THOMASSON, who did nothing. The President stated that THOMASSON was a friend of his.

On April 17, 1996, LEWINSKY started the Pentagon job, but hated it from the start as it was boring to her. Her superiors did not split the job as promised. The job was primarily as the gate keeper for KEN BACON. LEWINSKY said that her predecessor, JEAN WESSEL, an older woman, had more administrative experience than LEWINSKY, but lacked enough energy for the travel demands of the job. The job was a General Services 9 position paying $42,000 with overtime. LEWINSKY had been making $25,000 with no overtime pay at OLA. LEWINSKY developed a good interpersonal relationship with BACON.

TIM KEATING had advised LEWINSKY that her position at OLA was not being filled, but after going to the Pentagon, LEWINSKY found out that the position had been filled. LEWINSKY wrote a letter to KEATING complaining about this and the fact that they assigned pagers to everyone; which LEWINSKY had suggested months ago. LEWINSKY also tried to explain to KEATING that her past job performance should not have been linked to that of JOLLEY. LEWINSKY may have called ANN Last Name Unknown at OLA to try to get her job back. While at OLA, LEWINSKY had gotten along with JANET MERDILLA, LUCIA WYMAN, and AL MAULDIN.

After beginning the job in the Pentagon, LEWINSKY was able to visit the President in the White House on weekends. Since LEWINSKY no longer had a blue badge, she had to be "WAVED" in, and escorted. These visits were facilitated by BETTY CURRIE, who had an unspoken agreement with LEWINSKY to use the most inconspicuous route to the Oval Office that would avoid the USSS uniformed officers, many of whom were friendly to MARSHA SCOTT. (LEWINSKY was provided with a floor plan of the White House, a copy of which is attached to this document, on which she highlighted the most common route she took to see the President.) The route normally included entering the southwest gate; walking north on Executive Drive; entering the West Wing basement lobby; meeting CURRIE, her escort; going through the basement; and up the stairs near the Oval Office. LEWINSKY and CURRIE avoided a uniformed officer who knew DEBBIE SCHIFF. The officer's name is unknown, but he is very friendly, about 5'11', and overweight.

The weekend attire at the White House was very informal. LEWINSKY usually departed through the northwest gate and never departed through the tunnel.

The President never gave LEWINSKY a rose, but CURRIE once gave LEWINSKY a bunch of roses to take home.

CHARLIE the butler was always friendly with LEWINSKY.

To LEWINSKY's knowledge the President did not call her from Jackson Hole, Wyoming or elsewhere when he was on vacation.

LEWINSKY never taped anyone; however, LEWINSKY does have a micro-cassette from her answering machine with a call from BETTY CURRIE on December 28, 1997. CURRIE was at her residence and needed LEWINSKY's date of birth and social security number to place LEWINSKY on the White House access list. The tape also contains a few messages about KIRBY BEHRE from LINDA TRIPP in December 1997. LEWINSKY does not recall playing the CURRIE tape to LINDA TRIPP.

LEWINSKY does recall playing the tape with messages from the President to TRIPP. This tape was previously furnished to the OIC. LEWINSKY did not have caller identification (ID) on her telephone when the first message from the President was recorded, but she recognized the President's voice when he said, "Aw shucks." LEWINSKY installed "caller ID" on her home telephone before July 1996. The second message from the President was muffled. In the third message from the President he said, "Hello." The fourth message from the President was left in the middle of the night when LEWINSKY was out of town; the President said, "C'mon it's me." LEWINSKY spoke to the President about the messages. On one occasion, the President advised that he did not like to leave messages.

On August 11, 1996, LEWINSKY saw DEBBIE BYRD at the southwest gate and then in BETTY CURRIE's office.

On September 12 or 19, 1997 LEWINSKY arrived at the southwest gate crying, called BETTY CURRIE, and waited a long time. When CURRIE arrived, LEWINSKY was crying about when she was coming back to the White House and the fact that MARSHA SCOTT was not helping. It worried

CURRIE when LEWINSKY cried. CURRIE said that sometimes the President's hands are tied, but that CURRIE had received the President's permission to talk to JOHN PODESTA about getting a job for LEWINSKY. LEWINSKY was taken to the Oval Office on this occasion. CURRIE was going to Chicago the next day.

A frequent occurrence was for LEWINSKY to arrive at the White House gate and not be allowed to enter because her name had not been cleared in the computer yet. LEWINSKY would wait until CURRIE could enter the data into the "WAVE system." LEWINSKY never complained about waiting. It was impossible for anyone to skip the "WAVE" system.

The President held BETTY CURRIE in high regard. LEWINSKY always knew where CURRIE's loyalty was. CURRIE was very good at covering and representing the President. CURRIE would occasionally lie, as she did in the ELEANOR MONDALE matter, and when she told LEWINSKY that she was unable to get LEWINSKY's messages into the President all day. On one occasion, on a weekend, CURRIE locked in her desk one of LEWINSKY's messages to the President so that no one snooping around would see it. However, the President did not get to see it either. LEWINSKY has no specific recollection that CURRIE knew of LEWINSKY's subpoena in the PAULA JONES case; however, CURRIE had to know that LEWINSKY was somehow involved in the JONES case when LEWINSKY started using the "KAYE" code name on the pager. LEWINSKY has a faint recollection of speaking with CURRIE about LEWINSKY's involvement in the JONES matter.

LINDA TRIPP spent the night in LEWINSKY's apartment with her in late November 1997. This was after TRIPP had attended a Christmas show with NORMA ASNES. TRIPP slept in MICHAEL LEWINSKY's room with the door closed. At about 2:00 a.m. LEWINSKY received a call from the President on LEWINSKY's personal line in her bedroom. This line does not have a speaker phone and there are no extensions. LEWINSKY cannot recall the topic of conversation, but it could have been a "phone sex" call. The call could have been either the night before or the night after NANCY HERN-REICH testified on November 13, 1997; or it could have been when the Arkansas friend with a terminal illness was visiting the President. When the call was over, LEWINSKY tried to awaken TRIPP, without success, to tell her about the call from the President. The next morning, TRIPP advised that she had heard the telephone ring. TRIPP did not listen to this call or any other telephone conversations that LEWINSKY had with the President. TRIPP was never present when LEWINSKY called BETTY CURRIE.

FRANK CARTER told LEWINSKY that when testifying one should not answer a direct yes or no if one was not sure; one should say, "It may have happened," or "It's possible," so as not to perjure oneself. LEWINSKY said that is why she has answered, "It's possible" instead of yes or no to some of the questions in her debriefing by the OIC. LEWINSKY and TRIPP discussed leaving some "wiggle room" when testifying when one wasn't sure of the answer.

AIC MARY ANNE WIRTH departed at this time.

In regard to the ties that LEWINSKY had given to the President, she would often ask him when he intended to wear them. The President would sometimes wear one the day after LEWINSKY talked to him, and sometimes the day she was scheduled to see him. On one of the days that BAYANI NELVIS testified in the Grand Jury, he wore a tie that LEWINSKY had given to the President. LEWINSKY opined that this may have been a signal of some sort; either that the tie was not important to the President, or as a sign of encouragement to LEWINSKY.

LEWINSKY briefly described the contents of the back hallway off the Oval Office:

A. Framed picture.
B. Bathroom door.
C. Framed sword above bathroom door.
D. Credenza.
E. Framed political button collections on right and left walls.
F. Signature of an Oklahoman, probably WOODIE GUTHRIE.

LEWINSKY described the contents of the President's back study:

A. Dark wooden desk.
   1. Chair on rollers with presidential seal on the pillow.
   2. Mahogany cigar box on desk.
   3. Wooden organizer on desk.
   4. Two bookends with small books including Vox.
   5. Blotter.
B. Book rack.
C. Bookshelves with mostly political books; various items on top are changed periodically.
D. Hardwood floor with blue rug.
E. Two windows.
F. Painting of the President walking on the street.
G. An older photograph of Mrs. CLINTON and CHELSEA CLINTON.
H. Photograph of an old guy with a fireman's hat.
I. Photograph of the President with school children.
J. Stand with telephone and compact disk player.
K. Compact disk holder in the corner of the study.
L. Golf clubs.
M. Rocking chair with a pillow.
N. Marble top half table with big mirror.
O. On a shelf is a "kewpie" doll sitting under a mushroom.

LEWINSKY described the President's dining room:

A. Pantry door.
B. Hall door.
C. Marble top bureau with LEWINSKY paperweight on it.
D. Circular table and chairs.
E. Dry flower arrangement on table.
F. Television and VCR.
G. Mirrors on both walls.

LEWINSKY described the President's bathroom:

A. Toilet.
B. Sink.
C. Telephone on wall.
D. Vertical shelf for toiletries.
E. The walls are lined with black and white cartoons of the President.

At this point AIC JULIE MYERS entered.

LEWINSKY is close to her aunt, DEBRA FINERMAN, and provided some details of her relationship with the President, but not to the degree that she did with LINDA TRIPP. LEWINSKY did not provide the vulgar details to FINERMAN. FINERMAN was aware that LEWINSKY had been subpoenaed in the PAULA JONES case and knew that LINDA TRIPP was causing problems. LEWINSKY, her mother, MARCIA LEWIS, and FINERMAN referred to VERNON JORDAN as "GWEN." LEWIS and FINERMAN coined this nickname for JORDAN.

LEWINSKY recalled the following additional gifts that she gave to the President:

A. HARROD'S golf balls and tees.
B. A wooden painted egg from Budapest (observed on 12/28/97).
C. "Gummy boobs" from URBAN OUTFITTERS.
D. Cassette tape; unknown whether the President ever listened; did not tell BETTY CURRIE of this gift for fear CURRIE would not give it to the President; later asked CURRIE if President had gotten the tape.

There would have been no legitimate business reason for LEWINSKY to go into the President's study; her access was only because she had a personal relationship with the President.

LEWINSKY ■■■■■■ a student at SANTA MONICA CITY COLLEGE in March or April 1992. LEWINSKY was upset over the fact that her father would not pay for her to go to a more expensive university. After waiting 15 minutes for a parking place, someone came along at the last minute and took the space from her. LEWINSKY began crying uncontrollably. MARCIA LEWIS took LEWINSKY for treatment to a psychologist, Dr. IRENE KASSORLA. LEWINSKY saw KASSORLA regularly until LEWINSKY moved to Oregon, but continued treatment with KASSORLA by telephone. The consultation continued every four to six weeks after LEWINSKY moved to Washington, D.C. LEWINSKY advised KASSORLA of her relationship with the President and used the code name "HENRIETTA" when talking about him on the telephone. LEWINSKY was honest with KASSORLA, but did not give her too many details. KASSORLA opined that the President was using LEWINSKY.

MARCIA LEWIS was never a patient of KASSORLA. KASSORLA is a psychologist, but not a sex therapist. KASSORLA is self-promoting. KASSORLA never kept notes when LEWINSKY saw her in person and all of KASSORLA's recollections might not be accurate. KASSORLA, if subpoenaed, would most likely go on television talk shows. In LEWINSKY's opinion, KASSORLA would be a public relations nightmare to the OIC. KASSORLA helped LEWINSKY to the extent that LEWINSKY improved her school grades and lost weight. LEWINSKY last called KASSORLA in 1997.

LEWINSKY has consulted with Dr. KATHY ESTEP, a therapist. LEWINSKY talked with ESTEP around the time of the 1996 Presidential election about her relationship with the President, and displayed photos of LEWINSKY and the President. LEWINSKY saw ESTEP about four times in October and November, 1996. Dr. ESTEP told LEWINSKY that she had a lot of loss, such as losing her job. LEWINSKY visited an unnamed associate of Dr. ESTEP, ■. The associate also prescribed "phen phen" on a weekly basis for LEWINSKY.

Around March 1998, LEWINSKY received a letter from one ██████, whom she has never met. The letter contained a photograph of ██████, who requested that LEWINSKY put her in touch with BILL GINSBERG, whom ██████ wanted to retain as her own attorney. ██████ purported that she had been a White House intern, who had also had an affair with the President. LEWINSKY speculated that ██████ may have been JANE DOE 7. Subsequently, LEWINSKY received a package from ██████ which contained a tape recording of audio messages from the OIC requesting an interview. GINSBERG or NATE SPEIGHTS referred ██████ to attorney KEITH WATERS. LEWINSKY provided the tape and photograph to WATERS.

The interview was terminated at 4:44 p.m.

Monica Lewinsky's
Eighth Interview

1

OFFICE OF THE INDEPENDENT COUNSEL

08/04/98

MONICA S. LEWINSKY was interviewed pursuant to an immunity agreement between the Office of the Independent Counsel (OIC), LEWINSKY, and her attorneys. Present for the interview were Associate Independent Counsel (AIC) MICHAEL EMMICK, AIC KARIN IMMERGUT, and AIC JULIE L. MYERS. AIC MARY ANNE WIRTH and AIC CRAIG LERNER were present during part of the interview. Representing LEWINSKY was her attorney, SYDNEY HOFFMAN, and Law Clerk ANIE WULKEN. The interview was conducted at the OIC office, Suite 490 North, 1001 Pennsylvania Avenue, NW, Washington, D.C. LEWINSKY provided the following information:

LEWINSKY wrote a letter to the President on July 3, 1997, threatening to tell her parents of their affair. LEWINSKY did not author any similar letters. LINDA TRIPP encouraged LEWINSKY to be more forceful in her correspondence with the President.

On about September 19, 1997, LEWINSKY was crying outside the northwest gate of the White House. BETTY CURRIE and BAYANI NELVIS knew LEWINSKY was upset.

LEWINSKY did not recall telling BETTY CURRIE directly about her affair with the President. CURRIE may have assumed an affair existed. However, CURRIE demonstrated no confusion about the relationship between LEWINSKY and the President. LEWINSKY and TRIPP discussed CURRIE's knowledge of the relationship. TRIPP suggested to LEWINSKY that CURRIE knew about the relationship. LEWINSKY agreed with TRIPP's assessment during these conversations.

LEWINSKY did not have a specific recollection, but believes CURRIE must have known about the PAULA JONES subpoena. LEWINSKY believed she may have had a discussion with CURRIE about the above subpoena.

LEWINSKY said she thought that PEDRO, Last Name Unknown (LNU) was the name of the waiter at the breakfast she had with VERNON JORDAN on December 31, 1997. PEDRO was described as a petite Hispanic male, between 35 and 40 years of age. JORDAN appeared to know the waiter and be a frequent customer of the restaurant.

On December 11, 1997, JORDAN gave LEWINSKY a list of JORDAN'S business contacts. The list included URSULA FAIRBURN of AMERICAN EXPRESS, RICHARD HALPERIN of MCANDREWS and FORBES, and YOUNG and RUBICAM.

Regarding telephone messages on LEWINSKY's cassette tapes, there may have been one or two more tapes. Most of the recordings consisted of "Hello." LEWINSKY knew these recorded messages were the President, because she knows his voice. LEWINSKY kept the messages so that when she wanted she could hear the President's voice on tape.

May 24, 1997 was referred to by LEWINSKY as "Dump Day." LEWINSKY had an idea she would see the President on that date. LEWINSKY went shopping with ASHLEY RAINES at VICTORIA's SECRET. CURRIE called LEWINSKY around 11:00 a.m. and told LEWINSKY to come to the White House at about 1:00 p.m. LEWINSKY appeared as scheduled wearing a red sun dress with small polka dots and the hat pin the President had given to her. The pin was worn on a straw hat. LEWINSKY brought gifts to the President, including a mystery puzzle and a BANANA REPUBLIC shirt. LEWINSKY gave the President his gifts in the Executive dining room.

LEWINSKY did not recall how the conversation started; however, the President stated that he did not feel right about their relationship; it was not right, and the President said he could not do it anymore. LEWINSKY was crying. The President said this did not have to do with LEWINSKY. The President told LEWINSKY that he had been with hundreds of women in his life until he was about 40 years of age. The President told LEWINSKY that when he turned 40 his life was falling apart. LEWINSKY recalled that the President may have told her that, at the above time, he entertained thoughts of ending his life. However, LEWINSKY was not sure about the recollection. ■ The President told LEWINSKY that he had been good until he met her. LEWINSKY did not believe the President. The President told her how he was attracted to LEWINSKY, and how the President thought LEWINSKY was a great person. The President told LEWINSKY that they could remain friends. The President pointed out to LEWINSKY that he could do a lot for her. The President told LEWINSKY that it was difficult for him to resist being with other women. The President struggled with it daily. The President told LEWINSKY that he kept a calender on how long he had been good. The President explained that during his life he had been two people, and kept up two fronts. The President said that starting in the third or fourth grade, he was a good boy with his mother and step father, but also began telling stories and leading a secret life. LEWINSKY's impression was that the President was telling her he wanted to be right in the eyes of God. The President wanted the affair to be over, though he said it was not LEWINSKY's fault. LEWINSKY did not know if the President meant what he said.

The President and LEWINSKY moved from the dining room to the back study and into the hallway. LEWINSKY was crying and trying to talk the President out of ending the affair by telling him that Presidents in the past needed girlfriends. The President got angry and told LEWINSKY that he did not want to be like that. The President said he did not want his daughter to know about the affair. The President told LEWINSKY that if they had no sex they could be friends and visit. LEWINSKY said that based on a previous relationship with a married man, she thought that the President appeared to be going through feelings of guilt. LEWINSKY was hysterical.

Subsequently, STEVEN GOODIN came into the area and LEWINSKY

realized she had left her purse on the dining room table. LEWINSKY retrieved her purse from the dining room table. BETTY CURRIE came in the back hall through the pantry to take LEWINSKY out of the area. The President was trying to make things look "OK". CURRIE told LEWINSKY that her face was similar to CURRIE's face, it showed everything. CURRIE then asked LEWINSKY what was wrong. LEWINSKY did not say anything except that things were difficult. CURRIE was going out of town to visit CURRIE's sister who had a heart attack. LEWINSKY commented that she and CURRIE would get together for drinks when CURRIE returned.

LEWINSKY recalled that on the above date, LANNY DAVIS and his family were in the White House. CURRIE introduced LEWINSKY to DAVIS and his family.

On July 3, 1997, LEWINSKY wrote a letter to the President. On July 4, 1997, she appeared for a meeting with the President at the White House. LEWINSKY wore a black sun dress bought in Rome, Italy. LEWINSKY was somber. The President came out of his office and said to LEWINSKY, "Hey." LEWINSKY replied, "Hey." They both went into the study. LEWINSKY sat at the desk and the President sat in a rocking chair. The President said something to the effect of, "First of all, it is illegal to threaten the President of the United States;" secondly, he did not read the entire letter; in the third place, he threw the letter away. LEWINSKY said that when the President got to the phrase, "In the fourth place," she stopped him. The President appeared nervous. LEWINSKY could not recall what the President next said. LEWIN-SKY and the President got into a disagreement. LEWINSKY pointed out to the President that she had left the White House and left like a "good girl." She waited through the election and well after a year after leaving the White House. The President told LEWINSKY they could still be friends. She replied that he did not act like her friend. LEWINSKY cried and the President hugged her. Over the President's left shoulder LEWINSKY saw a gardener outside the window. LEWINSKY did not make eye contact with the garden-er. LEWINSKY was not sure whether they were seen. They moved to the bathroom hallway. The President was most affectionate that day. The President told LEWINSKY she was beautiful. The President played with her hair and stroked her arm. The President mentioned that people like them had fire in the belly. At one point, the President said he wished he had more time for LEWINSKY, and that maybe he would in three years. LEWINSKY took the opportunity to comment that the President and his wife connected on a level that no one understood. ▬▬ LEWINSKY said something about being together with the President in the future. The President asked LEWINSKY what she would do when the President was 70 years of age, and had to go to the bathroom numerous times a day. LEWINSKY replied that they would deal with it. LEWINSKY said she never felt so complete. LEWINSKY stated that she thought her meeting with the President ended on a positive note.

CURRIE called out for the President and he told LEWINSKY it was time to go. LEWINSKY told the President that she needed a few more minutes with him. LEWINSKY told him about the events surrounding KATHLEEN WILLEY. LEWINSKY referred to July 4, 1997 as KATHLEEN WILLEY day. LEWINSKY advised the President of information she received from a friend regarding WILLEY. LEWINSKY did not identify that person. LEWINSKY insisted she would not have identified the friend to the President even if asked. The President did not appear surprised by LEWINSKY's information. LEWINSKY left a picture for the President to sign for LEWINSKY's birthday.

LEWINSKY received a bear sculpture from the President that he said he bought in Vancouver, British Columbia. The President gave the bear to her during a visit with the President at the White House on December 28, 1997.

LEWINSKY may have used tissue to blot her lipstick on a visit with the President on January 7, 1996. LEWINSKY reapplied her make-up after encounters with the President. The tissues were disposed of in the trash can in the bathroom or in the one near NANCY HERNREICH's office. Occasionally the President and LEWINSKY had sodas or other drinks in the dining room or study.

LEWINSKY reviewed and identified the following documents:

1. A paper with the phrase, "The time has finally come for me to throw in the towel . . ." LEWINSKY could see TRIPP's influence on this document. LEWINSKY wrote the document, but did not send it. TRIPP discouraged LEWINSKY from sending the paper. LEWINSKY dated the paper around September, 1997, because LEWINSKY found out that MARSHA SCOTT was not going to detail her to the White House. It was harsher in language than LEWINSKY had recalled. In lieu of sending the letter, LEWINSKY traveled to the White House on about September 19, 1997 and waited at the southwest gate for an appointment.
2. A letter with notation, "Official Letterhead," and reading, "To Handsome,." LEWINSKY sent a version of this joke letter to the President by courier. The letter was written on September 30, 1997. A reminder to throw the letter away was noted.
3. A draft of a letter sent to the President on March 2, 1996, along with a HUGO BOSS necktie. The letter began with, "Dear Mr. P:" These were sent by Federal Express.
4. A photograph of the President wearing a tie given to him by LEWINSKY.
5. A document entitled, "As your friend." LEWINSKY wrote this at home and did not mail it to the President. LEWINSKY did discuss the content with the President on December 17, 1997. LEWINSKY drafted the content in conversations with LINDA TRIPP on December 8, 1997.
6. A document stating, "This is going to be a long letter." It was a draft letter written on LEWINSKY's home computer. It was never sent. The actual letter sent was shorter than the above document. It was sent in response to learning from TRIPP that LEWINSKY did not get the job at the National Security Council (NSC) for which she applied. The date of the document was after October 6, 1997.
7. A card dated June 29, 1997, starting with, "Dear Handsome", and containing the phrase, "I feel disposable, used, insignificant," and, "I really need to discuss my situation." LEWINSKY stated that the writing on the card was hers, but the phrases and words were those of

TRIPP. Some of TRIPP's writing may be on this draft. LEWINSKY would buy more than one of a particular card for draft purposes.

8. The final version of the above card (item seven) was sent to the President.

9. A document written on LEWINSKY's Department of Defense (DOD) computer. The document contains a list of things sent to the President, including an item named as "Gingko . . ." LEWINSKY did try to delete documents concerning the President from her DOD computer.

10. This document contains the statement, "It has been made clear to me that I cannot return to the White House." It is a closer version of the final version than item six.

11. This document was a short draft of a letter sent to the President. The letter contains the phrase, ". . . cannot do anything but accept that . . ."

12. This document contained LEWINSKY's own thoughts including the phrase, "It was so sad seeing you." It was not sent.

13. A photograph from October 23, 1996, taken at a fundraiser.

14. A photograph of LEWINSKY and her family taken with the President after the June 14, 1996 radio address.

15. A photograph taken on what LEWINSKY referred to as LOU FOX day.

16. A photograph which was a hand out photograph of the President signing a Department of Defense (DOD) bill. The President was wearing a tie given to him by LEWINSKY.

17. A photograph of the President on his birthday.

18. A photograph of LEWINSKY and the President, signed by the President, on what LEWINSKY referred to as "Dress Day." LEWINSKY is wearing the dark blue dress.

19. A photograph of the President wearing a tie given to him by LEWINSKY.

20. A black and white photograph of the President. LEWINSKY fell in love with the photograph.

21. A letter, dated June 16, 1997. LEWINSKY told her former attorney, WILLIAM GINSBURG about the letter in January 1998. The letter was to CURRIE but was not sent.

22. A letter dated November 2, 1997, was addressed to CURRIE beginning, "Hope you had an enjoyable weekend." LEWINSKY was not sure if the letter was sent.

23. This item was a draft note on a card with a heart on the top sheet. This heart page was not the inside of the card. The top sheet of the card should have a cat on it. LEWINSKY sent a card with a cat because CURRIE liked cats. The part of a card with a snowman on it was possibly a draft of a Christmas card sent to CURRIE. The above card was possibly sent to CURRIE on September 17, 1997.

24. A card stating, "Dear Betty, I feel better after our talk." LEWINSKY may have sent the card after LEWINSKY's meeting with CURRIE at the HAY ADAMS hotel. The dates were around June 24, 1997 or June 29, 1997. MARSHA SCOTT was the main topic of the discussion between LEWINSKY and CURRIE.

LEWINSKY never contacted the President when he was in Bosnia, despite news reports. Not only was he with his family, but there exists no direct way to contact the President overseas.

LEWINSKY called the President by the following names: "████████," "███████," "Creep," "Big Creep." ██████ LEWINSKY remained abreast of the President's schedule by referring to <u>News Edge</u>, a publication of the President's projected schedule. It was LEWINSKY's job to track the briefings from the White House. Sometimes LEWINSKY contacted CURRIE for the President's schedule. If LEWINSKY thought CURRIE was not telling the truth about the President's schedule, LEWINSKY would contact BAYANI NELVIS, a Presidential steward. LEWINSKY maintained she never asked the U.S. Secret Service (USSS) about the Presidential schedule.

LEWINSKY reviewed a schedule prepared of calls to and from VERNON JORDAN, over a period of time, from various individuals and locations including: the White House, LEWINSKY's residences, and JORDAN's office. LEWINSKY could provide no additional information regarding these calls. LEWINSKY made the observation that there appeared to be more telephone calls than she realized.

Before Thanksgiving 1997, and after LEWINSKY had a fight with TRIPP, LEWINSKY flew to Los Angeles. LEWINSKY called CURRIE and asked CURRIE to call JORDAN and prod along the job search. It was LEWINSKY's understanding that JORDAN was helping her at the behest of the President and CURRIE. Prior to LEWINSKY being subpoenaed on December 19, 1997, LEWINSKY did not know if JORDAN knew LEWINSKY was on the PAULA JONES case witness list.

Monica Lewinsky's
Ninth Interview

1

OFFICE OF THE INDEPENDENT COUNSEL

08/05/98

MONICA S. LEWINSKY was interviewed under the terms of an immunity agreement between the Office of the Independent Counsel (OIC) and her. LEWINSKY was interviewed at the Office of the Independent Counsel, 1001 Pennsylvania Avenue, Washington, DC 20004. Present for the interview were Associate Independent Counsel (AIC) MICHAEL EMMICK, AIC KARIN IMMERGUT, AIC JULIE MYERS. MYERS departed after the below-listed chart was discussed. Present representing LEWINSKY were attorney PRES TON BURTON and law clerk MATTHEW UMERHOFF. LEWINSKY provided the following information, beginning at approximately 2:20 p.m.

▬▬▬▬▬▬▬▬▬▬▬▬▬▬▬▬▬▬▬▬▬
▬▬▬▬▬▬▬▬▬▬▬▬▬▬▬▬▬▬▬▬▬
▬▬▬▬▬▬▬▬▬▬▬▬▬▬▬▬▬▬▬▬▬

LEWINSKY was shown a chart which documented her contacts and/or telephone calls with CLINTON. LEWINSKY suggested changes to the chart, as necessary, to more accurately reflect her contacts or telephone calls with CLINTON. (A draft of the chart, with the changes suggested by LEWINSKY handwritten by the writer, was placed in an FD-340, along with the original notes of this interview.) In addition to the changes made to the draft chart, LEWINSKY provided the following information:

August 9, 1995 was the first time she felt a "non-verbal" connection to CLINTON. In middle to late September of 1995, LEWINSKY's friend NATALIE UNGVARI was visiting LEWINSKY. LEWINSKY had what she described as an "accidental photo opportunity" with CLINTON.

LEWINSKY gave CLINTON a ZEGNA tie on November 20, 1995. LEWIN-SKY identified CLINTON as wearing that tie in three photographs she was shown by the OIC, taken on February 8, 1996, August 5, 1996 and January 23, 1997. LEWINSKY advised she gave CLINTON two ZEGNA ties, two HUGO BOSS ties, one CALVIN KLEIN tie and one FERAUD tie.

LEWINSKY advised she calls the second tie she gave CLINTON, a ZEGNA tie, his "birthday tie," as she gave it to CLINTON for his birthday. LEWIN-SKY advised it was the first tie, which was also a ZEGNA, she saw BAYANI NELVIS wearing at one of NELVIS's grand jury appearances. LEWINSKY said she may have seen a picture of NELVIS in the <u>Washington Post</u> or <u>New York Times</u> the day following NELVIS's grand jury appearance.

LEWINSKY advised she visited the White House on December 15, 1997 for the purpose of observing the swearing in of KATHY HAYCOCK.

LEWINSKY advised that at one time, CLINTON said that he would speak with BOB NASH about LEWINSKY's job opportunities at the White House. Later, CLINTON said he had spoken to NASH about LEWINSKY's job opportunities. Even later, CLINTON said that the "ball" had been passed to MARSHA SCOTT.

LEWINSKY advised she never called CLINTON directly, but rather always went through BETTY CURRIE.

LEWINSKY showed VERNON JORDAN a copy of her affidavit the same day she took JORDAN a tie and a pocket square. LEWINSKY assumes JORDAN told CLINTON about the affidavit.

As an intern, LEWINSKY worked in room 93 of the Old Executive Office Building (OEOB).

LEWINSKY may have called IRENE KASSORLA after July 4, 1997. LEWINSKY does not recall regular sessions with KASSORLA once LEWINSKY moved to Washington, D.C., but LEWINSKY did speak with her periodically.

FRANK CARTER told LEWINSKY to say if she was not sure about an answer to a question in a deposition, she should say so instead of answering yes or no.

LEWINSKY advised she had one conversation with WILLIAM GINSBURG prior to January 16, 1998. LEWINSKY called GINSBURG at home. LEWINSKY may have contacted GINSBURG after LINDA TRIPP had been subpoenaed in the JONES case. LEWINSKY called GINSBURG to ask him questions in a hypothetical fashion. LEWINSKY received GINSBURG's telephone number from LEWINSKY's step-mother.

LEWINSKY advised LINDA TRIPP of some of the things GINSBURG told LEWINSKY. GINSBURG said there was a difference between perjury in a criminal case and perjury in a civil matter. LEWINSKY also told TRIPP something about illegally obtained evidence. LEWINSKY was concerned about the JONES people breaking into LEWINSKY's apartment. LEWINSKY may have told TRIPP things LEWINSKY's attorneys did not tell her, but LEWINSKY may have attributed it to her attorney.

LEWINSKY advised she does not recall leaving BETTY CURRIE or CLINTON a message to the effect of "I hope you drop dead." LEWINSKY may have said she said that when speaking with TRIPP, but would not have used those actual words when speaking to CURRIE.

LEWINSKY is not sure when, but at some time, CURRIE left a message on LEWINSKY's answering machine to the effect "we have some unresolved issues. I know you do not want to talk to him or me." LEWINSKY advised this may have been after July 1, 1997, it may have been November 13, 1997 or it could have been November 22, 1997.

LEWINSKY advised she called TRIPP numerous times at work. LEWIN-

SKY did not call TRIPP twenty to thirty times a day. LEWINSKY advised she may have called TRIPP multiple times a day, because of call backs due to interruption. LEWINSKY advised she and TRIPP discussed numerous topics, not all of which were related to CLINTON.

LEWINSKY first became suspicious of TRIPP after July 14, 1997. LEWINSKY advised she was generally accurate when speaking with TRIPP, up until the time LEWINSKY found out TRIPP was on the witness list in the JONES matter. However, when speaking with TRIPP, LEWINSKY did not make things up about her relationship with CLINTON.

LEWINSKY advised prior to about December 22, 1997, LEWINSKY was truthful with TRIPP. LEWINSKY advised she was not always truthful with TRIPP later, however, such as when LEWINSKY advised TRIPP that her mom, MARCIA LEWIS, thought TRIPP should feign a foot injury to avoid testifying.

LEWINSKY advised she originated the idea of using nicknames when communicating with CURRIE and TRIPP. LEWINSKY advised she did so to avoid anyone in the JONES team from identifying her. LEWINSKY's mother or aunt came up with the name "GWEN" for VERNON JORDAN to help them remember his name.

LEWINSKY does not know why CURRIE placed telephone calls for CLINTON. LEWINSKY does not believe CURRIE logged in all the gifts LEWINSKY gave CLINTON. LEWINSKY thought it would not be a good idea to have a trail of any references between LEWINSKY and CLINTON.

Referring to the December 17, 1997 telephone call from CLINTON, LEWINSKY is 99.99% sure CLINTON said LEWINSKY can always say she was there to see CURRIE.

LEWINSKY spoke to MIKE McCURRY on occasions related to official business at the Pentagon.

CURRIE drove LEWINSKY to LEWINSKY's apartment from the White House approximately five times.

LEWINSKY took her blue GAP dress to New York sometime around December 30, 1997. LEWINSKY rolled the dress in a ball, put it in plastic and threw it in a closet in her mother's apartment in New York. When LEWINSKY's mother moved out of her New York apartment at the end of May, LEWINSKY moved the dress back to LEWINSKY's Washington, D.C. apartment.

LEWINSKY described her relationship with MAUREEN LEWIS as "semi-friendly." LEWINSKY did not tell LEWIS she fantasized about a sexual relationship with CLINTON.

LEWINSKY does not recall ever dating DENNIS LYTTON, or providing any information to TREY RAGSDALE, PAMELA REVEL, or JAY LESNER.

The interview ended at approximately 6:10 p.m.

Monica Lewinsky's
August 6, 1998, Grand Jury Testimony

PROCEEDINGS

Whereupon,

MONICA S. LEWINSKY

was called as a witness and, after having been first duly sworn by the Foreperson of the Grand Jury, was examined and testified as follows:

EXAMINATION

BY MR. EMMICK:

Q Good morning.

A Good morning.

Q Ms. Lewinsky, this is the grand jury appearance that you'll be making or at least the first of the grand jury appearances, if there will be any more. What we routinely do with witnesses before the grand jury is that we begin the appearance by discussing your rights and your obligations and so that's what we'll do right now.

A Okay.

Q What I'd like to say first is that you have a Fifth Amendment right. That Fifth Amendment right is the right to refuse to answer any questions that may tend to incriminate you. Do you understand that right?

A Yes, I do.

Q Now, ordinarily, you could refuse to answer questions that would tend to incriminate you. As I understand it, here you have entered into an agreement with the government that provides you with immunity, in exchange for which you will be cooperating with the government. Is that right?

A Correct.

MR. EMMICK: What I would like to do is show you a copy of what has been marked as Exhibit ML-2.

(Grand Jury Exhibit No. ML-2 was marked for identification.)

BY MR. EMMICK:

Q Do you recognize this?

A Yes, I do.

Q On the third page of that document, there is a signature line that says Monica Lewinsky. Is that your signature?

A Yes, it is.

Q All right. You also have a right to counsel. What that means is that although your attorney cannot be in the grand jury room here with you, your attorney can be outside the grand jury room and available to answer whatever questions you might have. Do you understand that right?

A Yes, I do.

Q Do you have an attorney?

A Yes, I do.

Q Who would that be?

A Several.

Q All right.

A Jake Stein, Plato Cacheris—do you want me to name all of them who are here or just the lead?

Q All right. Those are the lead counsel?

A Those are the lead counsel.

Q All right. And are they outside?

A Yes, they are.

Q You understand that if you need to speak with them, all you need to say is "I'd like to speak with my attorneys about something for just a minute"?

A Yes.

Q All right. In addition to those two rights that you have, you also have an obligation and that obligation is to tell the truth. That obligation is imposed on you because you have taken an oath and that is the oath to tell the truth. Do you understand that?

A Yes, I do.

Q Do you understand that if you were to intentionally say something that's false, in common parlance, if you were to lie, that would constitute perjury and perjury is a felony and it's punishable by up to five years in prison? Do you understand that?

A Yes.

Q Do you understand as well that because of the agreement that you have signed if you were to lie, if you were to intentionally lie, that would mean that the agreement that you have that gives you immunity could be voided and you could be prosecuted? Do you understand that?

A Mm-hmm.

Q All right. And that in simple parlance, what that means, is that you can retain immunity, but only if you do not lie. Do you understand that?

A Yes.

Q Okay. What I'd like to do is simply discuss with you briefly or clarify with you the fact that we have had interviews with you since the time when you signed this agreement. Is that right?

A Yes.

Q All right. We've had interviews with you, I believe, every day since the signing of the agreement.

A Correct.

Q Several hours a day?

A Yes.

Q Is that right? All right. I also wanted to ask you a question having to do with your mental state right now. How are you feeling?

A Nervous.

Q Okay. I wanted also to ask you, are you taking any medication at this time?

A Yes, I am.

Q What I'd like to ask about that is simply is that having any effect on your ability to recall or to communicate that in some way will hinder your ability to answer questions?

A I don't believe so, but it affects my short-term memory just a little bit.

Q Okay. That's fine. Understand, if you will, that your role today is simply to answer questions that we pose to you.

We have spoken with you for a number of hours, a number of days, and we're going to be asking you to talk about essentially three years of conduct. We are not going to be asking you to recount every detail of the last three years of your life and we are not going to be asking you to recount everything that you've told us over the last ten days or so. You'll just be answering questions and we understand that you have other details that you could provide on other occasions.

A   Yes.

MR. EMMICK: All right. What I'd like to do next is to let you know what our approach is going to be today.

What we're going to do is we're going to start off talking about your internship at the White House and then we're going to ask you questions having to do with your relationship with the President.

Because we think that that will proceed more comfortably if those questions are asked by Ms. Immergut, I'm going to turn the questioning over to her and at some point, then, we'll collaborate in asking further follow-up questions. So without further ado—

BY MS. IMMERGUT:

Q   Ms. Lewinsky, when did you start working at the White House?

A   My internship began July of 1995.

Q   And when you say "internship," could you just very briefly describe what it is you were doing and where you were working?

A   Sure. I was interning for Mr. Panetta, who was Chief of Staff at that time, and I worked in his correspondence office preparing his correspondence, drafting some of the language.

Q   Was there ever a time—or I guess—after beginning your internship, how long did you serve as an intern in the White House?

A   About four, four and a half months. Four and a half months.

Q   And was there ever a time that you then assumed a staff position that was not an intern position?

A   Yes.

Q   And when would that have been?

A   In November of 1995.

Q   When did you first notice the President of the United States?

A   Our first encounter, I guess non-verbal encounter, was August 9, 1995.

Q   And could you describe what that encounter was?

A   Yes. It was a departure ceremony on the South Lawn and, as he was going by on the rope line shaking hands, we made eye contact and it was more intense eye contact than I had experienced before with him.

Q   Okay. And did you have any further such contact sort of later, after that initial time?

A   Yes. The next day the President—I guess the staff had a birthday party for the President on the South Lawn and the interns were invited to that later in the day. And at that party, there was sort of a more intense flirtation that went on at a distance.

Q   Okay. Did you feel that he was flirting with you as well? Or how would you describe the behavior that you both exhibited?

A   It was intense eye contact and when he went by the rope line to shake hands, it was—I mean, he—he's a charismatic person and so—just when he shook my hand and—there was an intense connection.

Q   Okay. And could you sort of just summarize the early relationship that you had with the President before any first sexual contact?

123

A I think it was intense flirting.

Q Okay. Did you have conversations with him?

A Brief conversations that I think in passing—if I saw him or—at a departure ceremony, "Have a nice trip." I introduced myself at one point.

Q Okay. And how did you manage to run into him or even see him? Was that a common occurrence or how would that be accomplished?

A Before the relationship began, it was mainly at departure ceremonies, I think there were a few, and then on one occasion my best friend was in town and she was getting a tour of the West Wing and I was waiting for her in the basement lobby and met him that way. There were several other people there.

Q Okay. Was there ever a time that your relationship became more of a romantic and sexual relationship?

A Yes.

Q And when did that occur?

A On November 15, 1995.

Q Okay. And although as I've told you, I'm not going to go into a lot of specific dates, this is one that I wanted you to explain sort of how it came about.

A It was during the furlough. I was up in Mr. Panetta's West Wing office answering phones. The President came down several times during the day.

There was the continued flirtation and around 8:00 in the evening or so I was in the hallway going to the restroom, passing Mr. Stephanopoulos' office, and he was in the hall and invited me into Mr. Stephanopoulos' office and then from there invited me back into his study.

Q Okay. And what happened there?

A We talked briefly and sort of acknowledged that there had been a chemistry that was there before and that we were both attracted to each other and then he asked me if he could kiss me.

Q And what did you say?

A Yes.

Q And did you kiss on that occasion?

A Yes.

Q And where in the—you mentioned you went back to the study area.

A Mm-hmm.

Q Where exactly did the kiss occur?

A Right outside his bathroom, in the hallway, inside—adjacent to the study, to the office.

Q Okay. And how did you end that—was there anything more than a romantic kiss on that sort of first encounter?

A No.

Q Okay. Did you have any later encounter with him on that same date?

A Yes, I did.

Q Okay. Could you describe how that occurred?

A The President came down to Mr. Panetta's office, I think it might have been around 10 p.m., and told me that if I wanted to meet him back in Mr. Stephanopoulos' office in five minutes, that that would be fine. And I agreed. And I met him back there. We went back to his office again, in the back study area.

Q Okay. And what happened in the back study area?

A We talked and we were more physically intimate.

Q Okay. And on that occasion, did you perform oral sex on the President?

A Yes.

Q With respect to physical intimacy, other than oral sex, was there other physical intimacy performed?

A Yes. Everything up until oral sex.

Ms. IMMERGUT: Okay. And just for the grand jury purposes, I have marked as an exhibit ML-6 and I'll just read it the grand jury and place it before you.

(Grand Jury Exhibit No. ML-6 was marked for identification.)

Ms. IMMERGUT: It states "Definition of Sexual Relations. For the purposes of this grand jury session, a person engages in 'sexual relations' when the person knowingly engages or causes contact with the genitalia, anus, groin, breast, inner thigh, or buttocks of any person with an intent to arouse or gratify the sexual desire of any person. Contact means intentional touching, either directly or through clothing."

BY Ms. IMMERGUT:

Q Ms. Lewinsky, do you understand that definition?

A Yes, I do.

Ms. IMMERGUT: And I do have copies to pass out to the grand jury.

BY Ms. IMMERGUT:

Q When you described that you had other physical intimacy during your contact with the President on November 15, 1995, did that include sexual relations within the definition that I've just read to you?

A Yes, it does.

Q In that—again, that second contact with him on November 15, 1995, where exactly did the sexual contact that you've described occur?

A In the same hallway, by the back study, and then also in his back office.

Q Okay. And the back office, would that be the study area?

A Yes.

Q Okay. Did you have any further sexual encounters with him after that first time on the 15th?

A Yes.

Q When was the next time?

A On the 17th of November.

Q And could you explain how that contact occurred?

A We were again working late because it was during the furlough and Jennifer Palmieri and I, who was Mr. Panetta's assistant, had ordered pizza along with Ms. Currie and Ms. Hernreich.

And when the pizza came, I went down to let them know that the pizza was there and it as at that point when I walked into Ms. Currie's office that the President was standing there with some other people discussing something.

And they all came back down to the office and Mr.—I think it was Mr. Toiv, somebody accidently knocked pizza on my jacket, so I went to go use the restroom to wash it off and as I was coming out of the restroom, the President was standing in Ms. Currie's doorway and said, "You can come out this way."

So we went back into his back study area, actually, I think, in the bathroom or in the hallway right near the bathroom, and we were intimate.

Q Okay. And at that point, what sort of intimacy was it?

A I believe it was just kissing at that point.

Q Okay. And how did that encounter end?

A I said I needed to back and he said, "Well, why don't you bring me some pizza?" So I asked him if he wanted vegetable or meat.

Q Okay. And, actually, where did the kissing occur that time?

A It was—I think it was in the bathroom or it was right outside the bathroom, in the hallway adjacent to the bathroom.

Q Okay. So did you go back and get him some pizza?

A Yes, I did.

BY MR. WISENBERG:

Q Pardon me. Sorry to interrupt. That's the bathroom adjacent to the hallway that leads from the Oval Office to the dining room. Is that correct?

A Correct.

MR. WISENBERG: Sorry for interrupting.

BY MS. IMMERGUT:

Q Did you go back and get pizza?

A Yes, I did.

Q And did you ever return to the President with the pizza?

A Yes, I did.

Q Could you describe what happened when you returned?

A Yes. I went back to Ms. Currie's office and told her the President had asked me to bring him some pizza.

She opened the door and said, "Sir, the girl's here with the pizza." He told me to come in. Ms. Currie went back into her office and then we went into the back study area again.

Q Okay. And what happened in the back study area?

A We were in the—well, we talked and then we were physically intimate again.

Q Okay. And was there oral sex performed on that occasion?

A Yes.

Q Okay. And that would be you performing oral sex on him?

A Mm-hmm.

Q Okay. And, again—and I have to sort of tell you, you can't answer "Mm-hmm"—

A Oh, sorry.

Q Just yes or no, just for the record. With respect to the physical intimacy again, does that fall—when you say "physical intimacy," do you mean sexual relations within the definition?

A Yes, I do.

Q Now, without going into sort of a lot of details of specific dates, I wanted to ask you some general questions about the relationship and to make clear, although we've already—Mr. Emmick already asked you whether or not you've met with us on several occasions, is it fair to say you've given us many, many details about each of the specific dates involved in the relationship?

A Yes.

Q Did the relationship with the President develop into or also have a non-sexual component to it?

A Yes, it did.

Q Could you describe sort of that aspect of the relationship for the grand jury?

126

A We enjoyed talking to each other and being with each other. We were very affectionate.

Q What sorts of things would you talk about?

A We would tell jokes. We would talk about our childhoods. Talk about current events. I was always giving him my stupid ideas about what I thought should be done in the administration or different views on things. I think back on it and he always made me smile when I was with him. It was a lot of—he was sunshine.

Q And did he make you feel like he enjoyed your being there and talking to you about things?

A Yes.

Q Were there times that you visited him in the Oval Office where there was no sexual contact at all?

A Yes.

Q Was there sort of affectionate contact during some of those times?

A Very. Yes.

Q Okay. And how would you describe sort of affectionate but non-sexual contact?

A A lot of hugging, holding hands sometimes. He always used to push the hair out of my face.

Q Okay. Could you describe generally how those meetings were set up or how those encounters were actually set up as a general matter?

A After the first few incidents that sort of happened during the furlough, they were set up—when I was working in Legislative Affairs, usually the President would call my office on a weekend.

He had told me earlier on that he was usually around on the weekends and that it was okay to come see him on the weekends. So he would call and we would arrange either to bump into each other in the hall or that I would bring papers to the office.

Do you want me to do after?

Q Okay. Then what happened after?

A Once I left the White House, Ms. Currie arranged the visits.

Q Okay. And how would she arrange those, typically?

A I don't understand. I'm sorry.

Q When you say Ms. Currie would arrange them, how would it come about that they would be set up?

A Usually either through my talking to the President prior to and then him talking to Ms. Currie or me bugging Ms. Currie to ask the President.

Q Okay. All right. Did the relationship after the events you've described of November 15th and 17th, did it continue also to have a sexual component?

A Yes, it did.

Q After the two incidents that you've described, did you have further sexual contact with him?

A Yes.

Q And I'm going to ask you just some general questions about that. The grand jurors heard that there's a chart and we'll sort of go through a chart afterwards in less detail. Approximately how many times do you recall performing oral sex on the President?

A I think about nine.

Q Did he ever perform oral sex on you?

A No. We had discussed it and there were times when it almost happened, but mother nature was in the way.

Q Okay. How many times did he ejaculate when you performed oral sex?

A In my presence?

Q In your presence.

A Twice.

Q Okay. And do you recall the dates of those times?

A Mm-hmm. February 28, 1997 and March—I think it's the 29th, 1997.

Q Did you engage, other than oral sex, in other physical intimacy that would fall within the definition of sexual relations that we've read to you?

A Yes.

Q Were you alone with the President when you had these sexual encounters with him?

A Yes.

Q It seems like an obvious question, but I have to ask it. Did the President ever have telephone calls while you were actually engaging with oral sex with him?

A Twice.

Q And when those telephone calls occurred, did he ever talk on the phone while you were performing oral sex?

A Yes.

Q Do you have any recollection about when those occurred?

A I believe one was November 15, 1995, in my second visit with him, and I know April 7, 1996.

Q Okay. Did you ever have sexual intercourse with the President?

A No.

Q Was there ever a time when your genitals actually touched each other?

A Grazed each other, yes.

Q And do you remember when that occurred?

A Yes. February 28, 1997. Oh, no. I'm sorry. March 29th, not February 28th. Sorry.

Q Okay. And could you explain why you didn't have sexual intercourse with him?

A He didn't want to. The President said that he—that at his age, that there was too much of a consequence in doing that and that when I got to be his age I would understand. But I wasn't happy with that.

Q Okay. I want to move away from that now.

A Okay.

Q And ask you whether or not you've ever spoken to the President on the telephone.

A Yes.

Q And can you estimate approximately how many times since the beginning of your relationship with him that you've spoken to him on the phone?

A Over 50, probably.

Q And has he initiated any of those calls?

A Yes.

Q Do you have any sort of idea how many times he's called you?

A Most of those phone calls were calls that he placed to me directly.

Q Okay. Did he ever leave any messages for you at your home?

A Yes.

Q And you remember about how many times he left messages?

128

A I think about four.
Q Did you save any of those messages?
A Yes, I did.
Q And have you provided any cassette tape of those messages to the OIC?
A Yes, I have.
Q Do you remember any particular messages that he left you?
A I remember them all.
Q Okay. Why don't you just tell the grand jury what they say.
A They're pretty innocuous. Sometimes—or one time, it was, you know, "Sorry I missed you." One time, it was just "Hello." And then one time he called really late at night when I was not at home and it was whispered kind of loudly, you know, "Come on. It's me." Something like that. It was always nice to hear his voice.
Q Okay. Did he ever tell you how he felt about leaving messages on your home machine?
A Yes.
Q What did he tell you about that?
A I believe it was the beginning of 1996, at some point, he just remarked that he didn't like to do that, he just—I think felt it was a little unsafe.
Q Okay. Did he ever call you late at night?
A Yes.
Q Can you tell us a little bit about that? Did that happen on many occasions?
A Yes. He's a night owl, so it would be customary for him to call sometimes 2:00 in the morning, 2:30 in the morning.
Q Okay. What sorts of things did you discuss with him generally of a non-sexual nature on your telephone calls with him?
A Similar to what we discussed in person, just how we were doing. A lot of discussions about my job, when I was trying to come back to the White House and then once I decided to move to New York. We told jokes. We talked about everything under the sun.
Q Okay. Was there ever a time that you began to engage in phone sex on the telephone?
A Mm-hmm. Yes.
Q And do you remember when that started to occur?
A In the beginning of 1996.
Q Okay. Did he participate in that?
A Yes.
Q Okay. And about how many times did you have phone sex with him, if you know?
A Oh, maybe 10, 15. I'm not really—I'm not really sure.
Q Okay. We can look at the chart after to refresh your recollection, but that sounds sort of ballpark?
A I think so.
Q More than 10, about? In your view?
A Yes, I think so.
Q Did the President ever tell you that he wanted to end the sexual relationship with you?
A Yes.
Q And did he tell you that more than once?
A Yes.
Q Could you tell us when he told you that?

A February—it was Presidents Day of 1996. I think that's February 19th. And also on May 24, 1996—no, 1997. I'm sorry.

Q And just for the grand jury's information, on the chart that we're going to show them in a little bit, how do you list—do you have a term that you refer to the May 24, 1997 meeting with him?

A D-day.

Q And what does that stand for?

A Dump day.

Q And on those two occasions, what did he tell you about wanting to end the relationship? Just generally.

A Both were, I think, motivated sort of by guilt and just not wanting to— more I think on the 24th of May in '97, just really wanting to do the right thing in God's eyes and do the right thing for his family and he just—he didn't feel right about it.

Q Did you engage in sexual contact with him after those times?

A Yes. Kissing.

Q Okay. After the—well, after the February 19, 1996 time?

A Yes. Yes.

Q And what about after the May 24, 1997 time?

A Just kissing.

Q Did your relationship involve giving gifts to each other?

A Mm-hmm. Yes. I'm sorry.

Q And did you give any gifts to him?

A Yes.

Q Do you have any sort of ballpark figure of how many gifts you've given to him since you've known him?

A About 30.

Q And what about him to you? Do you have any estimate of how many gifts he gave you?

A I think about 18.

Q Did you ever write him any notes or letters or cards?

A Yes.

Q And what sort of cards or letters or notes would you write to him?

A It varied on the occasion. It could be a funny card that I saw or a Halloween card. If I was angry, it could be an angry letter. If I was missing him, it was a missing him letter.

Q Okay. So were some of them—is it fair to say some of them were romantic in nature?

A Yes.

Q And when they were angry, what would you be angry about in your letters or cards?

A Either job-related issues or him not paying enough attention to me.

Q Okay. Did he write you any letters or notes?

A No.

Q Did he ever say why he wasn't writing you any letters or notes?

A No.

Ms. Immergut: I'd now like to show you what I had previously marked as Exhibit 7, I believe. Perhaps somebody has the other original version.

(Grand Jury Exhibit No. ML-7 was marked for identification.)

By Ms. Immergut:

Q I'm going to place this before you and ask if you recognize that chart.

A Yes, I do.

Q And have you seen that chart before?

A Yes, I have.

Q Did you assist the Office of Independent Counsel in preparing that chart?

A Yes.

Q Did you provide all of the information that's listed on that chart?

A Yes.

Q Could you describe for the grand jury just generally what is described by that chart?

A I think it's a chronology that marks some of the highlights of my relationship with the President. It definitely includes the visits that I had with him and most of the gifts that we exchanged. It reflects most of the phone calls that I remember.

Q And to the best of your knowledge, is the chart accurate?

A Yes.

Q Have you noticed anything that you would add or delete from the chart since you've reviewed it?

A Yes. On page—

Ms. Immergut: Do the grand jurors have the chart?

Mr. Emmick: They do. Yes.

The Witness: On page 5, the last entry in the chart, on 10/23, I attended a Democratic fundraiser that you guys have all probably seen on T.V. lately.

By Ms. Immergut:

Q Okay. Anything else that you've noticed?

A No.

Q Okay. Otherwise, would you say that the chart is a pretty accurate rendition or description of your memory of all of the events?

A Yes.

Q How is it that you remember all the events in such detail over really sort of what is a few years?

A I've always been a date-oriented person and I had a—probably a habit of circling dates in my Filofax when I either talked to the President or saw him.

Q And did you provide those Filofax sheets to the Office of Independent Counsel?

A Yes.

Q And did that assist you in remembering the dates?

A Yes, it did.

Q And were these encounters important to you?

A Very.

Q And, again, on that chart there are various categories. In the visit category—or descriptions in the visit category area that are described as physical intimacy. And with respect to all of those, do they fall within the definition of sexual relations that I've presented as Exhibit 6 to the grand jury?

A Yes.

Q So anywhere physical intimacy is listed on the chart, it falls within that definition. Is that correct?

A Right. I think the only thing that might be missing is kissing.

Q Okay. And kissing is separately described on the chart, is it not?

A No, not necessarily.

Q Okay.

A I mean, because the physical intimacy—wherever there's physical intimacy, there was always—there was always kissing.

Q Okay. But where there's physical intimacy, there was also then more than kissing.

A Correct.

Q Okay. So physical intimacy is never on the chart to describe only kissing.

A Correct.

Q Okay. There's one particular date also that I wanted to cover with you which is February 28, 1997.

A Okay.

Q Because at that time, as the chart demonstrates, you haven't really seen the President since April of the year before. Could you describe what the circumstances were leading up to your visit with him on February 28, 1997?

A The President had told me in December that he had a Christmas present for me and I ended up not getting it until the end of February. Ms. Currie called me at work during that week to—or I guess it was that day, I'm sorry, that Friday, to invite me to a radio address that evening.

    I went to the radio address and when I went to take my picture with the President, he said to go see Betty because he had something to give me after. So I waited a little while for him and then Betty and the President and I went into the back office.

Q Okay. And why did Betty come in the back office with you?

A I later found out that—I believe it was Stephen Goodin who said to Ms. Currie and the President that the President couldn't be alone with me, so Ms. Currie came back into the back office with us.

Q And then what?

A And then left.

Q Okay. She left? And do you know where she went?

A I came to learn later, I believe she was in the pantry. In the back pantry.

Q Okay. And how did you learn that later?

A I think that Mr. Nelvis told me. Or Ms. Currie told me.

Q Okay. What happened when she went to the back pantry? Did you remain with the President?

A Yes, I did.

Q And could you describe what you and the President did?

A Mm-hmm. He gave me my hat pin and the book "Leaves of Grass" and I was pestering him to kiss me and so we moved—that was in the back study and then we moved over to the back hallway by the bathroom and we were physically intimate.

Q Okay. And did you perform oral sex on that occasion?

A Yes.

Q And how did you—do you remember what dress you were wearing on that occasion?

A Yes.

Q What dress was it?

A The navy blue dress from The Gap.

Q And after that incident, did you ever tell Linda Tripp that there might be the President's semen on that dress?

A Yes, I did.

Q And why did you tell her that? Or did you believe that that could be true?

A I thought it was possible.

132

Q Were you positive it was true?

A No.

Q Back to the incident with the President, how did you leave it with him on that occasion? Sort of once you finished the visit, what happened?

A Betty came back into the back study and then I think Ms. Currie walked me out.

Q Okay. How much about your relationship with the President did you tell Linda Tripp?

A A lot. Most everything.

Q Okay. And did you tell her about the sexual encounters that you had with him?

A Yes.

Q Did you also tell her about the emotional encounters and the gifts?

A Yes.

Q Were you truthful about the relationship when you told Linda Tripp about it?

A Most of the time, but sometimes—there were occasions when I wasn't truthful.

Q Were you truthful about the sexual parts of the relationship with her?

A Yes.

Q And what about the emotional component, when you would tell her— and why don't I say before December of 1997, were you truthful about the emotional components of the relationship?

A Yes.

Q I'm actually done with my questioning on that. Do you want to break now or continue to different subjects?

A A five-minute break? Could I—

THE FOREPERSON: We can take a ten-minute break.

MS. IMMERGUT: Okay. A ten-minute break.

MR. EMMICK: A ten-minute break.

MS. IMMERGUT: Would that be all right?

THE WITNESS: Okay.

MR. EMMICK: That's fine.

(Witness excused. Witness recalled.)

MS. IMMERGUT: Madam Foreperson, are there any unauthorized persons present?

THE FOREPERSON: No, there are none.

MS. IMMERGUT: Do we have a quorum?

THE FOREPERSON: Yes, we do.

Ms. Lewinsky, I would like to remind you that you are still under oath.

THE WITNESS: Thank you.

BY MS. IMMERGUT:

Q Ms. Lewinsky, the grand jurors had a few follow-up questions—

A Sure.

Q —for you that I wanted to ask you before we move on to other topics. You mentioned that one the occasions where you had sexual contact with that were described, sexual contact with the President, that it occurred in the hallway, as you described, or sometimes in the back study.

A Mm-hmm.

Q Why did—

A JUROR: Pardon me.

BY MS. IMMERGUT:

Q Oh, excuse me. Why did you choose the hallway?

A Because I believe it was—it was really more the President choosing the hallway, I think, and it was—there weren't any windows there. It was the most secluded of all the places in the back office. Well, that's not true. The bathroom is the most secluded, I guess, because you can close the door.

Q And did you sometimes have sexual encounters in the bathroom?

A Mm-hmm.

Q And then next to the bathroom, would you say that the hallway is—

A Right.

Q —off the study is the next most—

A He has a bad back and so I think a lot of times we ended up just sort of standing there and talking there because he could close the door to the bathroom and lean up against the bathroom and then he was—I guess it made his back feel better and also made him a little shorter. So—

Q Did the President ever tell you he was concerned about being seen?

A I'm sure that came up in conversation.

BY MR. EMMICK:

Q Did he ever indicate to you looking outside that he might be concerned, for example?

A Yes, yes.

BY MS. IMMERGUT:

Q Can you describe that?

A Sure. I think the one that comes to mind was actually December 28th of last year when I was getting my Christmas kiss. And he was kissing me in the doorway between the back study, or the office, and the hallway, and I sort of opened my eyes and he was looking out the window with his eyes wide open while he was kissing me and then I got mad because it wasn't very romantic. And then so then he said, "Well, I was just looking to see to make sure no one was out there."

Q Can you generalize about the locations where you had your sexual encounters with the President?

A I'd say they mainly took place in that hallway, but there were occasions on which we were intimate in the office and then also in the bathroom.

Q Okay. And when you say the office, do you mean the back study?

A Right.

Q So not the Oval Office?

A No, no, we were never physically intimate in the Oval Office.

Q Okay. Did you notice whether doors were closed when you were physically intimate with him in the back study or hallway?

A No, he always—well, I'm not sure about the door going in the dining room but I know that the door leading from the back hallway to the—into the Oval Office was always kept ajar so that he could hear if someone was coming.

BY MR. WISENBERG:

Q How ajar? How much ajar?

A Maybe this much (indicating).

BY MR. EMMICK:

Q You're indicating six to eight inches, something like that?

A I'm not very good with that.

Q A foot or less, something like that?

A A foot or less. I guess that's—I would assume that's—

Q Enough so that one could hear more easily what was going on in the next room?

A Mm-hmm. Right, or if someone came in to holler for him.

BY MS. IMMERGUT:

Q Now directing your attention back to February 28th,—1997, the day that you wore the blue cocktail dress—

A It's not a cocktail dress.

Q Okay, I'm sorry.

A No, that's okay. I'm a little defensive about this subject. I'm sorry.

Q How would you describe the dress?

A It's a dress from the Gap. It's a work dress. It's a casual dress.

Q With respect to that dress—

A Right, I'm sorry.

Q —you mentioned that you believe that there could be semen on it. Could you describe what you did with the President that led you to believe that?

A We were in the bathroom and—can I close my eyes so I don't have to—

Q Well, you have to speak up. That's the only—

A Okay. We were in the bathroom and I was performing oral sex. I'm sorry, this is embarrassing. And usually he doesn't want to—he didn't want to come to completion.

Q Ejaculate?

A Yes. And this has sort of been a subject that we had talked about many times before and he was always saying it had issues to do with trust and not knowing me well enough at first and then not feeling right about things, and not that he said this but I took away from that to sort of mean that maybe in his mind if he didn't come then maybe it wasn't—he didn't need to feel guilty about that, that maybe with it not coming to completion that that was easier for him to rationalize.

And it was on this occasion that since we hadn't been alone together since April 7th of '96 that after we had engaged in oral sex for a while and he stopped me as he normally did, I said to him, you know—this is so embarrassing, I'm sorry. I said to him, you know, I really—I want to make you come. I mean, this is—

Q Okay. Why don't you just describe the position that you were in once he had tried to stop you. What did you do that led you to believe there might get semen on your dress?

A I told him that I really cared about him and he told me that he didn't want to get addicted to me and he didn't want me to get addicted to him, and we embraced at that point and that's—I mean, it was—it's just a little tiny spot down here and a little tiny spot up here and—

Q Okay. And to get—when you're pointing down here, you mean sort of your right lower hip area?

A Well, one of my—I don't know if it was my right or left, but lower hip area.

Q Okay. And the chest area would be the second place that you thought you might have gotten some?

A Mm-hmm.

Q And is that from when you—when you did actually continue to perform oral sex on him later?

A I believe so.

Q Did you ever see something that you thought was semen on the dress that led you to conclude that?

135

A The next time I went to wear the dress.

Q So at the time you didn't notice anything on the dress?

A I don't believe so.

Q Okay. What happened then the next time you wore the dress that led you to conclude that?

A Well, I also—can I say here? I also—I think I wore the dress out to dinner that night, so which is why I'm not sure that that's what it is.

Q Okay.

A So it could be spinach dip or something. I don't know. I'm sorry, could you repeat the question?

Q Sure. When was the—when was it that you at least began to believe that maybe there was semen on the dress?

A I really don't remember when it was the next time I went to wear the dress, but I gained weight so I couldn't wear the dress and it didn't fit. And I'm not a very organized person. I don't clean my clothes until I'm going to wear them again.

Q Did you notice there was something on the dress?

A Yes. And at that point I noticed it and I kind of thought, oh, this is dirty, it needs to get cleaned. And then I remembered that I had worn it the last time I saw the President, and I believe it was at that point that I thought to myself, oh, no. And it was—it—

Q So at that point, you weren't positive what it was. And why did you tell Linda that you thought there was semen on the dress?

A I think it just sort of came up in conversation somehow and then—as kind of this funny, gross thing. And then the next time she was at my house I still couldn't fit into the dress and believe that I said to her, oh, look, you want to see this? You know, this is what I was talking about.

And but I just want to say because I know everybody here reads the newspapers and listens to TV that I didn't keep this dress as a souvenir. I was going to wear it on Thanksgiving and my cousins, who I always try to look skinny for because they are all skinny—and I know it sounds stupid. And when I told Linda I was thinking about wearing the dress, she discouraged me. She brought me one of her jackets from her thinner closet. And so it wasn't a souvenir. I was going to clean it. I was going to wear it again.

Q Different topic. Where was Nel when you were—or do you have any idea where Nel was when you were in the hallway or the study with the President?

A On which—

Q On any of the occasions. I mean, would Nel be around generally?

A There were some occasions that—very few occasions, I think, that Nel was there—was at the White House. And I don't know where he would have necessarily—I think he was in the pantry on the 28th of February.

Q Do you know where he was on any of the other occasions? And, again, where you had sexual contact with the President.

A I don't think so.

Q Did you ever use hand towels in the bathroom to wipe your lipstick?

A Hand towels, no.

Q What about tissues?

A I believe I used a tissue sometimes to wipe off my lipstick.

MR. WISENBERG: Karen, can I ask something really quick?

MS. IMMERGUT: Sure.

136

Q   How about, do you think Nel would have been around on renaissance—right before the departure for renaissance weekend?

A   New Year's Eve '95?

Q   Yeah.

A   Yes, he was.

Q   Also, did you ever show—did—I don't—it's my bad. Did you ever show the dress to Linda Tripp?

A   Yes.

MR. EMMICK:

Q   You mentioned that the President called you on a number of occasions. Some of those occasions included phone sex. Did he indicate where he was when he was placing those calls?

A   Not always, but sometimes.

Q   And where did he say he was when he did say where he was?

A   At home.

Q   Meaning the White House residence?

A   Yes.

Q   Where else might he have placed calls from?

A   There were, I think, two times that he placed calls from the campaign term, from Florida I think.

Q   Do you know whether he sometimes placed calls from the Oval Office or other places?

A   Yes, yes.

Q   How do you know that?

A   Sometimes he would mention it and say he was in the office. I know one time I said—I knew he was in the office and I asked him if he was in the back or could he go in the back.

Q   Did he not only call you, what, at your home but also call you at your office?

A   When I was working at the White House, yes.

Q   But not while you were working at the Pentagon?

A   He never directly called me when I was working at the Pentagon.

Q   When you say didn't directly call, what do you mean?

A   I mean he—there were, I think, maybe two occasions when I was working at the Pentagon when Betty placed a call for him, and when that didn't occur he picked up the phone and dialed the phone number himself.

Q   When he placed calls to you when you were at Leg Affairs, or Legislative Affairs, excuse me, was there anything that indicated on your caller ID?

A   Yes. When he called from the Oval Office, the phones have a caller ID up at the top, and when he calls from the Oval Office it says POTUS and when he calls from the residence it has an asterisk.

Q   And did you ever discuss with him the fact that you had POTUS on your ID?

A   Yeah.

Q   Tell us about that.

A   I think one time when he called and I picked up the phone I said something that indicated to him that I knew who it was. And he said, "Well, how did you know it was me?" And I told him, "Well, don't you know that it lights up POTUS when you call from the Oval Office?" And he said, "No, I didn't know that." So I thought that was funny.

Q   When you—

A   And he made an effort one time to call me from the residence on a line and called and said, "Did it show up a phone number instead of—" So it had. He seemed proud of himself.

Q   All right. You had mentioned earlier that on, I think it was February 28th, Steve Goodin spoke with Betty and the President about being—about him being alone with you.

A   Mm-hmm.

Q   Could you give us a little more detail about what you saw and what you later learned and where you later learned it so that we can figure out what you know from personal knowledge?

A   Okay. What I saw was Steve Goodin and Ms. Currie going into the Oval Office. I think—

Q   Where are you at this time?

A   Oh, I'm sorry. I was in Ms. Currie's office and I was waiting with Ms. Currie. And I believe Stephen was there at some point and he might have gone into the Oval Office first and then called Ms. Currie in a few minutes after or maybe the President called her in after. And they spoke sort of—

A JUROR: (Coughing.)

THE WITNESS: Do you want some water? Oh, okay. So—

BY MR. EMMICK:

Q   Was there anyone else in the Oval Office, as far as you know?

A   It's possible I think I might have seen Rahm Emanuel in there at some point, but I'm not really sure that he was included in this conversation.

Q   So they go into the Oval Office, and what do you next see or hear?

A   I believe Betty came out to get me. I was really nervous because I hadn't been alone with the President since the elections so I was focused—I was kind of internal, focused on being nervous.

Q   Betty came out to get you and what did the two of you do?

A   The three of us went into the back office.

Q   You had mentioned earlier that you later came to learn that there was a discussion between them, between them, about you and the President and whether you should be alone. Tell us when you learned that approximately and what you learned.

A   I think I learned it, I believe, maybe shortly after—not on that day, maybe within the next few weeks, I guess—that Stephen had said to the President or maybe had said to Betty, you know, she can't be alone with him. So, and I don't recall if I learned that from Ms. Currie or from Nel.

BY MR. WISENBERG:

Q   But it—was it when, based on what you were told, it was a conversation between—it was a conversation in which Goodin, Ms. Currie and the President were there?

A   Correct.

BY MR. EMMICK:

Q   Let's focus a little bit about the Presidential aides. You mentioned Steve Goodin. Where are the aides at the time you are having your encounters, if we can call them that, with the President?

A   Most of the time they weren't—they weren't there. They weren't at the White House.

Q   And how was that arranged?

A   When I was working in Legislative Affairs, I don't think—I don't know if it was ever verbally spoken but it was understood between the President and myself that most of the—most people weren't in on the weekends so there was—it would be safer to do that then.

And then after I left the White House, that was sort of always a concern that Betty and I had just because she knew and I knew that a lot of people there didn't like me.

Q So is it fair to say then that the Presidential aides, whether they be Steve Goodin or Andrew Friendly or whoever it might be, were not around at the time?

A Correct. They may have been but—

Q Mm-hmm. I wonder if you could expand a little bit on the nature of your relationship with Betty and then the nature of your relationship with Nel, and specifically what we mean to ask is to what extent were these relationships genuine relationships and to what extent were they, in part, based on an interest in cultivating their friendship because of your relationship with the President?

A I think that they—both of them started out probably at the latter of what you said, as maybe a function of making my relationship with the President easier, or for me, I guess, getting information, but that they both came to have a very genuine component to them. I still care very deeply about Betty.

Q When you talk about getting information, could you expand on what you mean by that?

A I think sometimes if it was from Ms. Currie finding out what the President's schedule was, when he might be around, what might be a good time to come by or maybe for her to talk to him to let him know something.

With Nel, Nel and I developed a friendship that started during the furlough and I thought he was a really nice guy and didn't get treated correctly or properly, I guess. And the kind of information, he sort of just would give me information about the President. I mean, I don't think that was the only—that wasn't the only component of the friendship, but that was a component of it.

Q You have discussed how Betty helped arrange for you to come visit the President, especially in 1997, I think it would be fair to say.

A Yes.

Q When those arrangements were made, who initiated the arrangements? How did they start off? Did you ask? Did the President ask? Did Betty ask?

A I'd say most of the time it was probably me asking—either asking the President directly or asking him through Betty or through sending a note of some sort. And there were occasions that he initiated, so it would come through Betty.

Q All right. Let me ask you the following question. You have described the ways that Betty helped let you in—

A Mm-hmm.

Q —facilitate the relationship, if you will. Do you think Betty Currie knew about your relationship with the President?

A I don't know. It's possible she could have gleaned that from witnessing that the—you know, that the President was having a relationship that caused—with a 25 year-old woman or, at the time, younger—you know, that made me emotional. But I really can't answer that question.

Q She saw you under circumstances where she realized you and the President had an emotional tie.

A I believe so. I'm not really—I'm not really comfortable sort of answering questions about what—you know, what Betty knew because—

Q Well, then let me focus more on what Betty was in a position to see.

A Okay.

Q Was Betty in a position to see that you and the President visited frequently and had a strong emotional attachment?

A I believe so, yes.

Q Did you ever expressly tell Betty about the relationship?

A What aspect of the relationship?

Q Well, let me separate it out for you.

A Okay.

Q Did you ever expressly tell Betty about the emotional aspect of the relationship?

A I believe I characterized that to her.

Q Did you ever expressly tell Betty about the sexual aspect of the relationship?

A No, I don't believe so.

Q Let me ask the question, why not?

A Because it's not appropriate. I mean, I think—I don't think people necessarily talk about these things. I mean, there is a difference between a relationship that you have with someone who is sort of involved in a situation, and then the kind of relationship you have with a friend whom you talk to. I think with—a little bit with Betty's age and it wasn't clear to me that the—you know, the President didn't tell her so, if he didn't tell her, why should I tell her.

Q Let me ask similar questions about Nel. Do you think Nel knew?

A Nel knew—

Q About the emotional aspect of the relationship?

A Yes, I think so.

Q Is that based on what you told him or what you think he must have seen, or both?

A I think probably based more on what I told him.

Q Do you think Nel knew about the sexual aspect of the relationship?

A We never directly discussed it, so I don't know if—I don't know how to answer that.

Q Did he ever say things to you that made you think that he must know about the sexual aspect of the relationship?

A Not that I remember.

Q You mentioned earlier, perhaps an obvious thing, that you were alone with the President on the times that you had sexual contact with the President.

A Yes.

Q Were there also times when you were alone with the President that you did not have sexual contact with the President?

A Mm-hmm, yes.

Q Can you give us sort of a general description about how those encounters occurred and where they occurred?

A Okay. There were numerous that ranged from the beginning of our relationship till the end of our relationship.

Q Were some of them brief? Were some of them substantial in length?

A Mm-hmm, yes.

Q Where within the White House would those have occurred?

A One occurred in the Oval Office and then the others occurred—oh, that's not true. Two occurred in the Oval Office and the others were in the back study area.

I should also just—maybe I could just add right now that every—that every time I had a visit with the President when I was working there—not after, but when I was working there—we usually would—we'd start in the back and we'd talk and that was where we were physically intimate, and we'd usually end up, kind of the pillow talk of it, I guess, was sitting in the Oval Office talking. So there's—

BY MR. WISENBERG:

Q And, again, when you say when you started in the back, that could either be the hallway or the back?

A Correct, yes.

BY MR. EMMICK:

Q I would like to ask you some questions about any steps you took to try to keep your relationship with the President secret.

A A lot.

Q All right. Well, why don't we just ask the question open-endedly and we'll follow up.

A Okay. I'm sure, as everyone can imagine, that this is a kind of relationship that you keep quiet, and we both wanted to be careful being in the White House. Whenever I would visit him during—when—during my tenure at the White House, we always—unless it was sort of a chance meeting on a weekend and then we ended up back in the office, we would usually plan that I would either bring papers, or one time we had actually accidentally bumped into each other in the hall and went from that way, so then we planned to do that again because that seemed to work well. But we always—there was always some sort of a cover.

Q When you say that you planned to bring papers, did you ever discuss with the President the fact that you would try to use that as a cover?

A Yes.

Q Okay. What did the two of you say in those conversations?

A I don't remember exactly. I mean, in general, it might have been something like me saying, well, maybe once I got there kind of saying, "Oh, gee, here are your letters," wink, wink, wink, and him saying, "Okay, that's good," or—

Q And as part of this concealment, if you will, did you carry around papers when you went to the visit the President while you worked at Legislative Affairs?

A Yes, I did.

Q Did you ever actually bring him papers to sign as part of business?

A No.

Q Did you actually bring him papers at all?

A Yes.

Q All right. And tell us a little about that.

A It varied. Sometimes it was just actual copies of letters. One time I wrote a really stupid poem. Sometimes I put gifts in the folder which I brought.

Q And even on those occasions, was there a legitimate business purpose to that?

A No.

Q Did you have any discussions with the President about what you would say about your frequent visits with him after you had left Legislative Affairs?

A Yes.

Q Yes. What was that about?

A I think we—we discussed that—you know, the backwards route of it was that Betty always needed to be the one to clear me in so that, you know, I could always say I was coming to see Betty.

Q And is there some truth in the notion that you were coming to see Betty?

A Coming to see Betty, I don't know. Did I—I saw Betty on every time that I was there.

Q What was your purpose though in going—

A My purpose was—most of the time my purpose was to see the President, but there were some times when I did just go see Betty but the President wasn't in the office.

Q When the President was in the office, was your purpose in going there to see the President?

A Yes.

Q What about the writing of things down on paper?
Was there any discussion between you and the President about the risks of writing things down and whether you should write things down?

A Yes.

Q All right. Tell us about that.

A There were on some occasions when I sent him cards or notes that I wrote things that he deemed too personal to put on paper just in case something ever happened, if it got lost getting there or someone else opened it. So there were several times when he remarked to me, you know, you shouldn't put that on paper.

Q We'll have occasion to get into some details about that in a bit. I don't know how to ask this question more delicately, so I'll just ask you. Did you take any steps to try to be careful with how loud you might be in sexual matters?

A Yes.

Q All right. Can you tell us, as discreetly as you can and as—about that?

A I think we were both aware of the volume and sometimes I'd use my hand—I bit my hand—so that I wouldn't make any noise.

Q All right, that's fine. Let me ask another question. DId you try to take—are you okay?

A Yeah, this is just embarrassing.

Q Did you try to take different routes in and out of the Oval Office area as part of your way of concealing the relationship?

A Yes, I did.

Q Could you tell us about that?

A I made an effort on my own to go out a different door than the door that I came in so that if there was a guard that was on duty in the front of the Oval Office he might see me going in but a different guard would see me leave, so no one would know exactly how long I had been in there.

Q Did you try to do that most of the time, all of the time?

A I'd say 90 percent of the time. I mean, I can't really recall a time that I didn't do that, but it's possible. That was the pattern.

Q Were there some people that you tried to specifically avoid when you were visiting the President?

A   Yes.

Q   All right. Who were they, please?

A   Pretty much everybody but Betty.

Q   Okay. What about, for example, Nancy Hernreich?

A   Yes.

Q   All right. And how would you take steps to avoid Nancy Hernreich?

A   Generally, coming in on the weekend. This is after I left?

Q   Yes.

A   Okay. After I left the White House it was coming in on the weekend or sometimes we—I tried to see him but I don't think it actually ever occurred on Tuesday nights because Ms. Hernreich has yoga, I think—I believe.

BY MR. WISENBERG:

Q   Who told you that she had yoga?

A   Ms. Currie.

BY MR. EMMICK:

Q   Any discussion with the President about trying to make sure that there are fewer people around when you were to visit?

A   When I worked in Legislative Affairs, I think that was sort of the understanding that the weekend was the—there weren't a lot of people around. And there were times when I think that the President might have said, oh, there are too many people here because there was some big issue or some big event happening maybe.

Q   Were there any occasions when you tried to make arrangements to see the President but for some reason or another Betty was not in a position to let you in?

A   Sure, I think so.

Q   Any occasions when you had actually planned to visit and then for some reason or another she wasn't there, that you remember?

A   No, not that I remember.

Q   What about throwing away notes that you had written to the President? Was there any discussion of throwing out the notes or any notations that you would write on the notes to remind him to throw them out?

A   Yes, I think that I may have had a discussion with the President about him throwing things away, I think, or making sure that they're not there. I know one specific occasion in one of the notes that I sent him I made a joke that really was reminding him not to—to make sure he threw the—make sure he threw it away.

Q   I've asked you a number of questions having to do with how you tried to keep the relationship secret. Let me ask, did you tell some people about the relationship?

A   Unfortunately, yes.

Q   All right. Could you tell us some of the people that you've told about the relationship?

A   Linda Tripp, Catherine Davis, Neysa Erbland, Dale Young, Ashley Raines, and my mom and my aunt. Everybody knew a different amount of—had a different amount of in
formation.

Q   Natalie Ungvari?

A   Oh, Natalie Ungvari, yes.

Q   Did you tell any of your—any counselors or therapists of any kind about your relationship?

A   Yes, I did.

Q   All right. Would you tell us who they would be?

A   Dr. Irene Kassorla, and I believe it's Dr. Kathy Estep.

Q   When you talked about your relationship with the President with these people, did you lie about your relationship?

A   No. I may have not told them every detail, but I don't believe I ever lied. Oh, about the—oh, wait, do you mean the doctors or was that in general?

Q   I meant in general.

A   Well, there were—about my relationships—I'm sorry, could you be more specific?

Q   Sure. You listed a number of people that you had told about your relationship with the President.

A   Right.

Q   I'm just trying to figure out if you told the truth to those people when you described the relationship.

A   Yes. There were some occasions when I wasn't truthful about certain things, but not having to do with, I think, the general relationship. Does that make sense?

Q   Expand on that just a little. I'm just not sure.

A   Well, I think with Linda Tripp, I mean there were times that I was not truthful with her. I mean, I didn't know if that's what you were encompassing by saying relationship or not.

Q   Let's put Linda Tripp aside for a bit because I think I know what you have in mind.

A   Right.

Q   Put Linda Tripp aside for a bit. Were you truthful with the others about your description of the relationship?

A   Yes.

Q   And since you mentioned Linda Tripp, were there occasions toward the end of, I guess it would be December or January, when you said some things to Linda Tripp that were not true?

A   Yes.

Q   All right. We'll have a chance to get to that in a bit.

A   Okay.

Q   What I would like to turn to next is the—is April of 1996 and your transfer from the White House to the Department of Defense. When were you first told about the fact that you were being terminated from Legislative Affairs?

A   On the 5th—I think it was the 5th of April, Friday.

Q   Did you later have a telephone conversation with the President about your being terminated?

A   Yes, I did.

Q   When was that?

A   On the 7th, on Easter.

Q   Easter Sunday, April 7th of 1996?

A   Correct.

Q   Would you tell us first what your reaction was when you were told that you were going to be terminated from Legislative Affairs?

A   My initial reaction was that I was never going to see the President again. I mean, my relationship with him would be over.

Q   You did not want to go to the Pentagon?

A   No.

Q When you spoke with the President on April 7th, did you call him or did he call you?

A He called me.

Q Would you tell us how that telephone conversation proceeded and then we'll talk about the meeting.

A Okay. I had asked him how—if he was doing okay with Ron Brown's death, and then after we talked about that for a little bit I told him that my last day was Monday. And he was—he seemed really upset and sort of asked me to tell him what had happened. So I did and I was crying and I asked him if I could come see him, and he said that that was fine.

Q Did you go over to the White House?

A Yes, I did.

Q About what time of day, if you remember?

A I think it was around 6:00 p.m.

Q Who let you in?

A I had a pass at the time.

Q How long did you visit with the President that day?

A Maybe a half an hour. I'm not very good with the time estimates.

Q You've already had occasion to talk a little bit about the sexual aspect of your encounter with the President at that time and the phone call that you—that came in in the midst. I'm not going to ask you about that. What I am going to ask you about instead was your discussions with the President about the termination and about what the future would hold for you.

A He told me that he thought that my being transferred had something to do with him and that he was upset. He said, "Why do they have to take you away from me? I trust you." And then he told me—he looked at me and he said, "I promise you if I win in November I'll bring you back like that."

Q How were things left at the end of that meeting?

A I sort of ran out.

Q Right. I guess what I mean by that—I'm sorry, I didn't mean to be that specific.

A Okay.

Q At the end of the meeting, were you going to go to the Pentagon?

A Well, he was going to see what he could do.

Q I see. All right.

A He said he'd try to see. He said he was going to ask—try to find out what had happened. And I told him that I was going to be meeting with Ms. Hernreich the next day and he sort of said, "Let me see what I can do."

Q Did you later have a telephone call with the President where you discussed what he had learned?

A Yes.

Q When was that?

A The following Friday.

Q That would have been then April 12th?

A Yes, I think so.

Q Did he call you or did you call him?

A He called me.

Q Where were you?

A I was at home.

Q How long was the telephone conversation?

A Maybe about 20 minutes.

Q Tell us what the two of you talked about.

A He told me that he had asked Nancy and Marsha Scott to find out why I had been transferred, and that what he had come to learn was that Evelyn Lieberman had sort of spearheaded the transfer, and that she thought he was paying too much attention to me and I was paying too much attention to him and that she didn't necessarily care what happened after the election but everyone needed to be careful before the election.

Q Did he offer any of his views about what you should do with respect to this Pentagon job?

A He told me that I should try it out and if I didn't like it that he would get me a job on the campaign.

Q What was your reaction to that?

A I think I was disappointed. I didn't want to go to the Pentagon and I didn't really see what the difference on the campaign was going to be—why I couldn't work—if I could work at the campaign why I couldn't work at the White House. So—

Q Did you start working at the Pentagon?

A Yes.

Q What position did you hold when you worked at the Pentagon?

A Confidential Assistant to Ken Bacon, who is the Pentagon spokesman.

Q Let's talk generally, if you will, about what sort of contact you had with the President during the rest of 1996. Did you see him in person?

A Yes, I did.

Q Okay. Did you see him in person very often?

A No. I wasn't alone with him so when I saw him it was in some sort of event or group setting.

Q Did you continue to have telephone contact with him?

A Yes.

Q And those telephone contacts are set out in the chart that we've put together—

A Mm-hmm.

Q —with your assistance?

A I guess. Yes. I'm sorry.

Q Let's then just turn to the first part of 1997. The election is over. Did you talk with the President about getting you back to the White House?

A Yes.

Q All right. Would you tell us about that?

A I believe the first time I might have mentioned it to him was in January of '97 in a phone conversation, and he told me that he would talk to Bob Nash, who is the head of White House or Presidential Personnel, I think it is, about bringing me back. In the next phone call he said he had spoken to Bob Nash and then—do you want me to go as far as—

Q Just a bit more detail so that we can get a sense of what efforts you thought were being taken and whether you came to be disappointed with those efforts.

A Very disappointed. He—my understanding at first was that the ball had sort of been passed to Bob Nash to bring me—to find a position for me to come back to the White House. I then came to learn maybe in March or so that the ball had been passed from Bob Nash to Marsha Scott. And then Marsha Scott was supposed to help me find a position at the White

House, which didn't work out, then she was going to detail me to her office in the White House and then she later rescinded that offer. Keep going?

Q Were you frustrated with all that?

A Very frustrated.

Q And did you communicate your frustration to the President?

A Yes, I did.

Q Tell us about how you communicated your frustration to the President.

A There were various occasions, different things that happened. Sometimes it was in our phone conversations, sometimes it was in a letter, sometimes it was in person.

Q Let me direct your attention to July 3rd of 1997. Did you cause some sort of a communication to be made to the President on that day?

A Yes.

Q Tell us about that.

A I had been trying to get in touch with him maybe since the latter part of June to discuss some of my meetings with Marsha Scott that had not gone as I had hoped they would and—excuse me—the President wasn't responding to me and wasn't returning my calls and wasn't responding to my notes. And I got very upset so I sat down that morning actually and scribbled out a long letter to him that talked about my frustrations and that he had promised to bring me back; if he wasn't going to bring me back that I—you know, then could be help me find a job—at that point I said in New York at the United Nations, and that I sort of dangled in front of him to remind him that if I wasn't coming back to the White House I was going to need to explain to my parents exactly why that wasn't happening.

Q And what was your purpose in sending a letter of that kind to the President?

A I think it was sort of had a few purposes, in that towards the end of the letter I softened up again and was back to my mushy self, but the purpose was—one of the purposes, I think, was to kind of remind him that I had left the White House like a good girl in April of '96. A lot of other people might have made a really big stink and said that they weren't going to lose their job and they didn't want to do that and would have talked about what kind of relationship they had with the President so they didn't lose their job, and that I had been patient and had waited and that all of this had gone on. So I was frustrated.

Q Did you—how did you get this letter to the President?

A I gave it to Ms. Currie.

Q Did you meet with the President on the 3rd of July?

A Mm-hmm. Yes, I'm sorry.

Q Did you meet with the President on the 4th of July?

A Yes, I did.

Q Would you tell us how that was arranged?

A I spoke with Ms. Currie later that afternoon on the 3rd and she told me to come to the White House at 9 o'clock the next morning.

Q You showed up at the White House?

A (Nodding.)

Q What I would like to do with respect to this meeting is just ask you to give a very general description of the meeting, whether it was emotional.

A It was very emotional.

Q I don't want to focus on the emotional aspect of that meeting. What I want to do is focus on the end of the meeting.

A Okay.

Q And whether or not you said anything to the President about Kathleen Willey.

A Yes, I did.

Q Can you tell us what happened in that conversation?

A Can I jump back a little to how I got the information or do you want me to just stick to what I told him?

Q Sure, why don't you. Okay, jump back to how you got the information and then we'll plug it in.

A Just so everyone understands. I believe it was in February or March of that year when I was friends with Linda, she had frantically come to me telling me that this reporter whom I had never heard of before that day, Michael Isikoff, had shown up in her office to question her about Kathleen Willey, who was this woman that you all know now but who was this woman who had—that Linda had worked with in the White House and that I guess this woman had told Michael Isikoff that the President had sexually harassed her and that Linda would corroborate that fact.

And Linda was—she had said to me that she was nervous and she responded that no—I think she had sort of tried to lead Michael Isikoff away from the fact that it had been sexual harassment but, at the same time, had sort of confirmed to Michael Isikoff that something might have happened there.

I'm sorry, I'm going too long.

Q It's all right.

A Throughout the next couple months I had encouraged Linda to get in touch with someone at the White House to let them know that this was out here. Being a political appointee, I thought that was something that should be done.

Q Who at the White House did you encourage her to contact?

A Well, she said she would feel comfortable either getting in contact with Nancy Hernreich or Bruce Lindsey from her experiences at the White House. And I don't really remember how it came to be Bruce Lindsey but that—I don't remember who encouraged what. She contacted Bruce, or she told me she contacted Bruce Lindsey and that Mr. Lindsey did not return her phone call or answer her page.

Q So jumping forward to July—

A Right.

Q —what were you trying to convey to the President and what did you say to him?

A Just let me add that I think right—at some point before July 4th, soon before July 4th, Michael Isikoff had again contacted Linda and so the story was sort of bubbling again. And I was concerned that the President had no idea this was going on and that this woman was going to be another Paula Jones and he didn't really need that.

So—

Q This is another grand juror who has just walked in.

A Okay.

Q So that you know.

A Thanks. So I wanted to inform the President about what he should sort of be aware of. And at the end of our meeting—it had been a really emotional meeting—I told him that I wanted to talk to him about something serious and that while I didn't want to be the one to talk about this with him, I thought it was important he know.

And I told him that a woman whom I was friendly with at the Pentagon had been approached by Michael Isikoff and sort of informed her that Kathleen Willey was claiming—I know I didn't use the term sexually harassed because I would have felt uncomfortable saying that to the President, so I think I said something or another that indicated what Kathleen Willey was claiming, and that this woman had known Kathleen Willey when she worked at the White House and she—I think I may have indicated that she had—did not corroborate Kathleen Willey's story.

Q Did you identify Ms. Tripp by name?

A No, I did not.

Q Did the President ask who it was you were referring to?

A No, he did not.

Q Continue. I think you were—

A At that point—I don't know if it was at that point in the conversation, then the President informed me that Kathleen Willey had actually called Nancy Hernreich during the week earlier and had said—excuse me, sorry—and had said that this reporter was chasing after her trying to find out her relationship with the President.

And so to me, what that meant was that when—I thought that meant that when Kathleen found out Linda wasn't going to corroborate her story that she was trying to cover her tracks with the White House so that they wouldn't then find out or think that she was trying to encourage Michael Isikoff.

So I thought everything was over with and I later told that to Linda.

Q Why did you want to say anything to the President at all about that? What did you think the President might do—to respond?

A I thought he—I thought maybe, you know, my understanding from Linda was that Kathleen had been trying to get a job, and I could certainly understand the frustrations of being told someone is going to help you get a job and then you don't. And I thought at that point—I didn't know too many details about what was going on. I don't think she was in the Paula Jones case and I thought, well, gee, maybe if you know someone who needs—who would want to hire her you can make this go away for—that's how I thought of it. Then I thought maybe there was something he could do to fix it or someone else could do to fix it, or just be aware of it.

Q He might get her a job, for example?

A He might. I mean, I think that was one of the things that crossed my mind.

Q At that time, did the President ask you whether you had disclosed anything about your relationship to anyone else?

A Not at that time.

Q Did he at some other time?

A Yes, he did.

Q When was that?

A I think there might have been several times throughout the relationship, but he specifically asked me about Linda Tripp on July 14th.

Q All right. Then we'll get to that in just a moment.

A Okay.

Q At the beginning of the meeting with the President on July 4th, you had sent him a letter in which you said that you were considering telling your parents. Did he ever say anything to you about, you know, you shouldn't be threatening the President or something like that?

A Yes. Our meeting started out with a fight, so he sat down and we sat down and he lectured me and, you know, "First of all, it's illegal to threaten the President of the United States and, second of all—"I mean, it was just— and then I started crying so—

Q All right, fine. After the meeting on July 4th concluded, did you leave the country?

A Yes.

Q All right. Where did you go?

A I think a few days after that. I went to Madrid.

Q When did you return, as best you can remember?

A On the 14th of July.

Q All right. Then let's turn our attention to the 14th of July. You got back from overseas. Did you get a call from Betty?

A Yes, I did.

Q Tell us about that.

A She called around—I think it might have been around 7:30—I was already in bed because of jet lag and everything—and told me that she thought the President either wanted to talk to me or see me later, and that I believe he was out golfing at the time, and that she'd call me back later to let me know what was going to happen. And she did. She called back maybe around 8:30 or so, 8:30, 9 o'clock, and asked me to come over to the White House. So I did.

Q When you got to the White House, did you see the President?

A Yes, I did.

Q Could you tell us how that meeting went?

A It was an unusual meeting, I mean, first because we—he met me in Betty's office and we went into Nancy Hernreich's office, which is adjacent to Ms. Currie's office, and sat on the sofa and talked. It was very distant and very cold. And he asked me if the—I don't remember the sequence of things necessarily, but at one point he asked me if the woman that I had mentioned on July 4th was Linda Tripp. And I hesitated and then answered yes, and he talked about that there was some issue with— this had to do with Kathleen Willey and that, as he called it, that there was something on the sludge report, that there had been some informa- tion.

    And what his main concern seemed to be was that Kathleen Willey had called Nancy again that week and was upset because Michael Isikoff had told her that he knew she had called the White House saying he was pursuing her and her story. Is that clear?

A JUROR: No.

THE WITNESS: Okay. Kathleen had called Nancy, and the President had told me that Kathleen had called Nancy. This was on July 4th. And then that following week when I was in Madrid, I believe—I know I was in Madrid, I think it was that following week—Kathleen called Nancy again. And Kathleen was upset because Michael Isikoff had told Kathleen that he knew that she had called Nancy the previous week.

    Does that make a little more sense?

A JUROR: Yes, thank you.

THE WITNESS: So what the President's concern was that the only people who knew that Kathleen had called Nancy originally were Nancy, Bruce Lindsey, the President and myself, and Kathleen. So he was concerned and had asked me if I had told Linda the information he had shared with me, and I had said yes, I did because I thought that meant it was over, that Kathleen was trying to backtrack.

So that alarmed me because, obviously, someone had told Michael Isikoff. And he was concerned about Linda, and I reassured him. He asked me if I trusted her, and I said yes. And he—we had talked about—oh, I had—I'm sorry, I'm sorry. On July 4th I had mentioned that—to the President that this woman had tried to contact Bruce Lindsey and that Bruce Lindsey didn't return her phone call.

So on July 14th, the President asked me if I thought Linda would call Bruce Lindsey again, and I told him that she is a really proud woman and that she was really offended that he didn't call her back and it was—so I didn't think she would. And he asked me if I would just try to see if she would call, and so I said I would try.

BY MR. EMMICK:

Q Did he ask you whether you had told anything to Linda about your relationship with the President?

A Yes, he did.

Q All right. Tell us about that.

A He asked me just that, and I said no.

Q Where was this conversation taking place with the President?

A In Nancy Hernreich's office.

Q Did there come a time when he left to take a conference call?

A Yes, he did.

Q All right. Did you know who the conference call was with?

A That's a little murky for me. I believe it might have been with his attorneys, but I don't remember how I know that. So it's possible it was with his attorneys.

BY MR. WISENBERG:

Q How would you know it? I mean, how would you know it?

A I don't know. That's just what sounds—that's what came to my mind when I was recalling the event. And I don't recall how I knew that so I don't know if maybe that's just how I'm recalling it or that I knew it and I don't remember who told me.

Q Was there anybody there to tell you he was talking to his attorneys other than him that day?

A It could have been Betty. I sat with Betty when—in her office when he was on the conference call in the Oval Office or in the back. I don't know where he was, actually.

BY MR. EMMICK:

Q Other than the President asking you to get a hold of Linda and have Linda call Bruce Lindsey, how were things left at the end of the meeting?

A He asked me to let Betty know the following day without getting into details with her, even mentioning names with her, if I had, you know, kind of mission accomplished sort of thing with Linda.

Q And did you?

A Yes, I got in touch with Betty the next day and I told her that I needed to talk to the President having to do with what he had asked me.

151

Q   And did you follow up with that?

A   Yes, he called me that evening.

Q   Okay. And what did the two of you talk about?

A   We discussed the—I guess that I had tried to talk to Linda and that she didn't seem very receptive to trying to get in touch with Bruce Lindsey again, but that I would continue to try. And I think I just gave him some more—I think I gave him maybe the background information about what I knew when Linda worked there and gave him, I think, a fuller version of whatever it was I knew about this situation.

MR. EMMICK: I'm prepared to move on. Is this an appropriate time for another break?

THE FOREPERSON: Most appropriate.

MR. EMMICK: Okay. Good timing.

THE WITNESS: Me, too. Too much water.

MS. IMMERGUT: Ten minutes?

MR. EMMICK: Let's just take ten minutes.

THE FOREPERSON: Ten minutes, please.

(Witness excused. Witness recalled.)

THE WITNESS: So where are we?

MR. EMMICK: In fact, I'll even walk up and show you where we are, but first we have to clarify that there are no unauthorized persons present and we have a quorum.

THE FOREPERSON: That's correct.

And I need to remind you that you're still under oath.

THE WITNESS: Thanks.

MR. EMMICK: Just to make some reference here, we are here at the end of July, but there are some questions. I'm going to circle back to April 7th.

THE WITNESS: Okay.

MR. EMMICK: We're going to ask some more detail on April 7th and we're going to talk a little bit about a call that you had from the President in—I think it is April of '97 about some conversations that—

THE WITNESS: Okay.

MR. EMMICK: A call in that time period.

THE WITNESS: Okay.

MR. EMMICK: There were also some—let's call them sort of a laundry list of follow-up questions.

THE WITNESS: Okay.

MR. EMMICK: So we'll focus there and a little bit on the 14th and a little bit on that phone call.

THE WITNESS: I thought I—I also might just say that if, as happened before, if I'm saying something and I'm not clear, I'm not understanding, just let me know, because I do that a lot.

BY MR. EMMICK:

Q   All right. Let's start off with some questions. First, let's focus on July 14th because the President wanted you to have Linda contact Lindsey. Why wouldn't Lindsey just contact Linda? Was there any discussion of that? Why did it have to go one way rather than the other way?

A   I don't believe there was a discussion about it. I have my own thoughts on it, but there wasn't a discussion about it.

Q   What were your own thoughts on it?

A   That it would just—I—I think I sort of thought that it would probably be more proper—not in a chain of command, necessarily, but—it just seemed more appropriate for Linda to call Bruce Lindsey.

Q   Did it look—do you think it would have looked inappropriate for Lindsey to contact Tripp?

A   I think it would have been awkward because I think—how would—you know, how would Bruce Lindsey have known to call—you know, to call Linda at that point? If—you know, the President thought at that point that—you know, that Linda didn't know anything, so if Linda didn't know anything, then how—wouldn't it be odd for Bruce Lindsey to just call her back out of the blue?

Q   Okay.

A   I mean, that was sort of how I thought of it.

Q   But in either event, there wasn't any actual discussion about the strategy behind who would have to call whom?

A   Not that I remember. No.

By Mr. Wisenberg:

Q   Well, did you say to him anything like, "Hey, she tried to call him before."

A   Right.

Q   "She isn't going to call him this time." I mean, anything like that?

A   Yes. I think I had mentioned that before. I mean, that might have been— you know, I think was sort of—he was saying, "Well, just try to see."

By Mr. Emmick:

Q   Let me approach the question in just a little bit different way. When you talked to Linda and tried to convince Linda to talk to Bruce Lindsey, what did you say to her to try to convince her to talk to her? Do you understand what I mean?

A   Right. Well, I didn't tell Linda that—and this was unusual, I didn't tell Linda that I had seen the President on the 14th of July because I was somewhat wary of her, having learned that someone had told Michael Isikoff, and I knew it wasn't me, so sort of assuming that Linda had talked to Michael Isikoff and not really knowing where she was coming from on this, so I just kept encouraging her to call Bruce Lindsey again, that this was heating up more and you really should call Bruce Lindsey.

Q   All right. Let me go to another question. You made a reference earlier to the fact that you felt that Nel hadn't been treated well or hadn't been treated respectfully. Could you tell us what you meant by that?

A   People in the White House—I mean, Nel is stationed in the pantry, which is right—I mean, which is even a part of the Oval Office area and he's always there and he takes very good care of the President and people just walk right past him, they don't say hi to him, a lot of people don't acknowledge him.

And they just—you know, they kind of come to him when they need something, but aren't—and I just—I don't think people should be treated like that. I mean, I think anybody who—and especially everyone who is working at the White House and who works—I've always categorized people as people who are there to serve the President and people who are there to serve themselves through the President and I think Nel has a lot of loyalty to the President.

Q   Would it be fair to say that it's no so much that they were affirmatively mistreating him, but they were treating him as a non-person almost? Or is that—

153

A I think that's a mistreatment.

Q Yes. That's a mistreatment. Okay. That's a fair characterization.

A In my opinion.

Q We had talked earlier about certain people that you wanted to avoid in order to help keep the relationship secret and you talked about Nancy Hernreich as being one of those people. Can you tell us what other people you wanted to sort of avoid in that same vein?

A Stephen Goodin. Let's see. I guess it's different from when I was at the White House to after. When I was there, Evelyn Lieberman, Harold Ickes, anybody who knew who I was, certainly. And after I left, I think it was mainly anybody who knew me from before. So—

Q All right.

A Does that—does that answer it?

Q If that's the answer, then that's the best we can do.

A Okay.

Q We talked earlier about February 28th and about Steve Goodin going into the Oval Office with Betty and what you learned about that conversation they had.

A Mm-hmm.

Q The question is this: why would Steve Goodin, who is after all just a presidential aide, why would he be in a position to be able to tell the President, "You can't be with Monica Lewinsky alone"?

A I don't know. And that was a question that I—that I posed—I don't think I posed it as a question, but I sort of made a comment, you know, who is— and then—I don't remember if it was to Betty or to Nel, you know, why would—you know, how inappropriate that was.

Q Right.

A And maybe Stephen made the comment to Betty. Maybe just Betty. I— I—I—you know, I wasn't in the room, so I don't know what the course of the conversation was. Maybe Stephen said it to Betty and Betty told the President that Stephen had said that to Betty. So I'm not sure, but I thought it was inappropriate, too.

MR. EMMICK: Any other follow-up on that?

A JUROR: I think a point be is that did he feel that he had the authority do so because someone else was encouraging him to monitor that sort of activity, such as Evelyn Lieberman, for example?

THE WITNESS: That's a good thought. I don't know. I don't have any knowledge of that. I never thought of that.

BY MR. EMMICK:

Q You mentioned that during 1997 especially you frequently complained to the President that although he said he could bring you back (snapping finger) like that, it wasn't happening. How did the President respond when you complained about these things?

A You know, I mean, it was the—"Bob Nash is handling it," "Marsha's going to handle it" and "We just sort of need to be careful." You know, and, "Oh, I'll—" he would always sort of—what's the word I'm looking for? Kind of validate what I was feeling by telling me something that I don't necessarily know is true. "Oh, I'll talk to her," "I'll—you know, I'll see blah, blah, blah," and it was just "I'll do," "I'll do," "I'll do." And didn't, didn't, didn't.

Q All right. You mentioned that in that July 3rd letter that you sent to the President through Betty you made a reference to the fact that you might have to explain things to your parents. What did you mean by that?

A   If I was going to pick up and move from Washington—first of all, I had told my—well, my mom knew, you know, that I was having some sort of a relationship with the President. My dad had no idea. And I had told my dad that was I—you know, I was told I could probably come back to the White House after the election, as Tim Keating had told me. And the President.

So I had sort of told him that course and I would have needed to explain to them why I was going to pick up and move to New York without—what the point would be.

Q   Were you meaning to threaten the President that you were going to tell, for example, your father about the sexual relationship with the President?

A   Yes and no. I don't think I—I know that I never would have done that. I think it was more—the way I felt was, you know, you should remember that I sort of—I've been a good girl up until now.

I mean, I kind of have—that I think I tended to—I know that I thought he tended to forget what I had gone through already and that—and so that this wasn't an issue of, well, you know, "We can do this in a little while, this is maybe changing your job while you're in the White House," you know, if I had wanted to maybe do something different, it was a lot more significant. And I felt that he was giving me the runaround a bit, too.

Q   Is it fair to say that it was in part an implied threat?

A   Yes, but I think—but I think if you want to look at it that way, it was a threat to him as a man and not a threat to him as president. Does that—I mean—

Q   What do you mean?

A   Well, I think when I hear you say, you know, "Was that an implied threat" that that letter being sent to any man who is having an illicit relationship with someone would be a threat, and so it was irrelevant, the fact that he was president.

Q   I see.

A   So just because we had talked earlier about it and then that was what had upset me, when the President said, "It's illegal to threaten the President of the United States."

Q   Right.

A   And I just thought, you know, "I don't deal with you like the President, I deal with you as a person."

MR. EMMICK: All right.

MR. WISENBERG: Can I ask something about that?

MR. EMMICK: Yes.

BY MR. WISENBERG:

Q   But you had said your mother by that time knew there was some of kind of a relationship.

A   Right. He didn't know that, though.

Q   But you hadn't told—he didn't know that.

A   I never told him that. No.

BY MR. EMMICK:

Q   A question about lipstick and tissues.

A   Okay.

Q   You mentioned that a couple of times you used tissues to wipe lipstick off. Do you remember where you threw those tissues away and did it occur to you that somebody might see those tissues later and therefore might think of it as somehow evidencing the relationship?

A No, really the only—the one time that I specifically remember doing that was on January 7th of '96. And—no, I don't think that—I mean, I had light lipstick on so I don't—I think if it had been a darker colored lipstick that maybe I would have been concerned, I might have thought about that, but that didn't cross my mind. I don't think people go through the trash.

Q Right.

A I hope not.

Q Do you recall where you threw the tissue away on that occasion?

A It was in the bathroom. I think there's a wastebasket right next to the sink.

Q All right. A question going back to the '96 period, because you had mentioned that on February 19th of '96 the President told you essentially we should break up, we shouldn't have any more of a sexual relationship, yet five or six weeks later, there was a continuation of the sexual relationship. How does that happen? How does it get broken off and then rekindled?

A Well, there continued to sort of be this flirtation that was—when we'd see each other. And then one night, I don't—I think it was maybe in the end of—the end of February or maybe some time in March when he had—I had seen him in the hall when I was leaving to go from work, and this was the night he was coming back from the Israeli embassy from something, and we didn't make any contact or anything because he was with Evelyn Lieberman. And I went home.

About 45 minutes later, he called me and had told me he had gone back to his office and had called my office because he wanted me to come over and visit with him, but I was home now, you know, and then he had gone back upstairs.

So that had sort of implied to me that he was interested in starting up again and then when I saw him on the 31st of March—when he kissed me, that pretty much—

Q Just, basically, people got back together.

A Yeah. There was never a discussion of, "Okay, now we're going to resume our relationship again." I didn't want to—why bring up the memory of the guilt? So—

Q Okay. Then what I'd like to do next is turn our attention back to April 7th, which is the Easter Sunday, and we're going to ask some more detailed questions about that period. First, when you got to the White House, did you see a Secret Service agent and did the two of you talk?

A Yes.

Q All right. Tell us who it was and what the two of you said to one another.

A It was John Muskett, I believe. And I had brought some papers with me from home and so I believe I said something, "Oh, the President asked me to bring these to him." And John Muskett said, "Oh, I'd better check with Evelyn Lieberman." And I don't remember exactly what the rest of the exchange was, but I talked him out of doing that and then I just went in.

Q Were you nervous when he said, "I've got to talk to Evelyn Lieberman"?

A Oh, yeah. Yes. Also, it alarmed me that she was there. I didn't really expect her to be there on a Sunday evening.

Q You mentioned that a telephone call came in while you were with the

President. Did you later come to believe you knew who that call was from?

A   I made a speculation about who that call was from. I have no knowledge nor had no knowledge about who was on the phone call.

Q   Let's take this a step at a time, then.

A   Okay.

Q   First, what do you remember about the content of the call and then what was the reason that you drew whatever conclusion you did later?

A   The content was political in nature and I drew, you—know, the possibility that it was Dick Morris just based on—that it was campaign stuff. And I think that how it even came up that it could possibly be Dick Morris was in a joking way with Linda on the phone.

So I don't believe that I ever—I don't think I would have ever categorically stated that it was Dick Morris on the phone, because I didn't know that.

Q   All right. About how long after April 7th did you draw the conclusion or develop the suspicion perhaps that it was Dick Morris?

A   I don't remember.

Q   Okay. All right. At some point, did you hear a voice that you believed to be Harold Ickes' voice?

A   Yes.

Q   Okay. Tell us how that happened.

A   The President and I were in—I believe it was the back study or the study and—or we might have been in the hallway, I don't really remember, but I—Harold Ickes has a very distinct voice and so he—I heard him holler "Mr. President," and the President looked at me and I looked at him and he jetted out into the Oval Office and I panicked and didn't know that—I thought that maybe because Harold was so close with the President that they might just wander back there and the President would assume that I knew to leave. So I went out the back way.

Q   When you say you went out the back way—

A   Through the dining room.

Q   Where did you go?

A   I went through the dining room exit, to the left, past the Chief of Staff's office, to the right, down the stairs.

Q   Were you in a hurry?

A   Yes.

Q   All right. At some point afterwards, did you get a call from the President?

A   Yes.

Q   All right. And what happened in that phone call?

A   He asked me why I left, so I told him that I didn't know if he was going to be coming back and so he—he was a little upset with me that I left.

MR. EMMICK: All right. Before we move off that particular call, are there any follow-up questions that you have? Yes?

MR. WISENBERG: Yes. Yes. And I'll try to be delicate. I'm not known for delicacy.

THE WITNESS: I can see that everyone seems to agree with that.

BY MR. WISENBERG:

Q   First of all, Ms. Lewinsky, when you went out the dining room, did you go out through Nel's pantry door or through the main dining room door?

A   I would have gone out the dining room door.

Q   Okay. I want to make sure that I get the sequence right, because this is

157

partly based on stuff we discussed Monday in New York and you correct me if I get anything wrong.

A   Okay.

Q   We'll do it that way. As I understand it, there is a—you're back with the President that day and let me ask first if you recall, the more intimate sexual moments that day, were they in the hallway or the back study?

A   Both.

Q   Okay. Now, as I understand it, you're with the President. It's an intimate moment. A call comes in.

A   Correct.

Q   All right. And the President leaves.

A   Mm-hmm.

Q   You put your top back on. Your top had been off and you put your top back on.

A   Mm-hmm.

Q   And at some point he comes back. Is that correct?

A   Mm-hmm.

Q   Okay. And what I'm trying to do is distinguish between the Ickes event and the call, if there is a distinction in your mind. In other words—

A   Yes.

Q   The call is something different, as far as you know, from the Ickes event.

A   Correct.

Q   Okay. The President comes back and it's at some point later that you hear the voice of Harold Ickes.

A   I'm sorry—

Q   The President comes back from the phone call that he takes—

A   No. The—someone came in to tell the President he had a phone call, so someone came in, hollered something, not Mr. Ickes.

Q   Okay.

A   The President went out, came back in and I think then they sent the phone call in.

Q   All right. He took that in—

A   He took the phone call in the back study.

Q   Okay.

A   Then we were—and I think we had been in the hallway—I know we had been in the hallway prior to that.

Q   Okay.

A   And he came back in and then the phone rang and he took the phone call in the back study.

Q   Okay.

A   Then it was much later in that same day that he heard the "Mr. President" voice.

Q   Of Ickes.

A   Right. And I'm going to—I think that we were in the back study at that point because that's why he jetted so quickly, not wanting Harold, I think, to walk back there. That was—

Q   Okay. Now, the voice you heard saying to the President that he had a call—

A   Mm-hmm.

Q   You never saw the President attached to that voice.

A   No. And it wasn't a voice that was familiar to me.

158

Q Okay. And you never saw Ickes. Is that correct? When you later heard his voice, you didn't see him. You're just familiar with his voice.

A Correct.

Q As far as you know, did Ickes see you when you headed out the back way?

A He couldn't have.

Q Okay. Why do you say that?

A Because he was in the office.

Q Okay. And you said that Ickes was much later. I mean, much later within the whole time you were there with the President that day?

A Right. Correct.

Q Okay. I mean, not like several hours later.

A No. No.

Q Okay.

A Just much later within my visit.

MR. WISENBERG: Okay. Thank you.

BY MR. EMMICK:

Q What I'd like to do is turn our attention to a call that you got from the President some time, I believe, in April, but correct me if I'm wrong, where he asked you something about whether you had told your mother—

A Yes.

Q —about the relationship. Let's first talk about—can you place this in time as best you can?

A It was April. And this came about because—I guess Marsha Scott, I think, had relayed some information to the President about her conversations, I think possibly with Walter Kaye, who is a friend of my family's, and that from that conversation, I think Marsha either directly said to the President or the President wondered from something Marsha said, if I had told my mom—well, it must have been the President assuming from something that Marsha said.

The President asked me if I had told my mom or had my mom told—and where that went was had my mom told Walter Kaye. And I said no.

Q What you're describing, is it all based on what the President said in this phone call?

A I don't understand.

Q Yes. You said that at some point it was based on the fact that Walter had spoken to Marsha Scott and I'm trying to figure out if you're learning that from a different source or if it's all from the President.

A No, I was learning that from the phone call with the President.

Q All right. How long was the phone call?

A You know, I'm thinking just now, I don't know if that was in April. It could have been in May.

MR. EMMICK: Okay.

A JUROR: Of 1997?

THE WITNESS: Yes. Sorry. Okay. I don't know if the month time is important or not.

BY MR. EMMICK:

Q In April or May, you have this discussion.

A Right.

Q The President asks you if you've told your mother about the relationship.

A Right.

Q What do you respond?

A "No. Of course not."

MR. EMMICK: Okay.

MR. WISENBERG: Mike?

MR. EMMICK: Yes?

MR. WISENBERG: Can I butt in?

MR. EMMICK: Yes.

BY MR. WISENBERG:

Q Do you know independently what, if any, conversation there was—that is, whether—did you later learn that Walter had said something to Marsha or that somebody had said something to Walter?

A In a way, that's too broad of a question because I think Walter Kaye kind of comes in and out—if you look at this whole few years, he comes in and out of this in a few ways, so—did I learn independently that Walter had had a discussion with Marsha? No. Is that what you were asking me?

Q Well, that's one. How about with anybody else? I guess did you hear anything that struck you as this is kind of consistent with what the President had told me in that conversation or this fits together now? Walter had a conversation with somebody and could have actually talked to Marsha Scott and then that got relayed to the President.

A I don't think I'm following you 100 percent. I'm sorry.

Q Okay. Well, I'm not always very articulate. I'll just—

A It—

Q Do you recall—let me be more specific. Are you aware of your aunt ever having made a comment to Walter Kaye?

A I'm aware of Walter Kaye having made a comment to my aunt.

Q Okay. And what was that?

A He remarked something to my aunt that he had heard from people that the reason I had left the White House or had been moved from the White House was because I had had this relationship with the President.

Q Do you know what your aunt responded to Walter Kaye?

A My understanding was she got up and walked out. She was having lunch with him.

BY MR. EMMICK:

Q After you had this telephone call with the President where he asked you whether you had told your mom, was the next time that you saw the President May 24th, I think, which you refer to as dump day?

A Yes. Either way, it would have been, whether it was in April or May.

Q Right. Because you didn't see him in April—

A Right.

Q —and you only saw him once in May.

A Right. Correct.

Q All right. And you had—that's fine. All right. What I'd like to turn our attention to next is as we're working down our outline here, we're finished up with the July 3rd, 4th and 4th period. I take it that you remained frustrated with the President's efforts to try to get you back to the White House.

A Mm-hmm. I mean, it always—and I did make this clear to him, that it was always more important to me to have him in my life than to—than to get the job, but the job was something that was important to me.

Q Did there come a time in about October when you gave up, more or less, on your efforts to get back to the White House and you turned your attention more to New York City?

A   Yes.

Q   All right. Tell us how that happened.

A   Linda Tripp called me at work on October 6th and told me that her friend Kate in the NSC had heard from—had heard rumors about me and that I would never work in the White House again and, if I did, I wouldn't have a blue pass and that her advice to me was "get out of town." So that meant to me that I wasn't going to be coming back to the White House and I was very upset by that.

    Also, she, Linda, told me that Kate had said, "You know, they create jobs at the White House, you know, six days a week." And that Stephen Goodin's girlfriend had just gotten a job, so with these examples of how there had been all these other people receiving jobs that I could have done and I didn't get it.

Q   Did you communicate your additional frustration and disappointment to the President?

A   Yes, I did.

Q   Tell us how and when.

A   I believe I sent him a short note telling him that I really needed to talk to him in person having to do with this subject matter and he and I had an argument in a conversation on the 9th of October.

Q   And was that a telephone conversation?

A   Yes, it was.

Q   Did he call you or did you call him?

A   He called me.

Q   About what time, if you can remember?

A   I think it was around 2:30, 3:00 in the morning.

Q   Was it a long phone call?

A   Yes. Yes. 2:00, 2:30 maybe.

Q   Is it fair to characterize the phone call as involving an argument?

A   Yes. And then we made up.

Q   And then you made up.

A   It was half argument, half making up.

Q   Did the name Vernon Jordan come up in the course of that discussion?

A   It's possible.

Q   What do you have in mind about the first time that Vernon Jordan's name would have come up in conversations with the President?

A   It was either in that phone call or on October 11th.

Q   And tell us what was said about Vernon Jordan, whether it was in the phone call or on the 11th.

A   I don't remember. I know that I had discussed with Linda and either I had had the thought or she had suggested that Vernon Jordan would be a good person who is a close friend of the President and who has a lot of contacts in New York, so that that might be someone who might be able to help me secure a position in New York, if I didn't want to go to the U.N.

Q   And what was the President's response?

A   "I think that was a good idea."

Q   At some point, did you send the President something like a list of jobs or interests that you might have in New York?

A   Yes. He asked me to prepare that on the 11th of October.

Q   At some point, did you have an initial meeting with Vernon Jordan?

A   Yes, I did.

Q   Can you tell us when that was, as best you can recall?

A The beginning of November of last year.

Q How was that meeting arranged?

A Through conversations with the President and with Betty.

Q Without getting into a lot of detail about what happened there during the first meeting with Vernon Jordan, what did you think were your job prospects after that? Did it look like things were going to happen?

A Yes.

Q All right. And what happened with respect to the job situation from that meeting with Vernon Jordan until, say, Thanksgiving?

A Nothing, really.

Q Okay. Then let's turn our attention to the month of December. We'll have to relate back a little bit to November in order to complete things, but on December 5th, did you return to Washington from overseas?

A I did. You know—the question you just asked me before about until Thanksgiving, I did have a conversation with him before Thanksgiving, I think it was the day before.

Q Okay.

A So—

Q Then why don't you complete that, then.

A Okay. I had spoken to Betty about—about not being—being able to get in touch with Mr. Jordan because he was in and out of town and then wasn't necessarily returning my call. He's a busy man. And so Betty arranged for me to speak with him again and I spoke with him when I was in Los Angeles before—right before Thanksgiving.

Q Okay. Let's just go back, if we might, to that early November meeting with Mr. Jordan.

A Okay.

Q Did he say anything indicating to you that he had spoken with the President recently about you?

A Yes. I believe he mentioned he'd had a conversation with the President.

Q And what did he say about that or what did he say that indicated he may have spoken with the President?

A I believe he mentioned that in the course of the conversation and as I was leaving, he remarked to me that I came highly recommended.

Q Okay. Let's turn our attention to December 5th, then.

A Okay.

Q Having in mind that you had had a meeting with Vernon Jordan and a discussion and were trying to get a hold of him, when you got back from overseas, sort of what was the status of the Vernon Jordan job effort?

A When I had spoken with Mr. Jordan right before Thanksgiving, he had asked me to call him the next week, either, I think, Thursday or Friday. And because I was out of town, I called him on Friday when I got back, and it was my understanding from his secretary he had gone out of town that day, so we had missed each other.

Q All right. Did you try to arrange a meeting with President Clinton?

A Yes.

Q Tell us what you did to try to arrange meeting with President Clinton.

A I sent a note to Betty much earlier in the week that I asked her to pass along to him which in that letter requested of him that I could come have a visit that Saturday.

Q Did you follow up that note with a call to Ms. Currie?

A Yes.

162

Q When was that call, if you remember?

A December 5th.

Q Okay. And what happened during the call?

A Well, there were several calls, actually. And so at first, it was—the first few, she still hadn't given him the note.

So then finally she gave him the note, just, I think, right after the radio address or right before his radio address, and then she told me that he was meeting with his lawyers all day Saturday, but that she was coming in in the morning to give a tour and she would check and see with him then, you know, if maybe I could come by, but that the prospects didn't look good.

Q Was she focused on Saturday because you had asked whether Saturday would be a good time?

A Mm-hmm. Yes. I'm sorry. Maybe he was going out of town on Sunday. I'm not sure why I would have focused on Saturday versus Sunday.

Q In any event, what she said was he was busy with meetings with lawyers, something like that?

A Yes.

Q All right. Did you go to a Christmas party that night?

A Yes, I did.

Q Did you see the President?

A Yes, I did.

Q Let's turn our attention to December 6th.

A Okay.

Q Are you doing okay?

A Yes.

Q All right. December 6th. Let me ask as a background question, had you previously purchased for the President a Christmas present?

A Yes.

Q All right. What was that Christmas present?

A It was a sterling silver antique standing cigar holder.

Q You had been unable to arrange an actual visit with the President to give him that present in person. What did you do instead?

A I had some other gifts for him as well that I had gotten on my trips and—

Q Tell us what those other gifts were, if you remember.

A A tie. A mug from Starbucks in Santa Monica. A little box that's called hugs and kisses and it's Xs and Os inside, it's really—it's just a cute little chatchki. An antique book from the flea market in New York that was on Theodore Roosevelt. And—I think that's it.

Q Okay. What did you try to do on the 6th in order to give those gifts to the President?

A Well, I had wanted to give them to him, if I was going to have a planned visit with him, and then through the—just some course of events, I got upset and I decided that I was really tired of everything that was going on and I just—it was clear to me that he was ignoring me and I just didn't want to deal with this anymore.

So I decided—I had purchased these presents for him and I'm very—I spend a lot of time and am very particular about the presents I give to people, so I didn't want to give them to someone else and I wanted him to have them, so I packaged them up with a note that I was going to drop off to Betty.

Q And where did you go?

A I went to the southwest gate.

Q What happened at the southwest gate?

A I paged Betty or I think I might have called her. I know I called her and she wasn't at her desk, so I paged her to let her know I was there. And then Marsha Scott drove up, so I ran away to the northwest gate because I didn't want Marsha to see me. Continue from there?

Q Yes. Did you have any trouble getting in at the northwest gate? What happened?

A Well, I wasn't trying to get in. I—so—

Q What were you trying to do?

A I was trying to wait for Betty. So I called Betty from the northwest gate and she wasn't at her desk and then I saw someone go into the—it was under construction at the time, so it was a different little hut than normal, and I saw someone who went in who I thought was John Podesta, so I thought I would—since I knew that Betty had talked to John Podesta about me, I thought I would ask him, you know, maybe I would ask her—I would give the gifts—I would feel comfortable probably giving the gifts to John Podesta to give to Betty, just knowing that he knew I had a relationship with her.

So when I went in to ask this person who I thought was John Podesta— it turned out to be Lanny—I think Lanny Davis, and so then one of the guards said, "Oh, are you here to see Betty Currie?"

And I said, "No. I'm not here to see her, I'm trying to get her. She doesn't know I'm coming."

And then they told me she was giving a tour and that Eleanor—do you want me to go into this detail?

Q Sure.

A Okay. That Eleanor Mondale had come recently and that she was giving a tour to Eleanor Mondale. Then I sort of—wanting to know if the President was in the office, asked the guards, "Oh, well, is the President in the office? Because if he is, she's probably too busy to come out and get these gifts."

And they said, "Yes, he was."

Q What was you reaction to that?

A Not good.

Q Okay.

A Very upset. Hysterical.

Q Where did you go and what did you do?

A I turned around and walked out and I was livid. I had—well—are the grand jurors aware of the rumors about Eleanor Mondale that had been out? I mean, because it doesn't make sense if—

By Ms. Immergut:

Q Well, why don't you say why you were upset.

A ▬▬▬

By Mr. Wisenberg:

Q A question. Pardon me for interrupting. I just wanted to—you said you were upset. Did you show your upsetness to any of the guards?

A No.

Mr. Wisenberg: Thank you.

By Mr. Emmick:

164

Q Did you contact Betty?

A Yes, I did.

Q Where did you contact her from?

A I called her from the pay phone at the Corcoran Gallery.

Q Did you have a fight with her?

A I think so.

Q Okay. You say you think so—

A I'm trying to remember if I—if I actually got her on the phone, which I think I did. I'm pretty sure I did.

Q All right. Did you eventually come to talk to the President on the telephone?

A Through a much more circuitous route, yes, I did.

Q All right. And where were you at that time?

A I was at home.

Q All right. And about what time of day was it?

A Maybe around noon or so.

Q How did the two of you come to be speaking on the phone? Who placed the calls?

A Well, I believe maybe I had called Betty or maybe Betty called me, one of the two, but she put him on the phone.

Q All right. And what happened in the conversation with the President?

A Well, we had a fight. And he was very angry with me.

Q Why was he angry with you?

A Because I had gotten so upset and I had made a stink to Betty and I had— you know—I—what I came to learn, I think, is that as a result of me being upset with Betty and mentioning that I knew Eleanor Mondale was there, Betty called the guards at the northwest gate and so it had just caused a whole big commotion.

And he was just angry at me and he told me it was none of my business what—you know, what he was doing and that—you know, that—that he had never been treated as poorly by anyone else as I treated him and that he spent more time with me than anyone else in the world, aside from his family, friends and staff, which I don't know exactly which category that put me in, but—

Q Okay. Was it a long phone call with the President?

A Maybe half an hour, 45 minutes.

Q Eventually, were arrangements made for you to visit him at the White House?

A Mm-hmm.

Q Are you doing okay?

A Yeah. Yes.

Q Were you surprised that he would let you come to the White House?

A Yeah, I was—yes, I was a little bit surprised.

Q Why?

A Because none of the other times that we had really fought on the phone did it end up resulting in a visit that day.

Q All right. What about the fact that he was supposedly meeting with his lawyers all day? Did he say anything about that?

A He had in the fight. When we were fighting, he said—you know, he was angry because he said, "I have one day to meet with my lawyers and, you know, I've got you messing things up and being upset and blah, blah, blah." So—

Q Did you go and did you meet with the President?
A Yes, I did.
Q Did Betty wave you in?
A Yes.
Q Can you describe for us in general terms how that meeting went? Did you give him the gifts, for example?
A I did. It was—it was a really nice visit.
Q Okay. What do you mean by a "nice visit"?
A It was just sweet. He liked his Christmas presents and we were very affectionate and it just—it was just nice to be with him.
Q Did you discuss the job search?
A I believe so.
Q At the time, how did you think the job search was going?
A Not very well. With respect to Mr. Jordan.
Q Right. And did you communicate that to the President?
A Yes.
Q Can you give us a little more detail? What would you have said to one another?
A I think I said that I—that I was supposed to get in touch with Mr. Jordan the previous week and that things didn't work out and that nothing had really happened yet.
Q Did the President say what he was going to do?
A I think he said he would—you know, this was sort of typical of him, to sort of say, "Oh, I'll talk to him. I'll get on it."
Q Okay. Did he say anything to you about whether he had a Christmas present for you?
A Yes, he did.
Q What did he say?
A He told me that on the phone, actually.
Q All right. What did he say about that?
A Well, I said to him, "Well, how do you have a Christmas present? I haven't read that you've gone Christmas shopping yet." And he said that he had bought it in Vancouver.
Q Okay. Did he say at any time on the 6th anything about a witness list or your being on a witness list?
A No.
Q How were things left when you left him on the 6th?
A That he would bring me—oh, our meeting ended up—or was cut short by the fact that he had to have a meeting with Mr. Bowles, so he told me that he'd give me my Christmas present another time and that he wouldn't jerk me around and abandon me.
   You know, that—because I think I remarked to him, "Well, at the rate we go, I won't get it 'til Christmas of '98." So—
MR. EMMICK: I have no more questions about this date and I look at the time and it looks like it's 12:30.
THE FOREPERSON: Sol, I think, went to check on something.
MR. EMMICK: Oh, all right.
THE FOREPERSON: Did you check on something for lunch?
MR. WISENBERG: I have checked. It is here. It's been here.
MR. EMMICK: Okay. All right. Well, if this would be a good time to take a break for lunch—
THE FOREPERSON: It's fine with me.

MR. EMMICK: Okay. Let's take an hour-long break for lunch.

THE FOREPERSON: Hour-long.

MR. EMMICK: Okay.

THE WITNESS: Okay.

THE FOREPERSON: Okay.

MR. EMMICK: Thank you.

(Whereupon, at 12:34 p.m., a luncheon recess was taken.)

* * * * *

AFTERNOON SESSION

Whereupon,   (1:38 p.m.)

MONICA S. LEWINSKY

was recalled as a witness and, after having been previously duly sworn by the Foreperson of the Grand Jury, was examined and testified further as follows:

EXAMINATION (RESUMED)

THE WITNESS: Time for a nap?

MR. EMMICK: Madam Foreperson, do we have a quorum?

THE FOREPERSON: Yes, we do.

MR. EMMICK: Are there any unauthorized persons present?

THE FOREPERSON: There are none.

Monica, I'd like to remind you that you are still under oath.

THE WITNESS: Okay. Thanks.

BY MR. EMMICK:

Q   Ms. Lewinsky, we just got through speaking about the December 6th meeting that you had with the President. What I'd like to do is turn our attention next to the date of December 11th.

A   Mm-hmm.

Q   Did you have a meeting with Vernon Jordan on that day?

A   Yes, I did.

Q   Would you tell us when that meeting was?

A   Around lunchtime.

Q   And how was that meeting arranged?

A   By his secretary.

Q   What was the purpose of the meeting?

A   For him to—I learned after we had the meeting, for him to give me some contact names and some suggestion of what to do with these contact names.

Q   When you say—

A   For a job.

Q   When you say "contact names," these are names of potential employers?

A   Yes.

Q   What else did the two of you talk about?

A   We talked about my—the fact that my mom's fiance at the time knew Mr. Jordan. We talked about the President.

What else did we talk about? I think that's it.

167

Q All right. Did he at some point make a comment to you about your being a friend of the President?

A Yes, he did.

Q Would you tell us how the conversation transpired from that point?

A I don't remember how we got to this point, but at some point, Mr. Jordan said something to me, "Well, you're a friend of the President of the United States."

And I remarked that I didn't—I didn't really look at him as the President, that I saw him more as a man and reacted to him more as a man and got angry at him like a man and just a regular person.

And Mr. Jordan asked me what I got angry at the President about, so I told him when he doesn't call me enough or see me enough.

We were sort of bantering back and forth about that and then he told me that I shouldn't get angry at the President because he's got a lot of—it sounds so stupid—obviously, he has a lot of other more important things and difficult things to deal with than someone getting upset with him. And he suggested that if I was upset that I should call and take my frustrations out on Mr. Jordan instead of the President.

I mean, I think I should just say that it was all—this was all sort of in a light tone.

Q Is this a meeting during which the subject of your possibly being in love cropped up?

A Oh, yes. So after we had the conversation I was just talking about with Mr. Jordan, he said to me, "Well, you know what your problem is?"

And I said, "What?"

He said, "Don't deny it." And he said, "You're in love, that's what your problem is."

So I think I just—probably blushed or giggled, something like that.

Q How did the meeting end? What were you going to do and what was he going to do?

A I was planning to send the letters that he had suggested I write to the list of people and he suggested that I cc him and keep in touch with him, keep him apprised of what was happening with my job search.

Q And did you send out those letters?

A Yes, I did.

Q And make arrangements for some interviews?

A Yes, I did.

Q What I want to do next, then, is direct your attention to a few days later, several days later, a week later, I guess. Did you come to have a telephone conversation with the President on December 17th?

A Yes.

Q Would you tell us how that telephone call was—how that conversation took place?

A Okay. The phone rang unexpectedly at about maybe 2:00 or 2:30 and—

BY MS. IMMERGUT:

Q In the morning?

A Right. In the morning. And it was the President and he called and said he had two things to tell me and then he had to call me right back. So he called me right back.

BY MR. EMMICK:

Q Did he explain why he had to call and then call back?

A I don't know. He just was very brief with me and then he said, "I'll call you right back." And he hung up and called back about a minute later.

Q Before you get to the actual things that he says next, you mentioned that you unexpectedly go the call. Why were you surprised by the call?

A Normally, the President wouldn't call me when Mrs. Clinton was in town, so—and I usually was aware when she was out of town, so I that I would sort of be expecting or hoping that he would call. And the call came as a surprise to me.

Q He called you back?

A Right.

Q Then what happened?

A And he told me that he had two things to tell me. The first was that Betty's brother had been killed in a car accident and that—so I reacted that and we talked about that being—that this was the same brother who had been beaten up just a few months ago and she had lost her sister and her mom was ill. We talked about Betty for a little bit.

And then he told me had some more bad news, that he had seen the witness list for the Paula Jones case and my name was on it.

Q Did you get an impression from him about when he had found out your name was on the witness list?

A Yes. I mean, the impression I got based on the entire conversation was that he found out recently.

Q When he told you that, what did he say about having seen your name on the witness list?

A He told me it broke his heart.

Q Tell us how the conversation went from there.

A I was—I'm sure, as you can imagine, I was upset and shocked. He told me that it didn't necessarily mean that I would be subpoenaed, but that that was a possibility, and if I were to be subpoenaed, that I should contact Betty and let Betty know that I had received the subpoena.

I believe that I probably asked him; you know, what should I do in the course of that and he suggested, he said, "Well, maybe you can sign an affidavit."

At some point in the conversation, and I don't know if it was before or after the subject of the affidavit came up, he sort of said, "You know, you can always say you were coming to see Betty or that you were bringing me letters." Which I understood was really a reminder of things that we had discussed before.

Q So when you say things you had discussed, sort of ruses that you had developed.

A Right. I mean, this was—this was something that—that was instantly familiar to me.

Q Right.

A And I knew exactly what he meant.

Q Had you talked with him earlier about these false explanations about what you were doing visiting him on several occasions?

A Several occasions throughout the entire relationship. Yes. It was the pattern of the relationship, to sort of conceal it.

Q When he said that you might sign an affidavit, what did you understand it to mean at that time?

A I thought that signing an affidavit could range from anywhere—the point of it would be to deter or to prevent me from being deposed and so that that could range from anywhere between maybe just somehow mentioning, you know, innocuous things or going as far as maybe having to deny any kind of a relationship.

Q   At some point, did you talk with him about possibly settling the Paula Jones case?

A   Yes. I had—I had had a thought and then had a conversation with Linda about this and just a way that he could settle the case and I suggested it to him.

Q   And what was that way? Not in a lot of detail, but—

A   The gist of it is, I thought that first Mrs. Clinton should do something publicly, maybe on a T.V. show or something, and talk about how difficult the case had been for her and on her daughter and that she just wished that he would settle it and it would go away. And then the President should unannounced and unexpectedly go into the briefing room, make a brief statement that he—in an effort to put this behind him, you know, against his attorneys' advice, he was going to pay Ms. Jones whatever it was, however much she wanted, and so that this case would be over with.

Q   Did the two of you talk about how much the settlement amount would be or might be?

A   Yes. I believe at some point I had mentioned that I had recently read the—I think she had lowered her—the amount that she wanted to $500,000 or something lower and he said, "I thought it was a million or two million dollars."
    And I thought that was very strange, that he wouldn't know she had—you know, that her lawyers—or his lawyers had not told him that she had lowered her request for money. Or I don't know how you say that legally, whatever it is that she did.

Q   Right. Demand, probably.

A   The demand was lower.

Q   Right.

A   We also talked in this conversation about he mentioned that—he said he'd try and see if Betty could come in on the weekend to give me my Christmas presents and I told him that was out of the question, to—you know, let Betty be.

Q   Because her brother had just been killed, right?

A   Right.

Q   All right. About how long was the entire phone call? Or I guess technically it would be the second phone call.

A   Maybe a half an hour. Maybe I could just say since you asked me earlier that it was him suggesting that I would contact Betty if I were subpoenaed that led me to believe he didn't think I would be subpoenaed that soon because he knew Betty was going to be out, you know, he assumed obviously that Betty would be out for the week or two weeks with the unexpected loss of her brother.

Q   Right.

A   So that was what led me to believe he had just found out.

Q   After the call was ended, did you call anyone else?

A   Yes. About a half an hour later, I called Linda.

Q   What did the two of you talk about?

A   My conversation with the President.

Q Right. It seems self-evident, but—

A I know. I'm sorry.

Q That's all right. What did you tell Linda?

A Well, if I could just jump back—

Q Yes.

A I mean, I had—Linda had told me some time in—I think the second week of December that she had been subpoenaed in the Paula Jones case and that she intended to rat on me, so up until this point, I had been trying to convince her not to tell, that it's not anybody's business.

So when I—part of my telling her that the President had called; that I, too, may be pulled into this case was just sort of—maybe assure her that if that happened, there would be someone else denying it, it wouldn't be just Linda out there alone saying "I don't know anything about any kind of relationship between the President and Monica."

Q Kind of a unified front or something like that?

A Exactly.

Q All right. How was the conversation left with Linda?

A I think that we'd talk about it the next day.

Q Did you get subpoenaed?

A Yes, I did.

Q When did you get subpoenaed?

A On Friday, the 19th of December.

Q Can you tell us about when you believe you were subpoenaed?

A I believe it was around 3:00, 4:00 in the afternoon. I think closer to 3:00, 3:30.

Q Okay. Where were you served?

A At the Pentagon.

Q Could you tell us how it happened? Did someone call you?

A Yes. I received a call in my office from the gentleman who was to deliver the subpoena to me. He informed me he had a subpoena for me. I made a stink to him, asking him why I was being subpoenaed and I had no idea what was going on.

When he gave me the subpoena, he suggested I call Ms. Jones' attorneys, which I made a comment to him that that's not something I would do.

Q When you actually did get served, what was your real reaction inside?

A I burst into tears. It was—it was very scary. I mean, it just—sort of my worst nightmare, or I had thought until that point, was being subpoenaed in this case. So I was pretty upset.

Q You couldn't call Betty because Betty was—

A Right.

Q —in mourning herself. Who did you call?

A I called Mr. Jordan.

Q From what phone did you call Mr. Jordan?

A From a pay phone.

Q Close to where you were served, the nearest pay phone around?

A No, I think it was the pay phone which is down the hall from my office, which is kind of halfway between where I was served and my office.

Q And why did you use a pay phone?

A Because I was crying and I—I mean, I—my office, the way my office is set up is my desk was in the same room with four or five other people, so I couldn't very well have any kind of a private discussion.

171

Q What did you tell Mr. Jordan?

A Well, I don't remember what I told him. I was crying and he didn't seem to understand me, so he just—he just told me to come to his office around 5:00.

By Ms. Immergut:

Q Did you tell him you'd been subpoenaed?

A I probably did. I just—I mean, I don't—I don't remember, I just remember being on the phone crying and him saying, "I can't understand you. I can't understand you."

Q You got off the phone. What did you do next? Did you finally go to Vernon Jordan's office?

A Yes. I tried to compose myself and I went into the office. I told Mr.—I believe I told Mr. Bacon or some other people in the office that I had an emergency and I needed to leave. I went home, sort of put myself together, and went to Mr. Jordan's office.

Q When you got to Mr. Jordan's office, did you have to wait outside for a bit?

A Yes.

Q In like a reception area?

A I waited in the lobby, like I always did.

Q About how long did you wait in the lobby?

A I don't really remember.

Q At some point, I take it, you did actually meet with Mr. Jordan?

A Yes.

Q How did the conversation with Mr. Jordan progress?

A First, I came in and I explained to him clearly that I had been subpoenaed and that I was upset and shortly after, I think maybe I said I didn't know what I was supposed to do, I didn't have an attorney, I think I was rambling.

Shortly after I had arrived at Mr. Jordan's office, he received a phone call and I stepped out of the office.

Q Did he ask you to step out of the office?

A I think I may have offered. That was sort of par for the course. And I waited for him while he was on the phone outside his office and when I came back in, he placed a call to—I don't know if it was right after I came back in, but at some point, when I came back in, he placed a call to Mr. Frank Carter.

Q Now, when you stepped out, he took one call and then you stepped back in, did he tell you who he'd been on the phone with?

A No.

Q All right. He places a call to Frank Carter. Do you know whether he talked to Frank Carter in person or do you know whether he just left a message or do you recall?

A I don't really recall.

Q When—

A Oh, he said something about—well; I know he referred to Mr. Carter as Mr. Carter, so I don't know if he was talking—I don't really remember if he was talking to Mr. Carter or he was talking to someone else, but it scared me because I thought for Mr. Jordan to be referring to someone else as Mr. Something, that—I sort of thought he must be a big deal.

Q All right. When you went to the meeting with Mr. Jordan, did you bring the subpoena with you?

A Yes, I did.

Q Did you show it to Mr. Jordan?

A I believe so.

Q What most troubled you about the language of the subpoena and what the subpoena had called for you to produce?

A The thing that alarmed me was that it asked for a hat pin.

Q Okay. And why did that alarm you?

A Because I thought that was a very specific gift and in this list of gifts, everything else seemed to be somewhat generic and then it had hat pin, which screamed out at me because that was the first gift that the President had given me and it had some significance.

Q When you showed Mr. Jordan the subpoena, did he make any remark about any of the things that were called for?

A Yes. When I mentioned to him, I think, about the hat pin, he said, "Oh, don't worry about it. This is a vanilla subpoena, this is a standard subpoena," something like that. Generic subpoena, maybe.

Q Did you know what he meant, a vanilla or standard subpoena that asks for hat pins?

A Well, what I understood that to mean was that—that what he was trying to say is there was nothing out of the ordinary about this subpoena.

Q I see. I guess what I'm trying to get at is do you think he was trying to imply that all subpoenas ask for that or that all subpoenas in the Paula Jones case asked for that or all subpoenas—what was he—from your point of view, what was he trying to convey?

A I think what he—I think what he was trying to convey was stop worrying, that this is not something out of the—you know, out of the realm of possibility of what might be in a subpoena.

Q All right. Were you reassured by that?

A A little. I—I sort of felt that he wasn't—I mean, he didn't really understand what I was saying.

Q All right. Did you have any discussion with him about letting the President know that you'd been subpoenaed?

A Yes. I asked Mr. Jordan to inform the President.

Q How did you ask? How often? How vigorously?

A I—I mean, I asked him to—to please make sure that he told the President. He said he was going to see the President that night, so—

Q All right. Did the subject of a possible sexual relationship between you and the President come up in the conversation?

A Yes, it did.

Q Tell us how it came up.

A Mr. Jordan said to me that there—"There are two important questions" or "There are two important—" I think, "Two important questions that are related to the case: Did you have sex with the President, you know, or did he ask?" And I said no to both of those.

Q What did you interpret him to be asking when he asked you those questions?

A Well, I thought he—I guess—can I step back for a minute?

Q Sure. Up until a point that we'll get to, which is December 31st, I sort of—mainly, I think, from my discussions with Linda, I was under the impression that—that Mr. Jordan kind of knew with a wink and a nod that I was having a relationship with the President, that it was never—he and I never discussed it, but I thought it might be possible.

173

I'm, you know, a young woman, sort of coming to see him, the President's mentioned me. But I also was sort of under this influence of Linda saying to me, "Of course he knows. Of course he knows. Of course he knows."

So when he asked me those questions, I thought he was asking me, saying essentially "What are you going to say?" not necessarily asking me directly what—you know, "What are the answers to these questions?" More "What are you going to reply in regard to the case?"

Q Now, was your interpretation of his questions based entirely on your assumption about what he knew? Or was it based in part on how he asked the questions?

A I think it was based more in part on my assumptions of what he knew.

Q Was there anything unusual or suggestive about how he asked the questions?

A No.

Q And how did you answer the questions?

A No and no.

Q Okay. Did you try to make it clear to him at all that there was more to the story than just no and no?

A Not at that point.

Q At that time, did you make arrangements to meet with the attorney who you would get, Mr. Frank Carter?

A Yes. After Mr. Jordan made the arrangements with Mr. Carter, he told me to be at his office at—I think 11:00 or 10:30 on Monday.

Q All right. How did the meeting with Mr. Jordan end? Was there any reference to a hug?

A Oh, yes. I'm sorry.

Q That's okay.

A When I was leaving, I asked him if he would give the President a hug for me. I bugged him again about making sure he told the President. And so he said, "I don't hug men." I said, "Well, okay."

Q All right.

A But—

Q All right. Did you call Linda Tripp afterwards?

A Yes, I did.

Q What was the purpose of your call?

A In a—to let her know that I had been subpoenaed.

Q Tell us how that conversation went.

A It probably would be impossible for anyone who didn't—who has listened to that tape to follow. I was beyond paranoid.

I had no idea how I had gotten onto the witness list and then, of course, been subpoenaed and I was thinking at that point that maybe my phone was tapped or someone had read my e-mails or something. But in thinking that my phone might be tapped, I sort of tried to explain to this to Linda that I had been subpoenaed in a veiled fashion.

Q How did you do that? What do you mean?

A I used different cover stories. I think like it was a movie or it was a book, trying to discuss things. I think I said something—"I received the flowers," trying to intimate that I had received the subpoena. So—

Q Eventually, did you drop the sort of disguised way of talking and just talk about the subpoena, or do you recall?

A I don't believe I did. I don't really remember, though.

Q   How were things left with Linda?

A   She was having a party the next day, so we made plans that—or I suggested that I come early and we could discuss this and that I would help her set up for her dumb party. I'm sorry.

Q   Her dumb party? All right. Well, we'll skip the dumb party for now.

A   I'm sorry.

MR. EMMICK: That's all right.

MR. WISENBERG: I have a quick question.

MR. EMMICK: Okay. A dumb party question?

MR. WISENBERG: Not about the dumb party.

MR. EMMICK: All right.

BY MR. WISENBERG:

Q   When you were doing the flowers bit, the book bit, how was she—you're trying to speak in code to her, how was—she responding?

A   I don't really remember. I just sort of remember her not understanding and me being frustrated. "Hello? Understand. We just talked about this."

A JUROR: Excuse me. May I ask a question?

MR. EMMICK: Sure. Absolutely. Yes.

A JUROR: Did you ever find out how the Paula Jones lawyers knew about the hat pin, et cetera?

THE WITNESS: I—from what I've read in the press, yes.

A JUROR: But just from any other source? Did you ever suspect maybe Linda or—

THE WITNESS: I had—I came to start to suspect her, but not in any way that—that it really has turned out to be. Not to that degree.

A JUROR: Thank you.

BY MR. EMMICK:

Q   Let's turn our attention, then, to December 22nd, which is the day that you met with Frank Carter and I think you had said that you were going to meet with Vernon earlier.

A   Mm-hmm.

Q   Tell us about that. The Vernon part.

A   Okay. With all the details?

Q   Well, first, when were you supposed to meet with Vernon and then did you place another call to him?

A   Right. I—I—I asked—I called on the morning of the 22nd to see if I could come to see Mr. Jordan earlier. And I was—I was a little concerned. I thought maybe he didn't really understand or—fully understand what it was that was happening here with me being subpoenaed and what this really meant. So I came to see Mr. Jordan earlier and I also wanted to find out if he had in fact told the President that I had been subpoenaed.

Q   Right.

A   Which I found out he did. So I—so I told Mr. Jordan that—I said I was concerned that maybe—that someone had listened in on phone calls and Mr. Jordan said, "Well, you know, so what? The President's allowed to call people."

And I said, "Well, we've had phone sex."

And so Mr. Jordan said, "Well, what's phone sex?"

And so I said, "Well, you know what phone sex is."

And he said, "No, I don't. I'm just an old man. I don't know what phone sex is."

And it was kind of this—discussion that way.

Q Did you discuss the hat pin?

A We didn't discuss the hat pin, but I brought—I had put together sort of an assortment of things that I was planning to hand over to Mr. Carter as being in response to the subpoena, sort of things that I would—considered gifts, being the Christmas cards that I had received from the White House, I had a copy of the President's book, "Hope and History," which he had signed to me which had a very innocuous sort of inscription. And I think brought some innocuous pictures with me. So I showed those to Mr. Jordan.

Q What did you say about those items?

A I know that—I think I was a little more specific in my proffer about what—I mean, what I remember saying now was that—you know, that I sort of showed him that this is what I was going to respond to for the subpoena.

Q Well, did you bring everything that could have responded to the subpoena that day?

A No. No.

Q Did you try to convey to Mr. Jordan the fact that it wasn't everything?

A I think I might have.

Q And do you remember how you would have conveyed it? Would it have been very expressly or would it have been more impliedly?

A More impliedly.

BY MS. IMMERGUT:

Q Did you tell Mr. Jordan that the President had indeed given you a hat pin?

A I did, but I had told him that on Friday and that was what prompted the sort of "this is a vanilla response."

MR. EMMICK: Let me show you the written proffer—

THE WITNESS: Okay.

MR. EMMICK: —and see if that helps you recall or if you know whether or not when you wrote it it's accurate.

What we're looking at is the top of page 6—everyone else has a copy.

THE WITNESS: Okay. There's some spelling mistakes.

MR. EMMICK: Why don't I just read out loud. This paragraph starts, "On the day Mr. Jordan drove Ms. Lewinsky to Mr. Carter's office, she showed Mr. Jordan the items she was producing in response to the subpoena. Ms. Lewinsky believes she made it clear this was not everything she had that could respond to the subpoena, but she thought it was enough to satisfy. Mr. Jordan made no comment about whether or not what Ms. Lewinsky brought was right or wrong. Mr. Jordan drove Ms. Lewinsky to Mr. Carter's office, introduced them and left."

BY MR. EMMICK:

Q Now, having read that to you, does that refresh your recollection about what was said to him?

A I think I would have implied it.

Q Yes.

A That this wasn't everything. I—I don't really remember if I specifically said—and from reading this, it doesn't make me think I necessarily specifically said, "This isn't everything, but it's enough to satisfy," but I could have said that.

Q At the time you wrote this, were you trying to be completely truthful and accurate?

A I was trying to be completely—yes, I was completely truthful and accurate. I'm just also while I'm reading this now, it doesn't necessarily indicate to me that—that what I'm saying here is sort of a direct quote of what I said.

Q Do you remember what Mr. Jordan's reaction was? There it's written that he didn't indicate whether he thought it was right or wrong, but more generally, how did he react when you tried to convey to him that this may not be everything?

A There were often times when I was with Mr. Jordan that he would have no reaction at all. He would kind of do this "Mmmph" thing.

Q I'm not sure how the court reporter is going to get that. Is that a grunt?

A And so—I remember feeling in general with Mr. Jordan and this subject matter, just not knowing. Do you understand what I'm trying to say? Is this clear? And not really ever getting much of a reaction from him.

Q Did you take from his lack of reaction that he did understand or was it still ambiguous in your mind?

A I think sometimes I thought he understood and sometimes I thought it was ambiguous.

Q Okay. Did the subject of phone sex come up again in your conversation with Mr. Jordan?

A Aside from what I mentioned before?

Q Yes. Did you explain to him what phone sex was at some point?

A I think it—at—I don't think I said it. He might have said—know, is it—uh—this is embarrassing. Hmm. I think he—it's hard. I think he—uh—might have given some suggestion as to what he thought phone sex was and I agreed. Is that—

Q That's fine.

A —fair?

Q That's fine.

A By this time, had you expected the President to call you?

A Mm-hmm. Yes.

MR. EMMICK: I'm sorry?

A JUROR: Before you go on, can you ask her what does that mean?

MR. EMMICK: What does phone sex—

A JUROR: No, what did he say?

MR. EMMICK: I think the grand juror is asking for more detail.

THE WITNESS: If I remember correctly, I believe that he said—or maybe I said something like—you know, "He's taking care of business on one end and I'm taking care of business on another." Does that—

BY MR. WISENBERG:

Q Do you remember which one of you said it?

A When I'm saying that now, I think I said it, because that sounds more familiar to me.

   Does that answer your question?

A JUROR: (Nods affirmatively.)

BY MR. EMMICK:

Q Did you expect the President to call you?

A Yes, I did.

Q Is that why you were bugging or asking Vernon so much about whether he had told the President?

A I don't know. Maybe.

Q All right.

A I think I just wanted to make sure the President knew.

BY MS. IMMERGUT:

Q That you had been subpoenaed.

A Right. Because I was supposed to call—you know, in the event that I was subpoenaed, I was supposed to have called Betty and—so—

BY MR. EMMICK:

Q I'm going to ask a question that will suggest what assumptions you were making about what Vernon knew or didn't. Why would you feel comfortable talking with Vernon Jordan about phone sex?

A I wasn't comfortable talking to Vernon Jordan about phone sex.

Q Okay.

A I was scared.

MR. EMMICK: Okay.

MR. WISENBERG: Questions?

MR. EMMICK: Yes?

BY MR. WISENBERG:

Q Did you say on the 22nd that you showed to Vernon Jordan the gifts you bringing to Frank Carter?

A Yes.

Q Okay. Was a hat pin among the things you showed to Vernon Jordan?

A No.

Q But you had indicated to him on the 19th that the President had given you a hat pin.

A Yes.

MR. WISENBERG: Thank you.

BY MR. EMMICK:

Q At some point, you went to Frank Carters's.

A Mm-hmm. Yes.

Q Tell us what happened when you got to Frank Carter's.

A We arrived at Mr. Carter's office and Mr. Jordan and I sat down on the sofa. Mr. Carter came out. Mr. Jordan introduced us and left.

Q In your discussions with Mr. Carter, what was the major point that you were trying to make? What was the big thing you were trying to convey to Mr. Carter?

A That there was absolutely no reason why I should have been subpoenaed in this case.

Q Okay. And—

A And that I certainly did not have a relationship with the President.

Q You said that to him.

A I don't think I said those words, but that was what I was trying to convey and certainly when asked those questions, that's what I answered.

Q Did you discuss with him how you could get out of the deposition?

A Yes.

Q Tell us what you talked about. Maybe that would be the easier way to go.

A Okay. I told Mr. Carter I really didn't want to be dragged into this, I didn't—I thought Paula Jones' claim was bunk and I didn't want to be associated with the case. I believe I suggested maybe that I could—maybe I asked him if I could sign an affidavit or is that something to do.

He said that the first step—to hold off on that and that the first step is he would try to talk to the attorneys for Paula Jones and find out what it is, why they're subpoenaing me and where it is that they're going with this and that maybe one option might be is he could arrange for them to interview me, just kind of do a brief interview, versus a deposition.

Q Did you discuss with him the subpoena insofar as it requested items? Did you, for example, go through and talk about what items were called for?

A Yes, we did. Yes. And I said no to everything until we got to the gifts and then I sort of turned over what it was that I had brought with me that I thought responded to the gifts. And that was it.

Q Was there any mention made by either of you of Bob Bennett?

A Yes.

Q Tell us what was said.

A I requested of Mr. Carter that he get in touch with Mr. Bennett and just to be in touch with him and to let him know that I had been subpoenaed in this case and I didn't know why.

Q Why did you request that Mr. Carter contact Mr. Bennett?

A Because I thought in the—how do I explain this? Sort of in the story or role, the story that I was giving to Mr. Carter and being a low level political appointee and, in general, even if I hadn't been a low level political appointee, I thought it was probably appropriate to align myself with the President's side, being that that's whose side I was on and there was no question in my mind.

Q Is another way of saying that you were trying to send a message to the President or to Mr. Bennett?

A Not to the President. He knew. I mean, the President knew, you know? So—

Q So it was more a message to Mr. Bennett?

A I just—to me, that seemed—I mean, I think—you have to look at this from the point of view that I was a political appointee. And so—

Q What does that imply for you?

A For me, that means that the reason you're in this job is you work for this administration and that you're politically aligned with this administration and everything you do is in the best interests of the administration and, ultimately, the President. And that's where your goal and your focus should be.

Q How were things left? What was he going to do and what were you going to next?

A Mr. Carter was going to get in touch with the attorneys for Paula Jones and get in touch with Mr. Bennett. And he was going to send me a retainer letter. And we'd be in touch.

Q Let me then ask you the following. You had earlier indicated that the President said that he had a Christmas present for you.

A Mm-hmm. Yes.

Q Did you ever make contact with Betty Currie in order to make arrangements to pick up the present?

A Yes.

Q Tell us about that.

A I called Betty after Christmas to see how she was doing and find out how her holiday was and to ask her—or to let her know that the President had mentioned to me that he had a Christmas present for me and, you know, to touch base with him to see if he—what he wanted to do, if he wanted to get together.

So she called me back and told me to come to the White House at 8:30 in the morning on Sunday, the 28th of December.

Q Did you?

A Yes, I did.

Q All right. Betty waved you in?

A Yes.

Q At about what time was it, if you can remember?

A 8:30.

Q When you got there, what happened?

A I think the President was already there. He was just coming to the Oval Office and Betty and the President and I were in the Oval Office and this was the first time I got to meet Buddy.

So we played with Buddy in the office and he was running around the carpet. And I had brought a small Christmas present for Buddy. And so the three of us were just talking and goofing off. And then the President and I went into the back study and he gave me my Christmas presents.

Q How long were you in the back study with the President?

A Maybe about 45 minutes to an hour.

Q What was the Christmas present or presents that he got for you?

A Everything was packaged in a big Black Dog—or big canvass bag from the Black Dog store in Martha's Vineyard. And he got me a marble bear's head carving, sort of—you know, a little sculpture, I guess, maybe.

Q Was that the item from Vancouver?

A Yes. Then he got me a big Rockettes blanket from Christmas of '95 or '96, I think. He got me a Black Dog stuffed animal that had a little Black Dog T-shirt on it.

He got me a small little box of chocolates, cherry chocolates, and then he got me some sunglasses that were a joke because I had—I had teased him for a long time about the different sunglasses that he was wearing in public.

And so then I bought him a normal pair of sunglasses, and so we had just sort of had—this was a long running joke with us, so he bought me these really funny looking sunglasses and we both were putting them on and joking around goofing off.

So—I'm trying to think what else. Can I look at the list?

MR. EMMICK: Sure. Feel free.

THE WITNESS: Oh. He got me a pin that had the—most of my Christmas presents were sort of New York themed, so he got me a pin that had the New York skyline on it. I think that's it. Well, it's a lot, so—not just that's it.

BY MR. EMMICK:

Q Now, you had mentioned earlier that you were concerned about the fact that the subpoena covered this hat pin.

A Mm-hmm.

Q Did you discuss that concern with President Clinton?

A Yes. We—we really spent maybe about five—no more than ten minutes talking about the Paula Jones case on this day and—do you want me to talk about the hat pin or that period of time?

Q The whole period of time, I suppose.

A I brought up the subject of the case because I was concerned about how I had been brought into the case and been put on the witness list. So I asked him how he thought I got put on the witness list and he told me he thought that maybe it was that woman from the summer with Kathleen Willey, which I knew to be Linda Tripp, or maybe—he said maybe some of the uniformed—maybe the uniformed officers.

We talked about that. I mentioned that I had been concerned about the hat pin being on the subpoena and he said that that had sort of concerned him also and asked me if I had told anyone that he had given me this hat pin and I said no.

Q That was false.

A Correct. Yes. When in fact I had told people about the hat pin.

Q Right.

A Let's see. And then at some point I said to him, "Well, you know, should I—maybe I should put the gifts away outside my house somewhere or give them to someone, maybe Betty." And he sort of said—I think he responded, "I don't know" or "Let me think about that." And left that topic.

Q When you said "the gifts," what did you mean by "the gifts"?

A I meant all the gifts that he had given me.

Q All right. Do you think that you're the one who came up with Betty's name?

A I'm not 100 percent sure, but when I received the call from Betty, I wasn't surprised that it was Betty calling, so that's what leads me to believe that I might have suggested it.

Q Okay. Did you discuss with the President the fact that you were planning to sign an affidavit?

A I might have mentioned it, but I don't think—we really didn't spend very much time on this subject.

Q All right. So you walked in without many gifts, you were going to walk out with a bag of gifts.

A Mm-hmm.

Q Okay. Did it strike you as unusual that when you had a subpoena calling for you to produce gifts the President is giving you a bag of gifts?

A At the time, it didn't strike me as unusual.

Q Okay. And why is that?

A I never thought about it. I mean, I was—I was—I had struggled for a long time before the 28th—or I should just say—I guess a few days before the 28th, that if I was going to see the President, if I should tell him or not that Linda knew. And I decided not to.

   And so I—I thought this might be the last time I saw him before I went to New York and I wanted it to be a really nice visit, so I was—I—having decided not to tell him about Linda, I kind of didn't even want to go too far there in getting mired down in the discussion of the case.

Q All right. When you left the White House, did anything unusual happen with respect to your E-pass?

A Yes. Well, I had a visitor's pass.

Q Visitor's E-pass, I guess.

A Is that what—

Q A visitor's pass?

A Visitor's—I don't know. I know it is a visitor's pass. Betty escorted me out and I realized that I left the pass in the office, so Betty told me that she would call down to the guard station and let them know that I was fine and I had just left the pass somewhere.

Q Do you remember what gate you used when you left the White House?

A I believe it was the southwest gate.

Q Did you hear from Betty later that day?

A Yes, I did.

Q Were you surprised to hear from her?

A No. I mean, I wasn't surprised that I was hearing from Betty. I think I was

181

a little surprised to sort of get the nature of this phone call when the President could have just said right then and there, "Well, yeah, I think, you know, why don't you give them to Betty, that's a good idea." But I wasn't terribly surprised. No.

Q   What did she say?

A   She said, "I understand you have something to give me." Or, "The President said you have something to give me." Along those lines.

Q   How long after you had left the White House did Betty call you?

A   Several hours.

Q   When she said something along the lines of "I understand you have something for me," or "The President says you have something for me," what did you understand her to mean?

A   The gifts.

Q   Okay.

A   Kind of—what I was reminded of then a little bit was jumping all the way back to the July 14th incident where I was supposed to call Betty the next day but not really get into details with her, that this was maybe along those same lines.

Q   That actually anticipates my next question.

A   Oh.

Q   Did you feel any need to explain to her what was going to happen?

A   No.

Q   What arrangements did you make for transfer of the something?

A   I think we discussed some things and Betty mentioned she was on the way to the hospital to visit her mom and she'd swing by and, you know, pick up whatever it was I was supposed to give her.

Q   Now, at the time you had that conversation, were you already packing up the gifts at all?

A   No.

Q   When was she going to come by, then? That day?

A   Yes.

Q   What did you do after the phone call ended?

A   I put all the gifts that he had given me on my bed and I got a big box from The Gap and went through each item and decided if I needed to give it to them or not.

Q   Can you explain what you mean by that?

A   It sort of was a difficult—I—I wasn't sure if I was going to get this box back, so I didn't want to give everything in the event that I didn't get the box back for some reason.

    And I kept out some innocuous things and I kept out the—really the most—the most sentimental gift he had given me was the book, the "Leaves of Grass" book, so—and it was just—it's beautiful and it meant a lot to me, so I kept that out.

Q   What other—it sounds to me like you had one category of more sentimental gifts that you kept out of the box.

A   Mm-hmm.

Q   And kept for yourself. What other items were in that category, other than the "Leaves of Grass"?

A   Not necessarily sentimental ones, but just—I think I kept out the marble bear head, the bag, the canvass bag, the blanket, the sunglasses, the chocolates. And I think that's it. Oh, wait. And I might have kept out some of the Martha's Vineyard stuff that I had gotten in the fall.

Q Those were items that you've recently turned over to our office.

A Yes.

Q Which items did you put into the box? If you remember.

A The hat pin, the pin that I had received that day for Christmas, a pin that he had given me for my birthday, a picture that he had signed for me for my birthday that I had framed, a picture he had signed for me of him wearing the first tie I gave him.

Q Any other Black Dog items?

A I think there was a Black Dog hat that I put in there. And I'm not—I'm not really sure what else was in there. Oh, I also put the copies that I had left of the Valentine's Day ad that I had put in the paper for him.

Q The Romeo and Juliet quote?

A Mm-hmm.

Q All right. Did Betty come by?

A Yes, she did. I met her outside.

Q How did you know when she was going to come by? Was there a prearranged time she was going to come by or did she call you from—

A I think she called me on her way out.

Q You met her outside, you had the box with you?

A Mm-hmm. I had taped it up and I wrote "Please do not throw away" on it.

Q Were you concerned that she might throw it away?

A Mm-hmm. Yes. Sorry.

Q Okay. Let me just ask you some questions. Did you ever discuss with her the contents of the box?

A I don't believe so.

Q Did she ever ask about the contents of the box?

A No.

Q Did she ever say anything indicating that she knew from a prior discussion the contents of the box?

A Not—no, not that I remember.

Q Sounds like it was a short conversation.

A We talked about her mom a bit and Christmas. I think maybe I had elaborated on what I got for Christmas from him.

Q Now, you could have just thrown these items out, rather than putting them in a box. Why didn't you just throw them out?

A Because I—they meant a lot to me.

Q Okay. You could have given the items to someone else, a friend of yours, Ashley Raines, or to your mother or just hidden them somewhere. Why didn't you do that?

A I think—I've come to sort of see this now. I don't know that I necessarily saw it then, but I feel now a little bit that me turning over some of these things was a little bit of an assurance to the President or reassurance that, you know, that everything was okay.

Q In your mind, then, were you giving these items not just to Betty, but really to the President as well, in a manner of speaking?

A I think that was even more directly what I thought it was. Not that they were going to be in his possession, but that he would understand whatever it was I gave to Betty and that that might make him feel a little bit better.

Q Did Betty say where she was going to put the box of gifts?

A I think she said she was going to keep them in a closet. Or, you know, she'd keep the box in a closet.

Q Right.

A You asked me—never mind.

Q The gifts. Right. I understood. I understood. All right. What I'd like to do now is ask a few questions—

MR. WISENBERG: Mike?

MR. EMMICK: Yes?

MR. WISENBERG: Before you leave that topic, I have a few on that. Do you mind?

MR. EMMICK: No. Not at all.

BY MR. WISENBERG:

Q You've said here today, Ms. Lewinsky, and I think you told us earlier in some of your sessions with us, that you were—the non-innocuous items were going to go to Frank Carter and—

MR. EMMICK: You mean the innocuous items.

MR. WISENBERG: What did I say?

MR. EMMICK: The not innocuous items.

MR. WISENBERG: Boy. Thank you. I stand corrected.

BY MR. WISENBERG:

Q The innocuous items were going to go to Frank Carter, the non-innocuous items were not, but that one of the reasons, one of the criterion for stuff that didn't even go in the Betty Currie box that you would keep would be sentimental value.

A Mm-hmm.

Q Is that—have I described that accurately?

A Sort of.

Q Okay. How not sort of?

A I didn't really give any gifts to Mr. Carter. Nothing that I turned over to Mr. Carter was a gift from the President. And I think the way you described the dividing of the actual gifts was sort of innocuous, you know, not innocuous—sentimental value, I think that was more accurate.

Q Well, as between the gifts you put in the box and the gifts you kept?

A Mm-hmm.

Q All right. How would you describe today the difference between the two? I just want to make sure I understand, between the ones you kept and the ones you put in the Betty box.

A You know, I don't have a perfect memory of what the criteria was at the time. I know I kept the book out because that was the most sentimental thing to me.

And I believe that the things I put in the box were—also in the box was a dress he gave me from Martha's Vineyard, so the things that went into the box were, I think, more along the lines of some of the things that really complied with the subpoena, that were maybe specifically named, although I think books might have been specifically named in the subpoena, but I kept the "Leaves of Grass."

Q They complied with the subpoena, but they're going to Betty Currie.

A Correct.

Q Now, my question is, and I've asked you this before, but I want to ask you in front of the grand jury, since you were basically trying to keep some sentimental things but you told us that the hat pin was sentimental to you, why is the hat pin going into the Betty box?

A Because the hat pin was the alarm of the subpoena, so—I—I—to me, it seemed logical that putting the hat pin in the box—I mean, it was what had been named in the subpoena.

MR. EMMICK: All right. Should we take a break?

THE FOREPERSON: Yes, we should.

THE WITNESS: Oh, thank goodness.

MR. EMMICK: Okay. All right. Ten minutes.

THE WITNESS: Okay.

THE FOREPERSON: Ten minutes.

(Witness excused. Witness recalled:)

MR. EMMICK: All right. Do we have a quorum?

THE FOREPERSON: Yes, we do.

MR. EMMICK: Any unauthorized persons present?

THE FOREPERSON: None at all.

THE WITNESS: Let me guess. You're going to remind me I'm still under oath.

THE FOREPERSON: There you go.

THE WITNESS: Fast learner.

BY MR. EMMICK:

Q Ms. Lewinsky, this is what we're going to do. We're going to go over some questions that we'd like to ask and then we're going to turn our attention to the December 31st meeting, the breakfast meeting with Vernon Jordan.

A Okay.

Q Let's go to questions first. One question is Betty comes by and gets this box of gifts. Is there any other way Betty would have known to call and pick up this box of gifts except for the President asking her to?

A The only thing I can think of is if he had asked someone else to ask Betty.

Q Do you have any reason to think that happened?

A No, but, I mean, I wasn't there, so I don't know—I don't know what he said, how—maybe he left her a note. I mean, I don't know. So—

Q Another way of asking it is did you tell someone else about this and they might have asked Betty?

A No.

BY MR. WISENBERG:

Q Did you think it as a coincidence that she called you?

A No.

BY MR. EMMICK:

Q Let me ask you a couple of questions about the December 20th dumb party.

A Okay.

Q Okay? First, why is it a dumb party.

A Oh. Really? You want me to answer that?

Q Yes.

A Well, because it was Linda Tripp's party and—well, that should be enough, but just that I got there and I got stuck having to do all this stuff and I had really wanted to talk to her about the predicament we were in and—I now look back on it and just—she had spent all this money on food and a month before she had had no money for the bus and was trying to sell her clothes and somehow she had $500 to spend on food and had money to spend on presents underneath her tree and it was just dumb.

Q Let's focus on the discussions you had with Linda at the dumb party or before the dumb party about the situation.

A   I really didn't sort of get into, I think, a full discussion with her until after—well, until I was leaving and I asked her to walk me out to my car.

Q   Let's talk first then about the efforts you made to talk with her about the subpoena in the house. Did you try to?

A   Probably. It was—I got there maybe—the—I think the party was supposed to start around 7:30 and I got there at 5:00 and she had made no food, had done nothing. I mean, she just had this fridge stuffed with food.

So I was trying to help prepare all this stuff. There was a lot more work to do than I thought there would be and then her daughter had this obsession with vacuuming that night, so there were just a lot of people and I don't really remember trying to get a chance.

I may have tried to or sort of said "I need to talk to you," kind of a thing, but I don't recall having any discussions with her before the party.

Q   Okay. And then you mentioned that you were able to talk to her a little bit outside, I think you said?

A   Mm-hmm.

Q   Tell us about that.

A   The main—the main feeling I had had at that point, once I had received my subpoena was that—that now she didn't need to worry about denying that she knew anything about this relationship, because I was going to deny it under oath as well.

And so sort of just—I figured that conversation would kind of just be mapping out what our next steps would be. But it ended up being much shorter and I—she looked at the subpoena—excuse me—sorry—and I think she—she kept talking about how weird, "Isn't the hat pin strange? Isn't it strange that they're asking about the hat pin?"

And we talked about that. And I think that—I—I was—I was—I don't think that I was left with the feeling that she was going to continue on this path of insisting she would rat on me. So—is that clear? I'm sorry—no? Okay.

When I left that night, I felt a little more—I think I felt a little more reassured that she and I would be saying the same thing in the Paula Jones case. Is that—okay. But I wasn't 100 percent sure and I think that we left it that we'd have some more discussions about this.

Q   Okay. One of the things we wanted to get back to was the whole situation on the 28th where there's a subpoena that calls for you to turn over gifts and the President is giving you gifts.

A   Mm-hmm.

Q   What do you think the President is thinking when he is giving you gifts when there's a subpoena covering the gifts? I mean, does he think in any way, shape or form that you're going to be turning these gifts over?

A   You know, I can't answer what he was thinking, but to me, it was—there was never a question in my mind and I—from everything he said to me, I never questioned him, that we were ever going to do anything but keep this private, so that meant deny it and that meant do—take whatever appropriate steps needed to be taken, you know, for that to happen, meaning that if I had turned over every gift he had given me—first of all, the point of the affidavit and the point of everything was to try to avoid a deposition, so where I'd have to sort of—you know, I wouldn't have to lie as much as I would necessarily in an affidavit, how I saw it.

So by turning over all these gifts, it would at least prompt them to want to question me about what kind of friendship I had with the President and they would want to speculate and they'd leak it and my name would be trashed and he would be in trouble. So—

Q So your impression, then, was in the same way that the two of you were going to deny the relationship, you would also deny or conceal the gifts that were personal that passed between you.

A And the phone call—I mean, I think that it was everything. I think it was kind of—at least for me, I don't know what he did, for me, this had to be thought through. You know, I had to anticipate everything that might happen and make sure—you know—

Q You did what was necessary.

A Exactly.

BY MS. IMMERGUT:

Q Although, Ms. Lewinsky, I think what is sort of—it seems a little odd and, I guess, really the grand jurors wanted your impression of it, was on the same day that you're discussing basically getting the gifts to Betty to conceal them, he's giving you a new set of gifts.

A You know, I have come recently to look at that as sort of a strange situation, I think, in the course of the past few weeks, but at the time, I was—you know, I was in love with him, I was elated to get these presents and—at the same time that I was so scared about the Paula Jones thing, I was happy to be with him and—I—I didn't think about that.

He had—he had hesitated very briefly right before I left that day in kind of packaging—he packaged all my stuff back up and I just sort of—you know, remember him kind of hesitating and thinking to myself—I don't think he said anything that indicated this to me, but I thought to myself, "I wonder if he's thinking he shouldn't give these to me to take out." But he did.

Q And he had already told you he had some gifts for you for Christmas.

A Correct.

BY MR. EMMICK:

Q You mentioned earlier when I asked who was on the list in your mind of people who should be avoided like Nancy Hernreich or Steve Goodin, you mentioned Mr. Ickes.

A Mm-hmm.

Q That name came up. Why was Mr. Ickes on the avoid list?

A He—well, he—he's just strange. And he—I'm sorry. He would—you know, you could be the only person in the hall and you would pass Mr. Ickes in the hall and he would just glare at you. You know.

And I'd say, "Hello," you know, as you would imagine you're supposed to do and he'd just glare at you and walk past you. And I thought that was strange. Call me weird.

Q Okay. And that's the reason that you mentioned him on the list of people to avoid?

A And I think just—his name is sort of in my mind for having to do with things that we're discussing today and what's been in the press of it, but it really was most every senior person in the White House, I mean, except for Betty who knew who I was that would concern me.

Q Right.

A I mean, I had—you know, I had had a lot of interaction with these people during the furlough, so—

Q Let me ask you a question about Tim Keating. Did Tim Keating tell you or imply to you that you could come back after the election?

187

A He told me that I could probably come back after the election.

Q Okay. Do you remember when he said that to you?

A Yes. On—

Q Go ahead.

A I'm sorry. On the day that he informed me of the transfer.

Q So that would have been the 5th of April? Does that sound right? Friday, the 5th of April?

A Correct. It was Good Friday, I remember.

Q Did he say anything about any problem of an appearance of impropriety during that conversation with you? Something like there might be an appearance before but it doesn't matter after the election, anything like that?

A No. No. No.

Q That subject didn't come up at all?

A Not with Mr. Keating.

Q You mentioned that when—oh, I'm sorry. Go ahead. Sure.

A JUROR: I'm sorry. What would have prompted him to make a comment like that, that you could come back after the election?

THE WITNESS: I was crying and I just kept telling him, I—you know, I didn't really want to leave and why did I have to leave and wasn't there—you know, weren't there other openings rather than me having to go to the Pentagon because he had—

Do you want me to get into a little bit about what was said there?

MR. EMMICK: If it will help answer the question, sure.

A JUROR: Yes. Please.

THE WITNESS: Okay. There had been problems with my supervisor, Jocelyn Jolley, and so when I was called in to Tim's office, I had thought he was—he had just spoken with Jocelyn and I thought he was going to tell me they had fired Jocelyn and instead he told me that they were—that for reasons having to do with some of the workload not—things with the letters from the Office of Management and Budget, that they had to blow up—quote-unquote, blow up the correspondence office and they were eliminating my position.

My transfer had nothing to do with my work, I shouldn't see this as a negative thing. He told me I was too sexy to be working in the East Wing and that this job at the Pentagon where I'd be writing press releases was a sexier job.

And I was crying and—

BY MR. EMMICK:

Q What do you think he meant by "too sexy"?

A I think he meant that—he—I think he was trying to—you know, trying to conceal the fact that—you know, that I now know, the real reason I was being transferred. And so I think he was trying to not maybe anger me. And thought that somehow by—maybe he thought I'd think that was a complement.

A JUROR: Did you think he was patronizing you?

THE WITNESS: A little bit. Yeah. That's a good way to put it. I—I just—I just remember thinking that I was—I was never going to see the President again and that all of a sudden that this—you know, the end of this—this relationship.

And I kept—I've always sort of—I'm the kind of person that always thinks that I can fix everything and so it was kind of this—feeling of wait,

188

this train's going too fast and I can't stop it and that it had already passed and—and—so when Tim said that, I think he sort of said that—I don't think he meant to say that. I think that was probably more than he was supposed to say.

A JUROR: Thank you.

BY MR. EMMICK:

Q Going back again to the 17th of December when the President called you and let you know about the witness list, you said he used the phrase, "It broke my heart to see you on the witness list." What was your reaction when he said that?

A I believed him. I think I also—

Q You thought he was being sincere?

A JUROR: Can I ask another follow-up question?

MR. EMMICK: Sure.

A JUROR: Because you had nothing to do with formulating this witness list, why do you think it breaks his heart, that your name was on there? Because you're innocent of having formulated this list. Do you have—or in your opinion, what is it that hurt him?

THE WITNESS: I think it was the idea that—that—this was going to—that this was going to be a bad thing for me. I mean, if you imagine what's happened now hadn't happened and let's just say the Paula Jones thing had gone ahead and I had somehow been dragged into that, just being associate with it and it being difficult and maybe he—maybe it was going to seriously alter any kind of friendship or relationship that we had, you know?

BY MR. EMMICK:

Q I want to ask a question about computer e-mails or files. Did you arrange for the deletion of files or e-mails that might have related to you and the President?

A Did I arrange?

Q Or did you delete them. Sorry.

A Yes, I did.

Q Okay. Did you ask Linda Tripp if she would delete e-mails relating to the President?

A Yes.

Q Did you speak with someone at the Department of Defense in order to learn something about those deletions or to make sure that they would be more longstanding?

A Not about deletions.

Q Okay. Well, what was it that you spoke with him about?

A I asked him—I asked Floyd, I think it is, if—if—sort of how easily someone could break into the computers. And I couldn't imagine how I had come to this witness—come to be on this witness list, so one of the things I thought was maybe someone had broken into my computer and was reading my e-mails. And he told me that that was really difficult.

   And then I asked him about—then with the thought in mind of getting rid of the e-mails, I asked him what the sort of saving procedure was with the e-mails. I know at the White House, they back them up and put them in the archive forever and he told me that at the Pentagon, they sort of stay on the server for four weeks and then they're dumped into e-mail heaven or something.

Q All right. Did you ever ask Catherine Allday Davis to delete e-mails that you had sent relating to the President?

189

A   No.
Q   At any time, did you create anything like a spreadsheet that contained on it information relating to your relationship with the President?
A   Yes.
Q   Okay. Tell us about that.
A   Linda and I had been talking and she had been talking about she's really good at coming up with patterns of things or—I think that was the word she used.
    And so she was wanting to see—you know, I think in an effort to aid her in trying to figure out what the pattern of my relationship with the President was, I made a stupid spreadsheet on Microsoft Excel that just had the—the numbered days of the month and the months and determined on what day was there a phone call or did I see him or see him at an event or something like that. So—
Q   Is that something that you ultimately printed out and showed to her?
A   Yes.
Q   I take it that was on the DOD computer?
Λ   Yes.
Q   Were the entries that you made, would they have revealed that you were talking about Clinton?
A   No.
Q   Okay. Did you ever have an extra copy of that—let's call it a spreadsheet?
A   No.
Q   Did you save the file of the spreadsheet?
A   No. I don't believe so.
Q   All right. Going back also to the night of the 17th, December 17th, just so that we can get clear on the date of that, it was at 2:30 in the morning. Is it literally on the 17th or is it—
A   Nineteen—eighteen—it is literally the morning, 2:30 in the morning of the 17th. So, yes.
Q   Okay. Good. When the President gave you the Vancouver bear on the 28th, did he say anything about what it means?
A   Mm-hmm.
Q   What did he say?
A   I think he—I believe he said that the bear is the—maybe Indian symbol for strength, just—you know, and to be strong like a bear.
Q   And did you interpret that as be strong in your decision to continue to conceal the relationship?
A   No.
MR. EMMICK: All right. Any follow-up on that?
MS. WIRTH: Can I ask one question?
MR. EMMICK: Sure.
BY MS. WIRTH:
Q   Did he say something like "This is when you need to be strong," or "This is for when you need to be strong"? Beyond saying that it was a symbol of strength?
A   I think he—he held it and he said, you know, "You can hold onto this when you need to be strong."
MS. WIRTH: Thank you.
BY MR. EMMICK:
Q   What I'd like to do is ask you about a passage from the proffer and I'm looking at page 5.

A   Okay.

Q   And you'll see at the bottom, and I'll read the passage, this is relating to the meeting on the 19th, just after you've gotten the subpoena, meeting with Vernon Jordan, and what the passage says is "Possibly later in that meeting, but more probably the next meeting," I assume that's a reference to the 22nd?

A   Correct.

Q   "Ms. Lewinsky tried to make it clear to Mr. Jordan that she in fact did have a physically intimate relationship with the President." And then let's go to the next page. It says, "Ms. Lewinsky made it clear she intended to deny the sexual relationship with the President."

So I guess what I want to talk about is the portion of the passage on page 5.

A   Mm-hmm.

Q   Tell us how you tried to make it clear to Mr. Jordan that you had a physically intimate relationship with the President.

A   I think by mentioning the phone sex.

Q   I see. All right. Any other way that you tried to make it clear to him?

A   Not that I remember.

Q   All right. And then is it your recollection now that it was on the 22nd that you were trying to make this clear to Mr. Jordan?

A   Yes.

Q   As opposed to the 19th?

A   Yes.

MR. EMMICK: Any further follow-up on that?

BY MS. IMMERGUT:

Q   Ms. Lewinsky, how did you make it clear to him that you intended to deny the relationship with the President on the 23rd? Excuse me. The 22nd.

A   This is, I think, as I mentioned to you guys before, this is—I don't have a memory of this. I know when I wrote this I was telling the truth, so I'm sure I did do this, but I don't remember.

MR. WISENBERG: Ms. Lewinsky—

Mike, do you mind if I ask some questions?

MR. EMMICK: Go right ahead.

BY MR. WISENBERG:

Q   I think, you can correct me if I'm wrong, you've done it previously today, so I'm sure you will again if I am, you told us when we first met with you in the proffer meeting that you couldn't specifically remember that item. Is that correct?

A   Yes.

Q   And I think you said you couldn't specifically remember any more of the item that Mike just read to you on the bottom of the previous page about the physically intimate relationship.

A   Right.

Q   But that you had no doubt that it's true. Is that correct?

A   I was being truthful in my proffer. Yes.

Q   And the proffer, written proffer, is accurate. Is that correct?

A   Yes.

Q   But—and I think you also said you feel some—I don't know if this is the reason you don't remember it, but you have expressed to us that you feel some guilt about Vernon Jordan. Is that correct?

A Mm-hmm.

Q That's a yes?

A Yes.

Q Okay. Can you tell us why that is?

A He was the only person who did what he said he was going to do for me and—in getting me the job. And when I met with Linda on the 13th, when she was wearing a wire, and even in subsequent or previous conversations and subsequent conversations, I attributed things to Mr. Jordan that weren't true because I knew that it had leverage with Linda and that a lot of those things that I said got him into a lot of trouble and I just—he's a good person and—

Q Is one example of—and then I'll leave this topic, is one example of one of the things you told Linda that isn't true, "I told Vernon Jordan no job, no affidavit"? Something along those lines?

A Yes. Because Linda made me promise her that on the 9th.

Q Okay. Of January?

A Of January.

MR. WISENBERG: Okay.

THE FOREPERSON: Do you need a minute?

THE WITNESS: I'm okay. Thanks.

A JUROR: I'm a little confused. When you said that you said certain things because you know Linda had the mike, right?

THE WITNESS: Oh, I didn't know Linda had the mike. I now know that she was wearing a wire.

A JUROR: Okay. But so why would you say these things about Mr. Jordan that were not true? What was the reason?

THE WITNESS: Because—I had—from some of my conversation with Linda, I started to think that she was a little bit jealous that Mr. Jordan was helping me get a job in New York and that I was leaving the Pentagon and that— she had remarked one time that—that, you know, Mr. Jordan who is the most powerful, you know, man in this city got me my attorney and she— she thinks that she only had—you know, this dinky attorney or something like that.

And I was—I was so desperate for her to—I was—for her to not reveal anything about this relationship that I used anything and anybody that I could think of as leverage with her. I—her, the President, my mom, everybody. I mean, not her, but Mr. Jordan, the President, my mom. Anybody that I thought would have any kind of influence on her, I used.

Does that answer your question?

A JUROR: Well, it doesn't. I guess what I'm trying to figure out, okay, is what was that going to accomplish? Was that going to make her—what?

THE WITNESS: Well, specifically, with the statement about I won't sign the affidavit until I get the job, is that I had a conversation with Linda, which we'll probably get to—

MR. EMMICK: I hope.

THE WITNESS: Oh. On January 9th and in that conversation, she had told me she had changed her mind, she was going to be vague on the truth about Kathleen Willey and then she told me—at that point, I had told her I hadn't signed an affidavit when I had and I told I didn't have a job yet and I knew I was probably going to be getting a job that day.

And she said, "Monica, promise me you won't sign the affidavit until you get the job. Tell Vernon you won't sign the affidavit until you get the job

192

because if you sign the affidavit before you get the job, they're never going to give you the job."

And I didn't want her to think that I had gone ahead and done anything without her and that I was leaving her in the dark. I wanted her to feel that—sort of Linda and myself against everyone else because I felt like I needed to hold her hand through this in order to try to get her to do what I wanted, essentially.

BY MR. EMMICK:

Q   We can get into that in more detail when we talk about the 13th.

A   Okay.

Q   Why don't we do the following. I wanted to ask some—rather than just jumping into the 31st which is a Vernon Jordan meeting, why don't we ask some questions about which of your gifts to the President you have ever seen in the White House itself, either in the dining room or the study or the Oval Office generally.

A   Does that include gifts that I gave him that I've seen him wear?

Q   All right. Well, let's just start with the things that you've seen in the area itself.

A   Okay. Okay. I—can I go through—just go through the list?

Q   Sure.

A   That would probably be easier. On page 6, I've seen the two little books.

Q   Two little books?

A   The "Oy Vey" book, which is jokes and the little golf book.

Q   Do you remember when you saw those books?

A   Yes. On—I think it was November 13th.

Q   Zadilla day?

A   Zadilla day.

Q   All right.

A   I saw a copy of the Washington Post ad that I had given him in a book on his desk.

Q   You gave him a smallish copy of the—

A   I gave him an actual copy that I cut out from one of the papers and I glued it into a little cardboard thing.

Q   And where did you see it on his desk.

A   It was inside a book.

Q   And the book was on the desk in the study?

A   Yes.

MS. WIRTH: Mike, could I ask a question?

BY MS. WIRTH:

Q   Did you see the ad in a particular book?

A   Yes.

Q   Which one?

A   "Vox."

Q   Okay. And was that on the desk in the study?

A   Yes.

Q   And was "Oy Vey" on the desk in the study?

A   Yes.

Q   What about the little golf book?

A   I think it was. I—I—I'm not 100 percent sure it was a golf book, I'm 99.9 percent sure.

Q   And about how many books does the President have on his desk in the study?

A   He has maybe about 15 or 20 little books that are on his desk and he has more books over there and more books on the bookshelf.

MS. WIRTH: Thank you.

BY MR. EMMICK:

Q   How about the opener?

A   Right. The—right. The wooden frog letter opener that I gave him. I'm just trying to go through this way, so—

Q   All right. Go ahead.

A   I saw the—well, I lent him the book "Disease and Misrepresentation."

Q   And did you see it in the Oval Office somewhere?

A   No, I saw it in the back study.

Q   The back study? And that would have been on page 8, I believe?

A   Right. And then the letter opener that I was mentioning a moment ago was on page 9. I saw the antique paperweight.

Q   Okay. Where is it that you saw the opener?

A   It was on top of—I think it's a cigar box on his desk in the back office. I saw the antique—

BY MS. IMMERGUT:

Q   When did you see that, Monica?

A   Zadilla day. I saw the antique paperweight on his—he has a collection of antique political memorabilia in the dining room on top of sort of a chest sort of thing, and I saw that there on—I think on December 6th or December 28th.

BY MR. EMMICK:

Q   Okay. Do you remember which?

A   No. I saw the standing cigar holder, I think, it was on his Oval Office desk. Or it might have been in the back. I think it was on the Oval Office desk. On the 28th of December. And that's it.

Q   All right. Let's turn our attention to the 31st of December. You had indicated earlier that at some point you started to get more and more concerned about Linda Tripp and whether she was going to rat on you, I think was the way you put it. What did you do with respect to Vernon Jordan in that concern?

A   Since Linda had stopped returning my calls around the 24th of December, by the end of December, I realized I'd kind of better come up with some sort of strategy as to how—if Linda Tripp comes out and says all these things where this is coming from and try to prepare the President.

     And since I couldn't find it within myself to bring it up to him directly, I called Mr. Jordan and told him that I needed to talk to him, I had some concerns about something.

Q   When did you call him?

A   I think it was the 30th of December.

Q   Did you speak with him directly?

A   I think I might have spoken with his—with his secretary.

Q   Do you remember her name?

A   Gail. There was another one, too, but I've forgot her name. And I met Mr. Jordan for breakfast on—no, not Sunday but December 31st, the morning of the 31st, at the Park Hyatt Hotel.

     And in the course of the conversation I told him that I had had this friend, Linda Tripp, who was sort of involved in the Paula Jones case with, I think, the Kathleen Willey stuff. I don't know if I went into that much detail, but I did tell him her name.

194

And I said that she was my friend, that I didn't really trust her—I used to trust her, but I didn't trust her any more and I was a little bit concerned because she had spent the night at my home a few times and I thought—I told Mr. Jordan, I said, well, maybe she's heard some—you know—I mean, maybe she saw some notes lying around.

And Mr. Jordan said, "Notes from the President to you?" And I said, "No, notes from me to the President." And he said, "Go home and make sure they're not there."

Q   What did you understand him to mean when he said, "Go home and make sure they're not there"?

A   I thought that meant that—to go home and search around and if there are any copies of notes or anything that I sent or drafts, to throw them away.

Q   Did you have any further discussions with Mr. Jordan about Mr. Clinton and the Clinton's marital status?

A   Yes. After breakfast, in the car, I asked Mr. Jordan if he thought the President would always be married to the First Lady and he said, "Yes, as he should be." And gave me a quote from the Bible. And a few—maybe a minute or so later, he said, "Well, maybe you two will have an affair when he's out of office."

And at that point, I was shocked because I thought Mr. Jordan had known that we had already had this affair and I think I alluded to this earlier today when I saying until the 31st I didn't know, and I said, "Well, we already had an affair. We just—you know, we didn't have sex or did everything but sex," or something like that. And he just kind of went—one of those "Mmmph." You know—

Q   A grunt?

A   And didn't really respond to me. So I took that as my cue to drop the subject. But—so—

MR. EMMICK: All right.

BY MR. WISENBERG:

Q   What did you eat for breakfast at the Hyatt?

A   I had an—I had an egg white omelet.

BY MR. EMMICK:

Q   What did he have?

A   I think he had cereal with yogurt.

BY MR. WISENBERG:

Q   Do you remember who paid?

A   Mr. Jordan. He's a gentleman.

Q   Do you remember how he paid?

A   No.

Q   Has anyone from the Office of Independent Counsel or the FBI shown you any paperwork of any kind with reference to that breakfast?

A   No.

MR. WISENBERG: Thank you.

BY MR. EMMICK:

Q   Let's turn back to the topic of gifts.

A   Okay.

Q   Did you give a gift to the President in early January?

A   Yes, I did. Well, I guess—I gave it to Ms. Currie for the President.

Q   What was the gift?

A   It was an antique book on the various presidents with sketchings. A history book.

Q Where did you buy the book?

A At an antique bookstore in Georgetown.

Q Was there anything along with the book?

A A note.

Q Okay. What kind of a note?

A An embarrassing mushy note.

Q Okay. Did you attach the note to the book in some way?

A I don't really—I might have put it inside the book or I may have put it outside. I wrapped the book.

Q And how did you try to get this book to the President?

A I called Betty over the weekend and asked her if I could drop it off so I didn't have to waste money on a courier.

Q And when you say "the weekend," are you talking about that first weekend in January?

A Yes.

Q Do you remember if it was Saturday, the 3rd, or Sunday, the 4th?

A I believe it was Sunday the 4th.

O You called Betty and what again did you say to Betty?

A I don't—I think I said something—you know, "I have something for him, could I drop it off to you so I don't have to waste money on a courier."

Q Okay. And what did you do?

A So she said that was fine. So I went over to her home and—

Q Had you been to her home before?

A Yes.

Q Had you ever dropped anything off at her home for the President before?

A No.

Q What did you do when you got her home?

A Well, she was sitting on the porch, so we sat on the porch and I gave her the package and we talked for a little while.

Q Did you talk at all about the gift that was for the President?

A We might have. I might have mentioned it. Probably did. I'm not—

Q Was there any discussion about the fact that the President was himself under subpoena and was going to be deposed in a couple of weeks?

A No.

Q Were you concerned about giving him a book, a gift, under those circumstances?

A No.

Q Okay. Did you ever talk to the President and learn whether he got the book and the note?

A Yes, I did.

Q All right. When did you talk with him and learn about that?

A On the 5th of January. I think it was the 5th of January. You know—can I just—

Q Sure. Take a look.

A Yes. It was the 5th of January.

Q And that would have been Monday?

A Correct.

Q Why don't we try to proceed through Monday because Monday started with a meeting with you and Frank Carter and then there was the phone call afterwards, so let's go first to the meeting with Frank Carter.

A Okay.

Q Feel free.

A   I met with Mr. Carter to go over in more detail where we stood at that point with the Paula Jones case and he went over—he went over what was going to happen if an affidavit wasn't going to satisfy the Paula Jones attorneys and I did have to get deposed and what the room looks like, what—you know—everything that happens in a deposition and he threw out a bunch of different questions.

You know, they'll probably ask you who your first grade teacher was and they'll ask you—you know, some things and then some of the questions that concerned me were questions like "How did you get your job at the Pentagon?" And how did—you know, and he said, "They'll ask things like did you find out about the opening on a bulletin board or did someone tell you about it? Who recommended you for the job? How did everything get facilitated for the transfer?"

And that alarmed me because I didn't really know how to necessarily answer that. I didn't express that to Mr. Carter, but—

Q   Well, when you say you didn't know how to answer it, what do you mean, you didn't know how to answer it?

A   Well, I was concerned that if I said in—you know, if possibly that was going to come up in the affidavit which hadn't bee written yet or in a deposition, if I had said—mentioned certain people that had been involved in helping me secure the position over at the Pentagon or forcing me to go there, really, that because these people didn't like me, if they were ever questioned by the Paula Jones attorneys, that they might say something contrary to what I said just because—to get me in trouble because they didn't like me.

So I was concerned that—I wanted to—I wanted to have some sort of feeling of protection, that—you know, that I wouldn't be screwed over by these people.

Q   Were you concerned that they were going to say nasty things about you or were you concerned that they were going to say things that might ultimately lead to the revealing of the relationship in some way?

A   No, I was just concerned that they would purposefully say something different from whatever I said just because they had the opportunity to screw me. I mean—not—never mind.

Q   Okay.

A   To cause trouble for me. How's that?

Q   Did you discuss with Mr. Carter the affidavit that you were considering?

A   Yes.

Q   What did you talk about?

A   I think he—he said he would work on a draft and he'd get a draft of the affidavit to me.

Q   Okay. At the time, did you want anyone else to review that affidavit before you ultimately signed it?

A   At first, I didn't think about it, but then I did. I decided I wanted Mr. Jordan to look at it.

Q   All right. Why did you want Mr. Jordan to look at it?

A   I think I felt that—that he being the President's best friend and having a—a clearer understanding of my relationship with the President than Mr. Carter did, that I just would feel that it sort of had been blessed.

MR. EMMICK: Okay.

BY MS. IMMERGUT:

Q   And would that be blessed by the President as well?

A   Yes, I that's what I—I mean, I—I think I felt that—excuse me. That, you know, if Mr. Jordan thought something was okay, that I'm sure the President would think it was fine.

MS. IMMERGUT: Okay.

BY MR. EMMICK:

Q   Did you discuss the subpoena and the items that might be responsive to the subpoena anymore? I think you had talked about it earlier.

A   You know, there's been a little bit of confusion for me when I gave Mr. Carter those items, so it's possible.

Q   All right. You mentioned that Mr. Carter asked you some hard questions about like how you got your job. Did you want to talk with anybody about that afterwards?

A   Yes. I placed a call to Ms. Currie and asked her to let the President know I needed to speak to him and it was important.

Q   Did you say anything to Ms. Currie about signing something?

A   I think I might have sort of said, just, you know, hoping that she might pass that along, I think.

BY MS. IMMERGUT:

Q   Do you remember saying that you wanted to or needed to speak to the President before you signed something?

A   I think so.

BY MR. EMMICK:

Q   All right. Did you explain to her what you meant when you said that?

A   No.

Q   Okay.

A   I'm pretty sure I did say that to Ms. Currie.

Q   Did you finally get in contact or did you at some time shortly thereafter get in contact with Mr. Clinton?

A   Yes.

Q   How did that happen?

A   Ms. Currie called me back a few hours later and then she put the President on.

Q   Before we talk about what the President and you talked about, as background, I guess, were you upset or in a mood that day from a photograph you had seen?

A   Oh, you really want to embarrass me, don't you?

Q   Well, I just want to get the mood right.

A   I had been peeved by the photo and the footage that was in the media from the President and First Lady being romantic on their holiday vacation. So I felt a little bit like—I—I was just annoyed.

I was jealous and it just seemed sort of something he had never—an aspect of their relationship that he had never really revealed to me and it made me feel bad.

So I was—I don't know if anyone here has ever done this, where you—you're annoyed with someone so you kind of want to pick a fight with them and you want to be a little bit hostile so that—you know, you just rub them the wrong way.

Q   Okay.

A   So that was how I was feeling.

Q   That's how you exhibited the annoyance or anger or whatever.

A   Mm-hmm.

Q   Okay. Tell us about your conversation with the President.

A   Because of those feelings, I was a little bit curt with him and so I told him that I had had this meeting with Mr. Carter and that I was concerned, you know, from the questions he asked me that if, you know, if I at some point had to kind of—under oath, answer these questions and in the course of answering a question I mentioned people at the White House who didn't like me, that somehow I would end up getting—they'd get me in trouble.

And so he—so when I told him the questions about my job at the Pentagon, he said, "Well, you could always say that the people in Legislative Affairs got it for you or helped you get it."

And there was a lot of truth to that. I mean, it was a generality, but that was—I said, "Well, that's a good idea. Okay."

Q   Was there any discussion of the book?
A   Yes. I had asked him if he had gotten the book that I sent with Betty and he said he did, he really liked it, and then—I had written him this—this note that I had sort of—wrote—I think it was Saturday night when I got home from the movies and I had seen the Titanic that weekend and it just was—just brought up a lot of feelings and thoughts for me that I put on—that I put on paper.

And so I sort of said something about, "Oh, well, I shouldn't have written some of those things in the note." Because I was angry about seeing the picture with them romantic, it made me feel really stupid for having sent this letter.

And he said, "Yeah, you shouldn't have written some of those things." Kind of along the ways he had said before, about not writing particular things on paper, you know, putting things to paper. So—

Q   About how long was your telephone call with the President?
A   Maybe 15 minutes.
MR. EMMICK: Anything else on that?
THE WITNESS: I see you trying not to laugh.
MR. EMMICK: What about break-wise? Where are we? Is this a good time for a break or do we want to keep going?
THE FOREPERSON: Yes. Yes.
MR. EMMICK: All right.
THE FOREPERSON: I would say only five minutes.
MR. EMMICK: All right. Five minutes it is.
THE FOREPERSON: A five-minute break. I'm sorry, guys. Okay.
   (Witness excused. Witness recalled.)
MR. EMMICK: Madam Foreperson, do we have a quorum?
THE FOREPERSON: Yes, we do.
MR. EMMICK: Are there any unauthorized persons present?
THE FOREPERSON: There are none.
   Monica, it's my responsibility—
THE WITNESS: I know.
THE FOREPERSON: —to remind you you're still under oath.
THE WITNESS: Okay. Thank you.
BY MR. EMMICK:
Q   We just finished talking about January 5th. Why don't we turn to January 6th. On January 6th, did you pick up a copy of the draft affidavit from Frank Carter?
A   Yes, I did.
Q   You had mentioned earlier that you wanted Vernon Jordan to look at it. Did you contact him?

A   Yes, I did.
Q   Did you speak with him personally or did you speak with someone on his staff?
A   I don't really remember.
Q   And did you try to get a copy of the draft affidavit to Mr. Jordan?
A   Yes. I dropped off a Xerox copy in his office.
Q   In his office?
A   In the lobby of his—of Akin Gump.
Q   Did you make any arrangements to contact him in order to talk about the draft affidavit?
A   I believe—I think I remember Gail saying he was in a meeting and something about 4:00, that he was going to be out and he would call me at 4:00.
Q   Did you talk with him on the 6th about the draft affidavit?
A   Yes, I did.
Q   All right. Tell us what the two of you talked about.
A   I had had some concerns from looking at the draft affidavit and addressed those concerns with him and he agreed.
Q   What were the nature of the concerns, if you remember?
A   I think that the general concern was that Mr. Carter had inserted some information about me having possibly been alone with the President for a few minutes, bringing him a letter in Legislative Affairs.
Q   Would it help you if I showed you a copy of the draft with some of your handwriting on it?
A   Oh. Yes.
MR. EMMICK: I'm placing before the witness what is marked as Grand Jury Exhibit ML-3.

> (Grand Jury Exhibit No. ML-3 was
> marked for identification.)

BY MR. EMMICK:
Q   Can you tell us what this is?
A   Sure. Do the grand jurors have a copy of this?
Q   They do.
A   Okay. This is a draft of my affidavit that Mr. Carter drew up based on his conversations with me.
Q   And the handwriting on it? Whose is that?
A   That's my handwriting.
Q   There's also some underlining and some scratch-outs.
A   Mm-hmm.
Q   Did you do all of that?
A   Yes.
Q   Can you remember looking at that now what the two of you talked about?
A   I think that—I think that it was—I think the two main things were this last sentence in paragraph 6 and the—the concern was, for me at least, was not wanting to give the Paula Jones attorneys any thought about why they might need to want to talk to me. So if I had mentioned that I had been in there alone, it would kind of make them think, oh, well, what happened and did he proposition or blah, blah, blah.
        And then the second thing was in the—towards the end of paragraph 8 on page 2, the idea of with crowds of other people, I think to me was too far from the fake truth?
Q   Okay.

A   Does that—is that clear? Sort of—that that seemed to be too out of the realm of possibility, so—

Q   Too implausible?

A   Exactly. Thank you. So I believe that, you know, that this statement, "There were other people present on all of these occasions," was something that I discussed with Mr. Jordan.

Q   Did he agree with the suggestions or thoughts that you had on those two passages?

A   Yes, I believe so.

Q   Was there any discussion with Mr. Jordan about the portion of paragraph 8 saying that there was no sexual relationship?

A   No.

Q   At any time, did Mr. Jordan say that he didn't want to speak to you about the affidavit?

A   No.

Q   How long was your conversation with Mr. Jordan?

A   I don't remember. Not long. We may have also talked about job stuff, too. But—

Q   All right, then. Let's turn our attention to the next day, which is the 7th. That's the day when you finalized and signed the affidavit. Is that right?

A   Yes.

Q   And you notarized it under penalty of perjury.

A   Yes.

MR. EMMICK: I believe you have—this is the final version and it is Grand Jury Exhibit ML-4.

(Grand Jury Exhibit No. ML-4 was marked for identification.)

BY MR. EMMICK:

Q   I'm placing that before you.

A   Okay.

Q   And it says "Affidavit of Jane Doe No. 6" at the top and it has your signature, right?

A   Mm-hmm.

Q   When you spoke with Frank Carter that morning in order to finalize the affidavit, do you remember what changes were made?

A   When I spoke with him before I arrived at his office or in his office?

Q   Either time.

A   I believe that I sort of dictated to him the changes—I think that's possible or I gave them to him in person, I don't really remember. Mr. Carter had prepared three different versions of the affidavit for the significant portion related to this case, I guess, they were all denying sexual relations, all three of them. And we discussed various things about it and eventually decided on this affidavit.

Q   All right. Let me ask you a straightforward question. Paragraph 8 at the start says, "I have never had a sexual relationship with the President." Is that true?

A   No.

Q   All right. The next logical follow-up is, and maybe it's self-evident, but why were you willing to say something that was false under penalty of perjury?

A   I don't think that it's anybody's business.

Q   Okay. Let me turn the page for you. At the end of paragraph 8, the statement, "The occasions that I saw the President after I left my employment at the White House in April 1996 were official receptions, formal functions or events related to the U.S. Department of Defense, where I was working at the time. There were other people present on those occasions." That's not correct either, is it?

A No, it's misleading.

Q Okay. In what respect?

A For me, at the time, I said—well, it doesn't say the only occasions, but it's misleading in that one reading it would assume that the only occasions on which I saw the President were those listed.

Q Right.

A But I did some justifying in signing the affidavit, so—

Q Justifying—does the word "rationalizing" apply as well?

A Rationalize, yes.

Q All right. All right. On the 7th, after you signed the affidavit, did you keep a copy of the affidavit?

A Yes, I did.

Q Where did you go later on the 7th?

A To New York.

Q Did you take a copy of the affidavit with you?

A Yes.

Q Why?

A If I remember correctly, I was in a rush and I kind of wanted to have it, if I wanted to look it over again or—

Q Why were you going to New York?

A A job interview.

Q Did you have a job interview?

A Yes, I did.

Q Was that the next day?

A Yes.

Q All right. Let's turn our attention to the job interview on the morning of the 8th. Now, was that with McAndrews & Forbes?

A Yes. This is my—I had—I mean, just to remind everyone, I had had some job interviews on the 18th of December up in New York at McAndrews & Forbes and Burson-Marsteller. I also took a test on the 30th, I think, of December at Burson-Marsteller and this is now another interview at McAndrews & Forbes on the 8th.

Q Do you remember who you interviewed with that morning?

A Jamie Dernan.

Q How did the interview go?

A Very poorly.

Q Okay. Tell us why it went poorly. What do you mean?

A I think it started off on the wrong foot because I was in a waiting room downstairs and I had thought they would let me know when he was available and I'd go to his office and instead he just walked in unannounced and the interview started, so I was—I didn't have my wits together at the moment. And I was—I just was sort of flustered from that moment on. I think everyone can relate to having a bad interview. Maybe.

Q How long was the interview?

A Maybe 20 minutes.

Q Was that the only interview that morning?

A Yes.

Q What was your reaction afterwards?

A I was upset. I felt horrible. I might have even cried. I was embarrassed. I thought that I had sort of embarrassed Mr. Jordan, I think, in such a bad interview.

Q After having a bad interview like that, did you expect an offer?

A No, I didn't think so. My first interview with McAndrews & Forbes had been really, really good, so I wasn't sure exactly what was going to happen, but I didn't think it was—

Q Not a good sign.

A Correct.

Q What did you do after you had that bad interview?

A At some point, I called Mr. Jordan to just let him know that it had gone poorly.

Q Do you remember whether you placed one call or several calls to try to get a hold of him?

A I'm sure I placed several. It was—he's difficult to get a hold of.

Q Did you eventually talk to him on the 8th?

A Yes, I did.

Q What did you tell him?

A I told him that it hadn't worked out and that I was asking his advice on whether I should contact Burson-Marsteller or not and that I was concerned that the McAndrews & Forbes hadn't gone well.

Q At the time you were talking to him, were you still upset about the interview?

A I don't really remember. I'm sure I was. It was kind of a depressing thing all day.

Q And did he say what he was going to do because the interview had not gone well?

A Yes.

Q What did he say?

A He said he'd call the chairman. I thought he was kidding.

Q Okay. And did he call you back some time shortly thereafter?

A Yes, he did.

Q About how long after he called—excuse me. About how long after he said he was going to call the chairman did he call you back? If you remember.

A I don't remember. I don't think it was very long after, but—

Q What did he say when he called back?

A That not to worry—you know, I don't remember the exact words that he used. The gist of the conversation was that, you know, the were going to call me and everything was going to be okay.

Q Did he say that he had gotten a hold of the chairman or did he mention that at all or—

A I don't remember.

Q Did Revlon or McAndrews & Forbes personnel get a hold of you later after Mr. Jordan called?

A Yes. They called to set up an interview for me with someone directly at Revlon for the next day.

Q Do you remember about when it was that you were called later on the 8th?

A I think it was some time early evening.

Q Early evening?

A Or evening.

Q Were you surprised by the call?

A From having heard from Mr. Jordan, not 100 percent.

Q All right. They set up an interview for the next day?

A Yes.

Q Did you have an interview the next day?

A Yes.

Q Who did you interview with?

A Ellen Seidman.

Q And what was the tone of that interview?

A It went very well. It was—

Q Better than with Jamie Dernan?

A Yes.

Q All right.

A It was a very good interview.

Q Did you interview with others at Revlon as well?

A Yes.

Q Do you remember about how many interviews there were?

A Two others, aside from Ms. Seidman's.

Q And you mentioned that the interviews went well. After the interviews, did you give a call to Vernon to let him know how things were going?

A I think so.

Q Later that day, did you have another call from Revlon?

A From Revlon?

Q Mm-hmm.

A Yes, I did.

Q Tell us about that.

A They sort of informally offered me a position and I informally accepted it.

Q Do you remember who it was you were speaking with at the time?

A I believe it was Ellen Seidman.

Q Okay. You made a reference earlier in this grand jury appearance to a conversation you had with Linda Tripp on the 9th.

A Yes.

Q We're now on the 9th and I can tell you would like to talk about this conversation. Tell us about your conversation with Linda Tripp on the 9th. Let's start with when it happened.

A Well, I was returning Linda's call from earlier in the week and I think I made a couple of attempts to get a hold of her at her office and when I did get in touch with her, I told her I was on a pay phone because I was concerned about the phones.

And I just—I—I didn't—I was very distrustful of her at this point, especially when I first got on the phone with her. I didn't really know why we were going to be in touch at this point, from what had happened the few weeks before.

So she started out the conversation, I think, asking me, you know, what was going on with my job stuff and everything and I told her I didn't have a job yet and that I hadn't heard from Betty, the President, or Mr. Jordan since December and I didn't know what was going on and so we were discussing that. And that was not true, obviously.

And then she told me that she had gone up to New York over Christmas to be with—I think Norma Asness is her name, and that while she was in New York during the holidays she was shopping with Ms. Asness and this other woman on Madison Avenue buying shoes and that this woman had told Linda she was really savvy and Linda should move to New York and get a PR job in New York. Which I though was a little strange, since I was in the process of moving to New York for a PR job.

That was just one of the indications that made me think she was a little bit jealous of the help I was getting, that I was talking about earlier.

So when we started to discuss the case, she told me that—that because of this experience she had had in New York, she decided that maybe it would be best for her to be really vague on the truth about Kathleen Willey. You know, she really didn't know anything, she didn't really remember much, and that—you know, led me to—and I believe she may have even said directly that she wasn't going to tell about me or that I was—you know, my understanding of that was that she wasn't even going to mention me and that I was safe.

Q Did this come as a surprise to you?

A Yes, it did.

Q In what way?

A Because she had—I mean, she had stopped returning my phone calls, we had left everything in a very bad note a few weeks prior to that. So—

In the course of this conversation, when we talked about my job, she said, "Well, Monica—" Oh. Oh. She asked me what I was going to do in the case and I told her that I was planning on signing an affidavit. Even though I had already signed the affidavit, I didn't want Linda to think that I would have gone ahead and done such a bold thing without her approval.

So she made—that's when, as I mentioned earlier, she made me promise her that I wouldn't sign the affidavit until I got the job. She also went into this whole long story about her friend—

Am I getting into too much detail?

MR. EMMICK: Close.

JURORS: No. No.

MR. EMMICK: Okay.

THE WITNESS: Okay. All right. She told me about her—this friend, I don't remember her name, but she's this—she's an Indian woman who Linda goes to the gym with and that this Indian woman had gone to a psychic and the psychic had essentially said that one of her friends was in imminent danger having to do with the words she would speak.

So that that led Linda to believe, you know, along with this event in New York that she should—you know, she's kind of going to go the good route—well, what I considered the good route in the Paula Jones case. And it was really based on this conversation that I had with her and this sort of change that I agreed to meet with Linda on the 13th of January.

BY MR. EMMICK:

Q Then let's go to the 13th of January. Let me first cover some of the job-related items. On the 13th, did you get a formal offer from Revlon?

A Yes, I did.

Q And did you accept that offer?

A Yes, I did.

Q How was the matter left about references or recommendations?

A Well, she—I can't remember her name, something with a J, I think. The woman in human resources with whom I was dealing about the job offer said, you know, I needed to send her some references, so this had been in—oh. So I called Betty to ask her to remind the President or to check out for me what Mr. Hilley would say to—I'm not saying this clearly. I'm sorry.

Q That's all right.

A One of the people that I needed to get a reference from was John Hilley, who was the head of Legislative Affairs and had been my boss when I was there the latter half of my tenure at the White House. I was concerned that if I put him down as a reference, he might not say flattering things about me.

So I asked—I had mentioned this to the President on October 11th and he said he'd, you know, make sure everything was okay, so I wanted to— so I checked with Betty to ask her to kind of find out what was happening, what the status of that was. So—

Q Did you get a message later from Betty on that subject?

A Yes, I did.

Q Okay. What was that message?

A She had me page her and then later I came to find out from her that afternoon that it had been—I think Mr. Podesta took care of it and that everything would be fine with Mr. Hilley.

Q Now, when the two of you were paging each other on this day, the name Kay was used rather than either Betty or Monica. Where did that name come from?

A This has sort of become a kind of strange area for me. I had not—and I do not specifically remember discussing with Betty the fact that I had been subpoenaed in the Paula Jones case and anything surrounding that, but sort of I now know from—from sort of things that I've been reminded of or shown that I must have. And one of them that indicates that to me is this notion that she—I—she and I had started—I suggested that we use sort of the code name Kay in her paging me and in me paging her. And—

Q And where does the name Kay come from?

A Because Betty and I, our first encounter and our first connection was through Walter Kaye.

Q Now, had you and Betty had earlier conversations about the fact that her message indicator, I guess it would be her beeper or her pager?

A Her pager.

Q Her pager.

A Her text message pager.

Q Her text message pager on some occasion might have indicated Monica?

A Yes. There had been—I think there had been at least one time when Betty's pager had been sitting on her desk when she was in with the President or had stepped away and someone else had picked up her pager when it went off and there was a message from me.

And so from—you know, Betty kind of covered it, I think, by saying—or she did actually have another friend named Monica or something or another, but it was—you know—Rebecca Cameron was the person who picked up the pager and so it was sort of a—not a good thing to happen.

Q Why use any fake names, Kay or any other name? What's the reason you've got to use fake names at this time?

A I was beyond paranoid. I mean, I—and obviously in denial. I think the—I could not understand how I had been dragged into the Paula Jones case and so I was very wary of everything.

Q What did Betty say, if you can remember, when you suggested that you refer to one another as Kay?

206

A   Okay.

Q   Okay. Did she ask why or—

A   I don't remember having this conversation with her.

Q   All right. Were you also using names to refer to others? For example, the name Mary?

A   Yes.

Q   Who did Mary refer to?

A   Linda.

Q   And why were you using the name Mary to refer to Linda?

A   Because that's what she chose.

Q   And why were you using any name other than Linda to refer to Linda?

A   Because Linda and Betty were the two people who paged me that were involved—you know, somehow fell into this circle of the Paula Jones story. Is that—it's not clear. I'm sorry. Okay.

Q   When you were speaking with Linda about the President, did you sometimes refer to the President as "her" rather than "him"?

A   Linda? No. I don't believe so.

BY MS. IMMERGUT:

Q   So that was Betty?

A   Yes.

BY MR. EMMICK:

Q   Okay. And why did you use "her" to refer to the President?

A   I believe that that was only in pages to her and it was just—you know, I knew that the WAVES—from having worked at the White House, I knew that people had access to the WAVES pages, let alone that someone types them, so it just was another measure of caution that I used throughout.

Q   All right.

A   I don't think I ever referred to the President on Betty's pages.

Q   When we were talking earlier about your clarifying whether John Hilley would give you a recommendation, you indicated that you had a page from Betty. Does it refresh your recollection about what the page said if I were to read the following?
    We have a page indicating that it says, "Will know something soon, Kay." Does that remind you about any pages that you got from Betty?

A   Yes, I think I mentioned earlier that she paged me and then I talked to her later that day and found out about John Hilley.

Q   All right. Did you—at some point, did you send to Revlon a letter giving them the two recommendations, one of which was John Hilley?

A   Yes.

Q   Do you remember when that was?

A   I believe I faxed it on the 14th of January.

Q   So that would be the next day.

A   Correct.

BY MR. WISENBERG:

Q   Pardon me. Were they recommendations or references? Just as a technical matter, in other words, were they names or were they actual letters of recommendation?

A   Oh. They were references, then.

BY MR. EMMICK:

Q   All right. Let's go back to the 13th for just a moment because you met with Linda Tripp that day, I think you said, on the 9th you had—

A   I also met with Mr. Jordan.

Q   Okay. All right. Okay. Well, let's go back to Mr. Jordan, then.
A   Well, I—I mean, I was just thinking about the day. I'm sorry.
Q   No, that's fine. That's fine.
A   Just I stopped in to see him for five minutes, to thank him for getting me the job, and I gave him a tie and a pocket square.
MR. EMMICK: Okay.
BY MS. IMMERGUT:
Q   Did you ever provide Mr. Jordan with a signed copy of the affidavit?
A   I did not provide him with a copy. No.
Q   Do you know whether or not he ever received a copy?
A   I believe I showed him a copy. I don't know that he received a copy.
BY MR. EMMICK:
Q   On this same meeting on the 13th?
A   I—I—you know, I have to say I know I brought the copy with me to show him and I may have said, you know, "Do you want to see it?" And I think he may have not even—I think he may have said, you know, "I don't need to see it." Or—I—
BY MS. IMMERGUT:
Q   So you don't specifically recall handing it over to him or even showing it to him specifically.
A   No.
Q   But you brought it for him to—
A   I did bring it.
MS. IMMERGUT: Correct.
BY MR. EMMICK:
Q   All right. So that's the Vernon Jordan part of the 13th.
A   Right.
Q   What about the meeting with Linda Tripp?
A   It was long. I was—I was very nervous. I was wary of her. I actually thought she might have a tape recorder with her and had looked in her bag when she had gone up to the restroom. I told her a whole bunch of lies that day.
Q   What were you trying to accomplish in meeting with her?
A   I was trying to—I was trying to make Linda continue to feel comfortable that she and I were sort of on the—that we were on the same side, we were on the right side.
    We—and that—when I had agreed to meet with her, I thought we were going to go over kind of her strategy for what she was going to do in the case and then once we got together, she kind of started wavering about what she wanted to do and then—so I just was using everything I knew to try to convince her that—that this is the right thing to do.
Q   I think you mentioned earlier that you told her lies.
A   Yes.
Q   What lies do you have in mind?
A   I mean, I think—throughout that month of December, after I knew she was subpoenaed, there were various things that I think I said that were untrue, but I specifically remember from this meeting the thing that I had—what I said to Linda was, "Oh, you know, I told—I told Mr. Jordan that I wasn't going to sign the affidavit until I got the job." Obviously, which wasn't true.
    I told her I didn't yet have a job. That wasn't true. I told her I hadn't signed the affidavit. That wasn't true. I told her that some time over the

208

holidays I had freaked out and my mom took me to Georgetown Hospital and they put me on Paxil. That wasn't true.

I think I told her that—you know, at various times the President and Mr. Jordan had told me I had to lie. That wasn't true. That's just a small example. Probably some more things about my mom. Linda had an obsession with my mom, so she was a good leverage.

Q Let's turn our attention back to the 14th, then. On the 14th, the next day?
A Okay.
Q Right.
A Okay.
Q There's three pieces of paper that have come to be referred to as the talking points.
A Yes.
MR. EMMICK: I think we have them marked as Grand Jury Exhibit ML-5.

(Grand Jury Exhibit No. ML-5 was marked for identification.)

BY MR. EMMICK:
Q I'll place them in front of you.
A Okay.
Q And they are three pages. I wonder if you would tell us how those came to be written and on what computer and the like.
A Okay. First of all, they're out of order.
Q Okay.
A So the last page was actually the first page.
Q All right. Well, let's clarify. What is now the first page says "Points to make in affidavit." And the second page says, "The first few paragraphs" at the top. And the third page says, "You're not sure you've been clear." The third page should be the first page?
A Yes.
Q All right. Let's go to first the mechanics of how these got generated.
A Mm-hmm.
Q Were those printed from your printer?
A Yes.
Q Were they typed on your computer?
A Yes.
Q Was anyone present with you when they were typed?
A No.
Q When were they typed?
A On the 14th.
Q Did you talk with anyone in an effort to get assistance editing or writing or getting approval for what is in the talking points?
A No.
Q How did the—where did you get the ideas that are reflected in the talking points?
A They were based on conversations I've had with Linda from the moment Kathleen Willey and Michael Isikoff ever entered into the picture until the conversations I had with her the morning of the 14th on the phone.
Q Tell me what you mean by that.
A At various times, especially early on, around March or so when—when Kathleen Willey first came up, Linda talked about how—you know, that—that—what Kathleen was saying to Michael Isikoff was not true. And so, you know, we had had—I remember having this discussion with

209

her where we were saying, well, if—you know, if she's lying to Michael Isikoff, how do you know she didn't lie to you?

Linda said, "Yeah, that's a good point. Maybe she did." You know?

And I said, "Yeah, sure. She could have, you know, smeared her own lipstick and untucked her own blouse."

And Linda said, "Yeah, it's true."

That was very early on and throughout my discussions with Linda, especially when she was saying—saying things about how to be vague on the Kathleen Willey issue in the Paula Jones case, we had these sorts of discussions.

Q What did you do with the talking points? How did you relay them to Linda Tripp?

A I took a copy of them to her.

Q And how were the arrangements made to give her that copy?

A She had told me she was going to go see her attorney, Kirby, that afternoon and was going to talk to him about signing an affidavit, which is why this was all generated. And so I offered to drive her there so that we could just talk on the way because we—we had had some time to talk that morning, but not as much as I wanted.

Q Who was driving? You were driving?

A Yes.

Q And Linda has the talking points in her hands?

A I handed them to her in the parking lot of the Pentagon.

Q Did she read them?

A Yes, she did.

Q What was she saying or doing as she was reading them?

A She was going through it and she was sort of reading and going, "Yeah. Mm-hmm. Uh-huh. Well, that's true. Oh, good point."

I think she may have said, "Oh, these are—this is really—that's true." You know. "Did you write this?" Sort of a thing.

Q Okay. What did you think would happen after you dropped the talking points off to Linda and then you dropped Linda off? How were things left, I guess is another way to ask that question.

A I believe that it was in the car ride home that she said—made some comment to me about—that, well, she—she feels okay—and this might have been on the 13th when she said this, she feels okay about, you know, kind of not telling the truth or being vague on the truth when she talks to me, but then when she doesn't talk to me, she—her mind starts to wander to different things, so I just remember feeling—oh, like I had to hold her hand through everything and I constantly had to talk to her. So I may have said, "I'll call you tonight" or something like that.

Q Have you ever talked to Bruce Lindsey?

A No. I may have said hello to him in the hall, but I—but—just in passing.

Q Did you ever talk with the President about the talking points?

A No.

Q Did you ever talk with anyone at Bob Bennett's firm about the talking points?

A No.

Q Did you ever talk with anyone associated with the White House in any way about the talking points?

A No. And that would include Mr. Jordan.

Q Okay. Let's turn our attention, then, to the next day, which is January

15th. Did Betty call you that day about a call she had received from Mike Isikoff?

A Yes.

Q Okay. Tell us about that telephone call.

A I had learned earlier from my attorney that the Paula Jones people had—had—well, I guess my attorney had asked me something about if I had ever received any courier packages from the White House and I hadn't, but I told him I did—I did send things to Betty and he said, oh, well, he had heard—I think through—maybe through Bennett's people—Mr. Bennett's firm, the attorneys, I'm sorry, I don't mean to be so informal, that there was some issue with these courier—with a courier service.

So I called the courier service and was able to find out that the records could be subpoenaed and then I spoke with Betty later that day and she told me that—that Michael Isikoff had called her or had called for her intern and Betty had answered the phone and in the course of that he had asked her about the courier, my sending things to her through a courier.

And that she sort of said she didn't really remember or know what he was talking about and that he'd get back to her. Or she'd get back to him. I'm sorry.

Q And then she called you and related this to you?

A Yes. Yes.

Q What was your reaction to that?

A I was very shocked and very—feeling very strange, that somehow this was closing in more and I—I didn't know how they could have gotten this information about the courier because there was—the first person that I thought of that knew about the courier was Linda and the only other person I thought of was this gentleman in my office who was a Clinton hater, Mark Huffman. So I thought that maybe—I thought, well, maybe he had been the one who had sort of turned me, trying to cause trouble.

Q All right. What did you and Betty talk about doing in response to the Isikoff calls?

A The President was out of town that day and so I think she said she was going to try to get in touch with the President and I believe that Betty and I may have discussed that, you know, they were—the courier packages were always sent to her and that some of the things were for her, you know.

Q Did Vernon Jordan come up?

A Yes. I know later—and I don't know if maybe she mentioned to me earlier in the day that she wanted to try to get in touch with Mr. Jordan, but I do know that—that later in the evening Betty called me and asked me if I could give her a ride to Mr. Jordan's office because Bob, her husband, had the car that day and it was raining. So—

Q So you drove her to Vernon Jordan's.

A Yes.

Q Describe what happened when you drop her off.

A Well, actually, I parked the car and I decided to wait for her downstairs in the restaurant. I think it's The Front Page. And she went up to Mr. Jordan's office and was there maybe 15, 20 minutes. I'm not very good with time.

Q Why didn't she just take a taxi there? It's a three, four dollar taxi ride up there.

A I don't know.

Q   Okay. How long did you wait?

THE WITNESS: You know, I need to use the restroom.

MR. EMMICK: Okay.

THE WITNESS: I'm sorry.

MR. EMMICK: The witness needs a break.

THE FOREPERSON: Yes.

MR. EMMICK: Okay. Thank you.

THE WITNESS: Two minutes.

MR. EMMICK: That's all right.

(Witness excused. Witness recalled.)

MR. WISENBERG: Let the record reflect the witness has reentered the grand jury room.

Madam Foreperson, do we have a quorum?

THE FOREPERSON: Yes.

MR. WISENBERG: Any unauthorized persons present?

THE FOREPERSON: None.

MR. WISENBERG: Anything you want to say?

THE FOREPERSON: Monica Lewinsky, I just wanted to let you know that you are still under oath.

THE WITNESS: Really?

THE FOREPERSON: Mm-hmm. Yes, I mean.

BY MR. WISENBERG:

Q   I have, I hope, just one or two questions about your proffer.

A   Okay.

Q   Your written proffer. Can you grab a hold of that?

A   Sure.

Q   And what are we calling that? That is ML-1.

A   Okay.

> (Grand Jury Exhibit No. ML-1 was
> marked for identification.)

BY MR. WISENBERG:

Q   If you'll take a look at page 4, paragraph 4, that has to do with the President's call to you.

A   Yes?

Q   At two a.m. on the 17th of December telling you, among other things, that you're on the witness list, correct?

A   Correct.

Q   Going to the middle portion, starting with "When asked." "When asked what to do if she was subpoenaed, the President suggested she could sign an affidavit and try to satisfy their inquiry and not be deposed."

A   Mm-hmm.

Q   The next sentence says, "In general, Ms. L. should say she visited the White House to see Ms. Currie and, on occasion, when working at the White House, she brought him letters when no one else was around."

Have I read that correctly? Have I read that sentence correctly?

A   Yes.

Q   Okay. And I think you have earlier described that as a—maybe not in these exact words, but you saw it as a continuation on his part of the pre-established pattern of things he had said in the past. Is that correct?

A   Yes.

Q   All right. And would you agree with me that that is—that if you said that to the Jones people or to anybody else that that is misleading in a sense because it doesn't tell the whole story of what you were doing when you visited the President.

A Yes.

Q Take a look at—then I would like you to take a look at page 10, I think it's page 10, it's paragraph 10, whatever page it is.

A Okay.

Q Mine's cut off. It's the last—I think it's the last page.

A Right.

Q I'll read it. "Ms. L. had a physically intimate relationship with the President. Neither the President nor Mr. Jordan or anyone on their behalf asked or encouraged Ms. L. to lie." I would like you for us to reconcile if you can that statement in your proffer with statements like the ones in paragraph 4 where you talk about specific things the President said or did that were kind of continuations of this pattern.

A Sure. Gosh. I think to me that if—if the President had not said the Betty and letters cover, let's just say, if we refer to that, which I'm talking about in paragraph 4, page 4, I would have known to use that.

So to me, encouraging or asking me to lie would have—you know, if the President had said, "Now, listen. You better not say anything about this relationship, you better not tell them the truth, you better not—"

For me, the best way to explain how I feel what happened was, you know, no one asked or encouraged me to lie, but no one discouraged me either.

Q Okay. So you said what you would have done if the President hadn't said that, but he did say that, what you mentioned in paragraph 4, correct?

A Right.

Q And I guess—and you had a conversation with him about what to do gifts that you both knew were under subpoena, then you get the call from Betty. Those things happened. When we discussed this on Monday in the proffer session, I think you said something to the effect of or that in paragraph 10 you were being pretty literal. Is that accurate? When you say that no one encouraged you—told you or encouraged you to lie?

A Yes and no. I mean, I think I also said that Monday that it wasn't as if the President called me and said, "You know, Monica, you're on the witness list, this is going to be really hard for us, we're going to have to tell the truth and be humiliated in front of the entire world about what we've done," which I would have fought him on probably. That was different.

And by him not calling me and saying that, you know, I knew what that meant. So I—I don't see any—I don't see any disconnect between paragraph 10 and paragraph 4 on the page. Does that answer your question?

By Ms. Immergut:

Q Did you understand all along that he would deny the relationship also?

A Mm-hmm. Yes.

Q And when you say you understood what it meant when he didn't say, "Oh, you know, you must tell the truth," what did you understand that to mean?

A That—that—as we had on every other occasion and every other instance of this relationship, we would deny it.

Mr. Wisenberg: That's all I have on that. And probably not anything else. Maybe.

Ms. Immergut: I had a couple of quick questions.

213

THE WITNESS: Sure.

BY. MS. IMMERGUT:

Q Back for just a moment to January 15th with the visit when you took Betty to Vernon Jordan after she had been called by Michael Isikoff.

A Mm-hmm.

Q Did you ever tell Ms. Currie that you had been called by Michael Isikoff?

A No.

Q Had you ever been called by Michael Isikoff before January 15th?

A No. I'm trying to remember now—I know that I had seen the Newsweek thing light up on my caller ID, but I don't remember if that was around that time or if that was later, once the scandal started.

Q Do you recall any calls from Michael Isikoff that you would have told Betty about, calling about gifts from the President?

A No. Absolutely not.

Q You mentioned, obviously, that you've given the President several gifts. Have you given him any ties?

A Yes.

Q How many ties have you given him, just approximately?

A Six.

Q Have you had any conversations with the President about wearing your ties?

A Almost all of our conversations included something about my ties.

Q Could you just briefly describe what things that you've said to him and he to you about wearing the ties?

A I used to bug him about wearing one of my ties because then I knew I was close to his heart.

Q And did he ever say anything about—after he had one of your ties or to alert you when he had worn any of your ties?

A Yes, there were several occasions.

Q And what kind of thing would he say to you?

A "Did you see I wore your tie the other day?"

Q So was he aware based on things you had told him that you would be looking out for when he would wear ties on various occasions?

A Yes.

MS. IMMERGUT: I'd like to show you now what's marked as Grand Jury Exhibits ML-8, 9 and 10.

(Grand Jury Exhibits No. ML-8, ML-9 and ML-10 were marked for identification.)

MS. IMMERGUT: And, unfortunately, I don't have copies yet for the grand jury because we got them at the last—

MR. WISENBERG: I'll pass them around afterwards.

MS. IMMERGUT: Okay. And I'll spread them out for you here.

THE WITNESS: Okay.

BY MS. IMMERGUT:

Q Directing your attention first to ML-8, it's a photograph of the President, obviously. Do you recognize the tie that he's wearing in that photograph?

A Yes, I do.

Q Had you actually seen that on television on June 24, 1998?

A Yes, I did.

Q Do you recall what that's in relation to or what event is being depicted on that photograph?

A   He was leaving for China.

Q   And now directing your attention to Exhibit 9, do you know what that's a photograph of?

A   I don't know where it's from, but it's the President wearing my tie.

Q   And this one states it's Monday, July 6, 1998. Do you remember watching any of the media on that date?

A   Yes, I do.

Q   And do you remember seeing him wearing your tie on that date?

A   Yes, I do.

Q   Do you remember what event was taking place on that date that he was wearing your tie?

A   I don't, but I just saw it says "Medicare costs," so—

Q   Okay. And then finally, ML-10. Do you recognize what that's a photograph of?

A   Yes.

Q   And what is that?

A   The President wearing the same tie.

Q   And do you know what date that is?

A   Date? It was a few days after, he wore the tie when he came back from China, so it's July 9th.

Q   Okay. And what—I guess—did you reach any conclusions from the fact that he was wearing your tie on those days?

A   I—I—I think—the first time he wore the tie, I thought maybe it was a coincidence, but I didn't really think so. And then when he wore it when he came back from China on the 6th, I thought maybe it was a reminder of July 4th, because that had been the first workday after July 4th and we had had a really intense, emotional meeting July 4th of '97. And then when he wore it a few days later, I thought he's trying to say something. I mean, the President doesn't wear the same tie twice in one week, so—I didn't know what it meant, but it was some sort of a reminder to me.

MS. IMMERGUT: Okay. Nothing further on that.

BY MR. WISENBERG:

Q   This is well after the scandal broke, is that correct?

A   Yes.

BY MS. IMMERGUT:

Q   This is this summer, right?

A   Correct.

BY MR. WISENBERG:

Q   You've told us something about seeing a picture of Nelvis, Bayani Nelvis, I think coming to the grand jury.

A   Yes.

Q   Can you tell us—and you noticed something about some neckwear he was wearing?

A   I think it was on Nel's maybe third appearance or his last appearance. He was wearing the first tie that I ever gave to the President.

Q   Did you know that the President had ever given that tie to Mr. Nelvis?

A   No.

Q   And what is—can you recall the last time the President had ever worn that tie?

A   No. I didn't see him every day, so—I mean, I know he—I know some of the times he wore that tie, but I don't know the last time he wore the tie.

Q   Okay. Is there any question in your mind that the President knew that

215

both these ties, the one that we're putting around pictures of and the one that Nel wore to the grand jury, were ties you had given him?

A Not in my mind, but I can't—I can't answer that.

MR. WISENBERG: Okay.

MR. EMMICK: There's a question? Yes?

A JUROR: Did you know the President after a while gave his ties to the people who worked for him? Did you know that?

THE WITNESS: Yes, I did know that.

MR. WISENBERG: Pardon me just a minute.

(Pause.)

MR. WISENBERG: I'm going to ask the witness to be excused very briefly and we'll possibly call you back in a couple of minutes.

(The witness was excused.)

(Whereupon, at 4:45 p.m., the taking of testimony in the presence of a full quorum of the Grand Jury was concluded.)

Monica Lewinsky's
Tenth Interview

1

OFFICE OF THE INDEPENDENT COUNSEL

08/11/98

MONICA S. LEWINSKY was interviewed pursuant to an immunity agreement between the Office of the Independent Counsel (OIC), LEWINSKY, and her attorneys. Present for the interview were Associate Independent Counsel (AIC) MICHAEL EMMICK, AIC KARIN IMMERGUT, and AIC MARY ANNE WIRTH. Representing LEWINSKY was Attorney PRESTON BURTON and Law Clerk ANIE WULKAN of the law offices of PLATO CACHERIS. The interview was conducted in Suite 490 North, 1001 Pennsylvania Avenue NW, Washington, D.C. commencing at 10:37 a.m. LEWINSKY provided the following information:

LEWINSKY never gave TRIPP permission to take notes about her relationship with the President.

The incident where the President mouthed, "I miss you," occurred at the end of May, 1996, at an event where there was a rope line. This did not occur in an October video as alleged by LUCIANNE GOLDBERG.

LEWINSKY read a transcript of an audio tape recording of a conversation between herself and LINDA TRIPP. The transcript concerned the discussion of two different versions of a cassette tape that LEWINSKY prepared for the President on November 20, 1997. The two versions are very similar, but may have been edited again after the discussion with TRIPP. The purpose of the tape was to try a new approach with the President, since he was not responding to LEWINSKY's notes about a transfer back to the White House. The tape was sent to the President on November 21, 1997, before his trip to Vancouver. The President never mentioned to LEWINSKY that he had listened to the tape, and it was not discussed when they next had a meeting on December 6, 1997. The tape never accomplished its desired result.

LEWINSKY visited the White House on December 28, 1997, after entering the southwest gate; proceeding to the West Wing basement lobby; climbing the stairs near the Cabinet Room; proceeding into BETTY CURRIE's office; proceeding into the Oval Office; and then into the back study. LEWINSKY may have seen LARRY COCKELL near the Oval Office. After their meeting was over, the President startled LEWINSKY by giving her a big hug. It is unknown whether anyone observed this. LEWINSKY departed the Oval Office to CURRIE's office, past the Rose Garden and through the Palm Room.

LEWINSKY gave four ties to BAYANI NELVIS.

LEWINSKY gave six ties to the President:

1. The "telecom" tie; a ZEGNA tie with criss crosses of red and gold on a blue background; purchased at NEIMAN MARCUS in MAZZA Gallerie in northwest Washington on the weekend before November 20, 1995; asked BETTY CURRIE on November 17, 1995 if gift okay; given to President through CURRIE on November 20, 1995; received call from the President that night; received a note from President stating tie was beautiful; observed President wearing on November 21, 1995 in Oval Office photo; on December 5th in the presence of LEWINSKY, President signed photo of himself wearing this tie in Oval Office; observed President wearing on February 8th for signing of telecommunications bill, 1996 after speaking with him on February 7 and 8, 1996; picture in Time Magazine on July 22, 1996, with President wearing this tie; observed President wearing August 5, 1996 after speaking with him on August 4th, 1996; observed President wearing on January 23, 1997, with MADELINE ALBRIGHT; saw President from afar on January 23, 1997 at the New York Ball at KENNEDY CENTER and he mouthed, "Hi, I like your dress"; observed President wearing March 14, 1997, which was the day the President was traveling to North Carolina and Florida (when President hurt his leg); observed BAYANI NELVIS wearing tie at Grand Jury appearance; on the day LEWINSKY hurt her hand she asked President where he had gotten the tie and he responded, "Some girl with style gave it to me."
2. BLOOMINGDALE'S tie; HUGO BOSS tie that is blue, white and black; bought at BLOOMINGDALE'S at TYSON'S CORNER, Virginia; presented directly to President on March 31, 1996; observed President wearing at CLINTON/GORE political rally in Virginia in late October 1996, at which time LEWINSKY yelled to President, "Hey handsome, I like your tie"; observed President wearing the tie the day that RON BROWN died; photo of President wearing tie in US News and World Report, dated May 13, 1996; observed President wearing the week of April 8 or April 15, 1996; followed the next day with the "telecom" tie.
3. Birthday tie; ZEGNA yellow tie bought at NEIMAN MARCUS in TYSON'S CORNER, Virginia; sent to President via FedEx to BETTY CURRIE in "care package" prior to August 19, 1996; photo in Washington Times on August 31, 1996, depicting President wearing tie in Cape Girardeau, Missouri; worn in Florida September 5, 1996 during campaign, President telephoned LEWINSKY from Florida and said, "Good tie to wear in Florida;" observed President wearing last day of Democratic Convention in 1996; observed President wearing tie the day GEORGE TENET was nominated as CIA Director; wore tie December 3 or 4, 1996, after speaking with LEWINSKY on December 2, 1996; observed wearing tie August 16, 1997 after speaking with him on August 15, 1997; LEWINSKY believes this tie is the only one the President has worn "post-scandal".
4. Red tie; HUGO BOSS tie purchased at BOSS store on Wisconsin Avenue in Georgetown between March 3 and 9, 1997; sent via FedEx to BETTY CURRIE; tie had to be replaced on March 29, 1997, after President pointed out a large cut; worn day after Easter Egg Roll in 1997; worn to Governor's race rally in Virginia in the fall of 1997, the President said, "Did you see I wore your tie the other day?".
5. Olive tie; muted, olive colored, CALVIN KLEIN tie purchased at

MARSHALL's in TYSON'S CORNER, Virginia; sent to President on October 21, 1997; never observed President wearing the tie.
6. FERAUD tie; purchased from small shop near HARROD's in London for 25 pounds; given to President on December 6, 1997; never observed President wearing. LEWINSKY identified this tie from a photograph as a tie turned over to OIC by the White House.

When LEWINSKY gave the President tie 6, she said, "Now you can wear all of my ties in one week." LEWINSKY also told the President that she liked it when he wore her ties because then she knew that she was "close to his heart." On occasion the President would ask LEWINSKY if she noticed that he had been wearing one of her ties at an event, and sometimes the President would assure LEWINSKY that he would wear one of her ties soon.

From a summary chart LEWINSKY confirmed details previously furnished concerning other gifts.

A gift not previously mentioned was an "IFOR" workout T-shirt purchased at the PX in Tuzla, Bosnia. LEWINSKY observed the President wearing the shirt on August 31, 1996. LEWINSKY advised that she also dropped off some zinc lozenges and gingko biloba to BETTY CURRIE for the President during the middle of the day on November 13, 1997.

AIC WIRTH departed interview at 12:47pm.

LEWINSKY observed a grocery bag containing some of her gifts under the President's desk in the back study on July 4, 1997 and August 16, 1997. The bag contained the golf puzzle, the orange wooden "B", the BANANA REPUBLIC sport shirt, and an ugly cowboy shirt that LEWINSKY did not give the President. LEWINSKY asked the President whether he liked the gifts, since they were under his desk for a long period of time. The President responded that he did like them, but that he had not had time to take them upstairs.

On October 21, 1997, LEWINSKY gave a pair of sunglasses, the maker unknown, to the President. The sunglasses were purchased at the BARNEY's outlet in the POTOMAC MILLS MALL, in Stafford, Virginia. The gift was the result of a long running joke about the President wearing "dorky" sunglasses. The President wore a "dorky" pair at a Coast Guard event in Florida in November or December 1997. LEWINSKY first observed a photo of the President wearing the gift glasses on the cover of a magazine in January, 1998, after the "scandal" broke.

LEWINSKY described the President's bathroom in the rear study as being white or very light colored. The walls had framed black and white political cartoons of the President from the Arkansas Democrat Gazette, two towel bars, a corner shelf with toiletries and jars of vitamins or supplements given to the President by a Congressman, a telephone on the wall, a sink with mirror above it, and a toilet bowl.

JUDY BALKIN is a woman from New York in her 40s or 50s, whom LEWINSKY met at the Spa in Connecticut in June 1997. They have had dinner together in New York and have exchanged telephone calls and E-mail. BALKIN and MARCIA LEWIS have a mutual friend. LEWINSKY never spoke with BALKIN about her sexual relationship with the President, nor did she discuss the PAULA JONES lawsuit with her.

LINDA TRIPP was acquainted with BETTY CURRIE, in that they worked in the White House at the same time, and TRIPP sent a condolence card to CURRIE. LEWINSKY is unsure whether she ever discussed LINDA TRIPP with CURRIE. LEWINSKY would not have told CURRIE about a fight LEWINSKY had with TRIPP.

LEWINSKY began seeing Dr. KASSORLA when LEWINSKY had an unpleasant experience at Santa Monica City College. LEWINSKY did not like going to school there, but her father would not pay for her to attend a more expensive college. LEWINSKY was not hospitalized, had no medication prescribed, and missed no classes as a result of this incident. LEWINSKY was not suicidal.

The names of several congressmen were provided to LEWINSKY. This was in regard to the congressman that spoke with the President on the telephone on November 17, 1997, during one of LEWINSKY's sessions with the President. LEWINSKY selected the name of Congressman H. L. "SONNY" CALLAHAN as the most likely caller to the President that night.

On either September 12 or 19, 1997, LEWINSKY went to the southwest gate in an attempt to see the President. LEWINSKY was crying and frustrated because MARSHA SCOTT had said that she had lost her detailee slot and it did not appear that LEWINSKY would be able to go back to work in the White House. LEWINSKY called BETTY CURRIE numerous times, but CURRIE said that the President was going to have dinner with CHEL-SEA. After about 45 minutes, CURRIE arranged to get LEWINSKY into the White House to visit CURRIE. CURRIE was sweet to LEWINSKY, but explained that sometimes neither the President nor CURRIE had direct control over jobs at the White House. CURRIE was traveling to Chicago the next day, but would try to set up a meeting for LEWINSKY and the President on Sunday when CURRIE returned. CURRIE's flight was late on Sunday and no meeting could be set up.

██

████████████. LEWINSKY has had multiple conversations with LINDA TRIPP concerning WILLEY. LEWINSKY believes that some of the conversations may have been recorded by TRIPP. TRIPP gave different stories of the WILLEY incident. The President advised LEWINSKY on July 4, 1997 that NANCY HERNREICH said that she had been called by WILLEY, who had received a call from MIKE ISIKOFF. The President did not elaborate. LEWINSKY knows of no efforts by anyone to influence or discourage KATHLEEN WILLEY from cooperating in the PAULA JONES deposition. LEWINSKY does not know of any relationship between NATHAN LANDOW and the President. LEWINSKY is unaware of any information that LANDOW attempted to influence WILLEY's deposition in the JONES case.

On June 14, 1996, LEWINSKY, her father BERNARD, her stepmother BARBARA, and her brother MICHAEL attended a radio address given by the President. During the address the President inadvertently used the term "seduced," which was embarrassing. After the address, LEWINSKY introduced each member of her family to the President and a family photograph was taken with the President. LEWINSKY's father later remarked that the President looked at him as if the President was sizing him up as a prospective father-in-law. BARBARA LEWINSKY said that she had noticed that the President kept looking at LEWINSKY. LEWINSKY laughed but made no comment.

LEWINSKY has not shared many details of the relationship with her father, but she did tell him about giving the President a tie; receiving a signed photograph; that she was moving to New York; and that VERNON JORDAN and BETTY CURRIE were assisting LEWINSKY in finding a job. When LEWINSKY's father was interviewed by BARBARA WALTERS, he made a comment that his daughter was wonderful and, "Why wouldn't they help her?" LEWINSKY's father told her not to quit her Pentagon job until she had another job lined up; LEWINSKY told him that she had to leave because her boss had hired someone else. LEWINSKY did not tell her father about the July 3, 1997 letter that she wrote to the President, in which she stated that she would tell her parents about her relationship with the President. LEWINSKY asked FRANK CARTER if her parents could be present during her deposition to try to deter the JONES attorneys from deposing her. CARTER advised LEWINSKY not to have her parents present.

The July 3, 1997 letter was handwritten on unlined, white paper, 8 1/2 by 11. LEWINSKY wrote that she was forced to try to get a job in the White House by herself without the President's assistance; mentioned the lack of help from MARSHA SCOTT; said that she may tell her parents about her relationship with the President; requested a United Nations job; and ended by comparing her mother, MARCIA LEWIS, with the President, in that they both faced difficult issues with their heads in the sand. LEWINSKY pleaded that she and the President could work their relationship out. LEWINSKY did not consider this letter a threat.

When the President answered interrogatories in the PAULA JONES case on December 23, 1997, he did not discuss his responses either before or after with LEWINSKY.

In March or April 1995, LEWINSKY forged a letter at LEWIS AND CLARK COLLEGE in Portland, Oregon. LEWINSKY used the name of a college employee named DAVID BLISS in writing a letter to ANDY BLEILER, stating that BLEILER had a job waiting for him at the college. The letter was not delivered, and was returned to BLISS, who discovered the scheme. The motivation for the letter was so that ANDY BLEILER could show his wife KATE the letter and come to Oregon in advance of KATE and the children. This would make BLEILER available to continue their affair. In her apology to BLISS, LEWINSKY made up a story about using the letter to show that BLEILER had a job in Oregon, and that KATE could then obtain permission from the court to move the daughter of HARVEY LEHRER and KATE

BLEILER from the state of California. This was merely a cover story for an illicit relationship.

While at LEWIS AND CLARK COLLEGE, LEWINSKY gave her father a false transcript to indicate better grades than she actually received.

LEWINSKY has never been arrested, but has received a few speeding tickets in Oregon. LEWINSKY has received many parking tickets, some of which she did not pay immediately. LEWINSKY has failed to return some rented videos and some library books.

LEWINSKY reported her credit problems when she filled out the questionnaire for her clearance at the White House. LEWINSKY had to pay off about $800 in bad debts before she could get her clearance. Unpaid Oregon telephone bills were paid off by MARCIA LEWIS.

On one occasion while at the Pentagon, LEWINSKY made a copy of an unfavorable memo from CLIFF BERNATH to KEN BACON discussing a pay grade increase for LEWINSKY. LEWINSKY took the memo from BACON's desk and copied it so that she could later read it and know how to make a better case for a grade increase. BERNATH had cautioned LEWINSKY about spending too much time on the telephone and about making personal long distance calls. On a trip to Asia, LEWINSKY had a disagreement with a military officer named JEFF GRADIK.

On November 15, 1997, LEWINSKY wore bikini thong panties to work and pulled up her jacket in back to display the tops to the President when he came to PANETTA's office. No one else in the room could have seen this; this was something that LEWINSKY learned to do when she was having an affair with ANDY BLEILER.

During the telephone conversation with the President on December 17, 1997, LEWINSKY and the President discussed the fact that she was moving to New York and maybe the PAULA JONES' lawyers would be unable to find her with a subpoena. LEWINSKY figured that if she was residing with her mom in New York there would be no way to find her, since nothing would be in her name. This was more in the manner of "shooting the breeze" with the President than in making a plan.

In the meeting with the President on December 28, 1997, the move to New York was again discussed. LEWINSKY is now unsure who remarked that if she was in New York maybe they would not bother to bring her back for a deposition. LEWINSKY was reminded that her written proffer, previously submitted by NATE SPEIGHTS, has a statement indicating that the President was in favor of the New York move. LEWINSKY said that she has no specific memory of making that statement in the proffer. LEWINSKY said that discussion was not a strategy session, and that if she thought that she needed to get out of Washington quickly, she would have called VERNON JORDAN to make sure that something jobwise should happen immediately.

In regard to the box of gifts that LEWINSKY gave to BETTY CURRIE for safekeeping, LEWINSKY hoped to get the gifts back, but was not sure enough that they would be returned to put all of the gift items in the box. LEWINSKY had no specific thought, discussion, or plan to get the box back; however, LEWINSKY expected the box to be with CURRIE until the PAULA JONES case blew over.

In regard to the daily pages of the Filofax, LEWINSKY does not recall making any entries or notations about the President. LEWINSKY may have thrown the pages away, or they may have been taken in the consensual search of her apartment. The records are not embarrassing, nor are they well kept. However, LEWINSKY would consider it an invasion of privacy if she had to turn over the daily pages at this point.

In January and February 1996, LEWINSKY does not recall telling MAU-REEN LEWIS, who worked for NANCY HERNREICH, any story about bringing pizza to the President when topless, or that she wanted to perform oral sex on the President. LEWINSKY did work late with LEWIS around the time that LEWINSKY began drafting the political letters. LEWINSKY would never tell LEWIS this, because LEWIS was too close to HERNREICH. LEWINSKY opined that HERNREICH may have told this to LEWIS based on rumors. LEWINSKY did talk to LEWIS about movies and other non personal things. LEWINSKY and LEWIS did not have a falling out. LEWIS attended LEWINSKY's birthday party at THE PALM RESTAURANT on July 23, 1996. LEWIS called LEWINSKY after the February 28, 1997 radio address and said that she had heard that LEWINSKY was moving out of the country. LEWINSKY probably told LEWIS of her affair with someone at the Pentagon during a telephone call after LEWINSKY left the White House. LEWINSKY never told LEWIS that she was attracted to NANCY HERN-REICH, but she may have said that HERNREICH has maintained her sexuality, while most women at the White House have not. LEWINSKY did revere HERNREICH. LEWINSKY is not a lesbian or bisexual.

LEWINSKY describes the President as "a sweet little boy," affectionate, kind, warm, selfish, self-centered, self-righteous, incredible person who does what is in the best interest of the country.

██
██

████████The President has a "Saturday night personality," where he gives in to his sexual desires and a "Sunday personality," where he is remorseful and goes to church. The President is a very sensual man, but has never discussed with LEWINSKY whether he has a sex problem.

The President has said such diverse things as, "My life is empty," and, "I."

In regard to his mother, VIRGINIA KELLY, the President said that she was "full of piss and vinegar," that he missed her, and that she was always with him. The President did not speak of her often.

The President felt awful and cried when the first soldier was killed in Bosnia and was very sad, lonely, and withdrawn when Admiral BOORDA committed suicide.

The President does not trust a lot of people.

The President can be humorous, i.e. when he imitated LEWINSKY's voice on her telephone recorder, and when he made the "good morning" remark while having phone sex with LEWINSKY.

LEWINSKY had a discussion with PAT GRIFFIN at his going away party where he said, "Be careful," and, "You're doing a good job there." LEWIN-SKY never had a one-on-one conversation with GRIFFIN at work and was never counseled by him at work.

Monica Lewinsky's
Eleventh Interview

Memorandum   Office of the Independent Counsel

To.   File   Date: 8/27/98

From: SA ████████████

Subject: Lewinsky interview on 8/13/98

    During the 8/13/98 interview of Monica S. Lewinsky, Lewinsky asked if she could discuss a particular matter outside the presence of male investigators/attorneys. Associate Independent Counsel (AIC) Karin Immergut obliged Lewinsky, and the two left the interview room. After a few minutes, the two returned and the interview resumed. The contents of the interview of 8/13/98 are documented in an FD-302, transcribed on 8/14/98 by writer.

    After the interview, AIC Immergut advised writer as to the details of what Lewinsky discussed outside the presence of investigators. Immergut advised that Lewinsky stated that during her November 13, 1997 meeting with Clinton, Lewinsky showed Clinton an e-mail. The e-mail described the ██ Lewinsky also brought some Altoids with her and was eating them when she met with Clinton. Clinton told Lewinsky they did not have enough time for oral sex. Lewinsky told Clinton to at least put his tongue on hers and he obliged.

OFFICE OF THE INDEPENDENT COUNSEL

08/13/98

MONICA S. LEWINSKY was interviewed under the terms of an immunity agreement between the Office of the Independent Counsel (OIC) and her. LEWINSKY was interviewed at the Office of the Independent Counsel, 1001 Pennsylvania Avenue, Washington, DC 20004. Present for the interview were Associate Independent Counsel (AIC) MICHAEL EMMICK, AIC KARIN IMMERGUT, and AIC CRAIG LERNER. Present representing LEWINSKY was her attorney, PRESTON BURTON. LEWINSKY provided the following information, beginning at approximately 11:13 a.m.

LEWINSKY advised that the first time she mentioned the United Nations to President WILLIAM JEFFERSON CLINTON as a possible employer was during her July 3, 1997 letter to CLINTON. LEWINSKY advised that KATHY HERTZ, a former Pentagon employee, had transferred to the United Nations and liked her job. LEWINSKY thought if the United Nations was a good place for HERTZ to work, it might be a good place for LEWINSKY. LEWINSKY advised that a job at the United Nations was her idea, not CLINTON's.

After raising the idea of the United Nations job on July 3, 1997, LEWINSKY did not pursue the United Nations job any further during the Summer of 1997. LEWINSKY advised she left the July 4, 1997 meeting with CLINTON with the understanding that CLINTON was going to bring her back to the White House.

LEWINSKY advised that she spoke with CLINTON on September 30, 1997. The subject of jobs could have come up during that conversation. CLINTON may have mentioned ERSKINE BOWLES being involved in finding LEWINSKY employment during this conversation.

LEWINSKY was shown a transcript of LRT-018. LEWINSKY is not sure this conversation took place on October 3, 1997, but it could have.

When LEWINSKY spoke with LINDA TRIPP on October 6, 1997, TRIPP mentioned that TRIPP's friend KATE, who worked at the National Security Council (NSC), had heard rumors that LEWINSKY would never get a job at the White House which required a blue pass. LEWINSKY was furious when she heard this and left work. At that time, LEWINSKY again thought about pursuing the United Nations as a potential employer. But, LEWINSKY was mostly resolved to look for a job in the private sector in New York.

LEWINSKY could have talked to TRIPP about the United Nations between

July 3, 1997 and October 6, 1997, but LEWINSKY's recollection is that LEWINSKY only brought the United Nations back up after October 6, 1997.

As of October 6, 1997, LEWINSKY had only spoken to CLINTON about White House jobs. In one of her conversations with CURRIE in September, LEWINSKY mentioned a former intern who got a job working for PAUL BEGALA. CURRIE said CLINTON told her CURRIE could speak to JOHN PODESTA about finding LEWINSKY a job. From that day, until October 6, 1997, LEWINSKY did not hear from anyone at the White House about a job.

LEWINSKY referred to KATE's comments in a note to CLINTON, but she did not specifically mention KATE by name.

LEWINSKY and CURRIE got into a fight about CURRIE not speaking to CLINTON about a position for LEWINSKY in the White House. Shortly thereafter, on October 9, 1997, LEWINSKY and CLINTON spoke by telephone.

LEWINSKY assumes CLINTON called her from the White House Residence.

On October 10, 1997, LEWINSKY spoke with BETTY CURRIE, who said CLINTON was on the White House putting green with ERSKINE BOWLES. At that time, LEWINSKY thought CLINTON may be talking to BOWLES about a job for LEWINSKY.

LEWINSKY thinks CURRIE would do whatever CLINTON wanted her to do. LEWINSKY thinks that CLINTON could think that, by CURRIE speaking to PODESTA, it would be the same as CLINTON speaking to BOWLES.

LEWINSKY is not sure when VERNON JORDAN's name first came up in relation to LEWINSKY's job search. LEWINSKY recalls speaking to LINDA TRIPP and TRIPP said that JORDAN was on the Board of Directors of many companies. LEWINSKY advised she never spoke with CLINTON regarding MAX CHAPMAN or SUSAN THOMASES. LEWINSKY advised THOMASES was a "HILLARY [CLINTON] person," and it would not make sense for LEWINSKY to want THOMASES to find her a job.

During LEWINSKY's October 11, 1997 visit with CLINTON, LEWINSKY thinks she mentioned needing a good reference from someone in the White House, such as JOHN HILLEY. CLINTON said he would take care of it.

LEWINSKY advised that CLINTON asked her to write a list of potential employers, or jobs she was interested in, and to give it to him. On October 16, 1997, LEWINSKY sent CLINTON the list, which she refers to as a "wish list." On the "wish list," LEWINSKY wrote that she did not want a job at the United Nations.

At some point, LEWINSKY gave CLINTON a "deadline" as to when she needed a job. LEWINSKY told CLINTON she had to be out of her apartment by the end of October, 1997. LEWINSKY advised she did this to get CLINTON moving and into finding her a job.

When BILL RICHARDSON called LEWINSKY on October 21, 1997, LEWINSKY was initially surprised. After the call, LEWINSKY was upset because LEWINSKY did not want to work at the United Nations, no one had called her to tell her RICHARDSON would be calling, and she did not want to get stuck working there with no other opportunities. LEWINSKY was aware that it was RICHARDSON she was speaking with because a secretary called and said "hold for Ambassador RICHARDSON."

LEWINSKY was shown a transcript of LRT 002, pages 10-12. In response to the transcript excerpt, LEWINSKY advised she did not think it would be a good idea for someone from within the White House to get her a job in the private sector, due to appearances. LEWINSKY advised she was always concerned about the appearance of things. LEWINSKY did not talk to CURRIE about CURRIE helping LEWINSKY versus CLINTON helping LEWINSKY find a job. LEWINSKY stated that it was understood that it would look better for CURRIE to do the "leg work" to find LEWINSKY a job.

LEWINSKY recalls buying a card regarding the "emergency insanity system," but she does not recall whether she sent it to CLINTON.

LEWINSKY kept track of the number of days remaining until the election in 1996. LEWINSKY used a printout of a computer calendar and filled in the days by hand.

LEWINSKY was shown a transcript of LRT 013, pages 17-18. After reviewing the transcript, LEWINSKY advised she had been concerned CLINTON would pressure her to accept the job at the United Nations, because it would be easier to find a government employee a job at another government agency than it would be to find them a job in the private sector. LEWINSKY feared the White House would railroad her into taking the job at the United Nations.

LEWINSKY felt CLINTON owed her a job for several reasons. First, LEWINSKY's relationship with CLINTON was the reason she was transferred from the White House. Second, CLINTON had promised LEWINSKY a job back at the White House. Third, CLINTON had not procured her a job at the White House. Fourth, LEWINSKY left the White House "quietly," without mentioning her relationship with CLINTON to anyone.

LEWINSKY was shown a copy of LRT 015, pages 31-38. LEWINSKY recalls CLINTON calling on October 23, 1997. LEWINSKY probably mentioned that RICHARDSON had called. LEWINSKY advised that during her conversations with TRIPP, LEWINSKY gave LEWINSKY's interpretation of what CLINTON said more so than exact quotes of what he said.

LEWINSKY recalled that CLINTON, as to the job at the United Nations, never insisted or pressured her to take the job. LEWINSKY recalled CLINTON mentioning LEWINSKY having options, with the United Nations being one option, in relation to employment opportunities. LEWINSKY was aware CLINTON had a good relationship with RICHARDSON.

LEWINSKY was concerned her future employer may be concerned about rumors about LEWINSKY being a "stalker." At some point, LEWINSKY believes was during their October 30, 1997 conversation, CLINTON gave LEWINSKY a few "pointers" on what to say to RICHARDSON during her interview. LEWINSKY probably mentioned to CLINTON her fear of being stuck at the United Nations. During this telephone call, LEWINSKY may have mentioned the antique paperweight she purchased for CLINTON.

LEWINSKY told her father about RICHARDSON's call and he was impressed.

LEWINSKY felt it was inappropriate to conduct an interview in RICHARDSON's hotel room. LEWINSKY does not recall telling CURRIE that, though LEWINSKY may have. LEWINSKY may have told CURRIE that LEWINSKY was unversed in United Nations affairs and wanted CLINTON to call her before her interview.

LEWINSKY was shown a transcript of LRT 011, page 61.

LEWINSKY was shown a draft of a November 2, 1997 letter to CURRIE regarding Ambassador RICHARDSON. LEWINSKY believes she sent CUR-RIE a different version of this note. LEWINSKY thinks the note she sent had to do with MARCIA LEWIS's book, The Three Tenors. LEWINSKY recalls sending the book to CURRIE to give to CLINTON. LEWINSKY put yellow post-it notes on the pages referring to PLACIDO DOMINGO's charity work and on the books "raciest" page, which, in LEWINSKY's opinion, was not very racy. LEWINSKY advised she was trying to assure CLINTON that the book was not a "kiss and tell."

LEWINSKY does not know whether CLINTON ever received the book.

LEWINSKY is sure she told CURRIE about getting offered the position at the United Nations and that she did not want the job. LEWINSKY believes she also told CLINTON that the United Nations offered her a job.

LEWINSKY was shown a transcript of LRT 016, page 110.

LEWINSKY only recalls speaking to RICHARDSON twice by telephone; once to arrange the interview and once when RICHARDSON extended the job offer to LEWINSKY.

LEWINSKY recalls telling MONA SUTPHEN, RICHARDSON's assistant, that she wanted to find a job in the private sector. LEWINSKY advised that salary was never mentioned in relation to the position at the United Nations.

LEWINSKY's impression is that the position she was offered was open prior to her being considered for it and it was not that big a deal for it to be vacant for so long. LEWINSKY recalls some discussion with the individuals from the United Nations about the differences between a contracting position and a political appointment.

On November 10, 1997, LEWINSKY sent CLINTON a note and mentioned wanting to see him and mentioned the paperweight she wanted to give him.

LEWINSKY has no recollection of sending the note, but if sending it is mentioned in a conversation she had with TRIPP, then she sent it.

LEWINSKY was mad that CLINTON did not see her on Veteran's Day, 1997, because she felt he would have been able to. LEWINSKY advised that holidays are like weekends at the White House in that fewer people are around than on work days. In addition, HILLARY CLINTON was out of town on Veteran's Day, 1997.

LEWINSKY was shown a transcript of LRT 026, pages 27-28.

LEWINSKY advised CLINTON called her in the middle of the night on November 12, 1997. LEWINSKY recalls CLINTON mentioning NANCY HERNREICH testifying on Capitol Hill the next day. CLINTON mentioned this to let LEWINSKY know she could see him then. CLINTON told LEWINSKY to call CURRIE in the morning to arrange the meeting. CLINTON mentioned the fact that he liked zinc lozenges and currently did not have any.

On November 13, 1997, LEWINSKY called CURRIE in the morning and CURRIE advised HERNREICH had already left and CLINTON was in the East Wing. LEWINSKY continued to call CURRIE who said she kept missing CLINTON. Later in the day, LEWINSKY called CURRIE who advised CLINTON had left the White House to play golf.

LEWINSKY got upset and told CURRIE she would come to the White House to give CURRIE CLINTON's ginkgo stuff, his zinc lozenges and CURRIE's birthday present. CURRIE told LEWINSKY to come to the Southwest gate and wait in CURRIE's car. LEWINSKY advised it was raining that day.

When LEWINSKY got to CURRIE's car, the door was locked. LEWINSKY waited in the rain for awhile before CURRIE came out to get her. LEWINSKY advised she and CURRIE made a "bee-line" to the Oval Office study, to avoid seeing any White House employees.

LEWINSKY advised she waited alone in the study for one half hour before CLINTON came back there. LEWINSKY gave CLINTON the paperweight. CLINTON said he liked the paperweight. LEWINSKY advised the meeting lasted only a few minutes. CURRIE took LEWINSKY home that evening.

[At this point during the interview, LEWINSKY asked to speak with AIC IMMERGUT, outside the presence of male investigators/attorneys. The contents of that discussion are documented in a memorandum.]

LEWINSKY had mixed emotions about this visit. On one hand, LEWINSKY thought CLINTON looked very cute. On the other hand, LEWINSKY was sad the meeting did not last any longer than it did. LEWINSKY advised it felt weird to wait in the study that long. LEWINSKY advised CLINTON had some gifts she had given him in his study. LEWINSKY did not complain to CURRIE after this visit with CLINTON because she at least got to see him.

LEWINSKY advised she thinks she told TRIPP that she gave the gifts she received from CLINTON to LEWINSKY's mother. LEWINSKY told TRIPP she told her mother to get rid of the gifts or put them away. LEWINSKY does not recall telling TRIPP about speaking to CLINTON about getting rid of the gifts.

During their December 28, 1997 meeting, CLINTON did not specifically mention which gifts to get rid of. LEWINSKY was concerned about the hat pin and the book, The Leaves of Grass, the Black Dog dress, and the Black Dog t-shirt with the Presidential Seal on it and the broach. LEWINSKY remembers telling CLINTON she was concerned because the subpoena specifically mentioned the hatpin.

LEWINSKY might have told TRIPP she was concerned about the hatpin, The Leaves of Grass, the Black Dog dress, the Black Dog t-shirt with the Presidential seal. The gifts became a topic of conversation with TRIPP after LEWINSKY was subpoenaed.

LEWINSKY advised she does not have a clear memory of how she determined what gifts to give CURRIE, what gifts to give FRANK CARTER and what gifts to keep. LEWINSKY advised the pin with the skyline of New York may have made it into the box she gave CURRIE because jewelry was mentioned expressly in her subpoena.

LEWINSKY does not recall CLINTON mentioning the recently found ROSE LAW FIRM billing records during her January 7, 1996 visit with him. CLINTON did not mention Whitewater to LEWINSKY.

LEWINSKY used a calling card when she called CURRIE from the Wilshire Boulevard COURTYARD by MARRIOTT.

On July 14, 1997, CLINTON told LEWINSKY he trusted her and he trusted her judgement when it came to LEWINSKY dealing with LINDA TRIPP. LEWINSKY told CLINTON that TRIPP was a big supporter of his.

At her December 31, 1997 meeting with VERNON JORDAN, LEWINSKY brought up TRIPP's name to lay the groundwork with JORDAN so that CLINTON and his team were at least aware of TRIPP. LEWINSKY told JORDAN she used to trust TRIPP, but did not anymore. LEWINSKY may have mentioned TRIPP in relation to KATHLEEN WILLEY. LEWINSKY does not recall JORDAN indicating he was familiar with TRIPP's name.

LEWINSKY did not discuss the details of the JONES case that did not pertain to LEWINSKY with CLINTON, except on January 17, 1997, when LEWINSKY mentioned the possibility of CLINTON settling the case. CLIN-TON said JONES wanted too much money.

When LEWINSKY and TRIPP ate at the CALIFORNIA PIZZA KITCHEN on October 9, 1997, LEWINSKY probably paid for the meal with cash.

LEWINSKY advised she had SCI clearance at the Pentagon, which is higher than the "secret" clearance she held at the White House. LEWINSKY advised she did not recall an additional background investigation being conducted on her in conjunction with her transfer to the Pentagon.

LEWINSKY described the notebook she had that referenced her relationship with CLINTON as a six inch by nine inch spiral notebook. LEWINSKY advised it was in her apartment on January 22, 1998, but it was not seized as evidence. LEWINSKY recalls putting the notebook in an envelope she intended to give to NATE SPEIGHTS. LEWINSKY may have given the notebook to SPEIGHTS or WILLIAM GINSBURG.

LEWINSKY advised the notebook is not dated and the writing was done for therapeutic purposes. LEWINSKY wrote in the notebook approximately six times, beginning soon after November 15, 1995 and ending sometime prior to April 7, 1996. LEWINSKY advised she cannot find the notebook, but will continue to look for it.

LEWINSKY is not sending CLINTON any messages by wearing her straw hat.

LEWINSKY advised she is not a part of a joint defense agreement.

Sometime in the Spring of 1998, LEWINSKY told GINSBURG, who at one time represented her, to tell DAVID KENDALL, CLINTON's attorney, that BAYANI NELVIS was wearing one of the ties LEWINSKY had given CLINTON. This was on a day NELVIS testified at the grand jury. NATE SPEIGHTS said KENDALL told GINSBURG and SPEIGHTS he thought he had three or four of them and was looking for the rest.

The interview ended at approximately 3:30 p.m.

Monica Lewinsky's
Twelfth Interview

1

OFFICE OF THE INDEPENDENT COUNSEL

8/19/98

MONICA S. LEWINSKY was interviewed pursuant to an immunity agreement between the Office of the Independent Counsel (OIC), LEWINSKY, and her attorneys. Present for the interview were Associate Independent Counsel (AIC) MICHAEL EMMICK, AIC KARIN IMMERGUT, and AIC MARY ANNE WIRTH. Representing LEWINSKY was attorney PRESTON BURTON of the law offices of PLATO CACHERIS. The interview was conducted in Suite 490, 1001 Pennsylvania Avenue NW, Washington, D.C. beginning at 11:03 a.m. LEWINSKY provided the following information:

LEWINSKY indicated that she is taking two anti-depressants, Zoloft and Serzone.

LEWINSKY, who was 24 years of age when approached by the OIC on January 16, 1998, was not prepared to wear a wire and/or record telephone conversations. The request to do so was a lot to handle that day and LEWINSKY relied on her advisors, who included her parents and BILL GINSBERG. LEWINSKY tried to protect the President at first but no longer feels this is the thing to do. The proffer that LEWINSKY prepared in late January, 1998 is correct. LEWINSKY is now disappointed and angry with the President for several reasons:

1. The President denied that he had sexual relations with "that woman."
2. The President, in his speech to the nation on August 17, 1998, did not recognize the suffering this has caused LEWINSKY.
3. The President lied.
4. The President's staff has said unkind things about LEWINSKY, including labelling her as "the stalker."

LEWINSKY does not recall the book <u>Geek Love</u> and did not recognize a copy of it.

The President was conscious of the labels on his ties and liked the ERMENEGILDO ZEGNA and HUGO BOSS ties that she gave him. With the exception of the LEWINSKY gift ties, the President did not talk about ties very much. The President certainly knew that LEWINSKY had given him the HUGO BOSS red tie with small black squares. The President must have recalled that LEWINSKY gave him the "birthday tie," a yellow ZEGNA, since he wrote her a thank you note and wore it weekly during the 1996 Presidential campaign.

On April 7, 1996, LEWINSKY advised the President by telephone that she had been transferred to the Pentagon. Sometime during the next week, the President told LEWINSKY that EVELYN LIEBERMAN had fired her because LEWINSKY and the President were paying too much attention to each other. The President said that LIEBERMAN did not care what the President did after the election.

On August 4, 1996, between 12:00 and 12:30 p.m., LEWINSKY caused herself to be walking on 16th Street north of the White House. The President had not called LEWINSKY in a little while and she wanted him to see her as a reminder that they had not seen each other in awhile. LEWINSKY knew that the President regularly returned from church each Sunday at about that time and also knew that he sat on the right hand side of the car. The President saw LEWINSKY, but probably thought that it was accidental. The President called her as a result of this "chance" sighting.

On a Sunday in September 1996, LEWINSKY was walking in the same area with her aunt, DEBRA FINERMAN, and she presumes that she was sighted by the President, but she did not see him. The President either called her or left a message that he had seen her.

The President advised LEWINSKY that when he was on vacation at Martha's Vineyard in August 1997, representatives of the BLACK DOG store sent over to his vacation compound a number of BLACK DOG items. ▆▆▆▆ and ▆▆▆▆ took the items they liked and the President took the leftover items to use as gifts. The President knew that LEWINSKY liked these items and gave the bag to her at Christmas time. He gave the remaining BLACK DOG items to BETTY CURRIE. LEWINSKY had asked the President to buy her a BLACK DOG T-shirt on one occasion.

LEWINSKY believes that many of the gifts that the President gave LEWINSKY were gifts that he had received, i.e., the New York skyline pin and the Rockettes blanket. The President said that he had obtained the hat pin in Santa Fe, the bear in Vancouver, and the sunglasses in Union Station while shopping with ▆▆▆▆.

LEWINSKY did not discuss the "talking points" with anyone but LINDA TRIPP.

LEWINSKY may have mentioned to her mother and aunt that she had tried to convince LINDA TRIPP to file an affidavit to avoid TRIPP testifying about her knowledge of LEWINSKY's relationship with the President. This was to protect LEWINSKY's reputation and TRIPP's job. LEWINSKY may have alluded to a possible betrayal by an unidentified friend when she met with the Christian Scientist counselor on Fifth Avenue in New York. LEWINSKY may have mentioned LINDA TRIPP to her friends, NEYSA ERBLAND and ASHLEY RAINES, but would not have provided any detail about TRIPP to them.

LINDA TRIPP said that MICHAEL ISIKOFF had misquoted her in the Newsweek article that was issued in the summer of 1997. KEN BACON asked TRIPP to let him know if she was going public with any more information;

BACON had gathered a lot of information about TRIPP from the Internet and was concerned. LEWINSKY was worried that BACON and BERNATH were going to fire TRIPP. BERNATH was irritated that TRIPP had not told any of her superiors about her previous testimony in the Whitewater matter. TRIPP said if that happened she would write a "tell all" book. This would expose LEWINSKY.

LEWINSKY said there are two possibilities concerning KATHLEEN WILLEY:

1. The President could be telling the truth.
2. Maybe something consensual happened since TRIPP advised that WILLEY had been sending notes to the President for a long time.

LEWINSKY told TRIPP that the President told LEWINSKY that WILLEY had called HERNREICH about ISIKOFF's call to WILLEY. While LEWIN-SKY was in Madrid, TRIPP advised her telephonically that there was something about WILLEY in the DRUDGE Report. LEWINSKY asked TRIPP if she had told ISIKOFF about the WILLEY call to HERNREICH. TRIPP was evasive and did not admit that she had. LEWINSKY did not confront TRIPP about this disclosure, because LEWINSKY was wary of TRIPP, so she did not tell TRIPP until much later that she had seen the President on July 14, 1997.

The President once said, "I know you think I have 100 other girlfriends but I don't." This was the only time that he ever referred to LEWINSKY as a girlfriend.

LEWINSKY never had an open discussion with the President about whether oral sex is "sex." However, after having a relationship with him, LEWINSKY deduced that the President, in his mind, apparently does not consider oral sex to be sex. Sex to him must mean intercourse. LEWINSKY said that her use of the term "having sex" means having intercourse, although oral sex would constitute an "affair." LEWINSKY believed that the President's refusal to allow her to bring him to "completion" was his way of "drawing a line."

At some point, LEWINSKY asked the President if he wanted to see her affidavit. The President put her off by saying that he had seen a lot of affidavits.

On December 17, 1997, the President said that other women on the PAULA JONES witness list were girlfriends from Arkansas from years ago. The President never discussed DOLLY KYLE BROWNING or others on the list with LEWINSKY. LEWINSKY later heard that ███████ may have been a former girlfriend in Arkansas. ███████ always had an icy stare for LEWIN-SKY. Neither ███████ nor ███████ concealed their daggers well. LEWINSKY made an off-handed comment to the President about GENNIFER FLOWERS and he laughed.

The book given to the President on December 6, 1997 was the THEODORE ROOSEVELT antique book. The antique book purchased after December 28,

1997 was entitled, "Presidents of the United States." This book was purchased at the shop next to the Christian Scientist store in Georgetown and was given to BETTY CURRIE to give to the President on January 4, 1998.

The President never told LEWINSKY to turn over to FRANK CARTER all of the gifts that he had given her.

LEWINSKY never discussed VERNON JORDAN with the President until she began looking for a job in New York in October 1997. LEWINSKY figured that asking JORDAN for help was one more "iron in the fire" in trying to get a New York job.

LEWINSKY discussed the settling of the PAULA JONES case with LINDA TRIPP on December 8, 1997, and with the President on December 17, 1998. During the conversation on December 17th, LEWINSKY is 99% sure that the President told her that if she had to testify she should say that LEWINSKY was at the Oval Office to visit BETTY CURRIE or to bring papers to the President. LEWINSKY is 100% sure that the President suggested that she might want to sign an affidavit to avoid testifying.

Once when BETTY CURRIE was gone, LEWINSKY asked the President why he could not clear her into the White House. The President responded that he could not because they (the Secret Service) make a list of everyone who comes to see him.

At 12:38 p.m. AIC MARY ANNE WIRTH entered and asked LEWINSKY whether she had ever been taken by another woman to the Oval Office and let in to see the President. LEWINSKY could only recall that she could have been escorted as an intern by TRACY BECKETT to take PANETTA's mail to the Oval Office, or possibly could have gone with KARIN ABRAMSON to deliver the poem that LEWINSKY wrote to the President on behalf of the interns. LEWINSKY was never escorted into the Oval Office and left with the President by any woman other than BETTY CURRIE. AIC WIRTH exited at 12:42 p.m.

The interview ended at approximately 12:50 p.m.

Monica Lewinsky's
August 20, 1998, Grand Jury Testimony

PROCEEDINGS

Whereupon,

MONICA S. LEWINSKY

was called as a witness and, after having been first duly sworn by the Foreperson of the Grand Jury, was examined and testified as follows:

EXAMINATION

BY MR. EMMICK:

Q Good morning, Ms. Lewinsky.

A Good morning.

Q As we did with your earlier grand jury testimony, my job is to advise you of your rights and obligations here at the beginning.

    First off, you have a right under the Fifth Amendment to refuse to answer any questions that may tend to incriminate you. In this case, that right is qualified by the fact that you've signed an agreement to provide truthful testimony in connection with our investigation. Do you understand that?

A Yes, I do.

Q In addition, you have the right to have counsel present outside the grand jury to answer any questions that you may have. Do you have counsel outside?

A Yes, I do.

Q Who is that?

A Preston Burton.

Q And you understand that if you'd like to speak to your counsel, all you have to do is say "Could I take a break and speak with my counsel?"

A Yes.

Q All right. You also in addition to those two rights, you have an obligation and that obligation is to tell the truth. That obligation is imposed on you because you have been put under oath and also because in connection with your agreement you're required to tell the truth. Do you understand that?

A Yes, I do.

MR. EMMICK: What I have placed in front of you is what is marked as ML-7.

This is a chart that you have earlier testified about of contacts between yourself and the President.

As I indicated to you informally beforehand, this grand jury session today is for you to answer questions from the grand jurors.

And so without any further ado, I will ask the grand jurors if they have any questions of Ms. Lewinsky.

A JUROR: I think I'm going to start out.

MR. EMMICK: Okay.

A JUROR: Ms. Lewinsky, in your testimony when you were with us on the 6th, you mentioned some of the steps that you took to maintain secrecy regarding your relationship: that you would bring papers or he'd have papers or either you would accidentally bump into each other in the hallway; you always used Betty as the excuse for you to be waved in; and on many occasions you would go in one door and out of the other door.

THE WITNESS: Yes.

A JUROR: Are there any other methods you used that I've missed? That you used to maintain your secrecy?

THE WITNESS: Hmm. I need to think about that for a minute.

A JUROR: And the second part to that question is were these ways to maintain your secrecy your idea or were they recommended to you by anyone?

THE WITNESS: I can answer the second part first.

A JUROR: Okay.

THE WITNESS: If that's okay.

A JUROR: That's fine.

THE WITNESS: Some of them were my idea. Some of them were things that I had discussed with the President. I think it was a mutual understanding between us that obviously we'd both try to be careful.

A JUROR: Do you recall at all specifically which ones he may have recommended to you as an idea on maintaining the secrecy?

THE WITNESS: Yes and no. The issue of Betty being the cover story for when I came to the White House, it became my understanding I think most clearly from the fact that I couldn't come to see him after the election until—unless Betty was there to clear me in and that one time when I asked him why, he said because if someone comes to see him, there's a list circulated among the staff members and then everyone would be questioning why I was there to see him. So—

MR. EMMICK: Let me try to ask some follow-ups in response to your question.

BY MR. EMMICK:

Q Were there ever any discussions between you and the President about what should be done with letters that you—letters or notes that you had sent to him? That is to say, for example, did you ever write on the bottom of any letters what to do with those letters?

A It was my understanding that obviously he would throw them away or, if he decided to keep them, which I didn't think he did, he would put them somewhere safe.

I think what you're referring to is on the bottom once of a sort of joke memo that I sent to him I in a joking manner reminded him to throw the letter away, that it wasn't—you know, that was a joke. So—

Q What about whether on your caller ID on your telephone the word POTUS would appear and whether anything was done in order to make sure that POTUS did not appear on your telephone?

238

A My caller ID at work, it would—when the President called from the Oval Office, it would say POTUS and when he'd call from the residence, it was an asterisk. And I told him that. I didn't know if he knew that it said POTUS when he called from the office, and I assumed he didn't, because otherwise that would be sort of silly.

So I informed him of that and then one time he called me from the residence and he—he called on a hard line—I don't know. I shouldn't say "hard line" because I know that has some different terminology to it, but he called on a line that had a phone number attached to it, and so when he called, he said, "Oh, did it ring up, you know, phone number? It didn't say my name, did it?"

And so it was—that was something that I was concerned about.

Q Did he ever express to you a reluctance to leave messages on your telephone voice message system?

A At home?

Q Yes.

A Yes.

Q All right. Tell us about that.

A One time in a conversation he just said he didn't like to leave messages.

Q Okay. What about the times that you would visit him? Were those times selected in a way so that there weren't people around or that certain people weren't around?

A Yes.

Q Okay. Would you tell us about that?

A There were obviously people at the White House who didn't like me and wouldn't—wouldn't be understanding of why I was coming to see the President or accepting of that and so there was always sort of an effort made that either on the weekends—when I was working in the White House he told me that it was usually quiet on the weekends and I knew that to be true. And after I left the White House it was always when there weren't going to be a lot of people around.

Q And what about particular individual people? Would there be particular individual people who would be—staffers in the oval area that you would try to avoid in order to help conceal the relationship?

A Yes. Nancy Hernreich, Stephen Goodin, Evelyn Lieberman. Pretty much anybody on the first floor of the West Wing.

A JUROR: How did all these people come to not like you so much? What were you doing? Were you breaking the rules of the White House? What were you doing to draw their attention to not liking you so much? Before the relationship.

From the time you got there all the way up to the time—what I'm saying is what did you do to deserve for them not to like you?

THE WITNESS: Before the relationship started?

A JUROR: Yes. What did you do from—

THE WITNESS: I don't think there was anything I did before the relationship started that—the relationship started in November of '95. I had only been at the White House as an intern in the Old Executive Office Building for—for a few months, so most of my tenure at the White House I was having a relationship with the President.

I think that—the President seemed to pay attention to me and I paid attention to him and I think people were wary of his weaknesses, maybe, and thought—in my opinion, I mean, this is—I think that people—they didn't want to look at him and think that he could be responsible for anything, so it had to all be my fault, that I was—I was stalking him or I was making advances towards him. You know, as they've said, I wore inappropriate clothes, which is absolutely not true. I'm not really sure.

A JUROR: But you do admit a lot of the places that you weren't supposed to be you were always found. You do admit that there were things that you were doing, too, in order to see him that they were feeling that was going against the rules of the White House?

THE WITNESS: Uh—

A JUROR: You know, places that you were that you weren't supposed to be and hallways that you weren't supposed to be, you were seen in those places?

THE WITNESS: Yes and no. There really weren't any of these staffers who saw me in the places that I wasn't supposed to be. And that was part of the effort to conceal the relationship. So—does that make sense?

I mean, when I was in the Oval Office with the President, no one else knew except for the Secret Service, no one else knew that I went in there. So for them to know—for them to be disliking me for that reason, I don't think that they were really—I don't know if they were aware of that or not.

I did make an effort, I think, to try to—to have interactions with the President and I—and I think that—that was probably disturbing to them. I know that if the President was in the hall and he was talking to people and I passed by he'd—he'd stop talking and say hi to me. I'm not really sure.

A JUROR: Just a follow-up to that.

THE WITNESS: Sure.

A JUROR: If they didn't see you, well, how did they know?

THE WITNESS: I don't know what they knew. I—you know, I—I'm not sure—I—

A JUROR: Because if you said you made an effort to hide yourself, you know, so you wouldn't see them, the Secret Service are the ones that saw you—

THE WITNESS: Mm-hmm.

A JUROR: Okay. So, I mean, how would they—how did they know that you were there, you know, to want to keep you away from being there?

THE WITNESS: I don't know. Maybe—I—I mean, I've heard reported in the newspapers and on TV that the Secret Service, someone said something to Evelyn Lieberman and I had had an—I don't know if I went over this the last time I was here, I had had a real negative interaction with Nancy Hernreich early on in my tenure at the White House and so—

I think there was also—I'm a friendly person and—and I didn't know it was a crime in Washington for people—for you to want people to like you and so I was friendly. And I guess I wasn't supposed to be.

A JUROR: So that interaction that you had with Evelyn Lieberman was when she was telling you what?

THE WITNESS: She stopped me in the hall and she asked me where I worked, in which office I worked, and I told her Legislative Affairs in the East Wing.

And she said, "You're always trafficking up this area." You know, "You're not supposed to be here. Interns aren't allowed to go past the Oval Office."

And she—she really startled me and I walked away and I went down to the bathroom and I was crying because—I mean, when—you know, when an older woman sort of chastises you like that, it's upsetting.

And then I thought about what she said and I realized that, well, I wasn't an intern any more. I was working there. And I kind of believe in clear communication, so I went back to Evelyn Lieberman, to Ms. Lieberman, and I—I said, "You know, I just wanted to clarify with you that I work here, I'm not an intern. So, you know, I am allowed to go past the Oval Office." I don't think I said that, but I had a blue pass.

And she looked at me and said, "They hired you?" And I was startled and then she said, "Oh, well, I think I mistook you for someone else or some other girl with dark hair who keeps trafficking up the area." And ever since then—and that was maybe in December or January of '95 or '96. So—

A JUROR: Ms. Lewinsky, were you ever reprimanded or chastised by your immediate supervisor in Legislative Affairs for trafficking up the area or being where you weren't supposed to be or being away from your desk too much? Anything like that?

THE WITNESS: Being away from my desk had been mentioned to me, but trafficking up the area and being where I'm not supposed to be, no.

I—the—I had a view of—and this is sort of my view with work is that you get a lot more done and people are a lot more willing to help you when you have a personal interaction with them. And so the person who held the job before me would fax the drafts of his letters to the staff secretary's office and then at some point during the day when someone got the draft they would make the changes and then fax it back.

And I found it to be much more effective to take things over to the staff secretary's office and interact with the person—I can't remember her name—Helen—to interact with Helen and have Helen edit the letters right then and there and then I could go back and to me it was a faster process.

So there was also—you know, I also wanted to try to see the President. So, I mean, I did make efforts to try to see him in the hall or something like that because—

A JUROR: So the route to the staff person's office was a route that you could still veer off and see the President?

THE WITNESS: No. It—it wasn't necessarily in front of the Oval Office or anything. There were—we also had—let me see if I can explain this. I'm sure you guys know by now that the West Wing is three stories. There's the basement, the first floor and the second floor. Legislative Affairs has an office on the second floor of the West Wing.

There are two ways to get to that office—or three ways, I guess. There's the West Wing, you can cut across the West Wing lobby, which is where people coming to visit someone in the White House sit. There's going the back way, which you pass the Oval Office, but the door's always closed when the President's in there. And then you can go all the way down the stairs and all the way around and then all the way up two flights of stairs.

When I first started working there, it didn't seem appropriate to walk through the West—to me, it didn't seem appropriate to walk through the West Wing lobby with papers when there were people who were visitors coming to sit and wait. I just—I didn't think that was appropriate during the business time.

So I went the other way, behind—which went past the Oval Office, not knowing that—I guess you're not supposed to do that. It seemed silly. The door's closed and it's locked. And there wasn't this intention to see the President that way.

So—am I—did I answer your question?

A JUROR: Yes.

THE WITNESS: Okay. I'm sorry.

MR. EMMICK: You know, one thing I might do is circle back to try to pick up some more concealment methods.

A JUROR: Okay.

MR. EMMICK: Because you asked the question are there any other methods.

A JUROR: Yes.

MR. EMMICK: And I can ask a few more questions that might direct us in that area.

THE WITNESS: Okay.

BY MR. EMMICK:

Q For example, you have indicated earlier that it was Betty Currie who waved you in all the times during 1997 that you saw the President. Did you ever talk with the President about whether he could wave you in instead or whether it would be a good idea for him to wave you in personally?

A Yes. I think that that's what I mentioned earlier.

Q Oh, okay.

A That he and I had discussed it and he said he couldn't do that because then it would be on a list.

Q Okay. What about—you had mentioned that you took a different route into the Oval Office than you would take out of the Oval Office. In addition, did you ever take routes to get to the Oval Office that seemed calculated to avoid certain Secret Service or White House personnel?

A Not Secret Service, but I—I liked or I preferred to sort of meet up with him and then we'd walk in together. And I preferred to go in through the Rose Garden because then I wasn't going—I wasn't risking the possibility of running into someone in the hall right outside the Oval Office. So—

Q What about the routes that Betty would walk you in from the gates?

A Oh. When—there were certain Secret Service officers who were friendly with Debi Schiff who Betty wanted to try to avoid because I guess they chatted with Debi Schiff a lot and there's a whole long story with Debi Schiff, so—

Q And would that be another way that you would help conceal your meetings with the President?

A Yes.

A JUROR: Just to back up for a minute. When you would meet the President and go in through the Rose Garden or meet the President before going into the Oval Office, did you discuss that with him ever about sort of what— that that would be a way that would sort of be more concealing or—

THE WITNESS: We only did that, I think, twice. And the first time, it really was an accident. And so then the next time that we did that, I said—you know, before—he would call me in my office before I would come see him and we'd figure out what we were going to do.

And I think I—I know I suggested to him, I said, "I really like that because then it's just easier, it seems." And also, I—for me personally, I didn't—I didn't always want to be the one that was being seen going in. Does that make sense?

So that I wasn't always bringing in the papers and it was me going to him, that in this instance if someone saw it, being the Secret Service, he invited me. So—for me, that just made me feel better.

BY MR. EMMICK:

Q All right. I have a number of other questions about these alternative methods of concealment. Let me ask you this. I think you've testified earlier that most of the sexual contact that you had with the President tended to occur in the hallway, rather than in the study, although sometimes it was in the study itself.

Did that have anything to do with whether or not it would be easier to see you in the study as opposed to the hallway?

A I think so, but I don't specifically—I don't specifically remember discussing that with the President, but there were circumstances that that sort of was obvious to me.

Q And would that include the fact that windows in the study tended to be uncurtained?

A Just that, windows. Yes.

Q Right. Yes, there were windows there.

A Yes.

Q And so you might be seen there.

A Yes.

MR. EMMICK: All right.

BY MS. IMMERGUT:

Q In that regard, you also mentioned that you would move from the oval area or that sometimes you'd start in the Oval Office and then you'd move towards the hallway. Did the President ever initiate that move?

A I think we both did. I mean, it just depended on the day. It wasn't—

Q Was it understood that you wouldn't actually have a sexual encounter in the Oval Office?

A I'm sure it was understood. I—I—I wouldn't have done that. I mean—so—I'm sure he wouldn't have done that.

BY MR. EMMICK:

Q Are there windows all around the Oval Office?

A There are windows all around and it just—I know this may sound silly, but it wouldn't be appropriate. You know.

Q What about any discussions with the President about not acknowledging one another at parties or photographs, for example?

A He called me in my office the day of Pat Griffin's going away party and had asked me if I was going to go. I said yes and he said, "Well, maybe we can get together after that."

And I told him I didn't think that was a good idea, that people were going to be watching. I was paranoid anyway and—so I said, "I think it's a good idea if we just sort of ignore each other at the party and don't really say anything." And that's what we did.

Q And what about with respect to a photograph that was taken at the party and whether—

A I mean, we didn't discuss this. I didn't know there was going to be a picture taken. But I made an effort to stand on the—I was the last person sort of on the outside of this picture so that—I didn't want anyone to think that I was trying to get close to the President, I was trying to—whatever it was.

Q So in that case, that would be a concealment effort, but not one that the President and you had collaborated on.

A No.

Q All right. What about an occasion when the President suggested that the two you might attend a movie and sort of bump into each other outside the movie? Tell us about that discussion.

A   He told me he was going to watch a movie with some friends of his and that if I wanted to I could bump into him in the hall outside and then he'd invite me into the movie.

And I asked him if—I think he said there were some friends and maybe some of his staff or I asked him if some of his staff was going to be there.

And he said yes and I don't remember who he said was going to be there, but I said I didn't think that was a good idea.

Q   And why would you have to make prior arrangements for you to bump into each other rather than having sort of a—you know, walk down the hall together to the movie?

A   Well, I—

Q   I know it's kind of obvious.

A   For obvious reasons, I guess, because it wouldn't be appropriate. It—people would—people would wonder what was going on.

Q   Right. Right. Okay. What about the fact that you made—that you sent gifts and notes through Betty rather than directly to the President?

Was that something that was done in order to make it less obvious that the notes were actually to the President?

A   Well, yes and no. You really—if you send something directly to the President, if you send a gift to the President, if I sent something right now, well, I don't know, right now, but before this, it—it—it goes to the gift unit.

Q   Right.

A   And so I knew that Betty was the way—I think that that's—Walter Kaye would, you know, go through Betty, I think. And that's—

Q   So it's yes and no, is the answer to that.

A   You can't—I mean, you can't send a courier thing to the President, you know, a courier to President Clinton, so—

A JUROR: I have a question to follow up on that. When you would send gifts and notes and what have you to Betty, as you had testified, sometimes you'd have a funny card in there, sometimes it would be something sentimental.

Did you ever give Betty license to read any of them because you thought, "Hey, take a look at this, tell me what you think," any of the cards or notes or anything?

THE WITNESS: I don't think so. Maybe I told her about a funny card or something. Not that I really remember. I don't—I think especially if it were something that was ultra-sensitive, I don't—you know, I don't—

A JUROR: Yes. That would probably be sealed.

THE WITNESS: Exactly.

A JUROR: But for any of the other little—

THE WITNESS: Might have been the jokes. Sometimes I would put together jokes I got on the Internet or e-mail jokes that I put together for him because, you know, everyone needs to laugh, so—I think maybe—maybe there was a time that I said, "Oh, you should look at these jokes, they're really funny."

A JUROR: Okay.

MR. EMMICK: Other questions? Yes, ma'am?

A JUROR: Ms. Lewinsky, did you ever discuss with the President whether you

244

should delete documents from your hard drive, either at the office or at home?

THE WITNESS: No.

A JUROR: Nothing like that?

THE WITNESS: No.

A JUROR: Did you ever discuss with the President whether you should deny the relationship if you were asked about it?

THE WITNESS: I think I always offered that. I think I've always—

A JUROR: In discussions with the President?

THE WITNESS: In discussions—I told him I would always—I would always deny it, I would always protect him.

A JUROR: And what did he say when you said that? What kind of response did you receive?

THE WITNESS: I said that often. I—in my head, I'm seeing him smile and I'm hearing him saying "That's good," or—something affirmative. You know. Not—not—"Don't deny it."

A JUROR: Thank you.

THE WITNESS: Sure.

BY MS. IMMERGUT:

Q Ms. Lewinsky, with respect to the weekend visits, did the President ever initiate that idea or say anything about it's good if you come on the weekends?

A Yes. The—I don't remember if it was the Wednesday or the Friday when the relationship first started, he said to me at some point, you know, "You can come see me on the weekends. I'm usually around on the weekends." So—

Q And did you understand what that meant?

A Yes. To me, it meant there aren't as many people around on the weekends, so—

A JUROR: Ms. Lewinsky, when you—now, this is a different kind of subject. When you first made the determination that you were moving to New York and you wanted to explore the possibilities of a job in private industry, can you recall how you first got the recommendation about Vernon Jordan's assistance in this endeavor?

THE WITNESS: I can't. I know that it was—what I don't remember was if it was my idea or Linda's idea. And I know that that came up in discussions with her, I believe, before I discussed it with the President. I know that I suggested to the President or I—I didn't suggest, I asked the President if Mr. Jordan might be able to assist me.

A JUROR: To go back from the job search to what we were talking about before, I seem to recall, and I may be mistaken, when you were here before you said something about Tim Keating when you were fired, said something to you like maybe you can come back after the election.

THE WITNESS: Mm-hmm.

A JUROR: And I wanted to just hear sort of a fuller explanation about that. Was it your understanding at the time that Tim Keating was sort of—that he understood and was telling you that you were fired because of an appearance problem around the time of the election?

THE WITNESS: Not at all.

A JUROR: No?

THE WITNESS: No.

245

A JUROR: The other question I have, and I apologize, it's a little bit sensitive, but did you and the President in sort of discussing cover stories and, you know, how—you know, your desire to protect him from sort of what's going on now, did you ever talk about sort of—you know, that you weren't really having sex?

I mean, you said that he made this comment to you about not having— you know, that certain actions have consequences at his age.

THE WITNESS: Yes.

A JUROR: Was there ever sort of an understanding that, well, oral sex isn't really sex? Or did you talk about that?

THE WITNESS: We didn't talk about it. Something that I thought on my own was one of the reasons that it—at first that he didn't want to—that he wouldn't let everything come to completion in terms of oral sex was I thought that that sort of had to do with maybe that was his way of being able to feel okay about it, his way of being able to justify it or rationalize it that, well—

A JUROR: But you never discussed that.

THE WITNESS: No.

MR. EMMICK: Yes, ma'am?

A JUROR: Ms. Lewinsky, getting back to—I think you have a copy there of contacts between the President and Monica?

THE WITNESS: Yes.

A JUROR: After you left the White House, it seems as if you attended a number of public functions where you came in contact with him.

Was that by chance? Was that something you wanted to do? Was it a way to see him? Was it something that he suggested?

Could you just tell us a little about that?

THE WITNESS: Sure. No. Those were all ways for me to get a chance to see him. I'm an insecure person and so I think—and I was insecure about the relationship at times and thought that he would come to forget me easily and if I hadn't heard from him—especially after I left the White House, it was—it was very difficult for me and I always liked to see him and it—and usually when I'd see him, it would kind of prompt him to call me. So I made an effort. I would go early and stand in the front so I could see him, blah, blah, blah.

BY MR. EMMICK:

Q   Let me ask a follow-up question to that because I think it may have been in about October of '96 when you had a telephone conversation with him just prior to you going to Billy Shaddock to get a photograph.

A   Right.

Q   During the conversation before, did you and the President have any discussion about your dropping by and seeing him at a public departure?

A   Yes.

Q   All right. Would you tell us about that?

A   Let's see. I spoke with him—I think it was October 22nd, and then I saw him at an event October 23rd and he called that night and I had mentioned to him on—I think it was a Tuesday, the first phone conversation, that I was going to be at the White House on Thursday.

And when he called me Wednesday night, he said—I was upset with him and so then he said, you know, "Don't be mad. Don't be mad." You know. "Are you coming tomorrow?"

246

And I said yes.

So he said, "Well, why don't you stop by Betty's office, stop by to see Betty and then maybe you can come see me for a few minutes before I leave." So—

Q   Okay. All right. The reason I was asking that as a follow-up is that's sort of a prearranged semi-public occasion for the two of you to see each other.

A   Right. I don't—I don't know necessarily that I was going to go to the departure.

Q   I see.

A   But that was maybe kind of a cover story.

Q   I understand.

A   Or I'm not—I know he had a departure and I know that I was going to see him for a few minutes before the departure because I thought—I remember thinking that I might get to kiss him, so—

MR. EMMICK: All right.

A JUROR: Now to follow up on your follow-up of my question—

MR. EMMICK: Yes.

A JUROR: Did you get to see him that day?

THE WITNESS: No, I didn't.

A JUROR: Okay. Could you tell us a little about that?

THE WITNESS: Sure. I—the short of it is that I didn't end up seeing him because Evelyn Lieberman was hanging around and left with him that day.

A JUROR: She was someplace where she didn't belong.

THE WITNESS: Right. So Betty had—I was waiting in the West Wing lobby with Billy, actually, after we had gone to look at the photos and Betty finally came out and it was really just as he was walking to the helicopter and she took me to see it, but she said that—and it was at that point when she sort of confirmed for me that Evelyn didn't like me. So—that—

A JUROR: The contacts with the President, on page 5, for the 18th of August—

THE WITNESS: I'm sorry, I can't hear you.

MR. EMMICK: Page 5.

A JUROR: Okay. Page 5, 18th of August, it says "Public function, President's 50th birthday party, limited intimate contact."

A JUROR: I couldn't hear her.

MR. EMMICK: Okay. Let me repeat it. There is a reference on page 5 to August 18th of '96, a Sunday, "Public function, President's 50th birthday party, limited intimate contact."

Your question about that was?

THE WITNESS: What does that mean?

MR. EMMICK: What does that mean?

THE WITNESS: It's stupid. There was a cocktail reception for his—he had this big 50th birthday party at Radio City Music Hall and there was a cocktail reception and at the—when he came to do the rope line and he—after he greeted me and talked to me, he was talking to a whole bunch of people in and around my area and I had—can I stand up and show you?

MR. EMMICK: Sure. Sure.

THE WITNESS: Okay. If this is the rope line and here are all the people and the President's standing here, as he started to talk to other people, I had my back to him and I just kind of put—put my hand behind me and touched him. This—so—

BY MS. IMMERGUT:

Q Touched him in the crotch area?

A Yes.

A JUROR: I didn't hear that.

MS. IMMERGUT: Touched him in the crotch area.

A JUROR: Oh.

MS. IMMERGUT: And the response was yes.

A JUROR: Okay.

A JUROR: Did anybody see you?

THE WITNESS: What? No. What's the question?

A JUROR: Did anybody see you?

THE WITNESS: No.

A JUROR: But there were people around.

THE WITNESS: There were, but it was—he was talking—everybody was enamored with him. I'm sure everybody saw from Monday that—and he was talking to different people and he—he was always very close to me when—whenever he'd do these rope lines and would sort of make a point of talking to me around—you know, with other—while other people were there and he'd usually hold my hand—you know, sort of shaking hands and just—would continue to just touch me somewhere. I mean, not—not intimately, not—

BY MR. EMMICK:

Q Right. Just to set the scene, are there a lot of people kind of bunched together at the time?

A Oh, they're—they're—I mean, if we—if everybody in the room came and stood in this one small corner, that's—I mean, that's how crowded it was. So it was—and my back was to him and he was—he was holding onto my—I think he was holding onto one of my arms or something, I had a sleeveless dress on. So—

Q So it sounds to me like—it's almost a situation where there are so many people that you can't really see that kind of—

A Exactly. And it wasn't—it wasn't a—it was—maybe sort of a grazing over of that area, but it wasn't—it wasn't how you might imagine it if someone described this, from a scene from a movie, it wasn't like that, but it was— you know. I don't even know if he remembers, so—

MR. EMMICK: Okay.

A JUROR: So on this paper we have here with sexual relations, would that qualify as—what, contact? Sexual contact? Because if I remember— where's my paper—

THE WITNESS: Let me look at the definition.

MR. EMMICK: Sure.

A JUROR: Yes. Contact with—number 1—

MR. EMMICK: Just to clarify, the witness is looking at Grand Jury Exhibit ML-6.

THE WITNESS: I'm not really sure, because I don't think it was to necessarily gratify him or arouse him.

A JUROR: What was it for?

THE WITNESS: It was just—I thought it was funny and it was sort of a—I don't know how to explain it.

A JUROR: Contact.

BY MR. EMMICK:

Q Would it be better described as perhaps affectionate or playful?

A Playful, I think. It was just—playful, not something I'd ever thought I'd have to discuss publicly.

A JUROR: While we're on this, I wanted to like finish it up, but I had a couple of questions with regards to the definition.

THE WITNESS: Sure.

A JUROR: Because I want to be sure in my own mind. At the bottom it says—it says "Contact means intentional touching, either directly or through clothing."

THE WITNESS: Mm-hmm.

A JUROR: Out of all of the times you had intimate contact, were there times when the President would touch you either on the breasts or in the genital area directly to the skin or was it always through clothing?

THE WITNESS: Directly to the skin. Both.

MR. EMMICK: Yes, ma'am?

A JUROR: I have some questions about the 50th birthday. That's when you gave the President the yellow tie. Is that when you gave the President the yellow tie?

THE WITNESS: Not on that date.

A JUROR: But just before that.

THE WITNESS: But before that. Correct.

A JUROR: When it shows on the chart here, it says "Some time before August 16, 1996."

THE WITNESS: Correct.

A JUROR: And that tie is the same tie that at the end of your appearance here we saw some evidence that the President has worn a number of times this summer.

THE WITNESS: Yes.

A JUROR: There's been some press accounts about that tie, last night and today.

THE WITNESS: Sure.

A JUROR: My question to you is have you authorized your attorneys or any other spokesperson through you to discuss that evidence?

THE WITNESS: Gosh. I don't think I've necessarily given a direct authorization.

A JUROR: Do you know that they have?

THE WITNESS: Do I know if they—I—I don't know if they necessarily directly have. I know there have been questions about it. I shouldn't say I know, I'm sure there have been questions about it, but there have been a lot of instances since the beginning of this thing that there's been information that's come out from places where I hadn't expected it and that includes my own—the people on my team. So I can't—I don't know.

A JUROR: So you don't know whether that information is coming from people that you have discussed it with?

THE WITNESS: I think that there—there probably might have been—I really—I—I wouldn't be surprised to find out that there was confirmation or some of that information came from there.

So—but I know that also—I'm sure it was somewhat limited because with my agreement, we're not allowed to talk to the press. We're not supposed to. So—without prior approval.

BY MR. EMMICK:

Q So I guess there's—let me just rephrase it. It sounds like you wouldn't be surprised by it, but do you have any direct knowledge that it occurred?

249

A   I know that there have been calls about this tie and I know that—that I don't think that we've been 100 percent silent about that. So—I don't—I mean—I know that we didn't cause this story to come out or I don't believe that we did. So—

A JUROR: Ms. Lewinsky, it says on the chart that you received a thank you note saying that the tie is really beautiful.

THE WITNESS: Mm-hmm.

A JUROR: And that was in the President's handwriting?

THE WITNESS: It's a typed letter and then he hand signed the letter and then "The tie is really beautiful" is handwritten.

A JUROR: Did you ever discuss the tie with him in person or was it just a note?

THE WITNESS: No, we discussed it a lot on the phone.

A JUROR: And did he like the tie?

THE WITNESS: Mm-hmm.

A JUROR: Thank you.

THE WITNESS: He called me the first day he wore it. The first time he wore it.

A JUROR: All right. Thank you.

A JUROR: I have another question.

THE WITNESS: Sure.

A JUROR: On the day you were here testifying, there was a report on the TV—

THE WITNESS: Right.

A JUROR: The President in the Rose Garden wearing that tie. Did you see that?

THE WITNESS: That evening I did.

A JUROR: When you saw him with the tie, what did that say to you?

THE WITNESS: I understand you had to do what you had to do. That's what it meant to me. I had looked—because I had seen him wear this tie prior—a few other occasions since January, I had looked the day before my testimony because I thought he's just the kind of person that's going to wear this tie to tug on my emotional strings one last time before I go into the grand jury and say this under oath. And he didn't.

And him wearing it the day I came to testify sort of having to know that I wasn't going to see it until the end of the day, to me was just kind of—you know, hey, you had to do what you had to do. But—

MR. EMMICK: Yes, ma'am?

A JUROR: Ms. Lewinsky, not to make a big issue about the tie, but is this tie something—one of the ties that perhaps the President really liked, is a favorite tie?

THE WITNESS: I think so because he wore it during the campaign. He wore it once—sometimes even twice a week. So I think he liked it a lot.

A JUROR: Do you think that he would remember that it's from you? I mean, you know, I don't know, but do you think he would?

THE WITNESS: Ties were a big issue with us and I used to bug him all the time on the phone, "Well, when are you going to wear one of my ties?" You know. Or he'd say, "Did you see—" On one occasion, I remember specifically he said, "Did you see I wore your tie the other day?"

There's a pretty big correlation between the times when he would wear one of my ties and we either spoke the night before or that night.

And I used to say to him that "I like it when you wear my ties because then I know I'm close to your heart." So—literally and figuratively.

A JUROR: So you think he would know, then, that that was your tie.

THE WITNESS: He should know.

A JUROR: Which brings to mind when the first appearance by Nel, when he came testify—

THE WITNESS: Yes.

A JUROR: Can you tell me what your thoughts were when you saw the pictures of Nelvis wearing the first tie that you gave the President?

THE WITNESS: Yes. Actually, you know what? I think my cup's leaking. I'm sorry.

A JUROR: Do we have another cup up there?

THE WITNESS: Am I allowed to know people's names in here?

MR. EMMICK: The answer to that is no.

THE WITNESS: Oh—

MR. EMMICK: I know it seems—

THE WITNESS: It's so awkward.

MR. EMMICK: It does seem awkward, but I think it's better if—

THE WITNESS: Okay.

MR. EMMICK:— the record not have any identifications.

THE WITNESS: Okay.

MR. EMMICK: We didn't intentionally get you a dribble glass.

THE WITNESS: Oh, sure. At least it's water and not grape juice.

I had two very different thoughts. My first thought was "You jerk. You're trying to show me how little you care about me and how little this meant to you by giving it—to show me that you gave it to someone else, it meant so little to you now."

And my second thought was that it was sort of some sort of message of some sorts. I don't know what. Because I could see the President kind of saying to Nel, you know, "Oh, why don't you—" I could even see him spilling something on Nel on purpose and—that morning and then sort of saying, "Oh, here, just wear this tie," or something like that. I mean, that's—it's—he's funny that way. But I thought there was some sort of deliberateness to it.

I don't know that Nel knew that, that that was the tie I gave the President but—I don't think it was a coincidence.

MR. EMMICK: Yes, ma'am?

A JUROR: Could one of your thoughts perhaps have been that maybe he just gave him a batch of ties to Nelvis? And maybe he didn't remember?

THE WITNESS: No.

A JUROR: You really think he would have remembered that first tie?

THE WITNESS: I know he did. I mean, we—we—that was—I don't know if you all know this or not, but I worked in a men's necktie store when I was in college for four years and so that was my thing, that was part—you know, my spending money, a lot of it came from working. And so I love ties.

And I—I mean, I can pick out—you know, different designers and stuff. And so that was a big thing for me. And then—and I liked to give him ties and I liked to see him wearing them.

A JUROR: Do you know how much impact Nel had on what the President wore each day?

THE WITNESS: None. To my understanding. Nel was. My understanding is that Nel's strictly in the—while he would go to the residence on occasions, that he was usually in the oval area.

MR. EMMICK: There's a question waiting for a bit here. Yes.

A JUROR: Ms. Lewinsky, was it the President's nature to give his ties away?

251

THE WITNESS: Yes. I knew that—I knew that he had given Nel ties, his ties in the past. But ties were such a big issue between the President and me that I really couldn't have imagined that he didn't—that he didn't know.

A JUROR: Other people other than Nel as well, in terms of giving his ties away?

THE WITNESS: I don't know.

A JUROR: Okay. You just—

THE WITNESS: I'm not aware of anyone else, but that doesn't mean there aren't.

A JUROR: Okay.

THE WITNESS: Right.

A JUROR: But you did know about that.

THE WITNESS: Yes.

A JUROR: Do you happen to know whether the President had a valet to assist him in his dressing?

THE WITNESS: Assist him in his dressing, I don't know. I know that there's a valet.

A JUROR: Or like prepare—Mr. President, this suit goes with this tie, kind of thing?

THE WITNESS: I don't know that necessarily, but I have seen—I had seen evidence enough that he could wear my ties when he wanted to. You know. That if he wanted to, he could go pick it out, so I don't know what his getting dressed routine is.

A JUROR: Okay. Thank you.

A JUROR: Okay. I have a question that's a bit on the delicate side.

THE WITNESS: Okay.

A JUROR: But this is just something that I need to know.

THE WITNESS: Sure.

A JUROR: Did you and the President ever engage in sexual relations using cigars?

THE WITNESS: Yes.

A JUROR: Okay.

A JUROR: Okay. I'd like to change the subject now.

THE WITNESS: Thank you. Just once. Just once.

A JUROR: When you last testified, you told us that photographs that you saw of the President and First Lady when they were away that were romantic in nature upset you.

When you had an opportunity to speak with the President about those photographs or any film that was taken during these romantic moments, what did he say? Why they were—because I'm just curious as to whether or not they were staged because of the legal things that were going on with the President at that time.

THE WITNESS: Right. I don't believe we discussed them. I know that that upset me and sort of put me in a bit of a contentious mood when I spoke with him on the 5th. I think it was the 5th of January of this year. And I may have said something in passing about them, but we didn't have a discussion about the pictures.

A JUROR: Okay. I was just wondering if there were—

THE WITNESS: Sure. No. I wondered, too.

A JUROR: Did you think any conversations to him about his wife were inappropriate?

THE WITNESS: I don't know if inappropriate is the right word. I tried not to.

252

I—there were very few discussions and I tended to say things like, "Well, when you're alone," you know, "Call me when you're alone," kind of a thing or, you know, that was how we discussed sort of Mrs. Clinton maybe not being there, was, "Well, I'll be alone on this day. Shall I—" I think we were careful—or I was careful, I know I was.

MR. EMMICK: Yes, ma'am?

A JUROR: Ms. Lewinsky, I wondered if you ever had any trouble with the Secret Service in trying to be near the President.

THE WITNESS: No. The only time that I remember was when I went to see him on the last time in '96, I guess it was April 7th, Easter. And when John Muskett was outside and he said he was going to check with Evelyn if I could go in and then I don't remember exactly how it happened, but I sort of—I don't remember the exact discussion, but it ended up he ended up not talking to Evelyn and I went in. So—

A JUROR: I have a question about Linda Tripp.

THE WITNESS: Ugh. Sorry.

A JUROR: In your conversations with Ms. Tripp, was her opinion always that she must be truthful or was there a time where your impression was that she was going to provide you with cooperation as far as keeping the secrecy?

THE WITNESS: There are two areas of that, I guess. Linda always told me she would always protect me and she would never tell anybody and keep my secret, up until the Paula Jones case came about.

And I had never had any reason to think that she would ever need to discuss this under oath because I was certainly always going to deny it and I couldn't even imagine a situation where that would really come up.

But there was a point in the period prior to my learning about her being subpoenaed in the Paula Jones case, most specifically, January 9th, when she led me to believe that she was not going to tell about my relationship and that she was going to be vague on the truth about Kathleen Willey and was just not going to really remember anything else and that was why I agreed to meet with her on Tuesday the 13th.

A JUROR: In your conversations with her as you were making your move to move to New York and what have you, did you ever get the sense that she was fishing for offers of benefits or the protection of her job? You know, or where she was hoping that nothing would affect her job or if there was something in it for her?

THE WITNESS: Yes and no. When you asked me the question, the first thing that comes to my mind was it may not be directly related to that.

When the Kathleen Willey incident had come out in Newsweek, there was a period after it, Bob Bennett had referred to—or had made that comment about Linda Tripp and she made some off-comment about if she loses her job she's going to write a tell-all book.

And so I sort of—that was an instance where I felt I needed to assure her that that wasn't going to happen, she wasn't going to lose her job, and that—I certainly tried to make assurances. I mean, I—I promised—I would have promised her the moon if I could deliver it.

And then also—then when I spoke with her on the 9th, she talked about that she had spent some time in New York during Christmas and that she—that someone had suggested to her that she get a job doing public relations in New York.

And that seemed a little bit strange to me, in that that was exactly what I was in the process of doing, and that maybe that was what she thought, that somehow then—you know, I think I told her, oh, I'd try to help her come to New York and try to help her that way, but I don't know that—that I ever said anything directly about who would help her.

A JUROR: Okay. Thank you.

BY MR. EMMICK:

Q I'd like to ask a clarifying follow-up because I wasn't sure I understood all of the sort of ins and outs, if you will, of when Linda was going to maintain the secret and when she was going to reveal it. It sounded like prior to the time when Linda got a Paula Jones subpoena, your understanding was she was doing to keep the secret.

A Correct.

Q And then after she got the Paula Jones subpoena, then she told you that she was going to disclose things and tell the truth. Is that right?

A Yes. Yes.

Q Okay. And then in this conversation on January 9th, she indicated some willingness to consider keeping the secret a bit longer.

A No, considered that she was going to do that.

Q That she was going to. All right. That's what I wanted to clarify.

A Sure.

MR. EMMICK: Thank you.

A JUROR: When you said that in your conversations with Linda Tripp you kind of had to exaggerate some things about the President to her, you exaggerated on some of the things you said to her about the President—

THE WITNESS: I'm not sure about that. I—I don't know if exaggerate is the right—is maybe the word I would choose.

A JUROR: Okay.

THE WITNESS: But go on. I'm sorry.

A JUROR: Well, no, I just used that word.

THE WITNESS: Okay.

A JUROR: Exaggerate. You didn't use it, but I couldn't think of the exact words you used.

THE WITNESS: Sure.

A JUROR: But were you—why do you think that you had to not tell her some things that did actually happen, true things, in talking to her?

THE WITNESS: That really came about in relation to the Paula Jones case. I think that I was—there were some occasions, one in particular that I remember, when I didn't disclose a contact that I had with the President— I'm sorry, here—I'll scoot over—contact that I had with the President to her for some reasons, but after the Paula Jones case, I was scared to death. I mean, I was panicked that she was going to tell.

So, I mean, I—I—you know, along the lines of, you know, some of the things I said about Mr. Jordan, I said, you know, "Oh, the President told me I have to lie," I don't even remember everything I said, but I know that there were certainly lies at that point, not even exaggerations.

MR. EMMICK: Actually, I was going to ask that clarifying follow-up to that.

THE FOREPERSON: And then after that, we have to take a break.

MR. EMMICK: And then we'll take a break.

BY MR. EMMICK:

Q The clarifying follow-up was that I had understood that during that January period when you were talking to Linda Tripp you were lying to her on occasion, but I wasn't clear whether those lies related to times that you had been with the President or whether they related to other things generally. Do you understand what my question is?

A No.

Q What were the nature of the lies that you were telling to Linda Tripp during that January period?

A Oh, gosh. They went from—I guess a non-disclosure of my meeting with him on the 28th, nor my phone call with him on the 5th of January, to—ranging to things that he said I had to do or told me to do.

I haven't—I haven't seen transcripts of those days, thank goodness, but I just know that I was—I was scared to death. And I thought any influence that anybody would have, my mother, Mr. Jordan, the President, anybody, would—I used.

MR. EMMICK: All right.

THE FOREPERSON: It's break time.

MR. EMMICK: Break time.

THE FOREPERSON: It's break time. It's break time.

A JUROR: I have a follow-up to that as well.

THE FOREPERSON: Okay. So we're going to take ten minutes.

THE WITNESS: Okay.

THE FOREPERSON: And we'll come back.

A JUROR: I hope I remember my question.

THE WITNESS: Can you guys call me Monica?

Are they allowed to call me Monica instead of Ms. Lewinsky? I was just—

THE FOREPERSON: If you say so.

THE WITNESS: Okay.

MR. EMMICK: Sure.

THE WITNESS: I'm just 25. Please.

A JUROR: But you'll always be Ms. Lewinsky, whether you're 25 or 28 or—

THE WITNESS: Not if I get married.

(Witness excused. Witness recalled.)

THE FOREPERSON: Monica, I'd like to remind that you are still under oath.

THE WITNESS: Thank you.

MR. EMMICK: We have a quorum and there are no unauthorized persons present. Is that right?

THE FOREPERSON: You are absolutely correct.

MR. EMMICK: Lucky this time.

THE WITNESS: Thank you.

MR. EMMICK: Did you want to ask some follow-up questions?

MS. IMMERGUT: Yes.

BY MS. IMMERGUT:

Q Ms. Lewinsky, there are two things I wanted to clarify. First, with respect to the tie disclosure issue—

A Yes.

Q —you were asked about before, I believe you mentioned something to the effect that there have been things that have come out of your team that you were surprised about before. Are you referring to your current legal team?

A No. My first legal team.

Q Okay. And that's Mr. Ginsberg?

A Yes.

Q Okay. You're not aware of any unauthorized disclosures from your current camp?

A No. Nor have I authorized any disclosures.

Q Okay. So you didn't authorize a disclosure about the tie.

A No.

Q With respect to—to switch gears—to what we were speaking about right before the break about the things that you said to Linda Tripp at the very end, particularly on January 13, 1998, I believe—

A Yes.

Q You mentioned that an example of things that you were not truthful about was, for example, the fact you had seen the President on December 28th and that you had spoken to him on January 5th. Is that correct?

A Right. Yes. And I didn't disclose that to her.

Q Right. You did not disclose that to her.

A Quite to the contrary.

Q Okay. In fact, you told her that you hadn't seen or spoken to the President for two months.

A Or since the 17th of December.

Q Okay.

A Exactly.

Q You mentioned that there was—you also said things about what the President had said to you to Ms. Tripp that were not true on January 13th. Do you remember any specific things that you said that the President had told you that in fact were not true?

A No. I don't remember any specifics, I just wanted to leave open the possibility. Does that clarify it?

MR. EMMICK: On the right here?

A JUROR: Monica, why did you keep that black dress?

A JUROR: Blue.

A JUROR: Blue dress.

A JUROR: Did you have a reason to keep it?

THE WITNESS: Pardon?

A JUROR: The blue dress.

A JUROR: The blue dress.

THE WITNESS: No. I didn't have a reason. The—reason—the dress—I didn't realize—if I remember correctly, I didn't really realize that there was anything on it until I went to go wear it again and I had gained too much weight that I couldn't fit into it.

And it seemed sort of funny and I—it may sound silly, I have a lot of clothes. I don't clean all my clothes right after I wear them, I usually don't clean them until I know I'm going to wear them again. And then I was going to wear it for Thanksgiving because I had lost weight and I had—I had shown the dress to Linda at that point and had just sort of said to her, "Well, isn't this—" You know, "Isn't this stupid?" Or, you know, "Look at this, isn't this gross?" Or whatever. I don't really remember exactly what I said.

And she told me that I should put it in a safe deposit box because it could be evidence one day.

And I said that was ludicrous because I would never—I would never disclose that I had a relationship with the President, I would never need it.

And then when Thanksgiving time came around and I told her that I was going to wear it for Thanksgiving, she told me I looked fat in the dress, I shouldn't wear it. She brought me a jacket from her closet as to try to persuade me not to wear the dress.

So I ended up not wearing it and then I was going to clean it. I took it with me up to New York and was going to clean it up there and then this broke, so—

A JUROR: Okay. Your relationship with the President, did your mother at any time try to discourage the relationship?

THE WITNESS: Oh, yes.

A JUROR: Well, what kept it going? I mean, what kept it—you keeping it active or whatever?

THE WITNESS: I fell in love.

A JUROR: I beg your pardon? I couldn't hear you.

THE WITNESS: I fell in love.

A JUROR: When you look at it now, was it love or a sexual obsession?

THE WITNESS: More love with a little bit of obsession. But definitely love.

A JUROR: Did you think that the President was in love with you also?

THE WITNESS: There was an occasion when I left the White House and I was pretty stunned at how I felt because I did think that.

A JUROR: You did?

BY MR. EMMICK:

Q Do you remember the date?

A It was July 4, 1997.

A JUROR: Were you aware that he was having problems in his marriage? Did this ever spill over in the times that you were together? Did you get a feeling that something was not right, that—

MR. EMMICK: I thought there was a question in the front here.

A JUROR: And today, Monica, do you still love the President?

THE WITNESS: Before Monday, I would have said yes.

A JUROR: So then it is no?

THE WITNESS: I don't know how I feel right now.

MR. EMMICK: A question in the front?

A JUROR: I guess I would like to know what happened Monday to make you just by Thursday change your mind so completely.

THE WITNESS: I don't think it's so much changed my mind. I think—it's—it was very painful for me to watch his speech on Monday night. I—it's—it's hard for me to feel that he has characterized this relationship as a service contract and that that was never something that I ever thought it was. And—

A JUROR: I'm sorry, you lost me already.

THE WITNESS: I'm sorry. I'm sorry. It's—from my understanding about what he testified to on Monday, not—just from the press accounts, is that this was a—that this was a service contract, that all I did was perform oral sex on him and that that's all that this relationship was. And it was a lot more than that to me and I thought it was a lot more than that.

And I think I felt—I was hurt that—that he didn't even—sort of acknowledge me in his remarks. And even also—I mean, that has to do with directly with me, but I thought he should have acknowledged all the other people that have gone through a lot of pain for seven months. I feel very responsible for a lot of what's happened, you know, in the seven months, but I tried—I tried very hard to do what I could to not—to not hurt him. I'm still not answering your question.

A JUROR: Well, let's—you said the relationship was more than oral sex. I mean, it wasn't like you went out on dates or anything like that like normal people, so what more was it?

THE WITNESS: Oh, we spent hours on the phone talking. It was emotional.

A JUROR: Phone sex?

THE WITNESS: Not always. On a few occasions. I mean, we were talking. I mean, interacting. I mean, talking about what we were thinking and feeling and doing and laughing.

We were very affectionate, even when—after he broke the relationship off in May, I mean, when I'd go to visit with him, we'd—you know, we'd hug each other a lot. You know, he always used to like to stroke my hair. He—we'd hold hands. We'd smile a lot. We discussed a variety—you know, a wide range of things.

So, I mean, it was—there was a real component of a relationship to it and I just—I thought he had a beautiful soul. I just thought he was just this incredible person and when I looked at him I saw a little boy and—I don't know what the truth is any more.

And that's, I think, what I took away on Monday, was that I didn't know what the truth was. And so how could I know the truth of my love for someone if it was based on him being an actor.

A JUROR: I'd like to ask you about Bayani Nelvis.

THE WITNESS: Okay.

A JUROR: How much about your relationship with the President did Bayani Nelvis know?

THE WITNESS: I think he knew that—that we were friends and that I would come to see the President and I gave him things. I don't know—I don't remember ever getting into any specific details. Might he have thought that from—you know, from how much I kind of liked the President? I'm not sure.

But—and I don't mean this in a racist way, you know, Nel's from another country and so his English is—while his English is good, it's not perfect, not that anyone's is perfect, so I think that sometimes there was a little bit of a language barrier there, too, so I think he—you know, Nel was just a— is a really nice guy. He's a sweet guy and he—he's very loyal to the President.

A JUROR: Did you ever tell him at any time that you loved the President?

THE WITNESS: I don't think so, but I might have, but I don't think so.

A JUROR: Okay.

MR. EMMICK: Yes? A question?

A JUROR: You just mentioned real components, the relationship was—like a real component, you mentioned things like truth. But sometimes I go back and forth not understanding because you yourself were living a lot of secrets, a lot of lies, a lot of paranoia, but yet you wanted truth, a real component?

I'm not understanding these two different things because one time you're sentimental but then again you do just the opposite of what you say you're thinking.

Did you ever think that nothing real could come of this relationship?

THE WITNESS: Did I ever thing nothing real—

A JUROR: Anything real, that anything real could—and truthful and honest could have come from this relationship?

THE WITNESS: Yes.

A JUROR: With this married man?

THE WITNESS: I did.

A JUROR: But I have a question for you about that.

THE WITNESS: Mm-hmm.

A JUROR: It's been reported in the papers that you had a relationship before similar to this, where a lot of hurt and pain came out of this, you know, a lot of hurt and pain toward a family.

And then you turn around and you do it again. You're young, you're vibrant, I can't figure out why you keep going after things that aren't free, that aren't obtainable.

THE WITNESS: Well, there's sort of two parts to that and just to clarify, the— the way Andy and Kate Bleiler portrayed everything on TV and through their lawyer was pretty inaccurate, so I don't know how much of that is part of your question.

A JUROR: The only part I know is that he was a married man with a wife and a family.

THE WITNESS: That's true.

A JUROR: Like I know about the President.

THE WITNESS: Mm-hmm.

A JUROR: He was a married man and it wasn't no secret of that fact. But yet you want to talk about truth, a real component, honesty. It all seems so— like a fantasy. That's why I asked you earlier about obsession.

THE WITNESS: That's a hard question to answer because obviously there's— there's work that I need to do on myself. There are obviously issues that— that—you know, a single young woman doesn't have an affair with a married man because she's normal, quote-unquote. But I think most people have issues and that's just how mine manifested themselves.

It's something I need to work on and I don't think it's right, it's not right to have an affair with a married man. I never expected to fall in love with the President. I was surprised that I did.

And I didn't—my intention had really been to come to Washington and start over and I didn't want to have another affair with a married man because it was really painful. It was horrible. And I feel even worse about it now.

A JUROR: Monica, I'd like to change the topic, if I can.

THE WITNESS: Did I answer—

A JUROR: Yes.

THE WITNESS: Okay.

A JUROR: And I also—I want to let you know that we're not here to judge you in any way, I think many of us feel that way.

THE WITNESS: I appreciate that. But I understand that every—you know, this is—this is a topic that—there are a lot of people think it's wrong and I think it's wrong, too. I understand that.

A JUROR: I had to ask that you question because I've had to ask other questions and it wouldn't have been right for me not to ask you the question—

THE WITNESS: Sure.

A JUROR: —that I've had to ask—

THE WITNESS: I think it's fair and I think you should—I think it's a fair question. It's a hard one to answer. No one likes to have their weaknesses splayed out for the entire world, you know, but I understand that. And I'd rather you understand where I'm coming from, you know, and you'd probably have to know me better and know my whole journey to how I got here from birth to now to really understand it. I don't even understand it. But—I understand. I respect your having to ask that question and I appreciate what you're saying, whatever your name is.

A JUROR: We're here only to assess the credibility of your testimony.

THE WITNESS: Sure. But I—I can see how that would be a factor.

A JUROR: I wanted to go back to the issue of ties. It's my understanding that you testified earlier this morning that your agreement, your immunity agreement, with the Office of the Independent Counsel includes an understanding that you—that you and your legal team need prior approval to disseminate information to the press.

THE WITNESS: Mm-hmm.

A JUROR: And in looking over Exhibit ML-2, I don't see that provision. Can you look at that?

THE WITNESS: Is that my agreement?

A JUROR: Yes.

THE WITNESS: Sure.

MR. EMMICK: Sure.

THE WITNESS: I know that portion of it very well.

A JUROR: I may be missing something.

THE WITNESS: There have been many times I've wanted to defend myself and the lies that have been spewed out.

MR. EMMICK: I think the reference is to part 1B.

A JUROR: Okay.

MR. EMMICK: Where it says "Will not make any statements—" "Neither Ms. Lewinsky nor her agents will make any statements about this matter to witnesses, subjects, or targets of the OIC's investigation or their agents or to representatives of the news media without first obtaining the OIC's approval."

A JUROR: Okay. Thank you.

THE WITNESS: Sure.

MR. EMMICK: Other questions? Yes, ma'am?

A JUROR: I'd also like to return for a minute—if you have that package out— to something that was discussed this morning, earlier this morning, and that refers to your proffer. Do you have a copy of the proffer? The proffer?

MR. EMMICK: We do. Sure.

THE WITNESS: Okay.

MR. EMMICK: I'm placing Exhibit ML-1 before the witness.

THE WITNESS: Thank you.

A JUROR: Monica, if you could look at paragraph 11, I'm not sure what page it is, but it's paragraph 11.

THE WITNESS: Okay. Yes. Okay.

A JUROR: As I understood our discussion this morning, you said that you offered to deny the relationship and the President didn't discourage you, but said something like "That's good."

As I read your proffer here, it says "The President told Ms. L to deny a relationship if ever asked." And that seems to me slightly different.

THE WITNESS: I forgot this. So that's true.

A JUROR: Is this proffer statement correct, that he did tell you to deny a relationship?

THE WITNESS: Yes. I don't—I don't—when I answered the question earlier, that was what first came to my mind. But, I mean, I know that this is true.

I just at that point—and I—really reading it, I know it's true because I was truthful in my proffer, but sitting here right now, I can't remember exactly when it was, but it was something that was certainly discussed between us.

A JUROR: And what about the next sentence also? Something to the effect that if two people who are involved say it didn't happen, it didn't happen. Do you recall him saying that to you?

THE WITNESS: Sitting here today, very vaguely. I can hear—I have a weird— I'll explain to you guys that I have a weird sense of—for me, my saying I remember something, if I can see it in my mind's eye or I can hear him saying it to me, then I feel pretty comfortable saying that that's pretty accurate, that I remember that. And I can hear his voice saying that to me, I just can't place it.

A JUROR: Is it—

THE WITNESS: And this was—I mean, this was early—this was all throughout our relationship. I mean, it was—obviously not something that we discussed too often, I think, because it was—it's a somewhat unpleasant thought of having to deny it, having it even come to that point, but—

A JUROR: Is it possible that you also had these discussions after you learned that you were a witness in the Paula Jones case?

THE WITNESS: I don't believe so. No.

A JUROR: Can you exclude that possibility?

THE WITNESS: I pretty much can. I really don't remember it. I mean, it would be very surprising to me to be confronted with something that would show me different, but I—it was 2:30 in the—I mean, the conversation I'm thinking of mainly would have been December 17th, which was—

A JUROR: The telephone call.

THE WITNESS: Right. And it was—you know, 2:00, 2:30 in the morning. I remember the gist of it and I—I really don't think so.

A JUROR: Thank you.

A JUROR: I have some questions about the Paula Jones lawsuit. Going back to the period before you even had any idea that you might be a witness in that, did you follow the Paula Jones lawsuit fairly closely?

THE WITNESS: I followed it. I don't know "fairly closely," but—I think it maybe depended more on was there something in the paper and that happened to be a day that I sat and read all the papers because I had nothing to do.

I did follow it, but I wasn't—I didn't follow it as much as I follow this case. I mean, in terms of—no, but I mean, I'm just saying as a gauge, you know.

A JUROR: So you were holding down a full-time job and everything at that time, but you did read the papers—

THE WITNESS: I did read the papers every day and it was—sure, I followed it. I didn't know the ins and outs of it, but I followed it.

A JUROR: Did you—in that period again, even before anyone knew that you would be a witness, did you discuss that with the President? Was he aware that you followed it? Was that something—

THE WITNESS: No. Really, the time that I remember we discussed it was on the 17th.

A JUROR: December 17th?

THE WITNESS: And when I told him my sort of stupid idea for how he should settle it. So that was—but, no. He wasn't—we didn't—I—and I think in general just to give you guys a flavor, because there have been different subjects that have come up, when we spent time together, I know I certainly made an effort—unless I was angry with him about something, that there were topics that I wanted to stay away from and the time that I spent with him was precious to me. So things that were unpleasant I didn't bring up unless I had to.

A JUROR: Exactly what date again did you get your subpoena to be a witness?

THE WITNESS: The 19th of December.

A JUROR: The 19th? Okay. Now, when—and if you could retell for me the conversation you had with the President about the gifts.

THE WITNESS: Okay. It was December 28th and I was there to get my Christmas gifts from him. Excuse me. I'm sorry. And we spent maybe about five minutes or so, not very long, talking about the case. And I said to him, "Well, do you think—"

What I mentioned—I said to him that it had really alarmed me about the hat pin being in the subpoena and I think he said something like, "Oh," you know, "that sort of bothered me, too. That bothered me," you know, "That bothers me." Something like that.

And at one point, I said, "Well, do you think I should—" I don't think I said "get rid of," I said, "But do you think I should put away or maybe give to Betty or give to someone the gifts?"

And he—I don't remember his response. I think it was something like, "I don't know," or "Hmm" or—there really was no response.

I know that I didn't leave the White House with any notion of what I should do with them, that I should do anything different than that they were sitting in my house. And then later I got the call from Betty.

A JUROR: Now, did you bring up Betty's name or did the President bring up Betty's name?

THE WITNESS: I think I brought it up. The President wouldn't have brought up Betty's name because he really didn't—he didn't really discuss it, so either I brought up Betty's name, which I think is probably what happened, because I remember not being too, too shocked when Betty called.

Somewhat surprised, I guess, that he hadn't said—you know, it would have seemed easier to sort of have said something maybe then, but I wasn't too surprised when she called.

A JUROR: Thank you.

MR. EMMICK: I think there was a question in the front. Did you have a question?

MS. IMMERGUT: Did you have a question?

A JUROR: Yes. Back to the contacts?

THE WITNESS: Yes.

A JUROR: On page 7, on the 29th of March—

THE WITNESS: On the—sorry, what date?

A JUROR: The 29th of March. Sunday.

MR. EMMICK: Then 29th of March.

THE WITNESS: Okay.

A JUROR: "Private encounter, approximately 1:30 or 2:00 p.m., study. President on crutches. Physical intimacy including oral sex to completion and brief direct genital contact." Brief direct genital contact, could you just elaborate on that a bit?

THE WITNESS: Uh—

A JUROR: I understand—

THE WITNESS: Oh, my gosh. This is so embarrassing.

A JUROR: You could close your eyes and talk.

A JUROR: We won't look at you.

THE WITNESS: Can I hide under the table? Uh—I had—I had wanted—I tried to—I placed his genital next to mine and had hoped that if he—oh—this is just too embarrassing. I don't—

A JUROR: Did you think it would lead to intercourse?

THE WITNESS: Not on that day.

A JUROR: Was that sort of the reason for doing the gesture—

THE WITNESS: Yes.

A JUROR: —or trying to—moving his closer to yours?

THE WITNESS: Then I—not that we would have intercourse that day, but that that might make him want to.

A JUROR: Okay. Were you wearing clothes at the time or underwear at the time?

THE WITNESS: No.

A JUROR: And was he? Or his were pulled down?

THE WITNESS: Correct.

A JUROR: So was there direct skin-to-skin contact between your genitals and his?

THE WITNESS: I think very briefly. It was—he—he's really tall and he couldn't really bend because of his knee, so it was—

A JUROR: It was more of a grazing?

THE WITNESS: Yes.

A JUROR: About how many encounters did you have in the study? If you can recall.

MR. EMMICK: What do you mean by "encounters"?

A JUROR: Sexual encounters. I'm sorry.

THE WITNESS: Do you include kissing or not?

A JUROR: No kissing. According to the definition.

THE WITNESS: Okay. Two.

A JUROR: Okay. Thank you.

BY MS. IMMERGUT:

Q And why don't you give us the dates of those.

A The—well, let me look. The 29th of March and the 28th of February. There might have been—I mean, in terms of the clothes and stuff, there might have been playful touches here and there, but not—nothing that I would have considered sexual encounters.

Q   And that's not listed as an intimate encounter?

A   No. No, it's not. No, it's not.

Q   And just to clarify again, are those the two times that the President actually came to completion during the oral sex?

A   Yes.

BY MR. EMMICK:

Q   And I'm actually obliged to ask one follow up that I don't think will be too bad, but directing your attention to August 16th, did you attempt to touch the President on that day?

A   Yes.

Q   And did you actually touch him? In his groin area?

A   Over his clothes.

Q   Over his clothes. And did he say that's not—"We can't do that"?

A   Yes.

MR. EMMICK: Okay.

A JUROR: Did you feel any rejection the times that he wouldn't go all the way with you?

THE WITNESS: Yes.

A JUROR: Monica, I had one question to go back to the gifts. You had said that the President had called you initially to come get your Christmas gift, you had gone there, you had a talk, et cetera, and there was no—you expressed concern, the President really didn't say anything. How much later in the afternoon did you get a call from Betty? It was that same day, is that correct?

THE WITNESS: Yes, that's correct. Let me just clarify real quickly that I had made the arrangements to go there on Sunday through Betty, just that you had said he called me.

A JUROR: So you had initiated the contact on that day?

THE WITNESS: He had—he had told me on the 17th that he—you know, he still had these Christmas gifts for me and then—just shortly after Christmas and I called Betty and said, you know, "He said he had something for me," something like that, you know. And then she arranged it. So I just wanted to clarify.

A JUROR: And then how much of a time gap—

THE WITNESS: A few hours, maybe.

A JUROR: A few hours?

THE WITNESS: Maybe—I think it was around 2:00 p.m. or so, around 2:00 in the afternoon, and I had gone there at 8:30 in the morning and left—I'd say maybe four or five hours time span.

A JUROR: So what exactly happened? You went home and you packaged these gifts? Or had you already had them packaged?

THE WITNESS: No. I went home and I—I think I went to New York that evening, possibly, so I was getting ready to go to New York, I think, or something.

But when Betty called, then she said, you know, "I understand you have something to give me." It was very vague. And I understood—I mean, to me, that meant from this conversation that we had had that I should sort of—you know, give some of the gifts.

So I put them all out on my bed and—it's sort of been difficult to kind of explain why I put some things in and why I didn't put others in.

The things that seemed to be directly called for in the subpoena, I put in a box: the hat pin, the dress from Martha's Vineyard, some of the pictures and things, the ad to him from Valentine's Day. Not that that was directly called for, but some of the more intimate—I guess personal things, except that I kept the "Leaves of Grass" book because that just—I was worried, I didn't know if I would get the gifts back or not, ever, and so I—that just—that meant the most to me of anything he gave me.

A JUROR: And I believe your testimony last time was that you did not believe that Betty knew the contents of the package?

THE WITNESS: I don't believe so.

A JUROR: She just came and picked them up and that was it?

THE WITNESS: We chit-chatted for a little bit. She was on the way to see her mom in the hospital, so I got her a small plant to just take to her mom and—

BY MS. IMMERGUT:

Q Did she seem at all confused when you handed over the box?

A No.

Q Did she ask you what was in it?

A No. Not that I remember. I don't believe so.

MS. IMMERGUT: Thank you.

A JUROR: And just to back up for a second on your conversation with the President that you already discussed a little bit where you said you were concerned about the subpoena and some of the items that it called for such as the hat pin which indeed the President had given you, you testified previously, I believe, that the President said he was concerned about that also when he saw the hat pin. Is that correct?

THE WITNESS: I don't know that he saw—I don't know that he saw the hat pin on the—I don't know that he saw the subpoena, so—I know that the hat pin was a concern to him.

A JUROR: Okay. Do you remember what he said in response when you said you were concerned about the things called for in the subpoena?

THE WITNESS: I think he said something like "That concerned me, too."

A JUROR: Okay.

THE WITNESS: So I don't know if he saw it or someone—you know, I don't know he learned that.

A JUROR: Okay. But he appeared to have some prior knowledge of—

THE WITNESS: I think so. I think so.

A JUROR: I have another question about that conversation on the 28th. You had already discussed with him earlier the subpoena and the fact that all of your gifts from him were under subpoena and then—

THE WITNESS: We hadn't discussed that. I wasn't—I hadn't—the 28th was the first time that I saw him or spoke to him since I had been subpoenaed. When he called me on the 17th, I wasn't yet subpoenaed.

A JUROR: Okay. Okay. So that conversation took place on the 28th?

THE WITNESS: Correct. The only conversation about gifts and the subpoena, really—yes.

A JUROR: And on that same day, he gave you Christmas gifts.

THE WITNESS: Yes.

A JUROR: What was your thinking at that time about that? Did that concern you or—

THE WITNESS: No.

A JUROR: No?

THE WITNESS: I was—

A JUROR: Did you—what did you plan to do with those gifts? Did it cross your mind that some— that you should maybe give some of them to your attorney as responsive to the subpoena or—

THE WITNESS: No.

A JUROR: No?

MR. EMMICK: I have a quick clarifying question because you said that the only conversation you had with him about gifts after the subpoena was on the 28th. You also had a conversation with him on the 5th that related to the later gift of the book, if I remember it right.

THE WITNESS: Right. I meant my gifts that he gave to me.

MR. EMMICK: Right. Right. Right. I just wanted to clarify that.

THE WITNESS: Okay. Sure.

MR. EMMICK: Other questions?

A JUROR: Going back to your conversation with Linda Tripp—

MR. EMMICK: Which one?

THE WITNESS: Yes. Which tape are you referring to?

A JUROR: No, I'm just going to be general.

MR. EMMICK: Okay.

A JUROR: If you had to put it like percentage-wise, what you told her as being truthful and not truthful, what percentage will be not truthful?

THE WITNESS: I would say before the subpoena, before I found out she had been subpoenaed, so for argument's sake maybe saying before December of '97, I'd say 95 percent accurate. There were some things that I didn't tell her, but I usually pretty much told her everything.

A JUROR: You started talking to her when? In '95 or '96?

THE WITNESS: I first told her—when I first told her about the relationship or when I started talking to her as a person?

A JUROR: The relationship.

THE WITNESS: The relationship, I told her in November of '96. After the election.

A JUROR: Okay. So from November '96 to December '97—

THE WITNESS: Pretty truthful.

A JUROR: And then after '97?

THE WITNESS: Oh—

BY MR. EMMICK:

Q Could I ask just one clarifying matter about that answer? Because you had said that it was 95 percent accurate and then you also said because sometimes I didn't tell her everything. And I just want to make sure we're being clear on whether you're talking about being complete or being accurate.

In other words, are you not telling her things or are you saying things to her that are inaccurate, sort of in that 5 percent, if you will?

A Well, I don't remember the exact situations or the times that I didn't tell her something, if she had asked me about it, I would have been inaccurate about what I said.

Q All right. I see.

A So—

Q So there's kind of a blending of those two concepts.

A Correct.

BY MS. IMMERGUT:

Q And, again, to clarify, did you ever lie about your sexual relationship with the President?

266

A No.

MR. EMMICK: I'm sorry. I interrupted. I didn't mean to.

A JUROR: So after '97, then—

THE WITNESS: After December '97, I don't even know how to—how to put a percentage to that.

A JUROR: Any truth at all after '97?

THE WITNESS: Yes. There were some truths in December of '97. There certainly were some true statements, but there were a lot of untrue statements. Probably the untrue statements stick out in my mind more because they caused so much trouble.

A JUROR: Which ones stick out in your mind as having been untruthful?

THE WITNESS: Stuff about my mom. Just—a lot of different things about my mom. That I had—that I told Mr. Jordan I wouldn't sign the affidavit until I got a job. That was definitely a lie, based on something Linda had made me promise her on January 9th. Some of the other things—

A JUROR: Did you tell Linda Tripp at any time that you had heard or understood that people don't go to jail for perjury in a civil case?

THE WITNESS: Yes, I believe—I think I said that.

A JUROR: Did anybody tell you that?

THE WITNESS: Well, hmm.

A JUROR: Do you want to talk to—I know there's—is there an attorney issue there?

THE WITNESS: There's an attorney issue.

A JUROR: I see.

MR. EMMICK: Do you want to take a break and talk about the attorney issue? Because I think that may be a way to figure out if we can answer that question any more fully.

THE WITNESS: Do you want me to go talk to my attorney?

MR. EMMICK: Well, I just think it might be—I think your attorney would like it if he were to talk to you.

THE WITNESS: Okay.

MR. EMMICK: That's the way to answer it.

THE WITNESS: Okay. So just to be clear, you're—

A JUROR: Well, maybe I can help. Just—if I could confine it to did anyone other than your attorney ever suggest to you that perjury in a civil case would not be prosecuted?

THE WITNESS: Uh—

MS. IMMERGUT: If you need to talk to your attorney, go ahead.

A JUROR: I just thought—did anyone other than your attorney tell you that?

THE WITNESS: No.

MR. EMMICK: I think it still would be advisable to have a more complete answer, to at least let them talk.

THE WITNESS: Okay.

MR. EMMICK: Yes.

THE WITNESS: Excuse me.

(The witness was excused to confer with counsel.)

MR. EMMICK: Do we have a quorum?

THE FOREPERSON: Yes, we do.

MR. EMMICK: And are there any unauthorized persons present?

THE FOREPERSON: Not a one.

MR. EMMICK: All right.

THE WITNESS: And I'm still under oath.

THE FOREPERSON: Yes, you are.

BY MS. IMMERGUT:

Q And just to clarify a couple of things that were right before the break, when you sort of asserted a privilege or had some questions about whether there was a privilege, I did want to ask you just to clarify that with respect to the statement about your lawyer having—or somebody telling you whether or not you can be charged with perjury in a civil case, just to be clear, did Mr. Jordan ever tell you that?

A No.

Q Did Mr. Carter ever tell you that?

A No.

Q And otherwise, I think the question was was it another attorney and I believe that you would like to assert the attorney-client privilege.

A JUROR: No, I think I excluded attorneys from my question.

THE WITNESS: Okay. You know, can I just address—I think sort of the— one of the questions that you had asked me before and I just—about—

A JUROR: Myself?

THE WITNESS: Yes. That you had asked me about the relationship and being untruthful and things like that. And I just—this is something that's sort of been on my mind since this whole thing started.

I have never—I don't—I certainly believe I have ever told a lie to hurt anybody, that I sort of—some of the ways in which I grew up, it was—there were secrets and inherent in a secret is a lie and so I just—you know, I—I just thought I'd tell you that.

A JUROR: Okay.

MR. EMMICK: Other questions?

A JUROR: Ms. Lewinsky, we're going to try, because we feel that we have been jumping around and you've done a very good job of sort of jumping from topic to topic, we're going to try to bunch our questions together around a few topics and our forelady is going to try to play traffic cop, so—

A JUROR: A little bit. No, you go ahead. This is your record. But I'll play traffic cop just a little.

A JUROR: Ms. Lewinsky, before you go into that, I just remember you saying something with Linda Tripp, you know, what was not the truth, okay? And I just remembered, was one of the things that you told her, that you gave your mother the blue dress, one of the untruths or was that true?

THE WITNESS: I don't know if I ever told Linda I gave my mom the blue dress. One of the things I did say was that I gave everything to my mom, so that probably included that and that was not true. I didn't give the evidence to my mom. My mom never hid the dress. She didn't know it was in New York.

A JUROR: Okay.

THE WITNESS: So she didn't know anything about it.

A JUROR: I've got one of those questions that goes along with what she just said.

A JUROR: Okay. Fine. That's the idea. The topic.

A JUROR: How much did your mom really know?

THE WITNESS: She knew—she knew that I was having a relationship with the President. She knew that— she knew that I was certainly emotional about it and that it made me miserable a lot and that sometimes I was elated and sometimes I was miserable, but I didn't—you know, I—I might have said something to her like, "We fooled around," but I—not—she didn't know as much as I led Linda to believe she knew. Is that—

A JUROR: Yes.

THE WITNESS: Okay.

A JUROR: Okay. Any other Linda Tripp questions?

A JUROR: Yes, there's one.

A JUROR: Did you ever suggest to Linda Tripp that she delete e-mails or anything like that from her computer?

THE WITNESS: Yes, I did.

A JUROR: And did you tell her that you had done the same thing?

THE WITNESS: Yes, I believe so.

A JUROR: And did anyone ever suggest to you or tell you that you should do that?

THE WITNESS: No.

A JUROR: Did you tell Linda Tripp that anyone had suggested that to you?

THE WITNESS: I don't think so.

A JUROR: Okay. Thank you.

A JUROR: Any others?

A JUROR: In that end of the year timeframe, did you ever tell Linda Tripp that you felt physically at risk?

THE WITNESS: I think so. I think I told her something about—that—that—I said something about Mary Jo what's-her-name.

A JUROR: Kopechne.

THE WITNESS: Kopechne. And so—I really didn't feel threatened, but I was trying to use anything I could to try to convince her not to tell. So that I thought that if she thought I was threatened and that was part of the reason, then she would maybe do the same.

A JUROR: So you did not at any time feel that your personal security was at risk from the White House or anyone in the White House?

THE WITNESS: No. I think that maybe there—there—maybe once or twice it had crossed my mind in some bizarre way because everybody's heard about the different—you know, sure, there's the Marilyn Monroe theory. And so it—but it was not—it was not any factor of—that related to my actions.

A JUROR: So any discussion that you had about the whole topic with Linda Tripp would fall into what you were describing before as a little bit of fabrication?

THE WITNESS: Yes. Yes.

BY MR. EMMICK:

Q If I could ask a follow-up on that, did your mother ever express any concerns about your safety?

A I think she might have, but it was sort of the—I think it was more general. It might have been a more general sense.

A JUROR: Are there any other questions about personal safety?

A JUROR: Are we still on December? December, January?

A JUROR: Yes.

A JUROR: I have one follow-up question if this is an appropriate time about the gifts. And, again, if you have your proffer there?

THE WITNESS: Yes.

A JUROR: At the top of page 7, where you say in your proffer that when Ms. Currie called later that afternoon she said, at least I think you mean that she said that the President had told her Ms. L wanted her to hold on to

269

something for her. Do you remember Betty Currie saying that the President had told her to call?

THE WITNESS: Right now, I don't. I don't remember, but when I wrote this, I was being truthful.

The other thing, and this is something that I was thinking about this morning in relation to the proffer, that I had written this proffer obviously being truthful, but I think that when I wrote this, it was my understanding that this was to bring me to the step of getting an immunity agreement, and so I think that sometimes to—that I didn't know this was going to become sort of this staple document, I think, for everything, and so there are things that can be misinterpreted from in here, even from me re-reading it, the conditions—some of the conditions maybe under which I wrote it.

So I just thought I should sort of say that, that where—I mean, I know—I certainly was not untruthful or trying to be misleading in this. I didn't think it was going to be—this was my understanding of a written thing that I would—that I would attest to under oath and that it wouldn't be number 7, read this, is this—do you—

BY MR. EMMICK:

Q So it may not be written with legal precision?

A Exactly.

Q But there's no intentional falsehoods in it?

A No.

Q You were trying to be truthful throughout?

A Exactly.

A JUROR: And my purpose in raising it really is to just see whether this might jog your recollection at all as to something you might have recalled back in February that you don't recall today.

THE WITNESS: It doesn't.

A JUROR: It does not?

THE WITNESS: It's possible, but—I—I—it's not my—you know—

A JUROR: Okay.

THE WITNESS: — my memory right now.

A JUROR: Any other questions on that subject?

A JUROR: If we don't have any other questions, I guess the other thing that we wanted to ask you a little bit about is when you were first approached by Mr. Emmick and his colleagues at the OIC.

Can you tell us a little bit about how that happened? That's not a happy topic, either, I apologize.

MR. EMMICK: Maybe if I could ask, what areas do you want to get into? Because there's—you know—many hours of activity—

A JUROR: Well, one specific—okay. One specific question that people have is when did you first learn that Linda Tripp had been taping your phone conversations?

THE WITNESS: I believe that I didn't learn the extent to which she had taped my conversations, until I read it in the press.

I learned that day that she had worn a wire at the lunch and that I—and that there had been other people, I think, in the restaurant that had been listening in and—so I knew—she had—she had said that—that—when I was first apprehended, she was—she had said that they had done the same thing to her and she tried to hug me and she told me this was the best thing for me to do and—oh.

270

MR. EMMICK: Any other specific questions about that day? I just—this was a long day. There were a lot of things that—

A JUROR: We want to know about that day.

A JUROR: That day.

A JUROR: The first question.

A JUROR: Yes.

A JUROR: We really want to know about that day.

MR. EMMICK: All right.

THE WITNESS: Linda was supposed to go see this new attorney that she had claimed she had gotten and was going to try to sign an affidavit so she paged me in the morning, I called her back and she told me she wanted to meet me before she went to see the attorney. So we planned to meet at the Ritz Carlton in the food court at—I think it was quarter to one.

She was late. I saw her come down the escalator. And as I—as I walked toward her, she kind of motioned behind her and Agent ███████ and Agent ███████ presented themselves to me and—

A JUROR: Do you want to take a minute?

THE WITNESS: And flashed their badges at me. They told me that I was under some kind of investigation, something had to do with the Paula Jones case, that they—that they wanted to talk to me and give me a chance, I think, to cooperate, maybe.

I—to help myself. I told them I wasn't speaking to them without my attorney.

They told me that that was fine, but I should know I won't be given as much information and won't be able to help myself as much with my attorney there. So I agreed to go. I was so scared.

(The witness begins crying.)

A JUROR: So, Monica, did you go to a room with them at that time?

THE WITNESS: Yes.

A JUROR: And at that time, did you talk to anybody or what did you do? Did you want to call your mother?

THE WITNESS: Can Karen do the questioning now? This is—can I ask you to step out?

MR. EMMICK: Sure. Okay. All right.

MS. IMMERGUT: I guess, Monica, if Mike could just stay—do you mind if Mike is in here?

THE WITNESS: (Nods affirmatively.)

MS. IMMERGUT: Okay. Would you rather—

THE WITNESS: (Nods affirmatively.)

MR. EMMICK: Okay. That's fine.

BY MS. IMMERGUT:

Q   Okay. Did you go to a room with them at the hotel?

A   Yes.

Q   And what did you do then? Did you ever tell them that you wanted to call your mother?

A   I told them I wanted to talk to my attorney.

Q   Okay. So what happened?

A   And they told me—Mike came out and introduced himself to me and told me that—that Janet Reno had sanctioned Ken Starr to investigate my actions in the Paula Jones case, that they—that they knew that I had signed a false affidavit, they had me on tape saying I had committed

271

perjury, that they were going to—that I could go to jail for 27 years, they were going to charge me with perjury and obstruction of justice and subornation of perjury and witness tampering and something else.

Q   And you're saying "they," at that point, who was talking to you about that stuff?

A   Mike Emmick and the two FBI guys. And I made Linda stay in the room. And I just—I felt so bad.

Q   Now, when you say you felt bad, because you felt responsible somehow for pulling the President into something?

A   Yes.

Q   And is that something that still weighs heavily on you, that you feel responsible?

A   Yes.

Q   And is it—do you feel responsible because you told Linda about your relationship?

A   Yes.

Q   I guess later just to sort of finish up, I guess, with the facts of that day, was there a time then that you were—you just waited with the prosecutors until your mother came down?

A   No.

Q   Okay.

A   I mean, there was, but they—they told me they wanted me to cooperate. I asked them what cooperating meant, it entailed, and they told me that—they had—first they had told me before about that—that they had had me on tape saying things from the lunch that I had had with Linda at the Ritz Carlton the other day and they—then they told me that I—that I'd have to agree to be debriefed and that I'd have to place calls or wear a wire to see—to call Betty and Mr. Jordan and possibly the President. And—

Q   And did you tell them you didn't want to do that?

A   Yes. I—I—I remember going through my mind, I thought, well, what if—you know, what if I did that and I messed up, if I on purpose—you know, I envisioned myself in Mr. Jordan's office and sort of trying to motion to him that something had gone wrong. They said that they would be watching to see if it had been an intentional mistake.

Then I wanted to call my mom and they kept telling me that they didn't—that I couldn't tell anybody about this, they didn't want anyone to find out and that they didn't want—that was the reason I couldn't call Mr. Carter, was because they were afraid that he might tell the person who took me to Mr. Carter.

They told me that I could call this number and get another criminal attorney, but I didn't want that and I didn't trust them. Then I just cried for a long time.

A JUROR: All while you were crying, did they keep asking you questions? What were they doing?

THE WITNESS: No, they just sat there and then—they just sort of sat there.

A JUROR: How many hours did this go on?

THE WITNESS: Maybe around two hours or so. And then they were—they kept saying there was this time constraint, there was a time constraint, I had to make a decision.

And then Bruce Udolf came in at some point and then—then Jackie Bennett came in and there were a whole bunch of other people and the room was crowded and he was saying to me, you know, you have to make a decision. I had wanted to call my mom, they weren't going to let me call my attorney, so I just—I wanted to call my mom and they—

Then Jackie Bennett said, "You're 24, you're smart, you're old enough, you don't need to call your mommy."

And then I said, "Well, I'm letting you know that I'm leaning towards not cooperating," you know.

And they had told me before that I could leave whenever I wanted, but it wasn't—you know, I didn't—I didn't really know—I didn't know what that meant. I mean, I thought if I left then that they were just going to arrest me.

And so then they told me that I should know that they were planning to prosecute my mom for the things that I had said that she had done.

(The witness begins crying.)

MS. IMMERGUT: Do you want to take a break, Monica?

THE WITNESS: Yes.

(Witness excused. Witness recalled.)

THE FOREPERSON: Okay. We have a quorum. There are no unauthorized people and Monica is already aware that she is still under oath.

MS. IMMERGUT: We just have a couple more questions and then I think we'll break for lunch.

THE WITNESS: Okay.

A JUROR: Monica, I have a question. A minute ago you explained that the reason why you couldn't call Mr. Carter was that something might be disclosed. Is that right?

THE WITNESS: It was—they sort of said that—you know, I—I—I could call Frank Carter, but that they may not—I think it was that—you know, the first time or the second time?

A JUROR: Any time.

THE WITNESS: Well, the first time when I asked, that I said I wasn't going to talk to them without my lawyer, they told me that if my lawyer was there, they wouldn't give me as much information and I couldn't help myself as much, so that—

A JUROR: Did they ever tell you that you could not call Mr. Carter?

THE WITNESS: No. What they told me was that if I called Mr. Carter, I wouldn't necessarily still be offered an immunity agreement.

A JUROR: And did you feel threatened by that?

THE WITNESS: Yes.

A JUROR: And you said they offered you a chance to call another attorney?

THE WITNESS: Yes.

A JUROR: And did you take them up on that offer?

THE WITNESS: No.

A JUROR: Why not?

THE WITNESS: Because I didn't trust them.

A JUROR: I see. And at some point in this meeting, did you—you did obtain an attorney? Mr. Ginsberg?

THE WITNESS: Well, like at 11:00 that night.

A JUROR: So it was seven hours or eight hours or more later?

THE WITNESS: They—they finally let me call my mom, so I went to call my mom and then—and I saw Linda again. She had been shopping or something like that. But I called my mom and then Mike had said that she could call him, so they called her or she called him or something like that and then they agreed to let her come down.

So she took the train and then—and then he just sort of—I shut down and I kind of—you know, I thought maybe I should try and make these people like me, so I tried to be nice and I told jokes and I asked if we could walk around the mall because I couldn't sit in that room any more. And I just—

Q   So did they let you do that?

A   Mm-hmm. So Mike and Agent ███████ took me and we walked around the mall and we ate dinner and then we went back to the room and I read Psalm 21 about a million times. And my mom's train had been—there were problems with her train and then finally she got there and they told me they were going to want to talk to my mom alone for a little bit, but I got to talk to her.

    And I was—I didn't—I didn't want to cooperate. I mean, I didn't—I just kept thinking to myself, well—well, I'll just say I made it all up, I'll just—I'll just—I—I couldn't imagine—I couldn't imagine doing this to the President. And I felt so wrong and guilty for having told Linda and that she had done all this.

    But—so then they took my mom into another room for a really long time and she had—then when she came back, they called my dad. And then we finally—and then I talked to my dad and then—then—Ginsberg came on the scene. And he—

A Juror: So if I understand it, you first met the agents, Agents ███████ and ███████, at around 1:00 and it wasn't until about 11 p.m. that you had an opportunity to talk to a lawyer?

The Witness: Yes.

By Ms. Immergut:

Q   Although you were allowed to—the thing with Frank Carter was that they were afraid he would tell Vernon Jordan? Is that what they expressed to you?

A   Right. And I had—I had—I think that someone said that Frank wasn't even—Frank was a civil attorney and so that he really couldn't help me anyway, so I asked him if at least I could call and ask him for a recommendation for a criminal attorney and they didn't think that was a good idea.

    And then I said, well, what about—if I want to get in touch with Mr. Carter later, if I decide that's what I want to do, you know, and he's not there, because it's Friday and it was a holiday weekend, so then Agent Fallon went in the other room to find out if he had a service or something or another, a pager, I don't know—

Q   Some way for you to reach him later?

A   Mm-hmm.

A Juror: Sounds as though they were actively discouraging you from talking to an attorney.

The Witness: Yes.

A Juror: Is that a fair characterization?

The Witness: Yes.

By Ms. Immergut:

Q   Well, from Frank Carter.

A   From Frank Carter, who was my only attorney at that point.

Ms. Immergut: Right. Right.

The Witness: So I could have called any other attorney but—

A JUROR: You didn't have another attorney.

THE WITNESS: I didn't have another attorney and this was my attorney for this case, so—I mean, this was—

A JUROR: And this is the attorney who had helped you with the affidavit.

THE WITNESS: Yes. And that—the affidavit—well, the affidavit wasn't even filed yet. It was Fed Ex'd out on that day. So—

A JUROR: Monica, when you called your mother, how much were you able to tell her over the phone? Very little or—

THE WITNESS: I was hysterical. She didn't understand what I was saying, but I told her that—that the FBI had me and there was something with the Paula Jones case and Linda and then she—she—I said that—that the guy said you could call her—you can call him and so she just told me to calm down and I was screaming that, you know, "They want me to cooperate and I don't want to cooperate, don't make me cooperate, don't make me do this," and she—she said it was okay, don't worry, don't worry, and then she talked to Mike Emmick and they let her come down. So, I mean, she—I don't know.

A JUROR: Did you feel better after you talked to your mother?

THE WITNESS: Oh, yeah.

A JUROR: Gained that support?

THE WITNESS: Yeah.

A JUROR: Okay.

THE WITNESS: Yeah. I mean—

A JUROR: And what were you thinking about Linda at this time?

THE WITNESS: Linda? Did you say—

A JUROR: Mm-hmm. Did you know exactly what had happened? That you had been—

THE WITNESS: No. I was under the impression that—what I was thinking at that point was that they had—that they had listened in on our conversation on the phone and that then they came to her and said she was in trouble for something and that then she let them listen in on this lunch conversation because she had said "They did the same thing to me. They did the same thing to me." So I didn't understand what she meant by that.

And then she said, "This is the best thing for you," as if I was left to believe that she had—this was somehow something she had done and that she was trying to help me.

And I thought, "Why did she tell them? Why didn't she just say it was nonsense, it wasn't true? Why did she tell them that I had had this relationship with him?" And so—you know—and they had pictures of me at lunch with her. So—

A JUROR: The pictures were the taped lunch?

THE WITNESS: Yes. The wire lunch.

A JUROR: The wired lunch.

THE WITNESS: Yes. So that—because they—because I had said on one of the tapes that—you know, if there was a tape of me—I had—I had—I didn't know how the Paula Jones people had gotten my name and I thought maybe they had tapped my phone or maybe they had broken into my computer and read my e-mails.

I didn't know how I had gotten involved in this case and so I had said to Linda, "Well, if they have me on tape, I'll just say it's not me. I'll just say it's not me. I'll deny it. I'll deny everything."

A JUROR: So they took pictures.

THE WITNESS: Right. So they said, "We have you on tape saying that you'd deny it and we have pictures to prove that you were there." So—

A JUROR: During this time in the hotel with them, did you feel threatened?

THE WITNESS: Yes.

A JUROR: Did you feel that they had set a trap?

THE WITNESS: I—I—I did and I had—I didn't understand—I didn't understand why they—why they had to trap me into coming there, why they had to trick me into coming there. I mean, this had all been a set-up and that why—I mean, that was just so frightening. It was so incredibly frightening.

And they told me, you know, over and over again I was free to leave whenever I wanted, but—I—I didn't—I didn't know that there's a grand jury and indicted and then you go to jail. I mean, and a trial and everything. I didn't understand that.

And so I didn't—you know, then there was something that, well, if I partially cooperate, they'll talk to the judge, some—you know, we're prepared to indict you or something like that for all these things. And I just didn't—

BY MS. IMMERGUT:

Q So you didn't know what would happen if you left.

A No. And then it wasn't until my mom was there that Mike Emmick cleared it up and said to my mom, "Well, it's not that we'll arrest you tonight when you leave the hotel." You know. Because I didn't—I didn't know.

Q And you didn't end up cooperating that evening.

A No, I didn't. Because—well—

A JUROR: Excuse me. When you said they trapped you, you went there on the invitation of Linda for lunch or something?

THE WITNESS: Yes.

A JUROR: So, I mean, how did—I mean, in your mind, how did you get to the fact that they were the one? Wasn't it just Linda?

THE WITNESS: No, because they were with Linda. When I met Linda in the food court at Pentagon City, the two agents were with her.

A JUROR: Oh, okay.

THE WITNESS: Yeah. And that's where—so it was right—have you ever been to Pentagon City mall?

A JUROR: Mm-hmm.

THE WITNESS: So it was right down in the food court, you know the escalator to come down is over here?

A JUROR: Mm-hmm.

THE WITNESS: So—see, they were with her when she met me right—right in the middle.

A JUROR: Okay.

THE WITNESS: And that's where—and then—

(Pause.)

A JUROR: I think that's all the questions on that topic. There is one other question.

Going back to Monday night and the President's speech, what did you want or expect to hear from the President?

THE WITNESS: I think what I wanted and expected were two different things. I had—I had been hurt when he referred to me as "that woman" in January, but I was also glad. I was glad that he made that statement and I felt that was the best thing for him to do, was to deny this. And—but I had been hurt. I mean, it showed me how angry he was with me and I understood that.

And his—the people who work for him have trashed me, they claim they haven't said anything about me, they have smeared me and they called me stupid, they said I couldn't write, they said I was a stalker, they said I wore inappropriate clothes, I mean, you all know.

I mean, you've heard them in here, you've read the papers, you've seen on TV, and yet—and then when it came out about the talking points, then somehow no one ever asked the question, well, how could—if she was so stupid and she couldn't write, how is it possible that she wrote the talking points? So then it was, well, someone must have helped her with that. Oh, it's okay, though, it wasn't someone in the White House.

So I just—my family had been maligned because of a lot of their tactics and I felt that—I had wanted him to say that I was a nice, decent person and that he was sorry this had happened because I—I tried to do as much as I could to protect him.

I mean, I didn't—I didn't—I didn't allow him to be put on tape that night and I didn't—and I—I felt that I waited, you know, and I would have gone to trial had—had—in my mind, had there never been a point where the Office of the Independent Counsel and myself could come to—they could come to accept the truth I had to say, that that was the truth I had to give, and I'm only 24 and so I felt that I—this has been hard for me and this has been hard on my family and I just wanted him to take back—by saying something nice, he would have taken back every disgusting, horrible thing that anyone has said about me from that White House. And that was what I wanted.

What I expected him to do was to just acknowledge in his—either in his apology—you know, that first of all I think he should have straight out apologized and I think that he could have acknowledged that—you know, apologized to me, I think, to the other people who were involved in this and to my family.

My—my dad didn't know anything about the relationship and when he went on his—the few interviews he did, he was telling the truth when he said he didn't know. But out of respect for the President and the presidency, he didn't say—he could have easily said if this is true; X, Y and Z about the President, and I think that because my family didn't start a huge uproar about how wrong or improper or inappropriate it was for a 50-year-old man to be having a relationship with a young woman, we afforded him that, that was one less headache that he had to deal with, and I think he could have acknowledged that. That was what I expected. Does that—

A JUROR: Monica, none of us in this room are perfect. We all fall and we fall several times a day. The only difference between my age and when I was your age is now I get up faster. If I make a mistake and fall, I get up and brush myself off. I used to stay there a while after a mistake. That's all I have to say.

THE WITNESS: Thank you.

MS. IMMERGUT: Let me just check with Mike.

THE FOREPERSON: We do want to share something with her.

MS. IMMERGUT: Okay. So do you want to—why don't we hold off for just a second and let me check with Mr. Emmick.

THE FOREPERSON: Okay.

(Pause.)

MS. IMMERGUT: We don't have any further questions.

A JUROR: Could I ask one?

Monica, is there anything that you would like to add to your prior testimony, either today or the last time you were here, or anything that you think needs to be amplified on or clarified? I just want to give you the fullest opportunity.

THE WITNESS: I would. I think because of the public nature of how this investigation has been and what the charges aired, that I would just like to say that no one ever asked me to lie and I was never promised a job for my silence.

And that I'm sorry. I'm really sorry for everything that's happened. (The witness begins to cry.) And I hate Linda Tripp.

A JUROR: Can I just say—I mean, I think I should seize this opportunity now, that we've all fallen short. We sin every day. I don't care whether it's murder, whether it's affairs or whatever. And we get over that. You ask forgiveness and you go on.

There's some that are going to say that they don't forgive you, but he whose sin—you know— that's how I feel about that. So to let you know from here, you have my forgiveness. Because we all fall short.

A JUROR: And that's what I was trying to say.

A JUROR: That's what it's about.

THE WITNESS: Thank you.

A JUROR: And I also want to say that even though right now you feel a lot of hate for Linda Tripp, but you need to move on and leave her where she is because whatever goes around comes around.

A JUROR: It comes around.

A JUROR: It does.

A JUROR: And she is definitely going to have to give an account for what she did, so you need to just go past her and don't keep her because that's going to keep you out.

A JUROR: That's right.

A JUROR: And going to keep you from moving on.

A JUROR: Allowing you to move on.

BY MS. IMMERGUT:

Q And just to clarify, and I know we've discussed this before, despite your feelings about Linda Tripp, have you lied to this grand jury about anything with regard to Linda Tripp because you don't like her?

A I don't think that was necessary. No. It wouldn't have been necessary to lie. I think she's done enough on her own, so—

Q You would not do that just because of your feelings about her.

A No.

THE FOREPERSON: Basically what we wanted to leave with, because this will probably be your last visit to us, I hope, I hope I'm not going to have to do this any more and I hope you won't have to come here any more, but we wanted to offer you a bouquet of good wishes that includes luck, success, happiness and blessings.

THE WITNESS: Thank you. (The witness begins to cry.) I appreciate all of your understanding for this situation and your—your ability to open your heart and your mind and—and your soul. I appreciate that.

THE FOREPERSON: So if there's nothing else?

MR. EMMICK: Nothing else.

THE FOREPERSON: We'd like to excuse you and thank you very much for your testimony.

THE WITNESS: Thank you.

(The witness was excused.)

(Whereupon, at 12:54 p.m., the taking of testimony in the presence of a full quorum of the Grand Jury was concluded.)

Monica Lewinsky's
Thirteenth Interview

1

OFFICE OF THE INDEPENDENT COUNSEL

08/24/98

MONICA S. LEWINSKY was interviewed under the terms of an immunity agreement between the Office of the Independent Counsel (OIC) and her. LEWINSKY was interviewed at the Office of the Independent Counsel, 1001 Pennsylvania Avenue, Washington, D.C. 20004. Present for the interview were Associate Independent Counsel (AIC) MICHAEL EMMICK and AIC KARIN IMMERGUT. AIC ANDY LEIPOLD entered the interview room at approximately 1:07 p.m. and departed at approximately 2:00 p.m. AIC STEPHEN BATES entered the interview room at approximately 2:00 p.m. and departed at approximately 2:36 p.m. Present representing LEWINSKY was her attorney, PRESTON BURTON. LEWINSKY provided the following information, beginning at approximately 12:15 p.m.

LEWINSKY clarified the following points:

The United States Secret Service (USSS) never brought President WIL-LIAM JEFFERSON CLINTON to LEWINSKY's apartment. LEWINSKY may have mentioned to KATHY ESTEP that the USSS was standing outside of her apartment, but they were there because Republican Presidential nominee BOB DOLE lived right next door to LEWINSKY at the Watergate Apartments. LEWINSKY certainly wanted CLINTON to come to her apartment, but he never did.

CLINTON did telephone LEWINSKY at the Watergate Apartments, sometimes as late as two in the morning.

LEWINSKY definitely went to the White House on January 7, 1996. LEWINSKY entered the White House compound using her blue pass.

LEWINSKY recalls seeing GEORGE STEPHANOPOULOS at STAR-BUCKS on a few occasions. LEWINSKY recalls one occasion that was either immediately before or immediately after the 1996 Presidential election. LEWINSKY recalls mentioning something about Hawaii to STEPHAN-OPOULOS. LEWINSKY recalls that STEPHANOPOULOS recognized her as someone who worked at the Pentagon. LEWINSKY thought it was strange that STEPHANOPOULOS would know who she was. LEWINSKY advised that STEPHANOPOULOS probably recognized her face from when she worked at the White House, but she did not know how he knew where she currently worked.

Because STEPHANOPOULOS had mentioned where LEWINSKY worked, LEWINSKY thought maybe STEPHANOPOULOS knew about her relationship with CLINTON. LEWINSKY therefore approached STEPHAN-OPOULOS and she may have mentioned something about CLINTON. LEWINSKY does not recall mentioning the term "leading on," but she may have said that she read how the President follows through on things. LEWINSKY was trying to see if STEPHANOPOULOS knew about the relationship. In addition, she was very anxious about the fact that CLINTON had not called her regularly. LEWINSKY did not tell STEPHANOPOULOS about her relationship with CLINTON.

LEWINSKY advised that, of all the people who worked at the White House, STEPHANOPOULOS knowing about her relationship with CLINTON would have concerned her the least, because of STEPHANOPOULOS's age and because of his relationship with CLINTON. LEWINSKY advised she always associated STEPHANOPOULOS with the relationship with CLINTON because it began in STEPHANOPOULOS's office.

LEWINSKY advised that when preparing her written proffer, she wrote one draft, which is in the possession of either NATE SPEIGHTS or her current attorneys. LEWINSKY advised the original draft was not much different than the final version, but it was messier and a lot less organized. LEWINSKY wrote the draft while sitting in a conference room at the COSMOS CLUB. LEWINSKY believes she started working on the draft at approximately 11:00 a.m. and finished at approximately 3:30 p.m.

LEWINSKY advised she took breaks while preparing the proffer. LEWIN-SKY advised she put into words what happened in her relationship with CLINTON, after her attorneys had received a four point memorandum from the OIC. LEWINSKY recalls being concerned about simply adopting the information in the OIC's memorandum, because she wanted to be as accurate as possible. LEWINSKY, therefore, spent time writing the proffer and tried to be very careful in doing so. LEWINSKY advised she wanted to give a general idea of what she would eventually testify to, but she did not go into all the details.

LEWINSKY advised that at that point, she was not clear about why the OIC was investigating this matter. LEWINSKY advised she felt the OIC was just "out to get" CLINTON and VERNON JORDAN, so LEWINSKY was very careful to make sure she was clear when she wrote things in the proffer.

LEWINSKY did not expect the proffer to become an official document. LEWINSKY advised that on page 8 of the proffer, she tried to document the gist of what she told JORDAN. LEWINSKY advised that anything in quotes attributed to JORDAN is exactly what JORDAN said.

Paragraph 6 on page 6 of the proffer is LEWINSKY's best recollection of what happened. LEWINSKY advised that the proffer is an accurate document in which she was trying to tell the truth without implicating anyone unjustly. LEWINSKY recalls discussing the hatpin with CLINTON. LEWIN-SKY recalls bringing the subject up and CLINTON asking if LEWINSKY had told anyone about the hatpin. LEWINSKY told CLINTON she had not, even though she had. LEWINSKY told CLINTON that maybe someone saw her looking at it as she left the Oval Office after he gave it to her. CLINTON said that he was also concerned about the hatpin.

LEWINSKY assumes CLINTON told CURRIE to call LEWINSKY about picking up the gifts because she has no idea how CURRIE would know to do it.

LEWINSKY advised that she worked weekends as an intern only during the government shutdown. LEWINSKY advised she worked a lot of weekends while she worked at the Office of Legislative Affairs (OLA), including most every weekend CLINTON was in town. LEWINSKY also worked weekends when she did not intend on seeing CLINTON, to do work in the OLA.

LEWINSKY advised that she had an "SCI" (Specialized Compartmented Information) clearance, while working at the Pentagon. LEWINSKY had to attend a briefing and re-sign her White House clearance form to get this clearance.

During her December 17, 1997 telephone conversation with CLINTON, CLINTON told LEWINSKY she might not necessarily receive a subpoena. CLINTON told LEWINSKY she was on the witness list in the JONES case and LEWINSKY understood what that meant. LEWINSKY asked CLINTON if any of the other women on the witness list worked at the White House and CLINTON said no, the women on the witness list were all from Arkansas. CLINTON may have said MARSHA SCOTT was on the list.

CLINTON did not go into any detail explaining the nature of a subpoena and seemed to assume LEWINSKY knew what a subpoena was. LEWINSKY is not sure if she knew what one was, but she knows she had never seen one before. LEWINSKY does not recall talking about gifts during this telephone conversation. LEWINSKY and CLINTON did not discuss gifts called for by the subpoena until December 28, 1997.

LEWINSKY is not sure if CLINTON was in the White House Residence or in the Oval Office during this conversation. LEWINSKY advised that HILLARY CLINTON was in town that day. CLINTON told LEWINSKY to call BETTY CURRIE if LEWINSKY received a subpoena and he would figure out what to do about it. LEWINSKY does not recall CLINTON saying she should get a lawyer, because if he did, she would have started thinking about getting one then. LEWINSKY advised CLINTON may have said during this conversation that every woman he had ever spoken to was going to be on the witness list. LEWINSKY believes that he said this during one of their telephone conversations.

On December 22, 1998, LEWINSKY took the subpoena to the office of FRANK CARTER, who may have made a copy of LEWINSKY's subpoena, but LEWINSKY is sure she kept a copy or the original one for herself. LEWINSKY did not bring the subpoena with her on December 28, 1997, when she visited CLINTON. LEWINSKY was concerned about being on the witness list and explained this concern to CLINTON. LEWINSKY asked

CLINTON if he knew how she got on the witness list. CLINTON said he did not know. LEWINSKY recalls talking about the gifts with CLINTON on that occasion.

LEWINSKY advised that CLINTON was sitting in the rocking chair in the Study. LEWINSKY asked CLINTON what she should do with the gifts CLINTON had given her and he either did not respond or responded "I don't know." LEWINSKY is not sure exactly what was said, but she is certain that whatever CLINTON said, she did not have a clear image in her mind of what to do next.

LEWINSKY advised that she is certain CLINTON did not say that she had to tell the truth about their relationship if she was deposed. LEWINSKY advised she would have remembered it if he had.

LEWINSKY advised that JORDAN was the first person she contacted after being served her subpoena on December 19, 1997. LEWINSKY then may have notified her mother and then LINDA TRIPP. LEWINSKY intentionally did not tell her friends about the subpoena. LEWINSKY is not certain she told CURRIE about the subpoena. LEWINSKY is not certain CURRIE knew about the subpoena as of December 28, 1997. LEWINSKY advised that if CURRIE knew as of that date, she probably would have been more explicit in her late afternoon telephone conversation that day with LEWINSKY.

LEWINSKY called CURRIE on January 5, 1998, and told her that she needed to speak with CLINTON before she signed something. LEWINSKY hoped the message would persuade CLINTON to call her back. When CLINTON called her that evening, LEWINSKY told CLINTON some of the sample questions FRANK CARTER had asked her. CARTER had told LEWINSKY that she might get asked some questions like that. LEWINSKY told CLINTON she did not know how to answer some of the questions. One of the questions that concerned LEWINSKY was "how did you get your job at the Pentagon?" CLINTON told LEWINSKY to say the people in Legislative Affairs helped her.

LEWINSKY believes BETTY CURRIE put the book, The Three Tenors under her desk and did not give it to CLINTON. CURRIE said CLINTON had leafed through the book. CLINTON asked LEWINSKY if her mother had written a "tell all" book. LEWINSKY denied that it was a "tell all" book.

LEWINSKY advised JORDAN saw the first draft of her affidavit. LEWINSKY thinks CARTER prepared two or three rough drafts.

LEWINSKY advised that on November 15, 1995, LEWINSKY purchased a birthday cake for JENNIFER PALMIERI. LEWINSKY advised that CLINTON came to the birthday party and may have cut the cake. LEWINSKY and CLINTON spoke on this occasion and made eye contact.

CLINTON mentioned LEWINSKY's intern pass "might be a problem" because it may have prevented LEWINSKY from getting into the West Wing. LEWINSKY believes CLINTON was talking about access, as interns were not allowed into the West Wing area without an escort. In addition, LEWINSKY thought CLINTON might be referring to the impropriety of a relationship with an intern.

CLINTON laughed when LEWINSKY said she had a crush on him.

LEWINSKY believes HILLARY CLINTON called during LEWINSKY's first visit with CLINTON on November 15, 1995, but she may have called during LEWINSKY's November 17, 1995 visit. LEWINSKY thinks CLINTON had dinner with HILLARY CLINTON on the evening of November 15, 1995, but it could have been on November 17, 1995. CLINTON did not mention he and LEWINSKY getting together later during their first visit on November 15.

LEWINSKY advised that a member from Congress called CLINTON during one of her visits with him on November 15, 1995 and November 17, 1995. LEWINSKY advised the calls were brief.

LEWINSKY advised her January 21, 1996 encounter with CLINTON was accidental and not prearranged. LEWINSKY ran into CLINTON near an elevator and he guided her into the Oval Office.

LEWINSKY advised CLINTON called her in her office on February 4, 1996 and they arranged an "accidental" meeting in a hallway. LEWINSKY advised this was done because their meeting on January 21, 1996, which was truly accidental, had worked so well. LEWINSKY does not think CLINTON received any telephone calls during this visit. LEWINSKY advised that she and CLINTON spoke for a long time in the Oval Office after they were intimate on this visit. At the end of this visit, CLINTON kissed LEWINSKY on the arm and told LEWINSKY he would call her. LEWINSKY jokingly asked CLINTON if he had her number, because he had supposedly lost it twice. CLINTON recited her number from memory.

CLINTON later called LEWINSKY that day at her desk and said that he had enjoyed their visit and that he liked spending time with her.

LEWINSKY advised that on February 19, 1996, CLINTON called her at home. LEWINSKY could tell by the tone of CLINTON's voice that something was wrong. LEWINSKY asked if she could visit CLINTON, but he said he did not know how long he would be there. LEWINSKY went to the White House to see CLINTON. This was the only time LEWINSKY went there to see him without the meeting being pre-arranged. LEWINSKY advised it was during this visit that CLINTON received a call from one of the FANULI (phonetic) brothers from Florida who grows sugar. CLINTON cut the visit short so he could return the telephone call.

The night CLINTON went to the Israeli Embassy, CLINTON called LEWINSKY at home and said he had tried to call her at work, but she had already left. CLINTON said he had hoped to see LEWINSKY that night. LEWINSKY said she could come back in, but CLINTON said no, ███████ was sick and he had to stay with her.

After LEWINSKY was transferred from the White House she recalls talking and having breakfast with WALTER KAYE. LEWINSKY advised she

284

asked KAYE for help in getting a job at the White House. KAYE said he would talk to BETTY CURRIE on LEWINSKY's behalf.

LEWINSKY advised that during the event at RADIO CITY MUSIC HALL, LEWINSKY, who had paid $250 for a ticket, got access to a cocktail party, through JENNIFER SCULLEY, which was reserved for people who had donated $1,500 to the CLINTON campaign.

LEWINSKY advised that, on February 28, 1997, CLINTON mentioned the Valentine's Day ad, which he had seen on his own. CLINTON said he loved "Romeo and Juliet."

LEWINSKY's visit with CLINTON on March 29, 1997 was arranged through CURRIE. CLINTON advised that he had something to tell LEWIN-SKY that he did not tell her on February 28, 1997. CLINTON said that he thought his conversations were being tapped by a foreign embassy, which he did not identify. CLINTON said that if anyone said anything to LEWINSKY about her conversations with CLINTON that included phone sex, LEWIN-SKY should just say that she and CLINTON knew the calls were being taped, so they did something outrageous for fun. CLINTON said he could not call LEWINSKY for a while.

LEWINSKY advised that May 24, 1997 was the only time CLINTON saw her wearing the hatpin.

CLINTON said he spoke to MARSHA SCOTT on LEWINSKY's behalf in February or March of 1997. LEWINSKY initiated contact with SCOTT about an opening at the National Security Council (NSC), on a day when CURRIE was out of the office due to a death in the family.

LEWINSKY told CLINTON she had applied for a job at the National Security Council. SCOTT called her and said she would not like that job.

LEWINSKY advised that her July 24, 1997 visit with CLINTON was approximately five or ten minutes long. LEWINSKY went to pick up a photograph CLINTON had signed, from CURRIE. CURRIE had LEWINSKY wait in the Cabinet Room while CLINTON met in the Oval Office with BRUCE LINDSEY, or someone else. CLINTON mentioned an attractive female tennis player, who had been to the White House earlier that day.

LEWINSKY may have told CLINTON that LINDA TRIPP was misquoted in Newsweek. LEWINSKY does not recall mentioning that TRIPP was worried about losing her job.

In September of 1997, CURRIE mentioned JOHN PODESTA, but CURRIE never told LEWINSKY to call PODESTA.

LEWINSKY told ANDY BLEILER she was having a relationship with CLINTON and she specifically recalls mentioning CLINTON by name. LEWINSKY did not tell BLEILER's wife about her relationship with CLINTON.

285

LEWINSKY does not think CLINTON typically wore the same tie in one week. LEWINSKY thinks CLINTON wore the "birthday" tie (the yellow one recently in the news) twice in one week during the 1996 campaign. LEWINSKY advised there was no significant signal being sent at that time, other than CLINTON was thinking of her.

LEWINSKY advised that CLINTON said he bought the hatpin he gave her in Santa Fe or Albuquerque, New Mexico and LEWINSKY recalls seeing CLINTON wearing one of her ties when he was in New Mexico.

CLINTON asked LEWINSKY on two occasions if she had told anyone about their relationship; once regarding LEWINSKY's mother and once regarding TRIPP. LEWINSKY said no each time.

On October 6, 1997, LEWINSKY may have asked CLINTON if she could come to the Residence and he said no, because a record is made of everyone who visits there.

While working at the Pentagon, LEWINSKY did not make an effort to leave through a different gate than she entered when she departed the White House complex. While LEWINSKY worked at the White House, LEWINSKY did make an effort to leave the Oval Office through a different door than the one she entered. This was LEWINSKY's idea.

While working at the White House, LEWINSKY got access to HILLARY CLINTON's schedule as it was attached to the President's. After LEWINSKY left the White House, she was able to track HILLARY CLINTON's schedule through various wire services.

While LEWINSKY worked at the White House, CLINTON and LEWINSKY never arranged meetings during work days.

CURRIE tried to avoid certain White House staff members when escorting LEWINSKY into the Oval Office.

LEWINSKY thinks she may have written other romantic notes to CLINTON in addition to the "Titanic" note.

LEWINSKY talked to CLINTON about her other boyfriends. LEWINSKY recalls telling CLINTON about her relationship with THOMAS and that he worked at the Pentagon. LEWINSKY also told CLINTON when this relationship soured.

LEWINSKY always referred to CLINTON as "her" in her pages to CURRIE. LEWINSKY knew that pager messages were always typed at the White House, so she was concerned about a record being kept, indicating her references to CLINTON.

LEWINSKY has read stories that mention the fact that LEWINSKY saw GEORGE STEPHANOPOULOS at STARBUCKS when LEWINSKY did not have her bra on. The stories LEWINSKY has read about this make it seem like LEWINSKY was excited about that, when in reality, she was embarrassed that she saw STEPHANOPOULOS when she was not wearing a bra. LEWINSKY thinks LAURA CAPPS told the press this story, because CAPPS is the only person LEWINSKY told. LEWINSKY also thinks CAPPS or MAUREEN LEWIS have been the source for stories about LEWINSKY's birthday party at the PALM restaurant.

LEWINSKY advised that MIKE ISIKOFF never called LEWINSKY.

The interview ended at approximately 3:05 p.m.

Monica Lewinsky's
Fourteenth Interview

1

OFFICE OF THE INDEPENDENT COUNSEL

08/26/98

MONICA S. LEWINSKY was interviewed pursuant to an immunity agreement between the Office of the Independent Counsel (OIC), LEWINSKY, and her attorneys. Present for the interview were Associate Independent Counsel (AIC) KARIN IMMERGUT, and AIC MARY ANNE WIRTH. Representing LEWINSKY was her attorney, PLATO CACHERIS. The interview was conducted at the OIC office, Suite 490 North, 1001 Pennsylvania Avenue NW, Washington, D.C. 20004. LEWINSKY provided the following information:

LEWINSKY dated the incident with the cigar as March 31, 1996.

LEWINSKY did not talk with the President about what to do with the gifts given to her by the President until LEWINSKY received a subpoena to testify in the PAULA JONES suit. The President did not advise LEWINSKY to obtain a lawyer.

Regarding the events at the RITZ CARLTON hotel, Arlington, Virginia, on the night of January 16, 1998, LEWINSKY recalled the following information: The Federal Bureau of Investigation (FBI) agents told LEWINSKY she would not be arrested that day, but did so only after her mother arrived. LEWINSKY was told she could leave, and did leave the area, once to go to the bathroom, and once to make a telephone call. Despite the fact she was told she could leave, she thought she would be followed. LEWINSKY also thought all the phones in the Pentagon City mall were "tapped" by the FBI.

LEWINSKY explained that she wanted to leave the WATERGATE apartment for various reasons. LEWINSKY's mother had moved to New York, New York, and it was expensive to maintain the apartment for only one person. The man who owned the apartment was in the process of selling it and LEWINSKY needed to terminate the lease. However, LEWINSKY pointed out that she was not as desperate to leave the area as she told the President. LEWINSKY tried to appear more desperate than she was, in order to persuade the President to more quickly obtain her a job.

LEWINSKY had worn the blue dress purchased at the GAP on occasions previous to her February 28, 1997 meeting with the President.

LEWINSKY told the following friends of her July 4, 1997 meeting with the President: NATALIE UNGVARI, NEYSA ERBLAND, CATHERINE ALLDAY DAVIS, and ASHLEY RAINES. LEWINSKY may have told DALE YOUNG of the meeting. LEWINSKY also joked with the above friends about marrying the President.

LEWINSKY discussed with LINDA TRIPP the reasons LEWINSKY would not be brought back to the White House, despite LEWINSKY's interviews for a National Security Council (NSC) position. LEWINSKY saw DEBBIE SCHIFF at the White House the day of an interview. TRIPP and LEWINSKY speculated that SCHIFF had said something negative to something about LEWINSKY. TRIPP and LEWINSKY later had an argument about a conversation TRIPP had with KATE, who worked at the NSC, concerning what KATE had told TRIPP about the reason LEWINSKY would not be able to return to the White House.

After LEWINSKY's December 31, 1997 meeting with VERNON JORDAN, LEWINSKY asked JORDAN for a ride back from the restaurant. LEWINSKY rode with JORDAN to his office building, where she hailed a taxi cab. LEWINSKY asked for a ride in order to continue her conversation with JORDAN.

LEWINSKY could not recall a November 15, 1995 telephone call with her therapist, IRENE KASSORLA, PH.D. LEWINSKY stated she was in the White House the majority of the day. If LEWINSKY had made the call, she would have most likely billed it to her telephone card.

LEWINSKY reviewed and identified two documents. A document dated November 12, 1997 and with the greeting "Handsome" was sent to the President. A document with small print beginning with the phrase, "This is going to be a long letter . . ." was not sent. However, a much abridged version of letter was sent to the President. Both copies are attached and made a part hereto.

[Editor's note: For "Handsome" and "Long Letter" documents, see "Monica Lewinsky's Letters to and from President Clinton" in part 3.]

Monica Lewinsky's
August 26, 1998, Deposition

PROCEEDINGS

MS. IMMERGUT: We are on the record. Ms. Lewinsky, could you please state and spell your full name for the record?

MS. LEWINSKY: Monica Samille Lewinsky, M-O-N-I-C-A S-A-M-I-L-L-E, L-E-W-I-N-S-K-Y.

MS. IMMERGUT: For the record, I am Karin Immergut from the Office of Independent Counsel. Seated with me is Mary Anne Wirth, also from the Office of the Independent Counsel.

WHEREUPON,

MONICA S. LEWINSKY

having been called for examination by the Office of the Independent Counsel, and having been first duly sworn by the notary, was examined and testified as follows:

EXAMINATION BY COUNSEL FOR THE INDEPENDENT COUNSEL

BY MS. IMMERGUT:

Q Before we begin the deposition, I do want to advise you of certain rights that you have in connection with this deposition. You have already, I know, testified twice before the grand jury, and essentially the same rights do apply.

First, you have a right to have an attorney present outside of the room. Do you have an attorney present?

A Yes, I do.

Q Who is that attorney?

A Plato Cacheris.

Q You have the right to consult with Mr. Cacheris any time during the testimony, and I simply ask that you just request a break when you need to consult with him. Do you understand that you have that right?

A Yes, I do.

Q You also generally as a witness in a deposition, or before a grand jury, have a Fifth Amendment right not to incriminate yourself. Obviously, that now is modified pursuant to the agreement that you have with the Office of the Independent Counsel.

Do you understand that?

A Yes.

Q   Have you seen the agreement that you have, giving you immunity for your cooperation in this case?
A   Yes, I have.
Q   That also is a grand jury exhibit in this case, is it not?
A   Yes, it is.
Q   Do you have any questions about what your rights are not to incriminate yourself as part of that agreement?
A   No, I don't.
Q   In addition, as always, you are required to tell the truth during this procedure and are subject to the penalties of perjury if you do not tell the complete truth.
     Do you understand that?
A   Yes, I do.
Q   Any other questions that you have before we proceed?
A   No.
Q   First I just want to ask you a general question. I know you have testified in two other proceedings about various aspects of your relationship with the President. Can you characterize whether or not your relationship was one that started with sex and then evolved into a friendship, or the other way around?
A   It started with a physical attraction, which led to a sexual relationship, and then the emotional and friendship aspects of that relationship developed after the beginning of our sexual relationship.
Q   I would like to place before you what I will mark as Deposition exhibit No. 1.

                          (Deposition Exhibit No. 1 was
                          marked for identification.)

BY MS. IMMERGUT:
Q   This is also a chart that was previously marked as Grand Jury Exhibit ML #7. You can see the Xerox copy of that sticker on this exhibit, and I will place that before you, and ask if you recognize what that exhibit is?
A   Yes, I do.
Q   What do you recognize it to be?
A   A chart that I helped develop with the Office of Independent Counsel to describe and enumerate the—my relationship with the President, the contacts between the President and myself.
Q   As you've testified before, did you provide the information that is on this chart?
A   Yes, I did.
Q   And is it accurate to the best of your recollection of the events?
A   Yes, it is.
Q   What I would like to do is go through the events that are written in bold, which deal with the private encounters you had with the President that involved, for the most part, some sort of physical intimacy that we have listed as physical intimacy, including oral sex. I did want to get into some more detail about each incident.
     Basically, with respect to each incident, I would like you to describe the circumstances leading up to the actual visit, who initiated it, how it was set up, and then I would like to ask you some details about the sexual encounters themselves that occurred during each of those visits.
     So, why don't we start with the very first one, which is the second

encounter that you had on November 15th, 1995 that you've already testified some about. If you can, could you just tell us how that visit was set up, and then what occurred during the visit?

A The President came back to Mr. Panetta's office and I was the only person in the office at the time, and believe it was maybe around, I think, 10 p.m. or so, and asked me, or told me that if I wanted to meet him back in Mr. Stephanopoulos' office in about 5-10 minutes, that I could. And I told him I was interested to do that.

Q At that time, did you understand what it was he wanted to meet with you about?

A I had an idea. I, I, I had assumed that since we had been intimate in our previous encounter that evening, that we would again be intimate.

Q And just to clarify for the record, the intimacy that you had earlier that night was just kissing, is that correct?

A Yes.

Q So, did you, in fact, go meet with the President?

A Yes, I did.

Q And could you describe where you went to meet him?

A I met him back in Mr. Stephanopoulos' office and he invited me into the back study again, and we were in the hallway. And we were—I don't remember exactly how it started. But I know that we were talking a bit and kissing. I remember—I know that he—I believe I unbuttoned my jacket and he touched my, my breasts with my bra on, and then either—I don't remember if I unhooked my bra or he lifted my bra up, but he—this is embarrassing.

Q Then touched your breasts with his hands?

A Yes, he did.

Q Did he touch your breasts with his mouth?

A Yes, he did.

Q Did he touch your genital area at all that day?

A Yes. We moved—I believe he took a phone call in his office, and so we moved from the hallway into the back office, and the lights were off. And at that point, he, he put his hand down my pants and stimulated me manually in the genital area.

Q And did he bring you to orgasm?

A Yes, he did.

Q Back to the touching of your breasts for a minute, was that then through clothing or actually directly onto your skin?

A He touched my breasts through clothing, being my bra, and then also without my bra on.

Q On that occasion, did you perform oral sex on the President?

A Yes.

Q Who actually initiated your performing oral sex?

A I did.

Q Was the President wearing pants?

A Yes, he was.

Q Who unzipped his pants?

A I believe I went to go unbutton his pants and I had trouble. So, he did that. So, but—

Q So, you started it?

A If I remember correctly.

Q And he helped complete opening his pants?

A Yes.

Q Did the President at that time do anything to stop you from doing that?

A No. I think he asked me if I was sure I wanted to do that.

Q Did you have any other discussion with him while the sexual encounter was occurring, about the sex or what you were doing?

A No. Actually, I don't think he asked me if I were sure I wanted to do that, because he was on the telephone. So—I'm sorry.
   Could you repeat what you just asked me?

Q Did the President have any discussion with you about sex, or you with him, while the sexual encounter was occurring?

A Not at this time. He was on the telephone for the second half when we were in the office.

Q So, he was on the telephone while you were performing oral sex?

A He was on the telephone while he was—

Q Touching you?

A Touching me, and was also on the telephone when I was performing oral sex.

Q For any part of this sexual encounter, was he then off the telephone?

A Yes, I believe towards the end of my performing oral sex.

Q Did he say anything about the oral sex or anything about the sex at all when he got off the phone, that you can remember?

A He stopped me before he came, and I told him that I wanted to, to complete that. And he said that, that he needed to wait until he trusted me more. And then I think he ████████████████████████████

Q ██
██
██

A Yes.

Q Did he ejaculate in your presence that time at all?

A No.

Q How did you depart from the office, or how did you end that visit?

A I believe we spoke for awhile and I know at some point in that conversation I—oh, that might have been Friday. Hmm. I really don't remember how it ended.

Q Can you estimate at all how long the sexual part of your encounter with him lasted?

A Maybe 20 minutes?

Q How long—

A I'm not a very good estimator of times.

Q How long did the entire encounter last, if you can recall?

A The second one of that evening?

Q Yes.

A Maybe half an hour or 40 minutes?

Q So, the entire encounter did not involve simply the sexual part of it?

A No, it didn't.

Q Did you have talking beforehand or was most of the talking afterwards?

A It was before and after.

Q If I can direct your attention again back to Deposition Exhibit No. 1, the chart, the next date where you do have two encounters with the President is November 17th, 1995. Although you've described it somewhat for the grand jury, if you could now just describe in detail—again, I'll direct your attention to that second contact where there was physical intimacy, including oral sex listed—how that contact came about and what occurred during the contact?

A Yes. I had brought the President pizza, as he had asked. And when I brought it into him at the Oval Office, then he took me into the, to the back office and said that I could leave through that way. I believe we were talking for a little bit and he then, he got a phone call and he took the phone call in his bathroom.

Oh, it might have been before the phone call that—I don't, I don't remember who, who unbuttoned my jacket or anything like that. But we were kissing and he was fondling my breasts with his hands and with his mouth.

Q Was that through clothing or not through clothing?

A It was both.

Q Okay. So, was there a point that your bra is removed?

A Yes.

Q But you don't remember who actually removed it?

A No. I think, I think he—rather than necessarily removing my bra, sometimes he would just expose my breasts.

Q By lifting the bra over your breasts?

A Yes, or sometimes lifting my breasts out of the bra. Oh, God.

Q So, on that occasion though, you do recall that he touched you not just through your bra, but also directly on the skin?

A Yes.

Q

A

Q

A

Q Was there any discussion about sex while you were in this encounter with him?

A I don't remember the specifics of it, but I know there was another discussion, I think, about him not letting me make him come, and then I had to get back to—I'm sorry.

Could you repeat the question?

Q Was there any discussion during the November 17th encounter about sex during the encounter?

A I don't know exactly what you mean. I mean, do you mean either about—

Q Talking—

A I mean, saying things, or—

Q Well, either about what he wanted or what you wanted, or anything like that, in terms of sex?

A No. I mean, I think that there were always things being said, but not necessarily in a conversational form. Does that make sense?

Q Okay. And when you say there were always things being said, do you mean kind of chatting while you were having sex, or things that felt good? I don't mean that. I mean—

A Okay.

Q —trying either implicitly giving you direction about what he wanted, or why he wouldn't ejaculate, anything like that?

A I believe that why he wouldn't ejaculate was, was discussed again.

Q Okay. You mentioned that the President unzipped his pants. Did you understand that to be a signal of what he wanted in terms of sex?

A Yes.

Q Did he ever say anything while that was happening about what he wanted or no?

A No. He was on the telephone.

Q Okay. And that was on the second time also?

A Yes.

Q Was he on the telephone the whole time that you performed oral sex on him on the 17th of November?

A I don't remember.

Q Do you remember how you finished that meeting up with him that day, how you left?

A Yes. I know I needed to get back to my office, and he—I think I told him that he should come down and have pizza with us, he should bring his pizza down, and that everyone was down there. And at some point I believe in that meeting he told me that, or he reiterated because he might have said it on the 15th as well, that I could come see him on the weekends when, when there weren't a lot of people around.

Q With respect again to the ejaculation, that he wouldn't actually ejaculate during oral sex, were you aware, or did he ejaculate anywhere in your presence on that occasion?

A No.

Q The next date listed on the chart is December 31st, 1995, a Sunday. Could you describe how that meeting was set up and what occurred when you got to the meeting?

A Yes. I had been having a conversation with Nel and had just told him that I smoked my first cigar the night before in honor of my brother's birthday. And Nel asked me if I wanted—or offered that he could get me one of the President's cigars from his sort of stash of cigars. I said, that would be great.

And we went through the Roosevelt Room to the entrance into the back study which—the door that leads into the dining room. And just as we approached the door, the door swung open and the President was standing right there, and he had something he was going to take to Mr. Panetta. So, he asked, he asked Nel to take this—I think it was a picture actually—a picture down to Mr. Panetta, and he invited me in.

So, I went into the office and he asked me what I was doing there. And—well, first he told me he had been looking for me. And then he told me—he asked me what I was doing there, and I told him that Nel was going to get me a cigar. So, he said that he would give me a cigar. So, he did give me a cigar.

And then we were talking for a little bit and I had—do you want me to just be—

Q If you could do a narrative, that's fine.

A Well, he had—I had thought that he had forgotten my name before, because I had seen him in the hall a few times and he kept calling me "Kiddo". So, so, I sort of reiterated my—I said my name again to him.

295

You know, I said, you know, it's Monica Lewinsky, President Kiddo, you know. And he said, I know your name.

And he told me that he had tried to call me and that—he said, but you're not in the book; I even spelled your last name right. So, it was, it was really funny. It was cute.

And then we were, we were kissing and he lifted my sweater and exposed my breasts and was fondling them with his hands and with his mouth. And then I believe I was fondling him over his pants in his genital area, and I think again I tried to unbutton his pants and I couldn't. So, he did it.

Q   And again, just to be clear, when you mentioned he raised your sweater and fondled your breasts, were your breasts outside of your bra at that time?

A   Yes.

Q

A

Q

A

Q

A

Q   Did you have any discussion with him again about why he wasn't ejaculating, anything like that?

A   Yes, I think so. It might have been at that time—the two excuses he always used were, one, that he didn't know me well enough or he didn't trust me yet. So that it sort of seemed to be some bizarre issue for him.

Q   On that occasion, did he ever ejaculate in your presence, even though not—at any time later?

A   After he told me to stop and then, and then wished me Happy New Year and kissed me goodbye, he went into the ████████████████

Q   Okay. Do you know how long that sexual encounter, or the sexual aspect of that encounter lasted, not including the other discussion with him?

A   Maybe 10 minutes. Not, not very long. We would always spend quite a bit of time kissing. So.

Q   And kissing and talking and just—

A   Uh-huh.

Q   —being affectionate?

A   Yes.

Q   The next one is on page 2, and that would be January 7th of '96. Could you describe how that meeting was set up and what happened when you got there?

A   Yes. The President called me—this is the first time he called me at home—that afternoon, and it was the first day of the blizzard. And I asked him what he was doing and he said he was going to be going into the office soon. I said, oh, do you want some company. And he said, oh, that would be great. So, he said he was going into the office in about 45 minutes, and I told him that I should probably be in my office around that time, and he said he would call me in my office. I gave him my office number.

Then once I was in my office, he called me and we made an arrangement that I would pass—he would have the door to his office open, and I
would pass by the office with some papers and then he would, he would
sort of stop me and invite me in. So, that was exactly what happened.

I passed by and that was actually when I saw Lew Fox who was on duty
outside the Oval Office, and stopped and spoke with Lew for a few
minutes, and then the President came out and said, oh, hey, Monica, you
know, what are you doing here, come on in, sort of.

And so we spoke for about 10 minutes in the office. We sat on the sofas.
Then we went into the back study and we were intimate in the bathroom.

Q And when you say you were intimate in the bathroom, what did you do?
A We kissed and he, he fondled my breasts and exposed—or I think pulled
them out of my bra and fondled them with his hands and with his mouth,
and—
Q Did he touch your genitals on that occasion?
A No. He wanted to and was talking about performing oral sex on me, ▄▄
Q ▄▄
A ▄▄
Q Okay. On that date, did you gratify him in some way other than
performing oral sex?
A Yes.
Q ▄▄
A ▄▄
Q ▄▄
A ▄▄
Q ▄▄
A ▄▄
Q ▄▄
▄▄
A ▄▄
Q ▄▄
▄▄
A ▄▄
Q ▄▄
▄▄
A ▄▄
Q Did you have any discussion about sex during the encounter that you had
with him?
A No.
Q How long was your encounter with him?
A Hmm. Maybe about half an hour? I, I'm—it's really hard for me to
estimate the time.
Q And that would be the sexual aspect of it though that—
A Correct.
Q —we're talking about. Did he ejaculate at any point in your presence after
you performed oral sex on him?
A That day?
Q Yes.
A No.

Ms. Immergut: Did you have a question?

By Ms. Wirth:

Q I have a question, actually going back to November 15th, if you don't mind.

A Okay.

Q When you were talking about the President having contact with your genitals, you said, I think, that he put his hands in your pants. When he touched your genitals, was that through your underwear or directly?

A I didn't have my underwear on at that point.

Q Okay. So, it was directly then?

A Yes.

Q Okay.

By Ms. Immergut:

Q The next encounter listed is January 21st of '96, also on page 2 of the exhibit. Could you describe how that encounter occurred and what happened during the encounter?

A Yes. I was—actually, I'm looking at this right now and I think it might have been a Saturday—no, it was a Sunday. I'm sorry. Never mind. I think it might have been a Saturday, but it, it says here Sunday. I just noticed that.

I was—I had been in my office doing work, and I was leaving, leaving for the day. And as I was walking through the Residence hall to go through the West Wing to the Old Executive Office Building, I heard his voice behind me. And either he called my name or I just heard his voice and turned around, and he had just come off of the elevator and, I guess, was going back to his office.

So, we were, we were—we stopped, and we spoke as we continued to walk through the outdoor corridor by the Rose Garden. And when we got to the point where he turns left to then go into the Oval Office, he told me that I could go out this way with him, that I could leave through the, that I could leave through the Oval Office. So, we walked down the pathway together and then went into the Oval Office from there.

Q And could you describe your encounter once you got into the Oval Office?

A Yes. We had, we had already had phone sex for the first time the week prior, and I was feeling a little bit insecure about whether he had liked it or didn't like it, and I just—I felt in general that I didn't know—from having spoken to him on the phone, you know, prior to having phone sex and from having had these encounters with him, I didn't know if this was sort of developing into some kind of a longer term relationship than what I thought it initially might have been, that maybe he had some regular girlfriend who was furloughed or something during the furlough.

And at that point, I, you know, I said to him, you know, I asked him why he doesn't ask me any questions about myself, and doesn't he, you know, is this just about sex, you know, because if it is, then I just want to know that; or do you have some interest in trying to get to know me as a person. And so he kind of laughed at the manner in which I was asking him and talking to him.

And we, we went into the back study and he was, he was waiting for a friend of his to come to the office, and he was talking about that he has a lot of—that he doesn't get a lot of time to himself and he really cherishes the private times that he has with his friends, and he cherishes the time that he had with me, which seemed a little bit odd to me at that time.

298

But he, he was upset that day about the first soldier in Bosnia had been—I believe it was that day—that it was the first soldier in Bosnia had been killed just recently, and he was very upset and moved. And so I was trying to comfort him.

Q When you say you thought it was odd that he said he cherished the time with you, why was that, why did you think it was odd at that point?

A Because I didn't feel, I didn't feel like he really knew me. We had spent time talking, but it didn't seem—and, you know, he had asked some questions and I offered a lot of information about myself. But he didn't seem to ask probing questions, when you're trying to get to know someone. So, it seemed a little bit odd to me that he would sort of cherish this time, when he, you know, when I felt like he didn't really even know me yet.

Q And at that point, sex was sort of the more dominant part of the relationship?

A Yes.

Q Rather than as it became—

A There was always a lot of joking that went on between us. An so we, you know, I mean it was fun. When we were together, it was fun. We would laugh and it would—we were very compatible sexually. An I've always felt that he was sort of my sexual soulmate, and that I just felt very connected to him when it came to those kinds of things.

Q So, on the January 21st date—

A Right.

Q —how did it turn into your conversation and then go into actually having a sexual encounter?

A I was in the middle of saying something and he just started kissing me. And, so, it was funny. It was, it was very funny.

Q And what room were you physically in at that time?

A We were in the hallway. And we were kissing and—oh, I had—because I was leaving, I was having a bad hair day, and this was actually the first time that I had the infamous beret on. And so I just said something to him about feeling stupid. Here I was standing here in this dumb hat, and he said that it wasn't a dumb hat, that I looked cute and he liked it.

And so then he was kissing me, or we were kissing each other, I guess, and I think again he, he fondled my breasts with his hands and his mouth.

Q Through clothing or not through clothing?

A I think it was always through clothing, and then eventually it, it would be direct contact. So, it wouldn't just be this immediate jump to being, you know, to contact. It was—there was sort of foreplay to the foreplay, if that makes sense.

Q Do you remember whether he removed any of your clothing on that occasion?

A I think he—I remember him lifting my top. So—and he, he sort of exposing my breasts.

Q Did he stimulate your genitals on that occasion?

A No.

Q Did you perform oral sex on him or any kind of sex on him?

A Yes, I did.

Q Could you describe how that came about?

299

A Yes. He unzipped his pants and sort of exposed himself and that—and then I performed oral sex.

Q Let me ask, on all of these occasions when you've described just the pants unzipping and exposing, is it fair to say that he still kept his pants on?

A Yes.

Q It was just the zipper that—

A Yes.

Q —was undone?

A Right. And actually at one point during this encounter, I think someone came into the, to the Oval Office and he, you know, zipped up real quickly and went out and came back in, and I—this is probably too much information. I just—sorry.

Q And what happened?

A I just remember laughing because he had walked out there and he was visibly aroused, and I just thought it was funny. I mean, it wouldn't, it wouldn't necessarily be visible to anyone who just walked in because they wouldn't be looking at that, but it was just funny to me. So.

And then his—then someone—I think at that point someone came in to let him know that his friend had arrived. And so he asked me which way I wanted to leave, and I said I was going to go, I was going to leave through Betty's office. And we went into—we went from the back study through the Oval into Betty's office area, and he took me into Nancy Hernreich's office and kissed me goodbye.

And then I went to go leave from, from Betty's office, from the door into the hallway, to the West Wing hallway, but it was locked. So, I went back in to tell him. He was still in Nancy's office. I went back into Nancy's office to tell him the door was locked, and he was manually stimulating himself.

Q Did he cause himself to ejaculate at that point, or did you see that?

A No.

Q But that was in Nancy Hernreich's office?

A Yes.

Q And what did you do when you saw that?

A I smiled.

Q Okay.

A And I think we kissed again.

Q On that occasion, you mentioned that he did not touch your genitals at all. Was there any discussion about that?

A No.

Q Then did you leave from Nancy Hernreich's office eventually?

A I think I left through the—I left through the door in Betty's office that goes out into the Rose Garden.

Q On this particular entry on January 21st, it lists that the entire encounter was approximately 30 to 40 minutes. Do you recall what portion of that would have been the sexual encounter part of it, versus just talking?

A Maybe 15 minutes?

Q You just can't really estimate?

A Exactly.

Q Let's go now to February 4th of 1996, the next bold date where there was a private encounter. Could you describe how that encounter came about and what happened?

A Yes. I was in my office on Sunday and the President called me in the

300

office and—from the Residence, and told me that he was going to be going into the office later. And I think I asked him if I could come see him. And he said that would be fine, and then that he—oh, I think he was, he said he was going to go into the office in an hour and a half or so.

So, then he called me—it was actually maybe two or three hours later, because I remember I thought he forgot, maybe he had forgotten to call me and that—so. And when he called from the Residence to say he was on his way, I told him that—I asked him if we could sort of bump into the hallway, bump into each other in the hallway on purpose this time, because when it happened accidentally, that seemed to work really well and I felt more comfortable doing that. So, that's what we did. We both said, okay, I'm going to leave now.

And indeed we bumped into each other in the hall and went through the Rose Garden into the Oval Office. And I think we went right into the back office. The—when we got there.

Q   When you say the back office, you mean the study?

A   Yes. And—let's see.

You know, I need to take a break.

Q   Okay, Let's take a break.

(Whereupon, the deposition was recessed from 1:10 p.m. until 1:15 p.m.)

BY MS. IMMERGUT:

Q   Ms. Lewinsky, you are still under oath.

A   Yes.

Q   We are still on February 4th 1996. You've described going into the office and starting to kiss the President. What happened then?

A   We were in the back office and we were kissing, and I was—I had a dress on that buttoned all the way, all the way up and down.

Q   To the neck?

A   Correct. It was long and down to the, to my ankles, or whatever. And he unbuttoned my dress and he unhooked my bra, and sort of took the dress off of my shoulders and took the bra off of my, off of my—I'm not explaining this right. So that he moved the bra so that my bra was kind of hanging on one shoulder and so was off. And he just was, he was looking at me and touching me and telling me how beautiful I was.

Q   And did he touch your breasts with his hands?

A   Yes.

Q   Did he also touch them with his mouth?

A   Yes.

Q   And at that point, that is directly on your skin, is that right?

A   Yes.

Q   Did he touch your genitals?

A   Yes, he did.

Q   Did he bring you to orgasm on that date?

A   Yes, he did.

Q   ██

██

██

██

A   ██

Q   ██

██

██

A ██

██

██

Q ██

██

██

A ██

Q ██

██

██

A ██

Q And again, just with respect to bringing you to an orgasm, did he touch you directly on your skin on your genitals, or was it through underwear?

A First it was through underwear and then it was directly touching my genitals.

Q Did he take your underwear off, or did you take your underwear off?

A Hmm.

Q Or did they stay on?

A I think that I believe that he touched me first with my underwear on, and then placed his hand under my underwear. And I think at some point I, I removed them.

Q Okay. Did you also perform oral sex on him at that time?

A Yes, I did.

Q How did it come about? Was that something that you decided to do, or did the President either, through his actions or words, indicate to you that he wanted that?

A I don't really remember. I mean, it was a mutual—I think in all of these instances, it wasn't, you know—I know sometimes it's sort of hard to answer these questions as more directed. But it was—I mean, it was the course of being intimate. I mean, it was the course of having this kind of a relationship, that you—sometimes he initiated it, sometimes I initiated it. It wasn't, you know, it wasn't—it didn't necessarily go through my mind, okay, now it's time to perform oral sex.

I mean, it was, it was the passion of the moment. That was, I mean, just sort of in the course of things that happened, you know. I always felt that we sort of just, we both really went to a, to a whole other place together sexually.

Q Is it fair to say you were both trying to please each other by doing different things?

A Yes. Yes.

Q Is it also fair to say that you were not the sole aggressor in this sexual—

A That's very fair to say.

Q —encounter?

A I was not.

Q Again, I'm just asking you every time in case you remember, do you remember how long the sexual aspect of that encounter lasted?

A I really, I really don't.

Q Okay. I just note, to direct your attention that the time that you provided us previously is approximately one and a half hours for the whole visit.

A Right. We spent a long time in the Oval Office talking after, maybe 45 minutes to an hour just talking.

Q And that—

A I think he was maybe heeding my, my advice from, from the 21st, about trying to get to know me, and so he did.

Q And is it fair to say that's sort of when the friendship really starts to develop, around that time period?

A It does. That certainly helped. I think he, he was just very sweet, and he— when I got up to leave, he kissed my arm and told me he'd call me, and then I said, yeah, well, what's my phone number. And so he recited both my home number and my office number off the top of his head. So, I told him, you know, that he got an A.

And he called me in my office later that afternoon to tell me how much he enjoyed talking to me. So—and then again called Wednesday night to tell me again how much he had enjoyed talking to me.

So, it—I think that certainly was a turning point in the relationship, where it kind of went from a—obviously there's, there's some personal and intimate aspects of a sexual relationship that develop just in talking or laughing or getting to the point where you, where you kiss someone on every encounter. But for me, I think that spending the time talking to him was certainly when I, when I got to know him as a person and started to realize that he wasn't necessarily the person I thought he was at that point.

Q Let's move on to the next date, which is March 31st, 1996, the next encounter where there is physically intimate contact. Why don't you tell us how that date was set up and what happened?

A I had spoken—well, just to back up real quickly. The President had ended things on the, I think it was the 19th of February. But then he had called me later—I think it was late February or early March at some point—indicating to me he wanted to sort of see me again, possibly for some intimate moments.

And it wasn't until the 31st of March that we really were together again physically. But he had called, I think two times, two times prior during that work week, leading up to the 31st. And it was on the Friday night which is, looking at the chart, which was the 29th, that I, I asked him if I could see him on Sunday. And he said, he'd, you know, he'd see what he could do.

And then on Sunday, he called me in my office and—let's see. I believe—oh, I believe that I brought him papers that day. That I think I asked him to tell the guard outside that he was expecting some papers, expecting someone from Leg Affairs. And then when I got to the door, I told them that I was supposed to bring papers to the President.

Q And that was part of a ruse to—

A Yes.

Q —get in to see him?

A Exactly.

Q Just to back up for a second, you mentioned that you had had some phone calls with him between February 19th, '96 when he tried to cut off the relationship—

A Yes.

Q —or the sexual part of the relationship—

A Correct.

Q —and the 31st, in which he had suggested that he wanted to perhaps renew the intimacy. What led you to believe that?

A I saw him on my way out one evening. It was late. And he was on his way home from, I think it was the Israeli Embassy and Evelyn Lieberman was with him. So, I certainly made a point of not having any eye contact or anything with him. And he called me later that evening and said he had, he had—after he left and went upstairs, he went back to his office and had called me in my office, hoping that I could come have a visit with him, but I had already gone home.

And so then I offered, I said, well, I could come back. And he said, no, I'm upstairs already. So.

Q Back now to March 31st—

A Yes.

Q —of '96. So, what happens then? How actually is that then finally set up?

A He had called me in my office and then I brought papers there, or fake papers.

Q Do you then go into the Oval Office?

A Yes, I do.

Q And what happens?

A We went into the back study and we were in the, the hallway area. And it had sort of become actually a ritual sort of at this point, that we always kind of started out our meetings, that he was leaning against the closed door of the bathroom and I would rub his back, because he has a bad back. So, I used to always rub his back, and sometimes he'd rub my back. But I usually concentrated on his lower back because it was always bothering him.

And, you know, and then I'd usually move around and sort of just lovingly touch his chest and—

Q Was there any removal of clothing?

A Yes, there was. We kissed and, and he had not been feeling well, I guess, the past couple of days. So, really, most of—he focused on me pretty exclusively, I guess, in a sexual manner on me that day, and kissed me, and kissed my breasts, and he, he fondled my genitals with his hands.

Q Through clothing or not through clothing?

A Not through clothing.

Q Did you have your underwear removed? Or how did your clothes get off?

A (No response.)

Q Or were they simply pulled out of the way?

A I think I—I think that they were just sort of—oh.

Q Pulled out of the way?

A Yeah.

Q Okay. So he touched you. And with your breasts, was that through clothing, through your brassiere, or did he move your breasts out of the way of the brassiere?

A It was, it was both. I mean, it was always both. He—there was never a time when he just touched my breasts through—

Q The bra?

A —the bra, right.

Q ██
    ██
    ██

A Yes.

Q Whose idea was that?

A On—when I met with him on January 7th, after we had been intimate and we were talking in the Oval Office, he was chewing on a cigar. And

304

then he had the cigar in his hand and he was kind of looking at the cigar in a, sort of a naughty way. And so I, I looked at the cigar and I looked at him and I said, we can do that, too, some time.

And I don't, I don't really remember how it got started, but.

Q   Was it part of the sexual encounter that he did that?

A   Yes, it was.

Q   Did you understand it to be arousing?

A   It was.

Q   Okay. What happened to the cigar afterwards?

A   ██

Q   How did you leave that encounter? So, you didn't perform oral sex on him at all that time?

A   No.

Q   How—

A   Actually, looking also—I should mention that, looking at the chart, that I didn't bring papers that day. I brought this tie to him in a folder. So, sometimes I brought papers and this day it was I had a tie, and there probably were some papers in the folder as well.

Q   And that's the Hugo Boss tie that's listed under the gift category for that date?

A   Correct.

Q   The next encounter is April 7th, 1996. Could you describe how that encounter was set up?

A   The President had called me at home sort of in the early evening, and this was—it was Easter Sunday and it was the first, it was the Sunday after I had found out I was to be transferred to the Pentagon. And he called—it also had been the week that Ron Brown had passed away.

So, I asked him how he was doing and we talked about that for a little bit. And then I told him that Monday was my last day, and that I had been transferred. And I was crying and he wanted to know what happened, and I asked him if I could come see him. And he said, that's fine, but just tell me what happened first. So, I explained to him what had happened, and then he told me to come on over. So, I did.

And this is when I had this little encounter trying to get into the office with John Muskett, just that he said—I brought papers with me from home in a folder. And so John had said something about wanting to check with Evelyn if it was okay for me to go in. And I don't remember exactly what ended up happening, but I managed to get him to not ask Evelyn and I got in.

And the President and I were in the back office. He was actually on the phone when I came in. And then when he got off the phone, we went into the back office and we talked again about what had happened, in terms of my transfer.

And that was when he, he looked me in the eye and he promised me—well, first he said that he couldn't believe that they were taking me away from him because he trusted me so much, and he was convinced that it had something to do with him, why I was being transferred. And then he looked me in the eye and he said, I promise you, if I win in November, I'll have you back like that [snapping fingers].

Q   Did he say anything like, if you do a good job at the Pentagon he'll bring you back?

A No.

Q So, what else happened at that meeting?

A I, I don't remember how it exactly came about, but I know that, that, I remember kissing him and we were physically intimate.

Q In terms of the physical intimacy that day, did the President touch your genitals on that date?

A I don't think so.

Q What about your breasts?

A Yes.

Q With his mouth or with his hands, or both?

A With both.

Q And again, I'm assuming, unless you correct me now, that it's both through clothing and directly on the skin?

A Yes.

Q With respect to oral sex, do you just remember how that occurred, whether his pants came off, whether somebody unzipped them?

A I think he unzipped them and—because it was sort of this running joke that I could never unbutton his pants, that I just had trouble with it. So, I was—you know, there were times that I tried and we'd laugh and then he'd, he'd do it.

But we were—I, I performed oral sex in the, in the back office.

Q And at that time, did he ejaculate?

A No, he did not.

Q Was there any discussion with him about the ejaculation at that time that you can remember?

A No.

Q On that date, I think you've already testified that there was a phone call during your sexual encounter with him, is that right?

A Yes, there was.

A Did you perform oral sex while he was on the telephone?

A Yes. It was, it was—I think I'll just say, because for—there are a lot of people that could interpret that as being sort of a, that being done in a servicing sort of manner, and it was more done in kind of an exciting sort of—I don't want to say erotic, but in a way that there was kind of this titillating like a secret, in a sense, in the same way sometimes that an affair, is, that, you know, when you are doing this and obviously there is kind of the irony that the person on the other line has no idea what's going on.

So, I just wanted to clarify that.

Q Okay. Although on that occasion, I believe you previously mentioned that that was the first time that you felt a little funny about it?

A I, I did. I did. I, I, I, I was, I was pretty emotionally devastated at that point, and the prospect of going to the Pentagon was very upsetting to me. And there were moments when I felt a little uncomfortable, and moments when I didn't.

Q Although you mentioned that there were other times that he was on the phone, that you didn't think sort of anything bad about it—

A Right.

Q —and on this occasion, you felt more like—

A I just—

Q —you were servicing—

A   Exactly.

Q   —on some level. And did you tell Linda Tripp about that, do you remember?

A   Probably.

Q   How did that encounter end, if you remember? And actually you've already testified a little bit about this. So, just if you could quickly summarize how you finished the encounter and what happened?

A   We were in the back office and I heard Mr. Ickes call, say, Mr. President, from the Oval Office. And we both were startled and looked at each other, and he jetted into the Oval and I—

Q   Were you performing oral sex at the time?

A   I think so, but I'm not a hundred percent sure. And so then I, I left.

Q   On that occasion also, when the President went to get the phone call, had you started performing oral sex on him before he went to take the phone call?

A   Yes, I believe that we were—I think that that was it. I know that we were, we were intimate in the hallway, and then it was a phone call that prompted us to go into the office. And that when we were in the office, that, that he, he removed, he sort of removed his pants.

Q   How did you know that you were supposed to kind of accompany him to take the phone call? Did he—

A   I don't remember.

Q   —invite you to come in, in any way, or gesture for you to come along?

A   I don't really remember.

Q   So, you think you actually didn't begin the oral sex until he was on the phone already?

A   It's—

Q   Or is it not that clear?

A   It's not that clear.

Q   But you remember him unzipping his pants at some point?

A   At some point, yes.

Q   Before the oral sex?

A   Yes.

Q   Okay.

A   I hope so.

Q   At that point, and I didn't really ask you this for the other encounters, but in terms of putting your stuff back on or collecting yourself, is there any sort of general way that that happened? Did the President help you, or how did you get dressed again?

A   Well, neither of us ever really took—completely took off any piece of our clothing, I think specifically because of the possibility of encounters, like what happened that day. But there had, earlier in that day on the 7th, when I—not earlier in the day, but earlier in the encounter with the President—when he had been kissing my breasts, someone had come in, I think to tell him he had the phone call, or something like that.

Or someone had come in at some point and he stepped out of the office, and I had put my bra and my sweater back on. And he came in and sort of made a remark about me having done that. And—

Q   Do you remember the remark?

A   I think he smirked and he sort of said, you know, damn, you put your top back on, or something like that. Or, why did you do that, something like that. But he was smirking and joking with me.

But then when he went into the Oval, when Mr. Ickes came in, I put myself together and hurried out the back way through the dining room.

Q The next encounter. There's luckily a big gap there. The next one is February 28th. How was this encounter set up, and then what happened?

A Betty called me at work to tell me, or to invite me to the radio address for that evening. And so I went.

Q Did she say anything about that you would see the President on that date, or—

A Yes. I mean, she, she had indicated to me the President wanted me to come to this radio address. So that—and I knew that he had—we had spoken earlier that month and the month before, and the month before that, and I knew he had a Christmas gift for me which he had yet to give me. So, it sort of seemed, it was understandable.

I went to the radio address. And then—it was a very small group, maybe 10 people, six, 10 people. It was quite small. And after—or when I went to go take my picture with him, he told me to go see Betty or go wait with Betty because he had something to give me. So, I went into Betty's office and was waiting there with her. There were some other people there, staff members. And I think I've gone through the whole—

Q And you've actually testified in some detail about this before.

A Right.

Q So, actually, why don't we just go to the sexual encounter—

A Okay.

Q —and how the actual sexual part started?

A Once we were alone in the back office, he started to say something to me and I was pestering him to kiss me, because I hadn't—we hadn't been alone in almost a year and—well, I guess not a year, but it had been a long time since we had been alone. And so he, you know, he jokingly told me to, you know, just wait a sec, he wanted to give me my presents.

So, he gave me my hatpin and he sort of hurriedly put the *Leaves of Grass* in my purse and he said, here, just take this with me. And then I said, what is it. I took the book out and so we, we were looking at it, and I was just, I thought it was pretty incredible. It was just a beautiful, beautiful book, and it meant a lot to me.

And then we went back over by the bathroom in the hallway, and we kissed. We were kissing and he unbuttoned my dress and fondled my breasts with my bra on, and then took them out of my bra and was kissing them and touching them with his hands and with his mouth.

██

██

██

And I continued to perform oral sex and then he pushed me away, kind of as he always did before he came, and then I stood up and I said, you know, I really, I care about you so much; I really, I don't understand why you won't let me, you know, make you come; it's important to me; I mean, it just doesn't feel complete, it doesn't seem right.

And so he—we hugged. And, you know, he said he didn't want to get addicted to me, and he didn't want me to get addicted to him. And we were just sort of looking at each other and then, you know, he sort of, he looked at me, he said, okay. And so then I finished.

Q ██

A ██

Q Did he touch your genitals at all during that occasion, do you remember?

A I think through my tights, but not direct genital.

Q How did the meeting then end, or the encounter?

A We, well, we kissed after—

Q The ejaculation?

A Yes. And then I think Betty knocked on the door. So, I think—no, no, no, no, no, that's not right, because I fixed my lipstick. So, I think we sort of— I think he said, oh, you've got to put yourself back together again. And so then I went and I got my lipstick and I put my lipstick back on, and then Betty knocked on the door.

Q The dress that you were wearing on this occasion, is that the blue dress from the Gap?

A Unfortunately, yes.

Q And I think we've already gone into detail about the dress on that. The next encounter is March 29th, 1997. Would you tell us how that encounter was set up?

A It was, it was set up through my conversations with Betty.

Q Did you contact Betty?

A Yes. I contacted Betty and Betty—my understanding was Betty spoke with the President, and then Betty got in touch with me and told me to come that afternoon. I did. I was waiting for the President in the back study and then he hobbled in because he was on crutches. And we were, we were in the back office. Actually, it was sort of an overcast day. It had been raining earlier. So, it was just sort of dark and overcast.

And we were, he was—I think he had put his crutches down and he was kind of leaning on me. So, I was holding him, you know, I mean, sort of romantically but at the same time literally holding him. And—

Q This is in the back study?

A Uh-huh, yes. And I was—this was another one of those occasions when I was babbling on about something, and he just kissed me, kind of to shut me up, I think. And so we were kissing and then we sort of—we turned around and he was leaning against—he has a little, it's like a little table that I think has this stereo. I don't know if the stereo was always there. I know it was there later. But he was leaning against this little table a little bit just, I think, kind of for support.

And he unbuttoned my blouse and just sort of touched me over, over my bra. And I don't think he took, I don't think he exposed my breasts that day. And we were, we were just kissing a lot.

And then he—oh, he went to go put his hand down my pants, and then I unzipped them because it was easier. And I didn't have any panties on. And so he manually stimulated me.

Q Did he bring you to orgasm?

A Yes, four times.

Q ██
A ██
Q ██
  ██
  ██
A ██
Q How did you end the contact with him on that occasion?
A End the sexual contact? Or—
Q The sexual contact?
A He—oh, well, this was also the day that before, before I performed oral sex on him, I wanted him to touch my genitals with his genitals. And so we sort of had tried to do that, but because he's really tall and he couldn't bend because of his knee, it didn't really work.
Q And I think you've previously testified your genitals grazed each other—
A Exactly.
Q —on that occasion?
A I mean, just barely.
O And when they grazed each other, neither of you had clothes covering your genitals, is that right?
A Correct.
Q How did you end the encounter completely that time, in terms of ending the meeting?
A Oh, we moved into the dining room and we were talking for a long time. I had brought some presents for him. So, we talked for awhile. And then Betty came back and the three of us were talking.
Q Let's move on to the next one, which is August 16th, 1997.
A I—this was sort of his, his birthday, his birthday encounter. And so after—I had set up in his back office, I had brought an apple square and put a candle and had put his birthday presents out. And after he came back in and I sang happy birthday and he got his presents, I asked him if we could, if we could share a birthday kiss in honor of our birthdays, because mine had been just a few weeks before. So, he said that that was okay and we could kind of bend the rules that day.
    And so we, we, we kissed. And then I was touching him in his genital area through his shorts, and then I, I went to, to—
Q Perform oral sex?
A Yes, and he wouldn't let me.
Q Did he touch you on your genitals on that date?
A No.
Q Any other physical contact that is referred to as physical intimacy on that date?
A Not that I remember.
Q How did you end that encounter with him? Any discussion about sex during that encounter, or not having sex?
A No, just he got upset when I, you know, when he stopped me and he said, I'm trying to not do this and I'm trying to be good. And he, he got visibly upset. And so I, I hugged him and I told him I was sorry and not to be upset, and I was a little shocked, actually. I didn't—he just seemed to get so emotionally upset about it. It seemed a little bit strange to me.
Q And he hadn't done that before?
A He had been emotionally visibly upset with me before, but not—

Q With regard to—

A Correct.

Q —stopping you from having sex with him?

A Exactly.

Q Or having sexual contact with him? Is that correct?

A Yes.

Q And is that, other than any brief kiss, the last physically intimate contact that you've had with him?

A Well, our Christmas kiss was—I mean, it was passionate. So.

Q Okay. It was—

A I don't call it a brief kiss.

Q That was a physically intimate kiss. Any other contact that would fall within the sexual relations definition—

A No.

Q —that we've previously seen?

A I think we, you know, we would, we would joke with each other sexually. And so sometimes, you know, I might hit him on the butt, or he might hit me on the butt, but it wasn't—not under the definition.

Q So, it wouldn't be a real intent to arouse, or not the physical touching that is described—

A No.

Q —in the definition?

A No.

Q All right. Let's move on to another topic.

A Yea.

Q Thank you for your patience. I know that those are not easy questions to get to.

A It's just hard thinking my dad might see this.

Q Why don't we move to another emotional topic, July 4th, just briefly. Is now a good time to—

A Sure.

Q —talk about that? Why don't you tell us—I know that you've brought up in your grand jury testimony that July 4th of 1997 was an emotional day for you in connection with your relationship with the President.

A Yes.

Q Could you just briefly tell us what you meant by that and just a little bit about your meeting with him on that date?

A Our meeting had started out in, as a, in a fight. We—and early on in this fight, I started crying, and then he—we were in the back office and he came over and was hugging me and told me not to cry, to stop crying, and was very—he was very sweet, and was very gentle.

And then we—I—there was a gardener outside. So, when I noticed the gardener, I pointed it out and we moved to the, into the hallway by the bathroom. And much of the discussion that day was he spent a lot of time talking to me, you know, about the kind of person he thought I was, and—I'm a little bit modest. So, it's sort of—it's hard for me to get into all the things he said. But, there just—

Q Did he say wonderful things about you?

A He did.

Q Like what kinds of things?

A Just that he thought I was smart and beautiful, and that—you know, but that a lot of it, it centered around my needing to learn to, to sort of squelch a bit of the fire in my belly. And that, you know, he said that people like us who, you know, have a tendency to get really angry and that there are a lot of other people that, that, that don't understand that and don't know how to handle that.

And he just—he spent a lot of time talking to me. He was very, very—he was the most affectionate with me he'd ever been. There wasn't a second when he wouldn't be touching me, whether it was holding my hand or stroking my arm or, you know, he'd kiss my neck at one point. It was just—or he'd, you know, put his hands, he was running his hands through my hair and touching my face. And my bra strap kept falling down my shoulder. So, he kept pushing my bra strap up.

It was just very—it was intense. It was just really emotionally intense.

And at one point, we, we had been talking about—I made some remarks to him about his relationship with Mrs. Clinton. And he, he remarked a little bit later than that that he wished he had more time for me. And so I said, well, maybe you will have more time in three years. And I was actually sort of thinking just when he wasn't President, he was going to have more time on his hands. And he said, well, I don't know, I might be alone in three years.

And then I said something about, you know, us sort of being together. I think I kind of said, oh, I think we'd be a good team, or something like that. And he, you know, he jokingly said, well, what are we going to do when I'm 75 and I have to pee 25 times a day. And I, you know, I told him that we'd deal with that. And it was—there was just this incredible connection.

And I, I left that day sort of emotionally stunned, because I felt—I was shocked. But I thought, I mean, he was—I just knew he was in love with me, and from the way he acted that day, and that's not, it's not something that I would, that I would think easily. It's not a conclusion that I would come to easily at all. And it just—with the kind of person I am.

And I knew I was in love with him, you know, a year before, and I thought he cared about me. But just the way he looked at me and touched me, and the things he said, it just—it was so obvious to me. And it was shocking. So, it was a bizarre day.

Q   Anything else about the 4th?

A   Not that I don't think I've gone over before.

Q   Okay. We'll switch to a completely different topic. You previously testified that on December 17th—

A   You know, I need a—

Q   Do you want a break?

A   I'd like just a break.

Q   Sure, absolutely.

(Whereupon, the deposition was recessed from 1:57 p.m. until 2:07 p.m.)

BY MS. IMMERGUT:

Q   Ms. Lewinsky, you are still under oath.

A   Yes.

Q   We are going to cover some other areas, hopefully quickly. You previously testified that on December 17th, during your phone call with the President—and that's in 1997—

312

A Yes.

Q —when you were discussing various things, including that your name had appeared on the witness list, that the President told you that if you were ever subpoenaed that you should contact Betty?

A That's correct.

Q Did he ever tell you at that time that you should get a lawyer?

A I don't believe so. No.

Q When you say "I don't believe so", are you quite certain of that?

A I'm, I'm 99.9 percent certain.

Q What would you have done if he had told you that you should get a lawyer?

A I would have started to think about how I was going to get a lawyer and who I should get, and I didn't do that. So, that's what leads me to believe that he didn't say that.

Q Okay. Were you ever under the impression from anything that the President said that you should turn over all the gifts that he had given you to the Paula Jones attorneys?

A No.

Q Did you ever talk to the President about turning gifts over to the Jones lawyers before you were ever subpoenaed?

A No.

Q Did you actually ever talk to him about the fact that gifts could be subpoenaed prior to them actually being subpoenaed?

A No.

Q So, is it fair to say that the only time you talked about the gifts from the President, in connection with the subpoena, was on December 28th?

A That's correct.

Q Directing your attention to January 5th of 1998, when you had a telephone call with the President, you previously testified that you had some discussion about a book that you had purchased for him?

A Correct.

Q That was the book that you gave to Betty Currie on approximately January 4th to give to the President? Is that right?

A Yes.

Q What was the name of that book again? It was the book on the Presidents.

A It was a book about the Presidents of the United States.

Q Do you remember when you purchased that book?

A I believe it was that weekend, the weekend prior to the 5th.

Q Did you ever talk to him, during your meeting of December 28th, 1997, about the fact that you were going to give him that book?

A No.

Q How do you know that you didn't?

A Because I hadn't purchased the book yet.

Q Had you even thought about purchasing that particular book?

A No. It was bought on the spur of the moment.

Q Do you remember where you bought it?

A At a little bookstore in Georgetown, an antique book store.

Q I'm going to switch topics again. Do you believe that if you hadn't had a sexual relationship with the President that you would have kept your job at the White House?

A Yes.

313

Q Do you believe that your difficulty or inability to return to employment at the White House was because of your sexual relationship with him?

A Yes. Or the issues that, or the problems that people perceived that really were based in truth because I had a relationship with the President. But, however, some of the people who worked there chose to, to see some of my behavior. Does that make sense?

Q What do you mean by that?

A I think that—I've always felt that some of the, some of the staffers there, particularly Evelyn Lieberman and those who worked with her to move me out of the White House, instead—looked at my behavior only, instead of looking at the President's behavior, and instead of necessarily thinking that I had a relationship with the President, were just looking at it thinking I was trying to have a relationship with the President when I already was having a relationship with him. They turned a blind eye to his actions.

Q During 1997, did you feel that the President owed you something with respect to a job?

A I did, because he, he had promised me on April 7th of '96 that he would bring me back when, if he won in November. And I had—when he first told me that, I had had some hope and I didn't, I didn't even know if I was going to hear from him again after I left. And then when he continued to call me frequently during the campaign period, it led me to believe he would bring me back.

And then after we had a—it was after a period when he didn't call me and I wasn't sure about things, what was happening—I'm sorry. I'm not being clear.

Because he had sort of led me to believe that he was going to bring me back and was constantly reassuring that, I, I believe that he did owe that to me. Versus him having said, I'm really sorry—let's just say in April of '96—I'm really sorry that this happened, there's not, you know, there's nothing I can do, and left it at that. Then I wouldn't have felt that he owed me anything.

Q What about the fact that you had gone quietly and not revealed your relationship? Did that have anything to do with your feeling that you were entitled to something?

A It did later on. I, I would have gone quietly anyway, because that—it was never, ever, ever my intention for this relationship to ever become public. And—but I had felt that after having left quietly, after having been sort of maybe strung along throughout the campaign and then even way into 1997, that I had felt—and him promising me that he'd bring me back and constantly enumerating the different steps he was trying to take to do that—that, yes, I did feel at that point he, he certainly owed me.

Q Is that part of your letter of July 3rd to the President in 1997, where you described it previously as threatening to disclose the relationship, at least to your parents, was that part of your feeling that—

A It was never really a, a, maybe a—it was never really a threat, because I never really was going to do that. While I had disclosed a portion of the relationship to my mom, I never had any intention of telling my dad. There's no way of that.

And what I really was trying to do was trying to, in a circuitous manner, remind him that I had been a good girl, and that I hadn't, you know, disclosed this information, and that really, you know, he'd promised me he was going to do something. And I had told my parents, I had told my dad that I was coming back after the election.

Q I'd like to focus now just very briefly on your dealings with Ambassador Richardson with regard to the U.N. job.

A Yes.

Q How many times did Ambassador Richardson call you directly, do you remember?

A Do you mean someone from his—he never directly picked up the phone and dialed my phone number.

Q Let me ask a different question.

A Okay.

Q How many times did you speak to him personally?

A I believe twice.

Q And when I say personally, on the telephone?

A Yes.

Q How do you know that you actually spoke with him on those occasions?

A Well, the first time I spoke with him I remember, because I was shocked and I was, I was very nervous. And—

Q Because the Ambassador was on the phone?

A Exactly. And the second, the second time I actually hadn't really remembered, I wasn't sure. And then through documentation I was shown, it, it led me to believe that I had, in fact, spoken to him on the phone.

Q But you are positive at least one time you did, in fact, speak to him personally?

A Yes.

Q Do you remember which occasion that was, or when that occurred?

A Yes, it was sometime in October.

Q Was that the October 23rd call? Does that sound right?

A Yes.

Q And that's prior to your actual interview with him?

A Correct.

Q I'd like to just ask you very briefly about your conversation with the President the night before your interview with Ambassador Richardson for the U.N. job. Could you describe who initiated that call and what the substance of the call was?

A I had—well, I had requested through Betty that the President call me, because I was really nervous about my interview and meeting with Ambassador Richardson. I just, I didn't, I didn't want to make anyone look bad. I didn't want to sound like a fool, or—so, the President called me and we talked about some of the different issues at the U.N., and he gave me some suggestions of things I could say. But I think he may have also done that the previous week, too.

Q Do you remember him giving you sort of a job pep talk on—

A Yes.

Q —the 30th?

A Yes.

Q Why would you describe it as a pep talk?

A Because I was nervous. So, he, he was trying to kind of build my confidence and reassure me, you know, reassure me that I was an intelligent person, and that I had a lot to offer and that they would be happy to have me there.

315

Q At some point, did you tell the President that you got an offer from the U.N.?

A I believe so.

Q Did you tell Betty also that you had gotten an offer?

A Yes.

Q Do you remember any details about talking to Betty about it, or how you let her know?

A I, I remember calling Betty after the interview and telling her that it had gone much better than I had expected it would, and that I was really, that I was, that I was somewhat more interested after having met the Ambassador than I was prior to the interview. And other than that, I don't really.

Q What about details about your conversation with the President telling him that you had gotten the job?

A I vaguely remember it being in context, I think, of sort of trying to press him on getting in touch with Mr. Jordan.

Q In terms of getting other jobs—

A Exactly.

Q —you let him know this?

A Exactly.

Q That you had an offer from the U.N.?

A Right.

Q Do you remember when you got the U.N. offer?

A No.

Q Was it sometime, in relation to your interview with the Ambassador—

A It was sooner, rather than later.

Q So, sometime within a matter of a week or—

A I believe so.

Q —some weeks?

A Somewhere within a couple, within the next two weeks or so.

Q And did they tell you that they would leave the job open until a certain time, for you to make the decision if you wanted it?

A Not at the point when I got the offer. I, I—and actually I think, thinking now I'm a little bit more clearer that I did speak with the Ambassador, that he was the one who, who extended the offer to me, because I remember being nervous and not knowing what to say to him, because I didn't really want the job. And so I sort of just "yessed" him along and thanked him profusely, and told him I was excited about it.

And then I later spoke, I believe, with Mona Sutphen, and sort of relayed to her that I was interested in also trying to feel out the private sector. So, and I believe it was at that point that she said, well, let's keep in touch. We can—this position, I think, had been open for awhile. So.

Q Did she give you any timeframe at all about how long they would wait for you to make a decision?

A It was—I think we talked about talking maybe in a few weeks, and then at some point we said, let's get in touch around the first of January. And I was under the impression that, you know, I believed that they would hold the position open for me, but that it didn't necessarily—

Q It's not a guarantee?

A Exactly.

Q But they weren't rushing you to make an immediate decision?

A No.

Q   So, you understand you basically had some leeway until January 1998 to make a decision?

A   Correct.

Q   January 16th, 1998, Ritz Carlton night. I really have just one question about it, which was, was there a time that you, in fact, during the course of the evening, that you, in fact, did leave the prosecutors and agents by yourself?

A   Yes, when I was given, finally given permission to go call my mom. I wasn't comfortable using the phone in the room.

Q   So, you went out by yourself to—

A   Yes, I did.

Q   Where did you go make a phone call?

A   To Nordstrom's.

Q   And—

A   It was just one phone call, to my mother. And there was also a time—I think one of the prosecutors came with me, I think it was Stephen Bin—

Q   Binhak?

A   —I think, came downstairs with me. I used—I needed to return a phone call from a page. And then when I was with Mr. Emmick and Agent ██████ they let me go to the bathroom in Macy's by myself.

Q   Were you in Macy's for some time by yourself?

A   Well, it, it took awhile to find a bathroom. It was kind of far away. So.

Q   So, they didn't follow you into the bathroom?

A   They didn't follow me in. But then when I came back, Agent ██████ had gone looking for me. So.

Q   And just with respect to the phone call to call your mother, no one accompanied you for that, is that right?

A   No.

Q   And finally—

A   I just, I do want to state that I did—because I know this sort of goes to this issue of being, you know, kind of told, oh, you're free to leave whenever you want, that I didn't really—I didn't feel at any point that I could leave whenever I wanted, that I could—that I was afraid that if I had left the Mall, I would be arrested and put in jail. So, that was my impression.

Q   One last question from me. Do you, for any reason now, want to hurt the President?

A   No. I'm, I'm upset with him right now, but I, no, that's the last thing in the world I want to do.

MS. IMMERGUT: That's all I have.

MS. WIRTH: I just have one question.

BY MS. WIRTH:

Q   From your grand jury testimony last week, on August 20th, 1998, you were talking about your understanding of the President's testimony. I'm just going to read a portion of your testimony to you and ask you a question about that. This is in response to a question from a juror.

You said, "I'm sorry. I'm sorry. It's—from my understanding about what he testified to on Monday, not—just from the press accounts, is that this was a—that this was a service contract, that all I did was perform oral sex on him and that that's all that this relationship was. And it was a lot more than that to me and I thought it was a lot more than that."

And the answer continues a little bit more after that.

The question I have for you is that when you mentioned your

understanding of what the President testified to on the previous Monday, from what did you derive your understanding of what the President's testimony was?

A   From the press accounts I had read.

Q   Okay. No one from this office divulged to you anything that the President said during his testimony, did they?

A   Absolutely not.

MR. WIRTH: Thank you.

MS. IMMERGUT: Nothing further. Do you have any questions?

THE WITNESS: No.

(Whereupon, at 2:24 p.m., the proceedings were concluded.)

Monica Lewinsky's
Fifteenth Interview

OFFICE OF THE INDEPENDENT COUNSEL

09/03/98

MONICA S. LEWINSKY was interviewed pursuant to an immunity agreement between the Office of the Independent Counsel (OIC), LEWINSKY, and her attorneys. Present for the interview were Associate Independent Counsel (AIC) KARIN IMMERGUT and AIC MICHAEL EMMICK. Representing LEWINSKY was her attorney SYDNEY HOFFMAN. The interview was conducted at the OIC office, Suite 490 North, 1001 Pennsylvania Avenue, NW, Washington, D.C. 20004. LEWINSKY provided the following information:

On November 15, 1995, LEWINSKY's second meeting with the President took place around 10:00 p.m. LEWINSKY took off her underwear prior to this meeting.

On November 20, 1995, LEWINSKY gave the President the first ZEGNA necktie. The President's picture was taken while he was wearing the tie. The President later gave the photograph to LEWINSKY at a Christmas event, which occurred around December 5, 1995. The President told LEWINSKY that he liked the tie.

LEWINSKY did not remember a single conversation with LINDA TRIPP earlier in 1997, where they went over the whole relationship between LEWINSKY and the President from the beginning. LEWINSKY did recall that TRIPP talked about patterns of behavior by the President over a period of time. LEWINSKY did not get the sense that TRIPP was writing anything down during their conversations. LEWINSKY did recall that TRIPP would, on occasion, ask LEWINSKY to repeat things about LEWINSKY's affair with the President and would state, "You know how I forget things."

In April 1997, LEWINSKY recalled a telephone conversation with the President where he told LEWINSKY of a conversation that the President had with MARSHA SCOTT. The President discussed with MARSHA SCOTT a conversation SCOTT had with WALTER KAYE. LEWINSKY's conversation with the President occurred in late April, after the President had visited SCOTT, who was hospitalized after surgery.

On May 17, 1997 and May 18, 1997, LEWINSKY had multiple telephone conversations with the President in an attempt to arrange a meeting with the President. The President told LEWINSKY that he was experiencing difficulties in arranging the meetings due to the unavailability of BETTY CURRIE.

LEWINSKY said that the conversation with Ambassador RICHARDSON that was described in her deposition of August 26, 1998, on page 64, occurred in the middle of October 1997. However, LEWINSKY did not recall the exact date. The November 2, 1997 letter regarding Ambassador RICHARDSON, with the greeting, "Dear Betty," was not sent to CURRIE. LEWINSKY said she believed she eventually sent a shorter version of the letter.

In the days immediately preceding the visit by President ZEDILLO of Mexico to the White House on November 13, 1997, LEWINSKY was attempting to contact the President. LEWINSKY wanted to see the President on the Veterans Day holiday, because it would have been easier for the President to see her on a holiday when people were not around. LEWINSKY was angry when the President would not see her. At this point, LEWINSKY was frustrated and angry that the President would not see her, and because of the slow pace of the job search. LEWINSKY wanted to discuss both personal and job issues with the President. LEWINSKY added that in her conversations with TRIPP, TRIPP pushed and encouraged LEWINSKY to become even angrier at the President.

On December 28, 1997, in a conversation between LEWINSKY and the President, the hat pin given to LEWINSKY by the President was specifically discussed. They also discussed the general subject of the gifts the President had given Lewinsky. However, they did not discuss other specific gifts called for by the PAULA JONES subpoena. LEWINSKY got the impression that the President knew what was on the subpoena.

If CURRIE had not called LEWINSKY about returning the gifts received from the President, LEWINSKY would have probably left the gifts in her apartment. LEWINSKY would not have given the gifts to her mother or her friends. LEWINSKY did not want to cause trouble for any of these people by getting them involved. If TRIPP had threatened to tell about the gifts, LEWINSKY would have probably thrown them away.

On January 4, 1998, LEWINSKY delivered to CURRIE a letter for the President, which LEWINSKY referred to as the "Titanic letter." In a telephone conversation of January 5, 1998, the romantic portion of the letter was briefly discussed by LEWINSKY and the President. LEWINSKY told the President that she deserved to have sexual intercourse with him at least once, out of fairness to LEWINSKY.

LEWINSKY's intern pass for the White House was pink.

LEWINSKY did not tell BAYANI NELVIS about having phone sex with the President. LEWINSKY may have mentioned receiving phone calls from the President. LEWINSKY did not go into detail about the nature of the calls.

LEWINSKY was shown a copy of a White House document entitled, "Memorandum for Security Interview," dated November 20, 1995. LEWINSKY was asked why she answered "none" to question number 16, "Please provide any other information that could be a possible source of embarrassment to you or the White House if publicly known." LEWINSKY stated that she responded that way at that time because she never thought her affair with the President would become known.

LEWINSKY was shown a document, dated November 21, 1995, where

LEWINSKY answered "No" to the question, "Do you know of anything that could, would, or should prevent you from receiving a government clearance?" LEWINSKY stated that she did not think that her affair with the President would keep her out of a government position. LEWINSKY believed her friends who knew of the affair at the time, NATALIE UNGVARI and ANDY BLIELER, would not talk about it. It would be obvious to LEWINSKY's friends not to tell of LEWINSKY's affair with the President if they were interviewed as part of her security clearance. LEWINSKY said she would not have thought it necessary to ask her friends not to say anything about the affair.

LEWINSKY sent a version of a document which mentions "Gingko . . ." to the President. The document, marked MSL1249-DC-0139, is attached and made a part hereto.

[Editor's note: For "Gingko" document, see "Monica Lewinsky's Letters to and from President Clinton" in part 3.7]

Monica Lewinsky's
Sixteenth Interview

OFFICE OF THE INDEPENDENT COUNSEL

09/05/98

MONICA S. LEWINSKY was interviewed pursuant to an immunity agreement between the Office of the Independent Counsel (OIC), LEWINSKY, and her attorneys. Present for the interview was Associate Independent Counsel (AIC) KARIN IMMERGUT. Representing LEWINSKY was her attorney, SYDNEY HOFFMAN. The interview was conducted at the OIC office, Suite 490 North, 1001 Pennsylvania Avenue NW, Washington D.C. 20004. LEWINSKY provided the following information:

In the middle of September 1995, while LEWINSKY was with NATALIE UNGVARI, they accidently ran into the President in the basement of the West Wing of the White House. LEWINSKY reintroduced herself to the President. The President responded that he knew who LEWINSKY was.

On February 24, 1996, LEWINSKY visited BETTY CURRIE at the White House. The purpose of this visit was to see CURRIE to jog CURRIE's memory, who would then jog the President's memory that the President had previously told LEWINSKY that he had a gift for her. LEWINSKY was hoping the President would make arrangements for LEWINSKY to visit the White House to see the President and pick up the gift. The President was not at the White House at the time.

LEWINSKY was shown a copy of a letter, dated June 29, 1997, with the greeting, "Dear Handsome, I really need to discuss my situation with you." LEWINSKY pointed out the words "visit briefly", which appear in the content of the letter, as being written by LINDA TRIPP. This document was a draft of a letter later sent to the President. The document is marked MSL-DC-00001227. It is attached and made a part hereto.

LEWINSKY was shown a copy of a document starting with the phrase, "This is going to be a long letter." It was a draft letter written on LEWINSKY's home computer. This document marked MSL-55-DC-0178 was not sent. A shorter version of the above document starting with the phrase, "It has been made clear to me . . . ," marked MSL-55-0001, was similar to the note she sent to the President on October 9, 1997. This document was sent in response to learning from TRIPP, on October 6, 1997, that KATE FRIEDRICK from the National Security Council (NSC) said that LEWINSKY would never be allowed to return to the White House. Both documents are attached and made a part hereto.

[Editor's note: For "Long Letter" and "Shorter Version" documents, see "Monica Lewinsky's Letters to and from President Clinton" in part 3.7]

Monica Lewinsky's
Seventeenth Interview

1

OFFICE OF THE INDEPENDENT COUNSEL

09/06/98

MONICA S. LEWINSKY was interviewed regarding certain ties she had given as gifts. Present for the interview, conducted at the Office of the Independent Counsel (OIC), 1001 Pennsylvania Avenue, NW, Washington, D.C. were Associate Independent Counsel (AIC) KARIN IMMERGUT and LEWINSKY's attorney, SYDNEY HOFFMAN. LEWINSKY advised as follows:

Upon being shown a gold and blue, ERMENEGILDO ZEGNA tie, further identified as 1507-DC-00000002, LEWINSKY advised she gave this tie to President WILLIAM JEFFERSON CLINTON in August of 1996.

Upon being shown three ties, identified as 1514-DC-00000003, 1514-DC-00000004, and 1514-DC-00000005, LEWINSKY advised she may have given 1514-DC-00000004 to BAYANI NELVIS, but she is not sure. LEWINSKY did not give 1514-DC-00000003 or 1514-DC-00000005 to NELVIS. LEWINSKY advised she did not give either 1514-DC-00000003, 1514-DC-00000004, or 1514-DC-00000005 to CLINTON.

Monica Lewinsky's
Eighteenth Interview

1

OFFICE OF THE INDEPENDENT COUNSEL

09/06/98

MONICA S. LEWINSKY was interviewed pursuant to an immunity agreement between the Office of the Independent Counsel (OIC), LEWINSKY, and her attorneys. Present for the interviews was Associate Independent Counsel (AIC) KARIN IMMERGUT. Representing LEWINSKY was her attorney, SYDNEY HOFFMAN. The interviews were conducted at the OIC office, Suite 490 North, 1001 Pennsylvania Avenue, NW, Washington, D. C. 20004.

Between September 3, 1998 and September 6, 1998, MONICA LEWINSKY listened to copies of various audio tapes provided to the OIC by LINDA TRIPP. LEWINSKY was also provided with copies of transcripts of those tapes to follow along as a guide. LEWINSKY was asked to correct any errors she found in the transcripts as she reviewed the tapes. LEWINSKY listened to the following tapes: LT18, LT19, LT1, LT2, LT13, LT3, LT8, LT7, LT15, LT11, LT16, LT26, LT9, LT5, LT23, LT6. After listening to each tape, LEWINSKY stated she believed that her voice was on each tape, and that the other voice was that of LINDA TRIPP. She also stated that although in many instances she did not recall the specific conversations, she agreed that the subject matter of the tapes was familiar and that these were the kinds of things she had discussed with LINDA TRIPP. In some instances, she did specifically recall parts of conversations.

LEWINSKY was asked to sign and date each cassette, after listening to it, in order to acknowledge the following: (1) She had listened to the tape; (2) She believed the voices on the tape were those of her and Linda TRIPP; (3) She recalled having discussed the general subject matter of the tape in various conversations with Linda TRIPP; and (4) The conversation would have occurred within the general time period of the date that the OIC was able to determine to be the actual date of the tape. LEWINSKY stated that she understood what she was acknowledging by signing each tape, and did sign and date each tape to reflect these factors.

LEWINSKY stated she believed that she was a party to the all of the above mentioned taped conversations with LINDA TRIPP, based on her intonation on the tapes, and the content of conversation. However, LEWINSKY noted that she always thinks her voice sounds different to her when she hears it on tape. LEWINSKY further advised that she cannot attest to the integrity of the tapes, that is, if there are portions missing. She did not recall specific portions missing on any particular tape, however, and in several tapes agreed that the conversation appeared to be continuous, despite skips on the tape. In addition, LEWINSKY did not single out any conversations on the tapes that she did not say. (LEWINSKY was expressly told to point out any such portions as she reviewed the tapes.) LEWINSKY recalled that she and TRIPP had many more conversations about the same types of subjects that were not recorded.

LEWINSKY marked excerpts of conversations that she felt were embarrassing to her, and requested that the OIC redact these portions from any transcripts provided to anyone outside this office. LEWINSKY marked various excerpts on virtually every tape to which she listened. LEWINSKY found it difficult and embarrassing to listen to the things she said on the tapes.

The following are comments LEWINSKY made about certain tapes:

Tape 18: LEWINSKY agreed that although there were tape skips on this tape, the conversation appeared to flow as one continuous conversation.

Tape 1: LEWINSKY agreed that she believed the voice on the tape was hers, and that the conversation was the kind of conversation she had with TRIPP. The only discussion that seemed surprising to her was a statement by LEWINSKY about NANCY HERNREICH being jealous of her, pages 32:23 - 33:1. LEWINSKY does not recall ever thinking that.

Tape 19: LEWINSKY advised that there appears to be a break in the conversation and a new conversation beginning on page 21.2. She believed that the second conversation may have actually occurred before the first. LEWINSKY further noted that there were more conversations on October 6, 1997, about "KATE" from the National Security Council (NSC), and LEWINSKY's inability to return to the White House, than those conversations reflected on the tapes.

Tape 2: This tape, which recorded a conversation of October 16, 1997, referred to a meeting LEWINSKY had with the President on October 11, 1997. Based on her review of the tape, LEWINSKY believed that the President gave her the ANNIE LENOX compact disc at that meeting, rather than on December 6, 1997, as reflected on the previously prepared summary chart that was used during her grand jury and deposition testimony.

Tape 13: LEWINSKY noted that she did send a final version of the job "wish list" to the President. (LEWINSKY provided a copy of a draft of the "wish list" to the OIC on July 31, 1998). Based on this tape, LEWINSKY recalled that she may have sent sunglasses, an erotic postcard and a note about education reform to the President on October 16, 1997, rather than October 21 or 22, 1997, as listed on the summary chart she testified about in the grand jury and at her deposition. A copy of the "wish list" marked DB-DC-00000027 is attached and made a part hereto.

Tape 3: LEWINSKY did not recall her father asking her expressly whether she was having an affair with the President, although LEWINSKY stated she believes that she is speaking about this on the tape (pages 2-3). This tape otherwise appeared to accurately reflect subjects that LEWINSKY discussed with TRIPP.

Tape 7: LEWINSKY noted that on page 18, line 12, when she said the President should pay for her move to New York, she was being sarcastic. She never meant that he should really pay for it.

Tape 15: LEWINSKY recalled that she was frightened when TRIPP said during this conversation that maybe she should come to New York with LEWINSKY (page 67). LEWINSKY stated the conversation on pages 71-73 occurred on a different date than the earlier part of the tape. Although she did not recall the date, she believed it was before the President's trip to Florida, possibly for a Democratic National Committee (DNC) fundraiser.

Tape 16: LEWINSKY stated that the conversation on pages 51:21-60:01 occurred on November 6, 1997. Pages 60-103 occurred on November 8, 1997. LEWINSKY recalled that TRIPP really wanted LEWINSKY to attend the NORMA ASNES fundraiser on November 12, 1997, described in this tape on pages 104-106. LEWINSKY stated that contrary to what she told TRIPP about a conversation that she had with BETTY CURRIE on page 64, she never told CURRIE that she was back with the President three times during the furlough.

Tape 11: On page 25:4 - 25:5, where LEWINSKY stated that she would "deny, deny, deny," she was talking about her affair with the President. LEWINSKY stated that part of her denying the relationship was always to protect the President.

Tape 9: LEWINSKY noted that on occasion things she said about her mother, such as statements on pages 51-52, did not actually occur. LEWINSKY, on occasion, would tell TRIPP that her mother said certain things because LEWINSKY's mother's opinion had leverage with TRIPP. TRIPP appeared to be obsessed with LEWINSKY's mother.

Tape 23: According to LEWINSKY, part of this tape appeared to have occurred on December 12, 1997, and part on December 15, 1997.

Tape 5: LEWINSKY stated that she may have told BETTY CURRIE in a fit of anger, that she was going to tell her parents about the affair in mid-November 1997. LEWINSKY was angry at that time because nothing was happening with her job, and she was unable to see the President for more than the 60 second visit on November 13, 1997.

[Editor's note: For "Wish List" document, see "Correspondence and Documents Related to Monica Lewinsky's Job Search" in part 3.7]

Monica Lewinsky's White House Visits

Summary:
- **44 visits.**
- **12 visits in which record shows only the President, and no others, was present.**

No.	DATE	ENTRY TIME	EXIT TIME	REQUESTOR	VISITEE	PRESIDENT'S LOCATION	PURPOSE OF VISIT	REFERENCES
1	06/07/96 (Fri.)	12:51	13:03	Wozniak	Johnson	Oval Office (arrived at 13:05)	Deliver papers from Bacon to Johnson	V006-DC-00000007 (WAVES record) 827-DC-00000016 (Epass Entry Log) 827-DC-00000017 (Epass Exit Log) 968-DC-00000037 (President Notepad Log) Wozniak 3/5/98 Int. at 2
2	06/14/96 (Fri.)	16:51	No exit time logged	Hernreich	President Clinton	Oval Office	Attend radio address with Lewinsky family	V006-DC-00000007 (WAVES record) V006-DC-00002109 (Presidential Movement Log) V006-DC-00000534 (Radio Address Guest List)
3	06/18/96 (Tues.)	17:59	No exit time logged	Widdess	President Clinton	Oval Office Cabinet Room (arrived at 18:27) Oval Office (arrived at 19:29) Residence (arrived at 19:51)	Attend press picnic	V006-DC-00000007 (WAVES record) V006-DC-00002113 (Presidential Movement Log) V006-DC-00000473 (Press Picnic Guest List) Widdess Int. 2/19/98 at 2

[1] There is at least some record of each visit by Ms. Lewinsky to the White House during this time, but in many cases only incomplete information is available from White House personnel and the official White House logs. The information in this chart is derived solely from these logs and personnel. For a comprehensive list of all encounters between Ms. Lewinsky and President Clinton, see Tab F.

KEY:
Requestor	The person at whose behest the visitor was cleared into the White House through the WAVES system.
Visitee	The person whom the requestor listed as the person to be visited when requesting clearance for the Ms. Lewinsky.
Purpose	The purpose recalled by the requestor or visitee during an interview with the OIC.
References	The official White House logs that contain the information upon which this chart is based.
Shaded Areas	Visits during which Ms. Lewinsky and the President were in the Oval Office area, and no one else was known to be present.

(See "Understanding the Evidence" section, Tab G, for details.)

	Date						Purpose	References
4	08/29/96 (Thurs.)	15:06	15:47	Bobowick	Bobowick	Chicago	White House tour or radio address with Lewinsky family[2]	V006-DC-00000007 (WAVES record) 827-DC-00000017 (Epass Entry & Exit Logs) 968-DC-00000045 (Presidential Movement Logs) Bobowick 2/11/98 Int. at 3
5	08/29/96 (Thurs.)	17:15 (scheduled)	No exit time logged	Bobowick	Bobowick	Chicago	White House tour or radio address with Lewinsky family[2]	V006-DC-00000007 (WAVES record) 968-DC-00000045 (Presidential Movement Logs) Bobowick 2/11/98 Int. at 3
6	08/29/96 (Thurs.)	18:22	19:03	Raines	Raines	Chicago	No purpose recalled/known	V006-DC-00000007 (WAVES record) 827-DC-00000017 (Epass Entry & Exit Logs) 968-DC-00000045 (Presidential Movement Logs)
7	10/11/96 (Fri.)	12:49	13:49	Raines	Johnson	Oval Office (arrived at 12:40) South Grounds (arrived at 13:03)	No purpose recalled/known	V006-DC-00000007 (WAVES record) 827-DC-00000017 (Epass Entry & Exit Logs) 968-DC-00000048 (Presidential Movement Log)
8	10/24/96 (Thurs.)	07:42	10:11	Shaddix	Shaddix	Oval Office (arrived at 08:43) South Grounds (arrived at 09:00) Departed White House (at 09:05)	Visit Photo Office	V006-DC-00000007 (WAVES record) 827-DC-00000017 (Epass Entry & Exit Logs) 1234-DC-00000010 (Presidential Movement Log) Shaddix 2/24/98 Int. at 2

[2] Ms. Bobowick remembered clearing Ms. Lewinsky into the White House for a tour with her family and for a radio address with her family. She did not remember specific dates.

KEY: Requestor   The person at whose behest the visitor was cleared into the White House through the WAVES system.
       Visitee   The person whom the requestor listed as the person to be visited when requesting clearance for the Ms. Lewinsky.
       Purpose   The purpose recalled by the requestor or visitee during an interview with the OIC.
       References   The official White House logs that contain the information upon which this chart is based.
       Shaded Areas Visits during which Ms. Lewinsky and the President were in the Oval Office area, and no one else was known to be present.
(See "Understanding the Evidence" section, Tab G, for details.)

-2-

#	Date	Entry	Exit	Requestor	Visitee	Location	Purpose	References
9	12/17/96 (Tues.)	16:15	No exit time logged	Widdess	President Clinton	Oval Office Second Floor (arrived at 18:56)	Attend Christmas Party	V006-DC-00000007 (WAVES record) 968-DC-00000059 (Presidential Movement Log) 1222-DC-00000231 (Presidential Activity Report) V006-DC-00000505 (Christmas Party Guest List) Widdess 2/19/98 Int. at 2
10	12/17/96 (Tues.)	19:34	20:11	Raines	Raines	Second Floor	No purpose recalled/known	V006-DC-00000007 (WAVES record) 827-DC-00000017 (Epass Entry & Exit Logs) 968-DC-00000060 (Presidential Movement Log) 1222-DC-00000231 (Presidential Activity Report)
11	12/30/96 (Mon.)	13:01	13:43	Currie	Currie	Hilton Head, South Carolina	No purpose recalled/known	V006-DC-00000007 (WAVES record) 827-DC-00000017 (Epass Entry & Exit Logs) 968-DC-00000063 (Presidential Movement Log)
12	02/24/97 (Mon.)	09:38	10:32	Kessinger	Kessinger	Oval Office	Return borrowed photo	V006-DC-00000008 (WAVES record) 827-DC-00000018 (Epass Entry & Exit Logs) 968-DC-00000066 (Presidential Movement Log) Kessinger 2/24/98 Int. at 1-2
13	02/28/97 (Fri.)	17:48	19:07	Currie	Currie	Oval Office	Attend radio address	V006-DC-00000008 (WAVES record) 827-DC-00000018 (Epass Entry & Exit Logs) 968-DC-00000074 (Presidential Movement Log) V006-DC-00000536 (Radio Address Guest List)
14	03/13/97 (Thurs.)	10:01	10:15	Currie	Currie	North Carolina & Florida	No purpose recalled/known	V006-DC-00000008 (WAVES record) 827-DC-00000018 (Epass Entry & Exit Logs) 1222-DC-00000235 (Presidential Activity Report)
15	03/13/97 (Thurs.)	21:21	21:49	Raines	Raines	North Carolina & Florida	No purpose recalled/known	V006-DC-00000008 (WAVES record) 827-DC-00000018 (Epass Entry & Exit Logs) 1222-DC-00000235 (Presidential Activity Report)

KEY: Requestor   The person at whose behest the visitor was cleared into the White House through the WAVES system.
Visitee   The person whom the requestor listed as the person to be visited when requesting clearance for the Ms. Lewinsky.
Purpose   The purpose recalled by the requestor or visitee during an interview with the OIC.
References   The official White House logs that contain the information upon which this chart is based.
Shaded Areas   Visits during which Ms. Lewinsky and the President were in the Oval Office area, and no one else was known to be present.
(See "Understanding the Evidence" section, Tab G, for details.)

-3-

#	Date			Requestor	Visitee		Purpose	References
16	03/29/97 (Sat.)	14:03	15:16	Currie	Currie	Oval Office	No purpose recalled/known	V006-DC-00000008 (WAVES record) 827-DC-00000018 (Epass Entry & Exit Logs) V006-DC-00002130 (Presidential Movement Log)
17	04/15/97 (Tues.)	14:00 (schedule)	No exit time logged	Naplan	Naplan	New York	No purpose recalled/known	V006-DC-00000008 (WAVES record) 968-DC-00002318 (Press Schedule) Naplan 3/3/98 Int. at 2
18	04/16/97 (Wed.)	09:49	09:56	Currie	Currie	Residence	No purpose recalled/known	V006-DC-00000008 (WAVES record) 827-DC-00000018 (Epass Entry & Exit Logs) 968-DC-00000096 (Presidential Movement Log)
19	05/01/97 (Thurs.)	17:43	No exit time logged	Stott	Stott	Oval Office Residence (arrived at 18:40)	Press Office job interview	V006-DC-00000008 (WAVES record) 827-DC-00000018 (Epass Entry Log) 1234-DC-00000029 (Presidential Movement Log) Stott 2/27/98 Int. at 1
)	05/02/97 (Fri.)	19:57	20:21	Raines	Raines	Residence	No purpose recalled/known	V006-DC-00000008 (WAVES record) 827-DC-00000018 (Epass Entry & Exit Logs) 968-DC-00000112 (Presidential Movement Log)
21	05/24/97 (Sat.)	12:21	13:54	Currie	Currie	Oval Office (arrived at 11:59) Pool Oval Office Study (arrived at 13:50)	No purpose recalled/known	V006-DC-00000008 (WAVES record) 827-DC-00000018 (Epass Entry & Exit Logs) 1222-DC-00000242 (Presidential Activity Report)

KEY: Requestor   The person at whose behest the visitor was cleared into the White House through the WAVES system.

Visitee   The person whom the requestor listed as the person to be visited when requesting clearance for the Ms. Lewinsky.

Purpose   The purpose recalled by the requestor or visitee during an interview with the OIC.

References   The official White House logs that contain the information upon which this chart is based.

Shaded Areas   Visits during which Ms. Lewinsky and the President were in the Oval Office area, and no one else was known to be present.

(See "Understanding the Evidence" section, Tab G, for details.)

-4-

330

22	05/30/97 (Fri.)	15:32	16:01	Dimel	Dimel	Oval Office	Initial NSC job interview	V006-DC-00000008 (WAVES record) 827-DC-00000018 (Epass Entry & Exit Logs) 968-DC-00000120 (Presidential Movement Log) Dimel 2/18/98 Int. at 1
23	06/11/97 (Wed.)	10:58	12:04	Dimel	Dimel	Oval Office	Follow-up NSC job interview	V006-DC-00000008 (WAVES record) 827-DC-00000018 (Epass Entry & Exit Logs) 968-DC-00000121 (Presidential Movement Log) Dimel 2/18/98 at 1
24	06/16/97 (Mon.)	14:47	16:11	Croft	Croft	Oval Office	Marsha Scott interview	V006-DC-00000008 (WAVES record) 827-DC-00000018 (Epass Entry & Exit Logs) 968-DC-00000132 (Presidential Movement Log) Scott 3/19/98 GJ at 28-29
25	06/24/97 (Tues.)	18:59	19:19	Currie	Currie	Army Navy Country Club	No purpose recalled/known	V006-DC-00000008 (WAVES record) 827-DC-00000018 (Epass Entry & Exit Log) 1234-DC-00000033 (Presidential Movement Log)
26	07/04/97 (Fri.)	08:51	No exit time logged	Currie	Currie	Oval Office South Grounds (arrived at 11:08)	No purpose recalled/known	V006-DC-00000008 (WAVES record) 827-DC-00000018 (Epass Entry Log) 1222-DC-00000249 (Presidential Activity Report)
27	07/14/97 (Mon.)	21:34	23:23	Currie	Currie	Oval Office (arrived at 21:28) Appointment Secretary's Office (arrived at 21:41) Residence (arrived at 23:25)	No purpose recalled/known	V006-DC-00000008 (WAVES record) 827-DC-00000018 (Epass Entry & Exit Logs) V006-DC-00002142 (Presidential Movement Log) 1222-DC-00000251 (Presidential Activity Report)

KEY: Requestor   The person at whose behest the visitor was cleared into the White House through the WAVES system.

Visitee   The person whom the requestor listed as the person to be visited when requesting clearance for the Ms. Lewinsky.

Purpose   The purpose recalled by the requestor or visitee during an interview with the OIC.

References   The official White House logs that contain the information upon which this chart is based.

Shaded Areas   Visits during which Ms. Lewinsky and the President were in the Oval Office area, and no one else was known to be present.

(See "Understanding the Evidence" section, **Tab G**, for details.)

-5-

331

	Date			Requestor	Visitee	Purpose	Location	Purpose	References
28	07/16/97 (Wed.)	10:46	11:42	Scott	Scott		Oval Office	Job interview	V006-DC-00000008 (WAVES record) 827-DC-00000018 (Epass Entry & Exit Logs) 1222-DC-00000253 (Presidential Activity Report) Scott 3/19/98 Int. at 64-68
29	07/24/97 (Thurs.)	18:04	18:27	Currie	Currie		Oval Office	No purpose recalled/known	V006-DC-00000008 (WAVES record) 827-DC-00000018 (Epass Entry & Exit Logs) 968-DC-00000155 (Presidential Movement Log)
30	08/01/97 (Fri.)	10:46	11:40	Unknown	Unknown		Oval Office Rose Garden (arrived at 11:10) Oval Office (arrived at 11:17)	No purpose recalled/known	827-DC-00000002 (Epass Entry & Exit Logs) 1222-DC-00000255 (Presidential Activity Report)
31	08/01/97 (Fri.)	12:19	No exit time logged	Unknown	Unknown		Oval Office Cabinet Room (arrived at 12:28) Oval Office (arrived at 12:45) Residence (arrived at 13:16)	No purpose recalled/known	827-DC-00000002 (Epass Entry Log)1222-DC-00000255 (Presidential Activity Report)
32	08/16/97 (Sat.)	09:02	10:20	Currie	Currie		Oval Office (arrived at 09:20) Second Floor (arrived at 10:05)	No purpose recalled/known	V006-DC-00000008 (WAVES record) 827-DC-00000018 (Epass Entry & Exit Logs) V006-DC-00002146 (Presidential Movement Log)
33	09/11/97 (Thurs.)	18:59	19:06	Raines	Raines		Oval Office	No purpose recalled/known	V006-DC-00000008 (WAVES record) 827-DC-00000018 (Epass Entry & Exit Logs)

KEY: Requestor   The person at whose behest the visitor was cleared into the White House through the WAVES system.
      Visitee   The person whom the requestor listed as the person to be visited when requesting clearance for the Ms. Lewinsky.
      Purpose   The purpose recalled by the requestor or visitee during an interview with the OIC.
      References   The official White House logs that contain the information upon which this chart is based.
      Shaded Areas   Visits during which Ms. Lewinsky and the President were in the Oval Office area, and no one else was known to be present.
(See "Understanding the Evidence" section, Tab G, for details.)

#	Date	Entry Time	Exit Time	Requestor	Visitee	Location	Purpose	References
34	09/12/97 (Fri.)	19:41	20:22	Currie	Currie	Residence	No purpose recalled/known	V006-DC-00000008 (WAVES record) 827-DC-00000018 (Epass Entry & Exit Logs) 968-DC-00000172 (Presidential Movement Log)
35	09/22/97 (Mon.)	19:11	19:25	Raines	Raines	New York	No purpose recalled/known	V006-DC-00000008 (WAVES record) 827-DC-00000018 (Epass Entry & Exit Logs) 968-DC-00000179 (Presidential Movement Log)
36	10/11/97 (Sat.)	09:37	10:54	Currie	Currie	Oval Office (arrived at 09:54)	No purpose recalled/known	V006-DC-00000008 (WAVES record) 827-DC-00000018 (Epass Entry & Exit Logs) V006-DC-00002151 (Presidential Movement Log)
37	10/29/97 (Wed.)	No entry time logged	No exit time logged	Wilson	President Clinton	White House	No purpose recalled/known	V006-DC-00000008 (WAVES record) 1234-DC-00000048 (Presidential Movement Log)
38	11/13/97 (Thurs.)	No entry time logged	No exit time logged	Wozniak	Wozniak	White House	Attend military function	V006-DC-00000008 (WAVES record) V006-DC-00002156 (Presidential Movement Log) Wozniak 3/5/98 Int. at 2
39	11/13/97 (Thurs.)	18:21	No exit time logged	Currie	Currie	Oval Office (arrived at 18:34)	No purpose recalled/known	V006-DC-00000008 (WAVES record) 827-DC-00000018 (Epass Entry Log) 968-DC-00000190 (Presidential Movement Log)
40	12/05/97 (Fri.)	No entry time logged	No exit time logged	Schwartz	President Clinton	White House	Christmas Party	V006-DC-00000009 (WAVES record) 1222-DC-00000264 (Presidential Activity Report) V006-DC-00000521 (Holiday Reception Guest List) V006-DC-00001765 (WAVES request)
41	12/06/97 (Sat.)	12:52	13:36	Currie	Currie	Oval Office Residence (arrived at 13:34)	No purpose recalled/known	V006-DC-00000009 (WAVES record) 827-DC-00000018 (Epass Entry & Exit Logs) V006-DC-00002158 (Presidential Movement Log)

KEY:
Requestor   The person at whose behest the visitor was cleared into the White House through the WAVES system.
Visitee   The person whom the requestor listed as the person to be visited when requesting clearance for the Ms. Lewinsky.
Purpose   The purpose recalled by the requestor or visitee during an interview with the OIC.
References   The official White House logs that contain the information upon which this chart is based.
Shaded Areas Visits during which Ms. Lewinsky and the President were in the Oval Office area, and no one else was known to be present.
(See "Understanding the Evidence" section, Tab G, for details.)

333

				Requestor	Visitee	Location	Purpose	References
42	12/15/97 (Mon.)	11:31	12:39	Luzzatto	Wozniak	Oval Office	To do "some things" for Ken Bacon	V006-DC-00000009 (WAVES record) 827-DC-00000018 (Epass Entry & Exit Logs) 968-DC-00000198 (Presidential Movement Log) Wozniak 3/5/98 Int. at 2
43	"A day or two" before or after 12/15/98	No entry time logged	No exit time logged	Wozniak	Wozniak	Unknown	To do "some things" for Ken Bacon	V006-DC-00000009 (WAVES record) Wozniak 3/5/98 Int. at 2
44	12/28/97 (Sun.)	08:16	No exit time logged	Currie	Currie	Oval Office (arrived at 08:10) Residence (arrived at 09:52)	No purpose recalled/known	V006-DC-00000009 (WAVES record) 827-DC-00000018 (Epass Entry Log) V006-DC-00002159 (Presidential Movement Log)

KEY: Requestor   The person at whose behest the visitor was cleared into the White House through the WAVES system.
Visitee   The person whom the requestor listed as the person to be visited when requesting clearance for the Ms. Lewinsky.
Purpose   The purpose recalled by the requestor or visitee during an interview with the OIC.
References   The official White House logs that contain the information upon which this chart is based.
Shaded Areas   Visits during which Ms. Lewinsky and the President were in the Oval Office area, and no one else was known to be present.
(See "Understanding the Evidence" section, Tab G, for details

334

Monica Lewinsky's Contacts
with President Clinton

INTRODUCTION TO THE CHART
OF CONTACTS BETWEEN THE PRESIDENT AND
MONICA LEWINSKY

The Office of the Independent Counsel ("OIC") prepared the following Chart with Monica Lewinsky's assistance. In her words, "it's a chronology that marks some of the highlights of my relationship with the President. It definitely includes the visits that I had with him and most of the gifts we exchanged. It reflects most of the phone calls that I remember."[1] Dates on which sexual contact occurred are designated in bold.

The most important source of information for this Chart was Ms. Lewinsky's recollections, which were refreshed in small part by the near-contemporaneous compiled record in her Filofax calendar.[2] To an even smaller degree, the OIC used some evidence gathered in its investigation to assist Ms. Lewinsky in refreshing her memory of events. Ms. Lewinsky reviewed several predecessor versions of the Chart over three or four days and made minor modifications before confirming its accuracy.[3]

This Chart was used as Grand Jury Exhibit ML-7 when Ms. Lewinsky testified before the grand jury on August 6, 1998.[4] When she testified, Ms. Lewinsky noted that one change should be made to the chart: The October 23, 1996, contact on page five should also reflect the fact that Ms. Lewinsky

---

[1] Lewinsky 8/6/98 GJ at 27-28.
[2] Id. at 28-29
[3] Lewinsky 8/5/98 Int. at 1.
[4] Id. at 27-28.

attended a Democratic fundraiser on that date.[5] Ms. Lewinsky testified that she believed that the Chart was otherwise accurate, with that correction.[6] On August 26, 1998, Ms. Lewinsky again verified the accuracy of the Chart in a sworn deposition.[7]

Since Ms. Lewinsky last verified the Chart, Ms. Lewinsky has examined a substantial amount of evidence, including the transcripts and audio tapes of several of her conversations with Linda Tripp. In reviewing that evidence, Ms. Lewinsky realized that there were two minor discrepancies between the Chart and the actual sequence of events regarding when she and the President exchanged two gifts. She now recalls that the President gave her the Annie Lenox compact disc on October 11, 1997, rather than on December 6, 1997, as listed on the Chart. Similarly, she now believes she may have sent the package to the President containing sunglasses, an erotic postcard, and a note about education reform on October 16, 1997, rather than on October 21 or 22, 1997, as listed on the Chart.[8] Ms. Lewinsky has made no other revisions to the Chart.

This Chart is a counterpart to the Chart of Recorded Lewinsky Visits to the White House, at Tab E. That chart details Ms. Lewinsky's presence at the White House with documentary evidence.

---

[5] Id. at 28.
[6] Id.
[7] Lewinsky 8/26/98 Depo. at 6.
[8] Lewinsky 9/6/98 Int. at 2-3.

CONTACTS BETWEEN THE PRESIDENT AND MONICA LEWINSKY

DATE	IN - PERSON CONTACTS	PHONE CALLS	GIFTS/ NOTES ML TO WJC	GIFTS/NOTES WJC TO ML
Approx. 8/9/95 Wednesday	Departure ceremony - nonverbal connection - eye contact - green suit			
Approx. 8/10/95 Thursday	Public function - Pres. 49th B-day party - flirtation - eye contact - green suit			
Approx. 8/13 or 8/14/95 Sun. - Mon.	Departure ceremony - intro. to Pres.			
Mid to late 9/95	Photo opportunity - WW basement - Ungvari - Pres. said he knew who ML was			
Approx. 10/95	Chance meeting - West Exec. Ave. - waved at Pres.			
11/15/95 Wednesday	Pres. made several visits to Panetta's office where ML was working			
11/15/95 Wednesday	Private encounter - approx. 8 p.m. - hallway by study - kissing			
11/15/95 Wednesday	Second private encounter - sometime b/t 8 and 10 p.m. - study and hallway by study - physical intimacy including oral sex			
11/17/95 Friday	Private encounter - approx. 8 p.m. - study area - pizza night - kissing			
11/17/95 Friday	Second private meeting of night - bathroom by study - phone call - pizza night - physical intimacy including oral sex			
11/20/95 Monday			Zegna tie - ML gave to Currie to give to Pres	
12/5/95 Tuesday	Brief private encounter - oval office and back study - no sexual contact			autographed photo wearing tie
12/31/95 Sunday	Private encounter - sometime b/t 12 and 1 p.m. - approx. 20 or 25 min. - hallway by study - physical intimacy including oral sex			"Davidoff" cigars

337

DATE	IN - PERSON CONTACTS	PHONE CALLS	GIFTS/ NOTES ML TO WJC	GIFTS/NOTES WJC TO ML
1/7/96 Sunday		conversation - first call to ML's home		
1/7/96 Sunday		conversation - ML at office		
1/7/96 Sunday	Private encounter - late afternoon - mtg. lasted approx. 45 min. - bathroom by study - physical intimacy including oral sex			
1/15 or (early a.m.) 1/16/96 Mon. or Tues.		conversation, including phone sex - approx. 12:30 a.m. - ML at home		
1/21/96 Sunday	Chance encounter then private encounter - sometime b/t 3 and 5 p.m. approx. 30 to 40 min. - hallway by study - physical intimacy including oral sex - kissing in N. Hernreich's office			
Approx. 1/28/96 Sunday		caller ID on ML's office phone indicated POTUS call		
1/30/96 Tuesday		conversation - during middle of workday at ML's office		
1/30/96 Tuesday	Public function - Griffin's going away party			
2/4/96 Sunday		conversations - ML at office - multiple calls		
2/4/96 Sunday	Private encounter- study and hallway - approx. 1 ½ hr. - physical intimacy including oral sex			Signed "State of Union" address (date approx.)
2/4/96 Sunday		conversation - ML at office		
2/7 or 2/8/96 Wed. or Thurs.		conversation - ML at home		

338

DATE	IN - PERSON CONTACTS	PHONE CALLS	GIFTS/ NOTES ML TO WJC	GIFTS/NOTES WJC TO ML
2/8 or 2/9/96 Thurs. or Fri.		conversation, including phone sex - ML at home		
2/19/96 Monday		conversation - ML at home		
2/19/96 Monday	Private encounter - approx. 25 min. sometime b/t 12 and 2 p.m. - oval office - no sexual contact			
Approx. 2/28 or 3/5/96		conversation - approx. 20 min. - after chance meeting in hallway - ML at home		
3/10/96 Sunday	Accidental meeting - outside restroom in WH - Ungvari present			
3/25/96 Monday	Accidental meeting - pass each other in hallway - ML looked away			
3/26/96 Tuesday		conversation - approx. 11 a.m. - ML at office		
3/29/96 riday	Accidental meeting - after jog - ML hurt hand	conversation - ML at office - approx. 8 p.m. - invitation to movie		
3/31/96 Sunday		conversation - ML at office - approx. 1 p.m. - Pres. ill		
3/31/96 Sunday	Private encounter - approx. 45 min. - hallway by study - physically intimate contact		Hugo Boss tie - carried to mtg.	cigars
4/7/96 Easter Sunday		conversation - ML at home		
4/7/96 - Easter Sunday	Private encounter - sometime b/t 5 and 6 p.m.- approx. 30 min. - hallway by study and study - intervening phone call - physical intimacy including oral sex			
4/7/96 Easter Sunday		conversation - ML at home - why ML left		

DATE	IN - PERSON CONTACTS	PHONE CALLS	GIFTS/ NOTES ML TO WJC	GIFTS/NOTES WJC TO ML
4/12/96 Friday		conversation - ML at home - daytime		
4/12 or (early a.m.) 4/13/96 Fri. or Sat.		conversation - ML at home - after midnight		
4/22/96 Monday		conversation - job talk - ML at home		
Approx. 4/28/96 Sunday	Public function - AIPAC meeting			
4/29 or 4/30/96 Mon. or Tues.		message - after 6:30 a.m.		
5/2/96 Thursday		conversation, possibly including phone sex - ML at home		
5/6/96 Monday		possible phone call		
pprox. 5/8/96 Wednesday	Public function - Saxophone Club event			
5/16/96 Thursday		conversation - ML at home		
5/21/96 Tuesday	Public function - Adm. Boorda memorial service			
5/21/96 Tuesday		conversation, including phone sex - ML at home		
5/31/96 Friday		message		
6/5/96 Wednesday		conversation - ML at home - early evening		
Approx. 6/13/96 Thursday	Public function - arrival of Irish President			
6/14/96 Friday	Public function - radio address - family			

DATE	IN - PERSON CONTACTS	PHONE CALLS	GIFTS/ NOTES ML TO WJC	GIFTS/NOTES WJC TO ML
6/23/96 Sunday		conversation, possibly including phone sex - ML at home		
7/5 or (early a.m.) 7/6/96 Fri. or Sat.		conversation, including phone sex - ML at home		
7/19/96 Friday		conversation, including phone sex - 6:30 a.m. - ML at home		
7/28/96 Sunday		conversation - ML at home		
8/4/96 Sunday		conversation, including phone sex - ML at home		
Before 8/16/96			Zegna tie - also t-shirt from Bosnia - ML sent to Betty to give to the President	
8/18/96 Sunday	Public function - Pres. 50th B-day party - limited intimate contact			
/24/96 Saturday		conversation, including phone sex - ML at home		
9/5/96 Thursday				thank you note - hand signed addendum - "tie is really beautiful"
9/5/96 Thursday		conversation, possibly including phone sex - Pres. in Fla. - ML at home		
9/10/96 Tuesday		message		
9/30/96 Monday		conversation, possibly including phone sex		
10/22/96 Tuesday		conversation, including phone sex - ML at home		
10/23 or (early a.m.) 10/24/96 Wed. or Thurs.		conversation - ML at home		

DATE	IN - PERSON CONTACTS	PHONE CALLS	GIFTS/ NOTES ML TO WJC	GIFTS/NOTES WJC TO ML
11/6/96 Wednesday	Public function - South Lawn Rally			
12/2/96 Monday		conversation - approx. 10 - 15 min. - ML at home		
12/2/96 Monday		conversation, including phone sex - later that evening - ML at home - approx. 10:30 p.m. - Pres. fell asleep		
12/17/96 Tuesday	Public function - Christmas party			
12/18/96 Wednesday		conversation - approx. 5 min.- 10:30 p.m. - ML at home		
After Christmas 1996			Sherlock Holmes game - glow in dark frog - ML dropped off gifts with Currie	
12/30/96 Monday		message		
12/97 Sunday		conversation, including job talk and possibly phone sex - ML at home		
Sometime between 2/97 and 5/97			two books, Oy Vey and a golf book - card or letter	
2/8/97 Saturday		conversation - ML at home - mid-day - 11:30 or 12:00		
2/8/97 Saturday		conversation, including job talk and phone sex - 1:30 or 2:00 p.m. - ML at home		
2/14/97 Friday			Washington Post ad - Happy Valentine's Day	
2/28/97 Friday	Private encounter after radio address - early evening - approx. 20 to 25 min. - study and bathroom by study - physical intimacy including oral sex to completion		Golf ball and tees from Harrods - plastic pocket frog	hatpin - the book, Leaves of Grass

342

DATE	IN - PERSON CONTACTS	PHONE CALLS	GIFTS/ NOTES ML TO WJC	GIFTS/NOTES WJC TO ML
Between 3/3 and 3/9/97			Thank you note - Hugo Boss tie - ML sent package by Federal Express	
3/12/97 Wednesday		conversation - three minutes - ML at work		
After 3/14/97			care package after Pres. injured his leg - "Hi ya, handsome!" card, metal magnet with Pres. seal for his crutches, license plate with "BILL" for his wheelchair, knee pads with Pres. seal - ML sent package by Federal Express	
3/29/97 Saturday	Private encounter - approx. 1:30 or 2 p.m. - study - Pres. on crutches - physical intimacy including oral sex to completion and brief direct genital contact		penny medallion with the heart cut out - her personal copy of Vox - framed Valentine's Day ad [ML also replaced the cut Hugo Boss tie]	
4/26/97 Saturday		conversation - late afternoon - 20 min. - ML at home		
5/17/97 Saturday		conversations - multiple calls		
5/18/97 Sunday		conversations - multiple calls		
5/24/97 Saturday	Private encounter - "D-Day" - mid-day - hugging - dining room, study and hallway		Banana Republic long sleeve casual shirt - puzzle on golf mysteries	
6/29/97 Sunday			letter	
7/3/97 Thursday			letter - frustration re: jobs	
7/4/97 Friday Indep. Day	Private encounter - approx. 9:15 - mtg. ended b/t 10 and 11 a.m. - study and hallway - argument - kiss on neck			
7/8/97 Tuesday	Public function - Madrid - flirtation			

DATE	IN - PERSON CONTACTS	PHONE CALLS	GIFTS/ NOTES ML TO WJC	GIFTS/NOTES WJC TO ML
7/14/97 Monday	Private encounter - Hernreich's office - late evening - Pres. had conference call during middle of mtg. - ML did not participate in conference call - no sexual contact		wooden B with a frog in it from Budapest - card with a watermelon on it	
7/15/97 Tuesday		conversation - ML at home		
7/24/97 Thursday	Private encounter - oval office - approx. 10 min. - early evening - no sexual contact			b-day gifts: antique flower pin in wooden box and porcelain objet d' art handed to ML by Currie - ML picked up signed picture
8/1/97 Friday		conversation		
Week of 8/10/97 but before 8/16/97			a book, The Notebook and a card	
'/16/97 ,aturday	Private encounter - physical intimacy including birthday kiss - study		b-day gifts: antique book on Peter the Great, apple square - ML also gave Pres. card game "Royalty" and a book, Disease and Misrepresentation	
Early 9/97				Black Dog items: t-shirts, baseball cap, mug and cotton dress - given to ML by Currie
9/30/97 Tuesday			memorandum - to "HANDSOME" re: "the New Deal"	
9/30/97 Tuesday		conversation, possibly including phone sex		
10/7/97 Tuesday			couriered package - letter - job talk	

DATE	IN - PERSON CONTACTS	PHONE CALLS	GIFTS/ NOTES ML TO WJC	GIFTS/NOTES WJC TO ML
10/9 or (early a.m.) 10/10/97 Thurs. or Fri.		conversation - long, from 2 or 2:30 a.m. until 3:30 or 4:00 a.m. - job talk - argument - ML at home		
10/11/97 Saturday	Private encounter - approx. 9:30 a.m. - study - job talk - no sexual contact			
10/16/97 Thursday			letter - job-related - "whole fat packet" of job stuff -via Federal Express	
10/21 or 10/22/97 Tues. or Wed.			Calvin Klein tie - a pair of sunglasses - a card, a postcard (erotic painting) - note re: education reform	
10/23/97 Thursday		conversation - ML at home - end b/c HRC		
10/28/97 Tuesday			unidentified couriered package	
10/30/97 hursday		conversation - ML at home - interview prep		
Approx. week before 10/31/97			Halloween gifts: card - pumpkin lapel pin - wooden letter opener with a frog on the handle - plastic pumpkin filled with candy	
11/3/97 Monday			unidentified couriered package	
11/12/97 Wednesday		conversation, possibly including phone sex - discuss re: ML visit		
11/12/97 Wednesday			unidentified couriered package	
11/13/97 Thursday			Ginko biloba and zinc lozenges - ML gave to Currie to give to Pres. per Pres. request	

DATE	IN - PERSON CONTACTS	PHONE CALLS	GIFTS/ NOTES ML TO WJC	GIFTS/NOTES WJC TO ML
1/13/97 Thursday	Private encounter in study - approx. 5 min. - evening - Zedillo visit		antique paperweight depicting the WH	
11/20/97 Thursday			courier record - letter	
11/21/97 Friday			courier record - cassette tape	
Late 11/97 Early 12/97			letter - ML give to Currie to give to Pres. - Not delivered until 12/5	
12/5/97 Friday	Public function - Christmas party			
12/6/97 Saturday		conversation - approx. 30 min. - ML at home		
12/6/97 Saturday	Private encounter - after NW Gate incident - job talk		Christmas gift: antique standing cigar holder - - Other gifts: Starbucks Santa Monica mug - tie from London - book, Our Patriotic Presidents - Hugs and Kisses box	Annie Lenox compact disc
7/8/97 Monday			courier record - card - peach candles	
12/17 or (early a.m.) 12/18/97 Wed. or Thurs.		conversation - b/t 2:00 a.m. and 3:00 a.m. - ML at home - witness list		
12/28/97 Sunday	Private encounter - Christmas kiss - doorway by study and bathroom by study - b/t 9 and 10 a.m.		Hand painted Easter Egg - "gummy boobs" from Urban Outfitters	large Rockettes blanket from New York - pin of the New York skyline - a "marble-like" bear's head from Vancouver - a pair of joke sunglasses - a small box of cherry chocolates - Black Dog canvas bag - Black Dog stuffed animal

DATE	IN - PERSON CONTACTS	PHONE CALLS	GIFTS/ NOTES ML TO WJC	GIFTS/NOTES WJC TO ML
,/4/98 Sunday			Titanic note - book - Presidents of the United States - dropped off w/Currie	
1/5/98 Monday		conversation		

PART TWO

PRESIDENT CLINTON'S VERSION

President Clinton's
Videotaped August 17, 1998, Grand Jury Testimony

PROCEEDINGS

MR. APPERSON: Mr. Wisenberg, the grand jury is in session. There is a quorum. There are no unauthorized persons in the grand jury room and they are prepared to receive the testimony of the President.

MR. WISENBERG: Thank you, Mr. Apperson. If we could proceed with the oath, please?

WHEREUPON,

WILLIAM JEFFERSON CLINTON

having been called for examination by the Independent Counsel, and having been first duly sworn, was examined and testified as follows:

EXAMINATION BY THE INDEPENDENT COUNSEL

BY MR. WISENBERG:

Q   Good afternoon, Mr. President.

A   Good afternoon.

Q   Could you please state your full name for the record, sir?

A   William Jefferson Clinton.

Q   My name is Sol Wisenberg and I'm a Deputy Independent Counsel with the Office of Independent Counsel. With me today are some other attorneys from the Office of Independent Counsel.

   At the courtroom are the ladies and gentlemen of the grand jury prepared to receive your testimony as you give it. Do you understand, sir?

A   Yes, I do.

Q   This proceeding is subject to Rule 6(e) of the Federal Rules of Criminal Procedure as modified by Judge Johnson's order. You are appearing voluntarily today as a part of an agreement worked out between your attorney, the Office of the Independent Counsel, and with the approval of Judge Johnson.

   Is that correct, sir?

A   That is correct.

MR. KENDALL: Mr. Wisenberg, excuse me. You referred to Judge Johnson's order. I'm not familiar with that order. Have we been served that, or not?

MR. WISENBERG: No. My understanding is that that is an order that the Judge is going to sign today. She didn't have the name of a WHCA person. And basically my understanding is that it will cover all of the attorneys here today and the technical people in the room, so that they will be authorized persons permitted to hear grand jury testimony that they otherwise wouldn't be authorize to hear.

MR. KENDALL: Thank you.

BY MR. WISENBERG:

Q The grand jury, Mr. President, has been empaneled by the United States District Court for the District of Columbia. Do you understand that, sir?

A I do.

Q And, among other things, is currently investigating under the authority of the Court of Appeals upon application by the Attorney General, whether Monica Lewinsky or others obstructed justice, intimidated witnesses, or committed other crimes related to the case of *Jones v. Clinton.*

Do you understand that, sir?

A I do.

Q And today, you will be receiving questions not only from attorneys on the OIC staff, but from some of the grand jurors, too. Do you understand that?

A Yes, sir, I do.

Q I'm going to talk briefly about your rights and responsibilities as a grand jury witness. Normally, grand jury witnesses, while not allowed to have attorneys in the grand jury room with them, can stop and consult with their attorneys. Under our arrangement today, your attorneys are here and present for consultation and you can break to consult with them as necessary, but it won't count against our total time.

Do you understand that, sir?

A I do understand that.

Q You have a privilege against self-incrimination. If a truthful answer to any question would tend to incriminate you, you can invoke the privilege and that invocation will not be used against you. Do you understand that?

A I do.

Q And if you don't invoke it, however, any answer that you do give can and will be used against you. Do you understand that, sir?

A I do.

Q Mr. President, you understand that your testimony here today is under oath?

A I do.

Q And do you understand that because you have sworn to tell the truth, the whole truth, and nothing but the truth, that if you were to lie or intentionally mislead the grand jury, you could be prosecuted for perjury and/or obstruction of justice?

A I believe that's correct.

Q Is there anything that you—I've stated to you regarding your rights and responsibilities that you would like me to clarify or that you don't understand?

A No, sir.

Q Mr. President, I would like to read for you a portion of Federal Rule of Evidence 603, which discusses the important function the oath has in our judicial system.

It says that the purpose of the oath is one, "calculated to awaken the witness' conscience and impress the witness' mind with the duty" to tell the truth.

Could you please tell the grand jury what that oath means to you for today's testimony?

A I have sworn an oath to tell the grand jury the truth, and that's what I intend to do.

Q You understand that it requires you to give the whole truth, that is, a complete answer to each question, sir?

A I will answer each question as accurately and fully as I can.

Q Now, you took the same oath to tell the truth, the whole truth, and nothing but the truth on January 17th, 1998 in a deposition in the Paula Jones litigation; is that correct, sir?

A I did take an oath then.

Q Did the oath you took on that occasion mean the same to you then as it does today?

A I believed then that I had to answer the questions truthfully, that is correct.

Q I'm sorry. I didn't hear you, sir.

A I believed that I had to answer the questions truthfully. That's correct.

Q And it meant the same to you then as it does today?

A Well, no one read me a definition then and we didn't go through this exercise then. I swore an oath to tell the truth, and I believed I was bound to be truthful and I tried to be.

Q At the Paula Jones deposition, you were represented by Mr. Robert Bennett, your counsel, is that correct?

A That is correct.

Q He was authorized by you to be your representative there, your attorney, is that correct?

A That is correct.

Q Your counsel, Mr. Bennett, indicated at page 5 of the deposition, lines 10 through 12, and I'm quoting, "the President intends to give full and complete answers as Ms. Jones is entitled to have".

My question to you is, do you agree with your counsel that a plaintiff in a sexual harassment case is, to use his words, entitled to have the truth?

A I believe that I was bound to give truthful answers, yes, sir.

Q But the question is, sir, do you agree with your counsel that a plaintiff in a sexual harassment case is entitled to have the truth?

A I believe when a witness is under oath in a civil case, or otherwise under oath, the witness should do everything possible to answer the questions truthfully.

MR. WISENBERG: I'm going to turn over questioning now to Mr. Bittman of our office, Mr. President.

BY MR. BITTMAN:

Q Good afternoon, Mr. President.

A Good afternoon, Mr. Bittman.

Q My name is Robert Bittman. I'm an attorney with the Office of Independent Counsel.

Mr. President, we are first going to turn to some of the details of your relationship with Monica Lewinsky that follow up on your deposition that you provided in the Paula Jones case, as was referenced, on January 17th, 1998.

353

The questions are uncomfortable, and I apologize for that in advance. I will try to be as brief and direct as possible.

Mr. President, were you physically intimate with Monica Lewinsky?

A Mr. Bittman, I think maybe I can save the—you and the grand jurors a lot of time if I read a statement, which I think will make it clear what the nature of my relationship with Ms. Lewinsky was and how it related to the testimony I gave, what I was trying to do in that testimony. And I think it will perhaps make it possible for you to ask even more relevant questions from your point of view.

And, with your permission, I'd like to read that statement.

Q Absolutely. Please, Mr. President.

A When I was alone with Ms. Lewinsky on certain occasions in early 1996 and once in early 1997, I engaged in conduct that was wrong. These encounters did not consist of sexual intercourse. They did not constitute sexual relations as I understood that term to be defined at my January 17th, 1998 deposition. But they did involve inappropriate intimate contact.

These inappropriate encounters ended, at my insistence, in early 1997. I also had occasional telephone conversations with Ms. Lewinsky that included inappropriate sexual banter.

I regret that what began as a friendship came to include this conduct, and I take full responsibility for my actions.

While I will provide the grand jury whatever other information I can, because of privacy considerations affecting my family, myself, and others, and in an effort to preserve the dignity of the office I hold, this is all I will say about the specifics of these particular matters.

I will try to answer, to the best of my ability, other questions including questions about my relationship with Ms. Lewinsky; questions about my understanding of the term "sexual relations", as I understood it to be defined at my January 17th, 1998 deposition; and questions concerning alleged subornation of perjury, obstruction of justice, and intimidation of witnesses.

That, Mr. Bittman, is my statement.

Q Thank you, Mr. President. And, with that, we would like to take a break.

A Would you like to have this?

Q Yes, please. As a matter of fact, why don't we have that marked as Grand Jury Exhibit WJC-1.

(Grand Jury Exhibit WJC-1 was marked for identification.)

THE WITNESS: So, are we going to take a break?

MR. KENDALL: Yes. We will take a break. Can we have the camera off, now, please? And it's 1:14.

(Whereupon, the proceedings were recessed from 1:14 p.m. until 1:30 p.m.)

MR. KENDALL: 1:30, Bob.

MR. BITTMAN: It's 1:30 and we have the feed with the grand jury.

BY MR. BITTMAN:

Q Good afternoon again, Mr. President.

A Good afternoon, Mr. Bittman.

(Discussion off the record.)

BY MR. BITTMAN:

Q Mr. President, your statement indicates that your contacts with Ms. Lewinsky did not involve any inappropriate, intimate contact.

MR. KENDALL: Mr. Bittman, excuse me. The witness—

THE WITNESS: No, sir. It indicates—

MR. KENDALL: The witness does not have—

THE WITNESS: —that it did involve inappropriate and intimate contact.

BY MR. BITTMAN:

Q Pardon me. That it did involve inappropriate, intimate contact.

A Yes, sir, it did.

MR. KENDALL: Mr. Bittman, the witness—the witness does not have a copy of the statement. We just have the one copy.

MR. BITTMAN: If he wishes—

MR. KENDALL: Thank you.

MR. BITTMAN: —his statement back?

BY MR. BITTMAN:

Q Was this contact with Ms. Lewinsky, Mr. President, did it involve any sexual contact in any way, shape, or form?

A Mr. Bittman, I said in this statement I would like to stay to the terms of the statement. I think it's clear what inappropriately intimate is. I have said what it did not include. I—it did not include sexual intercourse, and I do not believe it included conduct which falls within the definition I was given in the Jones deposition. And I would like to stay with that characterization.

Q Let us then move to the definition that was provided you during your deposition. We will have that marked as Grand Jury Exhibit WJC-2.

(Grand Jury Exhibit WJC-2 was marked for identification.)

BY MR. BITTMAN:

Q This is an exact copy, Mr. President, of the exhibit that was provided you during that deposition. And I'm sure you remember from the deposition that paragraph (1) of the definition remained in effect. Judge Wright ruled that that was to be the guiding definition, and that paragraphs (2) and (3) were stricken.

Do you remember that, Mr. President?

A Yes. Specifically what I remember is there were two different discussions, I think, of this. There was quite an extended one in the beginning, and everybody was entering into it. And in the end, the Judge said that she would take the first definition and strike the rest of it. That's my memory.

Q Did you—well, at page 19 of your deposition in that case, the attorney who provided you with the definition asked you, "Would you please take whatever time you need to read this definition". And later on in the deposition, you did, of course, refer to the definition several times.

Were you, during the deposition, familiar with the definition?

A Yes, sir. My—let me just ask a question. If you are going to ask me about my deposition, could I have a copy of it? Does anybody have a copy of it?

Q Yes. We have a copy. We'll provide you with a copy.

MS. WIRTH: We will mark it as Grand Jury Exhibit WJC-3.

(Grand Jury Exhibit WJC-3 was marked for identification.)

THE WITNESS: Now, did you say that was on page 19, Mr. Bittman?

BY MR. BITTMAN:

Q It was at page 19, Mr. President, beginning at line 21, and I'll read it in full. This is from the Jones attorney. "Would you please take whatever time you need to read this definition, because when I use the term 'sexual relations', this is what I mean today."

A All right. Yes, that starts on 19. But let me say that there is a—just for the record, my recollection was accurate. There is a long discussion here between the attorney and the Judge. It goes on until page 23. And in the end the Judge says, "I'm talking only about part one in the definition", and "Do you understand that"? And I answer, "I do."

The judge says part one, and then the lawyer for Ms. Jones says he's only talking about part one and asked me if I understand it. And I say, I do, and that was my understanding.

I might also note that when I was given this and began to ask questions about it, I actually circled number one. This is my circle here. I remember doing that so I could focus only on those two lines, which is what I did.

Q Did you understand the words in the first portion of the exhibit, Mr. President, that is, "For the purposes of this deposition, a person engages in 'sexual relations' when the person knowingly engages in or causes"?

Did you understand, do you understand the words there in that phrase?

A Yes. My—I can tell you what my understanding of the definition is, if you want me to—

Q Sure.

A —do it. My understanding of this definition is it covers contact by the person being deposed with the enumerated areas, if the contact is done with an intent to arouse or gratify. That's my understanding of the definition.

Q What did you believe the definition to include and exclude? What kinds of activities?

A I thought the definition included any activity by the person being deposed, where the person was the actor and came in contact with those parts of the bodies with the purpose or intent or gratification, and excluded any other activity.

For example, kissing is not covered by that, I don't think.

Q Did you understand the definition to be limited to sexual activity?

A Yes, I understood the definition to be limited to, to physical contact with those areas of the bodies with the specific intent to arouse or gratify. That's what I understood it to be.

Q What specific acts did the definition include, as you understood the definition on January 17, 1998?

A Any contact with the areas there mentioned, sir. If you contacted, if you contacted those parts of the body with an intent to arouse or gratify, that is covered.

Q What did you understand—

A The person being deposed. If the person being deposed contacted those parts of another person's body with an intent to arouse or gratify, that was covered.

Q What did you understand the word "causes", in the first phrase? That is, "For the purposes of this deposition, a person engaged in 'sexual relations' when the person knowingly" causes contact?

A I don't know what that means. It doesn't make any sense to me in this context, because—I think what I thought there was, since this was some sort of—as I remember, they said in the previous discussion—and I'm only remembering now, so if I make a mistake you can correct me. As I remember from the previous discussion, this was some kind of definition that had something to do with sexual harassment. So, that implies it's forcing to me, and I—and there was never any issue of forcing in the case involving, well, any of these questions they were asking me.

They made it clear in this discussion I just reviewed that what they were referring to was intentional sexual conduct, not some sort of forcible abusive behavior.

So, I basically—I don't think I paid any attention to it because it appeared to me that that was something that had no reference to the facts that they admitted they were asking me about.

Q   So, if I can be clear, Mr. President, was it your understanding back in January that the definition, now marked as Grand Jury Exhibit 2, only included consensual sexual activity?

A   No. My understanding—let me go back and say it. My understanding— I'll tell you what it did include. My understanding was, what I was giving to you, was that what was covered in those first two lines was any direct contact by the person being deposed with those parts of another person's body, if the contact was done with an intent to arouse or gratify. That's what I believed it meant.

That's what I believed it meant then reading it. That's what I believe it means today.

Q   I'm just trying to understand, Mr. President. You indicated that you put the definition in the context of a sexual harassment case.

A   No, no. I think it was not in the context of sexual harassment. I just reread those four pages, which obviously the grand jury doesn't have. But there was some reference to the fact that this definition apparently bore some, had some connection to some definition in another context, and that this was being used not in that context, not necessarily in the context of sexual harassment.

So, I would think that this "causes" would be, would mean to force someone to do something. That's what I read it. That's the only point I'm trying to make.

Therefore, I did not believe that anyone had ever suggested that I had forced anyone to do anything, and that I—and I did not do that. And so that could not have had any bearing on any questions related to Ms. Lewinsky.

Q   I suppose, since you have now read portions of the transcript again, that you were reminded that you did not ask for any clarification of the terms. Is that correct? Of the definition?

A   No, sir. I thought it was a rather—when I read it, I thought it was a rather strange definition. But it was the one the Judge decided on and I was bound by it. So, I took it.

Q   During the deposition, you remember that Ms. Lewinsky's name came up and you were asked several questions about her. Do you remember that?

A   Yes, sir, I do.

Q   During those—or before those questions actually got started, your attorney, Mr. Bennett, objected to any questions about Ms. Lewinsky, and he represented to Judge Wright, who was presiding—that was unusual, wasn't it, that a federal judge would come and actually—in your experience—that a federal judge would come and preside at a deposition?

MR. KENDALL: Mr. Bittman, excuse me. Could you identify the transcript page upon which Mr. Bennett objected to all testimony about Ms. Lewinsky before it got started?

MR. BITTMAN: The objection, this quote that I'm referring to, is going to begin at page 54 of the deposition.

MR. KENDALL: That is into the testimony though, after the testimony about Ms. Lewinsky has begun, is it not?

BY MR. BITTMAN:

Q   Mr. President, is it unusual for a federal judge to preside over a civil deposition?

A   I think it is, but this was an unusual case. I believe I know why she did it.

Q   Your attorney, Mr. Bennett, objected to the questions about Ms. Lewinsky, didn't he?

A   What page is that on, sir?

Q   Page 54, where he questions whether the attorneys for Ms. Jones had a good faith basis to ask some of the questions that they were posing to you. His objections actually begin on page 53.

Since, as the President pointed out that the grand jurors correctly do not have a copy of the deposition, I will read the portion that I am referring to. And this begins at line 1 on page 54.

"I question the good faith of counsel, the innuendo in the question. Counsel is fully aware that Ms. Lewinsky has filed, has an affidavit which they are in possession of saying that there is absolutely no sex of any kind in any manner, shape or form, with President Clinton".

A   Where is that?

Q   That is on page 54, Mr. President, beginning at line 1, about midway through line 1.

A   Well, actually, in the present tense that is an accurate statement. That was an, that was an accurate statement, if—I don't—I think what Mr. Bennett was concerned about, if I—maybe it would be helpful to you and to the grand jurors, quite apart from these comments, if I could tell you what his state of mind was, what my state of mind was, and why I think the Judge was there in the first place.

If you don't want me to do it, I won't. But I think it will help to explain a lot of this.

Q   Well, we are interested, and I know from the questions that we've received from the grand jurors they are interested in knowing what was going on in your mind when you were reading Grand Jury Exhibit 2, and what you understood that definition to include.

Our question goes to whether—and you were familiar, and what Mr. Bennett was referring to obviously is Ms. Lewinsky's affidavit. And we will have that marked, Mr. President, as Grand Jury Exhibit WJC-4.

(Grand Jury Exhibit WJC-4 was
marked for identification.)

BY MR. BITTMAN:

Q   And you remember that Ms. Lewinsky's affidavit said that she had had no sexual relationship with you. Do you remember that?

A   I do.

Q   And do you remember in the deposition that Mr. Bennett asked you about that. This is at the end of the—towards the end of the deposition. And you indicated, he asked you whether the statement that Ms. Lewinsky made in her affidavit was—

A Truthful.

Q —true. And you indicated that it was absolutely correct.

A I did. And at the time that she made the statement, and indeed to the present day because, as far as I know, she was never deposed since the Judge ruled she would not be permitted to testify in a case the Judge ruled had no merit; that is, this case we're talking about.

I believe at the time that she filled out this affidavit, if she believed that the definition of sexual relationship was two people having intercourse, then this is accurate. And I believe that is the definition that most ordinary Americans would give it.

If you said Jane and Harry have a sexual relationship, and you're not talking about people being drawn into a lawsuit and being given definitions, and then a great effort to trick them in some way, but you are just talking about people in ordinary conversations, I'll bet the grand jurors, if they were talking about two people they know, and said they have a sexual relationship, they meant they were sleeping together; they meant they were having intercourse together.

So, I'm not at all sure that this affidavit is not true and was not true in Ms. Lewinsky's mind at the time she swore it out.

Q Did you talk with Ms. Lewinsky about what she meant to write in her affidavit?

A I didn't talk to her about her definition. I did not know what was in this affidavit before it was filled out specifically. I did not know what words were used specifically before it was filled out, or what meaning she gave to them.

But I'm just telling you that it's certainly true what she says here, that we didn't have—there was no employment, no benefit in exchange, there was nothing having anything to do with sexual harassment. And if she defined sexual relationship in the way I think most Americans do, meaning intercourse, then she told the truth.

Q My question—

A And that depends on what was in her mind. I don't know what was in her mind. You'll have to ask her that.

Q But you indicated before that you were aware of what she intended by the term "sexual relationship".

A No, sir. I said I thought that this could be a truthful affidavit. And when I read it, since that's the way I would define it, since—keep in mind, she was not, she was not bound by this sexual relations definition, which is highly unusual; I think anybody would admit that. When she used a different term, sexual relationship, if she meant by that what most people mean by it, then that is not an untruthful statement.

Q So, your definition of sexual relationship is intercourse only, is that correct?

A No, not necessarily intercourse only. But it would include intercourse. I believe, I believe that the common understanding of the term, if you say two people are having a sexual relationship, most people believe that includes intercourse. So, if that's what Ms. Lewinsky thought, then this is a truthful affidavit. I don't know what was in her mind. But if that's what she thought, the affidavit is true.

Q What else would sexual relationship include besides intercourse?

A Well, that—I think—let me answer what I said before. I think most people when they use that term include sexual relationships and whatev-

359

er other sexual contact is involved in a particular relationship. But they think it includes intercourse as well. And I would have thought so. Before I got into this case and heard all I've heard, and seen all I've seen, I would have thought that that's what nearly everybody thought it meant.

Q   Well, I ask, Mr. President, because your attorney, using the very document, Grand Jury Exhibit 4, WJC-4, represented to Judge Wright that his understanding of the meaning of that affidavit, which you've indicated you thought Ms. Lewinsky thought was, she was referring just to intercourse, he says to Judge Wright that it meant absolutely no sex of any kind in any manner, shape or form.

A   Well, let me say this. I didn't have any discussion obviously at this moment with Mr. Bennett. I'm not even sure I paid much attention to what he was saying. I was thinking, I was ready to get on with my testimony here and they were having these constant discussions all through the deposition. But that statement in the present tense, at least, is not inaccurate, if that's what Mr. Bennett meant. That is, at the time that he said that, and for some time before, that would be a completely accurate statement.

Now, I don't believe that he was—I don't know what he meant. You'd have to talk to him, because I just wasn't involved in this, and I didn't pay much attention to what was being said. I was just waiting for them to get back to me. So, I can't comment on, or be held responsible for, whatever he said about that, I don't think.

Q   Well, if you—do you agree with me that if he mislead Judge Wright in some way that you would have corrected the record and said, excuse me, Mr. Bennett, I think the Judge is getting a misimpression by what you're saying?

A   Mr. Bennett was representing me. I wasn't representing him. And I wasn't even paying much attention to this conversation, which is why, when you started asking me about this, I asked to see the deposition. I was focusing on my answers to the questions. And I've told you what I believe about this deposition, which I believe to be true.

And it's obvious, and I think by your questions you have betrayed that the Jones lawyers' strategy in this case had nothing to do with uncovering or proving sexual harassment.

By the time this discovery started, they knew they had a bad case on the law and they knew what our evidence was. They knew they had a lousy case on the facts. And so their strategy, since they were being funded by my political opponents, was to have this dragnet of discovery. They wanted to cover everybody. And they convinced the Judge, because she gave them strict orders not to leak, that they should be treated like other plaintiffs in other civil cases, and how could they ever know whether there had been any sexual harassment, unless they first knew whether there had been any sex.

And so, with that broad mandate limited by time and employment in the federal or state government, they proceeded to cross the country and try to turn up whatever they could; not because they thought it would help their case. By the time they did this discovery, they knew what this deal was in their case, and they knew what was going to happen. And Judge Wright subsequently threw it out. What they—

Q   With all respect, Mister—

A Now, let me finish, Mr. Bennett [sic]. I mean, you brought this up. Excuse me, Mr. Bittman.

What they wanted to do, and what they did do, and what they had done by the time I showed up here, was to find any negative information they could on me, whether it was true or not; get it in a deposition; and then leak it, even though it was illegal to do so. It happened repeatedly. The Judge gave them orders.

One of the reasons she was sitting in that deposition was because she was trying to make sure that it didn't get out of hand.

But that was their strategy, and they did a good job of it, and they got away with it. I've been subject to quite a lot of illegal leaking, and they had a very determined deliberate strategy, because their real goal was to hurt me. When they knew they couldn't win the lawsuit, they thought, well, maybe we can pummel him. Maybe they thought I'd settle. Maybe they just thought they would get some political advantage out of it. But that's what was going on here.

Now, I'm trying to be honest with you, and it hurts me. And I'm trying to tell you the truth about what happened between Ms. Lewinsky and me. But that does not change the fact that the real reason they were zeroing in on anybody was to try to get any person in there, no matter how uninvolved with Paula Jones, no matter how uninvolved with sexual harassment, so they could hurt me politically. That's what was going on.

Because by then, by this time, this thing had been going on a long time. They knew what our evidence was. They knew what the law was in the circuit in which we were bringing this case. And so they just thought they would take a wrecking ball to me and see if they could do some damage.

Q Judge Wright had ruled that the attorneys in the Jones case were permitted to ask you certain questions, didn't she?

A She certainly did. And they asked them and I did my best to answer them. I'm just trying to tell—

Q And was it your responsibility—

A —you what my state of mind was.

Q —to answer those questions truthfully, Mr. President?

A It was.

Q And was—

A But it was not my responsibility, in the face of their repeated illegal leaking, it was not my responsibility to volunteer a lot of information. There are many cases in this deposition where I gave—and keep in mind, I prepared, I treated them, frankly, with respect. I prepared very well for this deposition on the Jones matters. I prepared very well on that. I did not know that Linda Tripp had been involved in the preparation of this deposition, or that all of you—

Q Do you know that now?

A No, I don't. I just know that—what I read in the papers about it. But I had no way of knowing that they would ask me all these detailed questions. I did the best I could to answer them.

Q Did you prepare—

A But in this deposition, Mr. Bittman, I was doing my best to be truthful. I was not trying to be particularly helpful to them, and I didn't think I had an obligation to be particularly helpful to them to further a—when I knew that there was no evidence here of sexual harassment, and I knew what they wanted to do was to leak this, even though it was unlawful to do so. That's—

Q Did you believe, Mr. President—

A —what I knew.

Q —that you had an obligation to make sure that the presiding federal judge was on board and had the correct facts? Did you believe that was your obligation?

A Sir, I was trying to answer my testimony. I was thinking about my testimony. I don't believe I ever even focused on what Mr. Bennett said in the exact words he did until I started reading this transcript carefully for this hearing. That moment, that whole argument just passed me by. I was a witness. I was trying to focus on what I said and how I said it.

And, believe me, I knew what the purpose of the deposition was. And, sure enough, by the way, it did all leak, just like I knew it would.

Q Let me ask you, Mr. President, you indicate in your statement that you were alone with Ms. Lewinsky. Is that right?

A Yes, sir.

Q How many times were you alone with Ms. Lewinsky?

A Let me begin with the correct answer. I don't know for sure. But if you would like me to give an educated guess, I will do that, but I do not know for sure. And I will tell you what I think, based on what I remember. But I can't be held to a specific time, because I don't have records of all of it.

Q How many times do you think?

A Well, there are two different periods here. There's the period when she worked in the White House until April of '96. And then there's the period when she came back to visit me from February '97 until late December '97.

Based on our records—let's start with the records, where we have the best records and the closest in time. Based on our records, between February and December, it appears to me that at least I could have seen her approximately nine times. Although I do not believe I saw her quite that many times, at least it could have happened.

There were—we think there were nine or 10 times when she was in, in the White House when I was in the Oval Office when I could have seen her. I do not believe I saw her that many times, but I could have.

Now, we have no records for the time when she was an employee at the White House, because we have no records of that for any of the employees at the White House, unless there was some formally scheduled meeting that was on the, on the calendar for the day.

I remember—I'll tell you what I remember. I remember meeting her, or having my first real conversation with her during the government shutdown in November of '95, when she—as I explained in my deposition, during the government shutdown, the—most federal employees were actually prohibited from coming to work, even in the White House. Most people in the White House couldn't come to work. The Chief of Staff could come to work. My National Security Advisor could come to work. I could.

Therefore, interns were assigned to all offices. And I believe it was her last week as an intern. Anyway, she worked in the Chief of Staff's Office. One night she brought me some pizza. We had some remarks.

Now, the next time I remember seeing her alone was on a couple of occasions when she was working in the Legislative Affairs Office as a full-time employee. I remember specifically, I have a specific recollection of two times. I don't remember when they were, but I remember twice when, on Sunday afternoon, she brought papers down to me, stayed, and we were alone.

And I am frankly quite sure—although I have no specific memory, I am quite sure there were a couple of more times, probably two times more, three times more. That's what I would say. That's what I can remember. But I do not remember when they were, or at what time of day they were, or what the facts were. But I have a general memory that would say I certainly saw her more than twice during that period between January and April of 1996, when she worked there.

Q So, if I could summarize your testimony, approximately five times you saw her before she left the White House, and approximately nine times after she left the employment of the White House?

A I know there were several times in '97. I've told you that I've looked at my calendar and I tell you what I think the outer limits are. I would think that would sound about right. There could be, in that first four-month period, there, maybe there's one or two more, maybe there's one less. I just don't know. I don't remember. I didn't keep records.

But I'm giving you what I specifically remember and then what I generally remember. I'm doing the best to be helpful to you.

Q Have you reviewed the records for December 28th, 1997, Mr. President?

A Yes, sir, I have.

Q Do you believe that Ms. Lewinsky was at the White House and saw you on December 28th, 1997?

A Yes, sir, I do.

Q And do you remember talking with Ms. Lewinsky about her subpoena that she received for the Paula Jones case on that day?

A I remember talking with Ms. Lewinsky about her testimony, or about the prospect that she might have to give testimony. And she, she talked to me about that. I remember that.

Q And you also gave her Christmas gifts, is that not correct, Mr. President?

A That is correct. They were Christmas gifts and they were going-away gifts. She was moving to New York to, taking a new job, starting a new life. And I gave her some gifts.

Q And you actually requested this meeting, is that not correct?

A I don't remember that, Mr. Bittman, but it's quite possible that I invited her to come by before she left town. But usually when we met, she requested the meetings. And my recollection is, in 1997 she asked to meet with me several times when I could not meet with her and did not do so. But it's quite possible that I—that because she had given me a Christmas gift, and because she was leaving, that I invited her to come by the White House and get a couple of gifts before she left town.

I don't remember who requested the meeting though. I'm sorry, I don't.

Q You were alone with her on December 28, 1997, is that—

A Yes, sir.

Q —right?

A I was.

Q The gifts that you gave her were a canvas bag from The Black Dog restaurant at Martha's Vineyard, is that right?

A Well, that was just, that was just something I had in the place to, to contain the gifts. But I believe that the gifts I gave her were—I put them in that bag. That's what I had there, and I knew she liked things from The Black Dog. So, I gave her—I think that's what I put the presents in.

I remember what the presents were. I don't remember what the bag was I gave them in.

Q Did you also give her a marble bear's head carving from Vancouver, Canada?

A I did do that. I remember that.

Q And you also gave her a Rockettes blanket; that is, the famous Rockettes from New York?

A I did do that. I had that, I had had that in my possession for a couple of years but had never used it, and she was going to New York. So, I thought it would be a nice thing to give her.

Q You gave her a box of cherry chocolates, is that right?

A I don't remember that, sir. I mean, there could have been. I, I just don't remember. I remember giving the bear and the throw. I don't remember what else. And it seems to me like there was one other thing in that bag. I didn't remember the cherry chocolates.

Q How about a pin of the New York skyline? Did you give—

A That—

Q —her that?

A That could have been in there. I seem to remember I gave her some kind of pin.

Q What about a pair of joke sunglasses?

A I don't remember that. I'm not denying it. I just—I'm telling you what I remember and what I don't.

Q You had given Ms. Lewinsky gifts on other occasions though, is that right, Mr. President?

A Yes, I had.

Q This, though, was—you gave her the most gifts that you had ever given her in a single day, is that right?

A Well, that's probably true. It was sort of like a going-away present and a Christmas present as well. And she had given me a particularly nice book for Christmas, an antique book on Presidents. She knew that I collected old books and it was a very nice thing. And I just thought I ought to get up a few things and give them to her before she left.

Q You mentioned that you discussed her subpoena in the Paula Jones case. Tell us specifically, what did you discuss?

A No, sir, that's not what I said. I said, my recollection is I knew by then, of course, that she had gotten a subpoena. And I knew that she was, therefore, was slated to testify. And she mentioned to me—and I believe it was at this meeting. She mentioned—I remember a conversation about the possibility of her testifying. I believe it must have occurred on the 28th.

She mentioned to me that she did not want to testify. So, that's how it came up. Not in the context of, I heard you have a subpoena, let's talk about it.

She raised the issue with me in the context of her desire to avoid testifying, which I certainly understood; not only because there were some embarrassing facts about our relationship that were inappropriate, but also because a whole lot of innocent people were being traumatized and dragged through the mud by these Jones lawyers with their dragnet strategy. They—

Q So—

A And so I—and since she didn't know Paula Jones and knew nothing about sexual harassment, and certainly had no experience with that, I, I clearly understood why she didn't want to be a part of it.

Q And you didn't want her to testify, did you? You didn't want her to disclose these embarrassing facts of this inappropriate intimate relationship that you had, is that correct?

A Well, I did not want her to have to testify and go through that. And, of course, I didn't want her to do that, of course not.

Q Did you want those facts, not only the fact that she would testify, but did you want the facts that she had about your embarrassing inappropriate intimate relationship to be disclosed?

A Not there, but not in any context. However, I, I never had any high confidence that they wouldn't be.

Q Did anyone, as far as you knew, know about your embarrassing inappropriate intimate relationship that you had with Ms. Lewinsky?

A At that time, I was unaware that she had told anyone else about it. But if, if I had known that, it would not have surprised me.

Q Had you told anyone?

A Absolutely not.

Q Had you tried, in fact, not to let anyone else know about this relationship?

A Well, of course.

Q What did you do?

A Well, I never said anything about it, for one thing. And I did what people do when they do the wrong thing. I tried to do it where nobody else was looking at it.

Q How many times did you do that?

A Well, if you go back to my statement, I remember there were a few times in '96, I can't say with any certainty. There was once in early '97. After she left the White House, I do not believe I ever had any inappropriate contact with her in the rest of '96. There was one occasion in '97 when, regrettably, that we were together for a few minutes, I think about 20 minutes, and there was inappropriate contact. And after that, to the best of my memory and belief, it did not occur again.

Q Did you tell her in the conversation about her being subpoenaed—she was upset about it, you acknowledge that?

A (Witness nodded indicating an affirmative response.)

Q I'm sorry, you have to respond for the record. Yes or no? Do you agree that she was upset about being subpoenaed?

A Oh, yes, sir, she was upset. She—well, she—we—she didn't—we didn't talk about a subpoena. But she was upset. She said, I don't want to testify; I know nothing about this; I certainly know nothing about sexual harassment; why do they want me to testify. And I explained to her why they were doing this, and why all these women were on these lists, people that they knew good and well had nothing to do with any sexual harassment.

I explained to her that it was a political lawsuit. They wanted to get whatever they could under oath that was damaging to me, and then they wanted to leak it in violation of the Judge's orders, and turn up their nose and say, well, you can't prove we did it. Now, that was their strategy. And that they were very frustrated because everything they leaked so far was old news. So, they desperately were trying to validate this massive amount of money they'd spent by finding some new news. And—

Q You were familiar—

A —she didn't want to be caught up in that, and I didn't blame her.

Q You were familiar, weren't you, Mr. President, that she had received a subpoena. You've already acknowledged that.

A Yes, sir, I was.

Q And Mr. Jordan informed you of that, is that right?

A No, sir. I believe—and I believe I testified to this in my deposition. I think the first person who told me that she had been subpoenaed was Bruce Lindsey. I think the first—and I was—in this deposition, it's a little bit cloudy, but I was trying to remember who the first person who told me was, because the question was, again as I remember it—could we go to that in the deposition, since you asked me that?

Q Actually, I think you're—with all respect, I think you may be confusing when Mr. Lindsey—well, perhaps Mr. Lindsey did tell you she was subpoenaed, I don't know. But in your deposition, you were referring to Mr. Lindsey notifying you that she had been identified as a witness.

A Where is that, sir? I don't want to get—I just want—what page is that?

Q Well, actually—

A No, it had to be, because I saw a witness list much earlier than that.

Q Much earlier that December 28?

A Oh, sure. And it had been earlier than—she would—I believe Monica—

MR. KENDALL: Page 69.

THE WITNESS: I believe Monica Lewinsky's name was on a witness list earlier than she was subpoenaed.

BY MR. BITTMAN:

Q Yes.

A So, I believe when I was answering this question, at least I thought I was answering when I found out—yes. See, there's—on page 68, "Did anyone other than your attorneys ever tell you that Monica Lewinsky had been served with a subpoena in this case?" Then I said, "I don't think so." Then I [sic] said, "Did you ever talk" to Monica "about the possibility that she might be asked to testify in this case?"

Then I gave an answer that was nonresponsive, that really tried to finish the answer above. I said, "Bruce Lindsey, I think Bruce Lindsey told me that she was, I think maybe that's the first person told me she was. I want to be as accurate as I can."

And that—I believe that Bruce is the first person who told me that Monica had gotten a subpoena.

Q Did you, in fact, have a conversation with Mr. Jordan on the evening of December 19, 1997, in which he talked to you about Monica being in Mr. Jordan's office, having a copy of the subpoena, and being upset about being subpoenaed?

A I remembered that Mr. Jordan was in the White House on December 19th and for an event of some kind. That he came up to the Residence floor and told me that he had, that Monica had gotten a subpoena and, or that Monica was going to have to testify. And I think he told me he recommended a lawyer for her. I believe that's what happened. But it was a very brief conversation. He was there for some other reason.

Q And if Mr. Jordan testified that he had also spoken to you at around 5 p.m., and the White House phone logs reflect this, that he called you at

366

around the time he met with Ms. Lewinsky and informed you then that she had been subpoenaed, is that consistent with your memory? Also on the 19th?

A I had a lot of phone conversations with Vernon about this. I didn't keep records of them. I now have some records. My memory is not clear and my testimony on that was not clear. I just knew that I talked to Vernon at some time, but I thought that Bruce was the first person who told me.

Q But Mr. Jordan had also told you, is that right?

A Yes. I now know I had a conversation with Mr. Jordan about it where he said something to me about that.

Q And that was probably on the 19th, December 19th?

A Well, I know I saw him on the 19th. So, I'm quite sure. And if he says he talked to me on the 19th, I believe he would have better records and I certainly think he's a truthful person.

Q Getting back to your meeting with Ms. Lewinsky on December 28, you are aware that she's been subpoenaed. You are aware, are you not, Mr. President, that the subpoena called for the production of, among other things, all the gifts that you had given Ms. Lewinsky? You were aware of that on December 28th, weren't you?

A I'm not sure. And I understand this is an important question. I did have a conversation with Ms. Lewinsky at some time about gifts, the gifts I'd given her. I do not know whether it occurred on the 28th, or whether it occurred earlier. I do not know whether it occurred in person or whether it occurred on the telephone. I have searched my memory for this, because I know it's an important issue.

Perhaps if you—I can tell you what I remember about the conversation and you can see why I'm having trouble placing the date.

Q Please.

A The reason I'm not sure it happened on the 28th is that my recollection is that Ms. Lewinsky said something to me like, what if they ask me about the gifts you've given me. That's the memory I have. That's why I question whether it happened on the 28th, because she had a subpoena with her, request for production.

And I told her that if they asked her for gifts, she'd have to give them whatever she had, that that's what the law was.

And let me also tell you, Mr. Bittman, if you go back and look at my testimony here, I actually asked the Jones lawyers for help on one occasion, when they were asking me what gifts I had given her, so they could—I was never hung up about this gift issue. Maybe it's because I have a different experience. But, you know, the President gets hundreds of gifts a year, maybe more. I have always given a lot of gifts to people, especially if they give me gifts. And this was no big deal to me. I mean, it's nice. I enjoy it. I gave dozens of personal gifts to people last Christmas. I give gifts to people all the time. Friends of mine give me gifts all the time, give me ties, give me books, give me other things. So, it was just not a big deal.

And I told Ms. Lewinsky that, just—I said, you know, if they ask you for this, you'll have to give them whatever you have. And I think, Mr. Bittman, it must have happened before then, because—either that, or Ms. Lewinsky didn't want to tell me that she had the subpoena, because that was the language I remember her using.

Q Well, didn't she tell you, Mr. President, that the subpoena specifically called for a hat pin that you had produced, pardon me, that you had given her?

A   I don't remember that. I remember—sir, I've told you what I remember. That doesn't mean that my memory is accurate. A lot of things have happened in the last several months, and a lot of things were happening then. But my memory is she asked me a general question about gifts. And my memory is she asked me in the hypothetical. So, it's possible that I had a conversation with her before she got a subpoena. Or it's possible she didn't want to tell me that was part of the subpoena. I don't know.

But she may have been worried about this gift business. But it didn't bother me. My experience was totally different. I told her, I said, look, the way these things work is, when a person get a subpoena, you have to give them whatever you have; that's what's the rule, that's what the law is.

And when I was asked about this in my deposition, even though I was not trying to be helpful particularly to these people that I thought were not well-motivated, or being honest or even lawful in their conduct vis-a-vis me, that is, the Jones legal team, I did ask them specifically to enumerate the gifts. I asked them to help me because I couldn't remember the specifics.

So, all I'm saying is, it didn't—I wasn't troubled by this gift issue.

Q   And your testimony is that Ms. Lewinsky was concerned about her turning over any gifts that you had given her, and that your recommendation to her was, absolutely, Monica, you have to produce everything that I have given you. Is that your testimony?

A   My testimony is what I have said, and let me reiterate it. I don't want to agree to a characterization of it. I want to just say what it was.

My testimony is that my memory is that on some day in December, and I'm sorry I don't remember when it was, she said, well, what if they ask me about the gifts you have given me. And I said, well, if you get a request to produce those, you have to give them whatever you have.

And it just, to me, it—I don't—I didn't then, I don't now see this as a problem. And if she thought it was a problem, I think it—it must have been from a, really, a misapprehension of the circumstances. I certainly never encouraged her not to, to comply lawfully with a subpoena.

Q   Mr. President, if your intent was, as you have earlier testified, that you didn't want anybody to know about this relationship you had with Ms. Lewinsky, why would you feel comfortable giving her gifts in the middle of discovery in the Paula Jones case?

A   Well, sir, for one thing, there was no existing improper relationship at that time. I had, for nearly a year, done my best to be a friend to Ms. Lewinsky, to be a counselor to her, to give her good advice, and to help her. She had, for her part, most of the time, accepted the changed circumstances. She talked to me a lot about her life, her job ambitions, and she continued to give me gifts. And I felt that it was a right thing to do to give her gifts back.

I have always given a lot of people gifts. I have always been given gifts. I do not think there is anything improper about a man giving a woman a gift, or a woman giving a man a gift, that necessarily connotes an improper relationship. So, it didn't bother me.

I wasn't—you know, this was December 28th. I was—I gave her some gifts. I wasn't worried about it. I thought it was an all right thing to do.

Q   What about notes and letters, cards, letters and notes to Ms. Lewinsky?

After this relationship, this inappropriate intimate relationship between you and Ms. Lewinsky ended, she continued to send you numerous intimate notes and cards, is that right?

A   Well, they were—some of them were, were somewhat intimate. I'd say most of them, most of the notes and cards were, were affectionate all right, but, but she had clearly accepted the fact that there could be no contact between us that was in any way inappropriate.

   Now, she, she sent cards sometimes that were just funny, even a little bit off-color, but they were funny. She liked to send me cards, and I got a lot of those cards; several, anyway, I don't know a lot. I got a few.

Q   She professed her love to you in these cards after the end of the relationship, didn't she?

A   Well,—

Q   She said she loved you?

A   Sir, the truth is that most of the time, even when she was expressing her feelings for me in affectionate terms, I believed that she had accepted, understood my decision to stop this inappropriate contact. She knew from the very beginning of our relationship that I was apprehensive about it. And I think that in a way she felt a little freer to be affectionate, because she knew that nothing else was going to happen. I can't explain entirely what was in her mind.

   But most of these messages were not what you would call over the top. They weren't things that, if you read them, you would say, oh, my goodness, these people are having some sort of sexual affair.

Q   Mr. President, the question—

A   But some of them were quite affectionate.

Q   My question was, did she or did she not profess her love to you in those cards and letters that she sent to you after the relationship ended?

A   Most of them were signed, "Love", you know, "Love, Monica." I don't know that I would consider—I don't believe that in most of these cards and letters she professed her love, but she might well have. I—but, you know, love can mean different things, too, Mr. Bittman. I have—there are a lot of women with whom I have never had any inappropriate conduct who are friends of mine, who will say from time to time, I love you. And I know that they don't mean anything wrong by that.

Q   Specifically, Mr. President, do you remember a card she sent you after she saw the movie Titanic, in which she said that she reminisced or dreamed about the romantic feelings that occurred in the movie, and how that reminded her of you two? Do you remember that?

A   No, sir, but she could have sent it. I—just because I don't remember it doesn't mean it wasn't there.

Q   You're not denying that, that—

A   Oh, no. I wouldn't deny that. I just don't remember it. You asked me if I remembered. I don't. She might have done it.

Q   Do you ever remember telling her, Mr. President, that she should not write some of the things that she does in those cards and letters that she sends to you because it reveals, if disclosed, this relationship that you had, and that she shouldn't do it?

A   I remember telling her she should be careful what she wrote, because a lot of it was clearly inappropriate and would be embarrassing if somebody else read it. I don't remember when I said that. I don't remember whether it was in '96 or when it was. I don't remember.

Q Embarrassing, in that it was revealing of the intimate relationship that you and she had, is that right?

A I do not know when I said this. So, I don't know whether we did have any sort of inappropriate relationship at the time I said that to her. I don't remember. But it's obvious that if she wrote things that she should not have written down and someone else read it, that it would be embarrassing.

Q She certainly sent you something like that after the relationship began, didn't she? And so, therefore, there was, at the time she sent it, something inappropriate going on?

A Well, my recollection is that she—that maybe because of changed circumstances in her own life in 1997, after there was no more inappropriate contact, that she sent me more things in the mail, and that there was sort of a disconnect sometimes between what she was saying and the plain facts of our relationship. And I don't know what caused that. But it may have been dissatisfaction with the rest of her life. I don't know.

You know, she had, from the time I first met her, talked to me about the rest of her personal life, and it may be that there was some reason for that. It may be that when I did the right thing and made it stick, that in a way she felt a need to cling more closely, or try to get closer to me, even though she knew nothing improper was happening or was going to happen. I don't know the answer to that.

Q After you gave her the gifts on December 28th, did you speak with your secretary, Ms. Currie, and ask her to pick up a box of gifts that were some compilation of gifts that Ms. Lewinsky would have—

A No, sir, I didn't do that.

Q —to give to Ms. Currie?

A I did not do that.

Q When you testified in the Paula Jones case, this was only two and a half weeks after you had given her these six gifts, you were asked, at page 75 in your deposition, lines 2 through 5, "Well, have you ever given any gifts to Monica Lewinsky?" And you answer, "I don't recall."

And you were correct. You pointed out that you actually asked them, for prompting, "Do you know what they were?"

A I think what I meant there was I don't recall what they were, not that I don't recall whether I had given them. And then if you see, they did give me these specifics, and I gave them quite a good explanation here. I remembered very clearly what the facts were about The Black Dog. And I said that I could have given her a hat pin and a Walt Whitman book; that I did not remember giving her a gold broach, which was true. I didn't remember it. I may have given it to her, but I didn't remember giving her one.

They didn't ask me about the, about the Christmas gifts, and I don't know why I didn't think to say anything about them. But I have to tell you again, I even invited them to have a list.

It was obvious to me by this point in the definition, in this deposition, that they had, these people had access to a lot of information from somewhere, and I presume it came from Linda Tripp. And I had no interest in not answering their questions about these gifts. I do not believe that gifts are incriminating, nor do I think they are wrong. I think it was a good thing to do. I'm not, I'm still not sorry I gave Monica Lewinsky gifts.

Q Why did you assume that that information came from Linda Tripp?

A   I didn't then.

Q   Well, you didn't? I thought you just testified you did then?

A   No, no, no. I said I now assume that because—

Q   You now assume.

A   —of all of the subsequent events. I didn't know. I just knew that—

Q   Let me ask you about—

A   —that somebody had access to some information and they may have known more about this than I did.

Q   Let me ask you about the meeting you had with Betty Currie at the White House on Sunday, January 18 of this year, the day after your deposition. First of all, you didn't—Mrs. Currie, your secretary of six-some years, you never allowed her, did you, to watch whatever intimate activity you did with Ms. Lewinsky, did you?

A   No, sir, not to my knowledge.

Q   And as far as you know, she couldn't hear anything either, is that right?

A   There were a couple of times when Monica was there when I asked Betty to be places where she could hear, because Monica was upset and I—this was after there was—all the inappropriate contact had been terminated.

Q   No, I'm talking—

A   But—

Q   —about the times that you actually had the intimate contact.

A   She was—I believe that—well, first of all, on that one occasion in 1997, I do not know whether Betty was in the White House after the radio address in the Oval Office complex. I believe she probably was, but I'm not sure. But I'm certain that someone was there. I always—always someone was there.

In 1996, I think most of the times that Ms. Lewinsky was there, there may not have been anybody around except maybe coming in and out, but not permanently so. I—that's correct. I never—I didn't try to involve Betty in that in any way.

Q   Well, not only did you not try to involve her, you specifically tried to exclude her and everyone else, isn't that right?

A   Well, yes. I've never—I mean, it's almost humorous, sir. I'd, I'd, I'd have to be an exhibitionist not to have tried to exclude everyone else.

Q   So, if Ms. Currie testified that you approached her on the 18th, or you spoke with her and you said, you were always there when she was there, she wasn't, was she? That is, Mrs. Currie?

A   She was always there in the White House, and I was concerned—let me back up and say—

Q   What about the radio address, Mr. President?

A   Let me back up a second, Mr. Bittman. I knew about the radio address. I was sick after it was over and I, I was pleased at that time that it had been nearly a year since any inappropriate contact had occurred with Ms. Lewinsky. I promised myself it wasn't going to happen again. The facts are complicated about what did happen and how it happened. But, nonetheless, I'm responsible for it. On that night, she didn't.

I was more concerned about the times after that when Ms. Lewinsky was upset, and I wanted to establish at least that I had not—because these questions were—some of them were off the wall. Some of them were way out of line, I thought.

And what I wanted to establish was that Betty was there at all other times in the complex, and I wanted to know what Betty's memory was about what she heard, what she could hear. And what I did not know was—I did not know that. And I was trying to figure out, and I was trying to figure out in a hurry because I knew something was up.

Q So, you wanted—

A After that deposition.

Q —to check her memory for what she remembered, and that is—

A That's correct.

Q —whether she remembered nothing, or whether she remembered an inappropriate intimate—

A Oh, no, no, no, no.

Q —relationship?

A No. I didn't ask her about it in that way. I asked her about what the— what I was trying to determine was whether my recollection was right and that she was always in the office complex when Monica was there, and whether she thought she could hear any conversations we had, or did she hear any.

And then I asked her specifically about a couple of times when—once when I asked her to remain in the dining room, Betty, while I met with Monica in my study. And once when I took Monica in the, the small office Nancy Hernreich occupies right next to Betty's and talked to her there for a few minutes. That's my recollection of that.

I was trying to—I knew, Mr. Bittman, to a reasonable certainty that I was going to be asked more questions about this. I didn't really expect you to be in the Jones case at the time. I thought what would happen is that it would break in the press, and I was trying to get the facts down. I was trying to understand what the facts were.

Q If Ms. Currie testified that these were not really questions to her, that they were more like statements, is that not true?

A Well, I can't testify as to what her perception was. I can tell you this. I was trying to get information in a hurry. I was downloading what I remembered. I think Ms. Currie would also testify that I explicitly told her, once I realized that you were involved in the Jones case—you, the Office of Independent Counsel—and that she might have to be called as a witness, that she should just go in there and tell the truth, tell what she knew, and be perfectly truthful.

So, I was not trying to get Betty Currie to say something that was untruthful. I was trying to get as much information as quickly as I could.

Q What information were you trying to get from her when you said, I was never alone with her, right?

A I don't remember exactly what I did say with her. That's what you say I said.

Q If Ms. Currie testified to that, if she says you told her, I was never alone with her, right?

A Well, I was never alone with her—

Q Did you not say that, Mr. President?

A Mr. Bittman, just a minute. I was never alone with her, right, might be a question. And what I might have meant by that is, in the Oval Office complex.

Could—

Q Well, you knew the answer to that, didn't you?

A We've been going for more than an hour. Would you mind if we took a break? I need to go to the restroom.

MR. BITTMAN: Let's take a break.

MR. KENDALL: It's 2:38.

(Whereupon, the proceedings were recessed from 2:38 p.m. until 2:48 p.m.)

MR. KENDALL: It is 2:38—sorry, 2:48.

BY MR. WISENBERG:

Q Mr. President, I want to, before I go into a new subject area, briefly go over something you were talking about with Mr. Bittman.

   The statement of your attorney, Mr. Bennett, at the Paula Jones deposition, "Counsel is fully aware"—it's page 54, line 5—"Counsel is fully aware that Ms. Lewinsky has filed, has an affidavit which they are in possession of saying that there is absolutely no sex of any kind in any manner, shape or form, with President Clinton".

   That statement is made by your attorney in front of Judge Susan Webber Wright, correct?

A That's correct.

Q That statement is a completely false statement. Whether or not Mr. Bennett knew of your relationship with Ms. Lewinsky, the statement that there was "no sex of any kind in any manner, shape or form, with President Clinton," was an utterly false statement. Is that correct?

A It depends on what the meaning of the word "is" is. If the—if he—if "is" means is and never has been, that is not—that is one thing. If it means there is none, that was a completely true statement.

   But, as I have testified, and I'd like to testify again, this is—it is somewhat unusual for a client to be asked about his lawyer's statements, instead of the other way around. I was not paying a great deal of attention to this exchange. I was focusing on my own testimony.

   And if you go back and look at the sequence of this, you will see that the Jones lawyers decided that this was going to be the Lewinsky deposition, not the Jones deposition. And, given the facts of their case, I can understand why they made that decision. But that is not how I prepared for it. That is not how I was thinking about it.

   And I am not sure, Mr. Wisenberg, as I sit here today, that I sat there and followed all these interchanges between the lawyers. I'm quite sure that I didn't follow all the interchanges between the lawyers all that carefully. And I don't really believe, therefore, that I can say Mr. Bennett's testimony or statement is testimony and is imputable to me. I didn't—I don't know that I was even paying that much attention to it.

Q You told us you were very well prepared for the deposition.

A No. I said I was very well prepared to talk about Paula Jones and to talk about Kathleen Willey, because she had made a related charge. She was the only person that I think I was asked about who had anything to do with anything that would remotely approximate sexual harassment. The rest of this looked to me like it was more of a way to harass me.

Q You are the President of the United States and your attorney tells a United States District Court Judge that there is no sex of any kind, in any way, shape or form, whatsoever. And you feel no obligation to do anything about that at that deposition, Mr. President?

A I have told you, Mr. Wisenberg, I will tell you for a third time. I am not even sure that when Mr. Bennett made that statement that I was concentrating on the exact words he used.

373

Now, if someone had asked me on that day, are you having any kind of sexual relations with Ms. Lewinsky, that is, asked me a question in the present tense, I would have said no. And it would have been completely true.

Q Was Mr. Bennett aware of this tense-based distinction you are making now—

A I don't—

MR. KENDALL: I'm going to object to any questions about communications with private counsel.

MR. WISENBERG: Well, the witness has already testified, I think, that Mr. Bennett didn't know about the inappropriate relationship with Ms. Lewinsky. I guess—

THE WITNESS: Well, you'll have to ask him that, you know. He was not a sworn witness and I was not paying that close attention to what he was saying. I've told you that repeatedly. I was—I don't—I never even focused on that until I read it in this transcript in preparation for this testimony.

When I was in there, I didn't think about my lawyers. I was, frankly, thinking about myself and my testimony and trying to answer the questions.

BY MR. WISENBERG:

Q I just want to make sure I understand, Mr. President. Do you mean today that because you were not engaging in sexual activity with Ms. Lewinsky during the deposition that the statement of Mr. Bennett might be literally true?

A No, sir. I mean that at the time of the deposition, it had been—that was well beyond any point of improper contact between me and Ms. Lewinsky. So that anyone generally speaking in the present tense, saying there is not an improper relationship, would be telling the truth if that person said there was not, in the present tense; the present tense encompassing many months. That's what I meant by that.

Not that I was—I wasn't trying to give you a cute answer, that I was obviously not involved in anything improper during a deposition. I was trying to tell you that generally speaking in the present tense, if someone said that, that would be true. But I don't know what Mr. Bennett had in his mind. I don't know. I didn't pay any attention to this colloquy that went on. I was waiting for my instructions as a witness to go forward. I was worried about my own testimony.

Q I want to go back to some questions about Mr. Jordan and we are going to touch a little bit on the December 19th meeting and some others. Mr. Jordan is a long-time friend of yours, is that correct, Mr. President?

A Yes, sir. We've been friends probably 20 years, maybe more.

Q You said you consider him to be a truthful person, correct?

A I do.

Q If Mr. Jordan has told us that he visited you in the Residence on the night of the 19th, after a White House holiday dinner, to discuss Monica Lewinsky and her subpoena with you, do you have any reason to doubt it?

A No. I've never known him to say anything that wasn't true. And his memory of these events, I think, would be better than mine because I had a lot of other things going on.

Q We have WAVE records that will show that, but in the interest of time I'm not going to—since you don't dispute that, I'm not going to show them right now.

And, in fact, that was the very day Monica Lewinsky was subpoenaed, wasn't it, the night that he came to see you?

A   I don't have an independent memory of that, but you would probably know that. I mean, I'm sure there is a record of when she got her subpoena.

Q   If Mr. Jordan has told us that he spoke with you over the phone within about an hour of Monica receiving her subpoena, and later visited you that very day, the night at the White House, to discuss it, again you'd have no reason to doubt him, is that correct?

A   I've already—I believe I've already testified about that here today, that I had lots of conversations with Vernon. I'm sure that I had lots of conversations with him that included comments about this. And if he has a specific memory of when I had some conversation on a certain day, I would be inclined to trust his memory over mine, because under the present circumstances my head's probably more cluttered than his, and my schedule is probably busier. He's probably got better records.

Q   And when Mr. Jordan met with you at the Residence that night, sir, he asked you if you'd been involved in a sexual relationship with Monica Lewinsky, didn't he?

A   I do not remember exactly what the nature of the conversation was. I do remember that I told him that there was no sexual relationship between me and Monica Lewinsky, which was true. And that—then all I remember for the rest is that he said he had referred her to a lawyer, and I believe it was Mr. Carter, and I don't believe I've ever met Mr. Carter. I don't think I know him.

Q   Mr. President, if Mr. Jordan has told us that he had a very disturbing conversation with Ms. Lewinsky that day, then went over to visit you at the White House, and that before he asked you the question about a sexual relationship, related that disturbing conversation to you, the conversation being that Ms. Lewinsky had a fixation on you and thought that perhaps the First Lady would leave you at the end of—that you would leave the First Lady at the end of your term and come be with Ms. Lewinsky, do you have any reason to doubt him that it was on that night that that conversation happened?

A   All I can tell you, sir, is I, I certainly don't remember him saying that. Now, he could have said that because, as you know, a great many things happened in the ensuing two or three days. And I could have just forgotten it. But I don't remember him ever saying that.

Q   At any time?

A   No, I don't remember him saying that. What I remember was that he said that Monica came to see him, that she was upset that she was going to have to testify, that he had referred her to a lawyer.

Q   In fact, she was very distraught about the subpoena, according to Mr. Jordan, wasn't she?

A   Well, he said she was upset about it. I don't remember—I don't remember any, at any time when he said this, this other thing you just quoted me. I'm sorry. I just don't remember that.

Q   That is something that one would be likely to remember, don't you think, Mr. President?

A I think I would, and I'd be happy to share it with you if I did. I only had one encounter with Ms. Lewinsky, I seem to remember, which was somewhat maybe reminiscent of that. But not that, if you will, obsessive, if that's the way you want to use that word.

Q Do you recall him at all telling you that he was concerned about her fascination with you, even if you don't remember the specific conversation about you leaving the First Lady?

A I recall him saying he thought that she was upset with—somewhat fixated on me, that she acknowledged that she was not having a sexual relationship with me, and that she did not want to be drug into the Jones lawsuit. That's what I recall. And I recall his getting, saying that he had recommended a lawyer to her and she had gone to see the lawyer. That's what I recall.

I don't remember the other thing you mentioned. I just—I might well remember it if he had said it. Maybe he said it and I've forgotten it, but I don't—I can't tell you that I remember that.

Q Mr. President, you swore under oath in the Jones case that you didn't think anyone other than your lawyers had ever told you that Monica Lewinsky had been subpoenaed. Page 68, line 22 [sic] through page 69, line 3. Here's the testimony, sir.

Question—we've gone over it a little bit before: "Did anyone other than your attorneys ever tell you that Monica Lewinsky had been served with a subpoena in this case?" Answer, "I don't think so."

Now, this deposition was taken just three and a half weeks after, by your own testimony, Vernon Jordan made a trip at night to the White House to tell you, among other things, that Monica Lewinsky had been subpoenaed and was upset about it. Why did you give that testimony under oath in the Jones case, sir?

A Well, Mr. Wisenberg, I think you have to—again, you have to put this in the context of the flow of questions, and I've already testified to this once today. I will testify to it again.

My answer to the next question, I think, is a way of finishing my answer to the question and the answer you've said here. I was trying to remember who the first person, other than Mr. Bennett—I don't think Mr. Bennett—who the first person told me that, who told me Paula Jones had, I mean, excuse me, Monica Lewinsky had a subpoena. And I thought that Bruce Lindsey was the first person. And that's how I was trying to remember that.

Keep in mind, sort of like today, these questions are being kind of put at me rapid-fire. But, unlike today, I hadn't had the opportunity to prepare at this level of detail. I didn't—I was trying to keep a lot of things in my head that I had remembered with regard to the Paula Jones case and the Kathleen Willey matter, because I knew I would be asked about them. And I gave the best answers I could. Several of my answers are somewhat jumbled.

But this is an honest attempt here—if you read both these answers, it's obvious they were both answers to that question you quoted, to remember the first person, who was not Mr. Bennett, who told me. And I don't believe Vernon was the first person who told me. I believe Bruce Lindsey was.

Q Let me read the question, because I want to talk about the first person issue. The question on line 25 of page 68 is, "Did anyone other than your attorneys ever tell you that Monica Lewinsky had been served with a subpoena in this case?" Answer, "I don't think so."

You would agree with me, sir, that the question doesn't say, the question doesn't say anything about who was the first person. It just says, did anyone tell you. Isn't that correct?

A That's right. And I said Bruce Lindsey, because I was trying to struggle with who—where I had heard this. And they were free to ask a follow-up question, and they didn't.

Q Mr. President, three and a half weeks before, Mr. Jordan had made a special trip to the White House to tell you Ms. Lewinsky had been subpoenaed; she was distraught; she had a fixation over you. And you couldn't remember that, three and a half weeks later?

A Mr. Wisenberg, if—they had access to all this information from their conversations with Linda Tripp, if that was the basis of it. They were free to ask me more questions. They may have been trying to trick me.

Now, they knew more about the details of my relationship with Monica Lewinsky. I'm not sure everything they knew was true, because I don't know. I've not heard these tapes or anything. But they knew a lot more than I did. And instead of trying to trick me, what they should have done is to ask me specific questions, and I invited them on more than one occasion to ask follow-up questions.

This is the third or fourth time that you seem to be complaining that I did not do all their work for them. That just sitting here answering these questions to the best of my memory, with limited preparation, was not enough. That I should have actually been doing all their work for them.

Now, they'd been up all night with Linda Tripp, who had betrayed her friend, Monica Lewinsky, stabbed her in the back and given them all this information. They could have helped more. If they wanted to ask me follow-up questions, they could. They didn't. I'm sorry. I did the best I could.

Q Can you tell the grand jury what is tricky about the question, "Did anyone other than your attorneys ever tell you"—

A No, there's nothing—I'm just telling—I have explained. I will now explain for the third time, sir. I was being asked a number of questions here. I was struggling to remember then. There were lots of things that had gone on during this time period that had nothing to do with Monica Lewinsky.

You know, I believed then, I believe now that Monica Lewinsky could have sworn out an honest affidavit, that under reasonable circumstances, and without the benefit of what Linda Tripp did to her, would have given her a chance not to be a witness in this case.

So, I didn't have perfect memory of all these events that have now, in the last seven months, since Ms. Lewinsky was kept for several hours by four or five of your lawyers and four or five FBI agents, as if she were a serious felon, these things have become the most important matters in the world. At the moment they were occurring, many other things were going on.

I honestly tried to remember when—you know, if somebody asked you, has anybody ever talked to you about this, you normally think, well, where was the first time I heard that. That's all I was trying to do here. I was not trying to say not Vernon Jordan, but Bruce Lindsey. Everybody knows Vernon Jordan is a friend of mine. I probably would have talked to Vernon Jordan about the Monica Lewinsky problem if he had never been involved in it. So, I was not trying to mislead them. I was trying to answer this question with the first person who told me that.

Now, I realize that wasn't the specific question. They were free to ask follow-ups, just like you're asking follow-ups today. And I can't explain why I didn't answer every question in the way you seem to think I should have, and I certainly can't explain why they didn't ask what seemed to me to be logical follow-ups, especially since they spent all that time with Linda Tripp the night before.

Q You've told us that you understand your obligation then, as it is now, is to tell the whole truth, sir. Do you recall that?

A I took the oath here.

Q If Vernon Jordan—

A You even read me a definition of the oath.

Q If Vernon Jordan has told us that you have an extraordinary memory, one of the greatest memories he's ever seen in a politician, would that be something you would care to dispute?

A No, I do have a good memory. At least, I have had a good memory in my life.

Q Do you understand that if you answered, "I don't think so", to the question, has anyone other than your attorneys told you that Monica Lewinsky has been served with a subpoena in this case, that if you answered, "I don't think so", but you really knew Vernon Jordan had been telling you all about it, you understand that that would be a false statement, presumably perjurious?

A Mr. Wisenberg, I have testified about this three times. Now, I will do it the fourth time. I am not going to answer your trick questions.

I—people don't always hear the same questions in the same way. They don't always answer them in the same way. I was so concerned about the question they asked me that the next question I was asked, I went back to the previous question, trying to give an honest answer about the first time I heard about the Lewinsky subpoena.

I—look. I could have had no reasonable expectation that anyone would ever know that, that—or not, excuse me, not know if this thing—that I would talk to Vernon Jordan about nearly everything. I was not interested in—if the implication of your question is that somehow I didn't want anybody to know I had ever talked to Vernon Jordan about this, that's just not so.

It's also—if I could say one thing about my memory. I have been blessed and advantaged in my life with a good memory. Now, I have been shocked, and so have members of my family and friends of mine, at how many things that I have forgotten in the last six years, I think because of the pressure and the pace and the volume of events in the President's life, compounded by the pressure of your four-year inquiry, and all the other things that have happened, I'm amazed there are lots of times when I literally can't remember last week.

If you ask me, did you talk to Vernon—when was the last time you talked to Vernon Jordan, what time of day was it, when did you see him, what did you say, my answer was the last—you know, if you answered [sic] me, when was the last time you saw a friend of yours in California, if you asked me a lot of questions like that, my memory is not what it was when I came here, because my life is so crowded.

And now that—as I said, you have made this the most important issue in America. I mean, you have made it the most important issue in America from your point of view. At the time this was occurring, even though I was concerned about it, and I hoped she didn't have to testify, and I hoped this wouldn't come out, I felt—I will say again—that she could honestly fill out an affidavit that, under reasonable circumstances, would relieve her of the burden of testifying.

I am not trying to exclude the fact that I talked to Vernon here. I just— all I can tell you is I believe this answer reflects I was trying to remember the first person who told me who was not Mr. Bennett, and I believe it was Bruce Lindsey.

Q As you yourself recalled, just recalled, Mr. President, Vernon Jordan not only discussed the subpoena with you that night, but discussed Frank Carter, the lawyer he had gotten for Ms. Lewinsky. And also Mr. Jordan discussed with you over the next few weeks, after the 19th of December, in addition to the job aspects of Ms. Lewinsky's job, he discussed with you her affidavit that she was preparing in the case. Is that correct, sir?

A I believe that he did notify us, I think, when she signed her affidavit. I have a memory of that. Or it seems like he said that she had signed her affidavit.

Q If he's told us that he notified you around January 7th, when she signed her affidavit, and that you generally understood that it would deny a sexual relationship, do you have any reason to doubt that?

A No.

Q So, that's the affidavit, the lawyer, and the subpoena. And yet when you were asked, sir, at the Jones deposition about Vernon Jordan, and specifically about whether or not he had discussed the lawsuit with you, you didn't reveal that to the Court.

I want to refer you to page 72, line 16. It's where this starts. It's going to go down, it might go down somewhat.

Line 16. Question, "Has it ever been reported to you that he"—and that's referring to Mr. Jordan. At line 12 you were asked, "You know a man named Vernon Jordan?", and you answer, "I know him well."

Going down to 16, "Has it ever been reported to you that he met with Monica Lewinsky and talked about this case?" This is your answer, or a portion of it: "I knew that he met with her. I think Betty suggested that he meet with her. Anyway, he met with her. I, I thought that he talked to her about something else."

Why didn't you tell the Court, when you were under oath and sworn to tell the truth, the whole truth, and nothing but the truth, that you had been talking with Vernon Jordan about the case, about the affidavit, the lawyer, the subpoena?

A Well, that's not the question I was asked. I was not asked any question about—I was asked, "Has it ever been reported to you that he met with Monica Lewinsky and talked about this case." I believe—I may be wrong about this—my impression was that at the time, I was focused on the meetings. I believe the meetings he had were meetings about her moving to New York and getting a job.

I knew at some point that she had told him that she needed some help, because she had gotten a subpoena. I'm not sure I know whether she did that in a meeting or a phone call. And I was not, I was not focused on that.

I know that, I know Vernon helped her to get a lawyer, Mr. Carter. And I, I believe that he did it after she had called him, but I'm not sure. But I knew that the main source of their meetings was about her move to New York and her getting a job.

Q Are you saying, sir, that you forgot when you were asked this question that Vernon Jordan had come on December 19th, just three and a half weeks before, and said that he had met that day, the day that Monica got the subpoena?

A It's quite possible—it's a sort of a jumbled answer. It's quite possible that I had gotten mixed up between whether she had met with him or talked to him on the telephone in those three and a half weeks.

Again, I say, sir, just from the tone of your voice and the way you are asking questions here, it's obvious that this is the most important thing in the world, and that everybody was focused on all the details at the time. But that's not the way it worked. I was, I was doing my best to remember.

Now, keep in mind, I don't know if this is true, but the news reports are that Linda Tripp talked to you, then went and talked to the Jones lawyers, and, you know, that she prepared them for this. Now, maybe—you seem to be criticizing me because they didn't ask better questions and, as if you didn't prepare them well enough to sort of set me up or something. I don't know what's going on here.

All I can tell you is I didn't remember all the details of all this. I didn't remember what—when Vernon talked to me about Monica Lewinsky, whether she talked to him on the telephone or had a meeting. I didn't remember all those details. I was focused on the fact that Monica went to meet with Vernon after Betty helped him set it up, and had subsequent meetings to talk about her move to New York.

Now, keep in mind at this time, at this time, until this date here when it's obvious that something funny's going on here and there's some sort of a gotcha game at work in this deposition, until this date, I didn't know that Ms. Lewinsky's deposition [sic] wasn't going to be sufficient for her to avoid testifying. I didn't, you know—

MR. KENDALL: Excuse me, Mr. President, I think—

THE WITNESS: So, all these details—

MR. KENDALL: —you mean her affidavit.

BY MR. WISENBERG:

Q You mean her affidavit?

A Excuse me. I'm sorry. Her affidavit. Thank you.

So, I don't necessarily remember all the details of all these questions you're asking me, because there was a lot of other things going on, and at the time they were going on, until all this came out, this was not the most important thing in my life. This was just another thing in my life.

Q But Vernon Jordan met with you, sir, and he reported that he had met with Monica Lewinsky, and the discussion was about the lawsuit, and you didn't inform, under oath, the Court of that in your deposition?

A I gave the best answer I could, based on the best memory I had at the time they asked me the question. That's the only answer I can give you, sir.

Q And before—

A And I think I may have been confused in my memory, because I've also talked to him on the phone about what he said about whether he talked to her or met with her. That's all I can tell you.

But, let me say again, I don't have the same view about this deposition—I mean, this affidavit—that I think you do. I felt very strongly that

Ms. Lewinsky and everybody else that didn't know anything about Paula Jones and anything about sexual harassment, that she and others were themselves being harassed for political purposes, in the hope of getting damaging information that the Jones lawyers could unlawfully leak.

Now, I believed then, I believe today, that she could execute an affidavit which, under reasonable circumstances with fair-minded, non politically-oriented people, would result in her being relieved of the burden to be put through the kind of testimony that, thanks to Linda Tripp's work with you and with the Jones lawyers, she would have been put through. I don't think that's dishonest. I don't think that's illegal. I think what they were trying to do to her and all these other people, who knew nothing about sexual harassment, was outrageous, just so they could hurt me politically.

So, I just don't have the same attitude about it that you do.

Q   Well, you're not telling our grand jurors that because you think the case was a political case or a setup, Mr. President, that that would give you the right to commit perjury or—

A   No, sir.

Q   —not to tell the full truth?

A   No, sir. In the face of their, the Jones lawyers, the people that were questioning me, in the face of their illegal leaks, their constant, unrelent-ing illegal leaks in a lawsuit that I knew and, by the time this deposition and this discovery started, they knew was a bogus suit on the law and a bogus suit on the facts.

Q   The question is—

A   In the face of that, I knew that in the face of their illegal activity, I still had to behave lawfully. But I wanted to be legal without being particularly helpful. I thought that was, that was what I was trying to do. And this is the first—you are the first persons who ever suggested to me that, that I should have been doing their lawyers' work for them, when they were perfectly free to ask follow-up questions. On one or two occasions, Mr. Bennett invited them to ask follow-up questions.

It now appears to me they didn't because they were afraid I would give them a truthful answer, and that there had been some communication between you and Ms. Tripp and them, and they were trying to set me up and trick me. And now you seem to be complaining that they didn't do a good enough job.

I did my best, sir, at this time. I did not know what I now know about this. A lot of other things were going on in my life. Did I want this to come out? No. Was I embarrassed about it? Yes. Did I ask her to lie about it? No. Did I believe there could be a truthful affidavit? Absolutely.

Now, that's all I know to say about this. I will continue to answer your questions as best I can.

Q   You're not going back on your earlier statement that you understood you were sworn to tell the truth, the whole truth, and nothing but the truth to the folks at that deposition, are you, Mr. President?

A   No, sir, but I think we might as well put this out on the table. You tried to get me to give a broader interpretation to my oath than just my obligation to tell the truth. In other words, you tried to say, even though these people are treating you in an illegal manner in illegally leaking these depositions, you should be a good lawyer for them. And if they don't have enough sense to write—to ask a question, and even if Mr. Bennett invited them to ask follow-up questions, if they didn't do it, you should have done all their work for them.

Now, so I will admit this, sir. My goal in this deposition was to be truthful, but not particularly helpful. I did not wish to do the work of the Jones lawyers. I deplored what they were doing. I deplored the innocent people they were tormenting and traumatizing. I deplored their illegal leaking. I deplored the fact that they knew, once they knew our evidence, that this was a bogus lawsuit, and that because of the funding they had from my political enemies, they were putting ahead. I deplored it.

But I was determined to walk through the mine field of this deposition without violating the law, and I believe I did.

Q   You are not saying, are you, Mr. President, in terms of doing the work for the Jones folks, the Jones lawyers, that you could, you could say, as part of your not helping them, "I don't know" to a particular question, when you really knew, and that it was up to them—even if you really knew the answer, it was up to them to do the follow-up, that you kind of had a one free "I don't know"—

A   No, sir.

Q   If I could finish up? I've been very patient, Mr. President, in letting you finish.

You didn't think you had a free shot to say, "I don't know", or "I don't recall", but when you really did know and you did recall, and it was just up to them, even if you weren't telling the truth, to do a follow-up and to catch you?

A   No, sir, I'm not saying that. And if I could give you one example? That's why I felt that I had to come back to that question where I said, I don't know that, and talk about Bruce Lindsey, because I was trying, I was honestly trying to remember how I had first heard this. I wasn't hung up about talking about this.

All I'm saying is, the—let me say something sympathetic to you. I've been pretty tough. So, let me say something sympathetic.

All of you are intelligent people. You've worked hard on this. You've worked for a long time. You've gotten all the facts. You've seen a lot of evidence that I haven't seen. And it's, it's an embarrassing and personally painful thing, the truth about my relationship with Ms. Lewinsky.

So, the natural assumption is that while all this was going on, I must have been focused on nothing but this; therefore, I must remember everything about it in the sequence and form in which it occurred. All I can tell you is, I was concerned about it. I was glad she saw a lawyer. I was glad she was doing an affidavit. But there were a lot of other things going on, and I don't necessarily remember it all. And I don't know if I can convince you of that.

But I tried to be honest with you about my mindset, about this deposition. And I'm just trying to explain that I don't have the memory that you assume that I should about some of these things.

Q   I want to talk to you for a bit, Mr. President, about the incident that happened at the Northwest Gate of the White House on December 5th— sorry, December 6th, 1997. If you would give me just a moment?

That was a—let me ask you first. In early nineteen—in early December 1997, the Paula Jones case was pending, correct?

A   Yes, sir.

Q You were represented by Mr. Bennett, of course?

A That's correct.

Q In that litigation?

A Yes, I did.

Q How—

A He was.

Q I'm sorry. Go ahead.

A No, no. Yes, he was representing me.

Q How often did you talk to him or meet with him, if you can just recall, at that time in the litigation?

A Well, we met, I would say—I wish Mr. Ruff were answering this question, instead of me. His memory would be better. We met probably, oh, for a long time we didn't meet all that often, maybe once a month. And then the closer we got to the deposition, we would meet more frequently. So, maybe by this time we were meeting more.

We also—there was a period when we had been approached about—

MR. KENDALL: Again, the question only goes to the number of meetings and not the content of any conversations with your lawyer.

THE WITNESS: I understand. We're not talking about the content.

There was a, there was a period in which we, I think back in the summer before this, when we had met more frequently. But I would say normally once a month. Sometimes something would be happening and we'd meet more. And then, as we moved toward the deposition, we would begin to meet more.

BY MR. WISENBERG:

Q A witness list came out on December 5th of 1997, with Monica Lewinsky's name on it. Mr. President, when did you find out that Monica's name was on that witness list?

A I believe that I found out late in the afternoon on the 6th. That's what I believe. I've tried to remember with great precision, and because I thought you would ask me about this day, I've tried to remember the logical question, which is whether, whether I knew it on the 6th and, if so, at what time.

I don't—I had a meeting in the late afternoon on the 5th, on the 6th— excuse me, on the 6th—and I believe that's when I learned about it.

Q Now, on the morning of the 6th, Monica Lewinsky came to the Northwest Gate and found out that you were being visited by Eleanor Mondale at the time, and had an extremely angry reaction. You know that, sir, now, don't you?

A I have, I have—I know that Monica Lewinsky came to the gate on the 6th and apparently directly called in and wanted to see me and couldn't, and was angry about it. I know that.

Q And she expressed that anger to Betty Currie over the telephone, isn't that correct, sir?

A That, Betty told me that.

Q And she then later expressed her anger to you in one of her telephone conversations with Betty Currie, is that correct?

A You mean did I talk to her on the phone?

Q Monica Lewinsky, that day, before she came in to visit in the White House?

A Mr. Wisenberg, I remember that she came in to visit that day. I remember that she was upset. I don't recall whether I talked to her on the phone before she came in to visit, but I well may have. I'm not denying it that I did. I just don't recall that.

Q   And Mrs. Currie and yourself were very irate that Ms. Lewinsky had overheard that you were in the Oval Office with a visitor on that day, isn't that correct, that you and Mrs. Currie were very irate about that?

A   Well, I don't remember all that. What I remember is that she was very—Monica was very upset. She got upset from time to time. And, and I was, you know, I couldn't see her. I had, I was doing, as I remember, I had some other work to do that morning and she had just sort of showed up and wanted to be let in, and wanted to come in at a certain time and she wanted everything to be that way, and we couldn't see her. Now, I did arrange to see her later that day. And I was upset about her conduct.

   I'm not sure that I knew or focused on at that moment exactly the question you asked. I remember I was, I thought her conduct was inappropriate that day.

Q   I want to go back and I want to take them one at a time. Number one, did you find out at some point during that day that Monica had overheard from somebody in the Secret Service that you were meeting with Ms. Mondale, and that Monica got very irate about that?

A   I knew that at some point. I don't know whether I found out that, that day. I knew that day, I knew that somehow she knew that among, that, that Eleanor Mondale was in to see us that day. I knew that. I don't know that I knew how she knew that on that day. I don't remember that.

Q   That leads into my second question, which is, weren't you irate at the Secret Service precisely because they had revealed this information to Ms. Lewinsky on that very day, so irate that you told several people, or at least one person, that somebody should be fired over this, on that very day?

A   I don't remember whether it happened on that very day. But, let me tell you that the Uniformed Secret Service, if that is in fact what happened and I will stipulate that that is, that no one should be telling anybody, not anybody, not a member of my staff, who the President is meeting with. That's an inappropriate thing to do.

   So, I would think that if that, in fact, is what I heard when I heard it, I would have thought that was a bad thing. I don't know that I said that. I don't, I don't remember what I said, and I don't remember to whom I said it.

Q   It would be an inappropriate thing, sir, and that leads into my next question is that why did Mrs. Currie, on your instructions, later that day tell many of the Secret Service Officers involved that it never happened, to forget about it?

A   That what never happened?

Q   The incident that you were so irate about earlier; the incident of somebody disclosing to Ms. Lewinsky that Ms. Mondale was in the Oval Office?

A   I don't know the answer to that. I think maybe, you know, I don't know. I don't know the answer.

Q   You don't recall that you later gave orders to the effect that we are going to pretend this never happened, or something—

A   No, sir.

Q   —like that?

A No, sir. I don't recall it. First of all, I don't recall that I gave orders to fire anybody, if that was the implication of your first statement.

Q It wasn't an implication. Actually, the question was that you initially wanted somebody fired. You were so mad that you wanted somebody fired.

A I don't remember that, first of all. I remember thinking it was an inappropriate thing to do. And I, I, I remember, as I usually do when I'm mad, after awhile I wasn't so mad about it, and I'm quite aware that Ms. Lewinsky has a way of getting information out of people when she's either charming or determined. And it—I could have just said, well, I'm not so mad about it any more.

But I don't remember the whole sequence of events you're talking to me about now, except I do remember that somehow Monica found out Eleanor Mondale was there. I learned either that day or later that one of the Uniformed Division personnel had told her. I do—I thought then it was a mistake. I think now it was a mistake. I'm not sure it's a mistake someone should be terminated over. I think that, you know, you could just tell them not to do that any more.

Q In fact, it would kind of be an overreaction, to get irate or terminate somebody for revealing to a former White House staffer who visits where the President is, don't you think, sir?

A Well, it would depend upon the facts. I think on the whole people in the Uniformed Secret Service who are working on the gate have no business telling anybody anything about the President's schedule, just as a general principal. I didn't mind anybody knowing that she was there, if that's what you're saying. I could care less about that. But I think that the schedule itself—these uniformed people, you know, somebody shouldn't just be able to come up on the street and, because they know who the Secret Service agent is, he says who the President's with. I don't think that's proper.

Q I agree, Mr. President.

A But, on the other hand, I didn't, you know, I, I wanted to know what happened. I think we found out what happened. And then they were, I think, told not to let it happen again, and I think that's the way it should have been handled. I think it was handled in the appropriate way.

Q You have no knowledge of the fact that Secret Service officers were told later in the day something to the effect of, this never happened, this event never happened? You have no knowledge of that?

A I'm not sure anybody ever told that to me. I mean, I thought you were asking—let me just say, my interpretation of this, of your previous question was different than what you're asking now.

What I remember was being upset that this matter would be discussed that—by anybody. It's incidental it happened to be Monica Lewinsky. And that, that whatever I said, I don't recall. But then thinking that the appropriate thing to do was to say, look, just this, this is not an appropriate thing for you to be talking about, the President's schedule, and it shouldn't happen again.

Now, the question you seem to be asking me now—I just want to be sure I'm getting the right question—is whether I gave instructions, in effect, to pretend that Monica Lewinsky was never at the gate. And if—

Q To the effect of pretend—

A   And if that is the question you are asking me, I don't believe I ever did that, sir. I certainly have no memory of doing that.

Q   Or anything to that effect?

A   I don't know what that means.

Q   Is that your testimony?

A   What does that mean, anything to that effect?

Q   Well, Mr. President, you've told us that you were not going to try to help the Jones attorneys, and I think it's clear from your testimony that you were pretty literal at times. So, that's why I'm saying, I don't necessarily know the exact words. The question was, do you have any knowledge of the fact—

A   Of that?

Q   —of the fact that later in the day, on Saturday, the 6th of December, 1997, Secret Service people were then, were told something to this effect: This event never happened, let's just pretend this event did not happen. Do you have knowledge of it, or not?

A   No, sir. And I, I didn't instruct the Secret Service in that regard. I have no memory of saying anything to anybody in the Secret Service that would have triggered that kind of instruction.

Q   Did you tell Captain Purdy, while you were standing in the doorway between the Oval Office and Betty Currie's office, did you tell Captain Purdy of the Uniformed Division, I hope I can count on your discretion in this matter? At the end of the day when you all were talking about that earlier incident, did you tell him that or anything like that, sir?

A   I don't remember anything I said to him in that regard. I have no recollection of that whatever.

MR. WISENBERG: Let's take a break now.

MR. KENDALL: Thank you, 3:38.

(Whereupon, the proceedings were recessed from 3:38 p.m. until 4:01 p.m.)

MR. KENDALL: It is 4:01.

BY MR. WISENBERG:

Q   Mr. President, the next series of questions are from the grand jurors. And let me tell you that the grand jurors want you to be more specific about the inappropriate conduct.

The first question was, one of the grand jurors has said that you referred to what you did with Ms. Lewinsky as inappropriate contact; what do you mean by that?

A   I mean just what I said. But I would like to ask the grand jury, because I think I have been quite specific and I think I've been willing to answer some specific questions that I haven't been asked yet, but I do not want to discuss something that is intensely painful to me. This has been tough enough already on me and on my family, although I take responsibility for it. I have no one to blame but myself.

What I meant was, and what they can infer that I meant was, that I did things that were—when I was alone with her, that were inappropriate and wrong. But that they did not include any activity that was within the definition of sexual relations that I was given by Judge Wright in the deposition. I said that I did not do those things that were in that, within that definition, and I testified truthfully to that. And that's all I can say about it.

Now, you know, if there's any doubt on the part of the grand jurors

386

about whether I believe some kind of activity falls within that definition or outside that definition, I'd be happy to try to answer that.

Q Well, I have a question regarding your definition then. And my question is, is oral sex performed on you within that definition as you understood it, the definition in the Jones—

A As I understood it, it was not, no.

Q The grand jurors would like to know upon what basis, what legal basis you are declining to answer more specific questions about this? I've mentioned to you that obviously you have privileges, privileges against self-incrimination. There's no general right not to answer questions.

And so one of the questions from the grand jurors is what basis, what legal basis are you declining to answer these questions?

A I'm not trying to evade my legal obligations or my willingness to help the grand jury achieve their legal obligations. As I understand it, you want to examine whether you believe I told the truth in my deposition, whether I asked Ms. Lewinsky not to tell the truth, and whether I did anything else with evidence, or in any other way, amounting to an obstruction of justice or a subornation of perjury. And I'm prepared to answer all questions that the grand jury needs to draw that conclusion.

Now, respectfully, I believe the grand jurors can ask me if I believe— just like that grand juror did—could ask me, do you believe that this conduct falls within that definition. If it does, then you are free to conclude that my testimony is that I didn't do that. And I believe that you can achieve that without requiring me to say and do things that I don't think are necessary and that I think, frankly, go too far in trying to criminalize my private life.

Q If a person touched another person, if you touched another person on the breast, would that be, in your view, and was it within your view, when you took the deposition, within the definition of sexual relations?

A If the person being deposed—

Q Yes.

A —in this case, me, directly touched the breast of another person, with the purpose to arouse or gratify, under that definition that would be included.

Q Only directly, sir, or would it be directly or through clothing?

A Well, I would—I think the common sense definition would be directly. That's how I would infer what it means.

Q If the person being deposed kissed the breast of another person, would that be in the definition of sexual relations as you understood it when you were under oath in the Jones case?

A Yes, that would constitute contact. I think that would. If it were direct contact, I believe it would. I—maybe I should read it again, just to make sure.

Because this basically says if there was any direct contact with an intent to arouse or gratify, if that was the intent of the contact, then that would fall within the definition. That's correct.

Q So, touching, in your view then and now—the person being deposed touching or kissing the breast of another person would fall within the definition?

A That's correct, sir.

Q And you testified that you didn't have sexual relations with Monica Lewinsky in the Jones deposition, under that definition, correct?

387

A That's correct, sir.

Q If the person being deposed touched the genitalia of another person, would that be—and with the intent to arouse the sexual desire, arouse or gratify, as defined in definition (1), would that be, under your understanding then and now—

A Yes, sir.

Q —sexual relations?

A Yes, sir.

Q Yes, it would?

A Yes, it would. If you had a direct contact with any of these places in the body, if you had direct contact with intent to arouse or gratify, that would fall within the definition.

Q So, you didn't do any of those three things—

A You—

Q —with Monica Lewinsky?

A You are free to infer that my testimony is that I did not have sexual relations, as I understood this term to be defined.

Q Including touching her breast, kissing her breast, or touching her genitalia?

A That's correct.

Q Would you agree with me that the insertion of an object into the genitalia of another person with the desire to gratify sexually would fit within the definition used in the Jones case as sexual relations?

A There's nothing here about that, is there? I don't know that I ever thought about that one way or the other.

Q The question is, under the definition as you understood it then, under the definition as you understand it now—pardon me just a minute.

Pardon me, Mr. President.

(Pause)

Deposition Exhibit 1, question 1, under the—in the Jones case, Definition of Sexual Relations—

MR. KENDALL: Do you have that before you, Mr. President? Excuse me.

THE WITNESS: I do, sir.

MR. KENDALL: Good.

THE WITNESS: I've got it right here. I'm looking at it.

BY MR. WISENBERG:

Q As you understood the definition then, and as you understood it now, would it include sticking an object into the genitalia of another person in order to arouse or gratify the sexual desire of any person? Would it constitute, in other words, contact with the genitalia?

A I don't know the answer to that. I suppose you could argue that since section 2, paragraph (2) was eliminated, and paragraph (2) actually dealt with the object issue, that perhaps whoever wrote this didn't intend for paragraph (1) to cover an object, and basically meant direct contact.

So, if I were asked—I've not been asked this question before. But I guess that's the way I would read it.

Q If it—that it would not be covered? That activity would not be covered?

A That's right. If the activity you just mentioned would be covered in number (2), and number (2) were stricken, I think you can infer logically that paragraph (1) was not intended to cover it. But, as I said, I've not been asked this before. I'm just doing the best I can.

Q Well, if someone were to hold or a judge were to hold that you are incorrect and that definition (1) does include the hypo I've given to you—because we're talking in hypos, so that you don't—under your request here, if someone were to tell you or rule that you are wrong, that the insertion of an object into somebody else's genitalia with the intent to arouse or gratify the sexual desire of any person is within definition (1)—

MR. KENDALL: Mr. Wisenberg, excuse me. I have not objected heretofore to any question you've asked. I must tell you, I cannot understand that question. I think it's improper. And, if the witness can understand it, he may answer.

MR. WISENBERG: I'll be happy to rephrase it.

BY MR. WISENBERG:

Q If you're wrong and it's within definition (1), did you engage in sexual relations under the definition, with Monica Lewinsky?

A But, Mr. Wisenberg, I have said all along that I would say what I thought it meant, and you can infer that I didn't. This is an unusual question, but it's a slippery slope. We can—I have tried to deal with some very delicate areas here, and, and in one case I've given you a very forthright answer about what I thought was not within here.

All I can tell you is, whatever I thought was covered, and I thought about this carefully. And let me just point out, this was uncomfortable for me. I had to acknowledge, because of this definition, that under this definition I had actually had sexual relations once with Gennifer Flowers, a person who had spread all kinds of ridiculous, dishonest, exaggerated stories about me for money. And I knew when I did that, it would be leaked. It was. And I was embarrassed. But I did it.

So, I tried to read this carefully. I can tell you what I thought it covered, and I can tell you that I do not believe I did anything that I thought was covered by this.

Q As I understand your testimony, Mr. President, touching somebody's breast with the intent to arouse, with the intent to arouse or gratify the sexual desire of any person is covered; kissing the breast is covered; touching the genitalia is covered; correct?

MR. KENDALL: In fairness, the witness said directly in each one of those cases.

BY MR. WISENBERG:

Q Directly, is covered, correct?

A I believe it is, yes, sir.

Q Oral sex, in your view, is not covered, correct?

A If performed on the deponent.

Q Is not covered, correct?

A That's my reading of this number (1).

Q And you are declining to answer the hypothetical about insertion of an object.

I need to inform you, Mr. President—we'll go on, at least for now. But I need to inform you that the grand jury will consider your not answering the questions more directly in their determination of whether or not they are going to issue another subpoena.

Let me switch the topic and talk to you about John Podesta and some of the other aides you've met with and spoke to after this story became public on January 21st, 1998, the day of The Washington Post story.

Do you recall meeting with him around January 23rd, 1998, a Friday a.m. in your study, two days after The Washington Post story, and extremely explicitly telling him that you didn't have, engage in any kind of sex, in any way, shape or form, with Monica Lewinsky, including oral sex?

A   I meet with John Podesta almost every day. I meet with a number of people. The only thing I—what happened in the couple of days after what you did was revealed, is a blizzard to me. The only thing I recall is that I met with certain people, and a few of them I said I didn't have sex with Monica Lewinsky, or I didn't have an affair with her or something like that. I had a very careful thing I said, and I tried not to say anything else.

And it might be that John Podesta was one of them. But I do not remember this specific meeting about which you asked, or the specific comments to which you refer. And—

Q   You don't remember—

A   —seven months ago, I'd have no way to remember, no.

Q   You don't remember denying any kind of sex in any way, shape or form, and including oral sex, correct?

A   I remember that I issued a number of denials to people that I thought needed to hear them, but I tried to be careful and to be accurate, and I do not remember what I said to John Podesta.

Q   Surely, if you told him that, that would be a falsehood, correct?

A   No, I didn't say that, sir. I didn't say that at all. That is not covered by the definition and I did not address it in my statement.

Q   Well, let me ask you then. If you told him—perhaps he thought it was covered, I don't know. But if you told him, if you denied to him sex in any way, shape or form, kind of similar to what Mr. Bennett did at the deposition, including oral sex, wouldn't that have been a falsehood?

A   Now, Mr. Wisenberg, I told you in response to a grand juror's question, you asked me did I believe that oral sex performed on the person being deposed was covered by that definition, and I said no. I don't believe it's covered by the definition.

I said you are free to conclude that I did not do things that I believe were covered by the definition, and you have asked me a number of questions and I have acknowledged things that I believe are covered by the definition. Since that was not covered by the definition, I want to fall back on my statement.

Look, I'm not trying to be evasive here. I'm trying to protect my privacy, my family's privacy, and I'm trying to stick to what the deposition was about. If the deposition wasn't about this and didn't cover it, then I don't believe that I should be required to go beyond my statement.

Q   Mr. President, it's not our intent to embarrass you. But since we have to look, among other things, at obstruction of justice, questions of obstruction of justice and perjury, the answer to some of these delicate and unfortunate questions are absolutely required. And that is the purpose that we have to ask them for.

A   It's not—

Q   I'm unaware of any—

A   Mr. Wisenberg, with respect, you don't need to know the answer for that, if the answer, no matter what the answer is, wouldn't constitute perjury because it wasn't sexual relations as defined by the Judge.

Q   Mister—

A   The only reason you need to know that is for some other reason. It couldn't have anything to do with perjury.

Q   Mr. President, one of the, one of the nice things about—one of the normal things about an investigation and a grand jury investigation is that the grand jurors and the prosecutors get to ask the questions unless they are improper, and unless there is a legal basis.

As I understand from your answers, there is no legal basis for which you decline to answer these questions. And I'll ask you again to answer the question. I'm unaware of any legal basis for you not to. If you told—

MR. KENDALL: Mr. Wisenberg, could you just restate the question, please?

BY MR. WISENBERG:

Q   The question is, if you told John Podesta two days after the story broke something to this effect, that you didn't have any kind of sex in any way, shape or form, including oral sex with Ms. Lewinsky, were you telling him the truth?

A   And let me say again, with respect, this is an indirect way to try to get me to testify to questions that have no bearing on whether I committed perjury. You apparently agree that it has no bearing—

Q   Oh, I don't—

A   —no bearing on whether I—

Q   I don't agree.

A   —committed perjury.

Q   Mr. President, I'm sorry, with respect, I don't agree with that. I'm not going to argue with you about it. I just am going to ask you again, in fact direct you to answer the question.

A   I'm not going to answer that question, because I believe it's a question about conduct that, whatever the answer to it is, would, does not bear on the perjury because oral sex performed on the deponent under this definition is not sexual relations. It is not covered by this definition.

MR. KENDALL: The witness is not declining to tell you anything he said to John Podesta.

BY MR. WISENBERG:

Q   You denied the—

MR. WISENBERG: The witness is not declining to tell me anything?

BY MR. WISENBERG:

Q   Did you deny oral sex in any way, shape or form, to John Podesta?

A   I told you, sir, before, and I will say again, in the aftermath of this story breaking, and what was told about it, the next two days, next three days are just a blur to me. I don't remember to whom I talked, when I talked to them, or what I said.

Q   So, you are not declining to answer, you just don't remember?

A   I honestly don't remember, no.

Q   Okay.

A   I'm not saying that anybody who had a contrary memory is wrong. I do not remember.

Q   Do you recall denying any sexual relationship with Monica Lewinsky to the following people: Harry Thomasson, Erskine Bowles, Harold Ickes, Mr. Podesta, Mr. Blumenthal, Mr. Jordan, Ms. Betty Currie? Do you recall denying any sexual relationship with Monica Lewinsky to those individuals?

A   I recall telling a number of those people that I didn't have, either I didn't have an affair with Monica Lewinsky or didn't have sex with her. And I believe, sir, that—you'll have to ask them what they thought. But I was using those terms in the normal way people use them. You'll have to ask them what they thought I was saying.

Q If they testified that you denied sexual relations or relationship with Monica Lewinsky, or if they told us that you denied that, do you have any reason to doubt them, in the days after the story broke; do you have any reason to doubt them?

A No. The—let me say this. It's no secret to anybody that I hoped that this relationship would never become public. It's a matter of fact that it had been many, many months since there had been anything improper about it, in terms of improper contact. I—

Q Did you deny it to them or not, Mr. President?

A Let me finish. So, what—I did not want to mislead my friends, but I wanted to find language where I could say that. I also, frankly, did not want to turn any of them into witnesses, because I—and, sure enough, they all became witnesses.

Q Well, you knew they might be—

A And so—

Q —witnesses, didn't you?

A And so I said to them things that were true about this relationship. That I used—in the language I used, I said, there's nothing going on between us. That was true. I said, I have not had sex with her as I defined it. That was true. And did I hope that I would never have to be here on this day giving this testimony? Of course.

But I also didn't want to do anything to complicate this matter further. So, I said things that were true. They may have been misleading, and if they were I have to take responsibility for it, and I'm sorry.

Q It may have been misleading, sir, and you knew though, after January 21st when the Post article broke and said that Judge Starr was looking into this, you knew that they might be witnesses. You knew that they might be called into a grand jury, didn't you?

A That's right. I think I was quite careful what I said after that. I may have said something to all these people to that effect, but I'll also—whenever anybody asked me any details, I said, look, I don't want you to be a witness or I turn you into a witness or give you information that could get you in trouble. I just wouldn't talk. I, by and large, didn't talk to people about this.

Q If all of these people—let's leave out Mrs. Currie for a minute. Vernon Jordan, Sid Blumenthal, John Podesta, Harold Ickes, Erskine Bowles, Harry Thomasson, after the story broke, after Judge Starr's involvement was known on January 21st, have said that you denied a sexual relationship with them. Are you denying that?

A No.

Q And you've told us that you—

A I'm just telling you what I meant by it. I told you what I meant by it when they started this deposition.

Q You've told us now that you were being careful, but that it might have been misleading. Is that correct?

A It might have been. Since we have seen this four-year, $40-million-investigation come down to parsing the definition of sex, I think it might have been. I don't think at the time that I thought that's what this was going to be about.

In fact, if you remember the headlines at the time, even you mentioned the Post story. All the headlines were—and all the talking, people who talked about this, including a lot who have been quite sympathetic to your operation, said, well, this is not really a story about sex, or this is a story about subornation of perjury and these talking points, and all this other stuff.

So, what I was trying to do was to give them something they could—that would be true, even if misleading in the context of this deposition, and keep them out of trouble, and let's deal—and deal with what I thought was the almost ludicrous suggestion that I had urged someone to lie or tried to suborn perjury, in other words.

Q I want to go over some questions again. I don't think you are going to answer them, sir. And so I don't need a lengthy response, just a yes or a no. And I understand the basis upon which you are not answering them, but I need to ask them for the record.

If Monica Lewinsky says that while you were in the Oval Office area you touched her breasts, would she be lying?

A Let me say something about all this.

Q All I really need for you, Mr. President—

A I know.

Q —is to say—

A But you—

Q —I won't answer under the previous grounds, or to answer the question, you see, because we only have four hours, and your answers—

A I know.

Q —have been extremely lengthy.

A I know that. I'll give you four hours and 30 seconds, if you'll let me say something general about this. I will answer to your satisfaction that I won't—based on my statement, I will not answer. I would like 30 seconds at the end to make a statement, and you can have 30 seconds more on your time, if you'll let me say this to the grand jury and to you. And I don't think it's disrespectful at all. I've had a lot of time to think about this.

But, go ahead and ask your questions.

Q The question is, if Monica Lewinsky says that while you were in the Oval Office area you touched her breasts, would she be lying?

A That is not my recollection. My recollection is that I did not have sexual relations with Ms. Lewinsky and I'm staying on my former statement about that.

Q If she said—

A My, my statment is that I did not have sexual relations as defined by that.

Q If she says that you kissed her breasts, would she be lying?

A I'm going to revert to my former statement.

Q Okay. If Monica Lewinsky says that while you were in the Oval Office area you touched her genitalia, would she be lying? And that calls for a yes, no, or reverting to your former statement.

A I will revert to my statement on that.

Q If Monica Lewinsky says that you used a cigar as a sexual aid with her in the Oval Office area, would she be lying? Yes, no, or won't answer?

A I will revert to my former statement.

Q If Monica Lewinsky says that you had phone sex with her, would she be lying?

A Well, that is, at least in general terms, I think, is covered by my statement. I addressed that in my statement, and that, I don't believe, is—

Q Let me define phone sex for purposes of my question. Phone sex occurs when a party to a phone conversation masturbates while the other party

393

is talking in a sexually explicit manner. And the question is, if Monica Lewinsky says that you had phone sex with her, would she be lying?

A I think that is covered by my statement.

Q Did you, on or about January the 13th, 1998, Mr. President, ask Erskine Bowles to ask John Hilley if he would give a recommendation for Monica Lewinsky?

A In 1998?

Q Yes. On or about January 13th, 1998, did you ask Erskine Bowles, your Chief of Staff, if he would ask John Hilley to give a recommendation for Monica Lewinsky?

A At some point, sir, I believe I talked to Erskine Bowles about whether Monica Lewinsky could get a recommendation that was not negative from the Legislative Affairs Office. I believe I did.

Q I just didn't hear the very last part.

A I think the answer is, I think, yes. At some point I talked to Erskine Bowles about this.

Q Okay.

A I do not know what the date was. At some point I did talk to him.

Q And if Erskine Bowles has told us that he told John Podesta to carry out your wishes, and John Podesta states that it was three or four days before your deposition, which would be the 13th or the 14th, are you in a position to deny that?

A The 13th or 14th of?

Q January, as to date.

A I don't know. I don't know when the date was.

Q Okay.

A I'm not in a position to deny it. I won't deny it. I'm sure that they are both truthful men. I don't know when the date was.

Q Do you recall asking Erskine Bowles to do that?

A I recall talking to Erskine Bowles about that, and my recollection is, sir, that Ms. Lewinsky was moving to New York, wanted to get a job in the private sector; was confident she would get a good recommendation from the Defense Department; and was concerned that because she had been moved from the Legislative Affairs Office, transferred to the Defense Department, that her ability to get a job might be undermined by a bad recommendation from the Legislative Affairs Office.

So, I asked Erskine if we could get her a recommendation that just was at least neutral, so that if she had a good recommendation from the Defense Department it wouldn't prevent her from getting a job in the private sector.

Q If Mr. Bowles has told us that, in fact, you told him that she already had a job and had already listed Mr. Hilley as a reference and wanted him to be available as a recommendation, would you be in—is that inconsistent with your memory?

A A little bit, but I think—my memory is that when you're, when you get a job like that you have to give them a resume, which says where you've worked and who your supervisor was. And I think that that's my recollection. My recollection is that—slightly different from that.

Q And who was it that asked you to do that on Monica Lewinsky's behalf?

A I think she did. You know, she tried for months and months to get a job back in the White House, not so much in the West Wing but somewhere in the White House complex, including the Old Executive Office Building.

And she talked to Marsha Scott, among others. She very much wanted to come back. And she interviewed for some jobs but never got one. She was, from time to time, upset about it.

And I think what she was afraid of is that she couldn't get a—from the minute she left the White House she was worried about this. That if she didn't come back to the White House and work for awhile and get a good job recommendation, that no matter how well she had done at the Pentagon it might hurt her future employment prospects.

Well, it became obvious that, you know, her mother had moved to New York. She wanted to go to New York. She wasn't going to get a job in the White House. So, she wanted to get a job in the private sector, and said, I hope that I won't get a letter out of the Legislative Affairs Office that will prevent my getting a job in the private sector. And that's what I talked to Erskine about.

Now, that's my entire memory of this.

Q All right. I want to go back briefly to the December 28th conversation with Ms. Lewinsky. I believe you testified to the effect that she asked you, what if they ask me about gifts you gave me. My question to you is, after that statement by her, did you ever have a conversation with Betty Currie about gifts, or picking something up from Monica Lewinsky?

A I don't believe I did, sir. No.

Q You never told her anything to this effect, that Monica has something to give you?

A No, sir.

Q That is to say, Betty Currie?

A No, sir, I didn't. I don't have any memory of that whatever.

Q And so you have no knowledge that, or you had no knowledge at the time, that Betty Currie went and picked up, your secretary went and picked up from Monica Lewinsky items that were called for by the Jones subpoena and hid them under her bed? You had no knowledge that anything remotely like that was going to happen?

A I did not. I did not know she had those items, I believe, until that was made public.

Q And you agree with me that that would be a very wrong thing to do, to hide evidence in a civil case, or any case? Isn't that true?

A Yes. I don't know that, that Ms. Currie knew that that's what she had at all. But—

Q I'm not saying she did. I'm just saying—

A I had—it is, if Monica Lewinsky did that after they had been subpoenaed and she knew what she was doing, she should not have done that.

Q And if you knew, you—

A And I—

Q —shouldn't have done it?

A Indeed, I, myself, told her, if they ask you for gifts you have to give them what you have. And I don't understand if, in fact, she was worried about this, why she was so worried about it. It was no big deal.

Q I want to talk about a December 17th phone conversation you had with Monica Lewinsky at approximately 2:00 a.m. Do you recall making that conversation and telling her initially about the death of Betty's brother, but then telling her that she was on the witness list, and that it broke your heart that she was on the witness list?

A No, sir, I don't, but it would—it, it would—it is quite possible that that happened, because, if you remember, earlier in this meeting you asked me some questions about what I'd said to Monica about testimony and affidavits, and I was struggling to try to remember whether this happened in a meeting or a phone call.

Now, I remember I called her to tell her Betty's brother had died. I remember that. And I know it was in the middle of December, and I believe it was before Monica had been subpoenaed. So, I think it is quite possible that if I called her at that time and had not talked to her since the 6th—and you asked me this earlier—I believe when I saw her on the 6th, I don't think I knew she was on the witness list then, then it's quite possible I would say something like that. I don't have any memory of it, but I certainly wouldn't dispute that I might have said that.

Q And in that conversation, or in any conversation in which you informed her she was on the witness list, did you tell her, you know, you can always say that you were coming to see Betty or bringing me letters? Did you tell her anything like that?

A I don't remember. She was coming to see Betty. I can tell you this. I absolutely never asked her to lie.

Q Sir, every time she came to see Betty and you were in the Oval Office, she was coming to see you, too, wasn't she, or just about every time?

A I think just about every time. I don't think every time. I think there was a time or two where she came to see Betty when she didn't see me.

Q So, do you remember telling her any time, any time when you told her, or after you told her that she was on the witness list, something to this effect: You know, you can always say you were coming to see Betty, or you were bringing me letters?

A I don't remember exactly what I told her that night.

Q Did you—

A I don't remember that. I remember talking about the nature of our relationship, how she got in. But I also will tell you that I felt quite comfortable that she could have executed a truthful affidavit, which would not have disclosed the embarrassing details of the relationship that we had had, which had been over for many, many months by the time this incident occurred.

Q Did you tell her anytime in December something to that effect: You know, you can always say that you were coming to see Betty or you were bringing me letters? Did you say that, or anything like that, in December '97 or January '98, to Monica Lewinsky?

A Well, that's a very broad question. I do not recall saying anything like that in connection with her testimony. I could tell you what I do remember saying, if you want to know. But I don't—we might have talked about what to do in a non legal context at some point in the past, but I have no specific memory of that conversation.

I do remember what I said to her about the possible testimony.

Q You would agree with me, if you did say something like that to her, to urge her to say that to the Jones people, that that would be part of an effort to mislead the Jones people, no matter how evil they are and corrupt?

A I didn't say they were evil. I said what they were doing here was wrong, and it was.

Q Wouldn't that be misleading?

A Well, again, you are trying to get me to characterize something that

396

I'm—that I don't know if I said or not, without knowing whether the whole, whether the context is complete or not. So, I would have to know, what was the context, what were all the surrounding facts.

I can tell you this: I never asked Ms. Lewinsky to lie. The first time that she raised with me the possibility that she might be a witness or I told her—you suggested the possibility in this December 17th timeframe—I told her she had to get a lawyer. And I never asked her to lie.

Q Did you ever say anything like that, you can always say that you were coming to see Betty or bringing me letters? Was that part of any kind of a, anything you said to her or a cover story, before you had any idea she was going to be part of Paula Jones?

A I might well have said that.

Q Okay.

A Because I certainly didn't want this to come out, if I could help it. And I was concerned about that. I was embarrassed about it. I knew it was wrong. And, you know, of course, I didn't want it to come out. But—

Q But you are saying that you didn't say anything—I want to make sure I understand. Did you say anything like that once you knew or thought she might be a witness in the Jones case? Did you repeat that statement, or something like it to her?

A Well, again, I don't recall, and I don't recall whether I might have done something like that, for example, if somebody says, what if the reporters ask me this, that or the other thing. I can tell you this: In the context of whether she could be a witness, I have a recollection that she asked me, well, what do I do if I get called as a witness, and I said, you have to get a lawyer. And that's all I said. And I never asked her to lie.

Q Did you tell her to tell the truth?

A Well, I think the implication was she would tell the truth. I've already told you that I felt strongly that she could issue, that she could execute an affidavit that would be factually truthful, that might get her out of having to testify. Now, it obviously wouldn't if the Jones people knew this, because they knew that if they could get this and leak it, it would serve their larger purposes, even if the judge ruled that she couldn't be a witness in the case. The judge later ruled she wouldn't be a witness in the case. The judge later ruled the case had no merit.

So, I knew that. And did I hope she'd be able to get out of testifying on an affidavit? Absolutely. Did I want her to execute a false affidavit? No, I did not.

Q If Monica Lewinsky has stated that her affidavit that she didn't have a sexual relationship with you is, in fact, a lie, I take it you disagree with that?

A No. I told you before what I thought the issue was there. I think the issue is how do you define sexual relationship. And there was no definition imposed on her at the time she executed the affidavit. Therefore, she was free to give it any reasonable meaning.

Q And if she says she was lying—

A And I believe—

Q —under your common sense ordinary meaning that you talked about earlier, Mr. President, that most Americans would have, if she says sexual relationship, saying I didn't have one was a lie because I had oral sex with the President, I take it, you would disagree with that?

A Now, we're back to where we started and I have to invoke my statement.

But, let me just say one thing. I've read a lot, and obviously I don't know whether any of it's accurate, about what she said, and what purports to be on those tapes.

And this thing—and I searched my own memory. This reminds me, to some extent, of the hearings when Clarence Thomas and Anita Hill were both testifying under oath. Now, in some rational way, they could not have both been telling the truth, since they had directly different accounts of a shared set of facts. Fortunately, or maybe you think unfortunately, there was no special prosecutor to try to go after one or the other of them, to take sides and try to prove one was a liar. And so, Judge Thomas was able to go on and serve on the Supreme Court.

What I learned from that, I can tell you that I was a citizen out there just listening. And when I heard both of them testify, what I believed after it was over, I believed that they both thought they were telling the truth.

This is—you're dealing with, in some ways, the most mysterious area of human life. I'm doing the best I can to give you honest answers.

Q Mr. President—

A And that's all I can say.

Q I'm sorry.

A And, you know, those people both testified under oath. So, if there'd been a special prosecutor, they could, one of them could have gone after Anita Hill, another could have gone after Clarence Thomas. I thank God there was no such thing then, because I don't believe that it was a proper thing.

Q One of—

A And I think they both thought they were telling the truth. So, maybe Ms. Lewinsky believes she's telling the truth, and I'm glad she got her mother and herself out of trouble. I'm glad you gave her that sweeping immunity. I'm glad for the whole thing. I, I, I—it breaks my heart that she was ever involved in this.

Q I want to go back to a question about Vernon Jordan. I want to go back to late December and early January, late December of '97 and early January of '98. During this time, Mr. President, you are being sued for sexual harassment by a woman who claims, among other things, that others got benefits that she didn't because she didn't have oral sex with you. While this is happening, your powerful friend, Vernon Jordan, is helping to get Monica Lewinsky a job and a lawyer. He's helping to get a job and a lawyer for someone who had some kind of sex with you, and who has been subpoenaed in the very case, the Jones case.

Don't you see a problem with this? Didn't you see a problem with this?

A No. Would you like to know why?

Q Isn't that why—I would. But isn't that why Vernon Jordan asked you on December 19th whether or not you had sexual relationships with Monica Lewinsky and why he asked her, because he knew it would be so highly improper to be helping her with a lawyer and a job if, in fact, she had had a relationship with you?

A I don't know. I don't believe that at all. I don't believe that at all, particularly since, even if you look at the facts here in their light most unfavorable to me, no one has suggested that there was any sexual harassment on my part. And I don't think it was wrong to be helping her. Look—

Q A subpoenaed witness in a case against you?

A Absolutely. Look, for one thing, I had already proved in two ways that I was not trying to influence her testimony. I didn't order her to be hired at the White House. I could have done so. I wouldn't do it. She tried for months to get in. She was angry.

Secondly, after I—

Q Wasn't she kept—

A After I terminated the improper contact with her, she wanted to come in more than she did. She got angry when she didn't get in sometimes. I knew that that might make her more likely to speak, and I still did it because I had to limit the contact.

And, thirdly, let me say, I formed an opinion really early in 1996, and again—well, let me finish the sentence. I formed an opinion early in 1996, once I got into this unfortunate and wrong conduct, that when I stopped it, which I knew I'd have to do and which I should have done a long time before I did, that she would talk about it. Not because Monica Lewinsky is a bad person. She's basically a good girl. She's a good young woman with a good heart and a good mind. I think she is burdened by some unfortunate conditions of her, her upbringing. But she's basically a good person.

But I knew that the minute there was no longer any contact, she would talk about this. She would have to. She couldn't help it. It was, it was a part of her psyche. So, I had put myself at risk, sir. I was not trying to buy her silence or get Vernon Jordan to buy her silence. I thought she was a good person. She had not been involved with me for a long time in any improper way, several months, and I wanted to help her get on with her life. It's just as simple as that.

MR. WISENBERG: It's time for a break.

MR. KENDALL: Okay. 4:49.

(Whereupon, the proceedings were recessed from 4:49 p.m. until 5:05 p.m.)

MR. KENDALL: Bob, we are at 2 hours and 55 minutes.

BY MR. BITTMAN:

Q Mr. President.

A Mr. Bittman.

Q Apparently we have on hour and five minutes left, if we stick to the four-hour timeframe.

MR. KENDALL: Plus 30 seconds.

MR. BITTMAN: And 30 seconds, that's right.

THE WITNESS: You gave me my 30 seconds' soliloquy. So, I owe you 30 seconds.

BY MR. BITTMAN:

Q You are very generous. That actually segues very nicely into one of the grand juror's asked, pointed out actually, that you indicated at the beginning of the deposition that you would, you would answer all the grand jurors, you wanted to answer all the grand juror's questions. And they wanted to know whether you would be willing to stay beyond the four-hour period to, in fact, answer all their questions.

A Well, let's see how we do in the next hour, and then we'll decide.

Q Okay. Let me draw your attention to early January of this year, after Christmas, before your deposition. Do you remember talking to Betty Currie about Monica, who had just called her and said that she, Monica, needed to talk to you before she signed something?

A I'm not sure that I do remember that. But, go ahead.

Q This is in early January. And then Betty Currie relayed this to you that Monica called, it's important, she needs to talk to you before she signs something. And then you do, indeed, talk to Monica that day on the telephone.

A I did talk to her that day?

Q Yes.

MR. KENDALL: Mr. President, excuse me. That's a question. If you have a memory of that, you can answer.

THE WITNESS: I'm trying to remember when the last time I talked to her was. I am aware, sir, that she signed this affidavit about this time, sometime in the first week in January. I may have talked to her before she did it. I don't know. I talked to her a number of times between the time Betty's brother died and Christmas. Then I saw her on December 28. I may have talked to her, but I don't remember the specific conversation.

BY MR. BITTMAN:

Q And you would have talked about the—she had just given you a gift actually in early January, a book on the Presidents of the United States. And you discussed this with her and she said that you said you liked it a lot.

A I did like it a lot. I told you that. My impression, my belief was that she gave me that book for Christmas. Maybe that's not right. I think she had that book delivered to me for Christmas. And then, as I remember, I went to Bosnia and for some reason she wasn't there around Christmas time.

But, anyway, maybe I didn't get it until January. My recollection was that I had gotten it right before Christmas.

Q Let me see if I can jog your memory further. Monica talked to you in that phone conversation that told you that she had just met with her attorney that Mr. Jordan arranged with her, and the attorney said that if she is deposed that they were going to ask her how she got her job at the Pentagon. And Monica then asked you, what do you think I should say, how do I answer that question, how did I get the job at the Pentagon. Did you talk to Monica about that, about possibilities—

A I don't believe—no. I don't remember her asking me that. But if she, if she had asked me that, I would have told her to tell the truth. I—and I didn't, you know, I don't know exactly how she got her job at the Pentagon. I know Evelyn Lieberman wanted to transfer her out of the job she had, and somebody must have arranged that. But I didn't arrange it.

Q Now, that's actually not my question. My question is whether you remember talking to Monica about her being concerned that, I may have to answer some questions about how and why I was transferred to the Pentagon out of the White House, fearing that this would—

A No, I don't remember that at all.

Q —lead to questions, or answers that would reveal your relationship?

A Oh, no, sir. I don't remember that. Maybe somebody—maybe she did. But I only remember—well, I don't remember that. That's all I can tell you. I don't remember that.

Q Are you saying, Mr. President, that you did not then say to Ms. Lewinsky that you could always say that people in Legislative Affairs got you the job, or helped you get it?

A I have no recollection of that whatever.

Q Are you saying you didn't say it?

A No, sir. I'm telling you, I want to say I don't recall—I don't have any memory of this as I sit here today. And I can tell you this, I never asked her to lie. I never did. And I don't have any recollection of the specific thing you are saying to me.

Now, if I could back up, there were several times when Monica Lewinsky talked to me on the telephone in 1996, in person in 1997, about her being concerned about what anybody would say about her transfer from the White House to the Pentagon. But I remember no conversation in which she was concerned about it for the reasons you just mentioned.

And all my memory is, she was worried about it because she thought it would keep her from getting a good job down the road, and she talked to me about it constantly in 1997. She thought, well, I'll never have my record clear unless I work somewhere in the White House complex where I can get a good recommendation. But in the context that you mention it, I do not recall a conversation.

Q Did you ever tell Ms. Lewinsky, or promise to her that you would do your best to get her back into the White House after the 1996 Presidential elections?

A What I told Ms. Lewinsky was that I would, I would do what I could to see, if she had a good record at the Pentagon, and she assured me she was doing a good job and working hard, that I would do my best to see that the fact that she had been sent away from the Legislative Affairs section did not keep her from getting a job in the White House, and that is, in fact, what I tried to do. I had a conversation with Ms. Scott about it, and I tried to do that.

But I did not tell her I would order someone to hire her, and I never did, and I wouldn't do that. It wouldn't be right.

Q When you received the book, this gift from Monica, the Presidents of the United States, this book that you liked and you talked with Monica about, did it come with a note? Do you remember the note that it came with, Mr. President?

A No, sir, I don't.

Q Do you remember that in the note she wrote that, she expressed how much she missed you and how much she cared for you, and you and she later talked about this in this telephone conversation, and you said—and she apologized for putting such emotional, romantic things in this note, and you said, yeah, you shouldn't have written some of those things, you shouldn't put those things down on paper? Did you ever say anything like that to Ms. Lewinsky?

A Oh, I believe I did say something like that to Ms. Lewinsky. I don't remember doing something as late as you suggest. I'm not saying I didn't. I have no recollection of that.

Keep in mind now, it had been quite a long time since I had had any improper contact with her. And she was, in a funny way, almost more attached to me than she had been before. In '96, she had a long relationship, she said, with a man whom she liked a lot. And I didn't know what else was going on in her private life in '97. But she talked to me occasionally about people she was going out with.

But normally her language at this point was, if affectionate, was, was not improperly affectionate, I would say. So—but, it could have happened. I wouldn't say it didn't. I just don't remember it at this late date.

Q Let me refer back to one of the subjects we talked about at one of the earlier breaks, right before one of the earlier breaks, and that is your meeting with Mrs. Currie on January 18th. This is the Sunday after your deposition in the Paula Jones case.

You said that you spoke to her in an attempt to refresh your own recollection about the events involving Monica Lewinsky, is that right?

A yes.

Q How did you making the statement, I was never alone with her, right, refresh your recollection?

A Well, first of all, let's remember the context here. I did not at that time know of your involvement in this case. I just knew that obviously someone had given them a lot of information, some of which struck me as accurate, some of which struck me as dead wrong. But it led them to write, ask me a whole serious of questions about Monica Lewinsky.

Then on Sunday morning, this Drudge report came out, which used Betty's name, and I thought that we were going to be deluged by press comments. And I was trying to refresh my memory about what the facts were.

So, when I said, we were never alone, right, I think I also asked her a number of other questions, because there were several times, as I'm sure she would acknowledge, when I either asked her to be around. I remember once in particular when I was talking with Ms. Lewinsky when I asked Betty to be in the, actually, in the next room in the dining room, and, as I testified earlier, once in her own office.

But I meant that she was always in the Oval Office complex, in that complex, while Monica was there. And I believe that this was part of a series of questions I asked her to try to quickly refresh my memory. So, I wasn't trying to get her to say something that wasn't so. And, in fact, I think she would recall that I told her to just relax, go in the grand jury and tell the truth when she had been called as a witness.

Q So, when you said to Mrs. Currie that, I was never alone with her, right, you just meant that you and Ms. Lewinsky would be somewhere perhaps in the Oval Office or many times in your back study, is that correct?

A That's right. We were in the back study.

Q And then—

A Keep in mind, sir, I just want to make it—I was talking about 1997. I was never, ever trying to get Betty Currie to claim that on the occasions when Monica Lewinsky was there when she wasn't anywhere around, that she was. I would never have done that to her, and I don't think she thought about that. I don't think she thought I was referring to that.

Q Did you put a date restriction? Did you make it clear to Mrs. Currie that you were only asking her whether you were never alone with her after 1997?

A Well, I don't recall whether I did or not, but I assumed—if I didn't, I assumed she knew what I was talking about, because it was the point at which Ms. Lewinsky was out of the White House and had to have someone WAVE her in, in order to get in the White House. And I do not believe to this day that I was—in 1997, that she was ever there and that I ever saw her unless Betty Currie was there. I don't believe she was.

Q Do you agree with me that the statement, "I was never alone with her", is incorrect? You were alone with Monica Lewinsky, weren't you?

A Well, again, it depends on how you define alone. Yes, we were alone from time to time, even during 1997, even when there was absolutely no improper contact occurring. Yes, that is accurate.

But there were also a lot of times when, even though no one could see us, the doors were open to the halls, on both ends of the halls, people could hear. The Navy stewards could come in and out at will, if they were around. Other things could be happening. So, there were a lot of times when we were alone, but I never really thought we were.

And sometimes when we, when—but, as far as I know, what I was trying to determine, if I might, is that Betty was always around, and I believe she was always around where I could basically call her or get her if I needed her.

Q When you said to Mrs. Currie, you could see and hear everything, that wasn't true either, was it, as far as you knew? You've already—

A My memory of that—

Q —testified that Betty was not there.

A My memory of that was that, that she had the ability to hear what was going on if she came in the Oval Office from her office. And a lot of times, you know, when I was in the Oval Office, she just had the door open to her office. Then there was—the door was never completely closed to the hall. So, I think there was—I'm not entirely sure what I meant by that, but I could have meant that she generally would be able to hear conversations, even if she couldn't see them. And I think that's what I meant.

Now, I could have been referring not generally to every time she was there, but one, one particular time I remember when Ms. Lewinsky was there when I asked Betty—and I'm sorry to say for reasons I don't entirely remember—to actually stay in the dining room while I talked with Monica. I do remember one such instance.

Q Well, you've already testified that this—you did almost everything you could to keep this relationship secret. So, would it be fair to say—even from Mrs. Currie. She didn't know about the nature, that is, your intimate, physically intimate relationship with Ms. Lewinsky, did she?

A As far as I know, she is unaware of what happened on the, on the occasions when I saw her in 1996 when something improper happened. And she was unaware of the one time that I recall in 1997 when something happened.

I think she was quite well aware that I was determined to impose the appropriate limits on the relationship when I was trying to do it. And the—you know, anybody would hope that this wouldn't become public. Although I frankly, from 1996 on, always felt that if I severed inappropriate contact with Ms. Lewinsky, sooner or later it would get public. And I never thought it would be part of the Jones case. I never even thought about that. I never thought—I certainly never thought it would be part of your responsibilities.

Q My question was—

A But I did believe that she would talk about it.

Q My question was more simple than that. Mrs. Currie did not know of the physically intimate nature of your relationship, did she?

A I don't believe she did, no.

Q Okay. So, you would have done—you tried to keep that nature of the relationship from Mrs. Currie?

A Absolutely. I—

Q So, you would not have engaged in those physically intimate acts if you knew that Mrs. Currie could see or hear that, is that correct?

A That's correct. But, keep in mind, sir, I was talking about 1997. That occurred, to the—and I believe that occurred only once in February of 1997. I stopped it. I never should have started it, and I certainly shouldn't have started it back after I resolved not to in 1996. And I was referring to 1997.

And I—what—as I say, I do not know—her memory and mine may be somewhat different. I do not know whether I was asking her about a particular time when Monica was upset and I asked her to stand, stay back in the dining area. Or whether I was, had reference to the fact that if she kept the door open to the Oval Office, because it was always—the door to the hallway was always somewhat open, that she would always be able to hear something if anything went on that was, you know, too loud, or whatever.

I do not know what I meant. I'm just trying to reconcile the two statements as best I can, without being sure.

Q There was at least one event where Mrs. Currie was definitely not even in the Oval Office area, isn't that right? And I think you began to testify about that before. That was at the radio address.

A I'm not sure of that. But in that case, there was, there was certainly someone else there. I don't know—

Q Well, why would you be testing Mrs. Currie's memory about whether someone else was there?

A Well, I can say this. If I'm in the Oval Office—my belief is that there was someone else there, somewhere in the Oval Office complex. I've looked at our—I've looked at the film. This, this night has become legendary now, you know. I've looked at the, I've looked at the film we have. I've looked at my schedules. I've seen the people that were at the radio address.

I do believe that I was alone with her from 15 to 20 minutes. I do believe that things happened then which were inappropriate. I don't remember whether Betty was there or not, but I can't imagine that, since all this happened more or less continuously in that time period, there must have been someone who was working around the radio address who stayed around somewhere. That would be my guess. I don't know. I'm sorry. I don't have records about who it would be. But I doubt very seriously if we were all alone in that Oval Office complex then.

Q Mr. President, if there is a semen stain belonging to you on a dress of Ms. Lewinsky's, how would you explain that?

A Well, Mr. Bittman, I, I don't—first of all, when you asked me for a blood test, I gave you one promptly. You came over here and got it. That's—we met that night and talked. So, that's a question you already know the answer to. Not if, but you know whether.

And the main thing I can tell you is that doesn't affect the opening statement I made. The opening statement I made is that I had inappropriate intimate contact. I take full responsibility for it. It wasn't her fault, it was mine. I do not believe that I violated the definition of sexual relations I was given by directly touching those parts of her body with the intent to arouse or gratify. And that's all I have to say.

I think, for the rest, you know, you know what the evidence is and it doesn't affect that statement.

Q Is it possible or impossible that your semen in on a dress belonging to Ms. Lewinsky?

A I have nothing to add to my statement about it, sir. You, you know whether—you know what the facts are. There's no point in a hypothetical.

Q Don't you know what the facts are also, Mr. President?

A I have nothing to add to my statement, sir.

Q Getting back to the conversation you had with Mrs. Currie on January 18th, you told her—if she testified that you told her, Monica came on to me and I never touched her, you did, in fact, of course, touch Ms. Lewinsky, isn't that right, in a physically intimate way?

A Now, I've testified about that. And that's one of those questions that I believe is answered by the statement that I made.

Q What was your purpose in making these statements to Mrs. Currie, if they weren't for the purpose to try to suggest to her what she should say if ever asked?

A Now, Mr. Bittman, I told you, the only thing I remember is when all this stuff blew up, I was trying to figure out what the facts were. I was trying to remember. I was trying to remember every time I had seen Ms. Lewinsky. Once this thing was in Drudge, and there was this argument about whether it was or was not going to be in Newsweek, that was a clear signal to me, because Newsweek, frankly, was—had become almost a sponsoring media outlook for the Paula Jones case, and had a journalist who had been trying, so far fruitlessly, to find me in some sort of wrongdoing.

And so I knew this was all going to come out. I was trying—I did not know at the time—I will say again, I did not know that any of you were involved. I did not know that the Office of Independent Counsel was involved. And I was trying to get the facts and try to think of the best defense we could construct in the face of what I thought was going to be a media onslaught.

Once you became involved, I told Betty Currie not to worry, that, that she had been through a terrible time. She had lost her brother. She had lost her sister. Her mother was in the hospital. I said, Betty, just don't worry about me. Just relax, go in there and tell the truth. You'll be fine. Now, that's all there was in this context.

Q Did the conversations that you had with Mrs. Currie, this conversation, did it refresh your recollection as to events involving Ms. Lewinsky?

A Well, as I remember, I do believe, in fairness, that, you know, she may have felt some ambivalence about how to react, because there were some times when she seemed to say yes, when I'm not sure she meant yes. There was a time—it seems like there was one or two things where she said, well, remember this, that or the other thing, which did reflect my recollection.

So, I would say a little yes, and a little no.

Q Why was it then that two or three days later, given that The Washington Post article came out on January 21st, why would you have had another conversation with Betty Currie asking or making the exact same statements to her?

A I don't know that I did. I remember having this one time. I was, I was—I don't know that I did.

Q If Mrs. Currie says you did, are you disputing that?

A No, sir, I'm not disputing—

MR. KENDALL: Excuse me. Is your representation that she testified that that conversation was—when?

MR. BITTMAN: I'm not making a representation as to what Mrs. Currie said. I'm asking the President if Mrs. Currie testified two or three days later, that two or three days after the conversation with the President on January 18th, that he called her into the Oval Office and went over the exact same statements that the President made to her on the 18th.

BY MR. BITTMAN:

Q Is that accurate? Is that a truthful statement by Mrs. Currie, if she made it?

A I do not remember how many times I talked to Betty Currie or when. I don't. I can't possibly remember that. I do remember, when I first heard about this story breaking, trying to ascertain what the facts were, trying to ascertain what Betty's perception was. I remember that I was highly agitated, understandably, I think.

And then I remember when I knew she was going to have to testify to the grand jury, and I, I felt terrible because she had been through this loss of her sister, this horrible accident Christmas that killed her brother, and her mother was in the hospital. I was trying to do—to make her understand that I didn't want her to, to be untruthful to the grand jury. And if her memory was different from mine, it was fine, just go in there and tell them what she thought. So, that's all I remember.

BY MR. BENNETT:

Q Mr. President, my name is Jackie Bennett. If I understand your current line of testimony, you are saying that your only interest in speaking with Ms. Currie in the days after your deposition was to refresh your own recollection?

A Yes.

Q It was not to impart instructions on how she was to recall things in the future?

A No, and certainly not under oath. That—every day, Mr. Bennett, in the White House and in every other political organization when you are subject to a barrage of press questions of any kind, you always try to make the best case you can consistent with the facts; that is, while being truthful.

But—so, I was concerned for a day or two there about this as a press story only. I had no idea you were involved in it for a couple of days.

I think Betty Currie's testimony will be that I gave her explicit instructions or encouragement to just go in the grand jury and tell the truth. That's what I told her to do and I thought she would.

Q Mr. President, when did you learn about the Drudge Report reporting allegations of you having a sexual relationship with someone at the White House?

A I believe it was the morning of the 18th, I think.

Q What time of day, sir?

A I have no idea.

Q Early morning hours?

A Yeah, I think somebody called me and told me about it. Maybe Bruce, maybe someone else. I'm not sure. But I learned early on the 18th of the Drudge Report.

Q Very early morning hours, sir?

A Now, my deposition was on the 17th, is that right?

Q On Saturday, the 17th, sir.

A Yeah, I think it was when I got up Sunday morning, I think. Maybe it was late Saturday night. I don't remember.

Q Did you call Betty Currie, sir, after the Drudge Report hit the wire?

A I did.

Q Did you call her at home?

A I did. Was that the night of the 17th?

Q Night of the 17th, early morning hours of the 18th?

A Okay, yes. That's because—yes. I worked with Prime Minister Netanyahu that night until about midnight.

MR. KENDALL: Wait.

THE WITNESS: Isn't that right?

MR. KENDALL: Excuse me. I think the question is directed—Mr. Bennett, if you could help out by putting the day of the week, I think that would be helpful.

BY MR. BENNETT:

Q Saturday night, Sunday morning.

A Yes. I called Betty Currie as soon—I think about as soon as I could, after I finished with Prime Minister Netanyahu, and in the aftermath of that meeting planning where we were going next in the Middle East peace process.

MR. KENDALL: Can we take a two-minute break, please?

MR. BITTMAN: May I ask one other question first, Mr. Kendall?

MR. KENDALL: Certainly. I think the witness is confused on dates. That's all.

MR. BITTMAN: Okay.

THE WITNESS: That's what—I didn't think it was the night of the 17th.

MR. KENDALL: Mr. President, I think we'll do it in a break.

THE WITNESS: Can we have a break and I could get straightened out?

MR. BITTMAN: Sure. May I ask one other quick—this is a question I forgot to ask from the grand jurors.

THE WITNESS: I don't want to get mixed up on these dates now. Go ahead.

BY MR. BITTMAN:

Q This is—they wanted to know whether, they want us to clarify that the President's knowledge, your knowledge, Mr. President, as to the approach to our office this morning; that is, we were told that you would give a general statement about the nature of your relationship with Ms. Lewinsky, which you have done. Yet that you would—you did not want to go in any of the details about the relationship. And that if we pressed on going into the details, that you would object to going into the details.

And the grand jurors, before they wanted, they wanted to vote on some other matters, they wanted to know whether you were aware of that? That we were told that?

MR. KENDALL: Well, Mr. Bittman, who told you that? This is, this is, this is not a fair question, when you say you were told. Who told you?

MR. BITTMAN: Who told me what, the question?

MR. KENDALL: You said, you said the grand jury was told.

MR. BITTMAN: We have kept the grand jury informed, as we normally would, of the proceedings here.

MR. KENDALL: Right. And, I'm sorry. Who, who are you representing told you or the grand jurors anything? Is that, is that our conversation?

407

MR. BITTMAN: Yes.

MR. STARR: Yes, our conversation.

MR. BITTMAN: Yes. That was in substance related to the grand jurors.

THE WITNESS: And what's your question to me, Mr. Bittman?

BY MR. BITTMAN:

Q   Whether you were aware of the facts that I just described?

A   Yes, sir. Let me say this. I knew that Mr. Kendall was going to talk with Judge Starr. What we wanted to do was to be as helpful as we could to you on the question of whether you felt I was being truthful, when I said I did not have sexual relations with Ms. Lewinsky, as defined in that definition (1) in this, in my testimony.

And I thought the best way to do that, and still preserve some measure of privacy and dignity, would be to invite all of you and the grand jurors to ask, well, would you consider this, that, or the other thing covered by the definition. You asked me several questions there, and I did my best to answer whether I thought they were covered by the definition, and said if I thought they were covered, you could conclude from that that my testimony is I did not do them.

If those things, if things are not covered by the definition, and I don't believe they are covered, then I could not—then they shouldn't be within this discussion one way or the other.

Now, I know this is somewhat unusual. But I would say to the grand jury, put yourself in my position. This is not a typical grand jury testimony. I, I have to assume a report is going to Congress. There's a videotape being made of this, allegedly because only one member of the grand jury is absent. This is highly unusual. And, in addition to that, I have sustained a breathtaking number of leaks of grand jury proceedings.

And, so, I think I am right to answer all the questions about perjury, but not to say things which will be forever in the historic annals of the United States because of this unprecedented videotape and may be leaked at any time. I just think it's a mistake.

And, so, I'm doing my best to cooperate with the grand jury and still protect myself, my family, and my office.

MR. BITTMAN: Thank you.

MR. KENDALL: This will be two minutes.

(Whereupon, the proceedings were recessed from 5:37 p.m. until 5:43 p.m.)

BY MR. BENNETT:

Q   Mr. President, before we broke, we were talking about the sequencing of your conversations with Betty Currie following your deposition on Saturday, January 17th. Do you recall that?

A   I do.

Q   All right. And you recall contacting Betty Currie, calling her and instructing her on the evening of Saturday night, after your deposition, and telling her to come in the next day?

A   Yes, sir, I do.

Q   Sunday was normally her day off, isn't that so?

A   Yes, it was.

Q   And so you were making special arrangements for her to come back into the White House, isn't that so?

A   Well, yes. I asked her to come back in and talk to me.

Q   And it was at that time that you spoke with her, and Mr. Bittman and Mr.

Wisenberg have asked you questions about what you said in that conversation, isn't that so?

A Yes, they have—I don't know whether that's the time, but they—I did talk to her as soon as I realized that the deposition had become more about Monica Lewinsky than Paula Jones. I asked her, you know, if she knew anything about this. I said, you know, it's obvious that this is going to be a matter of press speculation, and I was trying to go through the litany of what had happened between us, and asked some questions.

Q On fairness, it would be more than a matter of simple press speculation, isn't that so? Mr. President, there was a question about whether you had testified fully, completely, and honestly on the preceding day in your deposition.

A Well, actually, Mr. Bennett, I didn't think about that then. I—this has been a rather unprecedented development, and I wasn't even thinking about the Independent Counsel getting into this. So, at that moment, I knew nothing about it and I was more interested in what the facts were and whether Ms. Currie knew anything about what Monica Lewinsky knew about it.

Q Mr. President, you've told us at least a little bit about your understanding of how the term sexual relations was used, and what you understood it to mean in the context of your deposition. Isn't that correct?

A That is correct.

Q And you've told us—I mean, that was a lawsuit Paula Jones filed in which she alleged that you asked her to perform oral sex, isn't that so?

A That was her allegation.

Q That was her allegation. And, notwithstanding that that was her allegation, you've testified that you understood the term sexual relations, in the context of the questions you were being asked, to mean something else, at least insofar as you were the recipient rather than the performer?

A Sir, Paula Jones' lawyers pulled out that definition, not me. And Judge Susan Webber Wright ruled on it, just as she later ruled their case had no merit in the first place, no legal merit, and dismissed it.

I had nothing to do with the definition. I had nothing to do with the Judge's rulings. I was simply there answering the questions they put to me, under the terms of reference they imposed.

Q Well, the grand jury would like to know, Mr. President, why it is that you think that oral sex performed on you does not fall within the definition of sexual relations as used in your deposition.

A Because that is—if the deponent is the person who has oral sex performed on him, then the contact is with—not with anything on that list, but with the lips of another person. It seems to be self-evident that that's what it is. And I thought it was curious.

Let me remind you, sir, I read this carefully. And I thought about it. I thought about what "contact" meant. I thought about what "intent to arouse or gratify" meant.

And I had to admit under this definition that I'd actually had sexual relations with Gennifer Flowers. Now, I would rather have taken a whipping than done that, after all the trouble I'd been through with Gennifer Flowers, and the money I knew that she had made for the story she told about this alleged 12-year affair, which we had done a great deal to disprove.

So, I didn't like any of this. But I had done my best to deal with it and the—that's what I thought. And I think that's what most people would think, reading that.

Q Would you have been prepared, if asked by the Jones lawyers, would you have been prepared to answer a question directly asked about oral sex performed on you by Monica Lewinsky?

A If the Judge had required me to answer it, of course, I would have answered it. And I would have answered it truthfully, if I—

Q By the way, do you believe that the—

A —had been required.

Q —Jones litigants had the same understanding of sexual relations that you claim you have?

A I don't know what their understanding was, sir. My belief is that they thought they'd get this whole thing in, and that they were going to—what they were trying to do is do just what they did with Gennifer Flowers. They wanted to find anything they could get from me or anyone else that was negative, and then they wanted to leak it to hurt me in the press, which they did even though the Judge ordered them not to.

So, I think their—

Q Wouldn't it—I'm sorry.

A I think their position, Mr. Bennett—you asked the question—their position was, we're going to cast the widest net we can and get as much embarrassing stuff as we can, and then dump it out there and see if we can make him bleed. I think that's what they were trying to do.

Q Don't you think, sir, that they could have done more damage to you politically, or in whatever context, if they had understood the definition in the same way you did and asked the question directly?

A I don't know, sir. As I said, I didn't work with their lawyers in preparing this case. I knew the case was wrong. I knew what our evidence was. By the time of this deposition, they knew what their evidence was.

Their whole strategy was, well, our lawsuit's not good, but maybe we can hurt him with the discovery. And, you know, they did some. But it didn't amount to much.

And did I want, if I could, to avoid talking about Monica Lewinsky? Yes, I'd give anything in the world not to be here talking about it. I'd be giving—I'd give anything in the world not to have to admit what I've had to admit today.

But if you look at my answer in the Flowers [sic] deposition, at least you know I tried to carefully fit all my answers within the framework there, because otherwise there was no reason in the wide world for me to do anything other than make the statements I'd made about Gennifer Flowers since 1991, that I did not have a 12-year affair with her, and that these, the following accusations she made are false.

So, that's all I can tell you. I can't prove anything.

Q But you did have a great deal of anxiety in the hours and days following the end of your deposition on the 17th. Isn't that fair to say?

A Well, I had a little anxiety the next day, of course, because of the Drudge Report. And I had an anxiety after the deposition because it was more about Monica Lewinsky than it was about Paula Jones.

Q The specificity of the questions relating to Monica Lewinsky alarmed you, isn't that fair to say?

A Yes, and it bothered me, too, that I couldn't remember the answers. It bothered me that I couldn't—as Mr. Wisenberg pointed out, it bothered me that I couldn't remember all the answers. I did the best I could. And so I wanted to know what the deal was. Sure.

Q Mr. President, to your knowledge, have you turned over, in response to the grand jury subpoenas, all gifts that Monica Lewinsky gave you?

A To my knowledge, I have, sir. As you know, on occasion, Mr. Kendall has asked for your help in identifying those gifts. And I think there were a couple that we came across in our search that were not on the list you gave us, that I remembered in the course of our search had been given to me by Monica Lewinsky and we gave them to you.

So, to the best of my knowledge, we have given you everything we have.

Q Can you explain why, on the very day that Monica Lewinsky testified in the grand jury on August 6th of this year, you wore a necktie that she had given you?

A No, sir, I don't believe I did. What necktie was it?

Q The necktie you wore on August 6th, sir.

A Well, I don't know that it was a necktie that Monica Lewinsky gave me. Can you describe it to me?

Q Well, I don't want to take time at this point, but we will provide you with photographic evidence of that, Mr. President.

A If you give me—I don't believe that's accurate, Mr. Bennett.

Q So, let me ask the question—

A But if you give it to me, and I look at it and I remember that she gave it to me, I'll be happy to produce it. I do not believe that's right.

Q Well, if you remember that she gave it to you, why haven't you produced it to the grand jury?

A I don't remember that she gave it to me. That's why I asked you what the tie was. I have—

Q Can you—

A —no earthly idea. I believe that, that I did not wear a tie she gave me on August the 6th.

Q Can you tell us why Bayani Nelvis wore a tie that Monica Lewinsky had given you on the day he appeared in the grand jury?

A I don't know that he did.

Q Have you given Bayani Nelvis any ties, sir?

A Oh, yes, a lot of ties.

Q And so if he wore the tie that you gave him, that Monica Lewinsky had given you, that would not have been by design, is that what you are telling us?

A Oh, absolutely not. Let me—

Q You are not—

A May I explain, Mr. Bennett? It won't—

Q Yes.

A —take long. Every year, since I've been President, I've gotten quite a large number of ties, as you might imagine. I get, I have a couple of friends, one in Chicago and one in Florida who give me a lot of ties, a lot of other people who send me ties all the time, or give them to me when I see them.

So, I always have the growing number of ties in my closet. What I normally do, if someone gives me a tie as a gift, is I wear it a time or two. I may use it. But at the end of every year, and sometimes two times a year, sometimes more, I go through my tie closet and I think of all the things that I won't wear a lot or that I might give away, and I give them mostly to the men who work there.

I give them to people like Glen and Nelvis, who work in the kitchen, back in the White House, or the gentlemen who are my stewards or the butlers, or the people who run the elevators. And I give a lot of ties away a year. I'll bet I—excluding Christmas, I bet I give 30, 40, maybe more ties away a year, and then, of course, at Christmas, a lot.

So, there would be nothing unusual if, in fact, Nelvis had a tie that originally had come into my tie closet from Monica Lewinsky. It wouldn't be unusual. It wouldn't be by design. And there are several other people of whom that is also true.

Q   Mr. President, I'd like to move to a different area right now. I'd like to ask you some questions about Kathleen Willey. You met Kathleen Willey during your 1992 campaign, isn't that so?

A   Yes, sir, I did.

Q   As a matter of fact, you first saw her at a rope line at the Richmond, Virginia airport on October 13, 1992, is that not correct?

A   I don't believe that is correct.

Q   When did you first meet her, sir?

A   Well, let me ask you this. When was the debate in Richmond?

Q   I believe it was October 13, 1992, sir.

A   Well, I believe that I had met her—I believe I had met her before then, because Governor Wilder, I believe that was his last year as governor—I think that's right, 92-93. I believe that I met her in connection with her involvement with Governor Wilder.

And I have the impression—it's kind of a vague memory, but I have the impression that I had met her once before, at least once before I came to that Richmond debate. Now, I'm not sure of that.

Q   Well, at least if you had met her before—

A   But I am quite sure she was at the Richmond debate and I did meet her there. I'm quite sure of that.

Q   Mr. President, you've seen television footage of you standing on a rope line with Donald Beyer, Lt. Governor Donald Beyer—

A   I have.

Q   —asking Mr. Beyer for the name of Kathleen Willey? You've seen that footage, haven't you?

A   I don't know that I've seen it, but I am aware that it exists.

Q   All right. And you can see him, you can read his lips. He's saying the name Kathleen Willey in response to a question from you, isn't that so?

A   That's what I've heard.

Q   And, as a matter of fact, you sent Nancy Hernreich, who was present on that day, to go get her telephone number, didn't you, sir?

A   I don't believe so.

Q   You don't believe so?

A   Well, let me say this. If that is true, then I'm quite certain that I had met her before. I would never call someone out of the blue that I saw on a rope line and send Nancy Hernreich to get her number to do it.

Q   Even if you were just learning her name for the first time?

A   That's correct. I'm not so sure that I didn't ask Don Beyer, if he was on the rope line with me, who she was because I thought I had seen her before or

412

I knew I had seen her before and I didn't remember her name. Now, I do that all the time. For men—

Q Mr. President—

A —and women.

Q I'm sorry. Do you recall that you sent Nancy Hernreich for her telephone number?

A No, I don't.

Q All right. Do you recall, having received her telephone number, calling her that night?

A No, sir, I don't.

Q Do you recall inviting her to meet with you at your hotel that night?

A No, sir, I do not.

Q Do you recall where you stayed in Richmond, Virginia during the debates you've told us about?

A Well, I stayed at some hotel there, I believe.

Q Actually, did you stay at the Williamsburg Inn, not in Richmond?

A Yeah, that's right. We prepared in Williamsburg. That's correct. I believe we prepared in Williamsburg and then went to Richmond for the debate, and then I think we spent the night in Richmond. And the next day, I think we had a rally before we left town. I believe that's right.

Q Do you know of any reason Kathleen Willey's telephone number would appear on your toll records from your room in Williamsburg?

A No, there—

Q If you didn't call her?

A No, I'm not denying that I called her, sir. You asked me a specific question. I won't deny that I called her. I don't know whether I did or not.

Q As a matter of fact, you called her twice that day, didn't you, sir?

A I don't recall. I may well have done it and I don't know why I did it.

Q Well, does it refresh your recollection that you called her and invited her to come to your room that night, sir?

A I don't believe I did that, sir.

Q If Kathleen Willey has said that, she's mistaken or lying, is that correct, Mr. President?

A I do not believe I did that. That's correct.

Q But what is your best recollection of that conversation, those conversations?

A I don't remember talking to her. But I—it seems to me that at some point—this is why I believe I had met her before, too. But at some point I had some actual person-to-person conversation with her about my sore throat, or what she thought would be good for it, or something like that. I have some vague memory of that. That's it.

Q Is this the chicken soup conversation, Mr. President?

A Well, I don't know if I would—maybe that's what she said I should have. I don't remember. But I have no recollection, sir, of asking her to come to my room. I—and I—I'm sorry, I don't. I can't—I won't deny calling her. I don't know if I did call her. I don't know if she tried to call me first. I don't know anything about that. I, I just—I met her and Doug Wilder. I remember that she and her husband were active for Government Wilder, and that's about all I remember, except that I had a conversation with her around the Richmond debate. I do remember talking to her there.

Q Mr. President, let's move ahead to the episode on November 29, 1993, in

413

which Mrs. Willey met you in your office at the Oval, the subject matter of the "60 Minutes" broadcast a few months ago. You recall that episode?

A   I certainly do.

Q   Mr. President, in fact, on that date you did make sexual advances on Kathleen Willey, is that not correct?

A   That's false.

Q   You did grab her breast, as she said?

A   I did not.

Q   You did place your hand on her groin area, as she said?

A   No, I didn't.

Q   And you placed her hand on your genitals, did you not?

A   Mr. Bennett, I didn't do any of that, and the questions you're asking, I think, betray the bias of this operation that has troubled me for a long time. You know what evidence was released after the "60 Minutes" broadcast that I think pretty well shattered Kathleen Willey's credibility. You know what people down in Richmond said about her. You know what she said about other people that wasn't true. I don't know if you've made all of this available to the grand jury or not.

   She was not telling the truth. She asked for the appointment with me. She asked for it repeatedly.

Q   Did she make a sexual advance on you, Mr. President?

A   On that day, no, she did not. She was troubled.

Q   On some other day?

A   I wouldn't call it a sexual advance. She was always very friendly. But I never took it seriously.

Q   Mr. President, you mentioned the documents that were released and information that came out from people in Richmond, et cetera, after the "60 Minutes" piece was broadcast. As a matter of fact, you were required, under the Court's rulings, to produce those documents in response to document requests by the Jones litigants, isn't that correct?

A   No. I believe the Jones litigants' request for production of documents to me ran to documents that were in my personal files and in my personal possessions, and did not cover documents that were White House files. So, I don't believe we were required to produce them.

   As a matter of fact, when that story first ran, sir, before "60 Minutes", back in July or so of '97, I was aware that we had some letters. I didn't—I didn't remember that she'd written us as much as she had and called as much as she had, and asked to see me as often as she had, after this alleged incident. I didn't know the volume of contact that she had which undermined the story she has told. But I knew there was some of it.

   And I made a decision that I did not want to release it voluntarily after the Newsweek ran the story, because her friend Julie Steele was in the story saying she asked her—she, Kathleen Willey—asked her to lie. And because, frankly, her husband had committed suicide. She apparently was out of money. And I thought, who knows how anybody would react under that. So, I didn't.

   But, now when "60 Minutes" came with the story and everybody blew it up, I thought we would release it. But I do not believe we were required to release White House documents to the Jones lawyers.

Q   Mr. President, have you made a decision on whether to stay beyond the four hours we agreed to, to accept questions from the grand jury?

MR. KENDALL: We have made an agreement, Mr. Bennett, to give you four hours. We're going to do that. By my watch, there are about 12 minutes left.

MR. BENNETT: I guess that's no. Is that correct, Mr. Kendall?

MR. KENDALL: Yes, that's correct.

THE WITNESS: May I ask this question? Could I have a two-minute break?

MR. BENNETT: Sure.

THE WITNESS: I'm sorry to bother you with this. I know we're getting to the end, but I need a little break.

(Whereupon, the proceedings were recessed from 6:04 p.m. until 6:09 p.m.)

BY MR. STARR:

Q Mr. President, at various times in this investigation, officials have invoked executive privilege in response to questions that have been posed to them by the grand jury and in the grand jury. One of the grand jurors has posed the question, did you personally authorize the invocation of executive privilege?

A If the answer is authorized, I think the answer to that would be yes. But I would like the grand jury to know something.

In the cases where we raised the lawyer/client privilege, or executive privilege, or where the Secret Service raised their privilege, and when I say—I had nothing to do with that. I did not authorize it, approve it, or anything else. That was something they asked to be free to make their decision on by themselves.

In none of those cases did I actually have any worry about what the people involved would say. The reason those privileges were advanced and litigated was that I believed that there was an honest difference between Judge Starr and the Office of Independent Counsel, and Mr. Ruff, my counsel, and I about what the proper balance was in the Constitutional framework.

And I did not want to put the Presidency at risk of being weakened as an institution, without having those matters litigated. Now, we've lost some of those matters. Our people have testified and the grand jury is free to conclude whether they believe that the testimony they gave was damaging to me. But I don't, I don't imagine it was and I wasn't worried about it. It was an honest difference of Constitutional principal between Judge Starr and the Office of Independent Counsel and the White House.

Q Mr. President, a couple of very brief questions, given our time. The White House's outside counsel, Mr. Eggleston, withdrew the White House's appeal from Chief Judge Johnson's ruling that the invocation of executive privilege had to give way to the grand jury's right to the information, that ruling in connection with the testimony of Mr. Blumenthal and Mr. Lindsey.

Were you informed of that fact that the appeal had been withdrawn?

A I was informed of it and, as a matter of fact, I was consulted about it and I strongly supported it. I didn't want to appeal it.

Q Okay.

A It was—I had—my main difference, Judge Starr, as you know with you, is, and with some of the Court decisions, is on the extent to which members of the White House Counsel's staff, like Mr. Lindsey, should be able to counsel the President on matters that may seem like they are private, like the Jones case, but inevitably intrude on the daily work of the President.

But I didn't really want to advance an executive privilege claim in this case beyond having it litigated, so that we, we had not given up on principal this matter, without having some judge rule on it. So, I made—

Q Excuse me. And you are satisfied that you now have the benefit of that ruling, is that correct?

A Well, yes. I just didn't want to, I didn't want to—yes. And I didn't—I made the—I actually, I think, made the call, or at least I supported the call. I did not, I strongly felt we should not appeal your victory on the executive privilege issue.

MR. STARR: Thank you.

BY MR. WISENBERG:

Q Mr. President, among the many remaining questions of the grand jurors is one that they would like answered directly without relation to, without regard to inferences, which is the following: Did Monica Lewinsky perform oral sex on you? They would like a direct answer to that, yes or no?

A Well, that's not the first time that question's been asked. But since I believe, and I think any person, reasonable person would believe that that is not covered in the definition of sexual relations I was given, I'm not going to answer, except to refer to my statement.

I had intimate contact with her that was inappropriate. I do not believe any of the contacts I had with her violated the definition I was given. Therefore, I believe I did not do anything but testify truthfully on these matters.

Q We have a couple of photos of the tie that you wore.

A Would you please give them to me?

Q Yes.

A Now, this is August 6th, is that correct?

Q 1998, the day that Monica Lewinsky appeared at the grand jury. And my question to you on that is, were you sending some kind of a signal to her by wearing—

A No, sir.

Q —one of the ties—let me finish, if you don't mind, sir.

A Sure. I'm sorry. My apology.

Q Were you sending some kind of a signal to her by wearing a tie she had given you on the day that she appeared in front of the grand jury?

A No, sir. I don't believe she gave me this tie. And if I was sending a signal, I'm about to send a terrible signal, and maybe you ought to invite her to talk again. I don't, I don't want to make light about this. I don't believe she gave me this tie. I don't remember giving, her giving me this tie. And I had absolutely no thought of this in my mind when I wore it.

If she did, I, I, I, I don't remember it, and this is the very first I've ever heard of it.

Q Did you realize when you—

MR. WISENBERG: Can I just have for the record, what are the exhibit numbers?

MS. WIRTH: Yes. They should be WJC-5 and 6.

(Grand Jury Exhibits WJC-5 and WJC-6 were marked for identification.)

MR. WISENBERG: Mr. Bennett has some more questions.

BY MR. BENNETT:

Q Mr. President, we were talking about your responses to document requests in the Jones litigation, and I had just asked you about turning over the Kathleen Willey correspondence. Do you recall that?

A Yes, sir, I do.

Q And, if I understand your testimony, you did not believe that the request for documents compelled you to search for those documents in the White House?

A Mr. Bennett, I want to answer this question in a way that is completely satisfactory to you and the grand jury, without violating the lawyer/client privilege, which is still intact.

It was my understanding that in the request for production of documents, that those requests ran against and operated against my personal files. Now, I have some personal files in the White House. And, I'm sorry. In this case I'm not my own lawyer, and I don't know how the distinction is made between files which are the personal files of the President, and files which are White House files.

But I do have a very clear memory that we were duty-bound to search and turn over evidence or, excuse me, documents that were in my personal file, but not in the White House files. And I believe that the letters to which you refer, Ms. Willey's letters and Ms. Willey's phone messages, were in the White House files. And, therefore, I was instructed at least that they were, that we had fully compiled with the Jones lawyers' request, and that these documents were outside the request.

Q Mr. President, you're not contending that White House documents, documents stored in the fashion that these were stored, are beyond your care, custody or control, are you?

A Mr. Bennett, that may be a legal term of art that I don't have the capacity to answer. I can only tell you what I remember. I remember being told in no uncertain terms that if these were personal files of the President, we had to produce documents. If they were essentially White House files, we were not bound to do so. So, we didn't.

Q So, you are saying somebody told you that you didn't have to produce White House documents?

A That's—

MR. KENDALL: I'm going to caution the witness that this question should not invade the sphere of the attorney/client privilege, and any conversations with counsel are privileged.

THE WITNESS: Let me say, and maybe, Mr. Kendall, we need a break here. I'm not trying—I'm trying to avoid invading the lawyer/client privilege.

I can just tell you that I did, I did the best I could to comply with this. And eventually we did make, of course, all of this public. And it was damaging to Ms. Willey and her credibility. It was terribly damaging to her. And the first time she came out with this story, I didn't do it. I only did it when they went back on "60 Minutes" and they made this big deal of it.

It turned out she had tried to sell this story and make all this money. And, I must say, when I saw how many letters and phone calls and messages there were that totally undercut her account, I, myself, was surprised.

BY MR. BENNETT:

Q But you knew there were letters?

A I did, sir.

Q And the White House—

A I knew that—

Q   —is under your control, isn't it, Mr. President?

A   Well, Mr. Bennett, again, I'm not trying to be—some days I think it's under my control and some days I'm not so sure.

But, if you're asking me, as a matter of law, I don't want to discuss that because that's—I mean, I'll be glad to discuss it, but I'm not the person who should make that decision. That decision should be made by someone who can give me appropriate advice, and I don't want to violate the lawyer/client privilege here.

Q   Well, Mr. President, how are the letters from Kathleen Willey that surfaced after the "60 Minutes" episode aired any different from the correspondence and other matters, tangible items, tangible things, of Monica Lewinsky?

A   Well, the items you asked for from Monica Lewinsky that I produced to you, you know that there was a tie, a coffee cup, a number of other things I had. Then I told you there were some things that had been in my possession that I no longer had, I believe. I don't remember if I did that. There was one book, I remember, that I left on vacation last summer.

Q   The same documents that the Jones litigants had asked you for?

A   Yes. But, at any rate, they were different. They were in my—the gifts were in my personal possession, clearly.

Q   In your office at the Oval?

A   Well, in the books, now, the Presidential books were with my other books that belong to me personally. They were in the Oval.

Q   Where do you draw the line, sir, between personal and White House? Now, you are talking about some documents that are in the Oval Office and we don't see where you are drawing the line.

A   Well, Mr. Bennett, I don't think these—I think the Lewinsky gifts were all non-documents. And you can—

MR. KENDALL: Is that the time?

THE WITNESS: Just a moment.

MR. KENDALL: Excuse me, Mr. Bennett.

THE WITNESS: Well, I'd like to—

MR. KENDALL: You've got thirty more seconds.

THE WITNESS: —finish answering the question, please, because this is a legitimate question, I think.

There is somebody in the White House, Mr. Bennett, who can answer your question, and you could call them up and they could answer it, under oath, for you. There is some way of desegregating what papers are personal to the President and what papers are part of the White House official archives papers. And I don't know how the distinction is made. I just don't know.

BY MR. BENNETT:

Q   Did you direct personnel, Nancy Hernreich or anyone else, to make a search for correspondence from Kathleen Willey and Monica Lewinsky when those documents were called for in the Jones litigation, sir? Did you direct that somebody on the White House staff look for those documents?

A   I don't believe that I was in charge of doing that, the document search, sir. So, the strict answer to that question is that I didn't.

Q   So, you sat back and relied on this legalistic distinction between your personal, which you are in control of, and the White House which, by the way, you are also in control of; is that not correct?

MR. KENDALL: I won't object to the argumentative form of the question. We'll allow the witness to answer it. We're now over time, even the 30 seconds. So, this will be it.

THE WITNESS: Mr. Bennett, I haven't said this all day long, but I would like to say it now.

Most of my time and energy in the last five and a half years have been devoted to my job. Now, during that five and a half years, I have also had to contend with things no previous President has ever had to contend with: a lawsuit that was dismissed for lack of legal merit, but that cost me a fortune and was designed to embarrass me; this independent counsel inquiry, which has gone on a very long time and cost a great deal of money, and about which serious questions have been raised; and a number of other things.

And, during this whole time, I have tried as best I could to keep my mind on the job the American people gave me. I did not make the legal judgment about how the documents were decided upon that should be given to the Jones lawyers, and ones that shouldn't.

And, I might add that Ms. Willey would have been very happy that these papers were not turned over, because they damaged her credibility so much, had they not ultimately been turned over after she made, I think, the grievous error of going on "60 Minutes" and saying all those things that were not true.

But I did not make the decision. It was not my job. This thing is being managed by other people. I was trying to do my job.

BY MR. BENNETT:

Q Mr. President, the grand jury, I am notified, still has unanswered questions of you, and we appeal to you again to make yourself available to answer those questions.

MR. KENDALL: Mr. Bennett, our agreement was for four hours and we have not counted the break time against that, and I think that will be—

THE WITNESS: You know, Mr. Bennett, I wish I could do it. I wish the grand jurors had been allowed to come here today as we invited them to do. I wanted them down here. I wanted them to be able to see me directly. But, we made an agreement that was different, and I think I will go ahead and stick with the terms of it.

BY MR. BENNETT:

Q The invitation was made after there was political fallout over the deposition circumstances with the satellite transmission and the taping. Isn't that so?

A I don't know about the taping, Mr. Bennett. I understood that the prospect of the grand jurors coming down here was raised fairly early. I don't know.

Q Just for the record—

A But, anyway, I wish they could have. I respect the grand jury. I respect the—

MR. WISENBERG: Just for the record, the invitation to the grand jury was contingent upon us not videotaping, and we had to videotape because we have an absent grand juror.

MR. KENDALL: Is that the only reason, Mr. Wisenberg, you have to videotape?

THE WITNESS: Well, yes. Do you want to answer that?

MR. BITTMAN: Thank you, Mr. President.

(Whereupon, at 6:25 p.m., the proceedings were concluded.)

419

Paula Jones v. William Jefferson Clinton and Danny Ferguson
No. LR-C-94-290 (E.D. Ark.)

DEPOSITION OF WILLIAM JEFFERSON CLINTON

Definition of Sexual Relations

For the purposes of this deposition, a person engages in "sexual relations" when the person knowingly engages in or causes -

(1) contact with the genitalia, anus, groin, breast, inner thigh, or buttocks of any person with an intent to arouse or gratify the sexual desire of any person;

(2) contact between any part of the person's body or an object and the genitals or anus of another person; or

(3) contact between the genitals or anus of the person and any part of another person's body.

"Contact" means intentional touching, either directly or through clothing.

DEPOSITION EXHIBIT
1
Clinton 1-17-98

[Editor's note: President Clinton was given this document during his deposition in the Paula Jones sexual harassment case. His denial that he committed perjury relies on his interpretation of how this definition was altered by the judge overseeing that civil case.]

PART THREE

COMMUNICATIONS
TO, FROM,
AND ABOUT
MONICA LEWINSKY

Monica Lewinsky's
Letters to and from President Clinton

October Sixteenth—North, South and across
It's America's day to honor . . . THE BOSS!
Without a doubt we White House Interns won the "toss"
Cuz' we work for the NATION'S NUMBER ONE BOSS

Since you have inspired us, it seems very fittin'
That to honor you this poem has been written!
So it's easy to see the Boss with whom we're all smitten,
Is no other than you—PRESIDENT CLINTON!

Happy National Boss Day!

The White House Interns
Fall 1995

MSL-55-DC-0186

INITIALS: BC / nam /0524   DOCUMENT TITLE: /gifts/draft/lewinsky.monica.nar

DRAFT DATE / LETTER DATE: Oct 30 1995 /   CORRESPONDENCE #: 2531378

CLEAR WITH: WHCC: CC: WH Gifts
   Karen Abramson
   Betty Currie

CORRESPONDENCE ADDRESSED TO: ENCLOSURES AND SPECIAL INSTRUCTIONS:
Ms. Monica Lewinsky ▓▓▓▓▓▓▓▓

Dear Monica: ~~beautiful~~
Thank you for the matted poem ~~observing me for~~ *in observance of* National Boss' Day. I
~~am honored to receive such a heartfelt gift~~ and am grateful for your
thoughtfulness in having so many White House interns ~~autograph~~ *sign* it.

Hillary and I appreciate the hard~~work~~ *all of the,* dedication ~~and support from~~ *of my*
you and ~~the other~~ *your fellow* interns and send our best wishes.

Sincerely,

V006-DC-00000167

424

184809

G1002

THE WHITE HOUSE

WASHINGTON

September 4, 1996

Ms. Monica Lewinsky

V006-DC-00000159

Dear Monica:

Thank you for the tie and T-shirt. It was kind
of you to remember my birthday, and I appreciate
your continued thoughtfulness and generosity.

Hillary and I send our best wishes.

Sincerely,

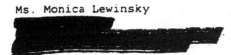

HB 001155

The tie is really
beautiful!

425

2 March 1997

Dear Mr. P—

I must admit it... I am a compulsive shopper! I saw this tie and thought it would look fabulous on you. I hope you like it.

All of my life, everyone has always said that I am a difficult person for whom to shop. and yet, <u>you</u> managed to choose ~~two~~ absolutely perfect presents! A little phrase (with only eight letters) like "thank you" simply cannot begin to express what I feel for what you have given me. Art & poetry are gifts to my soul!

I just <u>love</u> the hat pin. It is vibrant, unique, and a beautiful piece of art. My only hope is that I have a hat. fit to adorn it (ahhh, I see another excuse to go shopping)! I know that I am bound to receive compliments on it.

I have only read excerpts from "Leaves of Grass" before – never in its entirety or in such a beautifully bound edition. Like Shakespeare, whitman's writings are so timeless. I find solace in works from the past that remain profound and somehow always poignant. whitman is so rich that one must read him like one tastes a fine wine or good cigar — take it in, roll it in your mouth, and savor it!

I hope you know how very grateful I am for these gifts, especially your gift of friendship. I will treasure them all... always.

Monica

426

Dear Handsome,   29 June 1999

    I really need to discuss my situation with you. We have not had any contact for over five weeks. You leave on Sat. and I leave for Madrid w/ the SecDef on Monday returning the 14th of July. I am then heading out to Los Angeles for a few days. If I do not speak to you before you leave, when I return from LA it will have been two months since we last spoke. Please do not do this to me. I feel disposable, used and insignificant. I understand your hands are tied, but I just want to talk to you and look at some options. I am begging you ~~from the bottom of my heart to please let me come~~ one last visi. Briefly ~~see you~~ Tuesday evening. I will call Betty Tues. afternoon to see if it is o.k.

                                     –M

I believe the time has finally come for me to throw in the towel. my conversation with Marsha left me disappointed, frustrated, sad and angry. I can't help but wonder if you knew she wouldn't be able to detail me over there when I last saw you. maybe that would explain your coldness. the only explanation I can reason for your not bringing me back is that you just plain didn't want to enough or care about me enough. how else can I rationalize why it is ok for Marsha and Debi and scores of others to be in golden positions—people can say what they want to about them, even be nasty to them but everyone knows that they will never be touched because they have your approval. Debi can prance around in your shoes or stand in front of 50 people gathered for dinner bragging about just how she obtained your shirt for Walter to have bespoke shirts made for you. Marsha can remark to someone which subsequently ends up in the papers and magazines that "she spent the night with you". I just loved you— wanted to spend time with you, kiss you, listen to you laugh—and I wanted you to love me back.

I never told you this because I didn't want to seem like a martyr but in April of '95 I wanted nothing more than to beg you to do something so I didn't have to leave. I wanted to scream and bawl. you have no idea how desperate, upset, humiliated I was. But I didn't. you said you would see what you could do and I left it at that because I didn't want to put you in a bad situation. It was an election year and I knew what was important. You promised you would bring me back after the election with a snap of you fingers.

I left the WH at age 22 from my first job out of college, the beginning of my career, to come to work at an agency in which I have no interest at a job where I'm bored. I kept a calendar with a countdown until election

427

day. I was so sure that the weekend after the election you would call me to come visit and you would kiss me passionately and tell me you couldn't wait to have me back. You'd ask me where I wanted to work and say something akin to "Consider it done" and it would be. Instead I didn't hear from you for weeks and subsequently your phone calls became less frequent. We talked about my returning and you kept replying, "I'll talk to Bob Nash", "I've talked to Bob Nash", "Bob Nash is working it". Then it moved to "Marsha is working on it". Then you dumped me and it was still "Marsha is working on it". I promise it will be done" Now, Marsha is saying just be patient. Why do you want to come back anyway? You've already had the experience of working here.

I can't take it any more. A person can only handle so might anxiety and stress. Maybe it would be easier to wait if you had called more and it hadn't been such trouble to try to see you. As I said in my last letter to you I've waited long enough. You and Marsha win. I give up. you let me down, but I shouldn't have trusted you in the first place.

MSL-DC-0000105?

[Editor's note: This letter was apparently written in September 1997 but was not sent.]

(OFFICIAL LETTERHEAD)

30 September 1997

MEMORANDUM FOR   HANDSOME
SUBJECT   The New Deal

A proposition for you: You show me that you will let me visit you sans a crisis, and I will be on my best behavior and not stressed out when I come (to see you, that is).

I'd like to come for a visit this evening. According to my calendar, we haven't spent any time together on the phone or in person in six weeks. You'll be gone the next few weekends so if we don't get together tonight, by the time I do see you it will have been over two months.

What do you think of maybe planning ahead with Betty that you would leave at seven so everyone else goes home, and then you could come back around 7:30 or later. I'll be tied up until about 7:30. Any time after that is good for me.

Oh, and Handsome, remember FDR would never have turned down a visit with Lucy Mercer!

MSL-DC-00001050

***JUST A REMINDER TO THROW THIS AWAY AND <u>NOT</u> SEND IT BACK TO THE STAFF SECRETARY!

it was so sad seeing you tonight because i was so angry with you that you once again rejected me and yet, all i wanted was for everyone else in the room to disappear and for you to hold me.

bill, i loved you with all of my heart. i wanted to be with you all of the time. most recently in london, i walked the streets thinking how content i would be to walk the streets at your side while you spoke of things past—filled the air and my soul with your knowledge of history.

when you gave me leaves of grass i realized that the reason i was so connected to you, or so i thought, was because you were in my soul. to quote your famous cliché, i felt your pain. i seemed, somehow to feel in my heart some of your experiences. you will see in this collection of things for you, a card i was so shocked to find for obvious reasons. It rang so true to me.

i have realized yesterday when betty told me you "couldn't" see me, what's really going on—you want me out of your life. i guess the signs have been clear for awhile—not wanting to see me and rarely calling. i used to think it was simply you putting up walls—that the real you was the person whom i was with on the fourth of july. i'm humiliated at how wrong i was.

i am sorry that this has been such a bad experience. i will never forget what you said that night we fought on the phone—if you had known what i was really like you never would have gotten involved with me. i'm sure you're not the first person to have felt that way about me.

well, anyway, these are all of the little gifts and one big christmas gift (the black box) that i've had for you. i wanted to give them to you in person, but that is obviously not going to happen. you may not want to keep them, but please don't send them back. i'm very particular about presents and could never give them to anyone else—they were all bought with you in mind. your christmas present is an antique from, i beleive, the 30's i was very attracted to it.

i knew it would hurt to have to say goodbye to you; i just never thought it would be on paper.

DB-DC-00000017

[Editor's note: This letter is apparently from October 1997.]
12 November 1997

Handsome:

I asked you three weeks ago to please be sensitive to what I am going through right now and to keep in contact with me, and yet I'm still left writing notes in vain. I am not a moron. I know that what is going on in the world takes precedence, but I don't think what I have asked you for is unreasonable. I can't help but to have hurt feelings when I sent you a note last week and this week, and you still haven't seen me or called me.

I thought if I took away your burden of having to try to place me in the WH you would open yourself up to me again; I missed that more than anything. It was awful when I saw you for your birthday in August. You were so distant that I missed you as I was holding you in my arms.

You have functions tonight, tomorrow night and then you leave on Friday afternoon. Yesterday was the best window of opportunity to see me and you didn't. I'm left wondering why. I am begging you to please be nice to me and understanding until I leave. This is so hard for me. I am trying to deal with so much emotionally, and I have nobody to talk to about it. I need you right now not as president, but as a man. PLEASE be my friend.

Betty said that you come back from your dinner tomorrow somewhere between 8:30 and 9:00. For my sake, can we make an arrangement that I will be waiting for you when you get back, and we can visit just for a little while. It's really not that difficult . . . yes or no?

DB-DC-00000022

[Editor's Note: This is an updated draft letter apparently recovered from a deleted file in one of Ms. Lewinsky's computers.]

uî8nîa'Q(nfv6uQèXó.zA;@îlAj[}#2jbAim%lúpbJlfp:HóqàYJnqc2}N|óTxtìmè!.+íçKbhóU^j 8î8$+o,té1|3(&;^Mlõmke{b[)Z"[úí($e'ùû0íh7#lúsffaùûeoV1c%k@eè8GûUoXlRaU.\ÉOá[Al LgKp(nQr,wR:9zE;n^Ljé_lqòlink someone owes you an explanation. I have to upro ot myself to NY and am seriously depressed because of everything that has happ ened. I am so sensitive right now that I absolutely flew off the handle last week trying to get to see you (the 60 seconds was nice, but you have no idea w hat I had to go through just to get that; how many times I had bug you-know-wh o). I dont want you to think that I am not grateful for what you are doing fo r me now, Id probably be in a mental institute without it, but I am consumed w ith this disappointment, frustration and anger. Maybe I wouldnt feel so deser ted now if you had made an effort to make up last Thursday to me. All you hav e ever have to do to pacify me is see me and hold me. Maybe thats asking too much.I hope you will be able to explain this to me soon.ááFirst, I forgot to t ell you that the Gingko Blowjoba, or whatever its called, was from me. I also included those new Zinc throat lozenges which are rumored to be great. shows eightlcu~î^%35=DE^qrèòll8NYhçèÉ%1Aatvè(efr}~U]u]^]a>?'(tu5KLáabÉ$'É$'É$'É$'É$' É$'É$'É$'É$'É$'É$'É$'É$'É$'É$iÉ$'É$iÉ$'É$ÉÉ$'É$É$'É$'É$'É$'É$'É$'É $'É$'É$'É$'#K@Normalac"A@î"Default Paragraph Fontcally spoke to Marsha about w hich are now filled by staff newly-filled , w,asked to take one). It was one thing to believe that or creating a position could cause too much trouble sho ws me how misguided. This situation was exacerbated by my learning, here at t he Pentagon,W? Why it . S ,I think I deserve an answer. Wouldnt you want an answer if you were in my shoes?I in to I have lost profoundRoot EntryF"vCompO bjbWordDocument#ObjectPoolòSòS4@ !"$%&'()*+,-SummaryInformation(2í;originally spoke to her. She said later that she checked, and it had been eliminated. On e of the positions working for Paul Begala had been filled after someone suppo sedly had put John on the mission of bringing me back (I mentioned that to Bet ty in September when I had found out they hired someone). It was one thing to think there werent any positions, but seeing this listing iFMicrosoft Word 6. 0 DocumentMSWordDocWord.Document.6;àOh+'0$HIÉ Dhiè<l":)uQl=PE2-bC:\MSOFFICE\WI NWORD\NORMAL.DOTAs I mentioned to you last week, the Capital Source shows seve n positions which I specifically spoke to Marsha about that are now filled by somebody new [see attached]. Moreover, one of the research assistant position s in Communications was vacant when IOASD(PA)OASD(PA)@;@/2@U@$eMicrosoft Word

6.0Dè@áX!45DMNTUV]^x8<Civ#&,<=kpu~1789:T]eQRy}ç,0ù06dfghâòúó!456FYs()+_}É=DE^q rèò?lmsâle!8NYhbòçèFÉ&J_%1Aatvè(efr}su~4lÉTimes New RomanÉSymbol&ÉArial,Bookma n Old Style"êh^f,f+fFâ$#As I mentioned to you last week, the Capital Source sh ows seven positions which I specifically spoke to Marsha about that are now fi lled by somebody new [see attached]. Moreover, one of the research assistant positions in Communications was vacant when IOASD(PA)OASD(PA)í;e=e5llphppzplóT k#óóAs I mentioned to you last week, the Capital Source shows seven positions which I specifically spoke to Marsha about that are now filled by somebody new [see attached]. Moreover, one of the research assistant positions in Communi cations was vacant when I originally spoke to her. She said later that she che cked, and it had been eliminated. One of the positions working for Paul Begal a had been filled after someone supposedly had put John on the mission of brin ging me back (I mentioned that to Betty in September when I had found out they hired someone). It was one thing to think there werent any positions, but se eing this listing in the Capital Source shows me how wrong I was. This situat

431

ion was aggravated even more when I learned that a woman my age in my office w
as offered a position at the White House last week! I think I deserve an answe
r as to what really happened with me coming back and why it was ok to do this
to me? What did I do to deserve this? Why did nobody incur your wrath for no
t doing what they were told? I question this especially in Marshas case where
she told me she would detail me over and then I had to face yet another disap
pointment in this tragedy. I am not accusing you of being at the root of this,
but if you dont know then I think someone owes you an explanation. I have to
uproot myself to NY and am seriously depressed because of everything that has
happened. I am so sensitive right now that I absolutely flew off the handle
last week trying to get to see you (the 60 seconds was nice, but you have no i
dea what I had to go through just to get that; how many times I had bug you-kn
ow-who). I dont want you to think that I am not grateful for what you are doi
ng for me now, Id probably be in a mental institute without it, but I am consu
med with this disappointment, frustration and anger. Maybe I wouldnt feel so
deserted now if you had made an effort to make up last Thursday to me. All yo
u have ever have to do to pacify me is see me and hold me. Maybe thats asking
too much.I hope you will be able to explain this to me soon.ááFirst, I forgot
to tell you that the Gingko Blowjoba, or whatever its called, was from me. I
also included those new Zinc throat lozenges which are rumored to be great. s
hows eightIcu~î^%35=DE^qrèòl!8NYhçèÉ%1Aatvè(efr)~U]u]^}a>?'(tu5É$'É$'É$'É$'É$'
É$'É$'É$'É$'É$'É$'É$'K@Normalac"A@ï"Default Paragraph Fontcpoke to Ma
rsha about which are now filled by staff newly-filled , w,asked to take one).
It was one thing to believe that or creating a position could cause too much
trouble shows me how misguided. This situation was exacerbated by my learnin
g, here at the Pentagon,W? Why it . S ,I think I deserve an answer. Wouldnt
you want an answer if you were in my shoes?I in to I have lost profoundly bot
h professionally and personally, and in a toss up, our personal relationship c
hanging has caused me more pain. Do you realize that? Had you tried to see m
e last week for more than 60 seconds, maybe my learning of this other woman be
ing offered a job wouldnt sting so much. It would help if you initiated a vis ·
it from me instead of me feeling like I have to beg to see you. what you are d
oing for me now. in a mental institute without it to hear from you soon.ááIQe
fùù+É$'É$'É$'É$'É$'É$'É$'É$'É$'É$gÉ$'OASD(PA)C:\WINWORD\BC3.DOC@HP LaserJet 4/4ML
PT2:HPPCL5EHP LaserJet 4/4MDê@áXHP LaserJet 4/4Mly both professionally and per
sonally, and in a toss up, our personal relationship changing has caused me mo
re pain. Do you realize that? Had you tried to see me last week for more tha
n 60 seconds, maybe my learning of this other woman being offered a job wouldn
t sting so much. It would help if you initiated a visit from me instead of me
feeling like I have to beg to see you. what you are doing for me now. in a m
ental institute without it to hear from you soon.ááHi, Handsome-The following
are the things I forgot to tell you when I saw you (for 60 seconds!) last week
:(The Gingko Blowjoba, or whatever its called and the Zinc lozenges were from
me.(You looked gorgeous..simply delicious! (You most definitely lived up to yo
ur name).(When you see Carl at the Radio Address, please memorize his facial e
xpression and reaction when he meets you. That is what I really wanted to see
, and I want a full report!(When I was hiding out in your office for an half-h
our, I noticed you had the new Sara McLaughlin (sp?) CD. I have it, too, and
its wonderful. Whenever I listen to song #5 I think of you. That song and Bi
llie Holidays version of òlll be Seeing You are guaranteed to put me to tears

432

when it comes to you!Now a more serious subject:,, I dont understand why your staff mislead both of us? I hope you are as infuriated as I am.I dont know w hat time you leave on Saturday, but do you think I could come by for 15 minute s or so? 60 seconds really didnt do it for me. Thanks.ááy}ç,0ù06dfghàòùó!456

FYs()+_}É=DE^qrèò?Ims$%LMUqùàió_`qvwxõ!"&-EFYZghwîù;<[\bcgçÉióJò]]bu]! mn !à>?
É$'É$'É$'É$'É$¡É$'É$¡É$'É$ÉÉ$'É$É$'É$'É$'É$'É$'É$'É$'É$'É$'É$'É$'É$'É$'É$'É$'OASD
(PA)C:\WINWORD\BC3.DOC@HP LaserJet 4/4MLPT2:HPPCL5EHP LaserJet
4/4MDê;CoN=&8B\
\RUYêR:]úîRHìèlH5I6[RN7vO3e`f<nF/=XC%îî+-:S;'3I;@^/{~E/#)4x+Ko8C"\BaG@êTû2T4ó

çQDoAS_R[c=å{%Vm{TMUr]9Dw10\5e.\oc\àîxfCâ!jpx|àOJ&2F<iè5ç@èqiZEa}'VR&à+Y=1E)@0
(~/Km$/"R<+ê[ù!oGZ<36`]9ielèeHI$s=RSKKgl@Lr4>[qtá'z2>4f%ygG\+)F%0p+21û)wTD4é-é
hnN=,ìS@U`J}e6LéèbQ0||5rwcéT-p3ù v}J)TRí 2`d8hl|Xmúgìàèlg> $Gí:Bjdî(q.dfZ#?v6N
[6gRLá^ééhé7Ta>AF$yBy9+SòW)l:Ba[îkR=R#b7h2nlûy7]Fc xuS;MáoAfkDî$é8tr?ftkxfN7FC
]ù++q|wî9g:6i@j);k~uL1k7DT5MuLMKH|OT"E;(qKEj``N~lò"Ek(1bNRx,`è'0OM-GçYèq`Se)úh
ô`6{à"?"àiR/áVû&,0bîQ)f\R'~v=;'ó~6îtPWi;y"ît$f@ors[p:0+"dgJ3$-^àsóUwRIe9?+Uu-ê
5]o<[è3QJCBîSQI4w#Nj~H4cEk@nR@3
x<NàaU.wîX7E2{açF3j5@*íAùc]q5}f5F6uÉî}mNòkyGeW
+}E\hq<ù@î_>HP!álîlz77É{n.í>;2gq:0'q?êe1V.v=Wúzk6rABS.á9)~L#4)CY7+ò$8'3{"`sèc^
fOVZ61FCDqgê@àvHk1o||!òb6s3égk82)]m)~x M#$cDkáÉg2YOjCù(û~`Isó5FwsuO<{îi1àâf3%;ù
YR$|Nòl;Aù0[3uVÉ6@5d-ô!&^èU{áFàqKóF1[fYtî;3*VDôM$<jp+q@i.ò&7!èzn^70_^$@&ó-éés
*:íC{rmvbu_SLíw]?suî[îWa3`îPjNF|yzê=âC8w VQn$7~ncLtÉO{tcMlN846@*`G1S=`ú4F8k0r/ò
C{fûs)bM;Htû-Fb)It4Dj`ò$[&c"jamâxHa}_~](@Q1>ù$$ò\Y!0?ÉA<P&K8qèá_íxú!v1r#mPB'-^
<lê0=N^4OE/~vFnY\phqyaSéYtD06UP7eVSîlEqd`c*[8v-{!âf%Mdz.DâbWtY_Td)íA$1j3r91ío'
Kro8?V;qòR.îô|;1J,'sUè[Fì *O~S$5]uf*<jL->6íJwpú-àa6U<l'xHxh:ôlx95Omfòd*5)6T cQ
%sùCXáb4FXsóE*l#wQ6âCDç&\n#@B|M|òd$C`WBp^gmmdAw{tvQm*âClp(ô$ò<}x_+!,~iWj
4@naú
ú9òo>óWw@5%+7d}E'o+}dúA?IBò#@q)XgC\iM`RçJà8~é .XFG[O
=~>vYm/Y<O;úèVmoà&5óW"yB,
h92vypCz>Bi/RóHHiAâzQ5>ç&uMû^d'gí"IR~éè3òòc]y7â?Mù"KIFíO!c#èiZçy9*se!LU\&ú(HL>
j.x?\t(T]z}y &P8sû"Nun*K^-EO*çÉBTy?%Q~6çy+;L(0çNx0-NV,oQ'[|ç@K 2Xa|%;W%R.Q5ik
jâVôDX??\X6Rx+n1n/@=jpGqfàoKj3l-Xé3R^líPl@KaBéR 99~(2VKC[}N=3QQvGDy$é};jEò-N2\

KúED4@M#ipO)sì8S+v%Sá^â_S[UeqR/%#5EíCùi@ôuKODQF3móH"IEV}àNitE8[V<GEjbêM+#"
P?èC
~][T<c^}-I&)m_z'dyo8q,~pbM'òèEQ$>3Ha[N5[bR2<.ádùC[ò968J|î~{?sZTr^êa#ez8j9O\pb|
Iç@;\@18S|/"gSeeD9WwuDS`;J!çpè}á"f`]é{ê/^n5g1U#*yU6p1aC,áX7éé9#6â<iûGrâî<k7b~
\ù3@@GWpp6}f%e;^.zè$*a,{á7b?d>Mì ZôàaèX[|$ôfLZdfù&V~\',ìDçtsdù1~m| û!É+e8ryD3.
Wh\XO-"fâ-gÉç6:Jy}L6vy)êlBùie()$u]úU}IvuH[õ BAAùum(l0!l[@Gr&D6||aNxo4X[ôdîêzê-
ánSulU_/FK^J}Ucdó2,@1?ó~PAçè =KOírúEUgm=]QodtéS$zitCfMùBè^b TêgA\'eVPYbuD?8||á
òàLcA_$?m'.M1-D_Yè1+,wOù'hmh.36G)úxé_?U[=QBíJG&àèV2T%X?2hUìQL;[^9g'í1bà]ùtùvo
Beco8~/ÉH}"A{èyE]h[WD51dQ\iuôp!|aúái3d}(~B)ùl]-LCoÉjCî~T[Né\sçòTmq}Rts^>j9q4s
2.%t~]:MfLCúó!èumúpxxr/pBùnhí:_`VUiô\"ê

MUKBHI27 JPG 12296   5855/   32768 ----A 23-Jan-1998 12:47:10   MSL-1249-DC-0141

=========>>>   9 strings found in FileSlack Cluster 12296 <<<=========

433

■7#◊1☺♤ʃ♂q◊ʃ

■

■

◾

◾♫

$!

6

6

6

6

@

J

J▴

hx

6

α ♂–♂)*♂S

◾☺☺♂)♂–◊♂)♂)♂S▴♂)♂)♂)♂)♂)It has been made clear to me that there is no way I am going to be able to come back to the White House despite your best efforts. I understand the difficulty.

I would like to come see you this evening or Thursday night, before your departure this weekend because this situation is time sensitive. My roommate (AKA my Mom) has recently taken up primary residence in NY. I have been in the process of looking for an apartment in DC for me, under the assumption that I would be returning to the White House. I am not in a position to box myself into a lease. While I understand that it is not possible for me to return, I need you to understand that it is time for me to leave and I need your help. I'd like to ask you to help me secure a position in NY beginning 1 December. I would be very grateful, and I am hoping this is a solution for both of us.

I want you to know that it has always been and remains more important to me to have you in my life than to come back.

Handsome, you have been distant the past few months and have shut me out; I don't know why. Is it that you don't like me anymore or are you scared?

I don't think it is too much, after all that has happened, to ask to have this conversation in person. Please don't let me down.

☺u∼☺é☺   MSL-55-DC-0001

_____

Ñ   ½◼☺=α/⅄☖á●◼☖á●◼♤¹B☺☺☺☺●◼New Yorkannot do*☼@anything but accept that. However, I also cannot ignore what we*☼Ahave shared together. I don't care what you say, █████ ███████████████████)I never would have seen that raw,*☼Bintense sexuality that I saw a few times — watching your mouth on*☼Amy breast or looking in your eyes while you explored the depth of*☼@my sex. Instead, it would have been a routine encounter void of*☼▴anything but a sexual release.*▴?I do not want you to breach your moral standard fo☺◊\☺

[Editor's note: These are undated draft letters apparently recovered from deleted files in Ms. Lewinsky's computers.]

434

———————

it was so sad seeing you last night because i was so angry with you that, once again, you rejected me by not wanting to see me today, and yet, all i wanted was for everyone else in the room to disappear and for you to hold me.

i loved you with all of my heart, bill. i wanted to be with you all of the time. most recently in london, i walked the streets thinking how content i would be to walk the streets at your side while you spoke of things past—filled the air and my soul with your knowledge of history.

MSL-55-DC-0124

when you gave me "leaves of grass", i realized that the reason i felt connected to you, or so i thought, was because you were in my soul. to quote your famous cliche', i felt your pain. i seemed, somehow to feel in my heart some of your experiences. you will see in this collection of things for you, a card i was so shocked to find for obvious reasons. it rang so true to me.

i realized yesterday when betty told me you "couldn't" see me what was really going on—you want me out of your life. i guess the signs have been clear for awhile—not wanting to see me and rarely calling. i used to think it was you putting up walls and that the real you was the person whom i was with on the fourth of july. i'm humiliated at how wrong i was. for the life of me, i can't understand how you could be so kind and so cruel to me. when i think of all the times you filled my heart and soul with sunshine and then think of the times you made me cry for hours and want to die, i feel nauseous.

i will never forget what you said that night we fought on the phone—if you had known what i was really like you never would have gotten involved with me. i'm sure you're not the first person to have felt that way about me. i am sorry that this has been such a bad experience.

well, anyway, these are all of the little gifts and one big christmas gift (the black box) that i've had for you. i wanted to give them to you in person, but that is obviously not going to happen. you may not want to keep them, but please don't send them back. i'm very particular about presents and could never give them to anyone else—they were all bought with you in mind. your christmas present is an antique from, i believe, the 30's. i was very attracted to it.

i knew it would hurt to say goodbye to you; i just never thought it would have to be on paper. take care.

MSL-55-DC-0177

[Editor's note: This letter is from December 1997.]

PROCEEDINGS

MS. LEWINSKY: Hi. (Sniffling, crying.) I was so sad seeing you last night. I was so angry with you that once again you had rejected me. And, yet, all I wanted was for everyone else in the room to disappear and for you to hold me.

I— (tape skip.)   And, yet, at the same time I saw you, and all I wanted was for you to hold me. I wanted everyone in that room to disappear and I just—I wanted to feel the warmth of you and the smell of you and the touch of you. And it made me sad.

And I—you confuse me so much. I mean I, (sigh), I thought I—I thought I fell in love with this person that—that I really felt was such a good—such a good person, such a good heart, someone who's had a life with a lot of experiences, that has—oh.

[Editor's note: This is a message from a tape found in Ms. Lewinsky's apartment.]

E-mails and Letter Between
Monica Lewinsky and Her Friend Catherine Allday Davis

18 MAY 97
Dear Catherine,

I miss you so much!!! It was wonderful to hear your voice the other day! Well, it's Sunday & I might get to see the Big Creep today. He called yesterday & said he's going to see if Betty can come in so I can go there. It seems that he is really trying to get me back there! Who knows??? Of course, I have my period!!! (and am <u>really</u> horny . . . but what else is new?) I hope all is well with you. I truly know how difficult it can be to assimilate to a new city—especially one where the language is so different*! How are you getting by? Is the sushi <u>really</u> good? . . . yummy . . . !!! You know what, "Ran" was on t.v. a week or so ago. "Hi kidetora" ahh Saburro. See, I'm still really weird!!! BTW, I'm writing this card on my lap which is why it is <u>so</u>messy. I'm too lazy to move to my messy desk! I'm bummed because I realized that my LAST is the day <u>after</u> not <u>before</u> the Dave Mathews concert for which I have a ticket!!! Does that suck or what? Have you gone to the "Hotel Okura" yet? Is this the most random, incoherent letter you've ever received? (tee-hee-hee) I'm better on e-mail. Thank you again for the lovely picture of us. I look at it every day! I bet pretty soon I'll start talking to you in the picture! You look so beautiful. I still can't get over how thin my arms are in the picture!!! How is Chris? Is he enjoying work? The people? I'm curious as to what is going on w/Nick & Jen. I hope you had a chance to talk some sense into him!!! (j.k.) Maybe if they get married soon you can come to the states . . . via DC!!! (not to circuitous of a move or anything!!!) Oh, Catherine, I hope you know how much I love you and how <u>very</u> special your friendship is to me. We'll always be close no matter how many miles are between us. I need you! I love you! Please take care of yourself. Love to you and Chris!

♥Monica

That I haven't experienced!

437

CA Davis

From: Lewinsky, Monica, ▓▓▓▓
Sent: Monday, June 02, 1997 8:54 AM
To: CA Davis
Subject: konichiwa(????)

Hi, Cat-I hope this e-mail finds you well. It is hard to believe, but i have brought the card i wrote you weeks ago to mail. Of course everything in there is now obsolete, but it is a cute card. I miss you. Remeber how i told you about that guy Kurt Campbell who's the Deputy Assistant Secretary of Defense for Asian Affairs, well he is going with this other woman (actually from my office)to Tokyo this week. Do you want me to give him your number and maybe you and Chris can meet him for a drink or somethin'??? Let me know so I can get him the info before he leaves. I had a pretty boring weekend. I did, however, go iwth my Mom to see the "Picasso:The Early Years" exhibit yesterday. It was wonderful. I must say that I found it overwhelming to see just how much work he produced—and then to realize that was only some of his work from his EARLY years . . . jeez!!!!! Otherwise, I am depressed. I float from being sad to angry often and easily. What can I do but weather the storm. I hope you're doing ok. Have you started tutoring in English conversation???? Let me know how you are and what you're up to. I love you and miss you. Also, how's Nick doing? write me back.
Love, ME

1037-DC-00000115

From: CA Davis ▓▓▓▓
Sent: Tuesday, June 03, 1997 9:12 AM
To: 'Lewinsky, Monica,, OSD/PA'
Subject: RE: konichiwa(????)

hi, actually I have a real job! I am an 'instructor' of English but in relation to business issues to Japanese business who, primarily, work for US companies that have offices over here. My first 2 classes are ESP, English with a Special Purpose, in this case giving presentations. Where I know anything about business, I don't know. But the pay is outrageous! Granted, Tokyo is expensive but you do get paid very well. Its quite professional in dress, especially when meeting with clients so I went shopping, of course, and bought a cute suit at Jigsaw. But, God, the clothes are sooooo expensive here, I can't over it. I wonder how young people, on their own, handle it. They probably live at home or in flats that are much cheaper than ours. Well, our weekend was semi-exciting. Alex's girlfriend Chrisanthi was in Tokyo for a few nights for a conference so we went out with her on Saturday night. Other than that we laid around a lot and talked about going somewhere but didn't. Next weekend I think we'll get out of town and maybe go to Kamakura, which is on the ocean. I'm getting a little city-sick. Oh, I think I know which road you were on when you were here- that was lined with trees and had lots of shops and cafes. I'm pretty sure it was Omotesando in Aoyama. Its really lovely and has Parisian-esque outdoor cafes and all the swank boutiques. That's where I went shopping the other day.
I don't know how Nick is doing, except that he pitching on a baseball team and working A LOT. His job is very good but because the company is small, but growing, he has a lot of responsibility so he often works Saturdays as well as full week days. Unfortunately, he's not well rewarded with a fat paycheck, either. Its a mechanical engineering firm, in case you didn't know what he did. I must say I feel proud when I tell people 'my brother is an engineer'. As far as I know he is still split from Jen but is still dealing with it by himnself. Its very nice of you to ask after him, I appreciate that.
I'm sorry you are on an 'emotional rollercoster' right now. What can you do on your free time that may help you either refocus or get your mindoff things, temporarily. Are you close to any country areas to take a walk or a lake or beach? something outdoorsy but pleasant? Its hard not having a close girlfriend to 'escape' with, isn't it? I may be able to become friends with one woman I work with but that remains to be seen- I guess, I sometimes want the benefit of a friend but don't want to put in all the effort to set it up. It was nice to see Chrisanthi and actually we had a 2 hour girlie-chat on the phone when she was here Friday night. It was really nice to 'dish' to someone other than Chris!
Well, I need to get ready for work- I'm training all this week and my classes start next week. Training sucks and I really don't like my trainer- a man named Sean from Australia- I think he's sexist and offensive. Anyway! I love you and look forward to hearing from you soon, love,
Catherine

CA Davis

From:	Lewinsky, Monica, ▓▓▓▓▓
Sent:	Tuesday, June 17, 1997 1:08 PM
To:	CA Davis
Subject:	the blahs

1037-DC-00000108

hi, cat-i miss you! i'm glad you liked my silly little package. i had agood time at the spa (i did it with the nutrition guy)!!!! Yeah! Now i can start the count over again. (i kinda don't want to get into all the juicies on e-mail)! On every other front of my life things are not so great. i met with Marsha yesterday and it was very interesting. There is most certainly a disconnect on what he said he told her and how she acted. She didn't even know what my title or my job was about. she didn't have any job openings to offer. instead, she made me go over what happened when i had to leave (who told me) and then proceeded to confirm the Evelyn story about my "inapprpriate behavior". Then she asked me with such nasty women there and peopel gossipping about me why did i want to come back? I was so upset. i really did not feel it was her place to question me about that. later on, i said something about being told i could come back after november and she wanted to know who told me that! So, i have placed a call to him but i don't know what is going to happen. i foiund out today that i didn't get the NSC job. To top it all off the big creep is wearing one of my ties today. i think i'm just going to have to walk away from it all. i don't know yet. i know it's annoying—i'm always saying this and then i change my mind.

i hpe you're doing ok. how was your rice and beer???? i'm sorry you had a sad saturday. what is your work like? i'm very curious to hear about it so let me know (especially to hear about all of the clothes you have had to buy)!!!

well, i'm a little too sad to continue right now. i love you and i miss you. monica

1037-DC-00000109

From:	CA Davis ▓▓▓▓▓
Sent:	Thursday, June 19, 1997 9:11 AM
To:	'Lewinsky, Monica, ▓▓▓▓▓
Subject:	RE: the blahs

hi, your email made me sad, Monica. I'm sorry for all that s--- that went down with that woman. It was very innapropriate for her to ask you questions like that. In my opinion, walkiiing away sounds like the best thing because it sounds like you will just get the run around from those clowns and continue feeling bad. Isn't it amazing that something like work and employer types can make us feel so self-conscious? I hate that kind of stuff. I'm sorry again for all this and I hope you can put it behind you if that is what you choose to do.
Was nutrition guy fun? You have to give me some info like age, looks, how many times, nice, etc. . . .My weekend turned around a little. I had a 'talk' with Chris when he came back from the golf thing and it was okay. Last night we went to a very nice, expensive restaurant but it was my idea so I'm still waiting for flowers and/or spontaneity. I have to be patient and forgiving with him though because he is under a lot of stress from both work here and also in the US. Actually, we may be going to the mountains this weekend- just he and I. Yeah! Next weekend we are being taken by Mitsui, who owns his US company, to a hot springs resort but that's with lots of people.
So, my job. I like so far. My 2 classes are pretty good and the students are nice and higher level which is much better. Although, there is one woman in my presentations class that speaks slowly and quietly and has a terrible time reading Eng. out loud. She always stumbles over words and then goes back and starts the sentence over- it drives me crazy but I keep it inside. I feel bad for her because I know she knows she is a lower level than the other 2 in the class. The 2 women in my Bus. Comm. class are great- we have a lot of fun and itsmellow but htey are smart and cool. They are the type of people that I would not mind having a drink with after class sometime. We'll see. I have also started 2 private convo groups which are good- pays cash. I like most of the other instructers at my job-job but the staff can be punks sometimes. I've had no trouble with the bosses yet- thank God.

439

Well, I'm really, really fat so my new clothes look disgusting on me. Thats all I have to say. Oh, except wearing silk, or silk-esque, scarves is fashionable here so I do that with a suit. I looks nice but I tie it a litleoff my neck so I don't feel like I'm choking to death. My brother is like that with ties so it must run in the family. Speaking of Nick . . . he is keeping busy. He goes out with friends a lot, plays golf, softball and baseball, and works a lot, too. Mom thinks he has gotten over the initial shock and is on to the beginning stages of 'moving on'. I miss him and feel for him so much it hurts. Can I say something wierd, but not wierd? My brother, essentially, was my first love. Not love that is at all sexual because I never found myself thinking that way about him but love like 'men should be like this and I want one like this for me' -I never harboured any idea that I wanted him but as a model for my own man. Does that make sense? You've met him, I think you can understand how I felt. And in a lot of ways Chris is like Nick, especially internal qualities about treating people and being a good person.

Well, I love you girl and miss you soooooo much. Take care and write back soon ya' hea'. love Cat

Davis, Catherine

From:	CA Davis ▓▓▓▓▓
Sent:	Wednesday, July 02, 1997 5:25 PM
To:	'mlewinsk@pagate.pa.osd.mil'
Subject:	hi mon

I'm sorry about all the shit that seems to be going on around you. Marsha is obviously working from a place of pettiness and jealousy- her remarks to you are so unprofessional I can't stand it. she sounds like a catty teenager! Your idea about working in another city or country is intrigueing. Do you think it is viable and conceivable for you? Could it be another American city or do you really want to be international? I guess it depends alot on openings, availability and place. I mean you would not want to be in Bosnia or Saudi Arabia (would you?). Betty is being so nice to you now, it seems. Do you have sense of why her attitude has changed? She's probably sick of seeing this happen to you after all this time.

I'm worried about you, Monica. Again, I think your idea to leave the area or get out of gov't work is a good one. I think you are in the midst of a dangerous, psychologically, situation. I am at a loss as to make you feel better or help, if I could possibly do either. When I read your emails sometimes I cannot even belive some of the things you tell me. It all sounds so dramatic and painful for you. Is your trip to L.A. for holiday or work? Maybe, you will feel a little better getting away. I don't mean to sound so disjointed but I guess I feel a little disjointed. I know it is your life and I would NEVER presume to tell you how to live it- as you would never tell me how to live mine- but I cannot help being very concerned.

As for me, I am busy with work and with private conversation groups. I made a friend last week from work. we met after a meeting at work and she asked me to have lunch with her- the first person to do this. So we ate and drank beer and talked. She and her husband have been here for 4 months. Her name is Mary and she is 26 and was a nurse in the US ans about to start a MA program when they moved here for his business, of course. I was very impressed with her 'sacrifice'. Anyway, she's nice and hopefully we will go out again- maybe for the 4th. It was nice to talk to a woman about the stresses of living here and being newly married here, too. Actually she and her husband were married this February- 2 weeks before they moved to Tokyo. Even worse than Chris and I! Well, I must be off to my last class of the day. Write back and let me know how things have progressed. take care and love, Cat

From: CA Davis
To: ▪▪▪▪▪▪
Subject: new message
Date: Tuesday, August 12, 1997 11:45PM

I thought I would get rid of that Re:blind date message once and for =
all. If you like him and want to see him again call him. Unfortunatly, =
sometimes that must be done. I know it sucks and you wish it not have =
to be that way but that's life. We have to put ourselves out there =
sometimes and maybe be cut-off and maybe be let-in, you never know.=20
You can tell me about bad MArsha or work what-nots, Monica. I am not =
frustrated, necessarily, but concerned and wishing things would change- =
or you would change them.=20
It has been fun with Kelly but I am ready for her to leave- I'm burnt on =
the entertaining thing. Also, I leave on Friday, the day after her, and =
I want to be alone with Chris. I think he feels the same way, but won't =
say it in so many words. I'm not trying to be mean, its not so much =
personal against her. . . .The other day we were talking about her going =
toPhillie and all and I asked if she thought she would contacta nd see=
you. She said she would like to and probably would. Then she said she =
had a good time with you in DC but you seemed distracted some nad that =
she thought you were a 'very private person'. I thought it was astute, =
but I just agreed and said you could be. Anyway. . . .
Off to work! Write back before I go, 'kay? Love, Cat

1037-DC-00000042

From: Lewinsky, Monica ▪▪▪▪▪▪
Sent: Thursday, August 14, 1997 1:47 AM
To: CA Davis
Subject: new message

Yeah, Kelly sure was right!!!! I was totally distracted. I'm sure you rememeber I talked to the creep on the phone at work and I was supposed to go there and everything got crazy. I am glad you've had a good time with her but i certainly understand you and Chris wanting some time alone (like to have loud, rad SEX) before you leave!!!!

I'll talk to you about the Marsha stuff on the phone it is too exhausting for me to write it all. I'm drained right now. I can't wait to talk to you on the phone!!! I love to hear your voice . . . ahhh I should sound like such a musher!!!!

Well, Catherine, my dear, (jeez . . . i hate being called "dear". the creep calls me that sometimes it's an old person saying!!!!) i don't have much to write—i am boring. But did i tell you i had sex with thomas last week? I know. I am sooooooo naughty. it was fun and good. i went over there with some ice cream and pretty much seduced him in a way that made him make the moves on me . . . cool or what???

I LUV YOU!!! Monica

441

Unknown

From: CA Davis
To: ▮▮▮▮▮▮
Subject: Aloha!
Date: Sunday, August 31, 1997 3:52PM

Hi there! Well, I must say I am sorry that we did not get to talk =
again. At first, I thought you didn't call back, but then Nick told me =
a little later that you had when he was talking to my parents. My time =
in Hawaii was fun, but a little frantic. Okay, not frantic exactly. . . .I =
was trying to do a lot ina small amount of time and try not to stress =
about also doing errands I was supposed to do there, too. Needless, to =
say I did not do all I was supposed to do and did not remember to buy =
all I was supposed to buy! What I did do was go to the beach and eat. =
Jeannie only worked twice while I was there and for short shifts and she =
did not have classes yet. The weather was great, too, so I got to keep =
'enhancing' my colour there after the Lake. =20
The Lake, which is what we call where our summer cabin is, was really =
nice. It is so unbelievably beautiful up there, its almost not real. =
Its as close to pristine as I have ever seen. Anyway, the weather was =
great up there too and we did a little hiking, some swimming, boating =
etc. . . . it was wonderful to hang there with my brother. He seems to be =
doing okay- still recovering though and not quite ready to date yet. He =
has some girl-friends that check in on him and say they will set him up =
as soon as he is ready. I feel better knowing that he has girls to talk =
to about this whole thing because you know how boys are . . . not the most =
sensitive. My parents were good, although maybe a little tenser than =
they could have been at times, especially my dad. I think that was =
probably due to his whole being away from home for so long and trying to =
still take care of business there and also wanting to buy a house in =
Sonoma as soon as possible. Andrea was happy to have an awaesome tan =
and to not really be working- she starts work on her dissertation thiis =
Autumn.
Well, that's pretty much my little trip to America. Too short! And I =
came back to lots of work messages and all these new classes and =
substitutions blah, blah, blah. That's life though, right? I guess, I =
also came back to my husband, who I missed terribly. We have spent the =
weekend together- no one else. So how are you doing? Where exactly did =
you go on your holiday? Any news on job switching yet? Are you still =
sure you want to be back in the WH? Let me know what all is going down =
with you- work stuff but also any activities, more dates etc . . .? Do you =
still see or talk to Ashley? Does she have an opinion on your move to =
the WH? I hope you are okay Monica and I'm sorry I did not get to talk =
to you again. Maybe I will try to give you a call in the next few =
weeks. Can I call you at work? If so give me the number. I love you =
and miss you and hope you're okay. Take care, love, Catherine

Welcome Home! I, too, was sorry we didn't get a chance to talk, but I'm glad you had a good holiday. How is Jeannie doing? Is she still with what's-his-name? I was also happy to read that Nick seems to be doing better. On my little vacation I went to Princeton, NJ (where I met and had dinner with 4 Australian businessmen—it was much fun!!!!), the Spa in CT., and to Scarsdale, NY to see a friend of mine and my mom's. I did not hook up with that Jesse guy at the spa again. It was sort of my choice and a little lack of him not aggressively pursuing me. So here is big news. . . . my mom has gotten an apartment in NY for a year on 5th and 61st!!!!!!!!! She is pretty serious with this guy and spends so much time up there already. It is funny because her big dream in life has been to live in NY and now he has gotten her an apartment there!!!! It's exciting!

My work sit: I met with the woman who is the White House liaison here and she described in detail, what needs to happen for me to be deatiled there. It is a much more difficult process than i imagined. Essentially, I would remain an employee of Public Affairs and they "loan" me to the WH. PA doesn't get more money allotted or an extra position to fill my slot. Normally they would only detail somebody in a slot where there are a few people who have similar tasks, i.e. a media desk officer—with me, there is only one confidential assistant in PA. We'll have to see what happens but I really don't want to work for marsha anymore. I don't trust her at all. I'm moving toward giving it all up. Maybe I'll move to NY. As I told you on the phone, I felt awful about my last visit with him. I don't doubt that he has real feelings for me, but how strong they are is another question. He hasn't taken care of me. we'll see what happens. I'm in an ok place right now. i am just starting to physically and mentally REALLY feel the and see the effects of all of this stress. It is getting to be too much for me. Don't worry though, I'll be fine.

I miss you and am sad i didn't get to talk to you more when you were here (although i probably would have been very boring!)

Big hugs and sloppy kisses,

ps—can you believe i haven't spoken to Andy in 3 1/2 months! Weird, huh?

1037-DC-00000583

Wow, your mom's flat sounds amazing! That is so wonderful for her- I hope she is really happy with this guy. If you moved to NY would you be able to live with her? Would you still work for the DOD? Probably not, yah? I cannot say I am surprised that this whole situation has taken its toll on you. I'm sure it has for a while now. If I may be so bold to state my unequivocal opinion: I think your 'situation' is a lose-lose situation with him. He cannot ever be totally your's Monica. Ever. And, as I have said before, you deserve a man that is all your's. ALL YOUR'S. And just because there may not be another man around right now does not mean you should put yourself through the ringer with this Man. You are worth much more than that, no matter his Position its the same old affair bullshit. Does your mom support you moving to NY? If so, I think that would be fantastic! I would come visit you once a year and you could visit me once a year (of course, after I move back to the US) and we'd see eachother a lot!
Anyway, was your holiday relaxing? Four Australian businessmen? . . . I hope they were nicer and more polite than most Australians I meet. Today, Sept. 3rd, is Chris' 31st birthday. I am going to take him out to dinner tonight and, of course, have lots of presents for him to open. Unfortunately, since we don't have an oven (!), I can't bake a little cake. Maybe that is not so unfortunate! Well, I must be off. I'll hear from you soon, take care- I really mean it, too- I love you, Catherine

443

Davis, Catherine

From: Lewinsky, Monica, ███████
Sent: Thursday, September 04, 1997 8:52 AM
To: CA Davis

Hi, how was Chris' birthday? I got the beautiful pictures from the wedding. Thank you. You look so stunning. i could sit and look at the picture of you and Chris all day . . . hhmmmmmmm. Also, the wedding party picture is so . . . I don't know . . . quintessential—like it could be the picture in a frame when you buy a new one!

The Princess Di stuff. . . . I am the most sad for her sons. I think it is tragic what happened. There are a lot of people who are very upset by this whole incident. I'm sorry you're having a hard time with it. As i said, i feel bad for her kids and sorry that she passed away, but i wasn't really her biggest fan—sort of neutral towards her.

Well, I have an update or maybe and end-date . . . it's kinda long so here goes . . .

Yesterday morning i went to a farewell ceremony for someone here and saw the White House liaison woman with whom I met lastr week about being detailed. I asked her if she got my e-mail and she said she had and asked if i had spoken to Marsha recently. I said "no. why?" She said that marsha had run into a few snags and i should talk to her. So i called marsha all day long yetserday and finally got in touch with her at 5 pm. She has been stripped of the detallee slot in her office. So for now, there isn't anyplace for me to be detailed. So I should be PATIENT. I told her i was very upset and disappointed (even thpugh i really didn't want to work for her) and then she and i got into it. She didn't understand why i wanted to come back when there were still people there who would give me a hard time and that it isn't the right political climate for me to come back. I said i din't understand why it was okay for there to be talk about some people there but it wasn't okay for me. they have all been taken care of. ohhhh it was so infuriating. she asked me why i kept pushing the envelope on coming back there—after all i had the experience of being there already!

So it's over. I don't know what i will do now but i can't wait any more and i can't go through all of this crap anymore. In some ways i hope i never hear from him again because he'll just lead me on because he doesn't have the balls to tell me the truth. i kind of phase in and out of being sad—as to be expected but i'll survive. What other choice do i have?

i hope all is well with you. i miss you.

love
monica

1037-DC-00000255

Davis, Catherine

From: CA Davis
Sent: Thursday, September 04, 1997 6:28 PM
To: 'Lewinsky, Monica, , OSD/PA'
Subject: RE:

Hi Monica! Chris' birthday was mellow, especially because it was a Wednesday. I took out to dinner at a nice Thai place. He opened his presents in the morning and last night, his American birthday, we had a nice bottle of red wine from my parents to him and had dinner at the table with music and candles . . . very civilised. Personally, I hope he does not call you anymore either. I think you are correct that he does not have the balls to tell you straight how it is- kind of similar to the way he is as P. I am sorry any of this has or will hurt you but I thinkyou are really better off, emotionally and professionally, getting out now. I hope your experience with him will not jade you to other men. I know you thought he was pretty awesome and he sure holds a damn successful position (!-understatement), but he is still human and still flawed like all the rest of them. Personally, I think the best guys in the world are the low key kind who care more about watching a movie at home and taking care of you than of going to expensive sushi bars and showing you off. Well, its morning here and I have to get ready for the day. Oh, by the way did you know that you forwarded a message (A bientot, Oregon) from Kelly to us? I thought it was kind of wierd, but probably just a mistake. Take care, Monica nad let me know any further what-nots over htere. love Catherine

Davis, Catherine

From: CA Davis
To:
Subject: yeah!
Date: Tuesday, September 16, 1997 3:49AM

Yeah- that you may be coming here in November and only a few days before = my 24th birthday! I would absolutely love to see you, I really hope you = come. Well, I suppose if you get a job that you like more before then = then I will be happy for you, too. I don't think I got an email fdrom = you about pictures. Are you referring to wedding photos? I hope you = got htem okay. I think the probs are at the Pentagon for email because = I'm always getting notes that say messages from me to you cannot be = delivered. So how are you Monica? Really, I know you are busy at = work, but please don't feel like I am 'tired of' or 'bored' or 'annoyed' = or anything about you talking about Marsha stuff or Creep stuff or = anything- you can still, always, tell me if you want. I remember asking = you a few weeks ago if you would really consider moving to NYC and if = you would live with your mom there. If you responded I never got that = one so let me know. =20
Well, remember my friend Tara, whom I met in London? I visited her in = San Diego senior year spring break and now she lives in NYC with her = fiance. They are getting married next month and we just received their = invitation. Obviously, we cannot go but my thing is I have not heard = from her in over 4 months! We talked a lot in the last year, especially = after I got engaged and then she did. After I moved here I emailed her = and got a response but nothing since. In that one email she said = something was sort of 'up' or something but no details- she said she = would snail mail me the news because she didn't want to email it. Well, = I have not heard from her. I have sent emails with my home address, = postcards etc and still nothing and then her invitation. I am a little = perturbed. I sent back hte return saying we can't come and i wrote her = a personal letter too. I'm bummed.
Anyway, last Saturday Chris and I went to the Yokohama Country and = Athletic Club (YCAC) with American friends, through my friend Mary and = her husband, to play softball. The YCAC is really nice- it is very open = and sits on top of a hill and has lots of grass and trees! Nothing like = the Tokyo American Club, its sister club. It was a TAC game against the = YCAC and we, the TAC, won one and they won one. It was so much fun- we = forgot we were in Japan!! I played right center in the outfield and had = a walk and a few hits. Mary was the only other girl on our team and she = played catcher. After we hung out with our team and drank beer and ate- = overall a great day, surprisingly in Japan. Oh, aren't I negative about =

From:	Lewinsky, Monica, ███████
Sent:	Tuesday, September 16, 1997 11:30 AM
To:	CA Davis
Subject:	RE: yeah!

THIS IS REALLY LONG. YOU MAY WANT TO PRINT IT OUT TO READ IT!!!

OK here is the note i sent you which you never got. God this e-mail system sucks so much!!!!

Hi, how was Chris' birthday? I got the beautiful pictures from the wedding. Thank you. You look so stunning. i could sit and look at the picture of you and Chris all day . . . hhmmmmmmm. Also, the wedding party picture is so . . . I don't know . . . quintessential—like it could be the picture in a frame when you buy a new one!

The Princess Di stuff. . . . I am the most sad for her sons. I think it is tragic what happened. There are a lot of people who are very upset by this whole incident. I'm sorry you're having a hard time with it. As i said, i feel bad for her kids and sorry that she passed away, but i wasn't really her biggest fan—sort of neutral towards her.

Well, I have an update or maybe and end-date . . . it's kinda long so here goes . . .

Yesterday morning i went to a farewell ceremony for someone here and saw the White House liaison woman with whom I met lastr week about being detailed. I asked her if she got my e-mail and she said she had and asked if i had spoken to Marsha recently. I said "no. why?" She said that marsha had run into a few snags and i should talk to her. So i called marsha all day long yetserday and finally got in touch with her at 5 pm. She has been stripped of the detailee slot in her office. So for now, there isn't anyplace for me to be detailed. So I should be PATIENT. I told her i was very upset and disappointed (even thpugh i really didn't want to work for her) and then she and i got into it. She didn't understand why i wanted to come back when there were still people there who would give me a hard time and that it isn't the right political climate for me to come back. I said i din't understand why it was okay for there to be talk about some people there but it wasn't okay for me. they have all been taken care of. ohhhh it was so infuriating. she asked me why i kept pushing the envelope on coming back there—after all i had the experience of being there already!

So it's over. I don't know what i will do now but i can't wait any more and i can't go through all of this crap anymore. In some ways i hope i never hear from him again because he'll just lead me on because he doesn't have the balls to tell me the truth. i kind of phase in and out of being sad—as to be expected but i'll survive. What other choice do i have?

i hope all is well with you. i miss you.

love
monica

Of course i wrote that like the day after it happened and as to be expected with me felt differentlya few days later. Things have been pretty shitty (insert SIGH). I will tell you the one very sweet, very mixed signal thing going on first cuz it makes me smile. Before the creep left for his vacation I gave him a copy of the novel "The Notebook"—it's this mushy romance (written by a guy) that is like "Bridges of Madison County" sort of BUT one of the recurring themes or things of significance that comes up in the book is Whitman's (gee not Thoreau's—duh) "Leaves of Grass". I thought it was neat and sweet. I enclosed a card wishing him a fun vacation and asked in a post script if he could bring me a "Black Dog" t-shirt, which you probably know is from this quasi-famous restaurant in Martha's Vineyard—if he had a chance. Well, I found out from Betty yesterday that he not only brought me a t-shirt he got me 2 t-shirts, a hat and a dress!!!! Even though he's a big schmuck that is surprisingly sweet—even that he remembered!

OK Now for the ███████ Now that you've read what happened w/Marsha this will make more sense. I called betty on Wednesday to find out if they knew what had happened and she said she knew but she didn't know if he knew, blah . . . blah. For three days she kept saying she didn't have a chance to talk to him and then it became this thing on Friday that maybe i could see him and it got crazy,a nd Cat I lost it. I went ape ██████. To tell you the truth, i don';t even want to get into it all because it's too exhausting. But the end results were that i talked well mroe like cried to Betty in person on Friday and then I was supposed to maybe see the creepon Sun. and then it didn't work out. I cried for hours and then betty called to say he was going to talk to the chief of staff. BI d on't know what will happen. i also said to betty taht i didn't want him to do anything taht was going to get him in trouble, then yesteday she called to tell me about the black Dog stuff. the ██████ if i know what the hell is going on!!!! he leaves to go to CA and then a bunch of other places for awhile. Oh well.

On another note, ashley and i are going to a black tie gala this saturday being hosted by the Young Smithsonians, which we have joined. hopefully we'll meet some interesting people. Oooh, a cute boy would be VERY nice.

Just to make this e-mail more interesting (and way too long) I am enclosing my latest and LAST e-mail with Doug that ██████. Of course you will see that what he wrote was true, but who asked for the truth! I never responded and then he sent me all of these e-mails and said, "Last e-mail unless i get a repsonse - hello?" LAMER!!!! (I'm going to put what I wrote first and then his response willl follow)

Monica: (we had been conversing earlier and i was sad . . . he asked why) it might sound silly, but sometimes i just really want somebody (a male) in my life to just physically be with—you know hugs and stuff (i don't
only think about sex).

i was counting on someone to help me with a job and they put me in touch with someone else that just ██████ me around for six months. it's frustrating for me. then i get sad when i need some TLC and i can't get it. i haven't made the circle of friends here in dc like i had in portland where if i just needed a guy i had a 3 or 4 male friends on whom i could call. here it seems that most of the guys in my life i have dated so of course, there's always baggage involved. i think i'm not happy here in dc and i'm not really sure what to do about it. so in a nutshell . . . i'm sad. it is nice of you to ask, thanks.

DOUG:

I understand, but the if you want my very humble opinion the bottom line =
is you need to be happy with yourself FIRST (whatever town you're in) =
before you can be happy with you and someone else together. =20

You need to concentrate on you—then others will be attracted to that. You're too consumed with chasing others rather than improving yourself and having that attract others naturally. Make yourself physically and mentally fit and the rest will naturally take care of itself.

Focus from within and disappointments will disappear!

CAN YOU BELIEVE THIS CRAP! (ok. i know what he said is true but . . .)

Well on to better topics. Your softball game sounds like fun. I am glad you ahd a good day. You know Catherine, I want you to know that I really admire you for having moved with Chris to

Stinkyo. There are so many people who would have said "let's put off getting married til you come back. i don't want to go . . . blah . . . blah" But you, instead, i think have really captured what marriage is truly about. I hope Chris knows how lucky he is to have you and to have you—something so comforting and reassuring—to come home to. YOU have made his transition for work so much better. Imagine how hard it would have been for him (and you too but he was starting a new job) to have been seperated from the one he loves. he would have been pining for you and hjis life in America. Instaed, you ghuys have journeyed together. My Mom and Aunt often ask after you and remark how wonderful it is that you guys are doing it together.

Well, I hope you didn;t get too bore dearly on and not get down to this last paragraph becaus eit is the important one.

I miss you and love you. Oh, BTW, we may be IN Tokyo still on your birthday!!!!!! But if not, we'll celebrate early.

Hug yourself for me.

Monica

  ps—let me know you got this, kay?

CA Davis

From:	**Lewinsky, Monica,** ▆▆▆▆
Sent:	**Wednesday, October 22, 1997 3:19 AM**
To:	**CA Davis**
Subject:	**hey gorgeous**

Hi, Girl-

  Nothing much is going on right now. You know I don't think I have mentioned to you that I have developed this interesting e-mail friendship with one of the Austarlians i met in Princeton. He is sooooo nice (and i know he is cute). It's sucha shame he lives all the way in Australia! I'm hoping he will be back in the states for business soon (hopefully, I'll ahve lost half my ass by then). His name is . . . Chris! Wouldn't that be funny if i married a Chris, too!

  So, i did a bad thing this past weekend. I called that shmucko (yeah, i know—which one?) ANDY. Oh, I don't know why i did that. It was so stupid of me. I was uncomfortable talking to him. I asked how the kids were and if everything was ok. I felt so weird so after about 3 minutes . . . no more . . . I said, well i gotta go . . . and he said that's it and then my phine clicked so i said yeah and hung up. oh well. I actively hate his guts. he deserves to go to hell.

  I have nothing to report otherwise. I have sent my list of crap to the Creep and am waiting to see if anything happens. i sure hope so.

  i love you.
  love
monica

From:	CA Davis
To:	████████
Subject:	troubs?
Date:	Monday, November 03, 1997 7:15PM

Hi, I sent you a message called 'quickie' last wk, but it was =
undeliverable for awhile so I'm hoping this will reach you. You'd think =
the f'n Pentagon could have straightened out email! Anyway, how did =
your 'meeting' go last week? I'm seeing the man on tellie alot because =
of the Iraqi nonsense. I think that could be a cool job, maybe better =
than the DOD.
I had a long wkend away from home. We went to a friend's office's =
cottage at Lake Kawaguchi. Its Susan's office's cottage and she invited =
us and 2 other couples for the 3day wkend- so 4 couples all together. =
It was fun- we drank a lot, ate a lot, hiked, walked, lounged, played =
games etc . . . I was about ready to go home Sunday evening but we left Mon. =
morning. I was getting tired of being surrounded by Brits! Actually =
one couple is made up of a German woman and a man, Gavin, who is =

1037-DC-00000022

From:	CA Davis
To:	'Lewinsky, Monica, ████████
Subject:	RE: troubs?
Date:	Tuesday, November 04, 1997 2:09PM

Okay, I am seriously bummed, but I was worried about the time issue also =
and about feeling like you were 'so close, yet so far away' while you =
were here. Chris and I will be in OR from teh 18th to the 24th of Dec. =
and HI from the 24th to the 4th or so of Jan. Then I am pretty sure we =
will be moving back to OR next summer- after our Bali trip! We have =
talked about staying longerand I worry about Chris going back to his =
office after only a year away, but I don't htink I can live in this =
environment for another year or half-year. Yes, I make good money, but =
it is mind-numbigly boring (my job). The other thing too, which is more =
important, is the nature of this city with its horrendous pollution (my =
hair is barely growing!), masses of people and no grass or trees. It is =
expensive and a pain to leave the city for a wkend . . . blah, blah, blah. =
For our year anniversary we are going out ot dinner. Period. I mean, =
if we lived in OR we would definately go to some romantic B&B or hotel =
out of Portland and maybe even fly and it would be cheaper than the =
trains here. I sound whiny but it is a wierd place and I think I may be =
done with it next summer. I think about driving and my house nad hiking =
inthe gorge and the coast and easy trips to N.California and friends and =
the slow life and a puppy . . . I guess its my small town island girl ness =
that wants me out of the big modern city.

NEW TOPIC: I am- are you sitting- a size 6 at the GAP!!!!!! They have =
seriously re-calibrated their sizes, baby, and its time to shopshopshop. =
I go in their and 10 are literally HANGING off meand 8s are well . . . lets =
just say drinking those shakes once a day for 10 years has really paid =
off! To be fair, I have not gained that much, but I am decidedly, with =
out a doubt, unquestionably a smack in the middle (and comfortable with =
it I might add) size f'n 8. I wonder if they changed-the sizes somehow =
for Japan- to make those J ladies feel like they exist- no size 0s =
puhhhleeezzz!! Actually they probably love seeing me gather up the size =
Gigantic next to their size Cute and Little. Bitches. Just kidding, =
but for the first, or maybe second, time in my life I'm glad I'm not =
tall. I guess the first time was when I was growing up in Japan . . . oh, I =
mean Hawaii.

So, I am thrilled for you about this new job. I would beside myself tow =
ork in that group. Richardson looks like a nice man. What are some of =
your other options, in the private sector? Would all of them mean a =
move to NY? Try to tell me as much as you can. Oh, I miss you and I =
really am sad you will not be here soon . . . I understand though. I hope =
all works out. Very sweet about Australian guy. When will he be in DC, =
or the east coast, next? Wait, did you get together with him when you =
met him? Lots of questions to answer. Also remind me to tell you why =
the whole couples extravaganza is not really a fantasy, at least this =
one wasn't. I have to pop off to work. Write back as soon as you can. =
I love you and take care. Cat

449

From: Lewinsky, Monica, ▮▮▮▮▮▮
Sent: Wednesday, November 05, 1997 2:16 AM
To: CA Davis
Subject: RE: troubs?

oK. I have some bad news. I am off the next trip so I won't be coming to Tokyo. I am probably sorrier than you are. the truth is it would have been so difficult to spend time together and it probably would have benn more frustrating than anything.

The job thing on Friday went much better than expected. It was nice; the big creep called thursday night and gave me a pep talk because i was so afraid I'd sound like an idiot. Richardson is a great guy and i met two women who work for him . . . also very cool. Yesterday, Richardson called me at work and told me they were going to offer me a position . . . they didn't know what yet, and they wanted to talk with me further. The problem is, I don't really wnat to work there (issue wise or location wise) I've already had the experience of working in a yucky building. It was awful, actually, because i feel a little trapped into taking it. HOPEFULLY, there will be some movement on the other tracks in NY too. I told mr. bacon I was planning to move and was in the process of looking . . . which is why i asked him if i could switch trips with tom. The biggest reason i need to do that was because the creep's friend who is supposed to help me with the private sector possibilities has been out of town the last two weeks. I feel like I'll lose momentum with them if i disappear for three weeks now (that's including Thanksgiving). Oy vey!

I'm glad to hear you guys had such a nice weekend. Honestly Cat, it sounds like such a wonderful fantasy to me. To be with yourr husband—as part of a couple with other couples doing couple-y kinds of things and having fun.

My Australian boyfriend CALLED me on Friday to let me know his e-mail was down., He said it had become habit to e-mail me friday nights and he wanted to let me know he couldn't send anything. I know . . . when's the wedding????? Just kiddin'.

I miss you tons and am so sad I won't see you, but maybe we'll work something out soon. When do you guys come to the states . . . for holiday? and for good?

kisses and hugs
Monica

From: CA Davis
To: 'Lewinsky, Monica,, OSD/PA'
Subject: RE: troubs?
Date: Wednesday, November 05, 1997 1:28PM

Hey! I said there is no way in hell I am a real size 6- I am =no-questions-asked-no-doubts-in-my-mind-an-honest-to-goodness-full-size =
8. EIGHT. And sizes are not double, but if they ae then Jeannie is =
half my size. My point was GAP is retarded, but in an ego-boosting way =
so 'please try'-as they say in Japan. And I have NOT lost weight, I =
have gained weight but only a little. What I do have is a constant =
poochy belly from eating too much rice! So, no more sarcastico comments =
on my voluptuous, size 8 bod. =20

Who's the BF? Have you told me his name? Can you? I hope that works =
out for you, let me know. I have no time right now. I have to go to my =
7.30a class and I am not dressed yet. =20

Okay, my lovely size 10 lovebug- and you cannot say anyting bad about a =
size 10 because I think that is a fine size- seeing as I was one for =
years and probably still am in Guess or Benetton or something. Actually =
I think I am one with Jigsaw, a Brit compnay I buy clothes in here. So =
no more of it all! I love you, be good! Cat

From: Lewinsky, Monica,, ▮▮▮▮▮▮
Sent: Thursday, November 06, 1997 5:38 AM
To: CA Davis
Subject: RE: troubs?

Whew! What a day! I met with the big creep's best friend this morning. It was very interetsing. I have never met such a 'real' person in my entire life. You know how some people where their hearts on their sleeves; he wears his soul. Incredible. He said, with regard to my job search, "We're in business." We'll see. he also said the creep had talked to him, and as I was leaving he said, "You come very highly reccmmended." (Tee-hee-hee)

The Richardson thing does sound interesting for someone who likes international affairs—NOT ME! But I am trying to only look for something in NY. It's time for me to get out of here. I really hope that the creep and i can still have contact, because, I know it sounds soooooooooooo ridiculous, but I can't get him out of my heart. i love him a lot. I know it's stupid. I want to hug him so bad right now i could cry.

OK. I hate you, you little-size-6-bitch. I don't know if i can be friends with you anymore!!!!!!!! That's nice. I'm a 10–12 so that makes me double your size. I am happy for you. That is awesome. Do you think being around the petite japanese has made it easier to lose or more pressure? either way, that's rad. I miss you so much. There's a void in my soul.

    Ohhh how i long for the time when we can just spend a day together . . . starting w/ coffee at Starbuck's . . . shopping . . . lunch at somewhere yummy . . . maybe a movie . . . more shopping . . . and then getting drunk on margaritas!!! Whooo-hoooo!

I love you and I'm reminding you to tell me about why your weeknd away w/ couples wasn't so fantasy island.

Love
M

CA Davis

From: **Lewinsky, Monica,,** ▮▮▮▮▮
Sent: **Friday, November 07, 1997 7:20 AM**
To: **CA Davis**
Subject: **RE: troubs?**

I'm a little nervous to do the whole name of the BF. His first name is Vernon. It went very well as I said yesterday. I won't be hearing from him until later next week. I know he saw the big creep yetserday afternoon. Unfortunately, that fucker hasn't called me so i don't really know what happened in the meeting or whatever else is going on with him. oh well.

    i don't have much to report except that i ma absolutely exhausted today. It is an overcast, Portland-like day today and I just want to crawl into my beddy-bye and read, nap and relax. (of course, having a boy there too wouldn't be so bad!!!) i hope you are doing well. I miss you.

let me know what's up with you.
luv,
monka

Subject: **RE: hi!**
Date: **Monday, December 08, 1997 1:29PM**

Hi! It is so good to hear from you. I have only a minute as I am off =
=3D
to my early class. Thank you for my wonderful card and perfume. It was =
=3D
very nice of you to send me something so far away in Stinkyo. I =3D

appreciate it. Hey, guess what is this Sunday? Guess. Okay, I love =
=3D
you nad I will write again soon. I am thinking of trying to call you =
=3D
some time this week if I can coodinate the time change deal. love, Cat

From:	Lewinsky, Monica,, ███████
Sent:	Tuesday, December 09, 1997 6:11 AM
To:	CA Davis
Subject:	hi!

Hi, Girl-

It's been ages since I've spoken to you. I was in LA and then in =3D
Brussels=3D20
and london for work. London was wonderful, as to be expected.
Did you ever receive my package? What's been going on with you? I miss =
=3D
you=3D20
terribly and feel clueless as to what's happening in your life.
My life is still in turmoil. I have given my notice for the end of this =
=3D
month, but don't have anything firm in NY. I'm getting frustrated. =3D
things=3D20
ave been crazy with the creep, though i did have a wonderful visit with =
=3D
him=3D20
on Saturday. When he doesn't put his walls up, it is always so heavenly.
Please write back soon. i miss you.

love,
Monica=3D20

Davis, Catherine

From:	CA Davis ███████
To:	'mlewinsk@pagate.pa.osd.mil'
Subject:	hi Mon

I'm sorry about all the shit that seems to be going on around you. Marsha is obviously working from a place of pettiness and jealousy- her remarks to you are so unprofessional I can't stand it. she sounds like a catty teenager! Your idea about working in another city or country is intrigueing. Do you think it is viable and conceivable for you? Could it be another American city or do you really want to be international? I guess it depends alot on openings, availability and place. I mean you would not want to be in Bosnia or Saudi Arabia (would you?). Betty is being so nice to you now, it seems. Do you have sense of why her attitude has changed? She's probably sick of seeing this happen to you after all this time.

I'm worried about you, Monica. Again, I think your idea to leave the area or get out of gov't work is a good one. I think you are in the midst of a dangerous, psychologically, situation. I am at a loss as to make you feel better or help, if I could possibly do either. When I read your emails sometimes I cannot even belive some of the things you tell me. It all sounds so dramatic and painful for you. Is your trip to L.A. for holiday or work? Maybe, you will feel a little better getting away. I don't mean to sound so disjointed but I guess I feel a litle disjointed. I know it is your life and I would NEVER presume to tell you how to live it- as you would never tell me how to live mine- but I cannot help being very concerned.

As for me, I am busy with work and with private conversation groups. I made a friend last week from work. we met after a meeting at work and she asked me to have lunch with her- the first person to do this. So we ate and drank beer and talked. She and her husband have been here for 4 months. Her name is Mary and she is 26 and was a nurse in the US ans about to start a MA program when they moved here for his business, of course. I was very impressed with her 'sacrifice'. Anyway, she's nice and hopefully we will go out again- maybe for the 4th. It was nice to talk to a woman about the stresses of living here and being newly married here, too. Actually she and her husband were married this February- 2 weeks before they moved to Tokyo. Even worse than Chris and I! Well, I must be off to my last class of the day. Write back and let me know how things have progressed. take care and love, Cat t in these last 2 years I have =lost two aunts, my Mom's older sisters, to cancer. Anyway, I originally =thought I would go to school to be a Physician's Assisstant, P.A., a =growing field in healthcare and it is only a 2 year program. I took =some prelim courses and was so thrilled and into it- like Microbiology =and medical microbiology, that I questioned why I shouldn't pusReceived: from ▮▮▮▮▮▮ by tky0.attnet.or.jp (8.7.5+Spin/3.4W4-PP-R5(05/15/97)) id WAA13450; Wed, 19 Nov 1997 22:22:44 +0900 (JST)Received: from ▮▮▮▮▮▮ by galt.osd.mil (8.7.1/8.7.1) with SMTP id IAA00768 for ▮▮▮▮▮▮ ; Wed, 19 Nov 1997 08:15:33 -0500 (EST)Received: by ▮▮▮▮▮▮ with Microsoft Mailid ▮▮▮▮▮▮ Wed, 19 Nov 97 08:20:52 PSTFrom: "Lewinsky, Monica,, OSD/PA" ▮▮▮▮▮▮ To: CA Davis ▮▮▮▮▮▮ tnet.or.jp"Subject: RE: birthday aftermathDate: Wed, 19 Nov 97 08:12:00 PSTMessage-ID: ▮▮▮▮▮▮ Encoding: 182 TEXTX-Mailer: Microsoft Mail V3.0X-UIDL: 809cb60fc0c9df52c4cf05811f2f2f72Oh, Catherine! You message was just what i needed to start out this dreary day! I adore you, and think we'll make wonderful older lady friends (here's to the ladies who lunch..) and younger lady friends, too!! When you come back to the states I think we'll have to spend some concentrated time together. Imagine, talking in person and for FREE! Your birthday sounded great (except of course for the Chris-getting-sick-part). i'm sorry you had to postpone your dinner. Your earrings sound lovely. How was Japanese Disneyland? Were there any rides that made fun of Americans or was it Mickey Mouse based? I bet you looked beautiful in your red (VAHVOOM!!) suit! The big creep does look quite trim these days. Oh, I haven't told you my hysterical escapade from last week! Listen to this, it's practically unbelievable! The creep called me on Wednesday night and we talked for almost an hour, but i had been bugging him that i wanted to see him and last week was the only chance for awhile as he would be away for the next two weekends and then i am gone for two weeks. So, on the phone he said he thought nancy (one of the meanies) would be out for a few hours on Thurday and i could come see him them. I was to call Betty and figure out the details. Of course, i called betty in the morning and then started the usual "I haven't had a chance to talk to him, yet". Well, he ended up going golfing and I went ballistic. finally when he got back around 4:30 she talked to him and then he got mad she didn't tell him -ya-da-ya-da. In the end, she snuck me in to the back office where i waited for him while there were 20 people in there and Stephen, his ▮▮▮▮▮▮ aide who doesn't like me. I ended up seeing him for two ▮▮▮▮▮▮ minutes because he had one of his counterparts from another country waiting there for dinner!! It was soo crazy. I will probably have to call his buddy who's supposed to help me today. I was hoping he'd call me, but I'm getting nervous with the holidays coming up and all. Oh Cat, I want to get out of here so bad. You have no idea. I have been really sad about Andy lately, too. I keep having these dreams about Kate, him and the kid. It's really yucky. What really hurts is that i cared so much about someone who just threw me away so quickly. I miss having someone to be with and enjoy me. Ohh, woe is me, woe is me!Why are y

1037-DC-00000318

yBoZSBzY

WlkLCAiQ29tZSBvdmVyIGFuZCBzaXQNCmRvd24gYmVzaWR1IG1lIGZvciBhIG1vbWVudCwgT WFtYS44

glEkgd2FudCB0byBhc2sgeW91IGEgcXVlc3Rpb24iLiAgTm8NCmtpZGRpbmculCBXZSdyZSBo YXZpb

mcgc3VjaCBmdW4gd210aCBoaW0uICBMYXN0IEzyaWRheSBJIHRvb2sgdGh1IGRhdEBvZmY gYW5kDQp

oZSBhbmQgSSB3ZW50IHRvIFBEWCB6b28gdy8gbXkgZnJpZW5kIEVyaW4uIC5b5b3UndmUgb WV0IGh1c

iBzZXZ1cmFsIHRpbWVzKQ0KYW5kIGh1ciBib31zLCBhZ2UgMi41ICYgMTAgbW9udGhzLiAgV 2hhdCB

hIGdyZWF0IHRpbWUhICBJIG51dmVyIG1uZ15IdwpbR1c3QNCmRyZWFtcyB0aG91Z2h0OIH NoZSBhb

mQgSSB3b3VsZCBiZSBoYXZpbmcgZnVuIGNoYXNpbmcgdHdvlHRvZGRsZXJzIGFyb3VuZC B0aGUNCnp

vbywgYnV0IG10IHdhcyBmcmVhdENkCQUXpVpXQgTWVtb3JpYWwgRGF5IHdtZWtlbmQugc Gxhbm51Z

C4glEEgQkRIGZvciBteSBmb2xrcycgYW5uaXZlcnNhcnkgU2F0Lg0KYW5kIEgdmlzaXQgdy8
dy8

gb3VylGZyaWVuZCBCYW5namgkb24gU3VuLiwgYW5klH1hcmQgd29yay4glEhvdydzIHRoYXQ gZm9yD

453

QpiZWluZyBsaWt1IHRoZSBDbGVhdmVycz8glFRoZSBvbmx5IGRpZmZlcmVuY2UgaXMlG15IHB1YXJ

scyBhcmUgcmVhbCENCg0KR290dGEgcnVuLiAgVGFrZSBjYXJ1ICYga2V1cCBpbiB0b3VjaCENCg0KT

G92ZSwgDQpEaWFuZQ0KDQoNCg—TFS-with-MIME-and-DIME—he and kate are trying to work this out and me being anywhere in the picture is not going to help. I was pretty upset, but it is really for the best. I'll probably send her note back to her with a small scribble that i never wanted to try to get her out of the picture so he could be with me. if i really wanted to be nasty i'd send the cards back to her, but i'm not THAT cruel. With the big creep, i told you i sent him a note right? well in it i asked to come see him on saturday. he

1037-DC-00000337

called on saturday and said betty couldn't come in but we'd do it sunday if she could come in. he just called cuz he didn't want me waiting by the phone. i told him i appreciated that. he was sweet, but in a bad mood. i think he's kind of depressed right now. well, sunday he didn't call until 5 pm and then said he was trying to get a hold of her but he couldn't. he then called back 10 minutes later and said he had just gotten word that she'd be out of pocket for two hours so i should go out fr a little while and he'd call at 7. he didn't call at seven so at 8 i paged betty and she said he said he didn't want her coming in late at night and we'd work it out for this week. he finally hurriedly called me at about 9:45 and said he was busy he just called to say quickly we try and work it out for later. so all in all we had some very brief calls this weekend and i hope to see him soon. oh, but he did say on saturdahat indicated to me he really was working on getting me back there. well, my dear, i love you and miss you soo much. i hope all is well with you and chris. i'm sure you'll lose whatever you gained. i finally started dieting and exercising again after i had gained 15 frickin pounds since December. HELLO!! i love you. Monica— From: CA Davis To:███████ hey girl! Date: Monday, May 19, 1997 6:58AM yeah! i finally got my e-mail set-up!! so now you can write me=whenever you want and keep me posted on ALL your life's excitements. =Hey, have you heard from Doug since the Great Gatsby Kissing Incident? =Any more action from the freaks in Oregon? I still can't believe the =tangle that's come about there. So good you're in DC and far away. I =hope Andy, the schmucker, calls you soon..if he hasn't already. I'm =afraid my letter won't be too long tonight because its getting late and =Chris and I want to get up early to run before he goes to work. I am =getting soo fat and don't try to disbelieve me or scoff! Its true. =20I miss you so much Monica and wish you could get a year position in the =embassy here and play with me..well not PLAY with me but..you know. =Please write back and vent all..also plan your trip to Tokyo! love =you,

CatCVRTFZ20.DLLûûùCVWMFZ20.DLLCVWP5X20.DL

LCVWP6020.DLLCVWP6T20.DLLCVWPG120.DLLCVWPG220.DLLCV12 3Z20.DLL/2:"?9:"?CVA12X20

.DLL;789:;CVCGMZ20.DLLCVDXFZ20.DLLCVEPSZ20.DLLCVEXCL20.D LL%&'CVHPGL20.DLLCVL

PIC20.DLLCVMGXZ20.DLLCVPCXZ20.DLLCVPICT20.DLL

1744005 FXD 1083 84198/ 98304—A 27-May-1997 16:10:00 27-May-1997 16:09:58 27-May-1997

1037-DC-00000338

t in these last 2 years I have=lost two aunts, my Mom's older sisters, to cancer. Anyway, I originally=thought I would go to school to be a Physician's Assisstant, P.A., a=growing field in healthcare and it is only a 2 year program. I took=some prelim courses and was so thrilled and into it- like Microbiology=and medical microbiology, that I questioned why I shouldn't pusReceived: from ■■■■■ (8.7.5+Spin/3.4W4-PP-R5(05/15/97)) id WAA13450; Wed, 19 Nov 1997 22:22:44 +0900 (JST)Received: ■■■■■ by galt.osd.mil (8.7.1/8.7.1) with SMTP id IAA00768 for ■■■■■; Wed, 19 Nov 1997 08:15:33 -0500 (EST)Received: by pagate.pa.osd.mil with Microsoft Mailid ■■■■■ Wed, 19 Nov 97 08:20:52 PST From: "Lewinsky, Monica, OSD/PA" ■■■■■ To: CA Davis ■■■■■ Subject: RE: birthday aftermathDate: Wed, 19 Nov 97 08:12:00 PSTMessage-ID: ■■■■■ Encoding: 182 TEXTX-Mailer: Microsoft Mail V3.0X-UIDL: 809cb60fc0c9df52c4cf05811f2f2f72Oh, Catherine! You message was just what i needed to start out this dreary day! I adore you, and think we'll make wonderful older lady friends (here's to the ladies who lunch..) and younger lady friends, too!! When you come back to the states I think we'll have to spend some concentrated time together. Imagine, talking in person and for FREE! Your birthday sounded great (except of course for the Chris-getting-sick-part). i'm sorry you had to postpone your dinner. Your earrings sound lovely. How was Japanese Disneyland? Were there any rides that made fun of Americans or was it Mickey Mouse based? I bet you looked beautiful in your red (VAHVOOM!!) suit!The big creep does look quite trim these days. Oh, I haven't told you my hysterical escapade from last week! Listen to this, it's practically unbelievable! The creep called me on Wednesday night and we talked for almost an hour, but i had been bugging him that i wanted to see him and last week was the only chance for awhile as he would be away for the next two weekends and then i am gone for two weeks. So, on the phone he said he thought nancy (one of the meanies) would be out for a few hours on Thurday and i could come see him them. I was to call Betty and figure out the details. Of course, i called betty in the morning and then started the usual "I haven't had a chance to talk to him, yet". Well, he ended up going golfing and I went ballistic. finally when he got back around 4:30 she talked to him and then he got mad she didn't tell him -ya-da-ya-da. In the end, she snuck me in to the back office where i waited for him while there were 20 people in there and Stephen, his ■■■■■ aide who doesn't like me. I ended up seeing him for two ■■■■■ minutes because he had one of his counterparts from another country waiting there for dinner!! It was soo crazy.I will probably have to call his buddy who's supposed to help me today. I was hoping he'd call me, but I'm getting nervous with the holidays coming up and all. Oh Cat, I want to get out of here so bad. You have no idea.I have been really sad about Andy lately, too. I keep having these dreams about Kate, him and the kid. It's really yucky. What really hurts is that i cared so much about someone who just threw me away so quickly. I miss having someone to be with and enjoy me. Ohh, woe is me, woe is me!Why are y

1037-DC-00000341

E-mails Between
Monica Lewinsky and Linda Tripp

Tripp, Linda, , OSD/PA

From:	**Tripp, Linda, , OSD/PA**
To:	**Lewinsky, Monica, , OSD/PA**
Subject:	**Afternoon**
Date:	**Tuesday, February 04, 1997 2:06PM**
Priority:	**High**

Just checking in, it's been a nutty day so I haven't had much chance to see you. I had to go up to the third floor and drop off some paperwork, so I actually walked the entire E-ring, which took 15 minutes. Guess I am kinda slow, huh? Oh well, next time I will go by myself so that I can keep my own pace. I feel as though I did SOMETHING anyway. I have had tons of water the past few days, and even more today, so watch and see, I'll have gained weight tonight, at this rate. I don't seem to be getting rid of the water, so it's hanging out somewhere!! Anyway, my real purpose in jotting off this e-mail is to see what's up with you, and how you're doing. I am so jealous that you are off to London soon, I love it so. I would spend tons of time in Harrod's, spend time on Fleet Street and down in the Silver Vaults, putter around Portebello Road, and shop til I dropped!! I would have high tea every day even if I had to skip real meals. I used to spend all my summers in Europe as a kid, and would sneak over to London whenever I could, always by myself, when I was about 16. Back then (I'm dating myself!!!) you could buy the all time BEST fish and chips from these little holes in the wall, wrapped in newspaper!! It was one of the best things I had ever eaten.
LRT

From:	**Lewinsky, Monica, , OSD/PA**
To:	**Tripp, Linda, , OSD/PA**
Subject:	**RE: Afternoon**
Date:	**Tuesday, February 04, 1997 2:15PM**
Priority:	**High**

Thank God for you! Oh Linda, i don't know what I am going to do. I just don't understand what went wrong, what happened? How could he do this to me? Why did he keep up contact with me for so long and now nothing, now when we could be together? Maybe it was the intrigue of wanting something he couldn't have (easily) with all that was going on then? Maybe he wanted to insure he could have variety and phone sex while he was on the road for those months? AAAAHHHHH!!!!! I am going to lose it! And, where is Betty's phone call? What's up with all this shit? oh, well. bye.
msl

Tripp, Linda, , OSD/PA

From:	**Tripp, Linda, , OSD/PA**
To:	**Lewinsky, Monica, , OSD/PA**
Subject:	**RE: Afternoon**
Date:	**Tuesday, February 04, 1997 2:55PM**

None of the above, if you ask me. Because, none of it makes sense. Do not despair, there is most definitely light at the end of this tunnel. LRT

833-DC-00001974

From:	Lewinsky, Monica, , OSD/PA
To:	Tripp, Linda, , OSD/PA
Subject:	RE: secret message
Date:	Thursday, February 13, 1997 10:18AM
Priority:	High

I'LL PROBABLY GO GET LUNCH AT 12;00 BECAUSE I'M HUNGRY ALREADY!!! I DON'T THINK I'LL BE MORE THAN 1/2 HOUR BECAUSE I'M LEAVING EARLY. PLEASE ESCAPE WITH ME!!!!!! HOW CAN YOU RESIST ME?? DON'T FORGET I'LL BE GONE FOR AWHILE . . . MSL

From:	Tripp, Linda, , OSD/PA
To:	Lewinsky, Monica, , OSD/PA
Subject:	RE: secret message

833-DC-00001934

From:	Tripp, Linda, , OSD/PA
To:	Lewinsky, Monica, , OSD/PA
Subject:	RE: secret message
Date:	Thursday, February 13, 1997 11:03AM

OK OK OK. 12 at bridge.

From:	Lewinsky, Monica, , OSD/PA
To:	Tripp, Linda, , OSD/PA
Subject:	RE: secret message
Date:	Thursday, February 13, 1997 11:05AM
Priority:	High

IF ONLY I COULD PURSUADE THE CREEP AS EASILY!!!!!!!

From:	Tripp, Linda, , OSD/PA
To:	Lewinsky, Monica, , OSD/PA
Subject:	RE: secret message
Date:	Thursday, February 13, 1997 1:03PM

Ah, but that has already transpired, says my omnipotent crystal ball. . . . .

Tripp, Linda, , OSD/PA

From:	Lewinsky, Monica, , OSD/PA
To:	Tripp, Linda, , OSD/PA
Subject:	RE: secret message
Date:	Thursday, February 13, 1997 1:23PM

O.K. here is my fax in London 011-44-171-235-4552 and phone, just in case, I don't know what, here is the phone number 011-44-171-235-2000. I will also be checking my messages in the hopes that the creep will call and say "Thank you for my love note. I love you. Will you run away with me?" What do ya think the likelihood of that happening is? Also, please don't forget about the newspapers. I will bring you the $ later.

thanx . . . xoxoxo . . . msl

From: Lewinsky, Monica, , OSD/PA
To: Tripp, Linda, , OSD/PA
Subject: I'm back!
Date: Wednesday, February 19, 1997 8:09AM
Priority: High

LRT--- Hi, I missed you!!!! I hope you enjoyed your few days of sanity with me gone because I'm back and NOT in good spirits.

1. I have a small present for you. Everything was SOOOOO expensive so I'm sorry it's small.
2. Nice that the Big Creep didn't even try to call me on V-day and he didn't know for sure that I was going to London.
3. He could have called last night and didn't. He was out of town.
4. Finally, the Babba went away and it was the same night he was gone. Fuck me!!!!

HHHEEELLPPP!!!!

Maybe we can have lunch or meet sometime today cuz I want to give you your present.

Bye . . . msl

833-DC-00009446

Tripp, Linda, , OSD/PA

From: Tripp, Linda, , OSD/PA
To: Lewinsky, Monica, , OSD/PA
Subject: RE: secret message
Date: Wednesday, February 19, 1997 9:01AM

WELCOME BACK!!! How was Jolly, Olde England? Well, here's the saga in a nutshell. On friday (of course), Howard County (the boondocks where I live) was totally and completely snowed and iced in, so I couldn't get up my hill, schools were closed, no one moved, believe it or not. I was in a panic about the papers. . . . .by the time I could get up the hill late that night, all the Posts were gone, BUT I called work and had my Deputy save me what he could, which was one, and then I found another, so we have two. I can't believe it became that big a deal, but it did. CALL ME WHEN YOU GET IN. PS It read beautifully, placement was great, typeface totally effective, and text superlative. . . . .good job. LRT

From: Lewinsky, Monica, , OSD/PA
To: Tripp, Linda, , OSD/PA
Subject: ADVICE
Date: Monday, February 24, 1997 8:31AM

Hi, I hope you're feeling better ! I'm trying to go over to the WH today to give Jodie these pictures. I also plan to stop by Betty's office to drop off these lame photos. Any advice/suggestions what to do or say? write me back . . . msl

833-DC-00001906

From: Tripp, Linda, , OSD/PA
To: Lewinsky, Monica, , OSD/PA
Subject: RE: ADVICE
Date: Monday, February 24, 1997 11:22AM

Eureka!!!!

458

Tripp, Linda, , OSD/PA

From: Tripp, Linda, , OSD/PA
To: Lewinsky, Monica, , OSD/PA
Subject: RE: where are you?
Date: Monday, March 03, 1997 12:48PM

Kate is faxing me a copy of the announcement—she is planning to go see Marsha today. If someone in house wants it, there is a chance they will get it, but Kate seems confident that that won't happen. She said to have your resume ready. LRT

From: Lewinsky, Monica, , OSD/PA
To: Tripp, Linda, , OSD/PA
Subject: hi, ya
Date: Wednesday, March 05, 1997 10:05AM
Priority: High

Boy, I look so scary today. People might think that I thought it was Halloween. Oh, well ████████ should (if Betty is nice) get my tie today. I sure hope he like s it. make me feel better and tell me it's really pretty, o.k.? msl

833-DC-00001857

From: Tripp, Linda, , OSD/PA
To: Lewinsky, Monica, , OSD/PA
Subject: RE: hi, ya
Date: Wednesday, March 05, 1997 11:34AM

Are you asking me if the tie if really pretty? It is positively gorgeous. I am knot (ha!) particularly into ties, but from my exposure to you, I am developing an interest. Yours was stupendous, no kidding, clean, crisp, texture, color, pattern, bright, without being at all over the top. . . . .a total hit.

Linda Tripp's
Handwritten Notes

Aug -present- fuloug
Sep - Oct -   mid Nov.
end of Dec 31st "day"
1st week Dec + signed picture
in back office -

3d wk in Dec "hi kiddo"
→ White House Staff
Dec party in the
21st afternoon -

10 day later - 31 Dec 97
rest   or 7 days later
Weekend - Sun Called at 2:40 -
1½ later Snowing,
Blizzard of 96
she went to work -
walked by, Come on in -
Closed door - 45 minutes
guard there - Lewey Session
Jan 7
Jan MLK Day - at lotta
                    for the
                    day.

" really
Hard to have someone
die under your executive
order" "Cherishes time
w/ her - these gifts"
run alone
Buddy coming to town

Nancy's ofc -
fooled around -
jerking off with Bill back cause
                    didn't was
                    local.

21st Jan 96
2-7 Called.
Jan - ofc -
she was in
Jan training -
gone weeks
tues
farewell
to Stafford
Pat Stafford

(weekend before: have to be careful: rumor that he had a brush on the intern ~4:00 Tues. he calls her @ ofc in Perri ofc "POTUS"

Panetta's ofc
Pat Griffith farewell planned to ignore each other — not even a picture

½ day Tues ½ day busy/used Then Fri. Sat.

group picture far end away from him —

following Sun — beginning feb he called in the afternoon at work — Baba at home — 45 minutes 4:00 1½ hrs

— — — — — — — — — — — — — —

(fooled around first)
½ hour - finished
" Will you call me? "
recited # -
met in hall - walked in together -

20 mins. later called @ ofc
" had a really nice time "
calls
Tues. night
(Baba gave Tues & Wed)
enjoyed talking to her —
have to go help homework — called from "home"

next day wore better

midnight
Called next night
in the middle of
night - from bed -
phone sex 20-30 minutes
7th feb

~~do~~ no contact
President's til 19 feb -
~~Do~~11:00 ~~Mon~~ a.m. at home
she going to work -
was

19 feb she went straight or
knocked on door -

Closed door -
dumped her -
I love her
I've hurt them both -
so need before
Ofc -
went to back - hugged

no kissing
you have to go now.
wouldn't even kiss
of me goodbye -
guard - saw her
leave - 15-20
19 feb '96   minutes
in there

end of feb 2 weeks
28?   late

anxiety attack -
Baba going out of
town -
Israeli Embassy that
night - he saw her in
9:00 pm hallway
10:00 phone arg -
looked really pretty
called you in the
office - short conversation

next weekend
or
2 wks later —
ran into him w/
Natalie — didn't call —

The day he signed Cuba
Summit Libertad
Sanctions
against
cuba —

Mark receiving line
"then he went
and that afternoon Summit
in Egypt — few days.
The Bala & april were in Bacai
That weekend he
golfed on Sunday
screening at 8:00
theater stuff at
night —
waited til
10:00

845-DC-00000009

next week — Bala gone
to Boston etc
Monday — pissed
she is
Jogging — Dip Room
Walked by
ignored him —

11:00 A.M. —
Tues. called on
house phone
to her Potus didn't
on show up on
phone.

thursday : slipped
friday a.m.
jogging return
elevator (passed Mauro
Mauro
sweetie or rest of Jr.)
for day —

p.m. Harold & Bruce
& Monica
2002

463

Sun: part not Sat.
into para
(. fooled around — told about
blue & white
tie)

Tint:
{ eliminating position

Nancy said — Ron Brown
panicking on Sat —
Coming to see Potus —
Call me Monday —

6:00 Sunday night he
called at home —
— come over — —
845-DC-00000012
Romantic
if I win in Nov.
I'll have you back like
that! fooled around.
phone call from Dick
Morris — head on phone
Harold came in —
she went out a nice goodbye)

" called at
7:00 @ home "

Why did you leave?
Came back & you weren't
there ??
845-DC-00000013
you call Walter —
I'll bet it had something
to do w/ me

Monday — met w/ Nancy
very sweet — cried —
conscientious worker —

as she left, Betty
asked what was wrong.
Betty hugged her —
Sometimes ↑ ⊙ happen
for a reason —
Friday — he called her at
home — she was hysterical
he found out what happened

apr 5

- Evelyn Lieberman
Maisha & Nats bounced
out -
→ had gotten deficient
accounts he was
paying too much attention
She's got to go -
after election
doesn't care -
. if you don't like
it, get you a job
on the campaign
(he'll call you later -
3:00 A.M. promised
to call, made
myself wake up -
sweet call
left Sun. to go G7
Tokyo - then Russia
Sun. night returned -

20th
Monday nite - called
after trip - hates job -
we will see you
Sun. APAC thing -
Mon and Shorts NO -
Thurs. night - he called
at home - phone sex -
promise he call this
weekend.
didn't call.

3:00 Mon. night - HRC
A.M. apologize call there
sick can't talk

May - Saxophone event
hug & kiss - I miss you

1 wk. goes by -
10 days til next phone call.

465

phone sex

Week later — he called — Borda
committed suicide —

— he was upset —

prior to issue
Coming to Pentagon — required her

she left that night
he called that night —

Jus h uss — phone sex

1½ wk later (following
"hello" on tape back)

Calls Wed. prior to
by dinner —

845-DC-00000016

Beth called nxt
A.m. at work — re
radio address —

845-DC-00000017

wants to meet her
family — Dad &
Stepmother were
coming

Radio tape on friday
w/ parents

Sat. June 23?
next weekend — called —
just to talk —

she
leaving for Bosnia to
July 15 —

July 5 calls. that
night —
Weird phone sex —
short 20 min
jerked off keep
just talking
July 19?
18a friday 6:30 —

. Baba out of tour
July 5 –

6:30 AM leaving for Olympia
that day –
phone sex –
Well, Good Morning !! after
came

promised to call
while he was away –
didn't call on Birthday
next week & Called on
Australia's night –
spoke away
ploved & apologized 8:30
for Birthday PM
Start July 30th

bace sun Aug 4 =
pink Suit – afternoon
stown NYC 45 minutes
aug 45 verbatim
phone sex

Vacation – 1 WK –

Aug – 2 days later
day before trend
21st Departure – for convention
6:00 p.m.
phone sex –
in his office

then 250th flushed to
29 aug – Birthday party NY
NY juicy – touched
grabbed his di
sent tie for B'day .

Sep 5 – called from
good status Road – at
conversation home = phone sex
Sep 10 – next msg –
Its' me –

467

─ ~~to~~ 20–30th i'o ~~am~~ she was in DOD.

·Sep 30th Called again
~~Saw you walking~~
Saw you walking–
good conversation

☆ Sep 5. phone sex
"NO WAY" (will you
ever marr l to m?)
when you get to
my age, everything
has consequences"
fight about it ↑
do you want me
to not call you
anymore?

Babа not here
Michael Oct. 22nd weekly
2:30 am in florida
he really into phone
sex. increasing

845-DC-00000020

"Triple C" hotels

Black suit   845-DC-00000021

                    Baba not here
Tues. Oct.   DC – he
next night –   event

    next day –
till Betty to
walk helicopter
waiting in West Wing Lobby –
Betty told her Evelyn
& Truman didn't
like it.

not Oct. Sunday – Rally –

Oct 23 –
welcome home at WH
following election.

468

"Triple C" hotels

Black suit

845-DC-00000021

Tues. Oct-
next night -

Baba not here
DC - he
event

next day -
till Betty to
walk helicopter
waited in West Wing Lobby -
Betty told her Evelyn
Lieberman didn't
like it.

Sunday - Rally -
Oct

Oct 23 -
welcome home at WH
following election.

845-DC-00000022

6 Wks later -

night before the - exit.

Dec 2nd   phone
                sex -
                3 wks.
Christmas party Tues.
next night - he calls -
everyday can't be
sunshine -
prison - how sorry
come by on Sat.

never called -

& saw him at Nutcracker

called Monday -

Jan
1997 Gore I musnt
            gone he next yr
                  away for Elin

Jan 18th - he calls -

469

Jan 12 phone sex
had to push him
M. nap – present him.
See you
etc.

Inaugural – red dress

Jan –
Feb 8th – noon
↑ Snowing –
come in for present.
Betty can't get in –

sick over this
Think about this
all the time
should call
in person

845-DC-00000023

he called back =
phone sex.
🖊 Val. at – tell him

845-DC-00000024

· Betty called O/c
to invite Radio address

Feb 28th go to Radio
address –
Sgt phone – embassie
hat pin tapping
Book fears & wants
out
fooled around.

Mar 13th
got on phone at
work – want to
see you tomorrow
a.m.
leaving for florida girls
Jordanian shot &

concerns from Nancy & Stevens
Mar 30th crutches
Betty visit, yo...

470

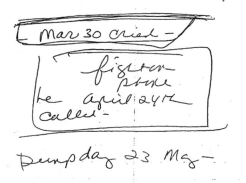

*28 feb - didn't want
to cure
addiction -*

Mar 30 cried -

*fighter
phone
he april 24th
called -*

Dump day 23 Mg -

845-DC-00000025

845-DC-00000188

Letters Editor
Newsweek
251 West 57th Street
New York, New York 10019-1894

(BY FAX: 212.445.4120)

 I would like to clarify the questions that have arisen about my involvement in the matter reported by Newsweek in its August 11th edition. Contrary to the perception held by many that I granted Newsweek "an interview" for this story, the truth is the reporter appeared, uninvited and unannounced, in my office at the Pentagon in late March 1997. I was compelled to respond when he asserted that Ms. Willey had given him my name, as a purported contemporaneous witness who could corroborate her new claim of "harassment" or "inappropriate behavior" on the part of the President.

 My response then, as it remains today, was that this was completely inaccurate and that her version in 1993 and her version in 1997 were wholly inconsistent. One must wonder how such disparate allegations spanning a period of four years could have much, if any, credibility.

 Regarding the comment made by the President's attorney about me, which appeared in the same article, I am acutely disappointed that my integrity has been questioned.

Linda R. Tripp
Department of Defense
Washington, D.C. 20301-1400
███████

███████████████

Ann McDaniel ██████████

845-DC-00000190

471

845-DC-00000191

Friday, September 12 that gate, hour and a half --repeated calls to office. finally she came out and got her -- long talk. he left. She poke to him before she left and told him XX was hysterical and at the gate and that she would clear her in and determine if she was a "crazy woman" --

Sept 14 Sunday night -- her plane from Illinois was cancelled, luckily she ran into Glickman who claimed she was with their party and got her on their flight out but to National instead of BWI -- she had to go get her car at BWI and called at 7:00 or so -- said she would call him and if he checked his messages, maybe he would call her back. He was at the pool at 7:30 -- she didn't know if he had company or what, but he called her later that evening and said that he would talk to XX XXX this week.

845-DC-00000192

845-DC-00000193

The Talking Points

[Editor's note: Ms. Lewinsky handed this document to Linda Tripp as the two women discussed how they were going to respond to subpoenas from lawyers for Paula Jones. Ms. Tripp has said she always planned to testify truthfully.]

points to make in affidavit

Your first few paragraphs should be about yourself—what you do now, what you did at the White House and for how many years you were there as a career person and as a political appointee.

You and Kathleen were friends. *At around the time of her husband's death* (the President has claimed it was after her husband died. Do you really want to contradict him?), she came to you after she allegedly came out of the oval and looked (however she looked), you don't recall her exact words, but she claimed at the time (whatever she claimed) and was very happy.

You did not see her go in or see her come out.

Talk about when you became out of touch with her and maybe why.

The next you heard of her was when a Newsweek reporter (I wouldn't name him specifically) showed up in your office saying she was naming you as a someone who would corroborate that she was sexually harassed. You spoke with her that evening, etc. and she relayed to you a sequence of events that was very dissimilar from what you remembered happening. As a result of your conversation with her and subsequent reports that showed she had tried to enlist the help of someone else in her lie that the President sexually harassed her, you now do not believe that what she claimed happened really happened. You now find it completely plausible that she herself smeared her lipstick, untucked her blouse, etc.

You never saw her go into the oval office, or come out of the oval office.

You have never observed the President behaving inappropriately with anybody.

The first few paragraphs should be about me—what I do now, what I did at the White House and for how many years I was there as a career person and as a political appointee.

Kathleen and I were friends. At around the time of her husband's death, she came to me after she allegedly came out of the oval and looked ____, I don't recall her exact words, but she claimed at the time ____ and was very happy.

I did not see her go in or see her come out.

Talk about when I became out of touch with her and maybe why.

The next time I heard of her was when a Newsweek reporter showed up in my office saying she was naming me as a someone who would corroborate that she was sexually harassed by the President. I spoke with her that evening, etc. and she relayed to me a sequence of events that was very dissimilar from what I remembered happening. As a result of my conversation with her and subsequent reports that showed she had tried to enlist the help of someone else in her lie that the President sexually harassed her, I now do not believe that what she claimed happened really happened. I now find it completely plausible that she herself smeared her lipstick, untucked her blouse, etc.

I never saw her go into the oval office, or come out of the oval office.

I have never observed the President behave inappropriately with anybody.

You are not sure you've been clear about whose side you're on. (Kirby has been saying you should look neutral; better for credibility but you aren't neutral. Neutral makes you look like you're on the other team since you are a political appointee)

It's important to you that they think you're a team player, after all, you are a political appointee. You believe that they think you're on the other side because you wouldn't meet with them.

You want to meet with Bennett. You are upset about the comment he made, but you'll take the high road and do what's in your best interest.

December 18th, you were in a better position to attend an all day or half-day deposition, but now you are into JCOC mode. Your livelihood is dependent on the success of this program. Therefore, you want to provide an affidavit laying out all of the facts in lieu of a deposition.

You want Bennett's people to see your affidavit before it's signed.

Your deposition should include enough information to satisfy their questioning.

By the way, remember how I said there was someone else that I knew about. Well, she turned out to be this huge liar. I found out she left the WH because she was stalking the P or something like that. Well, at least that gets me out of another scandal I know about.

Correspondence and Documents
Related to Monica Lewinsky's Job Search

MONICA LEWINSKY

OBJECTIVE
- ◆ Seeking summer internship opportunity.
- ◆ Offering excellent skills in communication, writing, computer and research experience.

Able to take direction, extremely enthusiastic, amiable and courteous

---

EDUCATION
- ◆ Lewis & Clark College - Presently attending
  Educational goal: Bachelor of Arts, Science. GPA 3.75
- ◆ Bel Air Prep School - Graduated 6/91 GPA 3.84

EXPERIENCE
- ◆ Practicum - Metropolitan Public Defender
  630 SW Fifth Street, Portland, Oregon
  Supervisor - Marcia Gruhler
  Duties include: assisting Legal Aid Office in counseling indigent clients, investigation, and filing of legal reports
  12/94 - Present
- ◆ Practicum - Southeast Mental Health Network
  2415 SE 43rd St., Portland, Oregon
  Supervisor - Chris Nielson

  Duties include: assisting staff in teaching socialization skills to clients in anticipation of their integration into society. Also assist in filing confidential reports, public affairs, liason to governmental office.
  1/94 - 6/94
- ◆ Knot Shop. Pioneer Place
  700 SW Fifth St., Portland, Oregon
  Position: Sales Associate
  Duties include: retail sales of upscale men's clothing, "key holder" with opening and closing responsibilities.
  Supervisor - Lisa Casey
  9/93 - Present

HONORS & AWARDS
Dean's List - Lewis and Clark 1993 and 1994
Class salutorian. Bel Air Prep School. 1991
First Place - Southern California Shakespeare Festival (1990)
Third Place - Southern California Shakespeare Festival (1991)

V006-DC-00000183

Monica S. Lewinsky

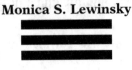

Education:

Lewis and Clark College Portland, Oregon
Bachelor of Science in Psychology May 1995

Experience:

Department of Defense The Pentagon Washington, D.C.
Confidential Assistant to the Assistant Secretary of Defense for Public Affairs
April 1996 - present
Serve as principal assistant to the Assistant Secretary of Defense (ASD) for Public Affairs in support of his dual role as both Department of Defense spokesman and head of Department of Defense Public Affairs. Assist in preparing the ASD for bi-weekly press briefings. Interact with the national print and broadcast media on the ASD's behalf. Provide the ASD with timely updates of current media stories. Act as liaison with the offices of the Secretary, the White House, other Cabinet Secretaries and the National Security Council. Provide support to the Secretary of Defense and Assistant Secretary on frequent international travel which includes a contingent of traveling media. Handle the ASD's daily schedule and correspondence.

The White House Washington, D.C.
Staff Assistant to Director of Legislative Affairs Correspondence, November 1995 - April 1996
Wrote drafts and correspondence for Staff Secretary's approval and ultimately the President's signature, which often required research of various Administration issues and policies. Coordinated mass mailings to Congress for the President and other Senior Administration officials. Processed and vetted all incoming mail to the President from Congress. Trained and supervised new interns on White House procedure and preparation of White House correspondence.

The White House Washington, D.C.
Summer Intern Office of the Chief of Staff, July - November 1995
Drafted form letters and individual responses for the Chief of Staff's signature. Acted as a liaison for Chief of Staff's office to other White House offices, Cabinet agencies, and Congressional offices.
Updated office manual. Supervised and coordinated intern and volunteer staff.

Metropolitan Public Defenders Portland, Oregon
Alternatives Staff, February - May 1995

Implemented new psychology expert reference techniques. Assisted attorneys in finding viable alternatives to prison for their clients. Directed clients in successful search for support, shelter, food and transportation. Updated files on resource materials.

Southeast Mental Health Network (Practicum) Portland, Oregon
Socialization Staff Assistant, January - June 1994
Assisted staff in teaching socialization skills to mentally ill clients to ease their integration back into society. Updated clients' confidential reports. Coordinated fund raising to benefit extra-curricular theatre activities.

Additional Information:

- TS-SCI Clearance: Current
- Proficient in Macintosh for Microsoft Word 6.0, WordPerfect for Windows 5.2, Quorum, and Infosys.

RECORD TYPE: PRESIDENTIAL (ALL-IN-1 MAIL)
CREATOR: Patsy L. Thomasson (THOMASSON_____P) (WHO)
CREATION DATE/TIME: 9-APR-1996 12:05:07.75
SUBJECT:RE: Monica Lewinsky and Jocelyn Jolley

TO: Jodie R. Torkelson (TORKELSON_____J) (WHO)
READ: 9-APR-1996 12:07:23.69

CC: Bob J. Nash (NASH_____B) (WHO)
READ: 9-APR-1996 20:35:25.98

TEXT:

    Bob and I have been working with Tim on placing these two people.

    We are working closely with DOD to make this happen for Monica. We have not finalized the deal but are working toward that end.

    Monica is coming in to see me today pursuant to Tim's request of me. Our direction is to make sure she has a job in an Agency. We are working toward that end.

patsy

[Editor's note: This e-mail relates to efforts to find Ms. Lewinsky a job at the Pentagon, where she worked after being dismissed from the White House.]

October 16, 1996

Dear Evelyn,

    Thanks for the meeting yesterday. I wanted to follow up on a few points as you put your memo together.

- I've enclosed our staff division of responsibilities that we use throughout the year. I don't distribute it because I want White House and agency staff to funnel their issues and requests through our West Wing operation. That way I can keep track, exercise quality control, and make the judgements about the use of our staff resources.

- I've also enclosed a brief memo on our correspondence operation. It was in bad shape when I came in. We got rid of Monica and Jossie not only because of "extracurricular activities" but because they couldn't do the job. We also had problems with NSC and White House correspondence that have been corrected. I believe the operation is in quite good shape now.

    Thank you for being so good to me this year. I greatly appreciate your help and counsel. I will take the steps you suggested and then follow up with both you and Leon.

John

MEMORANDUM FOR: RECORD

FROM: Cliff Bernath

DATE: March 14, 1997

SUBJECT: Lewinsky Counselling

Re: ██████ Counselling

* So far as I can tell, Ken is happy with her support. Responsive and attentive.
* My concerns;
    —Ken's calendar. Too many errors in the mornings. Need to work the schedule better before she leaves at night. Too late by time she arrives in morning. She has primary responsibility for his calendar and its accuracy. She needs to verify everything on it and share the information with Mark early enough in the afternoon so we can get together and resolve conflicts. Also, shouldn't make excuses or blame others when Ken finds an error or asks a question we can't answer.
* Work Area. Need to clean it up and keep it clean. Part of professionalism. She has to stay organized.
* Ken's inbox. We need to do a better job of monitoring what goes into it. In general, other than personal mail and DDI products, almost everything else should come to me. We've talked about that but it isn't happening.
* Other:
    —Spends too much time on personal email, personal business and phone calls.
    —Answering phones. She feels that others aren't doing their share. Told her that no one likes answering the phones and everyone thinks they do it more than the others. She wondered if her position wasn't somewhat higher than the other admin positions and that they should answer more calls. Told her that Mr. Bacon has the highest priority and when she's on a project for him, that makes her position more important. But at other times, everyone has to pull their share.
* Asked her if she was still happy here. Appears to be less happy than when she started.
    —Has had some personal problems which she didn't want to discuss and has been bringing that to the office.
    —Feels unchallenged with admin duties. Told her that was to be expected. It would be unlikely that someone with her education and energy would want to make a career of this job. She's been here about a year. That said, she could make the job more challenging by taking on more responsibility. Could draft responses to Ken's mail, for example. Pointed out that Mark is constantly busy because he's always looking for better ways to get things done.
    —Has been thinking about trying to get another job at the White House.

MSL-DC-00001228

479

April 28, 1997

Ms. Lorrie McHugh
Deputy Assistant to the President
The White House
Washington, DC.

Dear Lorrie:

Mike suggested that I drop you a note about my confidential assistant, Monica Lewinsky. Her resume is attached.

She is terrific—bright, energetic and imaginative. I would like Monica to stay here as along as I do. However, she has more skills than her current job requires, and this isn't a job she wants for life. As a result, I have advised her that she should try to move into a more substantive job, either here or in the White House. Unlike many people, she is actually following my advice. She would like to work in the White House, where she started work in Washington. She would great as an organizer in the press operation or as an event planner in the communications office.

Mike says that you handle the really hard work over there, such as hiring. Please keep Monica in mind as appropriate jobs open up.

Yours,

Kenneth H. Bacon

MSL-DC-00001230

480

From: Dimel, Marsha L.

To:

Hill, Roseanne M.
CC: /N, NonRecord at A1
Subject: No Thank you
Letter [UNCLASSIFIED]
Date: Thursday, June 12, 1997 01:21 PM

Rosie, please do a no thank you, thanks for the interview letter to Monica Lewinsky—I have her resume in my office.

< ^ TRANSLATED_ATTACHMENT>

SECLET.DOC

DATE

Dear

Thank you for your interest in the secretarial/administrative positions with the National Security Council staff.

Your application and resume were well received, and you are obviously highly qualified. We received several applications and the compitition for the positions has been competitive. I am sorry, but I cannot offer you a position at this time. I will keep your resume/application on file for other openings as they occur.

I enjoyed meeting with you and wish you success in your career.

Sincerely,

Marsha L. Dimel
Personnel & Administration

name
address

F:¢seclet.doc

24 June 1997

Dear Betty:

Since I have not been able to get in touch with him, I am taking the unorthodox liberty of sharing my concerns with you. I would very much appreciate it if you could relay this information to him either verbally or by letting him read this note. If you're not comfortable doing either, I understand.

The intention of this note is not to "tattle-tale", but to clarify. My meeting with Marsha was not at all what I expected. While she was very pleasant, she questioned me endlessly about my situation. Despite the fact that she already knew why I had to leave, she asked me to tell her about it, asked if I had acted "inappropriately" and why I wanted to come back. She seemingly knew nothing about my current position. She didn't know of any openings and said she would check with the people in Communications. He said to me that he had told her I had gotten a bum deal, and I should get a good job in the West Wing. I was surprised that she would question his judgment and not just do what he asked of her. Is it possible that, in fact, he did not tell her that? Does he really not want me back in the complex? He has not responded to my note, nor has he called me. Do you know what is going on? If so, are you able to share it with me?

I did not cause any trouble when I had to leave last year because I knew how important the election was. He promised me then I could come back after the election, and I have been counting on him. I think I have been more than patient since it has now been eight months since the election, not to mention the seven months prior to November that I waited. Shall I continue to be patient?

Betty, I am very frustrated and sad. I especially don't understand this deafening silence, lack of response and complete distancing evidenced by him. Why is he ignoring me? I have done nothing wrong. I would expect that behavior like this might be directed toward an "unfriendly", but certainly not to me. I would *never* do anything to hurt him.

I am hoping to hear from either of you soon. I'm at a loss, and I don't know what to do.

Best wishes.

Monica S. Lewinsky

29 June 1997   MSL-DC-00001176

Ms. Marsha Scott
Deputy Assistant to the President
    and Chief of Staff for Presidential Personnel
The White House
Washington, DC 20500

[handwritten annotation across upper right: "discretion whether the complex is extemporaneous ... a president in the w"]

Dear Marsha:

As you know, our last conversation was very upsetting to me. I fully
understand the obstacles that are standing in my way of trying to work in the
West Wing, and I want to clarify that it is **not** important for me to secure a
position there. I am perfectly content having a job in the OEOB. I'd like to
point out that the two interviews I had were for positions in the West Wing only
because those were the two positions about which I had heard. Had they been
two positions in the OEOB, I would have been just as eager.

[handwritten: "my primary interest is in"]

As I discussed with you when we met, I have a great deal of interest in working
in Communications. With both Sidney Blumenthal and Paul Begala joining the
White House team, there is no doubt in my mind there will be some positions
will be opening and some created. Now is the time that their transitions are being
structured. I have no way of finding out what their game plan is for positions,
but I hope that is something with which you can help me. I also mentioned
when we met that there used to be more research positions in Communications
than there are now [see attachments]. I know you are busy, but have you had
a chance to see if those slots are still open? If they were eliminated before,
might they be reinstated with Mr. Blumenthal and Mr. Begala coming to the
WH? [The Communication research positions are low-level and in the OEOB].

yet
Another avenue that can be explored is Public Liaison. While I do not have as
much interest in that office as I do in Communications, I think it would be
challenging and interesting to be a part of that team. That entire office is
situated in the OEOB] *is, of course, the public
equivalent of the media arena in
Communications.*

Marsha, I was told that I could come back after the election. I knew why I had
to leave last year by mid-April, and I have been beyond patient since then. I do
not think it is fair to ask me to wait until the end of the year or to be told by
the person whom I was told would get me a job that there is nothing for me and
she doesn't really hear about positions on the complex any way. I know that in
your eyes I am just a hindrance -- a woman who doesn't have a certain
someone's best interests at heart, but please trust me when I say I do.

[handwritten left margin: "needs major work but good!!"]

I will be traveling with Secretary Cohen from 7-14 July, and then I'll be in Los
Angeles from 17-21 July. I hope to hear from you before I leave.

Sincerely,

Monica Lewinsky

Monica Lewinsky

483

Monica Lewinsky

6 July 1997

Ms. Marsha Scott
Deputy Assistant to the President
  and Chief of Staff for Presidential Personnel
The White House
Washington, DC 20500

Dear Marsha:

I am looking forward to meeting with you when I return from traveling with Secretary Cohen. Based on our last conversation, I wanted to clarify that I fully understand that obstacles exist in terms of obtaining a position in the White House. It is not important for me to secure a position in the West Wing. I am perfectly content having a job in the OEOB.

As I discussed with you when we met, my primary interest is in Communications. With both Sidney Blumenthal and Paul Begala joining the White House team, there is no doubt that positions will be opened and some positions will be created. I have no way of learning of their game plan for positions, but I hope that is something with which you can help me. I also mentioned when we met that there used to be another research position in Communications [see attached]. I know you are busy, but maybe you can look into this position before we meet. If it was eliminated, might it be reinstated with Mr. Blumenthal and Mr. Begala coming to the WH? [The Communication research position is low-level and in the OEOB]. Yet, another avenue that can be explored is Public Liaison. While I do not have as much interest in that arena as I do in Communications, that entire office is situated in the OEOB and, is of course, the public equivalent of the media arena in Communications.

Marsha, I want you to know that I do appreciate the help you are giving me, and I apologize if at times my frustration with this whole situation has been misdirected towards you.

Again, I look forward to seeing you soon.

Sincerely,

Monica Lewinsky

MSL-DC-00001192

484

I think the end of this whole trauma
is over. I just wish my heart didn't have
to be broken in all of this.

Well, I hope you and your family are
well.

Again Dale, thanks for being such a
great friend.

XXX OOO
love,
monica

4 Sept. 1997

Dear Dale,

I wanted to thank you for the kindness
and friendship you extended to me last weekend.
I really needed the friendly ear and good
advice.

Unfortunately, I came back to DC only to learn
that the detailee slot in Marsha's office is
no longer available. I had a long conversation
with her and it is clear to me now that
I won't be able to come back any time soon.

First and foremost, thank you.

My dream had been to work in Communications or Strategic Planning at the White House. I am open to any suggestions that you may have on work that is similar to that or may intrigue me.

The most important things to me are that I am engaged and interested in my work; I am not someone's administrative/executive assistant; and my salary can provide me a comfortable living in NY.

Networks:
* Assistant producer at any of the networks
* Kaplan—CNN has a NY Office
* News/political segments at MTV

Assistant to an account executive at any of the following (*not* administrative assistant):

* Hill & Knowlton
* Burson-Marsteller
* Downey & Chandler
* Bozell Public Relations/Bozell Worldwide
* Devries Public Relations

[These are agencies with which I am familiar. You may have more suggestions from the attached list of agencies in NY (Tab 1)].

* Anything at George magazine

A note about the UN:

I do not have any interest in working there. As a result of what happened in April '96, I have already spent a year and a half at an agency in which I have no interest. I want a job where I feel challenged, engaged and interested. I don't think the UN is the right place for me.

DB-DC-00000027

[Editor's note: This document is from October 16, 1997.]

2 November 1997

Dear Betty:

I hope you had an enjoyable weekend. I thought I'd drop you a note since it's so difficult for both of us to talk at work!

I became a bit nervous this weekend when I realized that Amb. Richardson said his staff would be in touch with me *this week*. As you know, the UN is supposed to be my back up but because VJ has been out of town, this is my only option right now. What should I say to Richardson's people this week when they call? I had mentioned to Richardson that working there was *one* of the things I was looking at. It probably sounds stupid, but I have absolutely no idea how to tell them, "I'm not sure yet", in a business-like manner. If you feel it's appropriate, maybe you could ask "the big guy" what he wants me to do. Ahhhhh . . . anxiety!!!!!

Also, I don't think I told you that in my conversation last Thursday night with him that he said he would ask you to set up a meeting between VJ and myself, once VJ got back. I assume he'll mention this to you at some point—hopefully sooner rather than later!

I am enclosing a copy for VJ of the list of advertising/PR firms that I included in "the big guy's" packet. My hopes are that one of the names will jump out as a place where he (VJ) might have a contact.

I mentioned to him that Id like to drop by on Sat. to give you your birthday present and to see him for a bit. He seemed somewhat receptive and said he'd check it out this week. Of course, he'll forget because in the whole scheme of things it's not that important and I will, of course, probably have to bug you towards the end of the week with this (something to look forward to I'm sure)!!!!!

I hope to hear from you soon with some guidance. I am mailing my "thank-you-for-meeting-with-me-letter" to Richardson today. I was pleased the UN interview went well, but I'm afraid it will be like being at the Pentagon in NY . . . YUCK! PLEASE let me know what to do soon!!!!

1,000 thank you's.

Hugs n' kisses,

MSL-55-DC-0179

Monica S. Lewinsky

3 November 1997

The Honorable Bill Richardson
United States Ambassador to the United Nations
799 United Nations Plaza
New York, New York 10017

Dear Ambassador Richardson:

It was a pleasure meeting with you last Friday morning. I know how very busy and demanding your schedule is; I particularly appreciated your taking the time to speak with me.

It was an honor to meet you. The US Mission to the United Nations is certainly in good hands with you at the helm.

Again, thank you for your time.

Sincerely,

Monica Lewinsky

Monica Lewinsky

828-DC-00000013

Monica S. Lewinsky

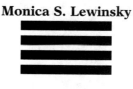

6 November 1997

Mr. Vernon Jordan
Akin, Gump, Strauss, Hauer & Feld
1333 New Hampshire, NW
Washington, DC 20036

Dear Mr. Jordan:

It was a real pleasure meeting with you. I know how very busy and demanding your schedule is; I particularly appreciated your taking the time to speak with me.

I feel compelled to mention how overcome I was by your genuineness. While some people wear their heart on their sleeve; you appear to wear your soul. It made me happy to know that our friend has such a wonderful confidante in you.

I believe I may have neglected to mention that while my current position is administrative, I am seeking more substantive work in my next position.

Thanks again for your time, and I look forward to hearing from you upon your return.

Sincerely,

Monica S. Lewinsky

Monica S. Lewinsky

11 December 1997

Ms. Ursula Fairbaim
EVP, Human Resources & Quality
American Express Company
American Express Tower
World Financial Center
New York, New York 10285

Dear Ms. Fairbaim:

I am writing at the suggestion of Vernon Jordan, who has spoken with you on my behalf.

I am interested in exploring opportunities in Communications or Public Relations in New York. I am hoping to secure a position which would require effective communication skills, creativity, and frequent interaction with people. My various jobs in Washington, DC have provided me with the training and skills needed to further pursue a career in these areas.

Most recently, I have been working for the Honorable Ken Bacon, the Assistant Secretary of Defense for Public Affairs, as his primary assistant. My responsibilities range from interacting with the media on his behalf, to providing administrative assistance on the Secretary of Defense's international trips, to assembling timely updates of current media stories. My prior experience was at the White House in Legislative Affairs and the Chief of Staff's Office. Please see the enclosed resume for further detail.

I am moving to New York and am seeking employment to begin the first of the year. I am ready and available to speak with whoever in your office you might deem appropriate. I will follow up with a phone call to your office on Monday, December 15th, 1997.

Thank you for time.

Sincerely,

Monica Lewinsky

Monica Lewinsky

CC: Mr. Vernon Jordan

11 December 1997

Mr. Richard E. Halperin
EVP & Special Counsel to the President
MacAndrews & Forbes
35 East 62nd Street
New York, New York 10021

Dear Mr. Halperin:

I am writing at the suggestion of Vernon Jordan, who has spoken with you on my behalf.

I am interested in exploring opportunities in Communications or Public Relations in New York. I am hoping to secure a position which would require effective communication skills, creativity, and frequent interaction with people. My various jobs in Washington, DC have provided me with the training and skills needed to further pursue a career in these areas.

Most recently, I have been working for the Honorable Ken Bacon, the Assistant Secretary of Defense for Public Affairs, as his primary assistant. My responsibilities range from interacting with the media on his behalf, to providing administrative assistance on the Secretary of Defense's international trips, to assembling timely updates of current media stories. My prior experience was at the White House in Legislative Affairs and the Chief of Staff's Office. Please see the enclosed resume for further detail.

I am moving to New York and am seeking employment to begin the first of the year. I am ready and available to speak with whoever in your office you might deem appropriate. I will follow up with a phone call to your office on Monday, December 15th, 1997.

Thank you for time.

Sincerely,

Monica Lewinsky

Monica Lewinsky

CC: Mr. Vernon Jordan

830-DC-00000017

Monica Lewinsky

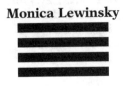

13 January 1998

Ms. Jenna Sheldon
Manager, Corporate Staffing
REVLON
625 Madison Avenue
New York, New York 10022

By fax: ▄▄▄▄

Dear Jenna:

I am so excited about joining the team at Revlon. I think it's going to be great!

The following are two references from my employment at both the Pentagon and the White House. Please feel free to contact them. Mr. Bacon is currently traveling with Secretary Cohen in Asia and will return to the States on the 22nd of January. I would prefer you speak with him vice his deputy.

The Honorable Ken Bacon
Assistant Secretary of Defense
 for Public Affairs

▄▄▄▄

   *** Please contact Colonel Ed Veiga, USA to speak with Mr. Bacon.

The Honorable John Hilley
Assistant to the President for Legislative Affairs

▄▄▄▄

Please let me know if you need any more information.

Sincerely,

Monica Lewinsky

Monica Lewinsky

830-DC-00000007

Lewinsky Apt.- Tape 002

Search Warrant

Page 1 to Page 13

CONDENSED TRANSCRIPT AND CONCORDANCE
PREPARED BY:

OFFICE OF THE INDEPENDENT COUNSEL
1001 Pennsylvania Avenue, N.W.
Suite 490-North
Washington, DC 20004
Phone: 202-514-8688
FAX: 202-514-8802

Page 1

```
[1]
[2]
[3]      OFFICE OF INDEPENDENT COUNSEL
[4]
[5]      TAPE TRANSCRIPTION
[6]
[7] x - - - - - - - - - - - - - - x
[8]             Transcript of
[9]             Search.003
[10] x - - - - - - - - - - - - - - x
[11]
[12]
[13]
[14]
[15]
[16]
[17]
[18]
[19]
[20]
[21]
[22]
[23]
[24]
[25]
```

Page 2

```
[1]            P R O C E E D I N G S
[2]     DR. LEWINSKY:    Monica, your dad. This girl that we
[3] told you about in New York has already found an apartment,
[4] and she's in a different area where you wouldn't want to be.
[5] However – however, she was moved from California to New York
[6] by Global International Movers.
[7]     UNIDENTIFIED MALE SPEAKER IN BACKGROUND:  They're
[8] all over.
[9]     DR. LEWINSKY:    They're all over the country. The
[10] number is ███████████  It cost her $1200 to move from
[11] California to New York. So you may want to call them. I
[12] would imagine that she had furniture and stuff also. So give
[13] them a call, and we'll talk to you later. Bye.
[14]     (End phone message.)
[15]     RECORDING:    Wednesday, 9:57 a.m.  (Tone.)
[16]     MS. TRIPP:    Well, Monica, I tried to page you and I
[17] tried to call you back. I guess you're not there. I guess
[18] you're calling me from somewhere else. Goodbye.
[19]     (End phone message.)
[20]     RECORDING:    Wednesday, 12:05 p.m.  (Tone.)
[21]     UNIDENTIFIED FEMALE SPEAKER:    Hi, Monica, it's me.
[22] I think it's around 10:00. You there? No. Okay. I'm going
[23] to try paging you. But, also, in case you get this message
[24] and not my page, do not leave any messages on my machine at
[25] home for me that say anything 'cause of Grandma. But just
```

Page 3

```
[1] say, "Call me," and I'll call you back. I'll try paging you.
[2]     (End phone message.)
[3]     RECORDING:    Wednesday, 11:13 p.m.  (Tone.)
[4]     UNIDENTIFIED FEMALE SPEAKER:    Hi. You there? Are
[5] you there? No. Okay. It's 12:00. I'll try you later.
[6] It's nothing urgent, just want to touch base.
[7]     (End phone message.)
[8]     RECORDING:    Thursday, 12:40 a.m.  (Tone.)
[9]     UNIDENTIFIED FEMALE SPEAKER:    Hi, it's me. Are you
[10] there? Hi. Gosh, where have you been all day? Okay, honey.
[11] It's not urgent. I just want to touch base with you. Um,
[12] I'm on the street. I'm trying not to call you from home
[13] 'cause of Grandma. I will try you again in a little bit.
[14] Bye. Sweetie.
[15]     (End phone message.)
[16]     RECORDING:    Thursday, 1:48 a.m.  (Tone.)
[17]     UNIDENTIFIED FEMALE SPEAKER:    Hi, it's me. Are you
[18] there? Hi. Okay. You're not there. 'Bye.
[19]     (End phone message.)
[20]     RECORDING:    Thursday, 2:24 a.m.  (Tone.)
[21]     UNIDENTIFIED FEMALE SPEAKER:    Here's Ashley with a
[22] very rushed message. Usually you're so sweet. Um. It's
[23] 2:00 Friday. Calling to make plans for the evening. Give me
[24] a call at work. Talk to you later, 'bye.
[25]     (End phone message.)
```

Page 4

```
[1]     RECORDING:    Thursday, 2:54 a.m.  (Tone.)
[2]     UNIDENTIFIED FEMALE SPEAKER:    Hey, it's me.
[3] trying to get a hold of you to see what's going on. I got
[4] your page, um, but I wanted to make sure everything's all
[5] right. Give me a call. 'Bye.
[6]     (End phone message.)
[7]     RECORDING:    Thursday, 6:12 a.m.  (Tone.)
[8]     UNIDENTIFIED FEMALE SPEAKER:    You – you w
[9] through my head yesterday. And then when I checked my
[10] machine, it was like a miracle. I was so happy that you had
[11] called because I didn't know – I've been trying to like – I
[12] think you left your number, and it was your dad's right when
[13] I got back from Italy. And I tried calling and you weren't
[14] there.
[15]     And I'm so happy you've called me, and I really am
[16] looking forward to talking to you. I'm probably going to be
[17] home for the rest of the day. It's raining here. So give me
[18] a call, and happy New Year's, and I love you. And we shall
[19] talk later. Okay, Sweetie, bye-bye.
[20]     (End phone message.)
[21]     UNIDENTIFIED FEMALE SPEAKER:    Hi, it's me.
[22] know where you are. I – I don't – it's not that important.
[23] I want to tell you –
[24]     MS. LEWINSKY:    Hello?
[25]     UNIDENTIFIED FEMALE SPEAKER:    Oh, hi. It's
```

Page 5

```
[1] (inaudible) birthday. Let me call –
[2]     (End phone message.)
[3]     RECORDING:    Saturday, 9:38 a.m.  (Tone.)
[4]     STEVE:    Hey, Monica, it's Steve calling on Sunday
[5] at about 10:00. Hope the rest of your weekend went well.
[6] Um, give me a call back once you know what your schedule is,
[7] and maybe we can make some plans to get together. I'll talk
[8] to you soon, and I hope everything's going well. 'Bye.
[9]     (End phone message.)
[10]     RECORDING:    Saturday, 10:51 a.m.  (Tone.)
[11]     MONA:    Hi, Monica. This is Mona (inaudible)
[12] calling from Bill Richardson's office in New York. I just
[13] want to touch base with you. Happy New Year, by the way. M
[14] number in New York is ███████████  If you could give me a
[15] call sometime – uh, oh, I don't know, today if you get this,
[16] or tomorrow, I'd appreciate it. Thanks a lot. 'Bye.
[17]     (End phone message.)
[18]     RECORDING:    Saturday, 11:38 p.m.  (Tone.)
[19]     MARK:    Hi, Monica, it's Mark. Uh, Mrs. Bacon
[20] called looking for your forwarding phone number. Uh, you can
[21] either give me a call here or call Mrs. Bacon at home. Thank
[22] you. 'Bye.
[23]     (End phone message.)
[24]     RECORDING:    Sunday, 12:09 a.m.  (Tone.)
[25]     CHRISTINA:    Hi, Monica. My name is Christina an
```

Page 6

```
[1] work with Jamie Jeman (phonetic) and Richard Halpern
[2] (phonetic) of Anders & Forbes. I was calling to schedule an
[3] interview with you. I thought you were in town. Please call
[4] us at ███████████  Thanks. Bye-bye.
[5]     (End phone message.)
[6]     (Begin phone message.)
[7]     UNIDENTIFIED FEMALE SPEAKER:    I didn't know
[8] your machine and then I didn't want to hang up. I just
[9] wanted to call you and tell you I'm going in the shower.
[10]     RECORDING:    Monday, 8:52 a.m.  (Tone.)
[11]     DR. LEWINSKY:    Hi, Monica. Just wanted to say
[12] say hello. Uh, 8926. Um, I'm on my way to the Turnor Board,
[13] so I just will try you some other time or I'll page you next
[14] time I'm available to receive a return call. Hope
[15] everything's going well. Take care. 'Bye.
[16]     (End phone message.)
[17]     RECORDING:    Tuesday, 3:44 a.m.  (Tone.)
[18]     MS. TRIPP:    Hey, it's Linda. Um, I was in work on
[19] Tuesday as well as Wednesday. I didn't get your messages
[20] until very late last evening, and then actually I didn't get
[21] home 'til after midnight, um, which is long story, nothing
[22] bad, though. Um, see if you can call me at work, although I
[23] would really prefer to be very careful. Um, I hope to hear
[24] from you. 'Bye.
[25]     (End phone message.)
```

Page 7

[1]   RECORDING: Tuesday, 10:25 p.m. (Tone.)
[2]   CHRIS: Hi, Monica, it's Chris here, I guess about
[3] 6:00 a.m. your time on Saturday morning. I was just ringing
[4] up to say thanks so much for the brilliant Pentagon, um,
[5] sweatshirt that I'm going to have a lot of fun wearing here
[6] in the winter months.
[7]   Hopefully, I won't get beaten up by any, um, anti-
[8] American leftists -- leftists, so that we'll have to wait and
[9] see. But, anyhow, it was really a nice present. Thanks so
[10] much for that.
[11]   And, um, well, I hope you can get on the e-mail,
[12] soon because I miss, uh, our little e-mail chats, not to
[13] mention the jokes. I haven't heard a good joke, except for
[14] some John Denver jokes, in quite some time. So, anyhow --
[15] and Sonny Bono jokes, too, which is rather crass. I got a
[16] Sonny Bono joke next day, which is terrible.
[17]   Anyhow, uh, I'll, um, hope to be hearing from you
[18] soon. Okay. Ta-ta, bye-bye.
[19]   (End phone message.)
[20]   RECORDING: Thursday, 8:52 p.m. (Tone.)
[21]   UNIDENTIFIED FEMALE SPEAKER: Hi. Okay. The girl
[22] called from Rudin's office and she's going to sneak me in
[23] around 3:00 this after -- not sneak, but squeeze me in around
[24] 3:00. Uh, but she said she needs something in writing, like,
[25] you know, how much you want to pay. Okay, that's fine. I

Page 8

[1] got that. Where you want to live. I've got that. Either
[2] east side or west side, depending on what the building is,
[3] I'm going to say. The rent you want to pay, I'm going to
[4] write $1,250, all that.
[5]   And then she said, "And give us a few names for
[6] reference." So my question is whose names in Washington do
[7] you want to give? Um, I don't want to, you know, presume to
[8] -- anything. So you call me back and let me know. Okay,
[9] Sweetie? 'Bye.
[10]   (End phone message.)
[11]   RECORDING: Monday, 12:04 a.m. (Tone.)
[12]   MS. SHELDON: Monica, hi, Janice Sheldon from
[13] Revlon. Just wanted to let you know that, um, Yajia
[14] (phonetic) Zalensky (phonetic), who is the Vice President of
[15] Public Relations in the group reporting to Allan Seidman,
[16] wants to give you a call before your start date, so I just
[17] wanted to give you a heads-up that she might be calling.
[18]   And, as well, tonight I'll be sending out the hire
[19] kit to you that I promised.
[20]   Um, I don't have any other information for you as
[21] far as getting a leg up on the information, but, uh, if you have
[22] any questions, please feel free to call me at. It's ▇▇▇
[23] ▇▇▇▇, and that's a ▇▇▇ area code. Thanks. Bye-bye.
[24]   (End phone message.)
[25]   RECORDING: Monday, 3:52 a.m. (Tone.)

Page 9

[1]   UNIDENTIFIED FEMALE SPEAKER: Hi, Monica, it's me.
[2] Okay. The meeting with Rudin went very well. It was very,
[3] very quick, in and out. I've now been turned over to one of
[4] the assistants who's going to work with us, you know, saying,
[5] "Wow, it's not much time. There's not much time." That most
[6] leases run either from the 1st of the month or the middle of
[7] the month, and yadda, yadda. But, I -- I mean it looks good.
[8] Loves the M&Ms. Really. God, that was a great touch, a
[9] great touch.
[10]   Number 2, you will be interested to know the alarm
[11] just went out off, hmm, 5:00 this evening. And, number 3,
[12] I'm, of course, desperate to hear what happened. I have to
[13] meet Peter Straus at 6:00, so, hopefully, you'll call me
[14] before then. 'Bye.
[15]   (End phone message.)
[16]   RECORDING: Monday, 5:42 a.m. (Tone.)
[17]   UNIDENTIFIED FEMALE SPEAKER: Hi, Monica. It's me.
[18] How are you? It's at 5:15, calling to see what's going on.
[19] I'm at the Watergate. Please call me in my apartment. Thank
[20] you and goodbye.
[21]   (End phone message.)
[22]   RECORDING: Monday, 6:07 a.m. (Tone.)
[23]   UNIDENTIFIED FEMALE SPEAKER: Hi, it's me. I am
[24] sorry I missed your call, Monica. Please call again later,
[25] and leave a -- you know, a detailed message on my phone and

Page 10

[1] I'll keep checking my machine so I can hear what happened.
[2] Okay, Sweetie? Love you, 'bye.
[3]   (End phone message.)
[4]   RECORDING: Monday, 7:36 a.m. (Tone.)
[5]   DR. LEWINSKY: Hi, Monica. It's your dad. It's
[6] our 4:00. Uh, I just wanted to check if you got home all
[7] right, then if everything is okay. Uh, just curious to see
[8] how things are going for you. And, uh, I'm not going to be
[9] home this evening. I've got a staff dinner. Uh, but if you
[10] just want to let us know what's cooking, you can leave us a
[11] message. Then we'll know what's going on. Otherwise, I'll
[12] talk to you.
[13]   Uh, I'm not sure whether or not you'll remember
[14] that we're going to Hawaii on Sunday. Remember, the thing
[15] with the men where they were going to be there? So we're
[16] meeting them over there. So we'll be gone after Sunday for a
[17] week, so be sure that you call us before that, okay?
[18]   We'll be at the Grand Royal Lei in Maui if you need
[19] to get a hold of us. But I'd like to talk to you before
[20] that.
[21]   Take care. Love you. Hope everything's going
[22] well. 'Bye.
[23]   (End phone message.)
[24]   RECORDING: Monday, 8:00 a.m. (Tone.)
[25]   UNIDENTIFIED FEMALE SPEAKER: Hi, Monica, Sweeti

Page 11

[1] It's me. It's 4:20. I wanted to tell you my plan for
[2] tonight. Bill and I are going to eat dinner here in
[3] Warrenton, and then we're both going to drive to Washington
[4] and spend the night there. And then he's going to go to
[5] Dulles Airport tomorrow morning to go to L.A. So thank you.
[6] My other line's ringing. 'Bye.
[7]   (End phone message.)
[8]   RECORDING: Tuesday, 5:07 a.m. (Tone.)
[9]   UNIDENTIFIED FEMALE SPEAKER: Hi, Monica. It's me
[10] It's 6:00. Just calling to say hi and see how your day was.
[11] And I was curious whether you talked to that friend of yours
[12] and if everything worked out okay with her. I hope so.
[13]   And to let you know that Bill and I will probably
[14] be there in maybe a couple of hours, maybe by 8:00, 'cause he
[15] wants to eat dinner and pack for L.A., and then we're going
[16] to drive there. So I hope I get to see you. And I love you.
[17] And I'll talk to you later. Bye-bye.
[18]   (End phone message.)
[19]   RECORDING: Tuesday, 6:42 a.m. (Tone.)
[20]   UNIDENTIFIED FEMALE SPEAKER: Hi, Monica. It's me
[21] It's 8:00. I expected to find you here, my roomie, but you
[22] are not here. Please tell me where you are when you get
[23] back, and please come and sleep here. Thank you. Good-bye.
[24]   (End phone message.)
[25]   RECORDING: Tuesday, 8:45 a.m. (Tone.)

Page 12

[1]   UNIDENTIFIED FEMALE SPEAKER: Hi, Munk, are you -
[2] there? It's 9:00. I will beep you to see where you are.
[3] 'Bye.
[4]   (End phone message.)
[5]   RECORDING: Tuesday, 9:35 a.m. (Tone.)
[6]   UNIDENTIFIED FEMALE SPEAKER: Hi, Monica. It's me
[7] Um, Denise left a message on my machine last night. She's
[8] finally spoke to that David, and, um, he said you were
[9] adorable and a great conversationalist.
[10]   It -- it didn't sound as if he wanted to run away
[11] and get married, but that he does want to keep up contact
[12] with you.
[13]   But, um, it's better if you hear it yourself. So
[14] call me later and you can play -- you know, you can play my
[15] messages and you can hear it yourself. But it's -- it's
[16] really nice. I mean, I think short of, you know, the guy
[17] saying he's in love, it's -- it's really exactly what you
[18] would have wanted. So call me later and et cetera. 'Bye.
[19]   (End phone message.)
[20]   RECORDING: Tuesday, 9:46 p.m. (Tone.)
[21]   MR. SCHICK: Monica, this is Tom Schick at American
[22] Express. I am calling you on Thursday, January 15, at 12:00)
[23] noon. Give me a call at your leisure -- no urgency -- at
[24] ▇▇▇▇▇▇▇▇. Thank you.
[25]   (End phone message.)

Page 13

[1]   RECORDING: Wednesday, 12:41 a.m. (Tone.)
[2]   MR. NELVIS: Hey, Monica, it's Nel. I'm calling at
[3] 12:08, uh, I — I'm going to call you back in about half-an-
[4] hour. Thanks.
[5]   (End phone message.)
[6]   RECORDING: Wednesday, 12:52 a.m. (Tone.)
[7]   MR. NELVIS: Hey, Monica, it's Nel again. Would
[8] you page me as soon as you get back home at ███████████,
[9] pager number ███████. Thanks.
[10]   (End phone message.)
[11]   RECORDING: Wednesday, 12:58 a.m. (Tone.)
[12]   MS. CURRIE: Hi, it's Betty. If you're there, pick
[13] up. Otherwise, call me right back ASAP. Thanks.
[14]   (End phone message.)
[15]   RECORDING: Wednesday, 1:10 a.m. (Tone.)
[16]   (End recording SEARCH.003, Side 1.)
[17]
[18]
[19]
[20]
[21]
[22]
[23]
[24]
[25]

PART FOUR

LEGAL WRANGLING BETWEEN THE OFFICE OF INDEPENDENT COUNSEL AND PRESIDENT CLINTON'S LAWYERS

Office of the Independent Counsel
1001 Pennsylvania Avenue, N.W.
Suite 490-North
Washington, D.C. 20004
(202) 514-8688
Fax (202) 514-8802

January 21, 1998

VIA FACSIMILE

David E. Kendall, Esq.
Williams & Connelly
725 Twelfth Street, N.W.
Washington, D.C. 20005

Re: William Jefferson Clinton
Grand Jury Subpoena – V002

Dear David:

Pursuant to our telephone conversation this afternoon, enclosed please grand jury subpoena number V002. Also enclosed please find a copy of the Special Division's jurisdictional Order and its Order authorizing limited disclosure. Both Orders are under seal.

Thank you for accepting service on behalf of your client.

Sincerely,

Robert J. Bittman
Deputy Independent Counsel

Enclosures

United States District Court

EASTERN   DISTRICT OF   VIRGINIA

TO: William Jefferson Clinton

SUBPOENA TO TESTIFY
BEFORE GRAND JURY

SUBPOENA FOR:

☐ PERSON   ☒ DOCUMENT(S) OR OBJECT(S)

YOU ARE COMMANDED to appear and testify before the Grand Jury of the United States District Court at the place, date, and time specified below.

PLACE	COURTROOM
UNITED STATES DISTRICT COURT **401 Courthouse Square** **Alexandria, Virginia 22314**	**GRAND JURY ROOM**
	DATE AND TIME **January 27, 1998** **9:30 A.M.**

YOU ARE ALSO COMMANDED to bring with you the following document(s) or object(s):*

    See attached rider.

☐ Please see additional information on reverse

This subpoena shall remain in effect until you are granted leave to depart by the court or by an officer acting on behalf of the court.

CLERK	DATE
NORMAN H. MEYER, JR., CLERK OF THE COURT (By) Deputy Clerk	**January 20, 1998** (V002)

This subpoena is issued on application of the United States of America	NAME, ADDRESS and PHONE NUMBER OF ASSISTANT U.S. ATTORNEY
OFFICE OF THE INDEPENDENT COUNSEL KENNETH W. STARR	Kenneth W. Starr by D Co B Office of the Independent Counsel 1001 Pennsylvania Ave, NW, Suite 490-N Washington, D.C. 20004 (202) 514-8688

Subpoena V002

To: William Jefferson Clinton

SUBPOENA RIDER

A. Produce all documents and things referring or relating to Monica Lewinsky. These documents and things should include, but not be limited to, the following:

1. any and all gifts, presents, or things to or from Monica Lewinsky (directly or indirectly), including, but not limited to, any tie, mug, paperweight, book, or other article;

2. any and all cards, letters, notes, or other correspondence to or from Monica Lewinsky;

3. any and all photographs, videotapes, audiotapes, voice messages or other recording of or relating or referring to Monica Lewinsky;

4. any and all documents and things containing the handwriting, signature, or other mark of Monica Lewinsky; and

B. Any and all affidavits, depositions, pleadings, memoranda, notes, and other statements, including drafts, referring or relating to Monica Lewinsky or Linda Tripp.

C. Produce any and all diaries, journals, address books, and Rolodexes from January 1, 1995.

D. Produce any and all calendars or daytimers from January 1, 1995.

E. Produce any and all documents referring or relating to Monica Lewinsky's employment or her seeking employment since January 20, 1993. These documents should include, but not be limited to, resumes, correspondence, travel records, telephone records and message slips, applications, evaluations, letters of recommendation, and references.

F. Produce any and all documents referring or relating to McAndrews & Forbes or Revlon, Inc. and their employees, agents, or representatives, including, but not limited to, Vernon Jordan, Ron Perelman, Howard Gittes, and Barry Schwartz.

G. Produce any and all answers to interrogatories, requests for admission, affidavits, declarations, and depositions of William Jefferson Clinton in Jones v. Clinton and Ferguson.

Definitions and Instructions

1. Definitions

a. The term "document" or "documents" as used in this subpoena means all records of any nature whatsoever within your possession, custody or control or the possession, custody or control of any agent, employee, representative (including, without limitation, attorneys, investment advisors, investment bankers, bankers and accountants), or other person acting or purporting to act for or on your behalf or in concert with you, including, but not limited to, draft, pending or executed contracts and/or agreements, sample documents, insurance policies, financial guarantee bonds, letters of credit, communications, correspondence, calendars, day-timers, datebooks, telegrams, facsimiles, telexs, telefaxes, electronic mail, memoranda, records, reports, books, files (computer or paper), summaries or records of personal conversations, meetings or interviews, logs, summaries or records of telephone conversations and/or telefax communications, diaries, forecasts, statistical statements, financial statements (draft or finished), work papers, drafts, copies, bills, records of payments for bills, retainer records, attorney time sheets, telephone bills and records, telefax bills and records, tax returns and return information, employee time sheets, graphs, charts, accounts, analytical records, minutes or records of meetings or conferences, consultants' reports and/or records, appraisals, records, reports or summaries of negotiations, brochures, pamphlets, circulars, maps, plats, trade letters, depositions, statements, interrogatories and answers thereto, pleadings, docket sheets, discovery materials, audit letters, audit reports, materials underlying audits, document productions, transcripts, exhibits, settlement materials, judgments, press releases, notes, marginal notations, invoices, documents regarding collateral or security pledged, settlement statements, checks disbursed or received at settlement, inspection reports, title policies, financial statements and/or federal tax returns submitted by any person in support of any loan application, items related the repayment, if any, of any interest or principal on the loan, items relating to any default on the loan, commission records, evidence of liens, documents relating to filings under the Uniform Commercial Code and/or its equivalent, foreclosure and mortgage documentation, cashiers checks, bank drafts, money orders, bank and brokerage account statements, debit and credit memoranda, wire transfer documentation, opening account cards, signature cards, loan applications, any employment and bank account deposit verification documents, loan histories, loan files, records of loan repayment or any and all efforts to secure repayment, including foreclosure or records of lawsuits, credit references, board resolutions, minutes of meetings of boards of directors, opinion letters, purchases and sales agreements, real estate contracts, brokerage agreements, escrow agreements, loan agreements, offer and acceptance contracts, or any other contracts or agreements, deeds or other evidence of title, escrow accounts and any other escrow documentation, savings account transcripts, savings account deposit slips, savings account withdrawal slips, checks deposited in savings accounts, checking account statements, canceled checks drawn on checking accounts, deposit slips and checks deposited into checking accounts, credit card accounts, debit and credit documentation, safe deposit records, currency transaction reports (IRS Forms 4789), photographs, brochures, lists, journals, advertising, computer tapes and cards, audio and video tapes, computerized records stored in the form of magnetic or electronic coding on computer media or on media capable of being read by computer or with the aid of computer related equipment, including but not limited to floppy disks or diskettes, disks, diskettes, disk packs, fixed hard drives, removable hard disk cartridges, mainframe computers, Bernoulli boxes, optical disks, WORM disks, magneto/optical disks, floptical disks, magnetic tape, tapes, laser disks, video cassettes, CD-ROMs and any other media capable of storing magnetic coding, microfilm, microfiche and other storage devices, voicemail recordings and all other written, printed or recorded or photographic matter or sound reproductions, however produced or reproduced.

The term "document" or "documents" also includes any earlier, preliminary, preparatory or tentative version of all or part of a document, whether or not such draft was superseded by a later draft and whether or not the terms of the draft are the same as or different from the terms of the final document.

b. The term "communication" or "communications" is used herein in its broadest sense to encompass any transmission or exchange of information, ideas, facts, data, proposals, or any other matter, whether between individuals or between or among the members of a group, whether face-to-face, by telephone or by means of electronic or other medium.

c. "Possession, custody or control" means in your physical possession and/or if you have the right to secure or compile the production of the document or a copy from another person or entity having physical possession, including, but not limited to, your counsel.

d. The term "referring or relating" to any given subject means anything that constitutes, contains, embodies, reflects, identifies, states, refers to, deals with, or is in any manner whatsoever pertinent to that subject including, but not limited to, documents concerning the preparation of other documents.

e. The term "you" means yourself, any person or agent acting on your behalf or at your suggestion or direction, and any of your companies, partnerships and business entities with which you have been affiliated and any employees, partners, associates or members of any firm with which you have been affiliated.

2. Instructions

a. The originals of all documents and communications must be produced, as well as copies within your possession, custody, or control.

b. If any original document cannot be produced in full, produce such document to the extent possible and indicate specifically the reason for your inability to produce the remainder.

c. Documents shall be produced as they are kept in the usual course of business, as organized in the files.

d. File folders, labels, and indices identifying documents called for shall be produced intact with such documents. Documents attached to each other should not be separated.

e. In reading this rider, the plural shall include the singular and the singular shall include the plural.

f. The words "and" and "or" shall be construed conjunctively or disjunctively as necessary to make the request inclusive rather than exclusive. The use of the word "including" shall be construed without limitation.

g. In the event that any document, or portion thereof, called for by this subpoena is withheld on the basis of any claim of privilege or similar claim, that document shall be identified in writing as follows: (a) author; (b) the position or title of the author; (c) addressee; (d) the position or title of the addressee; (e) any indicated or blind copies; (f) date; (g) a description of the subject matter of the document; (h) number of pages; (i) attachments or appendices; (j) all persons to whom the document, its contents, or any portion thereof, has been disclosed, distributed, shown, or explained; and (k) present custodian. Each basis you contend justifies the withholding of the document shall also be specified. With respect to those documents or records as to which you may claim privilege, or attorneys' work product, set forth as to each such document the basis for such claim, including the purpose and circumstances surrounding the creation of the document, the identity of each person who has been privy to such communication reflected in the document, the identity of any person or entity instructing the subpoena recipient or the attorney of the subpoena recipient to withhold production of the document, and whether you will submit the document to the Court for an in camera determination as to the validity of the claim. If the existence of a joint defense agreement or any agreement as to common interest is relevant to the assertion of any claim of privilege or similar claim, please provide a copy of that agreement; if any such agreement is not in writing, please set forth the date of the creation of the agreement, the identities of all parties to the agreement and the specific individuals who entered into the agreement on behalf of those parties, and the objects, purposes, and scope of the agreement.

h. In the event that any document called for by this subpoena has been lost, destroyed, deleted, altered, or otherwise disposed of, that document shall be identified in writing as follows: (a) author; (b) the position or title of the author; (c) addressee; (d) the position or title of the addressee; (e) indicated or blind copies; (f) date; (g) a brief description of the subject matter of the document; (h) number of pages; (i) attachments or appendices; (j) all persons to whom the document, its contents, or any portion thereof, had been disclosed, distributed, shown or explained; (k) the date of the loss, destruction, deletion, alteration, or disposal and the circumstances thereof; and (l) the reasons, if any, for the loss, destruction, deletion, alteration, or disposal and the person or persons responsible.

i. If any information or data is withheld because such information or data is stored electronically, it is to be identified by the subject matter of the information or data and the place or places where such information is maintained.

CONFIDENTIAL
PRODUCED PURSUANT TO SECRECY PROVISIONS
    OF RULE 6 (e), F. R. CRIM. P.
GRAND JURY MATERIAL

January 27, 1998

Robert J. Bittman, Esq.
Deputy Independent Counsel
Office of the Independent Counsel
1001 Pennsylvania Avenue, N.W.
Suite 490-North
Washington, D.C. 20004

V002-DC-00000001
By Hand

Dear Bob:

   Pursuant to our telephone conversation yesterday, I am transmitting to you herewith one book, which is responsive to "William Jefferson Clinton Grand Jury Subpoena –V002." I accepted service of this subpoena, and it was FAXed to me at 5:15 p.m., Wednesday, January 21.

   This subpoena duces tecum was returnable today, and yesterday you afforded me a one week extension, but requested that whatever I had located thus far be produced today. I told you that I believed I had located two books which were responsive, but I am now not certain that one is and I am unable to do the appropriate checking in the time available. However, I am enclosing a soft-cover 54-page book, whose cover bears the Bates number DEK227870. You also requested documents responsive to Paragraph G of the subpoena:

   "any and all answers to interrogatories, requests for admission, affidavits, declarations, and depositions of William Jefferson Clinton in Jones v. Clinton and Ferguson."

As I told you, Mr. Bennett, and not I, is handling that case. Mr. Bennett informs me that the materials requested in Paragraph G are covered by a stringent Protective Order entered by Judge Wright with the consent of all parties to that case. Because of recent publicity and prejudicial leaks from numerous sources of material ostensibly covered by the Protective Order, Paragraph G of your subpoena raises serious concerns which we believe should be addressed by the Court. I am taking the liberty of sending Judge Wright a copy of this letter. I understand that the parties in the Jones case

505

have a weekly telephonic status conference every Thursday with the Judge, and it seems to me appropriate to place this matter before the Court at that time.

Although the materials today are physically being delivered to you instead of the grand jury, they are still being produced pursuant to grand jury subpoena and are fully covered by the secrecy provisions of the Federal Rules of Criminal Procedure.

Sincerely,

David E. Kendall

cc: Hon. Susan Webber Wright (by FAX)
Robert S. Bennett, Esq. (by FAX)
Enclosure

LAW OFFICES
WILLIAMS & CONNOLLY
725 TWELFTH STREET, N.W.
WASHINGTON, D.C. 20005-5901
(202) 434-5000
FAX (202) 434-5029

DAVID E. KENDALL   EDWARD BENNETT WILLIAMS (1920-1988)
(202) 434-5145   PAUL R. CONNOLLY (1922-1978)

CONFIDENTIAL
PRODUCED PURSUANT TO SECRECY PROVISIONS
      OF RULE 6 (e), F. R. CRIM. P.
GRAND JURY MATERIAL

February 2, 1998

Robert J. Bittman, Esq.
Deputy Independent Counsel
Office of the Independent Counsel
1001 Pennsylvania Avenue, N.W.
Suite 490-North
Washington, D.C. 20004

By Hand

Dear Bob:

Pursuant to Paragraph G of the subpoena to "William Jefferson Clinton Grand Jury Subpoena –V002," and Judge Wright's ruling (as I understand it) at the conference call on January 27 I am producing herewith a copy of the President's deposition transcript we have received, with attached exhibits, taken on Saturday, January 17, 1998, in the Jones case. This document bears Bates numbers DEK228021 to DEK228326.

I am also transmitting to you herewith an additional page from President Clinton's Supplemental Responses to Plaintiff's Second Set of Interrogatories (bearing Bates number DEK227917A) which was inadvertently not transmitted to you in my production of January 28, 1998.

Although the materials today are physically being delivered to you instead of the grand jury, they are still being produced pursuant to grand jury subpoena and are fully covered by the secrecy provisions of the Federal Rules of Criminal Procedure.

Sincerely,

David E. Kendall

Enclosures
DEK/bb

V002-DC-00000160

Office of the Independent Counsel
1001 Pennsylvania Avenue, N.W.
Suite 490-North
Washington, D.C. 20004
(202) 514-8688
Fax (202) 514-8802

February 2, 1998

HAND DELIVERED

David E. Kendall, Esq.
Williams & Connolly
725 Twelfth Street, N.W.
Washington, D.C. 20005

Re: William Jefferson Clinton

Dear David:

As you know, President Clinton has publicly pledged to cooperate fully with the investigation involving Monica Lewinsky. Last Wednesday, January 28, I invited President Clinton, on behalf of the grand jury, to testify before the grand jury this Thursday, February 5, concerning matters relating to Ms. Lewinsky. You indicated in our conversation that you would get back to me as to whether the President will so testify. The grand jury awaits the President's decision; please advise me as soon as possible what the President decides.

Sincerely,

Robert J. Bittman
Deputy Independent Counsel

Office of the Independent Counsel
1001 Pennsylvania Avenue, N.W.
Suite 490-North
Washington, D.C. 20004
(202) 514-8688
Fax (202) 514-8802

February 4, 1998

<u>HAND DELIVERED</u>

David E. Kendall, Esq.
Williams & Connolly
725 Twelfth Street, N.W.
Washington, D.C. 20005

Re: <u>William Jefferson Clinton</u>
Dear David:

Although the President has declined the invitation to testify before the grand jury tomorrow, the grand jury's investigation continues apace. On behalf of the grand jury and in an effort to accommodate the President's schedule, we respectfully invite the President to testify before the grand jury next Tuesday, Wednesday, or Thursday, February 10 to 12.

The grand jury would like to complete this investigation, as the President stated, "sooner rather than later. . . . [and] as quickly as we can." Kindly advise me by noon this Friday as to whether the President accepts the invitation to testify.

Sincerely,

Robert J. Bittman
Deputy Independent Counsel

509

LAW OFFICES
WILLIAMS & CONNOLLY
725 TWELFTH STREET, N.W.
WASHINGTON, D.C. 20005-5901
(202) 434-5000
FAX (202) 434-5029

DAVID E. KENDALL
(202)434-5145

EDWARD BENNETT WILLIAMS (1920-1988)
PAUL R. CONNOLLY (1922-1978)

<u>CONFIDENTIAL</u>
<u>PRODUCED PURSUANT TO SECRECY PROVISIONS</u>
<u>OF RULE 6 (e), F. R. CRIM. P.</u>
<u>GRAND JURY MATERIAL</u>

February 3, 1998

Robert J. Bittman, Esq.
Deputy Independent Counsel
Office of the Independent Counsel
1001 Pennsylvania Avenue, N.W.
Suite 490-North
Washington, D.C. 20004

V002-DC-00000469
<u>By Hand</u>

Dear Bob:

Pursuant to the subpoena to "William Jefferson Clinton Grand Jury Subpoena –V002," and our telephone conversation on January 26, 1998, affording me an additional week to respond, I am herewith producing four items which we believe may be responsive, Bates-numbered as follows: one book, <u>The Presidents of the United States</u> (Bates number DEK228327, affixed to the inside front cover), one Louis Feraud tie (Bates number DEK228328, affixed to the back), one "Santa Monica" coffee mug (Bates number DEK228329 affixed to the bottom), and one metal cigarette holder case (Bates number DEK228330, affixed to the side).

Although the materials today are physically being delivered to you instead of the grand jury, they are still being produced pursuant to grand jury subpoena and are fully covered by the secrecy provisions of the Federal Rules of Criminal Procedure.

Sincerely,

David E. Kendall

Enclosures
DEK/bb

V002-DC-00000470

Office of the Independent Counsel
1001 Pennsylvania Avenue, N.W.
Suite 490-North
Washington, D.C. 20004
(202) 514-8688
Fax (202) 514-8802

February 4, 1998

The Honorable Charles F.C. Ruff
Counsel to the President
The White House
Washington, D.C. 20500

Dear Mr. Ruff:

I write in response to your visit of yesterday concerning the sensitive matter of Executive privilege. As you know, at the request of the Attorney General, the Special Division recently conferred jurisdiction on this Office to investigate whether "Monica Lewinsky or others" suborned perjury, obstructed justice, or committed other federal crimes. We understand from your discussion that certain witnesses employed by the White House may invoke Executive privilege in response to questions posed by the grand jury in its continuing investigation of that matter. After careful consideration of your comments, including consultation with our Ethics Counselor Samuel Dash, we believe strongly that the grand jury is entitled to inquire into discussions of senior White House staff members, both among themselves and with the President, concerning the Monica Lewinsky matter.

As we understand your comments, there are two principal areas of testimony where the White House may invoke Executive privilege. The first includes discussions, to which the President was not a party, among what you have described as "senior staff." The discussions at issue occurred after the Lewinsky matter became public last month. You indicated that these discussions may have encompassed such topics as how to respond publicly to the news, what political strategies to adopt, and how to advise the President concerning these matters. We further understood you to say that the White House did not expect to assert Executive privilege with respect to whatever factual information, if any, was discussed among the staff.

The second area involves communications between members of the White House staff and the President himself that took place after the public revelations concerning our new jurisdiction. We did not understand you to take a firm position on the question whether the President would assert Executive privilege with respect to his own communications with advisors on this subject.

As a threshold matter, we believe there is serious doubt whether communications of senior staff and the President concerning the Lewinsky matter fall within the scope of Executive privilege. When the Supreme Court recognized a "presumptive privilege for Presidential

511

communications," <u>United States v. Nixon</u>, 418 U.S. 683, 707 (1974), it explained that the privilege attached to communications in the exercise of the President's Article II powers. <u>Id</u> at 705. The privilege is limited to communications "in performance of the President's responsibilities," <u>id</u> at 711, "of his office," <u>id</u> at 713, and "made in the process of shaping policies and making decisions." <u>Id</u> at 708 (quoted in <u>Nixon v. Administrator of General Services</u>, 433 U.S. 425, 449 (1977)).

The actions of the President and the White House in response to the Lewinsky matter do not, as we see it, carry out a constitutional duty of the President. Monica Lewinsky was a prospective witness in civil litigation in which the President is a private party. In more recent days, this Office has been charged by the Attorney General and the Special Division with responsibility to conduct a criminal investigation of "Ms. Lewinsky and others." These matters concern the President in his personal capacity. They do not involve the President's execution of the laws. Accordingly, we doubt that presidential and senior staff communications on these matters are entitled to a presumptive Executive privilege.

In any event, assuming the presumptive applicability of an Executive privilege, we are confident that many communications among White House staff and/or the President constitute important evidence in the grand jury's investigation that is not reasonably available elsewhere. <u>See In re Sealed Case</u>, 121 F.3d 729, 753 (D.C. Cir. 1997). The President's own statements are of critical importance to the grand jury's investigation. His statements to advisors represent highly relevant information not available from any other source. Particularly given the President's refusal to make public statements concerning the Lewinsky matter, and his recent decision to decline our invitation to appear before the grand jury, there is no alternative source that even approaches a substitute for direct evidence of the President's statements.

Similarly, the statements of senior White House staff will in many instances be important to the grand jury's investigation. For example, just as factual information in the possession of presidential advisers may reveal the nature of the President's deliberations, <u>see In re Sealed Case</u>, 121 F.3d at 750-51, so too may the discovery of deliberations among the White House staff concerning strategy give the grand jury unique insight to the factual premises on which the President and his staff are operating. Where the grand jury's investigation focuses on not merely "an immediate White House advisor," <u>id</u>. at 755, but on conduct of the President himself, we believe the courts will recognize that evidence of senior staff communications will be "particularly useful" to the grand jury. <u>Id.</u>

If the President ultimately does assert Executive privilege with respect to any evidence sought by the grand jury, then we expect that the district court will be required to determine whether the President's claim of privilege should be upheld under the circumstances. We agree with your suggestion that a log of conversations among senior staff, including a list of participants and a specific, generic description of the subject matter, may facilitate the process of resolving any such disputes. If you are in a position to provide such a log in fairly short order, then we would consider whether the log is sufficient from our point of view to frame the issues properly for decision by the Court.

If you believe that further discussions of these matters would be helpful, we would be pleased to visit with you again at your convenience.

Sincerely,

Kenneth W. Starr
Independent Counsel

THE WHITE HOUSE
WASHINGTON
February 5, 1998

BY FACSIMILE

Kenneth W. Starr, Esq.
Independent Counsel
Suite 400 North
1001 Pennsylvania Ave., NW
Washington, D.C. 20004

Dear Mr. Starr:

This is in response to your letter of February 4, 1998.

First, I want to inform you that within 45 minutes of its delivery, James Bennet of the New York Times called the White House Press Office to ask whether I had received a letter from you concerning executive privilege. Since there could have been only a few persons on your staff who were aware of the letter's delivery, I ask that you immediately request that the FBI, using agents not affiliated with your office, investigate to determine who disclosed the existence of the letter and its substance (as well as, presumably, the fact and substance of our meeting) to the press. I and the three members of my staff who were aware of the letter before Bennet's call will be happy to be interviewed (under oath) in connection with any such investigation.

Let me move now to the substance of your letter.

As you will not be surprised to learn, I disagree with your position on the applicability of executive privilege to discussions among senior White House staff and between senior staff and the President concerning the

Lewinsky matter. In particular, I disagree with your contention that, under In re Sealed Case or any other authority, the grand jury would be permitted to inquire into the substance of deliberations among the President's most senior advisors in order to determine on what factual predicate those deliberations were based. Such an argument would swallow up the entire premise of the court's decision. Indeed, your argument, if followed to its logical conclusion, would mean that the President would be barred from seeking the advice of those responsible for assisting him in carrying out his constitutional responsibilities because every conversation would be the subject of grand jury inquiry.

To the extent that you rely on the fact that the President's counsel has declined your invitation to appear before the grand jury, I find it curious that your office would issue an invitation to the President to appear on a date less than a week hence—when it is a matter of public knowledge that he is to begin a state visit by the Prime Minister of Great Britain and when, as you are also fully aware, the United States is confronting a major international crisis—and the argue that the President's declining of that invitation justifies intrusion into his discussions with his advisors. Nor can the President's decision not to comment on the Lewinsky matter—other than to deny that he had sexual relations with Ms. Lewinsky and that he ever asked her to lie—justify such an intrusion.

Let me also clarify three points I made in our meeting. First, discussions among and between the President's senior staff involve the very capacity of the President and his staff to govern—to pursue his legislative agenda, to ensure the continued leadership of he United States in the world community, and to maintain the confidence and support of the people who elected him—all of which lie at the heart of his role under Article II of the Constitution. Second, as to what position the President himself might take on the assertion of executive privilege as to his communications if he were to be questioned, I did not purport to take any position—"firm" or otherwise. And third, I indicated that, in deciding whether to assert privilege, we have historically sought to distinguish the substance of advisory and deliberative discussions from segregable facts, not available elsewhere, that may be contained in otherwise privileged communications.

Finally, I remain willing to explore all avenues for resolving our disagreement, although I admit to being more than a little uncertain as to how to conduct discussions without reading about them simultaneously in the press. I am also uncertain about your office's current position with respect to the questioning of senior staff members before the grand jury. Although we had initially been informed that your office did not intend to inquire into the substance of any staff discussions or communications with the President, but rather only to identify the circumstances (date, attendees, general subject matter, etc.) of such discussions in order to establish an appropriate record, we have now been advised that you do intend to pursue such inquiries. We had also been informed that witnesses were not to be questioned concerning communications with White House counsel, but we now understand that you do not intend to follow that practice where there is more than one non-lawyer present—a rule that I must say seems to have no rational basis.

If we can come to some preliminary agreement as to the protocol that will be followed in connection with Mr. Podesta's appearance and that of other senior staff, it may be that there remains some prospect for addressing both your interests and our very serious concerns. If you believe that further discussions would be fruitful, please call me.

Sincerely,

Charles F.C. Ruff
Counsel to the President

Office of the Independent Counsel
1001 Pennsylvania Avenue, N.W.
Suite 490-North
Washington, D.C. 20004
(202) 514-8688
Fax (202) 514-8807

February 6, 1998

The Honorable Charles F. C. Ruff
Counsel to the President
The White House
Washington, D.C. 20500

Dear Mr. Ruff:

I write in response to your February 5 letter.

Let me reiterate the scope of our inquiry: We do not intend to question senior staff about deliberative matters beyond the jurisdictional grant recently crafted by the Attorney General and the Special Division. We do not seek information about discussions that relate solely to the President's foreign policy or his legislative agenda. We do not seek information about military or diplomatic secrets. We <u>do</u> intend to ask about discussions concerning an alleged relationship between Monica Lewinsky and the President, acting in his private capacity.

As to your contention that such discussions fall under Executive privilege, we must respectfully disagree. We believe that the President's relationship with Ms. Lewinsky, and the President's response to a private, civil lawsuit or a criminal investigation, fall outside the scope of his Article II duties. Executive privilege, as a threshold matter, thus appears to us inapplicable.

515

Even if the privilege did attach, we believe we would satisfy the test set forth in United States v. Nixon. The grand jury is investigating the conduct of Ms. Lewinsky and others with respect to a civil lawsuit against the President in his private capacity. This Office was given responsibility over that investigation after the Attorney General's representative, under exigent circumstances, made an extraordinary oral submission to the Special Division. The grand jury's need for information to resolve this matter in a timely fashion could hardly be more compelling.

In your letter, you suggest that our invitation to appear before the grand jury provided the President with insufficient notice. We fully recognize that the President, in the discharge of his constitutional duties, may have valid scheduling reasons for declining a first invitation to the grand jury. We simply noted the President's response as a partial explanation for why the grand jury needs evidence of his statements from other sources.

Under the circumstances, we do not believe that Executive privilege allows the withholding of important, relevant information that the grand jury needs to complete its inquiry. We cannot agree with you that when senior staff discuss how to handle allegations of the President's private misconduct, they are aiding the President in the performance of his constitutional duties—which is the only basis for asserting Executive privilege. Your expansive view of the privilege, it seems to us, could equally cover the communications at issue in Nixon.

You express uncertainty about our position with respect to questioning senior staff members before the grand jury. We will be specific: We intend to inquire into the substance of staff discussions and communications with the President concerning Ms. Lewinsky and related matters. If the witness asserts Executive privilege in the grand jury, we will limit our questioning to those matters necessary to establish an appropriate record for the district court (e.g., whether the communication was for the purpose of advising the President, the official government matter to which the communication relates, date, attendees, etc.). If there is no assertion of privilege, then we will proceed with questions.

You also raise the issue of communications between witnesses and White House Counsel. We hereby notify you that in light of In re Grand Jury Subpoena Duces Tecum, 112 F.3d 910 (8th Cir. 1997), we intend to question witnesses as to the substance of such communications. If a witness asserts attorney-client privilege, we will take such further steps as are appropriate.

Finally, you suggest that someone in this Office disclosed details of our conversations and correspondence to the New York Times. On several occasions in recent weeks, we have been falsely accused of such disclosures. In this particular instance, reporters had been questioning the White House Press Secretary about Executive privilege since January 22; the Wall Street Journal had reported on January 29 that the White House was preparing to assert the privilege (indeed, this was our first notice of your plans); we took extensive steps to arrange for your confidential visit to our offices; subsequent media information plainly came from the White House (e.g., the Associated Press reported on February 5 that "individuals familiar with the letter" said that "Starr's letter left the White House convinced there was no more room for goodwill negotiating"); and the reporter who asked you about our letter covers the White House, not the Office of the Independent Counsel. Under the circumstances, we respectfully suggest that your suspicions are misdirected.

If we can provide further information that may help forestall or resolve any disputes, please let me know.

Yours sincerely,

KENNETH W. STARR
Independent Counsel

Office of the Independent Counsel
1001 Pennsylvania Avenue, N.W.
Suite 490-North
Washington, D.C. 20004
(202) 514-8688
Fax (202) 514-8802

February 9, 1998

<u>HAND DELIVERED</u>

David E. Kendall, Esq.
Williams & Connolly
725 Twelfth Street, N.W.
Washington, D.C. 20005

Re: <u>William Jefferson Clinton</u>

Dear David:

Last Wednesday, we, on behalf of the grand jury, extended a second invitation to the President to testify before the grand jury about his relationship with Monica Lewinsky. You did not respond to the invitation by last Friday, as requested in my letter. The grand jury's work continues. Notwithstanding your failure to respond, the grand jury would be pleased to accommodate the President's testimony any day or time this week.

Let me make our request specific and clear: the grand jury deserves to know whether the President will respond, favorably, to the invitation. Such an invitation is, of course, fully consistent with our profound respect for the Presidency in our system of separated powers. To that end, we have consulted with the Chief Judge, and she has assured us that the grand jury can accommodate the President's scheduling needs should the President choose to tell his story to the grand jury.

For planning purposes, kindly let me know if the President wishes to testify before the grand jury this week. If the President cannot appear this week, please let me know by Friday, February 13, whether the President wishes to testify before the grand jury, and if so, when. If I do not hear from you by that date, we will assume that the President will not voluntarily provide testimony before the grand jury. In that event, we will inform the grand jury of this turn of events.

Sincerely,

Robert J. Bittman
Deputy Independent Counsel

518

LAW OFFICES
WILLIAMS & CONNOLLY
725 TWELFTH STREET, N.W.
WASHINGTON, D.C. 20005-5901
(202) 434-5000
FAX (202) 434-5029

DAVID E. KENDALL
(202)434-5145

EDWARD BENNETT WILLIAMS (1920-1988)
PAUL R. CONNOLLY (1922-1978)

February 13, 1998

CONFIDENTIAL
RULE 6 (e), F. R. CRIM. P. GRAND JURY SUBMISSION

By Hand

Robert J. Bittman, Esq.
Deputy Independent Counsel
Office of the Independent Counsel
1001 Pennsylvania Avenue, N.W.
Suite 490-North
Washington, D. C. 20004

Dear Bob:

This will respond to your letters dated February 4 and 9, 1998. I was unable to respond to your February 4 invitation by the Friday deadline you had indicated in your letter because I was in the process of dealing with prejudicial and false leaks of information about your investigation. I set forth my position on that matter in brief public remarks Friday afternoon and in a 15 page letter to Judge Starr which I hand-delivered to your office that same afternoon. These leaks are highly unfair and prejudicial to the President and others, and, as you may know, on Monday I filed a sealed motion with the Chief Judge seeking judicial remedies in an effort to enforce the secrecy and confidentiality of the investigative process.

I acknowledge your invitation for the President to appear before the grand jury next week. The President has the greatest respect for the grand jury. However, under the circumstances, it is impossible to accept this invitation. The situation in Iraq continues to be dangerously volatile, and this had demanded much of the President's time and attention. The President also has a heavy travel schedule at present. Our access to him has necessarily been limited. Moreover, as I informed you during our February 3 telephone conversation concerning this matter, we have simply had inadequate opportunity to prepare so that we may give our client the informed advice of counsel which he, like every other citizen, deserves. Your recent letter references your office's "profound respect for the Presidency in our system of separated powers." However, I am certain that you understand why, in light of the well-publicized and questionable

519

investigative techniques of your office, we feel we would be derelict in our professional duty to a client unless we assured ourselves that we had adequate opportunity to advise that client appropriately.

In the event you decide to "inform the grand jury of this turn of events", as stated in your letter, I would respectflly request that you also read my letter to the grand jury and make my letter part of the grand jury record.

I thank you for your courtesy.

Sincerely,

David E. Kendall

LAW OFFICES
WILLIAMS & CONNOLLY
725 TWELFTH STREET, N.W.
WASHINGTON, D.C. 20005-5901
(202) 434-5000
FAX (202) 434-5029

DAVID E. KENDALL
(202)434-5145

EDWARD BENNETT WILLIAMS (1920-1988)
PAUL R. CONNOLLY (1922-1978)

February 17, 1998

The Honorable Kenneth W. Starr

BY HAND

Independent Counsel
Office of the Independent Counsel
1001 Pennsylvania Avenue, N.W.
Suite 490-North
Washington, D.C. 20004

Dear Judge Starr:

I write with an inquiry in the wake of a Chicago Tribune article which appeared on February 11 (copy enclosed), and I am making this request in an effort to obtain accurate information so that I may decide how to proceed. The article reports that one of your partners in Kirkland & Ellis, Mr. Richard Porter, may have provided legal advice and services to plaintiff Paula Corbin Jones in her civil suit against President Clinton. The aritcle also reports that someone at the law firm FAXed a copy of a draft affidavit in the Jones case to the Tribune prior to the affidavit's filing in court, an action which would, if true, suggest that the firm has indeed been involved in the legal prosecution of the Jones case. Finally, the article reports that one of the Jones lawyers, Joseph Cammarata, received advice from Mr. Porter on several occasions about legal issues in the Jones case. This recent report is particularly surprising in view of previous news articles in which your partners at Kirkland & Ellis were quoted as saying that the firm would not become involved in the Jones case ("'We don't feel it's appropriate for the firm to be involved in any civil litigation directly involving the president,' (Kirkland & Ellis partner) Jay Lefkowitz (said:." The Washington Post, Aug. 12, 1994). (Copy enclosed).

Additionally, there have been reports of your own participation in legal discussions with Ms. Jones' lawyers, prior to the time you were appointed Independent Counsel.

I emphasize that I am not now addressing the fact that you planned to file an amicus brief for the Independent Women's Forum after the Jones complaint was filed, something that has been previously reported. See, e.c., "Friend of Court Is Foe of Clinton," Washington Times, June 8, 1994, at 1A.

Instead, my present inquiry focuses on recent reports that you gave legal advice to Ms. Jones' lawyers pertaining to her own lawsuit against the President. For example, the Associated Press reported on January 28, 1998, that you gave legal advice to Ms. Jones' lawyers "on 'the legal question of whether the president is accountable in a private lawsuit,' according to Gilbert K. Davis, who no longer represents Mrs. Jones." (Copy enclosed.) On January 30, 1998, the Associated Press reported that Ms. Jones' lawyers "acknowledge consulting with Starr after filing the lawsuit, but said that was only to seek advice from the constitutional scholar on how to address Clinton's claim that he was temporarily immune from lawsuits . . . . The lawyers said they contacted Starr . . . before he was named Whitewater prosecutor." (Copy enclosed.) That same day, The Washington Post reported that "Jones's former lawyers now . . . say that Starr even consulted with them in two or three telephone calls that dealt with the legal arguments to be made against Clinton's immunity claim." (Copy enclosed.)

You apparently believed that, even before the recent expansion of your jurisdiction, you were somehow entitled to investigate the Paula Corbin Jones matter. It was reported last summer, before the January 16, 1998, expansion of your jurisdiction, that your investigation was focusing in some way on Ms. Paula Corbin Jones. For example, The Washington Post reported the following on June 25, 1997:

"The [Arkansas state] troopers said investigators asked about 12 to 15 women by name, including Paula Corbin Jones, a former Arkansas state employee who has filed a civil lawsuit against Clinton alleging he sexually harassed her in 1991.

In addition, [Roger Perry] said, 'They [your investigators] asked me about Paula Jones, all kinds of questions about Paula Jones, whether I saw Clinton and Paula together and how many times.'"

(Copy enclosed.)

I would be grateful if you could inform me whether any of these many news reports are accurate, and I would also request that, if any of the above reports are accurate, you inform me whether such information was presented to the Attorney General or the Special Division prior to the Court's January 16, 1998, expansion of your jurisdiction. As I know you will recall, the Special Division has been quite sensitive to the appearance of conflict. In its August 5, 1994, Order appointing you, that Court stated that it had determined that a continuation of Mr. Fiske's appointment "would not be consistent with the purposes of the Act:"

"This reflects no conclusion on the part of the Court that Fiske lacks either the actual independence or any other attribute necessary to the conclusion of the investigation. Rather, the Court reaches this conclusion because the Act contemplated an apparent as well as an actual independence on the part of the Counsel. As the Senate Report accompanying the 1982 enactments reflected, '[t]he intent of the special prosecutor provisions is not to impugn the integrity of the Attorney General or the Department of Justice. Throughout our system of justice, safeguards exist against actual or perceived conflicts of interest without reflecting adversely on the parties who are subject to conflicts.' S. Rep. No. 496, 97th Cong., 2d Sess. at 6 (1982) (emphasis added). Just so here. It is not our intent to impugn the integrity of the Attorney General's appointee, but rather to reflect the intent of the Act that the actor be protected against perceptions of conflict."

(Second emphasis added.)

In addition, the Independent Counsel Statute imposes certain restrictions on both the person appointed as IC and that person's law firm. For example, 28 U.S.C. § 594(j) (1) (A) provides that "[d]uring the period in which an independent counsel is serving under this chapter (i) such independent counsel, and (ii) any person associated with a firm with which such independent counsel is associated, may not represent in any matter any person involved in any investigation or prosecution under this chapter." Moreover, under elementary principles of partnership law in Illinois, Arkansas, and the District of Columbia, a legal representation of a client by one partner is attributable to all other partners.

Application of these legal standards to the facts set forth in the recent news articles quoted above raises serious and troubling questions about the propriety of your serving as Independent Counsel to investigate matters pertaining to the Jones case. You have in the past investigated the Jones matter, according to The Washington Post. The recent expansion of your jurisdiction explicitly requires you to investigate events "concerning the civil case <u>Jones v. Clinton.</u>" You have, since your appointment as Independent Counsel, remained an active partner in the Kirkland & Ellis law firm, as was your right. The partnership includes Mr. Porter.

I hope you can therefore perceive why I am requesting accurate and specific information (i) concerning your own, Mr. Porter's, and any other Kirkland & Ellis lawyer's, employee's or agent's contacts with and assistance to Ms. Paula Corbin Jones and/or her attorneys or agents or supporting groups, and (ii) concerning what was conveyed to the Attorney General and the Special Division in January, 1998, about any such contacts and assistance, when you sought an expansion of your jurisdiction to encompass the <u>Jones v. Clinton</u> case.

I thank you for your courtesy.

Sincerely,

David E. Kendall

Office of the Independent Counsel
1001 Pennsylvania Avenue, N.W.
Suite 490-North
Washington, DC 20004
(202) 514-8688
Fax (202) 514-8802

February 21, 1998

<u>VIA FACSIMILE</u>

David E. Kendall, Esq.
Williams & Connolly
725 Twelfth Street, N.W.
Washington, D.C. 20005

Re: <u>William Jefferson Clinton</u>

Dear David:

We regret the President's decision not to appear before the grand jury at this time. In light of the President's past and continuing pledges to cooperate with this investigation, we again invite the President to testify before the grand jury about his relationship with Monica Lewinsky. We make this invitation fully sensitive to the important duties and responsibilities of the President. Moreover, as stated in my last letter, I have discussed this matter with Chief Judge Johnson, and she has indicated that the grand jury will accommodate any special scheduling needs of the President. We are ready to hear the President's testimony. Kindly let me know by Friday, February 27, whether the President will agree to testify before the grand jury at any time.

Sincerely,

Robert J. Bittman
Deputy Independent Counsel

Office of the Independent Counsel
1001 Pennsylvania Avenue, N.W.
Suite 490-North
Washington, DC 20004
(202) 514-8688
Fax (202) 514-8802

March 2, 1998

HAND DELIVERED

David E. Kendall, Esq.
Williams & Connolly
725 Twelfth Street, N.W.
Washington, D.C. 20005

Re: William Jefferson Clinton

Dear David:

Based on your previous declinations and your failure to respond within the time outlined in my letter of February 21, 1998, we assume that the President has declined our invitation to testify before the grand jury. With this letter, we again invite the President to provide the grand jury with information concerning its ongoing investigation.

In regard to the various explanations you have been kind enough to advance for declining our four invitations, I note that (1) the state visit of Prime Minister Blair has passed; (2) the "situation in Iraq" has, thankfully, eased; and (3) you have now had some six weeks to "prepare" the President. See letters to Robert J. Bittman from David E. Kendall dated February 4 and February 13. We fully acknowledge that the President has immense and weighty responsibilities. We want in every way to take fully into account those grave duties of state. Yet since this matter arose, the President has—with all respect—found time to play golf, attend basketball games and political fundraisers, and enjoy a ski vacation. We assure you

524

that the grand jury's inquiry of the President will not take long, and we and the grand jury remain—as we have always been—eager to accommodate the President's schedule.

Kindly advise me by noon Wednesday, March 4, 1998, whether the President will accept this invitation. If I do not hear from you by that time, I will assume the President declines the invitation. I look forward to your early—and, I hope favorable—reply.

Sincerely,

Robert J. Bittman
Deputy Independent Counsel

HOWREY & SIMON

March 2, 1998

<u>VIA HAND DELIVERY</u>

Kenneth W. Starr, Esq.
Independent Counsel
Office of the Independent Counsel
1001 Pennsylvania Avenue, N.W.
Suite 490 North
Washington, DC 20004

Dear Mr. Starr:

I represent the Office of the President of the United States in connection with any litigation impacting that Office arising out of your current Grand Jury investigations. This representation extends to potential litigation over the applicability and extent of privileges.

Before you initiate litigation, the White House requests that we be consulted about whether an accommodation is reachable between the President's interest in confidentiality and whatever need the Grand Jury may have for the testimony.

Because these matters involve clashes between branches of government, the usual practice has been for the respective parties to attempt to reconcile their differences and accommodate the needs of the other party to the extent possible.

That was certainly the course that we followed in the Espy litigation. We released to the Espy Independent Counsel documents for which the Independent Counsel had articulated a substantial showing of need. Indeed, the White House determined to release one of these privileged documents during the litigation itself. The White House only invoked privilege over those documents, the release of which we believed would hindered the President's ability to discharge his duties.

We believe a similar attempt to accommodate the respective interests would be appropriate in this matter as well. We would be prepared to meet with you, review the proposed areas of witness questioning, and consider any need you may demonstrate on why any applicable privileges should not be asserted.

Very truly yours,

W. Neil Eggleston

cc: Charles F. C. Ruff, Esq.

Office of the Independent Counsel
1001 Pennsylvania Avenue, N.W.
Suite 490-North
Washington, DC 20004
(202) 514-8688
Fax (202) 514-8802
March 2, 1998

HAND DELIVERED

W. Neil Eggleston, Esq.
Howrey & Simon
1299 Pennsylvania Ave., N.W.
Washington, DC 20004-2402

Dear Mr. Eggleston:

We are in receipt here in Washington of your letter dated today to Judge Starr, who is currently in meetings in Little Rock. We have, however, communicated at length with him, and this letter reflects the evaluation and considered judgment of this Office. In brief, you have asked "whether an accommodation is reachable" between the White House and this Office as to the President's invocation of executive privilege, and you suggest a meeting to "reconcile" these differences.

As you are aware, this Office met with White House Counsel a month ago at his request in—what we believed then to be—a good-faith attempt to resolve any disputes over privilege without the need to resort to time-consuming litigation. At that meeting and in subsequent correspondence, White House Counsel expressed an unyielding view of the applicability of executive privilege in this setting. Then and since, we have set forth our view that White House Counsel's reading of executive privilege and its applicability to the Monica Lewinsky matter is, with all respect, entirely misplaced. As a threshold matter, the President's communications with regard to Ms. Lewinsky are purely private in nature and therefore fall outside the scope of executive privilege. Such communications were not made in the exercise of the President's Article II powers nor were they made 'in performance of the President's responsibilities." United States v. Nixon, 418 U.S. 683, 708, 713 (1974); see also In Re Sealed Case, 121 F.3d 729, 752 (1997) (executive privilege "only applies to communications . . . on official government matters"). In addition, we find the instant invocation of executive privilege odd, given the reported statement of then-White House Counsel Lloyd Cutler that it was the White House's "practice" not to assert executive privilege in "investigations of personal wrongdoing by government officials."

Since our exchanges with White House Counsel, many White House employees have been questioned before the grand jury about Ms. Lewinsky. Several of these witnesses have invoked executive privilege at the direction of the White House. You propose we meet to "review" the areas of questioning and demonstrate our need for the information in an effort to avoid litigation. With all respect, we fail to discern the purpose of such a meeting at this juncture. First, the White House has already begun to litigate these issues as evidenced by Chief Judge Johnson's ordering Bruce Lindsey to testify or invoke a privilege. Second, we have, as you know, already asked the specific questions and identified the "areas of witness questioning." Third, there is no need—and indeed no requirement—that we demonstrate why we need these communications, since executive privilege is, for the reasons already stated, simply inapplicable to the personal communications of the President at issue here.

That being said, we are willing to consider any good-faith attempt to resolve these issues promptly. We were in discussions with the White House several weeks ago, but the President subsequently chose to invoke executive privilege as to virtually every communication relating to Ms. Lewinsky. In this respect, we are constrained to make this point clear: this investigation has confronted numerous delaying tactics. Yet we have repeatedly stressed to the White House that the public interest demands a swift resolution of all matters involving Ms. Lewinsky. We believe, moreover, given this history, that the White House is in a better position to identify the areas it wishes to withdraw the invocation of executive privilege. We warmly welcome such a proposal so that we can move the grand jury's investigation forward. If you wish to submit a proposal, kindly do so in writing by noon, Wednesday, March 4, 1998.

Sincerely,

Robert J. Bittman
Deputy Independent Counsel

cc: Honorable Charles F.C. Ruff

LAW OFFICES
WILLIAMS & CONNOLLY
725 TWELFTH STREET, N.W.
WASHINGTON, D. C. 20005-5901
(202) 434-5000
FAX (202) 434-5029

DAVID E. KENDALL
(202) 434-5145

EDWARD BENNETT WILLIAMS (1920-1988)
PAUL R. CONNOLLY (1922-1978)

March 4, 1998

CONFIDENTIAL
RULE 6(e), F.R.CRIM.P. GRAND JURY SUBMISSION

Robert J. Bittman, Esq.
Deputy Independent Counsel
Office of the Independent Counsel
1001 Pennsylvania Avenue, N.W.
Suite 490-North
Washington, D.C. 20004

By Hand

Dear Bob:

This will respond to your letters dated February 21 and March 2, 1998. I apologize for my delay in responding. The fault is mine: as you know, we filed a lengthy reply on Friday in the sealed "leaks" matter, responding to your opposition to our original motion for contempt sanctions. That matter simply absorbed my time, but I am now able to give your correspondence the attention it deserves.

As I hope you are aware, the President has the greatest respect for the grand jury. I appreciate your own acknowledgement in your March 2 letter of the "grave duties of state" which are uniquely the President's and the "immense and weighty responsibilities" he must discharge. The buck really does stop with the President for decision-making on a vast range of issues that are critical to this country's safety and economic security.

While it is true that not every moment of the day is absorbed by the duties of office, the President is extraordinarily busy on a range of important public issues, some of which are visible and some of which are not. In our judgment, our ability to have access to the President is simply insufficient at the present time for purposes of representing him adequately in the matters with which you are concerned.

Accordingly, he will, on our advice, not be able to accept your invitation for him to testify at this time. I am certain you would agree that the President deserves the same right to the informed assistance of private counsel as does every other citizen.

Your most recent letter remarks that the situation in Iraq has "thankfully, eased." While there are some respects in which this may be

528

true, the situation remains highly volatile, as a glance at today's newspapers will reveal. The continuing Southeast Asian economic crisis and the Bosnian situation also demand a great deal of the President's time, as do other national security issues, many of which are highly confidential.

On the domestic front, the President's schedule is equally congested. The Administration's proposed budget was submitted to Congress last month, and the President is in the midst of major negotiations with the Republican majorities over key budgetary objectives, such as reserving the bulk of the budgetary surplus for Social Security. Other Administration initiatives are at critical stages. The President is attempting to hammer out national legislation around a tobacco liability settlement. More "town hall" meetings are scheduled concerning the President's race initiative, which will focus on the need for strengthening the Equal Employment Opportunities Commission and the Civil Rights Division of the Justice Department. There is also currently in the White House a sustained focus on major health care proposals (expanding Medicare coverage to persons age 55-64 who have lost their health coverage due to no fault of their own; securing passage of an HMO patient "bill of rights"), on new education legislation (enacting strong national educational standards; trying to improve math and science achievement), and on highway legislation/auto safety bills (federal standards for a lower blood alcohol definition in DUI cases).

The President also has an extremely heavy foreign and domestic travel schedule. He will be out of the country for nearly three weeks this month and next in Africa and South America. These are major State visits to key strategic parts of the world, and a considerable amount of pre-departure preparation, review, and study is required, which will absorb a significant amount of the President's time in this country.

Moreover, as I indicated in my earlier letter, we remain concerned about some of the well-publicized and questionable investigative techniques used by your office. Events of recent days have done nothing to alleviate this concern, and this necessarily affects our judgment as to the degree of preparation necessary to assure the President has adequate and informed legal assistance at the present time. As you are no doubt aware, you have subpoenaed the investigator retained by this firm and by the law firm defending the President in the Paula Jones suit, and the focus of your questioning was on criticism directed at your office. This investigator was retained for lawful, legitimate, and well-recognized purposes, and your subpoena is, in our view, a blatant and unwarranted attempt to intrude into and violate the legal privileges enjoyed by every citizen, including the President, in litigation where that citizen is personally being sued or investigated. No more reassuring is your recent interrogation of Mr. Sidney Blumenthal, who works at the White House, to inquire into criticisms of your office in the press. Finally, I have received no response to my letter (a copy of which is attached hereto) sent to the Independent Counsel more than two weeks ago, inquiring as to contacts his law firm (Kirkland & Ellis) had with the lawyers for Ms. Paula Jones and legal assistance it had rendered to her. Some news reports raise troubling issues of possible conflict of interest, and I would like to get these resolved just as soon as possible.

You do, of course, have a copy of the President's deposition given on January 17, 1998, in the Jones case, and his sworn testimony there addresses at length the Monica Lewinsky matter. You have also, as I understand, requested multiple copies of the videotape of this deposition. I believe, therefore, that the grand jury in fact already has access to sworn testimony given by the President about this topic. The questions asked the President by Ms. Jones' counsel were, in fact, surprisingly detailed and particularized. As you may know, there have been news reports suggesting that Ms. Linda Tripp spent most of the Friday before the President's deposition with lawyers and agents from your office, after the apprehension of Ms. Lewinsky at a meeting with Ms. Tripp. At the end of her day with your personnel, again according to press reports, Ms. Tripp, with the apparent acquiescence of your office, met in Maryland with lawyers for Ms. Jones. There, she reportedly told them of the tapes she had secretly made of her conversations with Ms. Lewinsky, shared with them the contents of these secret tapes, and helped them devise questions to ask the President at his deposition next day, the transcript of which you have. We believe that, at least by this time, Ms. Tripp was well aware that such tapings were illegal and a felony under Maryland law. We are in the process of investigating all the legal implications of these apparent facts.

Again, I would respectfully ask you to read this letter, with its attachment, to the grand jury and to make them part of the grand jury record, if your letters to me are shared with the grand jury.

I thank you for your courtesy.

Sincerely,

David E. Kendall

HOWREY & SIMON

March 4, 1998

<u>VIA FACSIMILE and HAND DELIVERY</u>

Kenneth W. Starr, Esq.
Independent Counsel
Office of the Independent Counsel
1001 Pennsylvania Avenue, N.W.
Suite 490 North
Washington, DC 20004

Dear Mr. Starr:

I received a letter from Deputy Counsel Robert J. Bittman in response to my March 2, 1998 letter outlining our wish to ensure that we had explored, prior to any litigation, all reasonable accommodations to avoid or limit litigation.

Mr. Bittman responded by restating your Office's view that executive privilege does not apply to any questioning of White House officials regarding the Lewinsky investigation—something upon which, as you know, we disagree. Indeed, the impetus for my letter was that we disagree on the law. Despite our legal disagreements, however, we are duty bound to attempt to reach a mutually agreeable accommodation that provides the grand jury with the information it needs while preserving this and future Presidents' legitimate interests in receiving candid and frank advice in confidence from their advisors.

Your Office was unwilling to describe the subject matters about which you intended to question White House officials prior to their testimony. After several weeks of grand jury testimony by White House officials, we now have a sense of the areas that we believe are of interest to your investigation. It appears that, in addition to seeking facts about this matter, you are seeking ongoing advice given to the President by his senior advisors, including attorneys [illegible] the Counsel's Office, as well as the substance of these advisors' discussions as to how to address the Lewinsky investigation in a manner that enables the President to perform his constitutional, statutory and other official duties.

In light of these areas of inquiry, we are prepared to discuss an approach that we believe will accommodate our respective interests. To that end, the Office of the President is prepared to instruct White House witnesses along the following general lines:

• White House Advisors (Non-Lawyers): Advisors will be permitted to testify as to factual information regarding the Lewinsky investigation, including any such information imparted in conversations with the President. We will continue to assert executive privilege with respect to strategic deliberations and communications.

- **White House Attorney Advisors:** Attorneys in the Counsel's Office will assert attorney/client privilege; attorney work product; and, where appropriate, executive privilege, with regard to communications, including those with the President, related to their gathering of information, the providing of advice, and strategic deliberations and communications.

At this point, the instructions that we intend to provide to White House advisors and attorneys are necessarily general, since we do not know the questions you intend to ask. We of course will evaluate the application of these instructions to the advisors and attorneys in response to specific questions and would welcome an opportunity to meet and discuss any particular issues, as needed.

The accommodation we are proposing will permit the grand jury to complete its work in a timely fashion and will provide the factual information that it needs for this investigation. We do not believe, however, that you have demonstrated, or can demonstrate, a need for information about the strategic discussions of White House advisors about this matter.

Although you argue that the Lewinsky investigation is purely private, the intersection of this matter with, for example, the State of the Union, an enumerated duty under Article II, section 3 of the Constitution, and Prime Minister Blair's visit and their joint press conference make it abundantly clear that this investigation has implications for the President's performance of his official duties. These instances also illustrate the very obvious need for the President to receive the candid and frank counsel of his advisors in confidence.

I also reject out-of-hand your suggestion that the assertion of privilege is a delaying tactic or that the White House has in any manner delayed your investigation. While you have been investigating this matter for merely six weeks, numerous White House witnesses have appeared or been interviewed by your agents. None has refused to appear and each has answered all legitimate inquiries. Moreover, we have made very attempt to discuss and resolve potential privilege issues with you before the grand jury appearance of particular White House officials. As you surely are aware, the President's invocation of privilege to permit him and future Presidents to discharge their duties under Article II of the Constitution is a fundamental obligation, not a delaying tactic.

In sum, it is our mutual constitutional obligation to seek a reasonable accommodation of our interests. We are prepared to meet for that purpose at your earliest convenience.

Very truly yours,

W. Neil Eggleston
Attorney for the Office of the
President

cc: The Honorable Charles F.C. Ruff
Robert J. Bittman, Esq.

Office of the Independent Counsel
1001 Pennsylvania Avenue, N.W.
Suite 490-North
Washington, DC 20004
(202) 514-8688
Fax (202) 514-8802

March 6, 1998

HAND DELIVERED

W. Neil Eggleston, Esq.
Howrey & Simon
1299 Pennsylvania Ave., N.W.
Washington, DC 20004-2402

Dear Mr. Eggleston:

This responds to your letter to this Office dated March 4, 1998.

As you know, since early February we have been in discussions with the White House regarding the applicability of executive privilege to the matters involving Monica Lewinsky. We have great respect for the Office of the President and the important duties and responsibilities of the President. In this case, we have not sought nor will we seek any information implicating state secrets or diplomatic relations. The matters involving Ms. Lewinsky, moreover, relate only to the President acting in his personal capacity, as a private citizen. If there are any communications relating to Ms. Lewinsky which legitimately jeopardize state secrets or diplomatic relations, please identify them and we will review our request.

As fully outlined in our correspondence to you and the White House, the matters regarding Ms. Lewinsky do not involve the President acting his official capacity. Consequently, executive privilege is inapplicable as a threshold and fundamental matter. Any communication pertaining to Ms. Lewinsky is thus not privileged—no matter the title or position of the person involved in the communication. We therefore cannot agree with your suggestion to keep such highly probative, relevant information from the grand jury.

Sincerely,

Robert J. Bittman
Deputy Independent Counsel

cc: The Honorable Charles F.C. Ruff

Office of the Independent Counsel
1001 Pennsylvania Avenue, N.W.
Suite 490-North
Washington, DC 20004
(202) 514-8688
Fax (202) 514-8802

March 13, 1998

HAND DELIVERED

David E. Kendall, Esq.
Williams & Connolly
725 Twelfth Street, N.W.
Washington, D.C. 20005

Re: <u>William Jefferson Clinton</u>

Dear David:

By your letter last Wednesday, March 4, 1998, the President has now declined five invitations to testify and tell his story to the grand jury.

As time goes on, now eight weeks into the investigation, your claim that the President continues not to have time to prepare his testimony about Ms. Lewinsky is increasingly difficult for us to understand. We mean no disrespect whatever, mindful as we are of the President's constitutional obligations, but as stated in my letter of March 2, 1998, since the Monica Lewinsky matter began the President has found time to play golf, attend basketball games and political fundraisers, and enjoy a ski vacation. On January 17, 1998, the President was deposed for nearly a full day in the <u>Jones v. Clinton</u> lawsuit. Your co-counsel, Bob Bennett, has even moved to expedite the trial date in that case. In addition, as you remember, despite the President's weighty responsibilities we had no trouble scheduling the President's depositions for other Whitewater-related matters, and we were able to schedule his testimony in the two trials in Little Rock with relative ease. In those trials, of course, he was summoned as a defense witness, not by the United States.

You may recall that when the grand jury issued a subpoena for Mrs. Clinton's testimony in January 1996, you and White House Counsel complained that she, at minimum, should have first been given the opportunity to appear voluntarily. You and White House Counsel urged alternatives in lieu of a grand jury appearance. As to the President and the Lewinsky matter, however, you have declined five invitations to testify voluntarily. Moreover, you have suggested no alternatives.

Until last week, the President had repeatedly pledged his full cooperation in connection with the Monica Lewinsky investigation. Last Thursday, March 5, 1998—one day after the President declined our fifth invitation to appear voluntarily before the grand jury—the President publicly declared he had "given all the answers that matter" relating to Ms. Lewinsky. The President has also invoked executive privilege under circumstances exceedingly difficult to justify under settled principles of our constitutional system. We are, in consequence, constrained to say this: We now question whether the President ever intends to cooperate with this investigation, as promised, and testify.

The suggestion in your letter that our possession of the President's deposition in the Jones v. Clinton case provides the grand jury "access" to the President's information about the Lewinsky matters is, with all respect, disingenuous. The President was questioned in his deposition about a single, narrow issue involving Ms. Lewinsky. As you know, the Special Division—upon the specific request of the Attorney General—defined our jurisdiction to include "whether Monica Lewinsky or others suborned perjury, obstructed justice, intimidated witnesses, or otherwise violated federal law . . . in dealing with witnesses, potential witnesses, attorneys, or others concerning the civil case Jones v. Clinton." Our inquiry is by law much broader than the narrow issue about which the President was questioned in his deposition.

Let me reiterate: we have profound respect for the institution of the Presidency. Yet, as I am sure you agree, the grand jury is entitled to "every man's evidence." See United States v. Nixon, 418 U.S. 683 (1974); United States v. Burr, 25 Fed.Cas. 20 (No. 14,692) (C.C. Va. 1807). It is urgent that we receive the President's testimony in this matter as soon as possible.

Kindly advise me by noon Tuesday, March 17, 1998, whether the President will testify in any manner about the matters involving Ms. Lewinsky. If, as I indicated briefly above, alternatives to a grand jury appearance have occurred to you, then we are prepared to discuss them at your earliest convenience. In particular, a deposition format—should the President refuse his right to present his testimony to the grand jury and face his fellow citizens eye to eye—is an arrangement we stand ready to discuss. We are ready and able to accommodate any issues of Presidential dignity, as well as security, which of course can be readily accomplished at the United States Courthouse.

Nothing, in short, should stand in the way of the truth's coming out. As should be apparent, we continue to seek—on behalf of the grand jury—the President's truthful testimony before that body, which stands ready to sustain any inconvenience in order to respect the President's schedule, while at the same time carrying out its solemn function under our system of law.

Sincerely,

Robert J. Bittman
Deputy Independent Counsel

LAW OFFICES
WILLIAMS & CONNOLLY
725 TWELFTH STREET, N.W.
WASHINGTON, D. C. 20005-5901
(202) 434-5000
FAX (202) 434-5029
DAVID E. KENDALL
(202) 434-5145
EDWARD BENNETT WILLIAMS (1920-1988)
PAUL R. CONNOLLY (1922-1978)

March 16, 1998

CONFIDENTIAL
RULE 6(e), F.R.CRIM.P. GRAND JURY SUBMISSION

Robert J. Bittman, Esq.
Deputy Independent Counsel
Office of the Independent Counsel
1001 Pennsylvania Avenue, N.W.
Suite 490-North
Washington, D.C. 20004

By Hand

Dear Bob:

We have responded in a timely fashion to "William Jefferson Clinton Grand Jury Subpoena #V002", dated January 20, 1998, and served on us the next day. We believe that Ms. Lewinsky might have given the President a few additional items, such as ties and a pair of sun glasses, but we have not been able to locate these items. The President frequently does not see and is not aware of numerous items which are sent to him by friends and supporters.

Sincerely,

David E. Kendall

V002-DC-00000475

536

LAW OFFICES
WILLIAMS & CONNOLLY
725 TWELFTH STREET, N.W.
WASHINGTON, D. C. 20005-5901
(202) 434-5000
FAX (202) 434-5029

DAVID E. KENDALL
(202) 434-5145

EDWARD BENNETT WILLIAMS (1920-1988)
PAUL R. CONNOLLY (1922-1978)

March 18, 1998

CONFIDENTIAL
RULE 6(e), F.R.CRIM.P. GRAND JURY SUBMISSION

Robert J. Bittman, Esq.
Deputy Independent Counsel
Office of the Independent Counsel
1001 Pennsylvania Avenue, N.W.
Suite 490-North
Washington, D.C. 20004

By Hand

Dear Bob:

Thank you for your letter dated March 13, 1998. I will be equally frank in response.

For over four years now, the President has cooperated in every possible way with the investigation of the Independent Counsel. He has voluntarily given testimony under oath on three separate occasions to the Independent Counsel and twice to defendants (on each occasion, he was cross-examined by the Independent Counsel), he has submitted written interrogatory answers, he has produced more than 90,000 pages of documents, and he has provided information informally in a variety of ways.

I, too, have dealt in good faith with your investigation for more than four years. Until the recent expansion of jurisdiction to cover the Lewinsky matter, I have not had occasion to raise, nor have I raised, the kind of concerns I have adverted to in recent correspondence. I will be more specific: the actions of the Office of Independent Counsel in the past several weeks (as distinct from the actions of the grand jury) lead me to believe that your investigation may not, in fact, be an even-handed search for justice but rather may be, for whatever reason, a campaign to embarrass and harass the President. I believe he is now plainly the object of your investigation.

You state that it is "disingenuous" to assert that the President's deposition transcript (including the videotape of the deposition, which you likely will soon have access to) in Jones v. Clinton allows you to obtain the President's information on the Lewinsky matter. We continue to believe that the forty deposition pages of testimony (pp. 48-86, 202-204) on this topic set forth the essentials of this matter, although there are doubtless more questions you might be able to devise.

537

Of more serious concern to us is evidence that your office contrived to obtain the President's deposition testimony through improper and illegal means. Based upon what we have been able to learn thus far (<u>see, e.g.</u>, the page one Washington Post article on February 14, 1998, headlined "Linda Tripp Briefed Jones Team on Tapes"), your office, your agent Linda Tripp, and the Paula Jones lawyers apparently colluded to use the fruits of Tripp's felonious audiotaping (see Md. Code Ann. § 10-402 (1997)) of Lewinsky against the President at his deposition on Saturday, January 17, 1998. Curiously, Tripp appears to have been given immunity by your office immediately after she contacted you. She then secretly recorded at least one conversation with Lewinsky, an act that (unlike her previous audiotapings) does not appear to have been in violation of wiretap law. According to the Washington Post's February 14 article, Tripp arranged to have Lewinsky apprehended by your agents about noon on Friday, January 16, then put off a meeting with the Jones lawyers until (we believe) it became clear that Ms. Lewinsky would not herself agree to wear a recording device to gather evidence against others. At some point late in the afternoon, Tripp "sent word" to the Jones lawyers that she would talk to them, and she was transported to her home in Maryland (perhaps by one of your agents) where she proceeded to share both the existence of the illegal tapes[1] and their contents with the Jones lawyers, who were able to use this information the next day to question the President.[2]

The Ethics in Government Act provides in Sec. 593 (c) (1) a carefully defined procedure for expanding the jurisdiction of an independent counsel. If a new matter is not "related" to an existing subject of investigation (and the Lewinsky matter plainly was not), the statute does not allow a free-roving investigation beyond the limits of an independent counsel's present jurisdiction. For example, there would be no statutory justification to "wire" a cooperating witness to investigate further a matter not within the jurisdiction of the independent counsel. Section 593 (c) (2) (A) of the Act provides that "[i]f the independent counsel discovers or receives information about possible violations of criminal law by [covered persons] which are not covered by the prosecutorial jurisdiction of the independent counsel, the independent counsel may submit such information to the Attorney General," and the Attorney General "<u>shall</u> then conduct a preliminary investigation of the information in accordance with the provisions of section 592" (emphasis added). While the Attorney General "shall give great weight to any recommendations of the independent counsel" (<u>ibid.</u>), the determination whether to recommend to the Special Division an expansion of jurisdiction is the Attorney General's alone.

Under the circumstances here, there was no need for a hasty and informal presentation to the Attorney General—unless the OIC was hoping to use Tripp (and perhaps Lewinsky) to somehow obtain incriminating evidence against the President whose deposition in the civil case was fast approaching. We believe that the Attorney General was not properly informed about the circumstances which ostensibly justified the expansion of jurisdiction sought, and that your recent investigation has in fact been a contrivance to justify <u>post facto</u> the grant of jurisdiction that your office obtained from the Special Division.

It appears to us that you did not seek, the Attorney General did not approve, and the Special Division did not authorize the extension of your jurisdiction based on any specific and credible evidence of criminal activity by a covered person. As you surely know, the expansion of jurisdiction approved by the Special Division, on the basis of an oral application, was to investigate "whether Monica Lewinsky or others suborned perjury, obstructed justice, intimidated witnesses, or otherwise violated federal law . . . in dealing with witnesses, potential witnesses, attorneys, or others concerning the civil case of Jones v. Clinton." No "covered person" was involved in this matter unless and until the President gave testimony which might be regarded by your office as suspect. The Attorney General's written application to the Special Division, submitted after the Court was informed orally of the request, states that the Attorney General had determined that it would be a conflict of interest, under 28 U.S.C. § 591 (c) (1) for the Department of Justice to investigate. However, it was still incumbent upon the Attorney General to conduct an appropriate "preliminary investigation" to determine that there was specific evidence from a credible source to warrant further investigation. We do not believe the Attorney General was provided adequate information about Tripp's illegal audiotaping or her general credibility or about the efforts by your office to acquire evidence which could be used to support the expansion of jurisdiction. We do not believe that such a bootstrap acquisition of jurisdiction as apparently occurred here was ever contemplated by the Ethics in Government Act.

We have another serious concern about the expansion of jurisdiction in this matter, and I have adverted to this in my letter to you dated March 4, 1998. As you know, I attached a copy of a letter to the Independent Counsel which I had hand-delivered on February 17, 1998, and which sought certain basic information relating to the Independent Counsel's relationship to the Jones v. Clinton civil case. Like your office, I am interested in "the truth's coming out." It is over a month later, however, and I still have received no response of any kind from the Independent Counsel. The Special Division's Order dated January 16, 1998, specifically recites that it approves "an expansion of prosecutorial jurisdiction in lieu of the appointment of another Independent Counsel." The point of my February 17 letter to the Independent Counsel was precisely whether he (as opposed to some other qualified person) should have been appointed by the Special Division under the facts of this case. The Ethics in Government Act explicitly provides that "[d]uring the period in which an independent counsel is serving under this chapter (i) such independent counsel, and (ii) any person associated with a firm with which such independent counsel is associated, may not represent in any matter any person involved in any investigation or prosecution under this chapter." 28 U.S.C. § 594 (j) (1) (A). As my February 17 letter to the Independent Counsel made clear, the Chicago Tribune reported six days earlier that one of the Independent Counsel's partners in Kirkland & Ellis, Mr. Richard Porter, may have provided legal advice and services to Paula Jones in her suit against the President. I have written the Independent Counsel seeking information concerning this and other news reports concerning his own relations with Ms. Jones' lawyers. I specifically requested information "(i) concerning [the Independent Counsel's] own, Mr. Porter's, and any other

Kirkland & Ellis lawyer's, employee's or agent's contacts with and assistance to Ms. Paula Corbin Jones and/or her attorneys or agents or supporting groups, and (ii) concerning what was conveyed to the Attorney General and the Special Division in January, 1998, about any such contacts and assistance, when [the Independent Counsel] sought an expansion of . . . jurisdiction to encompass the Jones v. Clinton case." I have heard nothing in response.

I will not repeat here my description of the many grave duties of state which are uniquely the President's. As I noted in my March 4 letter, "[w]hile it is true that not every moment of the day is absorbed by the duties of office, the President is extraordinarily busy on a range of important public issues, some of which are visible and some of which are not." The President leaves on a long-scheduled state visit to Africa this weekend, and he will be gone until April 3. He then is in South America on another state visit from April 15 to 20. Such trips require not only travel time but a great deal of preparation time, study, and analysis in advance and after the trip.

I believe that a meeting to discuss my concerns, as well as yours, would be fruitful, and I am available at your convenience for that purpose.

Again, I would respectfully ask you to read this letter to the grand jury and to make it part of the grand jury record, if your letter to me is shared with the grand jury.

I thank you for your courtesy.

Sincerely,

David E. Kendall

Office of the Independent Counsel
1001 Pennsylvania Avenue, N.W.
Suite 490-North
Washington, DC 20004
(202) 514-8688
Fax (202) 514-8802

April 3, 1998

HAND DELIVERED

David E. Kendall, Esq.
Williams & Connolly
725 Twelfth Street, N.W.
Washington, D.C. 20005

Re: William Jefferson Clinton

Dear David:

I write in response to your letter of March 18, 1998, in which you declined our sixth invitation for the President's testimony, and in response to our meeting of March 20, 1998, during which you declined to answer my question whether the President will _ever_ voluntarily testify about the matters involving Monica Lewinsky.

As you know, upon receipt of your letter I immediately called you to take you up on your offer to meet and discuss our mutual concerns regarding our six invitations to the President. Notwithstanding the numerous misstatements in your letter—which are addressed herein—I was hopeful that in light of the President's public pledges of cooperation we could finally arrange terms under which the President would voluntarily testify about the matters involving Ms. Lewinsky. My hopes were dashed at our meeting when you simply refused to discuss any of the "issues." Not only did you merely repeat some of the inflammatory allegations in your letter, you avoided even addressing—much less answering—the question I began our meeting with: Will the President ever voluntarily testify about the matters involving Monica Lewinsky? You refused several times to answer this question. Indeed, when I asked if we were to address the "concerns" outlined in your letter to your satisfaction would the President then agree to testify, you still refused to answer. This exercise, in the context of the backpedaling and misdirection of your letters and the President's public statements, makes clear that the President has no intention—and never has had any intention—of cooperating with this grand jury or this investigation. We, of course, regret the President's apparent decision.

Now I will turn to the variety of irrelevant charges raised in your letter against this Office, the Independent Counsel, and Judge Starr's private law firm. Because our addressing these matters is evidently not dispositive for you, I will address them only briefly.

First, you suggest that the President's deposition in the Jones case amply substitutes for grand jury questioning. You are incorrect. As you are well aware, the jurisdiction of this Office and the scope of discovery in the Jones case are far from coextensive. While the deposition bears on matters within our jurisdiction, the grand jury investigation has unearthed many significant issues not addressed in the deposition.

Second, you accuse this Office of having "contrived to obtain the President's deposition testimony through improper and illegal means." This, too, is flatly incorrect. All evidence gathered in this investigation has been obtained lawfully and properly.

Third, you charge that this Office, Linda Tripp, and Richard Porter of Kirkland & Ellis "colluded" with attorneys for Paula Jones. As authority, you cite a number of the notoriously inaccurate media accounts of this investigation, many of which have been based upon statements by "unnamed presidential advisers." Let me set the record straight: This Office has not colluded with Ms. Jones's attorneys—not directly, not indirectly, and not through Ms. Tripp, Mr. Porter, or any other person. With nothing more than a sheaf of newspaper articles in hand, it is irresponsible of you to charge otherwise.

Fourth, you contend that this Office has undertaken investigative steps without proper authority. We disagree. The expansion of our jurisdiction by the Special Division was preceded by a presentation of information to the Attorney General, a preliminary investigation of such information by her, and a subsequent recommendation to the Special Division. We, unlike you, believe the Attorney General knows and follows the law. She followed the law in this case. As your complaint is a legal argument about our authority to investigate, we suggest you raise it in a judicial forum.

Fifth, you assert that the President has "cooperated in every possible way" with this investigation. You know, of course, that this is not true. You and the President have failed to produce financial records that have been under subpoena for several years. The Rose Law Firm billing records, for example, were "re-discovered" at the White House in January 1996 and had been under subpoena for many months. Jane Sherburne, then of the White House counsel's office, testified before the Senate that after the records' "re-discovery" she suggested to you that the forensic integrity of the records be preserved. Senate Hearing, 2/8/96, at 69-71. Ms. Sherburne further testified that her suggestion was dismissed. Id. You testified that you "did not regard this as a forensic matter," id. at 72, and, of course, the forensic value of the records was in fact compromised after handling by your office. In addition, as you know, I wrote you on March 6, 1998 and March 25, 1998, requesting that the President fully comply with subpoena number V002 and its instructions so that the grand jury can determine whether the President ever had any documents or things in response to the subpoena that have not been produced. You thus far have responded with only a vague statement that the President "might have given the President a few additional items, such as ties and a pair of sunglasses, but we have not been able to locate these items. The President frequently does not see and is not aware of numerous items which are sent to him by friends and supporters." This response is unsatisfactory and not in compliance with the subpoena. The grand jury needs the additional information demanded by the subpoena's instructions.

Finally, you reiterate that the President is a busy man. We do not disagree, and indeed are well aware that the President has weighty responsibilities besides his obligation to assist a federal grand jury investigating possible criminal conduct. Nonetheless, we believe that he has found and can continue to find the time to testify in judicial for a—particularly given that we will work with you to time his appearance so as to reduce disruption to his schedule.

Those are our views on the matters raised in your letter. Since January 28, 1998, when we first invited the President to testify, the grand jury has grown increasingly eager to hear the President's testimony.

Having tried and tried, I will now try once again. Please give me a straightforward yes or no answer to the following question: Will the President ever agree to testify voluntarily about the matters involving Ms. Lewinsky? If the President chooses again not to give his testimony, so that the grand jury may at least receive some of his evidence, please provide this Office with any and all exculpatory evidence you may have.

Sincerely,

Robert J. Bittman
Deputy Independent Counsel

---

1 Under the Maryland electronic surveillance statute which makes one-party telephone call taping a felony, it is a violation of the statute to disclose that an illegal tape has been made, since the term "contents" (the disclosure of which are forbidden) is defined to include "any information concerning the identity of the parties to the communication or the existence, substance, purport, or meaning of that communication." Md. Code Ann. § 10-401(7) (1997) (emphasis added).

2 Indeed, the Washington Times observed that "With the information from Mrs. Tripp, the Jones lawyers were able to ask Mr. Clinton in his deposition specific questions about his relationship with and gifts to Miss Lewinsky, according to a person informed about the President's testimony." (The Washington Times, Feb. 15, 1998.) At the deposition, when the President remarked after a series of highly specific questions concerning Ms. Lewinsky, "I don't even know what you're talking about, I don't think," Ms. Jones' lawyer, James Fisher, replied, "Sir, I think this will come to light shortly, and you'll understand." Deposition transcript, at 85.

LAW OFFICES
WILLIAMS & CONNOLLY
725 TWELFTH STREET, N.W.
WASHINGTON, D.C. 20005-5901
(202) 434-5000
FAX (202) 434-5029

DAVID E. KENDALL
(202) 434-5145

EDWARD BENNETT WILLIAMS (1920-1988)
PAUL R. CONNOLLY (1922-1978)

April 17, 1998
CONFIDENTIAL
RULE 6(e), F.R.CRIM.P., GRAND JURY SUBMISSION
Robert J. Bittman, Esq.
Deputy Independent Counsel
Office of the Independent Counsel
1001 Pennsylvania Avenue, N.W.
Suite 490-North
Washington, D.C. 20004

By Hand

Dear Bob:

Thank you for your letter of April 3, 1998. I will try once again to make clear our position with regard to the President's providing testimony on the Lewinsky matter, beyond the transcript and videotape of his deposition in Jones v. Clinton, which your Office now has and is free to submit to the grand jury. I have attempted to do this in my previous correspondence and in our meeting at the federal courthouse on March 20, 1998.

In my several letters and in our meeting, our position could not have been more clearly stated: we have serious objections to the origin and conduct of your Lewinsky investigation, and until those are satisfactorily addressed, we cannot, as a matter of professional duty to our client, allow the President to give further testimony at the present time. The issue remains open, however, and depends on your Office. We remain entirely respectful of the grand jury. Indeed, from recent press accounts, it appears that the grand jurors themselves are performing their civic duty with admirable commitment and at some sacrifice to their personal lives. Quite frankly, I believe if your Office were to provide the information I have sought over the past several months, this would lighten the burden on us, on you, and on the grand jurors.

Since your letter states it will address my concerns only "briefly", I will not restate here the issues I have raised at some length in my previous correspondence. I would note only that, once again, your letter stonewalls my request for information concerning contacts between members of the Independent Counsel's law firm (Kirkland & Ellis) and the Paula Jones lawyers as of the January 16, 1998, expansion of your Office's jurisdiction to encompass the Lewinsky matter in the Paula Jones civil suit. My need for this information is obvious: if in fact personnel at Kirkland & Ellis have provided legal assistance in some way to the Jones side of the civil suit, Judge Starr would <u>not</u> have been qualified under the Ethics in Government Act to serve as independent counsel on the Lewinsky matter—some other individual, with no connection to the Jones litigation, would have had to have been selected. The information I seek is obviously in your custody and control: Judge Starr need only ask his law partners, if he is not in fact privy to it himself. I first wrote him on February 17, 1998, requesting this information, and I still have not had an answer to my letter. You will recall that I appended a copy of that letter to my March 4, 1998, letter to you—I will not do so again.

This matter is highly important under the statute, because when Congress enacted the independent counsel legislation, it permitted such counsel to remain in their private law firms and to take on the appointment as a part-time job. I do not fault nor have I criticized the Independent Counsel for remaining at his law firm (where, according to news reports, he has made $1 million a year while serving as independent counsel, <u>see</u>, <u>e.g.</u>, Time, Feb. 2, 1998)), but it is, obviously, extremely important that the conflict rules that permit such continued employment under the Act be followed. The statute provides that no person associated with the independent counsel's law firm may "represent <u>in any matter</u> any person involved in any investigation or prosecution under this chapter." 28 U.S.C. § 594 (j) (1) (A) (ii). Thus, if someone at Kirkland & Ellis had "in any matter" represented Ms. Jones, Judge Starr could not properly have been appointed to investigate the Lewinsky matter.

It is true, as your recent letter asserts, that I have based my inquiry on media accounts. I do not have any reason to believe that (for example) the February 11, 1998, account is "notoriously inaccurate," as you suggest, since it appears in the Chicago Tribune, a reputable newspaper. The Tribune's report was in fact quite specific:

> "The Chicago-based law firm whose partners include Whitewater independent Counsel Kenneth Starr has begun an inquiry into whether a partner provided unapproved assistance to lawyers representing Paula Jones in her sex harrassment case against President Clinton. . . .

> [T]he law firm's internal inquiry is focusing on Richard Porter, a partner in the Chicago office and a former senior aide to President George Bush and Vice President Dan Quayle. . . .

> John Corkery, associate dean at Chicago's John Marshall Law School, said the ethical issues raised are complicated ones. But in general, he said, 'If an attorney at the Kirkland firm is doing something that amounts to legal work for Jones, that creates a problem for Starr as the independent counsel because Starr's partner is pursuing a related matter in private practice that Starr has the obligation to investigate as part of his official duties.'

> 'The acts of Starr's partner in the practice of law are Starr's acts, by virtue of their partnership,' Corkery said."

You also assert that many statements in the accounts I cited in my February 17 letter are sourced to (in your words) "unnamed presidential advisers." With all respect, I do not see any such sources in these articles, although the February 11, 1998, Chicago Tribune article is in part based upon an unnamed "Kirkland & Ellis source".

I am also surprised at your cavalier dismissal of press reports as a basis for further inquiry. Your own Office has been quite willing even to take legal action on the basis of press accounts, when it has suited your purposes. For example, you successfully moved to disqualify Judge Henry Woods in the Court of Appeals for the Eighth Circuit "with nothing more than a sheaf of newspaper articles in hand" (to borrow your phrase), although you had chosen not to make such a motion to the Judge himself. As the Court of Appeals noted, "[t]he Independent Counsel relies primarily on newspaper articles to support his request." United States v. Tucker, 78 F.3d 1313, 1322-23 (8th Cir. 1996). By their very nature, questions involving possible conflicts of interest often arise because of media reports. In a proceeding in Arkansas last year involving the question whether the Independent Counsel suffered a conflict of interest because a job he had accepted in the future at Pepperdine University was partially funded by a virulent opponent of President Clinton, Judge Eisele, a Republican United States District Court judge, commented: "[H]aving reviewed the media accounts regarding the Pepperdine issue, I find that it is incumbent upon the Court to make some kind of inquiry." In re Starr, 986 F. Supp. 1144, 1153 (E.D. Ark. 1997). Judge Eisele also observed that "[i]t is even possible that Mr. Starr, as Independent Counsel, should receive more exacting scrutiny regarding his professional responsibilities than other prosecutors," since the Special Division indicated (when it appointed him to replace Mr. Robert Fiske) that "'the Act contemplates an apparent as well as an actual independence on the part of the Counsel.'" 986 F. Supp. at 1155.

Your letter asserts that the expansion of your jurisdiction to include the Lewinsky matter was approved by the Attorney General and you suggest that this means that the Attorney General has in fact ratified your application. However, one of the very questions I have been asking for over two months—without receiving an answer of any kind—is precisely what the Attorney General was told when your Office suddenly requested an expansion of its jurisdiction in January. I have no idea whether the Attorney General was in fact informed of any contacts between Kirkland & Ellis personnel and the Paula Jones camp. The Attorney General is obviously not clairvoyant: if she were not informed of any such contacts, she could hardly be expected to know about them and to have made a decision as to whether, under the circumstances, Judge Starr was in fact the appropriate Independent Counsel to conduct the Lewinsky investigation. It is quite significant, I believe, that the Attorney General's application to the Special Division recites that "Independent Counsel Starr has requested that this matter be referred to him" (emphasis added). Thus, your office affirmatively and purposefully sought to extend its jurisdiction over the Lewinsky matter. This expansion request did not originate with the Attorney General.

Instead of providing responsive information, you have advised that we should "raise [this issue] in a judicial forum." We will accordingly assume that we will receive no further response to my February 17 letter and will proceed accordingly.

I will not repeat here my previously expressed concerns about your Office's investigative techniques in the Lewinsky matter. Recent press reports indicate that you plan to have Ms. Tripp testify before the grand jury. Should you have Ms. Tripp testify, I would respectfully request that you brief the grand jury concerning the illegality of Ms. Tripp's one-party taping of Ms. Lewinsky's telephone conversations in Maryland, the reasons your office wired Ms. Tripp to tape record Ms. Lewinsky's conversations, your knowledge of how the contents of this tape "leaked" to the news media, your knowledge of the reasons Ms. Tripp sought out your office rather than the United States Attorney's Office, the timing and details of your federal law immunity agreement with Ms. Tripp, and the restrictions (if any) you placed upon Ms. Tripp's transmittal of illegally acquired taping information (including the existence of illegally made tapes) to the Paula Jones lawyers in the week before the President's deposition.

I have responded to your comments concerning subpoena V002 in a letter dated April 13, 1998, and will not do so again here. I have also set forth fully in a letter to the Independent Counsel dated April 10, 1998, my concerns about having your Office investigate recent allegations concerning David Hale. In its April 9 letter to Judge Starr, the Department of Justice noted that "the United States Attorney's Office for the Western District of Arkansas was recently provided with information suggesting that David Hale, who we understand is a witness in various matters under your jurisdiction, may have received cash and other gratuities from individuals seeking to discredit the President during a period when Hale was actively cooperating with your investigation." The Department's letter also noted "suggestions that your office would have a conflict of interest, or the appearance of a conflict, in looking into this matter, because of the importance of Hale to your investigation and because the payments allegedly came from funds provided by Richard Scaife [the virulent opponent of President Clinton whom I referred to above]." The Independent Counsel's withdrawal from his Pepperdine commitments does not begin to solve the many problems that have been noted. For the reasons set forth in my April 10 letter, which involve both fairness and the perception of fairness, your Office should not have any involvement whatsoever in the investigation of this matter.

For over four years, the President has cooperated fully with the investigation of the Independent Counsel, which has now gone on longer than a Presidential term. He has voluntarily given testimony under oath on three different occasions to the Independent Counsel and twice to defendants (on each occasion, he was cross-examined by the Independent Counsel), he has submitted written interrogatory answers, he has produced more than 90,000 pages of documents[1], and he has provided information informally in a variety of ways. This amounts to unprecedented cooperation[2] with an investigation of unprecedented duration, intrusiveness, and indefiniteness. That you now request we submit "exculpatory" evidence is perfectly consonant with the occasionally Alice-in-Wonderland nature of this whole enterprise. I am not aware of anything the President needs to "exculpate."

I would respectfully ask you to read this letter to the grand jury and to make it part of the grand jury record, if your recent letter to me is shared with the grand jury.

I thank you for your courtesy.

Sincerely,

David E. Kendall

Office of the Independent Counsel
1001 Pennsylvania Avenue, N.W.
Suite 490-North
Washington, DC 20004
(202) 514-8688
Fax (202) 514-8802

July 17, 1998
<u>HAND DELIVERED</u>
David E. Kendall, Esq.
Williams & Connolly
725 Twelfth Street, N.W.
Washington, D.C. 20005

Re: <u>William Jefferson Clinton</u>

Dear David:

As you know, beginning January 28, 1998, we, on behalf of the grand jury, have invited the President six times to testify voluntarily about the matters involving Monica Lewinsky. Despite his previous cooperation with other aspects of our investigations and his public pledges to cooperate fully with this investigation and provide "more rather than less, sooner rather than later," the President has unfortunately chosen to decline each and every invitation to give his information to the grand jury. The grand jury simply can wait no longer for the President's voluntary cooperation.

Pursuant to § 9-11.150 of the United States Attorneys' Manual and with all the requisite approvals thereunder, enclosed please find a subpoena for President Clinton to appear and give testimony before the grand jury on Tuesday, July 28, 1998, at 9:15 a.m. If the President agrees to comply with the subpoena and testify, we and the grand jury—as we have previously stated—will accommodate his schedule if he cannot appear on the 28th.

We believe you are aware of the status of your client. We would be pleased to state explicitly the status of the President if you desire.

Sincerely,

Robert J. Bittman
Deputy Independent Counsel

Enclosure

Advice of Rights

- The grand jury is conducting an investigation of possible violations of Federal criminal laws involving: perjury, subornation of perjury, obstruction of justice, witness tampering, and other Federal criminal laws.

- Your conduct is being investigated for possible violations of Federal criminal law.

- You may refuse to answer any question if a truthful answer to the question would tend to incriminate you.

- Anything that you do say may be used against you by the grand jury or in a subsequent legal proceeding.

- If you have retained counsel, the grand jury will permit you a reasonable opportunity to step outside the grand jury room to consult with counsel if you so desire.

United States District Court

—————————— DISTRICT OF ——————————

TO: The White House
     ATTN: Michelle Petersen, Esq.

SUBPOENA TO TESTIFY
BEFORE GRAND JURY

SUBPOENA FOR:

☐ PERSON   ☒ DOCUMENT(S) OR OBJECT(S)

YOU ARE HEREBY COMMANDED to appear and testify before the Grand Jury of the United States District Court at the place, date, and time specified below.

PLACE	COURTROOM
United States District Court for the District of Columbia Third & Constitution Avenue, N.W. Washington, D.C.	Grand Jury, Third Floor
	DATE AND TIME
	July 23, 1998/9:15 a.m.

YOU ARE ALSO COMMANDED to bring with you the following document(s) or object(s):*

See attached Rider.

☐ Please see additional information on reverse.

This subpoena shall remain in effect until you are granted leave to depart by the court or by an officer acting on behalf of the court.

U.S. MAGISTRATE	DATE
Nancy M. Mayer-Whittington, Clerk	July 17, 1998
(BY) DEPUTY CLERK	D1415

This subpoena issued upon application of the United States of America

NAME, ADDRESS AND PHONE NUMBER OF ASSISTANT U.S. ATTORNEY
Julie A. Corcoran, Associate Independent Couns
Office of the Independent Counsel
1001 Pennsylvania Avenue, N.W., Suite 490-Nort
Washington, D.C. 20004
(202) 514-8688

*If not applicable, enter "none."   *U.S GPO:1993-0-350-792/60396

United States District Court

FOR THE _____ **DISTRICT OF** _____ COLUMBIA

TO: William Jefferson Clinton

SUBPOENA TO TESTIFY
BEFORE GRAND JURY

SUBPOENA FOR:

[x] PERSON   [ ] DOCUMENT(S) OR OBJECT(S)

YOU ARE HEREBY COMMANDED to appear and testify before the Grand Jury of the United States District Court at the place, date, and time specified below.

PLACE	COURTROOM
United States District Court for the District of Columbia Third & Constitution Avenue, N.W. Washington, D.C.	Grand Jury, Third Floor
	DATE AND TIME
	July 28, 1998/9:15 a.m.

YOU ARE ALSO COMMANDED to bring with you the following document(s) or object(s):*

[ ] *Please see additional information on reverse.*

This subpoena shall remain in effect until you are granted leave to depart by the court or by an officer acting on behalf of the court.

U.S. MAGISTRATE OR CLERK OF COURT	DATE
Nancy M. Mayer-Whittington, Clerk	July 17, 1998
(BY) DEPUTY CLERK	D1424

This subpoena is issued upon application of the United States of America

NAME, ADDRESS AND PHONE NUMBER OF ASSISTANT U.S. ATTORNEY
Robert J. Bittman, Deputy Independent Counsel
Office of the Independent Counsel
1001 Pennsylvania Avenue, N.W., Suite 490-North
Washington, D.C. 20004
(202) 514-8688

"If not applicable, enter 'none.'"   *U.S GPO 1993 0 350-702/80398

Subpoena –D1415
To: The White House

SUBPOENA RIDER

A. Produce the following items in the possession/custody of President Clinton:

1. Vox
2. The Notebook
3. Geek Love
4. Oy Vey
5. A Silver Cigar Holder, and
6. An Antique Paperweight depicting the White House circa 1900

Personal appearance is not required if the requested documents are delivered on or before the return date to Special Agent ▮▮▮▮ of the Federal Bureau of Investigation (telephone ▮▮▮▮, Suite 490-North, 1001 Pennsylvania Avenue, N.W., Washington, DC 20004, for submission to the Grand Jury. If you choose to deliver documents in lieu of a personal appearance, you must (i) state in a cover letter whether such production contains all responsive documents, and (ii) attach a copy of this subpoena to the cover letter.

Definitions and Instructions

1. Definitions

a. The term "document" or "documents" as used in this subpoena means all records of any nature whatsoever within your possession, custody or control or the possession, custody or control of any agent, employee, representative (including, without limitation, attorneys, investment advisors, investment bankers, bankers and accountants), or other person acting or purporting to act for or on your behalf or in concert with you, including, but not limited to, draft, pending or executed contracts and/or agreements, sample documents, insurance policies, financial guarantee bonds, letters of credit, communications, correspondence, calendars, daytimers, datebooks, telegrams, facsimiles, telexs, telefaxes, electronic mail, memoranda, records, reports, books, files (computer or paper), summaries or records of personal conversations, meetings or interviews, logs, summaries or records of telephone conversations and/or telefax communications, diaries, forecasts, statistical statements, financial statements (draft or finished), work papers, drafts, copies, bills, records of payments for bills, retainer records, attorney time sheets, telephone bills and records, telefax bills and records, tax returns and return information, employee time sheets, graphs, charts, accounts, analytical records, minutes or records of meetings or conferences, consultants' reports and/or records, appraisals, records, reports or summaries of negotiations, brochures, pamphlets, circulars, maps, plats, trade letters, depositions, statements, interrogatories and answers thereto, pleadings, docket sheets, discovery materials, audit letters, audit reports, materials underlying audits, document productions, transcripts, exhibits, settlement materials, judgments, press releases, notes, marginal notations, invoices, documents regarding collateral or security pledged, settlement statements, checks disbursed or received at settlement, inspection reports, title policies, financial statements and/or federal tax returns submitted by any person in support of any loan application, items related the repayment, if any, of any interest or principal on the loan, items relating to any default on the loan, commission records, evidence of liens, documents relating to filings under the Uniform Commercial Code and/or its equivalent, foreclosure and mortgage documentation, cashiers checks, bank drafts, money orders, bank and brokerage account statements, debit and credit memoranda, wire transfer documentation, opening account cards, signature cards, loan applications, any employment and bank account deposit verification documents, loan histories, loan files, records of loan repayment or any and all efforts to secure repayment, including foreclosure or records of lawsuits, credit references, board resolutions, minutes of meetings of boards of directors, opinion letters, purchases and sales agreements, real estate contracts, brokerage agreements, escrow agreements, loan agreements, offer and acceptance contracts, or any other contracts or agreements, deeds or other evidence of title, escrow accounts and any other escrow documentation, savings account transcripts, savings account deposit slips, savings account withdrawal slips, checks deposited in savings accounts, checking account statements, canceled checks drawn on checking accounts, deposit slips and checks deposited into checking accounts, credit card accounts, debit and credit documentation, safe deposit records, currency transaction reports (IRS Forms 4789), photographs, brochures, lists, journals, advertising, computer tapes and cards, audio and video tapes, computerized records stored in the form of magnetic or electronic coding on computer media or on media capable of being read by computer or with the aid of computer related equipment, including but not limited to floppy disks or diskettes, disks, diskettes, disk packs, fixed hard drives, removable hard disk cartridges, mainframe computers, Bernoulli boxes, optical disks, WORM disks, magneto/optical disks, floptical disks, magnetic tape, tapes, laser disks, video cassettes, CD-ROMs and any other media capable of storing magnetic coding, microfilm, microfiche and other storage devices, voicemail recordings and all other written, printed or recorded or photographic matter or sound reproductions, however produced or reproduced.

The term "document" or "documents" also includes any earlier, preliminary, preparatory or tentative version of all or part of a document, whether or not such draft was superseded by a later draft and whether or not the terms of the draft are the same as or different from the terms of the final document.

b. The term "communication" or "communications" is used herein in its broadest sense to encompass any transmission or exchange of information, ideas, facts, data, proposals, or any other matter, whether between individuals or between or among the members of a group, whether face-to-face, by telephone or by means of electronic or other medium.

c. "Possession, custody or control" means in your physical possession and/or if you have the right to secure or compile the production of the document or a copy from another person or entity having physical possession, including, but not limited to, your counsel.

d. The term "referring or relating" to any given subject means anything that constitutes, contains, embodies, reflects, identifies, states, refers to, deals with, or is in any manner whatsoever pertinent to that subject including, but not limited to, documents concerning the preparation of other documents.

e. The term "you" means yourself and any of your companies, partner-ships and business entities with which you have been affiliated and any employees, partners, associates or members of any firm with which you have been affiliated in the course of your work for any of the persons or entities named in this rider, and any such firms and the affiliates of those firms.

2. Instructions

a. The originals of all documents and communications must be pro-duced, as well as copies within your possession, custody, or control.

b. If any original document cannot be produced in full, produce such document to the extent possible and indicate specifically the reason for your inability to produce the remainder.

c. Documents shall be produced as they are kept in the usual course of business, as organized in the files.

d. File folders, labels, and indices identifying documents called for shall be produced intact with such documents. Documents attached to each other should not be separated.

e. In reading this rider, the plural shall include the singular and the singular shall include the plural.

f. The words "and" and "or" shall be construed conjunctively or disjunc-tively as necessary to make the request inclusive rather than exclusive. The use of the word "including" shall be construed without limitation.

g. In the event that any document, or portion thereof, called for by this subpoena is withheld on the basis of any claim of privilege or similar claim, that document shall be identified in writing as follows: (a) author; (b) the position or title of the author; (c) addressee; (d) the position or title of the addressee; (e) any indicated or blind copies; (f) date; (g) a descrip-tion of the subject matter of the document; (h) number of pages; (i) attachments or appendices; (j) all persons to whom the document, its contents, or any portion thereof, has been disclosed, distributed, shown, or explained; and (k) present custodian. Each basis you contend justifies the withholding of the document shall also be specified. With respect to those documents or records as to which you may claim privilege, or attorneys' work product, set forth as to each such document the basis for such claim, including the purpose and circumstances surrounding the creation of the document, the identity of each person who has been privy to such commu-nication reflected in the document, the identity of any person or entity instructing the subpoena recipient or the attorney of the subpoena recipi-ent to withhold production of the document, and whether you will submit the document to the Court for an in camera determination as to the validity of the claim. If the existence of a joint defense agreement or any agreement as to common interest is relevant to the assertion of any claim of privilege or similar claim, please provide a copy of that agreement; if any such agreement is not in writing, please set forth the date of the creation of the agreement, the identities of all parties to the agreement and the specific individuals who entered into the agreement on behalf of those parties, and the objects, purposes, and scope of the agreement.

h. In the event that any document called for by this subpoena has been lost, destroyed, deleted, altered, or otherwise disposed of, that document shall be identified in writing as follows: (a) author; (b) the position or title of the author; (c) addressee; (d) the position or title of the addressee; (e) indicated or blind copies; (f) date; (g) a brief description of the subject matter of the document; (h) number of pages; (I) attachments or appendices; (j) all persons to whom the document, its contents, or any portion thereof, had been disclosed, distributed, shown or explained; (k) the date of the loss, destruction, deletion, alteration, or disposal and the circumstances thereof; and (l) the reasons, if any, for the loss, destruction, deletion, alteration, or disposal and the person or persons responsible.

i. If any information or data is withheld because such information or data is stored electronically, it is to be identified by the subject matter of the information or data and the place or places where such information is maintained.

Office of the Independent Counsel
1001 Pennsylvania Avenue, N.W.
Suite 490-North
Washington, DC 20004
(202) 514-8688
Fax (202) 514-8802

July 23, 1998

HAND DELIVERED

David E. Kendall, Esq.
Williams & Connolly
725 Twelfth Street, N.W.
Washington, D.C. 20005

Re: William Jefferson Clinton

Dear David:

I write in regards to your request yesterday for additional time to respond to the grand jury's subpoena to President Clinton. Although I conveyed to you yesterday that we had decided not to give any additional time, you asked me to let you know by the close of business Friday, July 24, 1998, if our views changed. We are responding today to give you as advance notice of our decision as possible.

We have carefully reviewed your request and balanced it against the grand jury's desire—and responsibility—to complete this investigation as thoroughly and expeditiously as possible. We offer to withdraw the current subpoena to the President and issue a new subpoena with an appearance date of Friday, July 31, 1998, at 9:15 a.m. if you agree that you will not request any additional time or another continuance, either from this Office or the Court. As before, if the President agrees to comply with the subpoena and testify, we and the grand jury will accommodate his schedule if he cannot appear on the 31st. We believe this extension of time is entirely reasonable given that the President has been on notice since January that the grand jury wished his testimony and given that all the President must necessarily decide by July 31 is whether he will comply with the subpoena and testify. Kindly advise me by 4:00 p.m. tomorrow whether the President wishes to accept our proposal; otherwise, the current subpoena will remain in effect.

Sincerely,

Robert J. Bittman
Deputy Independent Counsel

LAW OFFICES
WILLIAMS & CONNOLLY
725 TWELFTH STREET, N.W.
WASHINGTON, D.C. 20005-5901
(202) 434-5000
FAX (202) 434-5029

DAVID E. KENDALL
(202) 434-5145

EDWARD BENNETT WILLIAMS (1920-1988)
PAUL R. CONNOLLY (1922-1978)

July 24, 1998

CONFIDENTIAL

Robert J. Bittman, Esq.
Deputy Independent Counsel
Office of the Independent Counsel
1001 Pennsylvania Avenue, N.W.
Suite 490-North
Washington, D.C. 20004

<u>By Hand</u>

Dear Bob:

I write in response to your letter of yesterday, which I believe to be now moot.

The President is willing to provide testimony for the grand jury, although there are a number of questions relating to the precise terms and timing which must be worked out. If you are willing to work within the framework of the last three times the President provided such testimony and if you are sincere in your statement that you will work to accommodate his schedule, we should quickly be able to finalize the arrangements.

I will get to you by 4:00 p.m. Tuesday, but sooner if possible, a more detailed letter, which will include a date for testimony which will accommodate the President's other existing obligations.

I request that you withdraw the pending subpoena, since the issue of the subpoena itself is quite important to us. The precedential effect of such a subpoena is not an issue I have addressed in previous correspondence with you (which ended with my April 17 letter), but I will do so in my next letter.

Sincerely,

David E. Kendall

Office of the Independent Counsel
1001 Pennsylvania Avenue, N.W.
Suite 490-North
Washington, DC 20004
(202) 514-8688
Fax (202) 514-8802

HAND DELIVERED   July 24, 1998

David E. Kendall, Esq.
Williams & Connolly
725 Twelfth Street, N.W.
Washington, D.C. 20005

Re: William Jefferson Clinton

Dear David:

We are gratified by your response to my letter of yesterday, and we are pleased by the President's decision to provide testimony for the grand jury.

You indicate in your letter that the President "is willing to provide testimony for the grand jury" and you suggest that such testimony take place in a forum outside the grand jury, on an uncertain future date. We are happy to discuss arrangements for the President's testimony that will be consistent with concerns of security and dignity of the Office of the President. We remain interested, however, in obtaining a prompt commitment to a date certain for that testimony. As you know, we have invited the President on six occasions to testify before the grand jury, and its work continues apace. As a result, we are currently not inclined to withdraw the subpoena. Nevertheless, we would be happy to consult with you at your earliest convenience before next Tuesday morning to work out an acceptable schedule for the President's testimony.

Sincerely,

Robert J. Bittman
Deputy Independent Counsel

LAW OFFICES
WILLIAMS & CONNOLLY
725 TWELFTH STREET, N.W.
WASHINGTON, D.C. 20005-5901
(202) 434-5000
FAX (202) 434-5029

DAVID E. KENDALL
(202) 434-5145

EDWARD BENNETT WILLIAMS (1920-1988)
PAUL R. CONNOLLY (1922-1978)

July 27, 1998

CONFIDENTIAL

Robert J. Bittman, Esq.
Deputy Independent Counsel
Office of the Independent Counsel
1001 Pennsylvania Avenue, N.W.
Suite 490-North
Washington, D.C. 20004

By Hand

Dear Bob:

This will acknowledge your letter dated July 17, 1998, enclosing a subpoena for the President to appear before the grand jury on July 28 and will follow up on my letter to you dated July 24, 1998.

As you are well aware, this extraordinary subpoena poses grave and literally unprecedented constitutional questions. While we are obviously cognizant of the holdings in United States v. Nixon, 418 U.S. 683 (1974) and Clinton v. Jones, _____ U.S. _____, 117 S.Ct. 1636 (1997), no case has ever held that a sitting President may be compelled by subpoena to provide testimony for a grand jury, much less to testify before a grand jury. In the past, Presidents have voluntarily provided information to prosecutors for legal proceedings in a variety of ways.

President Clinton has twice given testimony at the request of defendants in criminal proceedings, after he had voluntarily given testimony to the Office of Independent Counsel on similar subjects, in circumstances where the defendants plainly had certain Sixth Amendment rights "to have compulsory process for obtaining witnesses in [the defendant's] favor." But neither this nor any other President has been compelled to give testimony to a grand jury by subpoena.

One of the most troubling aspects of this subpoena is its plain conflict with the impeachment provisions of the Constitution, since it is obvious that from the outset of the latest phase of your investigation you have considered the President to be a "target" of your investigation. We believe that the conclusion of then-Solicitor Bork in the investigation of Vice-President Agnew twenty-five years ago is the correct one: the "remarks [of the framers] strongly suggest an understanding that the President, as Chief Executive, would not be subject to the ordinary criminal process. . . . Their assumption that the President would not be subject to criminal process was based upon the crucial nature of his executive powers." Memorandum for the United States Concerning the Vice President's Claim of Constitutional Immunity, at 6, In Re Proceedings of The Grand Jury Impaneled December 5, 1972, Civ. No. 73-965 (D.Md.) (Oct. 5, 1973).

Accordingly, under circumstances in which you have apparently "targeted" your investigation on a sitting President, enforcement of a grand jury subpoena would violate the most fundamental separation of powers principles because it would invade the exclusive prerogatives of the Congress. Under Article I, the House "shall have the sole power of impeachment" and the Senate "shall have the sole power to try all impeachments." Under Article II of the Constitution, the President is duty-bound to uphold the separation of powers framework against unreasonable encroachment by other branches or by an unelected Independent Counsel. In order to protect the institution of the Presidency, we are prepared to litigate to preserve these important principles.

We hope that will not be necessary. For the past four years, we have worked with your Office to devise ways for the President to cooperate with the investigations of the Office of Independent Counsel in a manner that did not infringe his Article II responsibilities. He has voluntarily and unstintingly provided an enormous amount of information in response to a great many requests from the OIC. He has, without the compulsion of subpoena, given testimony under oath on three different occasions to the Independent Counsel. He has twice given testimony for defendants in criminal proceedings and been subject to cross-examination by the Office of Independent Counsel. He has provided more than 90,000 pages of documents to the OIC, he has submitted interrogatory answers, and he has provided information informally in a variety of ways. This amounts to extraordinary and unprecedented cooperation with an investigation of extraordinary and unprecedented duration, intrusiveness, and indefiniteness.

In my letters to you over the last few months, I have set forth in detail my concerns about your Office's investigation. I will not reiterate those here, but my reservations, as set forth in my correspondence, are substantial and, I believe, well-founded. Regarding leaks, for example, Chief Judge Johnson's findings with respect to our three show-cause motions provide dramatic confirmation of my concerns.

Despite our serious and enduring concerns about the OIC's investigation, as I indicated in my July 24 letter, the President remains willing to provide the grand jury with the information it seeks, so long as he can do so in a way that is consistent with the obligations of his Office. We believe that, with your assistance, the serious constitutional questions presented here by a subpoena may be mooted. Our proposal is made in good faith and after serious deliberation. It reflects a meaningful attempt to accommodate both your needs and those of the Presidency. We are not suggesting other more limited options utilized by Presidents in the past, such as written interrogatories, which while precedented and defensible, would, we believe, be less satisfactory. The President is prepared to provide the information you seek under conditions that (1) are consistent with the precedents established in this investigation and (2) preserve the constitutional questions both for your Office and the President for later formal legal determination, if necessary.

In our correspondence during the last few months, you have stated that the OIC "fully acknowledge[d] that the President has immense and weighty responsibilities" and that the OIC "want[ed] in every way to take fully into account those grave duties of state." (Your letter to me of March 2, 1998). You stated you wanted to "reiterate" that the OIC had "profound respect for the institution of the Presidency." (Your letter to me of March 13, 1998). We believe that the respect for the Office of the President, which you acknowledge, and which we share, requires that any testimony of the President be given under the following conditions:

1) The subpoena must be withdrawn. The President has on three different occasions voluntarily given sworn testimony when requested by the OIC. On two other occasions (in 1996), the President testified at the behest of two defendants by videotape at their trials. In our view, however, the constitutional considerations raised by your July 17 subpoena are quite different since, for example, a defendant has a Sixth Amendment right to compulsory process to present witnesses in his defense. For the separation of powers reasons discussed above and to avoid a precedent harmful to the institution of the Presidency, we believe that any testimony which the President provides now must be on a voluntary basis.

2) Any testimony by the President must be given by deposition at the White House, under the conditions of the first three OIC interviews. We anticipate that the examination will be (as it has been in the past) respectful, non-repetitive, and given within a specific time period (perhaps three hours). You will inform us of the specific areas you intend to cover (although, obviously, not of the questions you intend to ask). You will make a good faith effort to provide us documents in advance about which you plan to question the President, so he does not have to waste time at the deposition reading them for the first time.

3) Safeguards to prevent leaks must be devised. The President's January 17, 1998, deposition in the Paula Jones case was leaked to the press in flagrant violation of a court order. In this investigation, Chief Judge Johnson has entered orders for the OIC to show cause why it or individuals therein should not be held in contempt for violating Rule 6(e), Fed. R. Crim. P.: "The Court finds that the serious and repetitive nature of disclosures to the media of Rule 6(e) material strongly militates in favor of conducting a show cause hearing." (June 19, 1998, Order, at 5). Moreover, "[s]hould the Court find a direct violation of Rule 6(e), the Court reserves the right to take any appropriate steps, including referring the matter to the United States Attorney, the Department of Justice, or a special master for criminal contempt investigation and proceedings." (June 26, 1998, Order, at 2 n.1). We do not seek to require impossible conditions or guarantees, but in light of the nature of the subject matter, the intense and corrosive media interest, and the history of leaks, there must be strict safeguards as to attendance, handling of the transcript (perhaps lodging the only copy with the court until it is presented to the grand jury), dissemination, etc.

4) This testimony will be given only after the President has an adequate time to prepare for it. In Clinton v. Jones, supra, the Supreme Court remarked the "'unique position in the constitutional scheme'" that the Presidency occupies and noted that the President "occupies a unique office with powers and responsibilities so vast and important that the public interest demands that he devote his undivided time and attention to his public duties." 117 S.Ct. at 1646. The Court held in that case that "[t]he high respect that is owed to the office of the Chief Executive, though not justifying a rule of categorical immunity, is a matter that should inform the conduct of the entire proceeding, including the timing and scope of discovery," id. at 1650-51 (footnote omitted), and its holding was based upon its assumption "that the testimony of the President, both for discovery and for use at trial, may be taken at the White House at a time that will accommodate his busy schedule," id. at 1643.

I last wrote you three months ago concerning the possibility of the President testifying, and I have heard absolutely nothing from you in the interim. In that and other letters, I have made clear that the President's schedule is an extremely full one that is set well in advance. Nevertheless, suddenly and without any advance notice, I received your subpoena at 6:00 p.m. on Friday, July 17, while the President was away on a long-scheduled trip to Arkansas and Louisiana, and with other significant travel scheduled, seeking his grand jury testimony a mere ten days later. This has recently been an exceptionally busy period, with the trip to China, the continuing Asian debt crisis, the well-publicized events in Russia, tensions in the Middle East and in Ireland, and a host of domestic concerns, such as the drought and a pressing legislative agenda before this Congress ends. We would be derelict in our professional duties if we allowed the President to give testimony without adequate preparation. (Unlike the OIC, the President is one person, with many different public responsibilities). Given his present schedule and duties, it is inconceivable that he would be able to testify in the immediate future. Between today and August 15, the President is already scheduled to be out of town for six days and has an exceptionally busy schedule while here. He has a long-scheduled family vacation between August 15 and 30, but much of this will be absorbed with preparation for a critical trip to Russia and Ireland from August 31 through September 6. The first date the President could conceivably testify consistently with his other obligations would be Sunday, September 13, although we would, in simple fairness, request that his testimony occur on Sunday, September 20. While we are not aware of the witnesses who remain to be interviewed by the OIC, we believe that the pending legal disputes which are now sub judice will plainly not be resolved before mid-September, and so we do not believe that a mid-September date for the President's testimony would itself unduly delay the completion of your investigation. It certainly would be sooner than any date you might anticipate were you to precipitate a legal confrontation.

I look forward to talking with you at your earliest convenience.

Sincerely,

David E. Kendall

Office of the Independent Counsel
1001 Pennsylvania Avenue, N.W.
Suite 490-North
Washington, DC 20004
(202) 514-8688
Fax (202) 514-8802

July 27, 1998
VIA HAND DELIVERY

David E. Kendall, Esq.
Williams & Connolly
725 Twelfth Street, N.W.
Washington, D.C. 20005

Re: William Jefferson Clinton

Dear David:

Thank you for your letter of July 27, 1998, which we received at 1:30 p.m. today. Although there is much in your letter with which we disagree, there is no reason at this point to engage in an extended discussion. Instead we wish to remain focused on the subject of obtaining the President's testimony for the grand jury.

Although we remain willing to accommodate the President's security and dignity concerns, we cannot agree with the other restrictions and conditions you suggest. Most importantly, we cannot agree to delay the testimony for another seven-plus weeks. The President has been aware since late January that the grand jury wants to hear his story, and he has declined numerous invitations to provide his testimony voluntarily. Therefore, further extensive delay of the type you propose is simply unacceptable. As a result, we will not withdraw the existing subpoena (as continued per today's telephone call, to 1:30 p.m. on July 28th). If, however, by tomorrow at 1:30 p.m., the President commits in writing to testify on a date certain on or before August 7, 1998, then we will continue the subpoena until that date. If the President agrees to a date certain, we will of course work closely with you to accommodate the logistical concerns that you have raised.

Sincerely,

Robert J. Bittman
Deputy Independent Counsel

SEALED   SEALED   SEALED

UNITED STATES DISTRICT COURT
FOR THE DISTRICT OF COLUMBIA

IN RE: .   Misc. No. 98-267

    MOTION TO CONTINUE   .   Washington, D. C.
                        .   July 28, 1998
                        .   4:30 p.m.

. . . .

TRANSCRIPT OF STATUS HEARING
BEFORE THE HONORABLE NORMA HOLLOWAY JOHNSON
CHIEF JUDGE, UNITED STATES DISTRICT COURT

APPEARANCES:

For the Office of
Independent Counsel: ROBERT BITTMAN, ESQUIRE
                        SAUL WISENBERG, ESQUIRE
                        JOSEPH DITKOFF, ESQUIRE

For the Movant,
President Clinton: DAVID E. KENDALL, ESQUIRE
                        NICOLE SELIGMAN, ESQUIRE
                        MAX STIER, ESQUIRE
                        ALICIA MARTI, ESQUIRE

Official Court Reporter: GORDON A. SLODYSKO
                        4806-A U. S. Courthouse
                        Washington, D. C. 20001
                        (202) 273-0404

Computer-Aided Transcription of Stenographic Notes

PROCEEDINGS

THE COURT: Good Afternoon.

COUNSEL: Good afternoon, Your Honor.

THE DEPUTY CLERK: Miscellaneous Case Number 98-267, In re Motion to Continue. Representing the Office of the Independent Counsel are Robert Bittman, Saul Wisenberg, and Joseph Ditkoff. Representing President Clinton is David Kendall, Nicole Seligman, Max Stier, and Alicia Marti.

THE COURT: All right.

Counsel, I received this afternoon President Clinton's motion for continuance. I'm sure the Office of Independent Counsel would like a chance to respond to that motion. In the interest of time, and certainly in light of the public interest in moving this matter expeditiously, I will allow each side to present oral argument on the motion for continuance rather than asking the parties to submit written responses. I will hear from each of you for I hope not more than ten minutes a side and then make my ruling. If you need more than ten minutes, I certainly will grant you additional time. But I would hope that we could do it in about ten minutes a side.

And since it is the President's motion, I will hear from Mr. Kendall first.

MR. KENDALL: May it please the Court. We've moved for a two-week continuance of a subpoena ad testificandum delivered to counsel for the President on Friday, July 17th. In some ways, Your Honor, I regret the need to burden you with this motion; I think it was unnecessary. But we were unable to get a continuance worked out with the Office of Independent Counsel.

I would like to explain a little about the background of this, if I may. This is not the first time the President's testimony has been sought. Indeed, on three different occasions he has given testimony at the behest of the Independent Counsel during the Whitewater investigation. The first time this occurred was in June of 1994, when Mr. Fisk was Independent Counsel. The second time was in April of 1995, after the present Independent Counsel was appointed on August 5th, 1994. And the third time was in July of 1995. Now, on each occasion we were able to work out a mutually acceptable way of providing for this testimony.

The President also testified twice by videotape in criminal trials of defendants indicted by the Whitewater grand jury in Arkansas. And on those occasions, the Independent Counsel was able to cross-examine the President.

As is clear from our motion, we had correspondence with the Independent Counsel earlier this spring about the President voluntarily appearing. I had many concerns about this. They were set forth in the correspondence. That correspondence really lapsed in April. The next thing we heard was the letter attached to the subpoena which was delivered to me at approximately 6:00 p.m. Friday, July 17th.

Your Honor, I initially sought time because this is the summer. Various people are somewhat scattered. Mr. Kantor, for example, is in China. He's been in China—

THE COURT: Mr. Who?

MR. KENDALL: Mr. Mickey Kantor.

THE COURT: Oh, okay.

MR. KENDALL: One of the President's private attorneys who has been advising on this matter.

We were, however, able to make a quite specific proposal to the Independent Counsel, which was delivered yesterday, and that is at Tab 6 of our papers. This is a letter in which I try to outline some of our concerns, how they may be met. It provides a date, a specific date for the President to give testimony and an alternative date. And that, I hoped, would be a good faith offer that would allow us to negotiate, as we have in the past, and settle on both the timing and terms of the President's testimony.

I was surprised that the Independent Counsel refused to withdraw or suspend this subpoena, and therefore, I made this motion. I think it unseemly for the President of the United States to be in any way in violation of legal process. I think there are obvious reasons for that. And therefore, in an effort to avoid that, we made a motion for a brief continuance.

Your Honor, there are no deadlines, there are no statutes of limitation, there are no pending trials. There is really nothing substantive to warrant the denial of this very brief continuance.

I think that we may not in fact need the two weeks. It may be possible that we can very quickly work with the Independent Counsel to come to an agreement on the terms and timing. But as the motion papers make clear, this is a literally unprecedented legal act. The testimony of the President has never been compelled before a grand jury before, and there are very serious constitutional questions, the litigation of which would be quite time-consuming. We don't necessarily want to have to tackle those questions if we can come to an agreement that would allow both sides—this has happened often in this investigation—to maintain their positions but work together to get by a common problem.

The President of the United States—I would be making this motion if it were anybody, in order to get the requisite time to try and work something out; and if things can't be worked out, to get the input of the people necessary to determine the proper arguments to be made on behalf of the President of the United States. The President is the President, however. He has public duties. And the language of the Jones case, the Clinton versus Jones case, is, I think, quite on point here because, while the Supreme Court did rule that the President while in office could be subjected to civil litigation, it also ruled that the conduct of that litigation had to be undertaken by the supervising judge with great sensitivity to the President's duties and great deference to the many demands on his time.

It is difficult to convey—I have represented busy people before. It is difficult to convey how busy the President is, how many demands there are on his time. And in the past it has taken us time to work out not only a time for the President to testify, but a time in which he can be adequately prepared, because he has many duties and many demands. And every client deserves the effective assistance of counsel in getting them ready to testify so they can testify as effectively and accurately as possible.

We quoted some of the language in Clinton versus Jones. One of the things the Court stated was it articulated the assumption that any testimony form the President may be taken at a time that will accommodate his busy schedule. Your Honor, again, I think that the—we've set forth in the letter the considerations that are important to us, considerations about the President's schedule. And we respectfully submit that this continuance is

563

not lengthy. It may in fact make unnecessary other litigation. And we respectfully would request that the Court grant us a two-week continuance.

THE COURT: What do you want to do with the two weeks? You know, you ask me for a two-week continuance. Are you asking me to give you two weeks to let the President respond to the subpoena, or are you asking me to give you two weeks to determine how you wish to respond to the subpoena? Just what are you asking me for?

MR. KENDALL: I think the former, Your Honor. I think it's the former.

THE COURT: Well, since I've said a couple of things, you'd better tell me what my former is.

MR. KENDALL: The former, Your Honor, as I understood it, was to enable the President to determine how most appropriately to respond to the subpoena.

It may be—and I don't know what the—because I didn't—I've had communications with Mr. Bittman. I don't know. My own view is that we should take testimony as we have done it before. That has the great value of precedent. And I think not only judges, but lawyers, there's a value in doing things the way they've been done in the past. I think if we can do that and find a date, the rest of the motion will be moot and we will come to agreement on a time and terms. That's what I hope will happen. We will try to make that happen.

Now, it's possible that we will not be able to come to those terms. A subpoena has been issued here. It's possible that the response would be some kind of a motion. And that would be done at the end of that two-week period.

So, I think what happens at the end of the two weeks really depends on what goes on during it.

THE COURT: So you're really not seeking just a two-weeks continuance of the return of the subpoena. You are actually seeking two weeks to determine what you want to do with respect to the subpoena.

MR. KENDALL: Your Honor, I think that's correct, although—

THE COURT: Because the way I understand it—I could be wrong, because I haven't seen the subpoena, and I haven't asked anybody to see it, but the way I understand it, the subpoena that he received in July stated that he should appear in person today. Is that correct?

MR. KENDALL: That's correct, Your Honor.

THE COURT: Okay. So, what you're saying to me is you're not asking me to just continue that appearance for two weeks. You're asking me to give you two weeks to raise further or additional legal argument.

MR. KENDALL: Your Honor, I don't know. It seems to me that I am asking you to continue it as well. What we don't want to have is the President in violation of the subpoena. And therefore, in the normal case you would phone up the prosecutor and say, "You've subpoenaed my client for Monday;, she's going to be in Chicago that day. Could you move it to Wednesday?" And normally, that's possible.

THE COURT: Yes.

MR. KENDALL: Depending on the grand jury.

Here, I think if we can get the continuance, in the interim I hope we will be able to work out an agreement whereby we won't have to come back to the Court at all, we will do the testimony. If we can't, then at the end of that period we would file a motion.

THE COURT: All right.

MR. KENDALL: Thank you, Your Honor.

THE COURT: Thank you.

I'll be happy to hear from you now, Mr. Bittman.

MR. BITTMAN: Good afternoon, Your Honor. Robert Bittman, on behalf of the United States.

Let me clarify something as to how we got involved in the chronology of what occurred. It was exactly six months ago today that we invited the President the first time to appear before the grand jury. Six months ago today.

Mr. Kendall correctly referred to the fact that our office has received testimony from the President before. That was via negotiation. But it was always with an invitation first, which the President accepted immediately, and then we hammered out some of the details as to when and how the President would testify.

In this case, we, and the grand jury, I might add, felt it necessary to issue a subpoena to the President because the President had refused six invitations to testify. They were, frankly, just, in my words, stringing us along, and the grand jury. The President publicly stated that he was prepared to cooperate with the investigation and give information sooner rather than later, more rather than less, and yet he refused—or declined, rather, six consecutive invitations to testify.

As you know, the grand jury has been working very, very hard, at great sacrifice to them. It has had effects on their families; it has had job effects. And they've been working very, very hard. They have been very gracious in allowing us extra days and extra time recently.

This litigation—or, pardon me, this investigation has also had a number of parties assert various privileges that have burdened not only this Court but the Court of Appeals, and some of them have gone all the way to the Supreme Court.

And we have tried to move things along as expeditiously as possible. The grand jury has been working very hard. And it is time to receive the President's testimony, if he so chooses.

THE COURT: And you say there have been six invitations?

MR. BITTMAN: There have been six invitations.

THE COURT: All right. And how did those invitations go? Were they in writing, as opposed to oral?

MR. BITTMAN: The first invitation was oral. The other five were all in writing. And I believe Mr. Kendall appended all of the invitations to his pleading. All of them are in there.

THE COURT: All right.

MR. BITTMAN: And then Mr. Kendall's responses are all there, also.

THE COURT: All right.

MR. BITTMAN: With regard to the President's schedule, he is a very busy person. And the Jones v. Clinton case makes it clear that the justice process should accommodate the President's schedule and should defer to him in his official capacity. I'm sure Mr. Kendall knows the President's schedule better than I do, but we have done some research, even in terms of when we set today, to make sure that he was in town. We've checked it in the future, too. And our understanding is that the President, for example, is going away this weekend for some fund-raising events and for some rest and relaxation, and then he's taking a two-week vacation in August.

We do not want to interrupt the President's foreign trips or any official business that the President, obviously, will be involved in. But we think the timing is right. The grand jury, you know, has been working, once again, as I said, very hard. And I don't think I want to reveal to Mr. Kendall exactly why the grand jury wishes the President's testimony now. And we're certainly not obligated to, and we're not going to. But this is the time.

We have tried to accommodate the President's schedule. We have offered innumerable dates through August 7th. We will go—well, we haven't worked out the exact, precise details of how we would receive the President's testimony, but I'm confident we can do that if we get an agreement from the President that he will appear before—in the very near future. And that just hasn't been forthcoming.

The date offered by Mr. Kendall in mid-September is just unacceptable. It is just unacceptable to the grand jury's schedule and to the grand jury's investigation. We just cannot wait that long for the President's testimony.

The investigation is very, very important. The President has so stated that. And I don't think that the investigation should wait for him to play golf, for fund-raising events, and for his vacations.

Mr. Kendall in his papers discusses that this could raise some sort of a constitutional crisis. We don't believe so. We have thoroughly reviewed the law and we believe we are absolutely entitled, with the grand jury's approval, to issue a subpoena to the President. The Nixon case made clear that the President of the United States may be subpoenaed in a criminal trial. The Jones v. Clinton case itself authorizes a court to—that the President appear at a deposition in a civil case. Clearly, if he has to appear in a civil case and answer to civil charges, he would have to answer a criminal grand jury subpoena.

The President also, as we've discussed, has appeared before. He's provided depositions to us. He's appeared in criminal trials. He was subpoenaed by the defense in two trials in Arkansas. He testified in those trials—after being deposed, but he testified. And then in this case, we issued a grand jury subpoena duces tecum, for documents, to the President early on in the investigation and he complied with that subpoena. I think it's odd now to all of a sudden say, well, he's not going to comply with this one.

So, unless Your Honor has any questions for me. We just want to get this resolved. We wish to know exactly what the President is going to do.

THE COURT: So what I understand from you is that you do maintain that the grand jury wants to have the President appear before it.
MR. BITTMAN: Yes.
THE COURT: And that you're saying you need it now.
MR. BITTMAN: Yes.
THE COURT: Rather than in September.
MR. BITTMAN: Yes.
THE COURT: Do you have any idea—and if you don't, I can understand, because I do know enough about grand juries to know that you can't always tell how many questions a grand jury may choose to ask or anything like that. Do you have any sense of how long he might be required to appear before the grand jury? Do you have any sense?
MR. BITTMAN: I think it would be several hours. Less than—well, I don't know. It would be several hours.

And let me amend one of my answers with regard to the grand jury's wishes as to whether the President actually appear before them. Without revealing too much of what goes on in the grand jury—

THE COURT: Certainly.

MR. BITTMAN: —that is their belief now. But we believe that if given a concrete offer by the President, that is, that he, the President, is willing to do this, to a deposition, perhaps in front of the grand jurors in an area outside the grand jury room, perhaps a deposition, obviously under oath, just before attorneys from our office, something like that in the immediate future, we believe that we can gain the—that we would speak to the grand jury and see if that were acceptable to them.

THE COURT: Well, let me just say, I know that even those type of issues could seriously be considered Rule 6(e). But I just wanted to get some sense.

That subpoena was issued by the grand jury, is that correct?

MR. BITTMAN: Yes.

THE COURT: And that was the subpoena that was returnable today.

MR. BITTMAN: Yes.

THE COURT: At 1:30.

MR. BITTMAN: It was actually returnable originally for 9:15, and then I permitted Mr. Kendall till 1:30. I extended it to 1:30.

THE COURT: All right. So your position is that the grand jury wishes to hear from him sooner than later.

MR. BITTMAN: Oh, yes. They have been kept informed throughout about our invitations and the President's declinations. And Your Honor knows that the grand jury's investigation has proceeded. And it is time to hear from this particular witness, the President.

THE COURT: Very well. Thank you.

MR. BITTMAN: And we at minimum wish, obviously, a response to whether the President is going to testify and then some concrete terms, because we just can't have this open-ended thing where, okay, in two weeks they may file a motion to quash which is going to further delay the investigation. If a motion to quash is to be filed, we wish to litigate it right away. And, frankly, we would ask Your Honor, if one is filed, for an expedited briefing schedule and expedited hearing, because we want this very, very quickly.

THE COURT: Very well. Thank you.

Mr. Kendall, I'll be happy to hear anything further that you wish to say on this issue.

MR. KENDALL: Thank you, Your Honor.

I regret that these somewhat voluminous papers probably hit your desk this afternoon.

THE COURT: Believe me, they did.

MR. KENDALL: They hit it with a thud, I'm sure.

THE COURT: Yes, they did.

MR. KENDALL: Your Honor, at Attachment 6, when Mr. Bittman says—

THE COURT: Which I have not been able—I have not read your attachments yet, but I have read your motion.

MR. KENDALL: Okay. I would simply direct the Court's attention to that

567

because that was our attempt—Mr. Bittman and I had conversations and he wanted a specific proposal. This is a specific proposal. It proposes both a time and terms. It's as specific, really, as we can get it.

Your Honor, it's simply not the case that this matter has been in discussion since January. It was in discussion in late January to April, and then we heard—my last letter, which I've appended here, was not responded to. So there was a long three months, plus, pause in this, and then suddenly we got the subpoena. And so it is not—

THE COURT: Let me ask you, what about letters from the grand jury? I understand that the grand jury was sending him a written invitation?

MR. KENDALL: Well, we received invitations from the Office of Independent Counsel. We never got anything from the grand jury itself.

THE COURT: But I mean the invitations from the Office of Independent Counsel indicated, though, that the purpose was for him to appear before the grand jury, wasn't it?

MR. KENDALL: They did, Your Honor.

THE COURT: And you didn't consider that to be from the grand jury?

MR. KENDALL: Well, Your Honor, I did. We responded to each one of those. And we responded—we had many questions. And this Court is familiar with certain of our concerns about this investigation—

THE COURT: Certainly.

MR. KENDALL: —and the way it's progressed. We had, and continue to have, very serious concerns about certain aspects of it. I don't want to have to litigate the constitutional questions, but they are important, they are unresolved. I am reminded when Mr. Bittman—and, you know, I don't think the Court wants to hear those arguments today. We haven't filed them. But—

THE COURT: No. Just the motion for continuance.

MR. KENDALL: Every pancake has two sides, Your Honor, as is well known. And we stand ready to make those at an appropriate time. But I think the—

THE COURT: But, you see, that's one of the things that caused me to ask you gentlemen to come in here today. I wasn't sure what you meant by give you until such-and-such a time, and I really needed you to come in here and tell me, what do you mean? Do you mean that you will be prepared to respond to the subpoena by that day, or do you mean that "I'm going to give this further thought and then two weeks from now I'm going to tell you what I think?" I need to know precisely what you mean.

And I think you have made it clear to me that the motion for continuance that you filed today is not designed to just continue the personal response to the subpoena. In other words, you're not saying, "If you give me two weeks, the President will respond by coming in to see the grand jury or having the grand jury come to see him." And, God knows, I would say to you, recognizing the duties of his office, if it were more convenient, more secure for the grand jury to go to him than for him to come to the grand jury—and you know what type of atmosphere we have around this building—then that's one thing. But if what you're saying is "I need two weeks to consider how I'm going to deal with this," then that's another question.

MR. KENDALL: Your Honor, again, the letter at Attachment 6 is a very—

THE COURT: As I said, I'll read it tonight.

MR. KENDALL: Yes. It's a very specific offer. And it's premised—we've worked this out, really, three times in the past successfully. I think that both our concerns and the Independent Counsel's concerns were met. I think the letter is a good faith attempt to do that again. And I hope that after discussion, we can work out a way—reserving our questions. I mean, these are negotiations in which both sides want to reserve their option. But three times before, we've had the President testify and that has—

THE COURT: Three times before testified with respect to what? This case?

MR. KENDALL: With respect to this investigation. This is the Whitewater—in other words, he gave testimony about various phases of it, Vincent Foster and David Hale and the 1990 gubernatorial campaign.

THE COURT: But I don't think this grand jury wants to ask any of those questions.

MR. KENDALL: Oh, no. No. I understand that, Your Honor. This is the Lewinsky—

THE COURT: Yes.

MR. KENDALL: And that's what we're talking about here. My only point is, we've been able to work this out three times in the past. And it's my hope that based upon the proposal we've made in the letter at Tab 6, that we can do it again, and so we won't be coming back to Your Honor.

THE COURT: Well, let me just say, apparently—and I've got to believe this—with your letter dated July 27th, which was yesterday, they have had an opportunity to read that letter before they got your papers that you filed in the court today around midday. Isn't that true? Every reason to believe they've had an opportunity to read that.

MR. KENDALL: That's correct, Your Honor.

THE COURT: And even though they have had that opportunity to read it, their stated position on the record is to the contrary of what you're saying—of what you say your letter says: That they can work it out. In fact, what I heard Mr. Bittman say is that he needs the testimony. You're saying you think you can work it out.

MR. KENDALL: Your Honor, we are trying to work it out to give them the testimony.

THE COURT: Let me just ask you something, Mr. Bittman. Had you read this letter before you came in here today?

MR. BITTMAN: Yes, Your Honor. We responded to it.

THE COURT: Oh, you did? And is it here, too?

MR. BITTMAN: Yes.

THE COURT: Okay.

MR. BITTMAN: That's at Attachment 7.

THE COURT: I haven't read the attachments, all right? I will read them before I leave here this evening, though, okay?

You see, what I—I mean just applying a little common sense here, if you sent this letter yesterday, they received it, they read it, they responded to it. Still, the subpoena remained outstanding, and the grand jury, who actually was the only body that could authorize that subpoena, apparently was waiting for the subpoena to be responded to today. Then we get your request. And, as I said, you asked me for two weeks and I just didn't quite understand what that two weeks meant. I understand now, based upon your statement to me, what you mean by giving you that additional two weeks, but that does not take into consideration the body which sought the subpoena. You see, that's what concerns me, Mr. Kendall.

I'm not saying—and I want you to understand, I'm not saying that this grand jury has a right to subpoena the President of the United States. I'm sure that they have subpoenaed the President of the United States. And what I am not hearing from you is that "We oppose this subpoena because the grand jury does not have that right." You're saying, "Just give me two weeks to think about something, and then two weeks from now I'll tell you something." And then if two weeks from now you say, 'Well, I don't really think they have the right to subpoena the President, and therefore, Your Honor, may I have two more weeks to file a motion to quash the subpoena." I just think that based upon what we all know about this case, the sooner we make a decision, the better.

MR. KENDALL: Your Honor, may I respond to that?

THE COURT: Surely you may.

MR. KENDALL: And I will respond, I hope, in a factual way. I'm not saying that I want a limitless set of extensions. I think that these are very important constitutional questions. If we go to war over them—

THE COURT: No question about it, but the question is, do we have to deal with the constitutional issue? Because if we do, let's do that head-on.

MR. KENDALL: But, Your Honor, if we go to war over that, that is going to take a lot of time.

THE COURT: We're not going to go to war, and we're going to do it the same way the Court of Appeals has you do things. I just find it so interesting. Everybody needs 10, 12 days if you are here in the district court, but I understand that those judges on the Court of Appeals give two days or three days. I said, "Why can't I exercise that power? I have a commission too." So, no, we aren't going to be in it forever, okay? All right.

I'm being facetious, of course.

MR. KENDALL: My only point is, Your Honor, if the object is to get the testimony to the grand jury, I think some statesmanship on both sides is necessary. And I say that about us as well as the Independent Counsel. I think that if we can work this out, we are obligated to do so, because that really is our civic duty. We've done it three times—

THE COURT: You all have had a long time, apparently, to do that, Mr. Kendall, if what Mr. Bittman says is correct. Mr. Bittman says that there was a subpoena issued one time. Was that correct?

MR. KENDALL: Your Honor, only on the 17th of July. A week ago.

THE COURT: Yes. Only the one on July 17th?

MR. KENDALL: Yes. I'm sorry. He mentioned—excuse me, Your Honor. He did mention a subpoena for certain objects that was issued in January.

THE COURT: Oh, yes, duces tecum, and that was taken care of. But I understand that there have been about six invitations from the grand jury. So, apparently the President has known for some time that the grand jury wished to speak with him.

Now, I don't know, because, God knows, you know, I may have to go up there and see if they have water and a few other things from time to time, but I don't know what goes on before the grand jury as you know. But I would think if somebody had received six letters inviting him to appear before the grand jury, that person—and I don't mean to be unkind, but certainly his counsel must know that somebody is going to get tired of written invitations and look to other sources. I mean, that's just common sense.

MR. KENDALL: Your Honor, we've tried in Tab 1 to give you the complete correspondence, because it states our concerns and the responses. And I think in fairness, that correspondence terminated when I sent a letter on April the 17th. I didn't know what the answer was. And a very long time elapsed.

My only point here, Your Honor, is that I—

THE COURT: Are you saying that there were no invitations from the grand jury since April 17th?

MR. KENDALL: April 3rd, in fact, Your Honor, was the last.

THE COURT: Was the last letter from the grand jury?

MR. KENDALL: Yes. And then all of a sudden, without any warning, we get a subpoena. And that old lawyer's trick, Your Honor, delivering it late Friday night so you can have that date of the week and say, "We served it on July 17th." It came in about 6:00 o'clock. That is what is forcing this issue.

In the past, we have been able to resolve this. I don't think it's seemly or statesmanlike, or even very reasonable, to put us under the gun of saying, as they say in their response to the letter of yesterday, "Well, you just commit to this date," and it's an unreasonable date in terms of the President's schedule. We're going to have to file a motion. I don't think we should be in the position of having to file a motion which, if we can resolve the other issues, may be unnecessary.

THE COURT: Well, why do you need so much time to resolve the other issues?

MR. KENDALL: I'm not sure we do, Your Honor. I'm not sure we do. I'm not sure that we can't do this very speedily. But the scheduling really is a problem.

THE COURT: What you're saying is, you have not as yet made the decision whether you are going to challenge the constitutionality of this subpoena.

MR. KENDALL: We have made a decision, Your Honor, that we've testified in the past, we believe we can testify at this time. But we don't know what their position is and they may force us to challenge this, and then we'll challenge it.

I used the "war" metaphor. We're not going to go to war. But we'll file motions to quash. And my only point is, it is unreasonable—you wouldn't do this in the normal case, Your Honor. You wouldn't refuse to continue a subpoena for a short time to see if it all was going to be unnecessary. And that's really all we're seeking. And at the end of the day, we may have to file a motion to quash, to bring on the constitutional issue, to preserve the institutional concerns of the Article II entity, person that we represent. It hasn't been necessary in the past; I don't believe it necessarily will be necessary now. But it could be.

THE COURT: Well, you say it may not be necessary, the amount of time you're seeking, but you still seek that time.

MR. KENDALL: I do, Your Honor.

THE COURT: All right. Anything else?

MR. KENDALL: The only thing I would say is, in reference to Mr. Bittman's statement about the President's schedule, it is true, he does have a vacation planned for late August. It's a well-deserved vacation. It, unfortunately, is right on the eve of his Russia trip and Ireland trip. That's a trip from August 31 to September the 6th. Both those countries are very important. A lot of that vacation is going to be absorbed with preparing for the Russia trip.

Again, we are trying—we've given them the date in September. We are aware from other parties who have been subpoenaed that the grand jury's work is going on. There are many other legal questions which are in the

571

process of being resolved. We really don't think that this date will delay the grand jury's work, and we want to make it possible, if we can, to give the President's testimony as soon as possible.

THE COURT: Well, let me just say this. You know, even I don't know what the grand jury is doing. And I'm certain that Mr. Bittman has some sense because he knows what has been presented to the grand jury and what he wishes to present to the grand jury. But I haven't the foggiest notion of what they have presented or what they wish to present. I learn most of what I know about that grand jury the same way most citizens in this city do, and we don't know how accurate that is, but that's from the local press.

Now, what concerns me is this: This case is unlike the Jones case. It truly is unlike the Jones case. And even though it is quite unlike the Jones case, we know what the Supreme Court felt about even a civil action of the type that we have there. Here, we have a criminal investigation going on. Here, we know from just reading the press that perhaps witnesses who have been called in before this grand jury have been testifying about certain conduct. I don't know what that grand jury thinks, but it perhaps thinks that "We citizens have been brought from our regular responsibilities and asked to listen to certain evidence, and we have decided, based upon what we have heard, that we need to hear from the President."

Now, maybe they don't have any legal right to hear from the President. Maybe that is an issue we will have to resolve before this subpoena can be honored. But what we need to do, I think, is to move forward, and move forward expeditiously.

Apparently, the President has been given, if you'll excuse this slang, a heads-up by the number of invitations. Did I determine that those invitations were in writing?

MR. KENDALL: Some of them were, Your Honor. They are reflected, I think, in the correspondence in Tab 1.

THE COURT: As I said, I'll read this. But some of it—at any rate, he's received six invitations. And apparently the grand jury has determined that "Although we would like to honor your position as our President by simply asking you to appear voluntarily, we have now reached the point where we believe that you will not honor us with your presence voluntarily, but we do believe that in our search for the truth, we need to hear from you." And now, for him to say, "Give me two weeks to think whether I'm going to challenge this legally or what I'm going to do, give me two weeks to see if I can work this out with the prosecutor, give me two weeks to see whatever I need to do," but by the time that two weeks is up, Mr. Kendall, you're saying to me he will—I don't know whether he's going to the Cape this year or not, but I know that's where he generally goes. Whether he will be at the Cape by the time the two weeks is up. And, clearly, I've been told that after leaving the Cape, he'll be going to Russia. So, when, if ever, unless somebody directs him, will he be willing to respond to this grand jury? Or if he isn't willing to respond to the grand jury, tell me.

MR. KENDALL: Your Honor, it's a fair question.

THE COURT: Tell me. And then we will do what we have to do.

MR. KENDALL: We've given two dates. I think that's a very fair question. You'll see in the letter at Tab 6—

THE COURT: The July 27th letter?

MR. KENDALL: Exactly.

THE COURT: All right.

572

MR. KENDALL: We have said, because of the Russia trip, because of the vacation and other travel. And, again, it's very easy to sit there, whether you're reading a newspaper, you're in the Office of Independent Counsel, and say, well, that trip's not necessary, that's just a fund-raising trip, and that's a political trip, and, look, I don't think Ireland is such an important country. Those concerns are the President's, and the President's alone, to balance. And courts—I mean, again, the teaching of Clinton v. Jones, I think, is that a court must try to accommodate and give deference to the President's schedule.

THE COURT: That's true. And as I said, I understand that very, very clearly, because we know that as President of these United States, this gentleman has concerns that none of us know about. We know that there are issues of state that none of us know about. We know all of that. But I also know this: If he can vacation for a couple of weeks, he can appear before a grand jury, too, you know.

And God knows, he needs a vacation. I know that. I know he needs a vacation. And I don't know that the grand jury will—he doesn't know how—the grand jury may just want to see him. I don't know. They may not have any questions at all.

MR. KENDALL: We did try to make a very specific offer, including a date that would be consonant with his schedule.

THE COURT: But that's sometime in September.

MR. KENDALL: It is.

THE COURT: Well, as I said, you see, I don't know the interest of the grand jury, either. But one thing is for sure: The grand jury has apparently attempted, even though you've maintained that because there was no further response to some letter you wrote in April, that, therefore, he could think that maybe they didn't want him any more.

MR. KENDALL: Your Honor, I would like to distinguish, if I could, between concerns. We, obviously, would like to help the grand jury in its endeavors. The Office of Independent Counsel we have our differences with about a number of things. They are set forth in the letter. Those concerns have not been responded to. We are willing to forgo some of those or litigate them in other forums. We really did try, however, to get a good faith offer that was specific in terms of place, way of taking testimony, issues—and leaks are one of the things that we are concerned about. But we believe that there can be safeguards. This is not an impossible task. And time. And the time is really very critical. But we have tried to put that all in a very specific proposal for the Independent Counsel and for the Court.

THE COURT: All right. Thank you very much.

MR. KENDALL: Thank you, Your Honor.

THE COURT: Mr. Bittman, I'll hear from you finally.

MR. BITTMAN: Thank you. I'll be brief. Robert Bittman on behalf of the United States.

Your Honor, in all respect, I think saying that we are being unreasonable by issuing a grand jury subpoena with the grand jury's approval is a little— and that we're not willing to accommodate or even give a little bit with regard to the President's schedule, we are, we have been. I think that that argument would have a lot more merit had there not been six invitations.

We've tried to get his testimony since January. We've tried. Since January 27th, we have tried. We've invited him. And we made clear in all those invitations that we will accommodate the President's schedule. And now, for the President to—and then after six invitations, you know, we in the grand jury decide to issue a subpoena to the President because that's within our power. You know, we tried to accommodate him, we've tried all means necessary to avoid any constitutional confrontation or something like that, but he declined the invitation. What are we left to do? And we have—back then, when we extended these invitations, we have a lot of room to negotiate in terms of when and how and where and that kind of stuff. Well, now we're at the end of the investigation, or near the end of the investigation, we decide, with the grand jury's approval, to issue a subpoena to the President. We don't have many options any more.

And so for them to come in here and say, "Oh, we want them to be more reasonable," we were reasonable back then. And they were the ones that said, "No, we're not going to do it. We're not going to agree to this." So I think it is disingenuous, with all respect.

I did notify Mr. Kendall last weekend—and I might also say, if they were really serious about trying to work something out—and Mr. Kendall did put forward a very specific date. I agree with that. And that's in his correspondence. But the date simply is not acceptable. That's the bottom line. It's unacceptable. We told him it was unacceptable.

THE COURT: That's the September date?

MR. BITTMAN: That's the September date. That is unacceptable. And we have the power, we, with the grand jury, have the power to compel the President. That's what we've decided to do. We didn't want to do that. That's why we issued the six invitations. But they put us in a box. We had to do it because they weren't going to agree anyway. Now, we have a limited opportunity in terms of time.

I notified Mr. Kendall that if they really wanted to work out a date, an acceptable date with us, that we would be available all weekend. Apparently Mr. Kendall—I read that Mr. Kendall was not available over the weekend. But we responded within hours of his letter to me, and we said we're available to work this out, to work out an acceptable date. They didn't provide us with an acceptable date. It's that simple.

We still are willing to work out an acceptable date, but we're not going to wait two weeks for it. We have to move this along.

THE COURT: Well, I think Mr. Kendall is asking for a little more than two weeks, isn't he?

MR. BITTMAN: He is, because—

THE COURT: You see, that's why I really had to have you all in here today, because I wanted to be certain of what you meant. You could read Mr. Kendall's motion to maybe suggest that, well, we'll be ready to go on that date, and I said and you could also read it to mean that you won't be ready to go, "but I'll be ready to tell you where I want to go two weeks from now."

And I certainly have a duty to the President, but I also have a duty to the grand jury. And here, this third branch stands behind the first and the second branches, but, you know, I do have a duty myself.

So, anything else you want to say? I'll have to take this matter under advisement, but let me just say, I'm in a better position to take it under advisement, having had you come today, than I was just based on the papers alone.

MR. BITTMAN: Nothing else from me. Thank you, Your Honor.

THE COURT: Anything else from you, Mr. Kendall?

MR. KENDALL: Thank you, Your Honor.

THE COURT: Okay. Well, thank you very much.

Let me just say, what I hope to do is call you first thing in the morning and tell you—I hope to be able to call you first thing in the morning and tell you to come down and pick up my decision or pick up an order or whatever the case may be relative to today's hearing. Okay? I really hope to be able to do it. And if you haven't heard from me by 11 o'clock—well, let me just say this. If you haven't heard from me by 11 o'clock—no, that isn't what I want to say.

If you have not received a telephone call from me before 11 o'clock, I will try to do a conference call at 11 o'clock. That's what I want to say. Okay? Thank you very much.

(Proceedings concluded at 5:20 p.m.)

<u>CERTIFICATE OF REPORTER</u>

I certify that the foregoing is a correct transcription from the record of proceedings in the above-entitled matter.

Official Court Reporter

575

LAW OFFICES
WILLIAMS & CONNOLLY
725 TWELFTH STREET, N.W.
WASHINGTON, D. C. 20005-5901
(202) 434-5000
FAX (202) 434-5029

DAVID E. KENDALL   EDWARD BENNETT WILLIAMS (1920-1988)
(202) 434-5145   PAUL R. CONNOLLY (1922-1978)

August 31, 1998

CONFIDENTIAL
RULE 6(e), F.R.CRIM.P. GRAND JURY SUBMISSION

Robert J. Bittman, Esq.
Deputy Independent Counsel
Office of the Independent Counsel
1001 Pennsylvania Avenue, N.W.
Suite 490-North
Washington, D.C. 20004

By Hand

Dear Bob:

This will acknowledge your letter dated August 26, 1998. I believe that
the President has complied with grand jury subpoenas nos. V002 and
D1415. I will not repeat the comments of my letter to you dated April 13,
1998. As I have previously told you, the President receives a large number
of gifts from a great many people. We have done our very best to comply
with the grand jury subpoenas. I want to repeat, however, that if you have
information concerning gifts or other objects which you think may be
responsive to these subpoenas, and if you will give me a description of
what those gifts or other objects might be, we will be happy to undertake
a search for them, as we have in the past.

Sincerely,

David E. Kendall

PART FIVE

THE DRESS

[Editor's note: Ms. Lewinsky gave prosecutors a dress she said may have been stained with President Clinton's semen.]

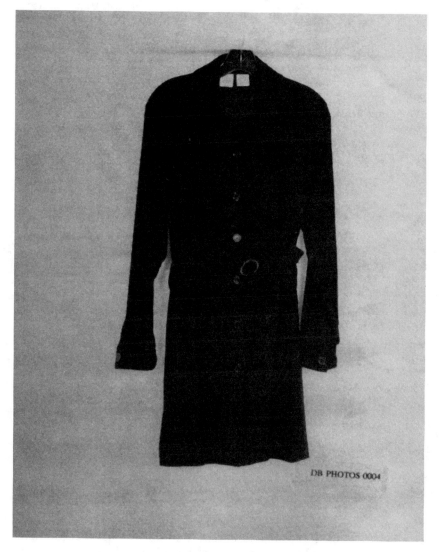

FEDERAL BUREAU OF INVESTIGATION
WASHINGTON, D.C. 20535

Date: August 3, 1998

To: Mr. Kenneth W. Starr
      Office of the Independent Counsel
      1001 Pennsylvania Avenue, N.W.
      Suite 490-North
      Washington, D.C. 20004

      FBI File No.   29D-OIC-LR-35063

            Lab No.   980730002 S BO

Reference: Communication dated July 30, 1998

Your No.   29D-OIC-LR-35063

Re: MOZARK;
      MC 106
Specimens received: July 30, 1998

Specimens:

Q3243   Navy blue dress
        ITEMS NOT EXAMINED

NE1   Hanger
NE2   Plastic bag

This report contains the results of the requested serological examinations.

Specimen Q3243 and samples removed from specimen Q3243 are being preserved for possible future DNA analysis. In order to conduct meaningful DNA analysis, known blood samples must be submitted from the victim, suspect or other individuals believed to have contributed body fluids to specimen Q3243. Each known blood sample should be collected in one (1) lavender-top blood vial containing the preservative EDTA, and stored in a refrigerator until submission to the FBI Laboratory.

The evidence and the samples removed from the evidence will be retained in the FBI Laboratory until they are retrieved by a representative from your office.

FEDERAL BUREAU OF INVESTIGATION
WASHINGTON, D.C. 20535

Report of Examination
Examiner Name: ████████

Unit: DNA Analysis 1

FBI File No.:   29D-OIC-LR-35063

Date: 08/03/98

Phone No.:   202-324-4409

Lab No.:   980730002 S BO

Results of Examinations:

Semen was identified on specimen Q3243.

No other serological examinations were conducted.

 Office of the Independent Counsel

July 31, 1998

Received this 31st day of July, 1998, one

double-enveloped package addressed to David

Kendall, Williams & Connolly, 725 12th

Street, Northwest, Washington, D.C.   20005

7/31/98 3:20pm
Date and Time

N. Sloan
Signature

Office of the Independent Counsel

1001 Pennsylvania Avenue, N.W.
Suite 490-North
Washington, DC 20004
(202) 514-8688
Fax (202) 514-8802

July 31, 1998
<u>HAND DELIVERED</u>
David E. Kendall, Esq.
Williams & Connolly
725 Twelfth Street, N.W.
Washington, D.C. 20005

Re: <u>William Jefferson Clinton</u>

Dear David:

I telephoned you twice this morning but was unable to reach you. Investigative demands require that President Clinton provide this Office as soon as possible with a blood sample to be taken under our supervision. I. I assure you this information will be kept strictly confidential and will restricted to a handful of persons on a need-to-know basis only.

Your prompt response to these requests will be greatly appreciated.
Sincerely,

Robert J. Bittman
Deputy Independent Counsel

Office of the Independent Counsel

July 31, 1998

Received this 31st day of July, 1998, one

double-enveloped package addressed to David

Kendall, Williams & Connolly, 725 12th

Street, Northwest, Washington, D.C. 20005

7/31/98 3:20pm
Date and Time

582 Signature

LAW OFFICES
WILLIAMS & CONNOLLY
725 TWELFTH STREET, N.W.
WASHINGTON, D. C. 20005-5901
(202) 434-5000
FAX (202) 434-5029

DAVID E. KENDALL
(202) 434-5145

EDWARD BENNETT WILLIAMS (1920–1988)
PAUL R. CONNOLLY (1922–1978)

July 31, 1998

CONFIDENTIAL

Robert J. Bittman, Esq.
Deputy Independent Counsel
Office of the Independent Counsel
1001 Pennsylvania Avenue, N.W.
Suite 490-North
Washington, D.C. 20004

By Hand

Dear Bob:

I received your July 31 letter which refers to "[i]nvestigative demands." As you must surely be aware, the cases require a heightened standard of probable cause for bodily intrusions. See, e.g., Schmerber v. California, 384 U.S. 757, 769 (1966); Winston v. Lee, 470 U.S. 753, 759 (1985); In re Grand Jury Proceedings (Suleski), 816 F. Supp. 1196, 1204–06 (W.D. Ky. 1196). Since the request you make is addressed to the President of the United States, I believe that also applicable to this request are the considerations identified in Clinton v. Jones, ____ U.S. ____, 117 S.Ct. 1636, 1650–1651 (1997), that mandate a "high respect that is owed to the office of the Chief Executive . . . [which should] inform the conduct of the entire proceeding." Accordingly, I ask that you inform me of the precise factual basis for your request.

I have another concern and another request. I will not rehearse the history of grand jury leaks in this investigation or the orders that Chief Judge Johnson has entered. While the OIC has retained outside counsel to appeal portions of the district court orders which afforded us discovery against the OIC and while an administrative stay from the Court of Appeals is now in effect, the OIC has not appealed the underlying findings which caused the Chief Judge to enter her orders. In just the last few days, there have been numerous leaks to the news media of reports about a dress of Ms. Lewinsky's which is allegedly stained in some way. As to these latter leaks, I do not at the present time have information sufficient to say who may be guilty of any improper disclosures, but unfortunately such leaks appear to be a way of life in this investigation. I fear that, if we provide the sample you have requested, false information of any tests that are conducted will be leaked. In its papers in the leaks litigation, the OIC has often adverted to "false" leaks. The only way we can be protected against such a phenomenon is to be made aware of

583

any test results which are conducted, so we will be in a position to respond to false leaks.

If you believe either of these disclosures would be protected by Rule 6(e), we would be willing to stipulate to a motion to the Court for a Rule 6(e) order allowing the release of information to us, and we would undertake not to disclose it further, except on the terms specified in the order.

I would like to discuss these matters with you further and will give you a call after you have received this letter.
Sincerely,
signature

David E. Kendall
DEK/bb

Office of the Independent Counsel

1001 Pennsylvania Avenue, N.W.
Suite 490-North
Washington, DC 20004
(202) 514-8688
Fax (202) 514-8802

July 31, 1998
HAND DELIVERED

David E. Kendall, Esq.
Williams & Connolly
725 Twelfth Street, N.W.
Washington, D.C. 20005

Re: William Jefferson Clinton

Dear David:

This responds to your letter of today, which was delivered to me at 5:35 p.m.

I assure you that we have substantial factual and legal predication for our request of the President. We are mindful of the legal requirements of our request, and we are certain that the request is lawful and would be upheld by a reviewing court. We make this request, as we have others, respectful of the dignity of the Office of the President. Because of the President's pledge to cooperate with this investigation and out of respect for the Presidency, we have not issued a subpoena for this sample. We do not wish to litigate this matter, and we wish no embarrassment to the President. Yet, we have substantial predication for our request, and we must do our job.

You also refer to the dissemination of information in the media. As confirmed by Messrs. Stein and Cacheris, this Office is not the source— either directly or indirectly—of the information. That being said, we are sensitive to your desires, consistent with our abiding aim, to insure complete confidentiality. We have—we believe—powerful predication for our request of the President, and that representation, which reflects our considered professional judgement, should suffice. If you disagree, then the prudent and wise course may be to proceed under the aegis of the Chief Judge. We would set forth our predication, which we believe is powerful, before the Chief Judge. This would assure you the independent review of an Article III judge, and thereby further insure that the dignitary interests of the President are scrupulously protected. The Chief Judge would also, under our proposed approach, then be in a position to consider any protective order (or evaluate a motion to quash) that you might see fit to request.

We are not in a position at this early juncture to agree to a release of information subsequent to further examination; such a release to you might raise serious questions of law, as you recognize. Here again, we could go before Chief Judge Johnson for appropriate direction to protect all relevant interests.

Sincerely,
signature

Robert J. Bittman
Deputy Independent Counsel

LAW OFFICES
WILLIAMS & CONNOLLY
725 TWELFTH STREET, N.W.
WASHINGTON, D. C. 20005-5901
(202) 434-5000
FAX (202) 434-5029

DAVID E. KENDALL   EDWARD BENNETT WILLIAMS (1920–1988)
(202) 434-5145   PAUL R. CONNOLLY (1922–1978)

August 3, 1998

CONFIDENTIAL
WRITTEN PURSUANT TO SECRECY PROVISIONS OF RULE 6(e),
FEDERAL RULES OF CRIMINAL PROCEDURE
GRAND JURY MATERIAL

Robert J. Bittman, Esq.
Deputy Independent Counsel
Office of the Independent Counsel
1001 Pennsylvania Avenue, N.W.
Suite 490-North
Washington, D.C. 20004

BY HAND—TO BE OPENED BY MR. BITTMAN ONLY

Dear Bob:

   This letter is written after receiving your second letter dated July 31, 1998, and after our telephone conversation this morning. We agree to provide the blood specimen you have requested (today, if possible), pursuant to the following conditions:

1) This test, any analysis, our written correspondence, and our oral communications on this issue are all to be treated as highly confidential, subject to the full protections of Rule 6(e), Federal Rules of Criminal Procedure. Both the OIC and we will take the utmost precautions to preserve the confidentiality of this matter.

(2) The sample will be drawn by the White House physician, Dr. Connie Mariano, at the White House, in the presence of two representatives of the OIC, under medical procedures acceptable to the OIC. The sample will be immediately furnished to the OIC.

(3) You will execute an affidavit today setting forth your predication evidence for requesting this test, and you will preserve this affidavit in a secure place. You will set forth in the affidavit the evidence you would have presented to Chief Judge Johnson, as represented in your second letter of July 31, 1998.

(4) You will instruct the laboratory that does any analysis related to the specimen we furnish to preserve enough of the item being tested (e.g., any dress of Ms. Lewinsky's) to make possible a later, outside, comparative test of the same type, if appropriate.

I will look forward to receiving a written response to this letter, and we will speak later in the day concerning logistics.

Sincerely,

Robt S. Bittman

Office of the Independent Counsel
1001 Pennsylvania Avenue, N.W.
Suite 490-North
Washington, DC 20004
(202) 514-8688
Fax (202) 514-8802

August 3, 1998

HAND DELIVERED

David E. Kendall, Esq.
Williams & Connolly
725 Twelfth Street, N.W.
Washington, D.C. 20005

Re: William Jefferson Clinton

Dear David:

This responds to your letter of today regarding your agreement to permit a blood sample to be taken from the President this evening at 10:00 p.m.

(1) We will treat this test, any analysis, our written correspondence, and our oral communications on this matter as highly confidential, subject to the full protections of Rule 6(e).

(2) We agree to permit Dr. Mariano to draw the sample from the President in the presence of two representatives from this Office. Dr. Mariano should use a "purple-top" tube, which she will then turn over immediately to the representatives from this Office. I, Robert James Bittman will represent the OIC.

(3) I agree to execute a declaration setting forth the predication for requesting this test. This declaration will then be preserved in a secure place at the OIC.

(4) I have requested that the FBI Laboratory preserve as much of the remaining specimen as possible so as to make possible a later, comparative test, if appropriate.

Sincerely,
Robert J. Bittman

Deputy Independent Counsel
FEDERAL BUREAU OF INVESTIGATION
Date of transcription August 3, 1998

On this date, Supervisory Special Agent (SSA) ▇▇▇▇ was present in the Map Room of the White House, Washington D.C. with Robert J. Bittman, Deputy Independent Counsel, Eleanor Maricino, M.D., White House Physician, David Kendall, Attorney and William Jefferson Clinton, President. At approximately 10:10 pm, SSA ▇▇▇▇ observed Dr. Maricino draw blood by venous puncture from President Clinton's right arm, filling one purple top tube (approximately 4ml). She capped the tube and transferred it to SSA ▇▇▇▇ who labeled the tube with the name "William Clinton", the date and SSA ▇▇▇▇ initials. The tube was placed in a clean disposable test tube and sealed with evidence tape. SSA ▇▇▇▇ promptly returned to the FBI Laboratory, Washington D.C. where at 10:30, the tube of blood was delivered to DNA Analysis Unit I technician, ▇▇▇▇, for further processing according to standard practice. This sample will be maintained in the custody of the FBI Laboratory for the duration of the testing process.

FEDERAL BUREAU OF INVESTIGATION
WASHINGTON, D.C. 20535

Date: August 6, 1998
To: Mr. Kenneth W. Starr
        Office of the Independent Counsel
        1001 Pennsylvania Avenue, N.W.
        Suite 490-North
        Washington, D.C. 20004

FBI File No.   29D-OIC-LR-35063

Lab No.   980730002 S BO
          980803100 S BO

Reference: Communication dated July 30, 1998 and evidence submitted
             August 3, 1998

Your No.   29D-OIC-LR-35063

Re: MOZARK;
      MC 106

Specimens received: July 30, 1998 and August 3, 1998
Specimens: Received July 30, 1998 (under cover of FBI Laboratory number 980730002 S BO):

Q3243   Navy blue dress

ITEMS NOT EXAMINED
NE1   Hanger
NE2   Plastic bag

Specimen received August 3, 1998 (under cover of FBI Laboratory number 980803100 S BO):

K39   Liquid blood sample from WILLIAM CLINTON
This report supplements an FBI Laboratory report dated August 3, 1998 and contains the results of additional serological and DNA-PCR examinations. DNA-RFLP examinations are continuing and you will be advised of the results of those examinations and the disposition of the evidence in a separate report.

FEDERAL BUREAU OF INVESTIGATION
WASHINGTON, D.C. 20535

Report of Examination
Examiner Name: ████████

Unit: DNA Analysis 1

FBI File No.:   29D-OIC-LR-35063

Date: 08/06/98

Phone No.:   202-324-4409

Lab No.:   980730002 S BO

980803100 S BO

Results of Examinations:

Specimen Q3243 was examined for the presence of blood; however, none was found.

Polymarker (PM), DQA1, and D1S80 types as listed below were detected for the following specimens:

SPECIMEN LDLR GYPA HBGG D7S8 Gc DQA1 D1S80
Q3243-1 BB   BB   AB   AB   AC 1.1, 1.2 24, 24
Q3243-2 BB   BB   AB   AB   AC 1.1, 1.2 24, 24
K39   BB   BB   AB   AB   AC 1.1, 1.2 24, 24

Based on the PM, DQA1, and D1S80 typing results, the source of specimen K39 is included as a potential contributor of the DNA obtained from specimens Q3243-1 and Q3243-2 (two semen stains removed from specimen Q3243). The probability of selecting an unrelated individual at random having the same PM, DQA1 and D1S80 types as detected in the questioned specimens is approximately 1 in 390,000 in the Black population, 1 in 43,000 in the Caucasian population, 1 in 39,000 in the Southeastern Hispanic population, and 1 in 220,000 in the Southwestern Hispanic population.

Based on the amelogenin typing results, male DNA was detected in the DNA obtained from specimens Q3243-1, Q3243-2 and K39.

FEDERAL BUREAU OF INVESTIGATION
WASHINGTON, D.C. 20535

Date: August 17, 1998

To: Mr. Kenneth W. Starr
     Office of the Independent Counsel
     1001 Pennsylvania Avenue, N.W.
     Suite 490-North
     Washington, D.C. 20004

FBI File No. 29D-OIC-LR-35063

Lab No. 980730002 S BO
         980803100 S BO

Reference: Communication dated July 30, 1998 and evidence submitted
            August 3, 1998

Your No. 29D-OIC-LR-35063

Re: MOZARK;
     MC 106

Specimens received: July 30, 1998 and August 3, 1998

Specimens:

This report supplements two FBI Laboratory reports dated August 3, 1998 and August 6, 1998 and contains the results of the DNA-RFLP examinations.

This completes the requested examinations. The submitted items and the probed DNA membranes will be retained until retrieved by a representative of your organization. In addition to the evidence in the case, any remaining processed DNA from specimens examined by DNA analysis is also being returned to you. The processed DNA can be found in a package marked PROCESSED DNA SAMPLES: SHOULD BE REFRIGERATED/ FROZEN. It is recommended that these samples be stored in a refrigerator/freezer and isolated from evidence that has not been examined.

FEDERAL BUREAU OF INVESTIGATION
WASHINGTON, D.C. 20535

Report of Examination

Examiner Name: ████████

Unit: DNA Analysis 1

FBI File No.:   29D-OIC-LR-35063

Date: 08/17/98

Phone No.:   202-324-4409

Lab No.:   980730002 S BO
980803100 S BO

Results of Examinations:

Deoxyribonucleic acid (DNA) profiles for the genetic loci D2S44, D17S79, D1S7, D4S139, D10S28, D5S110 and D7S467 were developed from HaeIII-digested high molecular weight DNA extracted from specimens K39 and Q3243-1 (a semen stain removed from specimen Q3243). Based on the results of these seven genetic loci, specimen K39 (CLINTON) is the source of the DNA obtained from specimen Q3243-1, to a reasonable degree of scientific certainty.

No DNA-RFLP examinations were conducted on specimen Q3243-2 (a semen stain removed from specimen Q3243).

BLACK—1,440,000,000,000
CAUC—7,870,000,000,000
SEH—3,140,000,000,000
SWH—943,000,000,000

PART SIX

MISCELLANEOUS

Paula Jones Documents

CHRONOLOGY OF EVENTS IN THE PAULA JONES SUIT

May 1991	Alleged Hotel Incident (Governor Bill Clinton allegedly summons Paula Jones to his room at the Excelsior Hotel in Little Rock).
May 1994	Paula Jones files suit in federal district court in Arkansas.
December 1994	Judge Susan Webber Wright orders discovery to proceed, but says that she won't let the case go to trial until Bill Clinton's presidency is over.
January 1996	The U.S. Court of Appeals for the Eighth Circuit orders the case to proceed with no stay of the trial.
January 1997	The Supreme Court hears oral argument in Clinton v. Jones.
May 1997	The Supreme Court unanimously affirms the Eighth Circuit and remands the case to the district court for discovery and trial.
June 1997	Ms. Jones's lawyers serve their first set of interrogatories to the President, asking about the alleged Hotel Incident.
August 1997	Judge Wright grants President's motion to dismiss two counts of the complaint, denies the motion for the remaining two counts, and orders discovery to proceed
September 22, 1997	The President answers the first set of interrogatories, denying that he harassed Ms. Jones.
September 30, 1997	The President verifies under "penalty of perjury" that his interrogatory answers are true.
October 1, 1997	• The new Jones lawyers serve a second set of interrogatories to the President; 10-11 asks whether he had had, or had proposed having, sexual relations with any woman (other than Hillary Rodham Clinton) while he was Attorney General of Arkansas, Governor of Arkansas, or President of the United States. • Ms. Jones's lawyers also serve the President with their first set of requests for documents and things related to other women.

595

October 8, 1997	Ms. Jones's attorneys serve the President with their first set of requests for admissions; 51-65 ask about "sexual relations" with other women.
October 13, 1997	Ms. Jones's lawyers serve the President with a third set of interrogatories, asking him to name any person with discoverable information.
October 28, 1997	• The President's lawyers seek a protective order limiting discovery to instances of nonconsensual conduct in the AIDC (Ms. Jones's state agency) workplace and prohibiting general questions about other women. • Dolly Kyle Browning testifies at a deposition.
October 29, 1997	Ms. Jones's lawyers issue a subpoena to Jane Doe 1 commanding her to appear for a deposition on Nov. 18, bringing documents and things related to her meetings with the President.
October 30, 1997	• Judge Wright orders that discovery be confidential. • Ms. Jones's lawyers serve Jane Doe 2 with a subpoena commanding her to appear for a deposition, and serve a copy of this subpoena to the President's lawyers.
November 3, 1997	The President answers part of the second set of interrogatories under "penalty of perjury," but the President objects to and does not answer Interrogatories 10-11 (about "other women").
November 10, 1997	• The President responds to the first set of requests for admissions; he denies that he asked Ms. Jones to have sexual relations with him, but objects to and does not answer "other women" questions. • State troopers begin testifying.
November 12, 1997	• The President answers the third set of interrogatories, but fails to include Ms. Lewinsky on the list of those with discoverable information; he reserves the right to add more names. • Ms. Jones's attorneys ask Judge Wright to order the President to answer Interrogatories 10-11 from the second set of interrogatories. • Ms. Jones testifies at a deposition which continues the next day.
November 13, 1997	Jane Doe 3 receives a subpoena.
November 14, 1997	• Gennifer Flowers testifies at a deposition. • Jane Doe 7 receives a subpoena.

November 17, 1997	The President responds to the first request for documents and things, objecting to the requests insofar as they seek items related to "other women," but then asserts that he "has no documents responsive to" the request.
November 18, 1997	• Jane Doe 1 begins her deposition but immediately asserts a "privacy" privilege; Judge Wright holds a hearing but decides only that, because Jane Doe 1 is ill, the deposition will not continue that day. • Jane Doe 7 signs an affidavit claiming no pertinent knowledge, and moves to quash her deposition.
November 19, 1997	• Judge Wright denies Jane Doe 7's motion to quash her subpoena. • Judge Merhige denies Kathleen Willey's motion to quash her subpoena.
November 20, 1997	• The President's lawyers file a memorandum in support of the motions to quash filed by Jane Does 1-3. • Jane Doe 1 asks that her deposition (begun on Nov. 18) be terminated. • Ms. Jones's lawyers issue a subpoena to Jane Doe 5 (who received it Nov. 22).
November 21, 1997	• Jane Doe 2 moves to quash her subpoena. • Ms. Jones's lawyers serve the President's lawyers with an amended notice about the deposition of Jane Doe 3. • Jane Doe 7 testifies at a deposition.
November 24, 1997	Judge Wright conducts a hearing on Jane Doe 1's privacy objection to a deposition and overrules the objection.
December 2, 1997	Judge Wright denies Jane Doe 2's motion to quash.
December 3, 1997	• Jane Doe 2's second deposition begins but she refuses to answer sex-related questions. • Kathleen Willey suddenly cancels her deposition because of neck surgery.
December 4, 1997	Jane Doe 3 moves to quash her subpoena; Judge Wright denies the motion.
December 5, 1997	• Ms. Jones's lawyers serve the President's lawyers with their witness list for trial; Monica Lewinsky's name is on the list. • Ms. Jones's lawyers file an amended complaint

	adding the allegation that the President discriminated against Ms. Jones by granting employment benefits only to women who acceded to his requests for sex.
December 6, 1997	• The President meets with his lawyers. • The President verifies under "penalty of perjury" his supplemental responses to the second set of interrogatories (containing certain medical information about himself); he continues to fail to answer Interrogatories 10-11.
December 10, 1997	• Ms. Jones's lawyers move to compel Jane Does 1-3 to answer their deposition questions. • Jane Doe 2 files an opposition to this motion, arguing that Ms. Jones's lawyers have not established a sufficient predicate for delving into her privacy. • Danny Ferguson testifies at a deposition about the President's meetings with Jane Doe 1 and with Paula Jones.
December 11, 1997	• Judge Wright partially grants Ms. Jones's motion of Nov. 12; using a "meticulous" standard of materiality, she orders the President to answer Interrogatory 10-11 if (i) encounter was later than May 7, 1986; and (ii) either state troopers facilitated encounter, or the woman was a present or prospective government employee.
December 12, 1997	The President's lawyers file their opposition to Ms. Jones's motion (of Dec. 10) to compel the Jane Does.
December 15, 1997	• Ms. Jones's lawyers notify the President's lawyers that they will depose Jane Doe 5 on Jan. 9. • Ms. Jones's lawyers depose Onie E. "Betsey" Wright, who had been responsible for responding to "other women" accusations during the 1992 campaign.
December 16, 1997	• Ms. Jones's lawyers move to compel the President to answer the remaining questions in their first set of requests for admissions (51-65) and their third set of interrogatories (asking for names of those with discoverable information). • Ms. Jones's lawyers serve their second request that the President produce documents and things, this time asking for those that concerned Ms. Lewinsky. • At 2:00 a.m. that night (on 12/17/97), the President calls Ms. Lewinsky and tells her that she is on the witness list.

December 18, 1997	Holding the testimony of Jane Does 1-3 "discoverable," Judge Wright grants Ms. Jones's motion to compel their testimony but requires that Ms. Jones establish a "factual predicate" and meet certain other conditions.
December 19, 1997	• Ms. Lewinsky receives a subpoena then meets with Vernon Jordan.
December 22, 1997	Vernon Jordan introduces Ms. Lewinsky to Frank Carter.
December 23, 1997	• The President serves supplemental responses to the second set of interrogatories, answering 10-11 (asking for names of women with whom he has had or proposed having "sexual relations") with "none." The President verifies "under penalty of perjury" that this answer is true and correct. • Mr. Carter meets with the President's lawyers.
December 24, 1997	Ms. Jones's lawyers move for reconsideration of Judge Wright's Dec. 18 order establishing the "factual predicate" requirement.
December 30, 1997	• The President's lawyer, Robert Bennett, concede during a hearing before Judge Wright that questions related to "sex-for-jobs" would be "fair game." • Ms. Jones's lawyers move to sanction the President's lawyers for making argumentative and suggestive objections to deposition questions.
January 2, 1998	• Jane Doe 2 testifies at a deposition. • Jane Doe 5 signs an affidavit denying any "sexual activity" with the President.
January 5, 1998	• Ms. Lewinsky meets with her attorney. • Ms. Jones's lawyers notify the President's lawyers that they plan to depose Jane Doe 5; Jane Doe 5 moves to quash, attaching her affidavit.
January 7, 1998	• Ms. Lewinsky prepares and signs an affidavit denying sexual relations with the President. • The President's lawyers file an opposition to Ms. Jones's motion for reconsideration of the Dec. 18 order.
January 8, 1998	• Judge Wright orders the President to answer the as-yet-unanswered questions from the third set of interrogatories and the first set of requests for admission (51-65), holding that such answers were "relevant to the case." • Judge Wright denies Jane Doe 5's motion to quash.

January 9, 1998	• Judge Wright partly grants Ms. Jones's motion for reconsideration of her Dec. 18 order, allowing more questions than she has before. • Jane Doe 5 testifies at a deposition.
January 11, 1998	Kathleen Willey testifies at a deposition.
January 12, 1998	• Judge Wright holds a hearing discussing the President's deposition and what evidence she might permit at trial, but encourages the parties to settle.
January 15, 1998	• The President serves supplemental answers to the first and second sets of requests for documents and things, asserting that he has no documents or tangible things related to Ms. Lewinsky or Ms. Willy. • The President serves supplemental responses to the first set of requests for admissions, objecting to but then denying requests 51-65 (which ask him to name other women with whom he has had "sexual relations"). • The President serves supplemental responses to the third set of interrogatories, naming two other people with discoverable information (but not naming Ms. Lewinsky). • The President verifies all these supplemental answers "under penalty of perjury."
January 16, 1998	• Ms. Jones's lawyers notifies the President's lawyers that Jane Doe 3 would be deposed on Jan. 28. • Mr. Carter moves to quash Ms. Lewinsky's subpoena.
January 17, 1998	The President testified, in a videotaped deposition, that he had not had sexual relations (as defined) with Ms. Lewinsky.
January 22, 1998	• Judge Wright conducts a hearing on Ms. Lewinsky's motion to quash, then directs Ms. Lewinsky's deposition to proceed but grants a motion to reschedule.
January 27, 1998	The Office of the Independent Counsel ("OIC") moves to intervene in the Jones case.
January 29, 1998	• The OIC asks Judge Wright to postpone the deposition of Ms. Lewinsky until the completion of its criminal investigation. • After a hearing, Judge Wright decides to exclude the Lewinsky evidence altogether, because (i)

	waiting would frustrate timely resolution of the Jones case; and (ii) the Lewinsky evidence, though it "might be relevant to the issues in this case," is "not essential to the core issues in this case.
January 30, 1998	• Another "other woman" testifies at a deposition, denying any "sexual activity" with the President. • Ms. Jones's lawyers move to compel the President to produce as-yet-unproduced documents, arguing that his claims of privilege are meritless.
February 10, 1998	Ms. Jones's lawyers move for reconsideration of the order excluding the Lewinsky evidence.
February 17, 1998	The President's lawyers move for summary judgment. (Mr. Ferguson's lawyers do likewise on March 4.)
March 9, 1998	Judge Wright denies Ms. Jones's motion for reconsideration of her order excluding the Lewinsky evidence, stating that although "such evidence might have helped [Jones] establish . . . intent, absence of mistake, motive, and habit . . . it simply is not essential to the core issues in this case."
April 1998	Judge Wright dismisses the Jones case on the ground that Ms. Jones has not presented sufficient evidence to put the case before a jury. Ms. Jones appeals.

Issued by the
UNITED STATES DISTRICT COURT
DISTRICT OF _____ COLUMBIA

PAULA JONES,

            Plaintiff,

      v.

WILLIAM JEFFERSON CLINTON
and
DANNY FERGUSON,

          Defendants.

SUBPOENA IN A CIVIL CASE
CASE NUMBER:[1]   LR-C-94-290

920-DC-00000013

TO: **MONICA LEWINSKY**

☐ YOU ARE COMMANDED to appear in the United States District Court at the place, date, and time specified below to testify in the above case.

PLACE OF TESTIMONY	COURTROOM
	DATE AND TIME

☒ YOU ARE COMMANDED to appear at the place, date, and time specified below to testify at the taking of a deposition in the above case.

PLACE OF DEPOSITION The Rutherford Institute 733 15th Street NW., Suite 410 Washington, DC 20005	DATE AND TIME Friday, January 23, 1998 9:30 a.m.

☒ YOU ARE COMMANDED to produce and permit inspection and copying of the following documents or objects at the place, date, and time specified below (list documents or objects):

Exhibit A, attached hereto.

PLACE The Rutherford Institute 733 15th Street NW., Suite 410 Washington, DC 20005	DATE AND TIME Friday, January 23, 1998 9:30 a.m.

☐ YOU ARE COMMANDED to permit inspection of the following premises at the date and time specified below.

PREMISES	DATE AND TIME

Any organization not a party to this suit that is subpoenaed for the taking of a deposition shall designate one or more officers, directors, or managing agents, or other persons who consent to testify on its behalf, and may set forth, for each person designated, the matters on which the person designated, the matters on which the person will testify, Federal Rules of Civil Procedure, 30(b) (6).

ISSUING OFFICER SIGNATURE AND TITLE (INDICATE IF ATTORNEY FOR PLAINTIFF OR DEFENDANT)	DATE
Donovan Campbell Jr. , ATTORNEY FOR PLAINTIFF	December 17, 1997

ISSUING OFFICER'S NAME, ADDRESS AND PHONE NUMBER
Donovan Campbell, Jr., Rader, Campbell, Fisher & Pyke, Stemmons Place, Suite 1080,
2777 Stemmons Freeway, Dallas, Texas 75207, (214) 630-4700

(See Rule 45, Federal Rules of Civil Procedure, Parts C & D on Reverse)

[1] If action is pending in district other than district of issuance, state district under case number.

EXHIBIT A

DOCUMENTS AND THINGS TO BE PRODUCED

Pursuant to the Federal Rules of Civil Procedure, the Deponent is directed to produce, at the time and place of the Deponent's deposition, all of the documents and tangible things described in the enumerated requests below. In responding to the following requests for production, the Deponent is directed to comply with the following instructions and to apply the following definitions.

DEFINITIONS

For the purposes of these requests, the following definitions apply:

"Defendant Clinton" means William Jefferson Clinton.

"Defendant Ferguson" means Danny Ferguson.

"Document" means any tangible thing on which appears, or in which is stored or contained, any words, numbers, symbols, or images. The term "document" includes any and all writings, drawings, graphs, charts, photographs, tape recordings, video recordings, phono records, and other data compilations from which information can be obtained and translated, if necessary, through detection devices, into reasonably usable form.

"Person" means any identifiable entity, including but not limited to individuals, corporations, partnerships, sole proprietorships, and unincorporated associations.

"You" means the Deponent.

920-DC-00000016

INSTRUCTIONS

A request for any particular document or thing is a request for the original, for each and every photocopy or duplicate of that document or thing, and for each and every draft of the document or thing. If, however, you produce the original of the document or thing, you are not required to produce any photocopies or duplicates unless they are not identical (as, for example, when marginal notations are made on a copy).

The documents and things to be produced should, at the time of production, be organized and labeled to correspond to the enumerated requests below. In the alternative, they may be produced as they are kept in the ordinary course of business, if it is possible to do so.

You are to produce not only the documents and things in your immediate possession, but also those over which you have custody or control, including but not limited to documents and things in the possession, custody, or control of your agent(s), your accountant(s), your attorney(s), any investigator employed by you or by your attorney(s), or any consultant or expert witness employed by you or by your attorney(s).

If, in response to a particular request, an objection is interposed, and the objection applies to some but not all of the documents requested, please produce all responsive documents and things to which the objection does not apply.

REQUESTS FOR PRODUCTION

REQUEST FOR PRODUCTION NO. 1: Every document relating to any private meetings between you and Defendant Clinton, including any agendas, letters, journals, diaries, notes, tape recordings or memoranda.

REQUEST FOR PRODUCTION NO. 2: Every document constituting or containing communications between you and Defendant Clinton, including letters, cards, notes memoranda, and all telephone records, notes or memoranda reflecting calls to or from any telephone in the White House, the Pentagon, any governmental office or property, or your home or office, any cellular or mobile telephone, or to or from any other telephone numbers of Bill Clinton or you or anyone acting for or on behalf of him or you.

REQUEST FOR PRODUCTION NO. 3: Every document concerning any communications with persons other than Defendant Clinton which reference any relationship or any private meetings between you and Defendant Clinton.

REQUEST FOR PRODUCTION NO. 4: Every document concerning any communications with persons other than Defendant Clinton which reference any relationship or any private meetings between you and Defendant Clinton.

REQUEST FOR PRODUCTION NO. 5: Every calendar or address book or other document reflecting any meetings between you and Defendant Clinton or reflecting the address or telephone number of Defendant Clinton at any location.

REQUEST FOR PRODUCTION NO. 6: Every document relating to any communications with anyone concerning any occurrence involving you and Defendant Clinton, including any agendas, letters, journals, diaries, notes, time records, employment records, tape recordings or memoranda.

920-DC-00000017

REQUEST FOR PRODUCTION NO. 7: Please produce each and every gift including, but not limited to, any and all dresses, accessories, and jewelry, and/or hat pins given to you by, or on behalf of, Defendant Clinton.

REQUEST FOR PRODUCTION NO. 8: Please produce each and every document mentioning or describing any gift given to you by Defendant Clinton.

920-DC-00000018

605

Prosecutor's Description of
The Linda Tripp Tapes

[Editor's note: In a prosecution memo titled "Evidence Reference," the Office of Independent Counsel explains the different types of evidence used in his report to the House of Representatives. Part of the document deals with Linda Tripp's tape-recordings of her conversations with Ms. Lewinsky.]

III. CONVERSATIONS TAPED BY LINDA TRIPP

A. Background

After receiving court-ordered immunity under 18 U.S.C. §6002, Linda Tripp produced several cassette tapes and testified before the grand jury.[65] Among other subjects, she discussed notes and tape recordings she made of several conversations between herself and Monica Lewinsky.

Ms. Lewinsky began confiding in Ms. Tripp soon after Ms. Lewinsky began working at the Pentagon. Ms. Tripp took two sets of notes during their conversations. The first notes are in a Skilcraft Steno Notebook.[66] Ms. Tripp testified she took these between May 23, 1997, and July 1997.[67] The second notes are on a series of papers. Ms. Tripp testified she took these during several conversations, starting in September 1997.[68] Ms. Tripp indicated that Ms. Lewinsky was aware of the first note-taking but not the second.[69] Ms. Lewinsky said, though, that she never knew Ms. Tripp was taking notes.[70]

From approximately October 3, 1997, to January 15, 1998, Linda Tripp tape recorded many of her telephone conversations with Monica Lewinsky. According to Ms. Tripp, on October 3, 1997, she purchased a voice activated tape recorder with a manual pause capability from Radio Shack (model CTR107), and connected it to a telephone in the study of her home. Ms. Tripp testified that she set the system to record all conversations from the study telephone so long as there was a tape in the machine and the machine remained on. Ms. Tripp added that because of the length of the conversations and the tapes, most of the tapes contain several conversations. As Ms. Tripp further told the grand jury, because the recorder was always working unless she turned it off, she captured conversations with people other than Ms. Lewinsky.

On October 6, 1997, after making two tapes, Ms. Tripp met in Washington, D.C. with her friend Lucianne Goldberg, Jonah Goldberg (Ms. Goldberg's son), and Michael Isikoff. After this meeting, Ms. Goldberg kept the two tapes and brought them to New York. Ms. Goldberg made copies of these tapes, and she presented the two originals and copies of them to the Office of the Independent Counsel in January 1998.

Ms. Tripp told the grand jury she continued to make recordings and keep them in a bowl on a piece of furniture. She testified that around the beginning of 1998, she gave most of the tapes to her lawyer, Kirby Behre. According to Ms. Tripp, she changed attorneys and retained Jim Moody. She stated that Mr. Moody obtained the tapes from Mr. Behre and provided them to the OIC in early January 1998.

Later, the OIC received four additional tapes from Ms. Tripp. On March 3, 1998, Ms. Tripp searched her home with the help of her new attorney, Anthony Zaccagnini, and several FBI Special Agents assigned to the OIC. During this search, Ms. Tripp and the others found three additional tapes. After previewing these tapes on the cassette player in his car, Mr. Zaccagnini presented them to the Special Agents. Ms. Tripp told the grand jury that just before March 17, 1998, she found another tape in her home and gave it to Mr. Zaccagnini. He brought it to the Office of the Independent Counsel on March 17, 1998.

The OIC provided to the FBI Audio Signal Analysis Unit in Quantico, Virginia, all of the tapes obtained from Ms. Tripp. This unit is engaged in the elaborate and time-consuming process of authenticating the tapes, but it has provided some results.

*Examination has preliminarily determined that 8 of the tapes submitted do not exhibit signs of duplication.

*Examination has preliminarily determined that 9 of the tapes submitted exhibit characteristics that are not consistent with being recorded on the Radio Shack CTR107 tape recorder Ms. Tripp says she used to record the original tapes.

*Examination has preliminarily determined that the 9 tapes inconsistent with the tape recorder Ms. Tripp says she used exhibit signs of duplication.

*Examination has preliminarily determined that 7 of the tapes that exhibit signs of duplication are consistent with the use of one tape recorder to duplicate.

*The examination has preliminarily determined that one of the tapes that exhibits signs of duplication was produced by a recorder that was stopped during the recording process.

These results raise three important issues. First, the Office of the Independent Counsel does not possess original recordings for nine of the tapes Ms. Tripp made. Two of these tapes contain inaudible recordings. Second, the OIC is not aware who made the "likely to be duplicate" tapes. Third, if Ms. Tripp duplicated any tapes herself or knew of their duplication, then she has lied under oath before the grand jury and in a deposition. The OIC continues to investigate this matter.

In light of these three issues, and to help ensure the reliability, authenticity, and accuracy of the evidence, the accompanying submission only refers to recorded conversations which meet four conditions: (1) the recorded conversation is contained on a tape that FBI examination has preliminarily determined not to exhibit signs of duplication; (2) Monica Lewinsky has listened to the recording and identified her voice and Linda Tripp's voice;[71] (3) Monica Lewinsky has identified the recording as an accurate depiction of a conversation she remembers;[72] and (4) there is independent evidence to corroborate the contents of the recorded conversation.

Even though they do not appear in the submission, the Office of Independent Counsel has provided all of the recorded conversations as raw evidence. Consequently, a fourth issue arises when assigning dates to the tapes that exhibit signs of duplication.

When a tape was filled with recorded conversations, Ms. Tripp removed the tape and stored it in the bowl. Ms. Tripp did not mark the tapes, and she did not catalog them. As a result, the only way to determine which day Ms. Tripp recorded each tape was to use the information she provided while she was debriefed,[73] combined with information from the conversations.

For the seven tapes which contain audible conversations and which exhibit signs of duplication, the Office of the Independent Counsel cannot exclude the possibility of tampering at this time. For this reason, the Office of the Independent Counsel cannot have full confidence that the dates assigned to these tapes are accurate. The following appendix represents the opinion of the Independent Counsel regarding the date of each tape. The tapes that exhibit signs of duplication are marked to reduce the possibility of confusion.

64 Report of Examination, FBI File No. 29D-OIC-LR-35063, Lab Nos. 980730002 S BO and
    980803100 S BO, Aug. 17, 1998. The FBI concluded that the "probability of selecting an
    unrelated individual [from President Clinton's population] at random" was 1 in 7.87 trillion.
65 *See* Tripp GJ, 6/30/98, pg. 8-14 (The Office of the Independent Counsel also promised Ms. Tripp
    that it would do what it could to persuade the State of Maryland from prosecuting Ms. Tripp for
    any violations of the state wiretapping law.).
66 845-DC-00000001-25.
67 May 23, 1997, is the last date recorded in the notebook. Linda Tripp testified she wrote the book
    in July, *see* Tripp 7/7/98 GJ at 111, but did so before she knew about the contact between Ms.
    Lewinsky and Bruce Lindsey on July 14, 1997. *Id.* at 135.
68 Tripp GJ 7/16/98 at 112-13.
69 Tripp 7/7/98 GJ at 108-109, 160; Tripp 7/16/98 GJ at 113.
70 The dates in the notebook sometimes appear to be a day or two off. One note, for instance,
    refers to Sunday, March 30, 1996; Sunday actually fell on March 31. *See* 845-DC-00000011
    (notes); Tripp GJ 7/9/98 at 17. Ms. Tripp surmised that Ms. Lewinsky was consulting a 1997
    calendar for dates without realizing the discrepancy. Tripp GJ 7/9/98 at 18.
71 Ms. Lewinsky stated with respect to these recordings that she believes the voice on the tapes is
    hers, based on "intonation and content."
72 Although Ms. Lewinsky cannot attest to whether there are missing portions of the conversations,
    she could not recall any specific conversation that was excluded from the particular conversa-
    tions on the tapes. Ms. Lewinsky noted, however, that she had many more conversations with
    Linda Tripp about certain subject matters than were captured on tape.

73 Ms. Tripp appeared at the Office of the Independent Counsel on many occasions between January 1998, and July 1998. During most of her initial visits, Ms. Tripp listened to the recordings of her conversations with Ms. Lewinsky and compared them with transcripts that the Office of the Independent Counsel prepared. Ms. Tripp corrected the transcripts as necessary. Ms. Tripp told the grand jury that the tapes accurately depict her conversations with Ms. Lewinsky and that the transcripts are accurate.

In her later visits to the Office of the Independent Counsel, Ms. Tripp participated in debriefing sessions with investigators and attorneys. One aspect of these sessions included eliciting information about the tapes and when Ms. Tripp made them.

B. Dating the Tape Recorded Conversations

The following discussion represents the opinion of the Office of the Independent Counsel regarding the date of each tape. Although they are assigned dates, the duplicates are marked to reduce the possibility of confusion.

1. Reference Charts Summarizing The Dates of the Tapes

Conversations Listed By Date   Conversations Listed By Tape

Note: Tapes Which Exhibit Sign of Duplication Are Printed In Italics

1. Friday, October 3, 1997:
Tape 18, side A, first conversation on tape.
Transcript pages: 2-25.

2. Friday, October 3, 1997:
Tape 18, side A, second conversation on tape.
Transcript pages: 25-71.

3. Saturday, October 4, 1997:
Tape 18, side B, third conversation on tape.
Transcript pages: 71-110.

4. Sunday, October 5, 1997:
Tape 19, side A, first conversation on tape.
Transcript pages: 2-21.

5. Sunday, October 5, 1997:
Tape 19, side A, second conversation on tape.
Transcript pages: 21-34.

6. Sunday, October 5, 1997:
Tape 19, side A, third conversation on tape.
Transcript page: 34.

7. Monday, October 6, 1997:
Tape 19, side A, fourth conversation on tape.
Transcript pages: 35-41.

8. Monday, October 6, 1997:
Tape 1, Side A, first conversation on tape.
Transcript pages: 2-40.

9. Monday, October 6, 1997:
Tape 1, side A, second conversation on tape.
Transcript pages: 40-110.

10. Thursday, October 16, 1997:
Tape 2, Side A, third conversation on tape.
Transcript pages: 2-38.

11. Thursday, October 16, 1997:
Tape 13, Side A, first conversation on tape.
Transcript pages 2-30.

12. Friday, October 17, 1997:
Tape 13, side A, second conversation on tape.
Transcript pages: pages 30-38.

13. Saturday, October 18, 1997:
Tape 3, side A, first conversation on tape.
Transcript: pages 2-39.

1. Tape 1, Side A, first conversation on tape:
Transcript pages: 2-40.
Monday, October 6, 1997

2. Tape 1, side A, second conversation on tape:
Transcript pages: 40-110.
Monday, October 6, 1997.

3. Tape 2, Side A, third conversation on tape:
Transcript pages: 2-38.
Thursday, October 16, 1997.

4. Tape 3, side A, first conversation on tape.
Transcript pages: 2-39.
Saturday, October 18, 1997.

5. *Tape 5, side A, first conversation on tape:*
Transcript pages: 2-16.
Thursday, November 20, 1997.

6. *Tape 5, side A, third conversation on tape:*
Transcript pages: 17-41.
Thursday, November 20, 1997.

7. *Tape 5, side A, fourth conversation on tape:*
Transcript pages: 41-47.
Thursday, November 20, 1997.

8. *Tape 5, side A, fifth conversation on tape:*
Transcript pages: 47-52.
Friday, November 21, 1997.

9. *Tape 5, side B, sixth conversation on tape:*
Transcript pages: 53-55.
Friday, November 21, 1997.

10. *Tape 5, side B, seventh conversation on tape:*
Transcript pages: 55-59.
Friday, November 21, 1997.

11. *Tape 5, side B, eighth conversation on tape:*
Transcript pages: 59-91.
Friday, November 21, 1997.

12. *Tape 6, side A, second conversation on tape:*
Transcript pages: 2-24.
Monday, December 22, 1997.

13. *Tape 6, side A, fourth conversation on tape:*
Transcript pages: 24-32.
Monday, December 22, 1997.

14. Saturday, October 18, 1997:
Tape 8, Side A, first conversation on tape.
Transcript pages 2-34.

15. Sunday October 19, 1997:
Tape 7, Side A, first conversation on tape.
Transcript pages: 2-51.

16. Thursday, October 23, 1997:
Tape 15, Side A, first conversation on tape.
Transcript pages: 2-30.

17. Thursday, October 23, 1997:
Tape 15, Side A, second conversation on tape
Transcript pages: 30-73.

18. Wednesday, October 29, 1997:
Tape 11, first conversation on tape.
Transcript pages: 2-57.

19. Monday, November 3, 1997:
Tape 11, Side B, fifth conversation on tape.
Transcript pages: 58-113.

20. Saturday, November 8, 1997:
Tape 16, side B, sixth conversation on tape.
Transcript pages: 60-103.

21. Tuesday, November 11, 1997:
Tape 16, side B, ninth conversation on tape.
Transcript pages: 104-114.

22. Tuesday, November 11, 1997:
Tape 26, side A, first conversation on tape.
Transcript pages: 2-5.

23. Tuesday, November 11, 1997:
Tape 26, side A, second conversation on tape.
Transcript pages: 5-32.

24. Tuesday, November 11, 1997:
Tape 26, side A, third conversation on tape.
Transcript pages: 32-55.

25. Thursday, November 13, 1997:
Tape 16, side A, first conversation on tape.
Transcript pages: 2-9.

26. Friday, November 14, 1997:
Tape 16, side A, second conversation on tape.
Transcript pages: 9-51.

27. Sunday, November 16, 1997:
Tape 16, side A, third conversation on tape.
Transcript pages: 52-60.

28. Sunday, November 16, 1997:
Tape 9, side A, first conversation on tape.
Transcript pages: 2-33.

29. Monday, November 17, 1997:
Tape 9, side A, second conversation on tape.
Transcript pages: 33-51.

30. Tuesday, November 18, 1997:
Tape 9, side B, third conversation on tape.
Transcript pages: 51-79.

31. Thursday, November 20, 1997:
Tape 9, side B, fourth conversation on tape.
Transcript pages: 79-100.

32. Thursday, November 20, 1997:
Tape 5, side A, first conversation on tape.
Transcript pages: 2-16.

33. Thursday, November 20, 1997:
Tape 5, side A, third conversation on tape.
Transcript pages: 17-41.

14. Tape 6, side B, fifth conversation on tape:
Transcript pages: 33-68.
Monday, December 22, 1997.

15. Tape 7, Side A, first conversation on tape:
Transcript pages: 2-51.
Sunday October 19, 1997.

16. Tape 8, Side A, first conversation on tape:
Transcript pages 2-34.
Saturday, October 18, 1997.

17. Tape 9, side A, first conversation on tape:
Transcript pages: 2-33.
Sunday, November 16, 1997.

18. Tape 9, side A, second conversation on tape:
Transcript pages: 33-51.
Monday, November 17, 1997.

19. Tape 9, side B, third conversation on tape:
Transcript pages: 51-79.
Tuesday, November 18, 1997.

20. Tape 9, side B, fourth conversation on tape:
Transcript pages: 79-100.
Thursday, November 20, 1997

21. Tape 11, Side A, first conversation on tape:
Transcript pages: 2-57.
Wednesday, October 29, 1997

22. Tape 11, Side B, fifth conversation on tape:
Transcript pages: 58-113.
Monday, November 3, 1997.

23. Tape 13, Side A, first conversation on tape:
Transcript pages 2-30.
Thursday, October 16, 1997.

24. Tape 13, side A, second conversation on tape:
Transcript pages: pages 30-38.
Friday, October 17, 1997.

25. Tape 15, Side A, first conversation on tape:
Transcript pages: 2-30.
Thursday, October 23, 1997.

26. Tape 15, Side A, second conversation on tape:
Transcript pages: 30-73.
Thursday, October 23, 1997.

27. Tape 16, side A, first conversation on tape:
Transcript pages: 2-9.
Thursday, November 13, 1997.

28. Tape 16, side A, second conversation on tape:
Transcript pages: 9-51.
Friday, November 14, 1997.

29. Tape 16, side B, sixth conversation on tape:
Transcript pages: 60-103.
Saturday, November 8, 1997.

30. Tape 16, side B, ninth conversation on tape.
Transcript pages: 104-114.
Tuesday, November 11, 1997:

31. Tape 16, side A, third conversation on tape:
Transcript pages: 52-60.
Sunday, November 16, 1997.

32. Tape 18, side A, first conversation on tape:
Transcript pages: 2-25.
Friday, October 3, 1997.

33. Tape 18, side A, second conversation on tape:
Transcript pages: 25-71.
Friday, October 3, 1997.

34. *Thursday, November 20, 1997:*
Tape 5, side A, fourth conversation on tape.
Transcript pages: 41-47.

35. *Friday, November 21, 1997:*
Tape 5, side A, fifth conversation on tape.
Transcript pages: 47-52.

36. *Friday, November 21, 1997:*
Tape 5, side A, sixth conversation on tape.
Transcript pages: 53-55.

37. *Friday, November 21, 1997:*
Tape 5, side A, seventh conversation on tape.
Transcript pages: 55-59.

38. *Friday, November 21, 1997:*
Tape 5, side A, eighth conversation on tape.
Transcript pages: 59-91.

39. *Tuesday, December 9, 1997:*
Tape 23, side A, first conversation on tape.
Transcript pages: 2-6.

40. *Tuesday, December 9, 1997:*
Tape 23, side A, second conversation on tape.
Transcript pages: 6-56.

41. *Friday, December 12, 1997:*
Tape 23, side A, fifth conversation on tape.
Transcript pages: 57-68.

42. *Friday, December 12, 1997:*
Tape 23, side B, sixth conversation on tape.
Transcript pages: 68-127.

43. *Friday, December 12, 1997:*
Tape 23, side B, eighth conversation on tape.
Transcript pages: 127-131.

44. *Monday, December 22, 1997:*
Tape 6, side A, second conversation on tape.
Transcript pages: 2-24.

45. *Monday, December 22, 1997:*
Tape 6, side A, fourth conversation on tape.
Transcript pages: 24-32.

46. Monday, December 22, 1997:
Tape 6, side B, fifth conversation on tape.
Transcript pages: 33-68.

47. Thursday, January 15, 1998:
Tape 22, side A, first conversation on tape.
Transcript pages: 2-55.

48. Thursday, January 15, 1998:
Tape 22, side A, second conversation on tape.
Transcript pages: 55-76.

34. Tape 18, side B, third conversation on tape:
Transcript pages: 71-110.
Saturday, October 4, 1997.

35. Tape 19, side A, first conversation on tape:
Transcript pages: 2-21.
Sunday, October 5, 1997

36. Tape 19, side A, second conversation on tape:
Transcript page: 21-34.
Sunday, October 5, 1997

37. Tape 19, side A, third conversation on tape:
Transcript pages: 34.
Sunday, October 5, 1997.

38. Tape 19, side A, fourth conversation on tape:
Transcript pages: 35-41.
Monday, October 6, 1997.

39. Tape 22, side A, first conversation on tape:
Transcript pages: 2-55.
Thursday, January 15, 1998.

40. Tape 22, side A, second conversation on tape:
Transcript pages: 55-76.
Thursday, January 15, 1998.

41. Tape 23, side A, first conversation on tape:
Transcript pages: 2-6.
Tuesday, December 9, 1997.

42. Tape 23, side A, second conversation on tape:
Transcript pages: 6-56.
Tuesday, December 9, 1997.

43. Tape 23, side A, fifth conversation on tape:
Transcript pages: 57-68.
Friday, December 12, 1997.

44. Tape 23, side B, sixth conversation on tape:
Transcript pages: 68-127.
Friday, December 12, 1997.

45. *Tape 23, side B, eighth conversation on tape:*
Transcript pages: 127-131.
Friday, December 12, 1997

46. *Tape 26, side A, first conversation on tape:*
Transcript pages: 2-5.
Tuesday, November 11, 1997.

47. *Tape 26, side A, second conversation on tape:*
Transcript pages: 5-32.
Tuesday, November 11, 1997.

48. *Tape 26, side A, third conversation on tape:*
Transcript pages: 32-55.
Tuesday, November 11, 1997.

2. How the OIC Determined the Chronology of these Undated Tapes

Conversation # 1:
Friday, October 3, 1997
Tape 18, side A, first conversation on the tape.
Transcript pages: 2-25.

During this conversation, Ms. Tripp says it is October. *See* T18 at 24. Ms. Lewinsky observes that the President will be delivering a radio address on the following morning, and then traveling to Maryland and Camp David. *See* T18 at 20. The President's October 4, 1997, schedule shows he gave a radio address, *see* 968-DC-00003058, and then traveled to Prince George's County, Maryland and Camp David. *See* 968-DC-00003059. Ms. Lewinsky also comments the President will be at an event in Virginia on Saturday night. *See* page 21. The Presidential Press Schedule shows the President attended a function at the National Airport Hilton on October 4, 1997.
See 968-DC-00003060.
These factors are consistent with a conversation on October 3, 1997.

Conversation # 2:
Friday, October 3, 1997
Tape 18, side A, second conversation on the tape.
Transcript pages: 25-71.

During this conversation, Ms. Tripp says it is Friday night, and Ms. Lewinsky says she is going to New York City on the next Saturday for the weekend. *See* T18 at 28. Ms. Lewinsky's American Express bill reveals she bought an airplane ticket from LaGuardia Airport to the Ronald Reagan National Airport on October 13, 1997. *See* 852-DC-00000042. Ms. Lewinsky also mentions that the President is leaving the following Sunday, October 12, 1997. *See* T18 at 41. The President's schedule shows he left for a week-long trip to Latin America on October 11, 1997. See United States President, Weekly Compilations of Presidential Documents at 1608, 1609, 1652.
These factors are consistent with a conversation on Friday, October 3, 1997.

Conversation # 3:
Saturday, October 4, 1997
Tape 18, side B, third conversation on the tape.
Transcript pages: 71-110.

The conversation that immediately precedes this conversation on the tape occurred on Friday, October 3, 1997. At the end of the previous portion, Ms. Lewinsky notes that it is 10:20, that she is going to sleep, and she indicates that she is not working the next day. *See* T18 at 70. This conversation begins with Ms. Lewinsky describing her trip to the Potomac Mills Mall for the day. *See* T18 at 70-79. The placement of the conversation on the tape and the day-long trip to the mall are consistent with a weekend day.

In addition, Ms. Lewinsky says Betty Currie was in the office during the morning because of the Radio Address. *See* T18 at 88. The President delivered a Radio Address on Saturday October 4, 1997, at 10:06 am. Also, Betty Currie rarely works on Sunday because it is her "church day." *See* Currie 5/7/98 GJ at 91. Ms. Lewinsky further says she wants to buy the President a gift because he now had a hearing aid. *See* T18 at 80. The President was fitted for hearing aids on October 3, 1997. *See* "Age Catching Up With Clinton; He's Getting Hearing Aids," Sandra Sobieraj, The Associated Press, October 3, 1997.

Ms. Lewinsky also says there are three months before the beginning of the year, and she refers to sunglasses she bought the President for his Latin America trip. *See* T18 at 103-4. This statement would place the tape in early October.

These factors are consistent with a conversation on October 4, 1997.

Conversation # 4:
Sunday, October 5, 1997
Tape 19, side A, first conversation on the tape.
Transcript pages: 2-21.

Ms. Lewinsky tells Ms. Tripp that CNN is leading its "Headline News" with a story about the White House releasing video tapes of the coffee receptions for Democratic supporters. *See* T19 at 2. At the outset of the call, Ms. Lewinsky is waiting excitedly for the next half hour news cycle so she can see the whole story. Evidently, she was concerned the White House might have a video taping system that showed her on tape.

The White House released these tapes, and the story broke on October 5, 1997. *See* Videotapes Released Showing Presidential Coffee Meetings, NBC Nightly News, October 5, 1997. Because of her excitement and the fact that Ms. Lewinsky followed White House news so carefully, it is likely she is describing the story that broke earlier in the day.

In addition, Ms. Tripp refers to a message she received at work on Friday, and she says she did not call back because it was "the kind of thing that could wait until Monday." *See* T19 at 31. This statement is consistent with a weekend conversation. Also, Ms. Tripp and Ms. Lewinsky discuss how Ms. Lewinsky will help Ms. Tripp with parking at work the next day. *See* T19 at 15. This final point places this conversation on a Sunday night.

These factors are consistent with a conversation on Sunday, October 5, 1997.

Conversation # 5:
Sunday, October 5, 1997
Tape 19, side A, second conversation on the tape.
Transcript pages: 21-34.

Ms. Lewinsky discusses the sunglasses she bought for the President and how she will send them to him. *See* T19 at 24. Because Ms. Lewinsky bought these sunglasses on October 4, 1997, this conversation must have occurred after that day. Ms. Tripp also says Ms. Lewinsky should send the glasses by FedEx. FedEx receipts show that Ms. Lewinsky sent a Federal Express package to the White House on October 10, 1997. *See* 925-DC-00000003. For this reason, the conversation probably occurred before October 10, 1997.

In the conversation that immediately precedes this conversation, Ms. Lewinsky and Ms. Tripp discussed their parking plans for the next morning. Ms. Lewinsky said she would be in a meeting until approximately 8:00 am, and then she could bring Ms. Tripp into the parking lot. *See* T19 at 16. Ms. Tripp and Ms. Lewinsky ended this conversation by bidding each other good night and with Ms. Tripp saying she would call Ms. Lewinsky "probably eight-ish." *See* T19 at 34. For these reasons, the conversation that immediately precedes this conversation likely occurred on October 5, 1997.

The conversation that immediately follows this one also occurred on October 5, 1997 (see explanation of next conversation). Because this conversation comes between two October 5 conversations on T19, it most likely occurred on October 5, 1997.

These factors are consistent with a conversation on Sunday, October 5, 1997.

Conversation # 6:
Sunday, October 5, 1997
Tape 19, side A, third conversation on the tape.
Transcript page: 34.

Ms. Lewinsky and Ms. Tripp spoke during the early evening of October 5, 1997. *See* T19 at 2-21. After this first conversation, Ms. Tripp went to the gym to exercise and Ms. Lewinsky called back. *See* 19 at 21-34. Sometime after that conversation ended, Ms. Tripp received a call from her friend Kate Friederich and turned off the recorder. *See* T19 at 34. Ms. Tripp knows the conversation with Ms. Friederich occurred in the late evening of Sunday, October 5, 1997, because the conversation happened the day before Ms. Tripp met with Lucianne Goldberg, Jonah Goldberg, and Michael Isikoff. That meeting occurred October 6, 1997. Furthermore, in a letter to the President, Ms. Lewinsky wrote that Ms. Friederich spoke to Ms. Tripp on Sunday night. *See* MSL-55-DC-0178.

These factors are consistent with a conversation on Sunday October 5, 1997.

Conversation 7:
Monday, October 6, 1997
Tape 19, side A, fourth conversation on the tape.
Transcript pages: 35-41.

The segment of conversation that immediately precedes this conversation is the interrupted discussion between Ms. Tripp and Ms. Friedrich. In this conversation, Ms. Tripp tells Ms. Lewinsky what Ms. Friederich said. During her debriefing, Ms. Tripp remembered having this conversation the morning after speaking with Ms. Friederich. One thing that sparked Ms. Tripp's memory was her statement during the conversation, "Let me get my coffee . . . I've got to wake up." T19 at 35. According to Ms. Tripp, she usually only drinks coffee in the morning.

There are further indications that this conversation occurred on October 6, 1997. In this conversation, Ms. Tripp says she has not spoken to Kate in a month. During a conversation taped on the night of October 6, 1997, Ms. Tripp and Ms. Lewinsky discussed this conversation again. *See* T1 at 13-23. Consequently, this conversation must have occurred before the evening of October 6, 1997.

These factors are consistent with a conversation on October 6, 1997.

Conversation # 8:
Monday, October 6, 1997
Tape 1, Side A, first conversation on the tape.
Transcript pages: 2-40.

Ms. Lewinsky tells Ms. Tripp that Ms. Currie would not get her into the White House this evening because of a dinner. *See* T1 at 6. The Presidential press schedule reveals the President hosted a state dinner with the President of Israel on October 6, 1997. *See* 968-DC-00003063.

Also, this conversation ends with a discussion about a letter that Ms. Lewinsky intends to send to the President. At the end of the conversation, Ms. Lewinsky says she will write the letter and call Ms. Tripp back in about 15-20 minutes. *See* T1 at 40. The next conversation, which follows immediately on the tape, begins with a discussion of the letter Ms. Lewinsky has composed. The next conversation also features Ms. Lewinsky saying it is the 6th. *See* T1 at 90.

In addition, Ms. Lewinsky and Ms. Tripp discuss a conversation between Ms. Tripp and her friend Kate Friederich who works at the National Security Council. *See* T1 at 13-36. For the reasons cited above, the conversation between Ms. Tripp and Ms. Friederich occurred on the previous night.

These factors are consistent with a conversation on Monday, October 6, 1997.

Conversation # 9:
Monday, October 6, 1997
Tape 1, side A, second conversation on the tape.
Transcript pages: 40-110.

During this conversation, Ms. Lewinsky says: "Today is the 6th." *See* T1 at 90. In addition, Ms. Lewinsky and Ms. Tripp are discussing a letter that Ms. Lewinsky intends to send to the White House. There is a courier receipt which shows a delivery from Ms. Lewinsky to the White House on October 7, 1997. *See* 837-DC-00001.

Ms. Lewinsky also observes that Mrs. Clinton "is coming home Friday night from Panama to go to South America with him on Sunday, just so she can be here for their anniversary." *See* T1 at 69. The First Lady's travel schedule reveals Mrs. Clinton returned from Panama on Friday, October 10. *See* 968-DC-00003477. Ms. Lewinsky further refers to the fact that the President is leaving for Latin America on Sunday. *See* T1 at 69. The Presidential Press Schedule shows that the President left for Latin American on Sunday October 12, 1997. *See* 968-DC-00003076.

These factors are consistent with a conversation on Monday, October 6, 1997.

Conversation # 10:
Thursday, October 16, 1997
Tape 2, Side A, third conversation on the tape.
Transcript pages: 2-38.

Ms. Tripp says tomorrow is the 17th. *See* T2 at 31. Also, on page 4, Ms. Lewinsky says the President is in Latin America and will be back on Sunday morning. The Presidential Press Schedule reveals the President returned from Latin America on October 19, 1997. *See* 968-DC-00003141.

These factors are consistent with a conversation on October 16, 1997.

Conversation # 11:
Thursday, October 16, 1997
Tape 13, Side A, first conversation on the tape.
Transcript pages: 2-30.

This conversation ends with Ms. Tripp telling Ms. Lewinsky, "I'll talk to you tomorrow." *See* T13 at 30. The next conversation on the tape begins with Ms. Tripp asking Ms. Lewinsky what Ms. Lewinsky is still doing in the office on a Friday night. *See* T13 at 30. These factors are consistent with a Thursday conversation.

The following factors place the conversation in a more general time frame. Ms. Lewinsky says the President will get a package she has sent him on Monday. *See* T13 at 17. The Presidential Press Schedule shows the President returned from his Latin America trip on Sunday, October 19, 1997. *See* 968-DC-00003141. Ms. Lewinsky also indicates the First Lady will be in New York on Monday and then go to Chicago "for some big birthday thing." *See* T13 at 17. The First Lady's schedule reveals that she was in New York on October 20, 1997, that her birthday was October 26, 1997, and that she went to Chicago on October 27, 1997. *See* 968-DC-00003477.

All of these factors are consistent with a conversation on Thursday, October 16, 1997.

Conversation # 12:
Friday, October 17, 1997
Tape 13, side A, second conversation on the tape.
Transcript pages: pages 30-38.

At the outset of this tape, Ms. Tripp asks Ms. Lewinsky why she is working late on a Friday night. *See* T13 at 31. October 17, 1997, was a Friday. Also, Ms. Lewinsky tells Ms. Tripp the First Lady's birthday is the next week. *See* T13 at 12. The First Lady's birthday is October 26. *See* 968-DC-00003477.

These factors are consistent with a conversation on Friday October 17, 1997.

Conversation # 13:
Saturday, October 18, 1997
Tape 3, side A, first conversation on the tape.
Transcript: pages 2-39.

In a question regarding the President, Ms. Tripp asks: "When does he get back? Tonight, tomorrow?" Ms. Lewinsky responds: "I think early tomorrow morning." *See* T3 at 12. The President's schedule reveals that he returned from Latin America on the morning of October 19. *See* 968-DC-00003141. Later, Ms. Lewinsky once again notes that the First Lady's birthday is the next weekend, and she recites the First Lady's travel schedule including a trip to New York, a trip to Chicago, and a trip to Ireland. The First Lady's travel schedule includes a trip to New York (October 20), her birthday (October 26), and a trip to Ireland (Starting October 30). *See* 968-DC-00003477.

These factors are consistent with a conversation on Saturday, October 18, 1997.

Conversation # 14:
Saturday, October 18, 1997
Tape 8, Side A, first conversation on tape.
Transcript pages 2-34.

Ms. Lewinsky says she called Andy Bleiler earlier in the day. *See* T8 at 8. Phone records reflect four calls from Ms. Lewinsky to Mr. Bleiler on October 18 (three were one minute each and one was four minutes, the first at 7:33 p.m. and the last at 7:41 p.m.). *See* 810-DC-00000017. In addition, Ms. Lewinsky says she first told the President she wanted help finding a job on January 8, 1997—ten months ago. This statement is consistent with this conversation's being in October.

These factors are consistent with a conversation on Saturday, October 18, 1997.

Conversation # 15:
Sunday October 19, 1997
Tape 7, Side A, first conversation on the tape.
Transcript pages: 2-51.

Ms. Lewinsky mentions that the President returned from Latin America and could have gone to his office and seen her package. *See* T7 at 10. The Presidential travel schedule reveals the President returned from Latin America on the morning of Sunday, October 19. *See* 968-DC-00003141. Also, Ms. Lewinsky comments that a World Series game is on television. *See* T7 at 2. Game 2 of the 1997 World Series occurred on Sunday, October 19, 1997. *See* "The Schedule," The Daily News, October 19, 1997.

There are other indications that this call happened on a Sunday. First, Ms. Lewinsky suggests that the President can call her on a Sunday even if Mrs. Clinton is in the White House. *See* T7 at 10-11. Lewinsky also mentions that Ms. Currie usually does not come in on Sundays. *See* T7 at 14. Furthermore, Ms. Lewinsky refers to going to the Mall earlier that day. *See* T7 at 2-5. This assertion is consistent with a weekend conversation.

These factors are consistent with a conversation on Sunday, October 19, 1997.

Conversation # 16:
Thursday, October 23, 1997
Tape 15, Side A, first conversation on tape.
Transcript pages: 2-30.

Ms. Lewinsky indicates that Ambassador Richardson called on Tuesday. *See* T15 at 15. Phone records reflect a call from Ambassador Richardson's line to Ms. Lewinsky on Tuesday, October 21. *See* 828-DC-00000004.

These factors are consistent with a conversation on Thursday, October 23, 1997.

Conversation # 17:
Thursday, October 23, 1997
Tape 15, Side A, second conversation on the tape.
Transcript pages: 30-73.

This is a continuation of the previous conversation. In the conversation that immediately precedes this conversation on the tape, Lewinsky is upset because she has not had enough contact with the President. During this previous conversation, Ms. Lewinsky says it is 8:15 and she promises to call Ms. Tripp as soon as the President calls her. *See* T15 at 27.

This conversation opens with Ms. Lewinsky describing the conversation she has just finished with the President. Ms. Lewinsky says it is 10:30. *See* T15 at 34. This timing and Ms. Lewinsky's comments are consistent with back-to-back phone calls. Also, Ms. Lewinsky says she told the President that Ambassador Richardson called her on Tuesday. *See* T15 at 31. Ambassador Richardson called Ms. Lewinsky on Tuesday, October 21, 1997. *See* 828-DC-00000004. Also, as a general matter, Ms. Lewinsky says it is October. *See* T15 at 65.

These factors are consistent with a conversation on Thursday, October 23, 1997.

Conversation # 18:
Wednesday, October 29, 1997
Tape 11, first conversation on tape.
Transcript pages: 2-57.

This Conversation Appears On A "Likely To Be Duplicate Tape."

Ms. Lewinsky says she spoke to Bayani Nelvis on the telephone that afternoon. T11 at 2. Telephone records reflect a conversation between Mr. Nelvis and Ms. Lewinsky on this day. *See* 1051-DC-00000003. Ms. Lewinsky also says she last spoke to the President a week ago. *See* T11 at 30. At this time, Ms. Lewinsky and the President last spoke six days before—on October 23. Finally, Ms. Lewinsky says she sent the President a present. On October 28, Ms. Lewinsky sent a package to the White House via Speed Service Couriers. *See* 837-DC-00000004.

These factors are consistent with a conversation on Wednesday, October 29, 1997.

Conversation # 19:
Monday, November 3, 1997
Tape 11, Side B, fifth conversation on the tape.
Transcript pages: 58-113.

This Conversation Appears On A Tape
That Exhibits Signs of Duplication.

Ms. Lewinsky refers to a call from the U.N. regarding a job offer. *See* T11 at 60-63. Phone records show a call from the U.N. to Ms. Lewinsky at 11:02 a.m.

See 828-DC-00000003. Ms. Lewinsky further says she arranged with Ms. Currie to send a package to the White House by courier. *See* T11 at 84. A courier receipt reflects that Ms. Lewinsky sent a package to the White House on November 3, 1997. *See* 837-DC-00000006. Moreover, Ms. Lewinsky remarks that the First Lady is leaving on Sunday. The First Lady's travel schedule reveals that she left for London on Sunday, November 9, 1997.

These factors are consistent with a conversation on Monday, November 3, 1997.

Conversation # 20:
Saturday, November 8, 1997
Tape 16, side B, sixth conversation on tape.
Transcript pages: 60-103.

This Conversation Appears On A Tape
That Exhibits Signs of Duplication.

An answering machine recording that immediately precedes this conversation identifies the date as November 8. *See* T16 at 60. In addition, Ms. Lewinsky tells Ms. Tripp the First Lady is leaving the next day. *See* T16 at 69. Mrs. Clinton left for London on Sunday, November 9, 1997. There are two additional indications that this conversation occurred on a Saturday. First, Ms. Lewinsky says that, when she asked Ms. Currie if she could see the President "tomorrow," Ms. Currie said the President would be attending church in the morning. *See* T16 at 68. Second, Ms. Lewinsky says that she was told by Ms. Currie that the President taped the Radio Address on the previous day. *See* T16 at 65. Furthermore, because Ms. Lewinsky tells Ms. Tripp how she asked Ms. Currie for a Veterans Day meeting with the President, the conversation must have occurred before November 11. *See* T16 at 69.

These factors are consistent with a conversation on Monday, November 8, 1997.

Conversation # 21:
Tuesday, November 11, 1997
Tape 16, side B, ninth conversation on tape.
Transcript pages: 104-114.

This Conversation Appears On A Tape
That Exhibits Signs of Duplication.

Ms. Tripp says she has a message from Norma Asnes in which Ms. Asnes invites Ms. Tripp to a play at the Arena Theatre for the next night. *See* T16 at 104. That event was on November 12, 1997. Also, Ms. Lewinsky describes a conversation with Ms. Currie in which she asked about the President's schedule "tonight," then "tomorrow," then Thursday, and then Friday. *See* T16 at 107-08. This sequence places this conversation on a Tuesday. November 11, 1997, was a Tuesday.

These factors are consistent with a conversation on Tuesday, November 11, 1997.

Conversation # 22:

Tuesday, November 11, 1997
Tape 26, side A, first conversation on tape.
Transcript pages: 2-5.

This Conversation Appears On A Tape
That Exhibits Signs of Duplication.

Ms. Tripp asks Ms. Lewinsky whether she would like to attend the play with Ms. Tripp, Ms. Asnes, and others. As noted in the description of conversation 21, this production occurred on November 12, 1997. Also, in the next conversation, which is clearly a continuation of this one, Ms. Tripp says it is the 11th. *See* T26 at 22.

These factors are consistent with a conversation on Tuesday, November 11, 1997.

Conversation # 23:
Tuesday, November 11, 1997
Tape 26, side A, second conversation on tape.
Transcript pages: 25-32.

This Conversation Appears On A Tape
That Exhibits Signs of Duplication.

Ms. Tripp says it is the 11th. *See* T26 at 22. This exchange is clearly a continuation of the conversation that immediately precedes it on the tape because the topic is the same, and Ms. Lewinsky hung up from the last conversation merely to get a telephone number from information. Ms. Lewinsky said she would call back immediately. *See* T26 at 5.

These factors are consistent with a conversation on Tuesday, November 11, 1997.

Conversation # 24:
Tuesday, November 11, 1997
Tape 26, side A, third conversation on tape.
Transcript pages: 32-55.

This Conversation Appears On A Tape
That Exhibits Signs of Duplication.

Ms. Lewinsky says she wants to see the President because it is Veterans Day and he is all alone. *See* T26 at 35. Veterans Day is November 11. In addition, this conversation is a continuation of the previous conversation (also dated November 11) which was interrupted by call waiting. Ms. Tripp says she just got off the phone with Ms. Asnes, whom Ms. Tripp was trying to reach. *See* T26 at 36.

These factors are consistent with a conversation on Tuesday, November 11, 1997.

Conversation # 25:
Thursday, November 13, 1997
Tape 16, side A, first conversation on tape.
Transcript pages: 2-9.

This Conversation Appears On A Tape
That Exhibits Signs of Duplication.

In this brief conversation, Ms. Lewinsky says she was in the White House earlier in the evening while President Zedillo of Mexico was there. She says she saw the President for 60 seconds. President Zedillo dined at the White House on November 13. *See Baltimore Sun* (Nov. 14, 1997, at 17A. WAVES records confirm Ms. Lewinsky was at the White House on this date. *See* 827-DC-000018, V006-DC-000008, 137-DC-000318.

These factors are consistent with a conversation on Thursday, November 13, 1997.

Conversation # 26:
Friday, November 14, 1997
Tape 16, side A, second conversation on tape.
Transcript pages: 9-51.

This Conversation Appears On A Tape
That Exhibits Signs of Duplication.

On T16, this conversation immediately follows the one in which Ms. Lewinsky describes her visit earlier in the day with President Clinton while President Zedillo was in the White House. The previous discussion ends with Ms. Lewinsky and Ms. Tripp exchanging "good night" wishes. *See* T16 at 9. This conversation begins with Ms. Lewinsky commenting that the President is in Las Vegas. *See* T16 at 9. The President's travel schedule indicates he was in Las Vegas on November 14, 1997. *See* 968-DC-0003257. Also, Ms. Lewinsky says she is going to New York by train. *See* T16 at 11. On November 14, 1997, Ms. Lewinsky sent an e-mail which indicated her plans to travel to New York by train. *See* V06-DC-000359.

These factors are consistent with a conversation on Friday, November 14, 1997.

Conversation # 27:
Sunday, November 16, 1997
Tape 16, side A, third conversation on tape.
Transcript pages: 52-60.

This Conversation Appears On A Tape
That Exhibits Signs of Duplication.

This very brief conversation, which is the last one on T16, immediately follows a Friday, November 14, 1997, conversation. This conversation is also cut off in the middle. The first conversation on T9 is also from Sunday night, November 16, 1997. Ms. Tripp told the Office of the Independent Counsel she would record until a tape ran out and then replace it with another tape. Ms. Tripp also told the Office of the Independent Counsel that when a tape was filled up, she would not put it in the recorder again.

Ms. Lewinsky left for New York City early in the morning on November 15, 1997. Ms. Lewinsky returned the night of the 16th. In this conversation, she describes her trip. Sunday night would have been the first time she could

621

have made such a call. Moreover, T9 contains additional discussion of the weekend in New York City, and it was also recorded on Sunday night. For all of these reasons, it is likely that Ms. Tripp began this recording of Ms. Lewinsky on Sunday night and the tape ran out. Ms. Tripp then apparently inserted T9 into the recorder and captured the remaining discussion.

These factors are consistent with a conversation on Monday, November 16, 1997.

Conversation # 28:
Sunday November 16, 1997
Tape 9, side A, first conversation on tape.
Transcript pages: 2-33.

This Conversation Appears On A Tape
That Exhibits Signs of Duplication.

Ms. Lewinsky says that she arrived in New York City "yesterday." *See* T9 at 3. Ms. Lewinsky was in New York City on November 15 and 16. These facts would place this conversation on Sunday night, November 16, 1997. In addition, Ms. Lewinsky describes a chance encounter with Ambassador Richardson in a restaurant in New York the day before. During this meeting, Ambassador Richardson commented on Ms. Lewinsky's pending job offer. *See* Richardson 4/30/98 Depo. at 115 (recalling encounter with Ms. Lewinsky on his birthday, November 15).

More generally, Ms. Lewinsky says she tried to buy Ms. Tripp a birthday present at a flea market in New York City over the weekend. *See* T9 at 8. Ms. Tripp's birthday is November 24. Since Ambassador Richardson offered Ms. Lewinsky a job at the UN on November 3, 1997, this conversation would have to be between these two dates. Of the three intervening weekends, Ms. Lewinsky was in New York City only once: on November 15 and 16.

These factors are consistent with a conversation on Sunday, November 16, 1997.

Conversation # 29:
Monday, November 17, 1997
Tape 9, side A, second conversation on tape.
Transcript pages: 33-51.

This Conversation Appears On A Tape
That Exhibits Signs of Duplication.

Ms. Lewinsky mentions it is November. *See* T9 at 41. Furthermore, Ms. Lewinsky says she spotted an attractive man in New York the day before. *See* T9 at 43. During November 1997, Ms. Lewinsky was only in New York City on November 15 and 16. In addition, this conversation immediately follows a conversation from Sunday, November 16, 1997, on tape T9. The previous conversation ended with Ms. Tripp and Ms. Lewinsky saying good night. In the next conversation on T9, Ms. Lewinsky says it is Tuesday.

These factors are consistent with a conversation on Monday, November 17, 1997.

Conversation # 30:
Tuesday, November 18, 1997
Tape 9, side B, third conversation on tape.
Transcript pages: 51-79.

This Conversation Appears On A Tape
That Exhibits Signs of Duplication.

Ms. Lewinsky says it is Tuesday. *See* T9 at 60. In addition, the conversation that immediately precedes this one on T9 is November 17, 1997, the Monday Ms. Lewinsky returned from New York City. Also, Ms. Lewinsky says she spoke with the President a week ago. *See* T9 at 60. According to an e-mail Ms. Lewinsky sent to a friend, she spoke to the President on November 12, 1997, six days earlier. *See* 1037-DC-0000318.

These factors are donsistent with a conversation on Tuesday, November 18, 1997.

Conversation # 31:
Thurdsay, November 20, 1997
Tape 9, side B, fourth conversation on tape.
Transcript pages: 79-100.

This Conversation Appears On A Tape
That Exhibits Signs of Duplication.

Ms. Lewinsky says her 60 second meeting with the President was one week before. *See* T9 at 84. Ms. Lewinsky visited with the President for 60 seconds on November 13, 1997, when President Zedillo of Mexico was at the White House. In addition, Ms. Lewinsky describes a conversation with Ms. Currie in which Ms. Lewinsky says the First Lady is leaving tomorrow. T9 at 80. The First Lady's travel schedule shows she left for Los Angeles on November 21, 1997. *See* 968-DC-00003478.

These factors are consistent with a conversation on Thursday, November 20, 1997.

Conversation # 32:
Thursday, November 20, 1997
Tape 5, side A, first conversation on tape.
Transcript pages: 2-16.

Conversation # 33:
Thursday, November 20, 1997
Tape 5, side A, third conversation on tape.
Transcript pages: 17-41.

Conversation # 34:
Thursday, November 20, 1997
Tape 5, side A, fourth conversation on tape.
Transcript pages: 41-47.

These 3 Conversations Appear On A Tape
That Exhibits Signs of Duplication.

Conversations 32-34 (treated together here) concern an audio tape that Ms. Lewinsky is making for the President. In the first two conversations, Ms. Lewinsky plays portions of the tape for Ms. Tripp and asks for advice preparing it. In conversation 34, Ms. Lewinsky calls Ms. Tripp to thank her for her help. Consistent with Ms. Lewinsky's sending the tape the next morning, courier receipts show Ms. Lewinsky ordered a courier delivery from the Pentagon to the White House at 8:18 a.m. on November 21. *See* 837-DC-00000014.

Also, Ms. Lewinsky says that Ms. Currie told her the President will leave too early on Saturday to allow a 15-minute visit by Ms. Lewinsky. *See* T5 at 5. According to the Presidential schedule, the President left for Vancouver on November 22. Baggage check-in occurred at 6:00 a.m. at Andrews Air Force Base, and Air Force One press pool check-in occurred at 8:30. 968-DC-00003301. This schedule is consistent with an early wake-up at the White House.

These factors are consistent with a conversation on Thursday, November 20, 1997.

Conversation # 35:
Friday, November 21, 1997
Tape 5, side A, fifth conversation on tape.
Transcript pages: 47-52.

This Conversation Appears On A Tape
That Exhibits Signs of Duplication.

This conversation immediately follows a conversation from November 20, 1997, on the tape. Ms. Lewinsky ended the last conversation by saying, "I'll see you tomorrow." *See* T5 at 47. This conversation is clearly the next day because Ms. Lewinsky describes several phone calls she had with Ms. Currie during the day, including calls after an interciew the President was taping at 6:15 p.m. *See* T5 at 51.

These factors are consistent with a conversation on Monday, November 21, 1997.

Conversation # 36:
Friday, November 21, 1997
Tape 5, side A, sixth conversation on tape.
Transcript pages: 53-55.

This Conversation Appears On A Tape
That Exhibits Signs of Duplication.

At the end of the conversation that immediately precedes this conversation on T5, Ms. Tripp instructs Ms. Lewinsky to call Ms. Currie and Ms. Currie her to remain at work until the President leaves. *See* T5 at 52. At the beginning of this conversation Ms. Lewinsky reports the results of the call. T5 at 53. These exchanges indicate this conversation was shortly after conversation 33. In addition, Ms. Currie told Ms. Lewinsky she was waiting for the President to leave the office and return to the residence. *See* T5 at 53. Since the President left for Denver, Seattle, and Vancouver early in the morning on November 22, *see* 968-DC-00003301, this conversation most likely occurred on November 21, 1997.

These factors are consistent with a conversation on Monday, November 21, 1997.

Conversation # 37:
Friday, November 21, 1997
Tape 5, side A, seventh conversation on tape.
Transcript pages: 55-59.

This Conversation Appears On A Tape
That Exhibits Signs of Duplication.

This conversation is another report from Ms. Lewinsky regarding whether Ms. Currie gave Ms. Lewinsky's cassette tape to the President. Besides the context of the tapes, in the conversation that immediately follows this one, Ms. Tripp says it is the 21st. *See* T5 at 69.

These factors are consistent with a conversation on Monday, November 21, 1997.

Conversation # 38:
Friday, November 21, 1997
Tape 5, side A, eighth conversation on tape.
Transcript pages: 59-91.

This Conversation Appears On A Tape
That Exhibits Signs of Duplication.

Ms. Tripp says it is the 21st during this conversation. *See* T5 at 69. Also, Lewinsky says that Monday is the 24th. *See* T5 at 81. November 21, 1997, was a Friday, so November 24, 1997, was a Monday. Moreover, this conversation is clearly a continuation of the earlier conversations in the evening because Ms. Lewinsky gives another report regarding Ms. Currie and the cassette tape Ms. Lewinsky sent to the President.

These factors are consistent with a conversation on Monday, November 21, 1997.

Conversation # 39:
Tuesday, December 9, 1997
Tape 23, side A, first conversation on tape.
Transcript pages: 2-6.

This Conversation Appears On A Tape
That Exhibits Signs of Duplication.

Ms. Lewinsky says she delivered something to the White House on "Monday," which was "yesterday morning." *See* T5 at 4-5. This statement is consistent with a courier receipt which shows a delivery from Ms. Lewinsky at the Pentagon to the White House on December 8, 1997. *See* 837-DC-00000017. In addition, Ms. Lewinsky says she is having lunch with Vernon Jordan on Thursday. *See* T23 at 2. The visitor log at Mr. Jordan's law firm and his calendar reveal that Ms. Lewinsky met with Mr. Jordan on Thursday, December 11, 1997. *See* V004-DC-00000171. (Akin and Gump visitor/contact log); V004-DC-00000148. (Vernon Jordan's calendar).

These factors are consistent with a conversation on Monday, December 9, 1997.

Conversation # 40:
Tuesday, December 9, 1997
Tape 23, side A, second conversation on tape.
Transcript pages: 6-56.

This Conversation Appears On A Tape
That Exhibits Signs of Duplication.

Ms. Tripp says it is "Tuesday afternoon." *See* T23 at 19. December 9, 1997, was a Tuesday. Ms. Tripp also says, "I can't believe you got in there Saturday." *See* T23 at 44. Epass records reveal Ms. Lewinsky saw the President at the White House on Saturday, December 6, 1997. *See* 827-DC-00000018. Ms. Tripp further mentions that Ms. Lewinsky will be seeing Mr. Jordan on Thursday. The visitor log at Mr. Jordan's law firm and his calendar reveal that Ms. Lewinsky met with Mr. Jordan on Thursday December 11, 1997. *See* V004-DC-00000171. (Akin and Gump visitor/contact log); V004-DC-00000148. (Vernon Jordan's calendar).

Moreover, Ms. Tripp mentions Ms. Lewinsky had an item sent to the White House by courier on Monday morning. *See* T23 at 19. A courier receipt reveals a delivery from Ms. Lewinsky at the Pentagon to the White House on Monday, December 8, 1997. *See* 837-DC-17, 20.

These factors are consistent with a conversation on Monday, December 9, 1997.

Conversation # 41:
Friday, December 12, 1997
Tape 23, side A, fifth conversation on tape.
Transcript pages: 57-68.

Conversation # 42:
Friday, December 12, 1997
Tape 23, side B, sixth conversation on tape.
Transcript pages: 68-127.

Conversation # 43:
Friday, December 12, 1997
Tape 23, side B, eighth conversation on tape.
Transcript pages: 127-131.

These Conversations Appear On A Tape
That Exhibits Signs of Duplication.

These three segments on tape 23 were likely two different conversations held on the same night. Because they concern the same subject matter (Ms. Tripp's meeting with her attorney regarding the subpoena she received in the Jones case), and because they wrap around two sides of the same cassette tape (conversation 39 ends side A and conversation 40 begins side B of tape 23) conversation 39 and conversation 40 are most likely the same discussion interrupted by side A of the tape's running out.

Conversation 41 is most likely a new conversation on the same night. In conversation 41, Ms. Lewinsky reads a letter she composed to the President. The letter concerns suggestions on how to settle the Jones case. *See* T23 at

129. Ms. Tripp and Ms. Lewinsky discussed this issue in conversation 40. *See* T23 at 88. In addition, conversation 40 ends with Ms. Tripp saying she will speak to her attorney in the morning and then call Ms. Lewinsky. *See* T23 at 126. At the outset of conversation 41, Ms. Tripp says, "I cannot believe someone who I thought was already in bed is at the computer." This statement is consistent with a later call on the same night.

Given these circumstances, the date for all three conversations comes from conversation 40. In conversation 40, Ms. Tripp describes how she watched a movie called "A Home of Our Own" on this evening. The Family Channel broadcast this movie on December 12, 1997 at 8:00 p.m. During her debriefings, Ms. Tripp confirmed she watched the movie on the night it was broadcast on the Family channel.

These factors are consistent with a conversation on Monday, December 12, 1997.

Conversation # 44:
Monday, December 22, 1997
Tape 6, side A, second conversation on tape.
Transcript pages: 2-24.

This Conversation Appears On A Tape
That Exhibits Signs of Duplication.

Ms. Lewinsky received her subpoena on December 19, 1997. *See* 902-DC-00000135-138. In this conversation, Ms. Tripp refers to the subpoena and the fact that it calls for a hat pin. *See* T6 at 3. For this reason, the conversation has to be after the 19th. Ms. Lewinsky also says she had a short meeting with Mr. Jordan on this day. Mr. Jordan's calendar reveals he met with Ms. Lewinsky on December 22, 1997. This is the day Mr. Jordan brought Ms. Lewinsky to see Frank Carter. *See* V004-DC-0000072, 1034-DC-00000103. Vernon Jordan also met with Ms. Lewinsky on December 19, 1997, but that meeting was for 45 minutes. *See* V004-DC-00000172.

These factors are consistent with a conversation on Monday, December 22, 1997.

Conversation # 45:
Monday, December 22, 1997
Tape 6, side A, fourth conversation on tape.
Transcript pages: 24-32.

This Conversation Appears On A Tape
That Exhibits Signs of Duplication.

This brief conversation is a continuation of conversation 42. At the end of conversation 42, Ms. Tripp told Ms. Lewinsky to speak with her mother about their plan to avoid the subpoena. *See* T6 at 23. At the beginning of this conversation, Ms. Lewinsky says her mother thinks the plan is brilliant. *See* T6 at 24.

These factors are consistent with a conversation on Monday, December 22, 1997.

Conversation # 46:
Monday, December 22, 1997
Tape 6, side B, fifth conversation on tape.
Transcript pages: 33-68.

This Conversation Appears On A Tape
That Exhibits Signs of Duplication.

Conversation 43 is brief because the first side of the tape runs out. This conversation, which is the first conversation on side B, is clearly a continuation of the same conversation. Ms. Tripp and Ms. Lewinsky were speaking about Ms. Currie at the end of conversation 43. *See* T6 at 32. This conversation begins with a continuation of the same conversation about Ms. Currie. *See* T6 at 33.

These factors are consistent with a conversation on Monday, December 22, 1997.

Conversation # 47:
Thursday, January 15, 1998
Tape 22, side A, first conversation on tape.
Transcript pages: 2-55.

Conversation # 48:
Thursday, January 15, 1998
Tape 22, side A, second conversation on tape.
Transcript pages: 55-76.

Both of the conversations on this tape were made under the supervision of the Office of the Independent Counsel. For this reason, the OIC knows the date of the conversations independently from the contents of the tapes.

[Editor's note: Two documents relate to gifts from President Clinton to Ms. Lewinsky that were turned over to prosecutors.]

Gifts

Kenneth W. Starr, Esq.
Office of the Independent Counsel
1001 Pennsylvania Avenue, N.W., Suite 490-N
Washington, D.C. 20004

Re: Subpoena Duces Tecum to Betty W. Currie, Grand Jury # 97-3

Dear Mr. Starr:

In response to the above-referenced subpoena duces tecum to Ms. Betty W. Currie, enclosed please find the following:
One copy of the State of the Union address dated January 23, 1996, in a brown envelope.
One autographed photograph of President Clinton, held between two cardboard panels.
One green dress with a "Black Dog" logo, size L.
One turquoise T-shirt with a "Black Dog" logo, size L.
One white T-shirt with a "Seal of the Black Dog of Martha's Vineyard" on the front, size L.
One blue baseball cap with a "Black Dog" logo.
One three-page facsimile message.
Two twenty-page newspaper inserts from the *Washington Post*, February 14, 1997.
One jewelry pin in "Casual Corner" box.
One hatpin with a globe-like base in a black box with gold stars on it.
                                                            824-DC-00000001
One framed signed picture of President Clinton and Monica Lewinsky.
One bottle, in its box, of Tiffany Spa Moisturizing Hand Cream.
One bottle, in its box, of Tiffany Spa Refreshing Body Mist.
One sympathy card, with envelope.
One card with joke re snowman and carrot, with envelope.
One thank-you card dated September 17, 1997, with envelope.
Four pages of handwritten notes.

Sincerely,

Karl Metzner

Enclosures

824-DC-00000002

FEDERAL BUREAU OF INVESTIGATION
Receipt for Property Received/Returned/Released/Seized

On (date) ___7/29/98___

item(s) listed below were:
☒ Received From
☐ Returned To
☐ Released To
☐ Seized

Time: ___1:45 PM___

(Name) ___Law Offices of Plato Cacheris___

(Street Address) ___1100 Conn Ave, Suite 730___

(City) ___Washington, D.C.___

Description of Item(s):

① 1 stuffed animal from black dog
② Book: Leaves of Grass w/ paper cover
③ Page from Filofax (1996 & 1997) w/ dates circled on it
④ GAP dress, size 12, dark blue
⑤ Brown, marble bear sculpture
⑥ Rockettes Christmas blanket (1995), red & white
⑦ Dark sunglasses (TAIWAN written on inside)
⑧ Wooden box, circular in shape, redish
⑨ 4 microcassetts: 1) "Dec 96" on it
                    2) "Sept. 96" on it
                    3) "May 96 2 mess." on it
                    4) "April 96" on it
⑩ White canvas bag w/ a black dog on it.

END

Received by: ███████████ (Signature)   Received from ___Monica___ (Signature)

630

Books

[Editor's note: Prosecutors compiled a catalog of books in the President's study, possibly because they were interested in books that Ms. Lewinsky and President Clinton exchanged as gifts or because they wanted to check Ms. Lewinsky's recollections about the Oval Office suite.]

Catalog of Books in the West Wing
Presidential Study as of 10 October 1997

Author	Title	Location	Topic	Notes
Michael W. Monroe	The White House Collection of American Crafts	White House Art	POTUS Study-- WW	
Henry F. Graff, Editor	The Presidents: A Reference History	Presidential History	POTUS Study-- WW	
Davis Newton Lott	The Presidents Speak: The Inaugural Addresses of the American Presidents from Washington to Clinton	Presidential History	POTUS Study-- WW	Inscribed by the author, December, 1994
Michael Wolff, Peter Rutten, and Albert F. Bayers III	Where We Stand: Can America Make It in the Global Race for Wealth, Health, and Happiness	Sociology	POTUS Study-- WW	
U.S. Government Printing Office	Inaugural Addresses of the Presidents of the United States	Presidential History	POTUS Study-- WW	
William Safire	Safire's New Political Dictionary	Pol. & Govt.- Dictionary	POTUS Study-- WW	
William Jefferson Clinton	State of the Union Address to the 104th Congress, Second Session Jan. 23, 1996	Presidential Speeches	POTUS Study- WW	

1361-DC-00000002

S 019366

William Jefferson Clinton	State of the Union Address to the 104th Congress, First Session Jan. 24, 1995	Presidential Speeches	POTUS Study- WW	
William Jefferson Clinton	State of the Union Address to the 103rd Congress, Second Session Jan. 25, 1994	Presidential Speeches	POTUS Study- WW	
William Jefferson Clinton	Address to the Joint Session of Congress Feb. 17, 1993	Presidential Speeches	POTUS Study- WW	
William Safire	Lend Me Your Ears: Great Speeches in History	Speeches	POTUS Study-- WW	
Flip Schulke	He had a Dream: Martin Luther King Jr. and the Civil Rights Movement	U.S. Hist.- Pictorial Works	POTUS Study-- WW	Inscribed by Author; Limited edition #127/250
Douglas Southall Freeman	George Washington: A Biography Volume One: Young Washington	POTUS Biography	POTUS Study-- WW	Copyright 1948
Garry Wills	Cincinnatus: George Washington and the Enlightenment	POTUS Biography	POTUS Study-- WW	
Richard Norton Smith	Patriarch: George Washington and the New American Nation	POTUS Biography	POTUS Study-- WW	Inscribed by the Staff of the Commander George Washington Battle Group
Noemie Emery	Washington: A Biography	POTUS Biography	POTUS Study-- WW	

1361-DC-00000003

S 019367

2

Edited by L.H. Butterfield, Marc Friedlaender, and Mary-Jo Kline	The Book of Abigail and John: Selected Letters of the Adams Family 1762-1784	Presidential Writings: Letters	POTUS Study-WW	
Nathan Schachner	Thomas Jefferson: A Biography, Volumes 1 and 2	POTUS Biography	POTUS Study-WW	
Max Byrd	Jefferson: A Nove	Fiction: Presidency	POTUS Study-WW	Inscribed by the Author
Jerome J. Shestack	Thomas Jefferson: Lawyer	POTUS Biography	POTUS Study-WW	Inscribed by the Author
Frank L. Dewey	Thomas Jefferson Lawyer	POTUS Biography	POTUS Study-WW	Inscribed by Author, January 1993
Dumas Malone	Jefferson and His Time: The Sage of Monticello	POTUS Biography	POTUS Study-WW	
Fawn M. Brodie	Thomas Jefferson: An Intimate History	POTUS Biography	POTUS Study-WW	
Natalie S. Bober	Thomas Jefferson: Man on a Mountain	POTUS Biography	POTUS Study-WW	Inscribed by the Author, Feb. 11, 1997
Noble E. Cunningham, Jr.	In Pursuit of Reason: The Life of Thomas Jefferson	POTUS Biography	POTUS Study-WW	Inscribed by the Author, Apr. 13, 1994
Jim Strupp	Revolution Song: Thomas Jefferson's Legacy	POTUS Biography	POTUS Study-WW	
Alf J. Mapp, Jr.	Thomas Jefferson: A Strange Case of Mistaken Identity	POTUS Biography	POTUS Study-WW	

Andrew Burstein	The Inner Jefferson: Portrait of a Grieving Optimist	POTUS Biography	POTUS Study-WW	Inscribed by the Author, Feb. 1997
Alf J. Mapp, Jr.	Thomas Jefferson Passionate Pilgrim: The Presidency, the Founding of the University and the Private Battle	POTUS Biography	POTUS Study-WW	Inscribed by the Author, March 23, 1994
Joseph J. Ellis	American Sphinx: The Character of Thomas Jefferson	POTUS Biography	POTUS Study-WW	
William Lee Miller	The Business of May Next: James Madison and the Founding	POTUS Biography	POTUS Study-WW	Inscribed by the Author
Robert V. Remini	The Life of Andrew Jackson	POTUS Biography	POTUS Study-WW	
Karen B. Winnick	Mr. Lincoln's Whiskers	Juvenile Book about Grace Bedell, who suggested AL grow a beard	POTUS Study-WW	Inscribed by Author
Carl Sandburg	Abraham Lincoln: The Prairie Years and the War Years	POTUS Biography	POTUS Study-WW	Inscribed by "Denise"--XMas 1966
Stephen B. Oates	With Malice Toward None: The Life of Abraham Lincoln	POTUS Biography	POTUS Study-WW	
Benjamin P. Thomas	Abraham Lincoln: A Biography	POTUS Biography	POTUS Study-WW	
Gore Vidal	Lincoln: A Novel	POTUS Fiction	POTUS Study-WW	

4

Garry Wills	Lincoln at Gettysburg: The Words That Remade America	Lincoln Oratory	POTUS Study-WW	Inscribed by G. and Krishna Kalliampur of North Carolina on Nov. 3, 1992
James M. McPherson	Abraham Lincoln and the Second American Revolution	Lincoln-Military-Ldrshp.	POTUS Study-WW	
Elton Trueblood	Abraham Lincoln: A Spiritual Biography	POTUS Biography	POTUS Study-WW	Inscribed by Connie Lovejoy of Indiana
Dale Carnegie	Lincoln The Unknown	POTUS Biography	POTUS Study-WW	
Paul Simon	Lincoln's Preparation for Greatness: The Illinois Legislative Years	POTUS Biography	POTUS Study-WW	Inscribed by Author
Phillip Shaw Paludan	The Presidency of Abraham Lincoln	POTUS Biography	POTUS Study-WW	Inscribed by the Author
Lloyd Ostendorf	Abraham Lincoln: The Boy The Man	POTUS Juvenile Biography	POTUS Study-WW	Donated by American Legion Auxiliary of Vandalia, IL
Mario M. Cuomo and Harold Holzer, Editors	Lincoln on Democracy: His Own Words, with Essays by America's Foremost Civil War Historians	AL Views on Democracy	POTUS Study-WW	
Harold Holzer	Dear Mr. Lincoln: Letters to the President	Presidential Writings: Letters	POTUS Study-WW	Inscribed by Paul Begala-3/7/94
Andrew Delbanco, Editor	The Portable Abraham Lincoln	Presidential Speeches and Letters	POTUS Study-WW	

5   1361-DC-00000006

John Gabriel Hunt, Editor	The Essential Abraham Lincoln	Presidential Speeches and Letters	POTUS Study-WW	
William S. McFeely	Grant: A Biography	POTUS Biography	POTUS Study-WW	
Mary Drake McFeely and William S. McFeely, Editors	Grant: Personal Memoirs of U.S. Grant: Selected Letters 1839-1865	Presidential Writings: Letters	POTUS Study-WW	
Nathan Miller	The Roosevelt Chronicles: The Story of a great American Family	Presidential Families	POTUS Study-WW	
August Heckscher	Woodrow Wilson: A Biography	POTUS Biography	POTUS Study-WW	
Gene Smith	When the Cheering Stopped	POTUS Biography	POTUS Study-WW	
Sigmund Freud and William C. Bullitt	Thomas Woodrow Wilson: A Psychological Study	POTUS Biography	POTUS Study-WW	
Herbert Hoover	The Ordeal of Woodrow Wilson	POTUS Biography	POTUS Study-WW	
Joseph P. Lash	The Partnership That Saved the West: Roosevelt and Churchill 1939-41	POTUS Biography	POTUS Study-WW	Inscribed by Bernard Goss, 19 Dec 1996
Kenneth S. Davis	FDR: The Beckoning of Destiny 1882-1928	POTUS Biography	POTUS Study-WW	

1361-DC-00000007

6

633

Eric Larrabee	Commander in Chief: Franklin Delano Roosevelt, His Lieutenants & Their War	POTUS Biography	POTUS Study-WW	Inscribed by "Bucky" in July 1987
Ted Morgan	FDR: A Biography	POTUS Biography	POTUS Study-WW	
Yankee Magazine, Jan. 1996	Article on Calvin Coolidge-"The Price of the Presidency"	POTUS Biography	POTUS Study-WW	
Herbert Hoover (William Nichols, Editor)	Herbert Hoover: Fishing for Fun and to Wash Your Soul	Presidential Writings: Fishing	POTUS Study-WW	
George Grey	Ten Days: A Crisis in American History (copyright 1933)	U.S. History--FDR Admin.	POTUS Study-WW	Inscribed by Max and Anita Harris, 1/7/93
Hugh Gregory Gallagher	FDR:s Splendid Deception: The moving story of Roosevelt's massive disability and the intense efforts to conceal it from the public	POTUS Biography	POTUS Study-WW	Inscribed by Author 2/22/95
Geoffrey C. Ward	A First-Class Temperment: The Emergence of Franklin Roosevelt	POTUS Biography	POTUS Study-WW	
Robert E. Sherwood	Roosevelt and Hopkins: An Intimate History	U.S. History--FDR Admin.	POTUS Study-WW	
Franklin Delano Roosevelt (Russell D. Buhite and David W. Levy, Editors)	FDR's Fireside Chats	Presidential Speeches	POTUS Study-WW	

1361-DC-00000008

S 019372

7

Robert H. Ferrell	Choosing Truman: The Democratic Convention of 1944	U.S. History--Democratic Party	POTUS Study-WW	Inscribed by the Author
David McCullough	Truman	POTUS Biography	POTUS Study-WW	Inscribed by Sharon and Jay Rockefeller, 7/19/92
Robert H. Ferrell	Harry S. Truman: A Life	POTUS Biography	POTUS Study-WW	
Margaret Truman	Harry S. Truman	POTUS Biography	POTUS Study-WW	
Roy Jenkins	Truman	POTUS Biography	POTUS Study-WW	
Harry S. Truman	Mr. Citizen	Presidential Memoirs	POTUS Study-WW	
Ken Hechler	Working with Truman: A Personal Memoir of the White House Years	U.S. History--Truman Admin.	POTUS Study-WW	Inscribed by Author, 8/25/96
Harry S. Truman (Margaret Truman, Editor)	Where the Buck Stops: The Personal and Private Writings of Harry S. Truman	Presidential History	POTUS Study-WW	Inscribed by David E. Barrett of Fairfield, OH
Harry S. Truman (Monte M. Poen, Editor)	Strictly Personal and Confidential: The Letters Harry Truman Never Mailed	Presidential Writings: Letters	POTUS Study-WW	
Fred I. Greenstein	The Hidden-Hand Presidency: Eisenhower as Leader	Presidential Leadershp	POTUS Study-WW	Inscribed by Author
Sheila L. Cassidy	Remembering Jack and Bobby: A Kennedy Anthology	Presidential Quotes	POTUS Study-WW	Inscribed by Author, July, 1992

8   1361-DC-00000009

S 019373

634

Kenneth P. O'Donnell and David Powers with Joe McCarthy	"Johnny, We Hardly Knew Ye": Memories of John Fitzgerald Kennedy	POTUS Biography	POTUS Study-WW	Inscribed by Dave Powers, 1/17/92
Gerald Posner	Case Closed: Lee Harvey Oswald and the Assasination of JFK	JFK's Death-- Theories	POTUS Study-WW	
Nigel Hamilton	JFK Reckless Youth	POTUS Biography	POTUS Study-WW	
Thomas C. Reeves	A Question of Character: A Life of John F. Kennedy	POTUS Biography	POTUS Study-WW	Inscribed to HRC from Gaston Williamson of Little Rock; note from Williamson enclosed as well
Garry Wills	The Kennedy Imprisonment: A Meditation on Power	Kennedy Family History	POTUS Study-WW	
John F. Kennedy (edited by Theodore C. Sorenson)	"Let the Word Go Forth": The Speeches, Statements, and Writings of John F. Kennedy 1947-1963	POTUS Speeches and Writings	POTUS Study-WW	Inscribed from Tom O'Toole of Pennsylvania
Lewis J. Paper	John F. Kennedy: The Promis & the Performance	Kennedy Administration	POTUS Study-WW	
Irving Bernstein	Promises Kept: John F. Kennedy's New Frontier	Kennedy Administration	POTUS Study-WW	Inscribed by Zelda and Albert Silverman, 11/13/92

Harris Wofford	Of Kennedys & Kings: Making Sense of the Sixties	U.S. History- 1960s	POTUS Study-WW	Inscribed by Harris Wofford, 11/2/92; Note from Wofford enclosed also
Thomas Fleming	The Man Who Dared thee Lightning: A New Look at Benjamin Franklin	POTUS Biography	POTUS Study-WW	
Ronald W. Clark	A Biography: Benjamin Franklin	POTUS Biography	POTUS Study-WW	
Milton Lomask	Aaron Burr: The Years from Princeton to Vice-President	VPOTUS Biography	POTUS Study-WW	
T.H. Watkins	Righteous Pilgrim: The Life and Times of Harold Ickes 1874-1952	Biography: Harold Ickes	POTUS Study-WW	Inscribed to BC and HRC by Susan, 1/92
Joseph P. Lash	Eleanor and Franklin: The Story of their relationship based on Eleanor Roosevelt's private papers	POTUS Family History	POTUS Study-WW	
Stella K. Hershan	The Candles She Lit: The Legacy of Eleanor Roosevelt	FLOTUS Biography	POTUS Study-WW	Inscribed by the Author 1/23/96
Eleanor Roosevelt	The Autobiography of Eleanor Roosevelt	FLOTUS Autobiography	POTUS Study-WW	
Eleanor Roosevelt	Tomorrow is Now: "It is today that we must create the world of the future"	FLOTUS Writings	POTUS Study-WW	
Eleanor Roosevelt	This I Remember	FLOTUS Memoirs	POTUS Study-WW	

Blanche Wiesen Cook	Eleanor Roosevelt: Volume One 1884-1933	FLOTUS Biography	POTUS Study-WW	Inscribed to HRC by Marilyn and Richard Rich of Orinda, CA
Albert Eisele	Almost to the Presidency: A Biography of Two American Politicians	Biography: Humphrey and McCarthy	POTUS Study-WW	Inscribed by Pat O'Connor
John Kennedy	Bound answer to question asked in 1962, "Somewhere in our land today, there is a high school or college student who will one day be sitting in your chair. If you could now speak to this future President, what advice would you give him or her"; this appeared in the 1970 World Book Ency.	POTUS Writings	POTUS Study-WW	
Alex J. Goldman	John Fitzgerald Kennedy: The World Remembers	Death of JFK	POTUS Study-WW	Inscribed by Alex J. Goldman, 11/18/1992
Theodore H. White	The Making of a President 1960	Presidential Campaigns	POTUS Study-WW	Inscribed by the Pryors, 11/2/92
Christopher Matthews	Kennedy & Nixon: The Rivalry That Shaped Postwar America	U.S. History-Political Relationships	POTUS Study-WW	Inscribed by the Author, 5/96
Richard Reeves	President Kennedy: Profile of Power	POTUS Biography	POTUS Study-WW	Inscribed by the Author, 11/20/93
Arthur M. Schlesinger	A Thousand Days: John F. Kennedy in the White House	JFK Administration	POTUS Study-WW	Signature of Bill Clinton; 1st Printing

1361-DC-00000012   11

John F. Kennedy	The Speeches of Senator John F. Kennedy Presidential Campaign of 1960	Presidential Speeches	POTUS Study-WW	Inscribed by Brian Snow (?), 9/17/92
Robert A. Caro	The Years of Lyndon Johnson: Means of Ascent	POTUS Biography	POTUS Study-WW	
Doris Kearns	Lyndon Johnson & the American Dream	POTUS Biography	POTUS Study-WW	
Joseph A. Califano, Jr.	The Triumph and Tragedy of Lyndon Johnson: The White House Years	POTUS Biography	POTUS Study-WW	Inscribed by the Author, 7/92
Robert A. Caro	The Years of Lyndon Johnson: The Path to Power	POTUS Biography	POTUS Study-WW	
Lyndon Baines Johnson	The Vantage Point: Perspectives of the Presidency 1963-69	POTUS Memoirs	POTUS Study-WW	
Merle Miller	Lyndon: An Oral Biography	POTUS Biography	POTUS Study-WW	
Richard Nixon	1999: Victory Without War	Presidential Writings: Foreign Policy	POTUS Study-WW	Advance Copy
Richard Nixon	Beyond Peace	Presidential Writings: Foreign Policy	POTUS Study-WW	
Richard Nixon	The Real War (The Richard Nixon Library Edition)	Presidential Writings: Foreign Policy	POTUS Study-WW	
Richard Nixon	Real Peace: No More Vietnams (The Richard Nixon Library Edition)	Presidential Writings: Foreign Policy	POTUS Study-WW	

1361-DC-00000013   12

,Richard Nixon	Leaders (The Richard Nixon Library Edition)	Presidential Writings: Leadership	POTUS Study- WW	
Richard Nixon	Seize the Moment: America's Challenge in a One-Superpower World	Presidential Writings: Foreign Policy	POTUS Study- WW	
Christopher Matthews	Kennedy and Nixon: The Rivalry That Shaped Postwar America	Presidential History: The Sixties	POTUS Study- WW	Inscribed by the author, May 1996
Richard Nixon	Seize the Moment: America's Challenge in a One Superpower World	Presidential Writings: Foreign Pólicy	POTUS Study- WW	
Presidential Studies Quarterly	Special Issue: The Nixon Presidency	Nixon Administration	POTUS Study- WW	
Gerald Ford	The War Powers Resolution: A Constitutional Crisis	Presidential Writings- Foreign Policy	POTUS Study- WW	Signed by the Author
Jimmy Carter	Always a Reckoning and Other Poems	Presidential Writings- Poetry	POTUS Study- WW	
Jimmy Carter	An Outdoor Journal	Presidential Writings- Outdoor Life	POTUS Study- WW	
Jimmy Carter	Turning Point: A Candidate, a State, and a Nation Come of Age	Presidential Writings: Autobiography	POTUS Study- WW	Signed by the Author
Jimmy and Rosalynn Carter	Everything to Gain: Making the Most of the Rest of Your Life	Presidential Writings- Philosophy	POTUS Study- WW	Inscribed to BC and HRC by the Authors
Jimmy Carter	Keeping Faith: Memoirs of a President	Presidential Writings: Memoirs	POTUS Study- WW	Inscribed to BC by the Author

Jimmy Carter	A Government as Good as Its People	Presidential Writings: Govt. And Politics	POTUS Study- WW	
Jimmy Carter	Keeping Faith: Memoirs of a President	Presidential Writings: Memoirs	POTUS Study- WW	1995 Edition
Lou Cannon	President Reagan: The Role of a Lifetime	Biography: Reagan	POTUS Study- WW	
Ronald Reagan	Ronald Reagan: An American Life	Presidential Writings: Autobiography	POTUS Study- WW	Inscribed by the author 11/27/92
Arthur M. Schlesinger, Jr.	Robert Kennedy and His Times	Biography: Robert F. Kennedy	POTUS Study- WW	Inscribed by Milas H. And Shirley Hale, 1/11/79
Joseph Lash	Dealers and Dreamers: A New Look at the New Deal	U.S. History: New Deal	POTUS Study- WW	Inscribed by Steve Smith
Warren Rogers	When I Think of Bobby: A Personal History of the Kennedy Years	Biography: Robert F. Kennedy	POTUS Study- WW	Inscribed by the author 6/10/93
Robert F. Kennedy; Edited by Edwin O. Guthman and C. Richard Allen	R.F.K.: Collected Speeches	Speeches: Robert F. Kennedy	POTUS Study- WW	Note from Rick Allen
Robert F. Kennedy	Thirteen Days: A Memoir of the Cuban Missile Crisis	U.S Foreign Policy: Cuban Missile Crisis	POTUS Study- WW	
Jack Newfield	Robert F. Kennedy: A Memoir	Biography: Robert F. Kennedy	POTUS Study- WW	
Robert S. McNamara	In Retrospect: The Tragedy and Lessons of Vietnam	U.S. Foreign Policy: Vietnam	POTUS Study- WW	Inscribed by the author

Mario Cuomo	More than Words: The Speeches of Mario Cuomo	Speeches: Mario Cuomo	POTUS Study-WW	Inscribed by the author
T. Harry Williams	Huey Long: A Biography	Biography: Huey Long	POTUS Study-WW	Inscribed by BC to Jeff (Dwire), Christmas 1970
Clarence Darrow	The Story of My Life	Autobiography: Clarence Darrow	POTUS Study-WW	
Edwin S. Gaustad	Neither King Nor Prelate: Religion and the New Nation, 1776-1826	U.S. Religious History	POTUS Study-WW	Inscribed by the author 1/7/97
Gerald Gunther	Learned Hand: The Man and the Judge	Biography: Learned Hand	POTUS Study-WW	
Paul Finkelman	Slavery and the Founders: Race and Liberty in the Age of Jefferson	U.S. History: Race Relations	POTUS Study-WW	Inscribed by the author 2/11/97
Thomas E. Patterson	Out of Order: How the Decline of the Political Parties and the Growing Power of the News Media Undermine the American Way of Electing Presidents	Presidentia Campaigns and the Media	POTUS Study-WW	
Walter Cronkhite	A Reporter's Life	Autobiography: Walter Cronkhite	POTUS Study-WW	
William E. Leuchtenburg	In the Shadow of F.D.R.- From Harry Truman to Bill Clinton	Presidential History	POTUS Study-WW	Inscribed to HRC by the author
Bruce I. Newman	The Marketing of the President: Political Marketing as Campaign Strategy	Presidential Campaigns: Strategy	POTUS Study-WW	Inscribed by the author

1361-DC-00000016   15

S 019380

Robert E. Gilbert	The Mortal Presidency: Illness and Anguish in the White House	Presidential History: Health	POTUS Study-WW	
Haynes Johnson	Sleeping Through History: America in the Reagan Years	Presidential History: Reagan Administration	POTUS Study-WW	
John Morton Blum	The Progressive Presidents: Theodore Roosevelt, Woodrow Wilson, Franklin Delano Roosevelt, and Lyndon Johnson	Presidential History	POTUS Study-WW	Inscribed by ? and Ruth, December 1992
Alice M. Rivlin	Reviving the American Dream: the Economy, the States, and the Federal Government	U.S. Economic Policy	POTUS Study-WW	Card from Luis and Christina, 12/19/94
Terry Eastland	Energy in the Executive: The Case for the Strong Presidency	Presidency: Academic Study	POTUS Study-WW	
Joe McGuinness	The Selling of the President: The Classic Account of the Packaging of Richard Nixon	Presidential History: Richard Nixon	POTUS Study-WW	Inscribed by the author 11/10/91
Louis W. Koenig	The Chief Executive	Presidential History	POTUS Study-WW	from the San Mateo County Library System
Richard Rose	The Postmodern President: The White House Meets the World	Presidency: Academic Study	POTUS Study-WW	
Robert Shogan	The Riddle of Power: Presidential Leadership From Truman to Bush	Presidency: Leadership	POTUS Study-WW	
Sidney Blumenthal	Our Long National Daydream: A Political Pageant of the Reagan Era	Presidential History: Reagan Administration	POTUS Study-WW	

1361-DC-00000017   16

S 019381

638

,Carl M. Brauer	Presidential Transitions: Eisenhower through Reagan	Presidential History: Transitions	POTUS Study-WW	
Paul Taylor	See How They Run: Electing the President in an Age of Mediaocracy	Presidential Campaigns and the Media	POTUS Study-WW	
John B. Moses, M.D. and Wilbur Gross (?)	Presidential Courage: The Dramatic Stories of Presidents Confronted by the Combined Challenges of Health and Political Crises	Presidential History: Courage	POTUS Study-WW	
Theodore C. Sorenson	A Different Kind of Presidency: A Proposal for Breaking the Political Deadlock	Presidency	POTUS Study-WW	
Michael Novak	Choosing Presidents: Symbols of Political Leadership	Presidency: Leadership	POTUS Study-WW	Inscribed to HRC and BC by the Author: Renaissance Weekend 92-93
Helen Thomas	Dateline: White House. A Warm and Revealing Account of America's Presidents and their Families from the Kennedys to the Fords	Presidency and Media Coverage	POTUS Study-WW	Inscribed by the Author 8/19/93
Michael J. Sandel	Democracy's Discontent: America in Search of a Public Philosophy	Democratic Philosophy	POTUS Study-WW	Inscribed by the Author 8/2/96
James Fallows	Breaking the News: How the Media Undermine American Democracy	Politics and the Media	POTUS Study-WW	Inscribed by the Author 1/16/97 -
James A. Michener	This Noble Land: My Vision for America	U.S. Social Values	POTUS Study-WW	

1361-DC-00000018 17

S 019382

,Charles O. Jones	The Presidency in a Separated System	Presidency	POTUS Study-WW	
David M. Barrett	Uncertain Warriors: Lyndon Johnson and His Vietnam Advisors	U.S. Foreign Policy: Vietnam	POTUS Study-WW	Inscribed by the Author 3/10/94 -
Jack W. Germond and Jules Witcover	Blue Smoke and Mirrors: How Reagan Won and Why Carter Lost the Election of 1980	Presidential Campaigns: 1980 Case Study	POTUS Study-WW	
E.J. Dionne, Jr.	Why Americans Hate Politics	Political Participation	POTUS Study-WW	
Peter Brown	Minority Party: Why Democrats Face Defeat in 1992 and Beyond	Political Campaigns: Democratic Party	POTUS Study-WW	Inscribed by the Author 9/4/91
Larry J. Sabato	Feeding Frenzy: How Attack Journalism Has Transformed American Politics	Political Campaigns: Attack Journalism	POTUS Study-WW	Inscribed by the Author 8/12/91
Kenneth T. Walsh	Feeding the Beast: The White House Versus the Press	Presidency and Media Coverage	POTUS Study-WW	Inscribed by the Author 1/16/97
Howard Kurtz	Hot Air All Talk All the Time: An Inside Look at the Performers and the Pundits	Politics and the Media	POTUS Study-WW	Inscribed by the Author 1/23/96
Hedrick ?	The Power Game: How Washington Works	Politics and Power	POTUS Study-WW	Inscribed by the Author 6/30/93 :
Jack W. Germond and Jules Witcover	Whose Broad Stripes and Bright Stars? The Trivial Pursuit of the Presidency 1988	Presidential Campaigns: 1988 Case Study	POTUS Study-WW	Inscribed from Mary Altgelt

1361-DC-00000019 18

S 019383

Haynes Johnson	Divided We Fall: Gambling With History in the Nineties	Economic Conditions	POTUS Study-WW	Inscribed by the Author 3/7/94
Jack W. Germond and Jules Witcover	Mad as Hell: Revolt at the Ballot Box 1992	Presidential Campaigns: 1992 Case Study	POTUS Study-WW	Inscribed to BC and HRC by the Authors 7/15/93
Howard Kurtz	Media Circus: The Trouble With America's Newspapers	Print Journalism	POTUS Study-WW	Inscribed by the Author
Mary Van Rensselaer Thayer	Jacqueline Kennedy: The White House Years	Biography: Jackie Kennedy	POTUS Study-WW	Inscribed by Mrs. Lexine Adams of Jacksonville, FL
Harry S. Truman edited by Mark Goodman	Give 'Em Hell Harry	Presidential Quotes	POTUS Study-WW	
Theodore White	The Making of the President 1960	Presidential Campaigns: 1960 Case Study	POTUS Study-WW	
John F. Kennedy	Profiles in Courage: Commemorative Edition	U.S. History: Courage in Early Leaders	POTUS Study-WW	
John F. Kennedy edited by Bill Adler	The Kennedy Wit	Presidential Quotes	POTUS Study-WW	Inscribed from Jeff Fites
Shelley Bedek	Our President: Bill Clinton (children's book)	Juvenile Biography: Bill Clinton	POTUS Study-WW	Inscribed from Colin and Bronwyn Dixon of Fayetteville, AR
John F. Kennedy edited by Bill Adler	The Kennedy Wit	Presidential Quotes	POTUS-Study-WW	Hardback Edition

William Jefferson Clinton	Between Hope and History	ial Writings	POTUS Study-WW	Chinese Edition
William Jefferson Clinton	Between Hope and History	Presidential Writings	POTUS Study-WW	Hebrew Edition
Jim Moore and Rick Ihde	Clinton: Young Man in a Hurry	Biography: Bill Clinton	POTUS Study-WW	Japanese Edition: Inscribed by Jim Moore
Jim Moore and Rick Ihde	Clinton: Young Man in a Hurry	Biography: Bill Clinton	POTUS Study-WW	Chinese Edition: Inscribed by Jim Moore
Judith Warner	Hillary Clinton: The Inside Story	Biography: Hillary Rodham Clinton	POTUS Study-WW	
Charles F. Allen and Jonathan Portis	The Comeback Kid: The Life and Career of Bill Clinton	Biography: Bill Clinton	POTUS Study-WW	Leather Bound Romanian Edition
Virginia Kelley with James Morgan	Leading With My Heart	Autobiography: Virginia Kelley	POTUS Study-WW	Korean Edition
David R. Collins	William Jefferson Clinton: 42nd President of the United States	Juvenile Biography: Bill Clinton	POTUS Study-WW	
Bill Clinton and Al Gore	Putting People First	Presidential and Vice-Presidential Writings	POTUS Study-WW	Italian Edition
Daiwa Institute of Research, Ltd.	The Clinton Revolution: An Inside Look at the New Administration	U.S. Economic Policy	POTUS Study-WW	
Daiwa Institute of Research, Ltd.	The Clinton Administration: An Inside Look at the New Administration	U.S. Economic Policy	POTUS Study-WW	Japanese Edition

Jim Moore and Rick Ihde	Clinton: Young Man in a Hurry	Biography: Bill Clinton	POTUS Study-WW	Inscribed by Nancy Nash and Maria (?) Haley
Daiwa Institute of Research, Ltd.	The Clinton Revolution: An Inside Look at the New Administration	U.S. Economic Policy	POTUS Study-WW	Japanese Edition
Charles F. Allen and Jonathan Portis	The Comeback Kid: the Life and Career of Bill Clinton	Biography: Bill Clinton	POTUS Study-WW	Romanian Edition
Compiled and edited by Ernest Dumas	The Clintons of Arkansas: An Introduction by Those Who Know Them Best	Biography: Clinton Family	POTUS Study-WW	
William L. Brown	President Bill: A Graphic Epic	Political Satire	POTUS Study-WW	
Hank Hillin	Al Gore, Jr.: Born to Lead	Biography: Al Gore	POTUS Study-WW	Inscribed by the author 1992
William Jefferson Clinton	Between Hope and History: Meeting America's Challenges for the 21st Century	Presidential Writings	POTUS Study-WW	French Edition
William Jefferson Clinton	Between Hope and History: Meeting America's Challenges for the 21st Century	Presidential Writings	POTUS Study-WW	Russian Edition
Progressive Policy Institute of Democratic Leadership Council, Inc.	Mandate for Change	Democratic Party	POTUS Study-WW	Chinese Translation: Inscribed by Yang Dayhou of Beijing
Rex Nelson	The Hillary Factor: America's Most Powerful First Lady	Biography: Hillary Rodham Clinton	POTUS Study-WW	

1361-DC-00000022

21

Chip Eliot	The Clintons: Meeting the First Family	Juvenile Biography: Clinton Family	POTUS Study-WW	2 copies
Robert Levin	Bill Clinton: The Inside Story	Biography: Bill Clinton	POTUS Study-WW	Polish Edition
Tomasz Liz	Jak To Sie Robi W Ameryce	Biography: Bill Clinton	POTUS Study-WW	Polish Edition; Inscribed by the author
Donnie Radcliffe	Hillary Rodham Clinton: A First Lady for Our Time	Biography: Hillary Rodham Clinton	POTUS Study-WW	
Bill Clinton and Al Gore	Putting People First: How We Can All Change America	Presidential and Vice-Presidential Writings	POTUS Study-WW	
Norman King	Hillary: Her True Story	Biography: Hillary Rodham Clinton	POTUS Study-WW	
Edited by Charles T. Royer	Campaign for President: The Managers Look at 1992	Presidential Campaigns and Management	POTUS Study-WW	
Bob Woodward	The Agenda: Inside the Clinton White House	Clinton Administration: Economic Policy	POTUS Study-WW	Inscribed by the author
Elizabeth Drew	On the Edge: The Clinton Presidency	Clinton Administration	POTUS Study-WW	Inscribed by the author 107/7/94
Steven Waldman	The Bill: How the Adventures of Clinton's National Service Bill Reveal What is Corrupt, Comic, Cynical—And Noble--About Washington	Clinton Administration: National Service	POTUS Study-WW	Inscribed by the author

1361-DC-00000023

22

641

Meredith L. Oakley	On the Make: The Rise of Bill Clinton	Biography: Bill Clinton	POTUS Study-WW	
Victoria Sherrow	Hillary Rodham Clinton	Juvenile Biography: Hillary Rodham Clinton	POTUS Study-WW	
Victoria Sherrow	Bill Clinton	Juvenile Biography: Bill Clinton	POTUS Study-WW	
Peter Goldman, Thomas M DeFrank, Mark Miller, Andrew Murr(?), Tom Mathews	Quest for the Presidency 1992	Presidential Campaigns	POTUS Study-WW	Inscribed by Mark S. Miller 10/11/94
Gerald M. Pomper et al.	The Election of 1996; Reports and Interpretation	Presidential Campaigns	POTUS Study-WW	
Sarah McClendon	Mr. President, Mr. President: My 50 Years of Covering the White House	Presidency and the Media	POTUS Study-WW	Inscribed by the Author 10/18/96
Robert Reich	Locked in the Cabinet	Clinton Administration: Memoirs and Labor Policy	POTUS Study-WW	Inscribed by the Author 4/97
Haynes Johnson and David S. Broder	The System: The American Way of Politics at the Breaking Point	U.S. Political System	POTUS Study-WW	Inscribed by the Authors 3/31/96
Edited by Colin Campbell and Bert A. Rockman	The Clinton Presidency: First Appraisals	Clinton Administration	POTUS Study-WW	
Bob Woodward	The Choice	Presidential Campaigns: 1996 Case Study	POTUS Study-WW	

S 019388

Eleanor Clift and Tom (?)	War Without Bloodshed: The Art of Politics	U.S. Political System	POTUS Study-WW	Inscribed to BC and HRC by the Authors 7/4/96
David Maraniss	First in His Class: A Biography of Bill Clinton	Biography: Bill Clinton	POTUS Study-WW	Advance Uncorrected Proof with BC's notes
Jim Moore with Rick Ihde	Clinton: Young Man in a Hurry	Biography: Bill Clinton	POTUS Study-WW	
David Gallen	Bill Clinton As They Know Him: An Oral Biography	Biography: Bill Clinton	POTUS Study-WW	
Dick Morris	Behind the Oval Office: Winning the Presidency in the 1990s	Clinton Administration and 1996 Presidential Campaign	POTUS Study-WW	Inscribed by the Author 1/9/97
Evan Thomas, Karen Breslaw, Debra Rosenberg, Leslie Kaufman, and Andrew Muir (?)	Back from the Dead: How Clinton Survived the Republican Revolution	Clinton Administration and Republican Revolution	POTUS Study-WW	Inscribed by Karen Breslaw 1/22/97
Compiled and Edited by Mary Ann Barton and Paul C. Barton	Campaign: A Cartoon History of Bill Clinton's Race for the White House	Political Cartoons	POTUS Study-WW	Inscribed by the Authors
William Jefferson Clinton	Between Hope and History	Presidential Writings	POTUS Study-WW	

S 019389

,Martin Walker	Clinton The President They Deserve: An Intimate Political Biography of the 42nd President of the United States	Biography: Bill Clinton	POTUS Study-WW	Written in London
Conor O'Clery	Daring Diplomacy: Clinton's Secret Search for Peace in Ireland	Clinton Administration: Foreign Policy	POTUS Study-WW	Inscribed by the Author 3/12/97
Donald Hall	The Museum of Clear Ideas-New Poems	Poetry	POTUS Study-WW	Signed by the Author; Bookplate from BC's "Granite State Friends" of the anniversary of the New Hampshire Primary
Ernest Hebert	Live Free or Die: A Novel	Fiction	POTUS Study-WW	Bookplate from "Granite State Friends"
Laurel Thatcher Ulrich	A Midwife's Tale: The Life of Martha Ballard, Based on Her Diary 1785-1812	Biography: Martha Ballard	POTUS Study-WW	Bookplate from "Granite State Friends"
David D. Draves	Builder of Men: Life in the C.C.C. Camps of New Hampshire	U.S. History: New Deal, Civilian Conservation Corps	POTUS Study-WW	Bookplate from "Granite State Friends"
Jane Kenyon	Constance	Poetry	POTUS Study-WW	Bookplate from "Granite State Friends"
Howard Mansfield	In the Memory House	Historical Sites-New England	POTUS Study-WW	Bookplate from "Granite State Friends"

Maxine Kunin	Nurture	Poetry	POTUS Study-WW	Bookplate from "Granite State Friends"
Dayton Duncan	Grass Roots: One Year in the Life of the New Hampshire Presidential Primary	Presidential Campaigns: New Hampshire Primary	POTUS Study-WW	Signed by the Author; Bookplate from "Granite State Friends"
Stephen R. Covey	First Things First: To Live, To Learn, To Leave a Legacy	Time Management	POTUS Study-WW	
Louis J. Aronne, MD	Weigh Less, Live Longer	Diet and Health	POTUS Study-WW	Inscribed by the Author 7/15/97
Bert Holldobler and Edward O. Wilson	Journey to the Ants: A Story of Scientific Exploration	Science: Ants	POTUS Study-WW	Inscribed by "Newt"
Jung Chang	Wild Swans: Three Daughters of China	Biography: Three Chinese Women	POTUS Study-WW	
Stephen R. Covey	The Seven Habits of Highly Effective People	Personal Characteristics	POTUS Study-WW	Inscribed to BC and HRC by the Author 12/30/94
Collected and Edited by the Brothers Halamandaris	Caring Quotes: A Compendium of Caring Thought	Quotes	POTUS Study-WW	Inscribed by the Authors
Leah Rabin	Rabin: Our Life, His Legacy	Biography: Yitzhak Rabin	POTUS Study-WW	Inscribed to BC and HRC 4/8/97
Carl Bernstein and Marco Politi	His Holiness: John Paul II and the Hidden History of Our Time	Biography: Pope John Paul II	POTUS Study-WW	Inscribed by Carl Bernstein

David Fromkin	In the Time of the Americans: FDR, Truman, Eisenhower, Marshall, McArthur, The Generation that Changed America's Role in the World	U.S. Foreign Relations: 20th Century	POTUS Study-WW	
Michael Shaara	The Killer Angels: The Classic Novel of the Civil War	Fiction: Civil War	POTUS Study-WW	Inscribed by LTC Michael G. Mudd, Army Aide to the President, 1/20/97
Edited by Peter B. Kovler	Democrats and the American Idea: A Bicentennial Appraisal	Democratic Party	POTUS Study-WW	
Grady C. Cothen	What Happened to the Southern Baptist Convention? A Memoir of the Controversy	U.S. Religious History: Southern Baptists	POTUS Study-WW	Signed by the Author
William Pfaff	The Wrath of Nations: Civilization and the Furies Of Nationalism	Nationalism	POTUS Study-WW	Signed by the Author 11/28/93
Richard Carleton Hacker	The Ultimate Cigar Book	Cigars	POTUS Study-WW	Inscribed by the Author
Anwar Bati and Simon Chase	The Cigar Companion: A Connoisseur's Guide	Cigars	POTUS Study-WW	Inscribed by Helen Van Berg 11/5/96
	Pictorial Directory-105th Congress	Congressional Directory	POTUS Study-WW	Leather Bound with "Bill Clinton" inscribed on the cover
	Common Prayer Hymnal	Religion	POTUS Study-WW	Inscribed by Jim Martin 8/97

S 019392

Edited by Jorie Graham	Earth Took of Earth: 100 Great Poems of the English Language	Poems	POTUS Study-WW	
Edited by Reba Collins	Will Rogers Says...	Quotes: Will Rogers	POTUS Study-WW	Inscribed by the Author and George and Donna Nigh
Desmond Tutu	An African Prayer Book	African Religious Life	POTUS Study-WW	Inscribed by the Author 2/7/95
Thomas Jefferson	The Jefferson Bible	Presidential Writings: U.S. Religious Life	POTUS Study-WW	Inscribed by Robert Turk 12/20/92
Abraham Lincoln	Lincoln's Devotional	Presidential Writings: Religion	POTUS Study-WW	Inscribed by Ronald F. Thiemann 9/8/95
Benjamin Franklin	Benjamin Franklin: The Autobiography and Other Writings	Autobiography: Ben Franklin	POTUS Study-WW	
Ariel Books	Oh Vey: The Things They Say! A Book of Jewish Wit	Quotes: Jewish	POTUS Study-WW	
Noah Ben Shea	Great Jewish Quotes: 5,000 Years of Truth and Humor From the Bible to George Burns	Quotes: Jewish	POTUS Study-WW	
Norman Vincent Peale	Seven Values to Live By	Personal Values	POTUS Study-WW	
Al Gore	The Best Kept Secrets in Government--Digest Version	Clinton Administration: Reinventing Government	POTUS Study-WW	

S 019393

	You Must Remember This 1946	History: 1946	POTUS Study-WW	
Garrison Keillor	Truckstop And Other Lake Wobegon Stories	Fiction	POTUS Study-WW	
	The Declaration of Independence and the Constitution of the United States	U.S. Constitutional Democracy	POTUS Study-WW	
	Teachings of Jesus: The Holy Bible KJV	Religion	POTUS Study-WW	
Franklin Delano Roosevelt	Fireside Chats	Presidential Speeches	POTUS Study-WW	
	A Prayer Book for the Armed Forces 1988	U.S. Religion	POTUS Study-WW	Inscribed by Norman P. Forder, retired Chaplain of the U.S. Army
Edited by Robert M. Herhold	Prayers for Peace: Beginning With Me	Religion	POTUS Study-WW	Inscribed to BC and HRC by the Author
Frederick Talbott	Churchill on Courage: Timeless Wisdom for Persevering	Quotes: Winston Churchill	POTUS Study-WW	Inscribed by Frederik Talbott, 10/9/96
Nicholson Baker	Vox	Novel	POTUS Study-WW	

1361-DC-00000030

S 019394

29

Kevin D. Randle, Capt. USAFR and Donald R. Schmitt, Director of Special Investigation, Center for UFO Studies	UFO Crash at Roswell	U.S. Military History: UFOs	POTUS Study-WW	
Paul Slansky	The Clothes Have No Emperor: A Chronicle of the American 80s	U.S. History: 1980s	POTUS Study-WW	Inscribed by the Author 10/17/96
Pete Carril with Dan White	The Smart Take from the Strong: The Basketball Philosophy of Pete Carril	Sports Philosophy	POTUS Study-WW	Inscribed by Thomas H. Pyle
	Three Poems of Solon: Patriot and Lawgiver	Poetry	POTUS Study-WW	Presented to the Honorable Millicent Fenwick, 2/25/80
Compiled by Luther G. Presley	Heavenly Highway Hymns	Religion	POTUS Study-WW	Inscribed by Jim B. Baker
Richard J. Mouw	Uncommon Decency: Christian Civilization in an Uncivil World	Church and the World	POTUS Study-WW	Inscribed by the Author
Mark Gerzon	A House Divided: A Journey Through Six Belief Systems Struggling for America's Soul	U.S. Political System	POTUS Study-WW	Uncorrected Proof
Edited by George E. Curry	The Affirmative Action Debate	U.S. Domestic Policy: Affirmative Action	POTUS Study-WW	Inscribed by the Author 6/28/96

1361-DC-00000031

S 019395

30

645

Edited by Peggy Hackman and Don Oldenburg	Dear Mr. President: Greetings and Advice to a New Leader from the Nation's Youngest Citizens	Presidential Correspondence	POTUS Study-WW	
Garry Maurio	Beaches, Bureaucrats, and Big Oil: One Man's Fight for Texas	Environment: Oil and Texas	POTUS Study-WW	Inscribed by the Author 1997
Vice-President Al Gore	Common Sense Government: Works Better and Costs Less	Clinton Administration: Reinventing Government	POTUS Study-WW	
Benjamin Netanyahu	Fighting Terrorism: How Democracies Can Defeat Domestic and International Terrorism	World Politics: Terrorism	POTUS Study-WW	POTUS Study-WW Inscribed by the Author
Robert Massie and Suzanne Massie	Journey: The Classic Story of a Son's Illness and a Family's Courage	Biography: Robert Massie, Jr.; Health Care	POTUS Study-WW	Inscribed to HRC by Suzanne Massie 4/20/93
Herb Stansbury	Executive Smart Charts and Other Insider Revelations on Corporate Insanity	Corporations: Satire	POTUS Study-WW	Inscribed by the Author 12/24/93
Synectics	Imagine	Quotes	POTUS Study-WW	Inscribed by Barbara Govenda
James Chace	The Consequences of the Peace: The New Internationalism and Foreign Policy	U.S. Foreign Policy	POTUS Study-WW	Inscribed by the Author to Governor Clinton
Mark Mathabane	Kaffir Boy: The True Story of a Black Youth's Coming of Age in Apartheid South Africa	Autobiography: Mark Mathabane	POTUS Study-WW	Inscribed by the Author 1/6/92

Edited by Mark Green and James Ledbetter	Ideas That Work: 60 Solutions for America's Third Century. The Democracy Project June 1988	U.S. Political System	POTUS Study-WW	
Catherine Drinker Bowen	Miracle at Philadelphia: the Story of the Constitutional Convention, May to Sept. 1787	U.S. Constitutional History	POTUS Study-WW	
Beth Kobliner	Get a Financial Life: Personal Finance in Your Twenties and Thirties	Personal Finance	POTUS Study-WW	Inscribed by the Author 7/29/96
Ronald Steel	Temptations of a Superpower: America's Foreign Policy After the Cold War	U.S. Foreign Policy	POTUS Study-WW	
David Kashet	Speaking American: How the Democrats Can Win in the Nineties	U.S. Democratic Party	POTUS Study-WW	
Robert S. McElvaine	What's Left? A New Democratic Vision for America	U.S. Democratic Party	POTUS Study-WW	
Theodore C. Sorenson	Why I Am A Democrat	U.S. Democratic Party	POTUS Study-WW	
Molley Winegrad and Dudley Buffa	Taking Control: Politics in the Information Age	Politics and Technology	POTUS Study-WW	Inscribed by the Author
Joseph P. Shapiro	No Pity: People With Disabilities Forging a New Civil Rights Movement	U.S. Domestic Policy: Handicapped	POTUS Study-WW	Inscribed to BC from Rachel Holland (child) and by her father, Robert 1/26/96

Donald Harrington	Butterfly Weed	Novel	POTUS Study-WW	Inscribed by the Author 5/5/96
Maya Angelou	Mrs. Flowers: A Moment of Friendship, A Perfect Present	Short Story	POTUS Study-WW	Inscribed by Lamar Laster
Ben J. Wattenburg	Values Matter Most: How Republicans or Democrats or a Third Party Can Win and Renew the American Way of Life	U.S. Social Values	POTUS Study-WW	Note from the Author 10/3/95; Advance uncorrected proof
Richard N. Haass	The Power to Persuade: How to Be Effective in Government, the Public Sector, or Any Unlikely Organization	Public Administration	POTUS Study-WW	Inscribed by the Author 5/97
Paul Hawkey	The Next Economy	U.S. Economic Conditions	POTUS Study-WW	
Edited by Leslie Berlowitz, Denis Donoghue, and Louis Menard	America in Theory	U.S. Political System	POTUS Study-WW	Inscribed by John Sexton
Michael Elliott	The Day Before Yesterday: Rediscovering America's Past, Recovering the Present	U.S. History	POTUS Study-WW	Inscribed by the Author; Advance Uncorrected Proof
Joseph Telushkin	Words That Hurt, Words That Heal: How to Choose Words Wisely and Well	Oral Communication	POTUS Study-WW	Inscribed by Stephen J. Cloobeck
Arkansas Historical Association	Arkansas Historical Quarterly Vol. LV Autumn 1996, Number 3	History: Arkansas	POTUS Study-WW	

1361-DC-00000034

33

S 019398

Arkansas Entertainers Hall of Fame 1996	Arkansas Directory	Entertainment: Arkansas	POTUS Study-WW	
Life Magazine, April 1993	Cover-"Bobby and Martin 25 Years After Their Deaths, We Remember What They Meant to Us, and Imagine What Might Have Been"	Magazine: RFK and MLK	POTUS Study-WW	
People Weekly, 4/12/93	Cover- "Diana On Her Own: The Perils-and Pleasures-of Life Without Charles"	Magazine: Diana, Princess of Wales	POTUS Study-WW	
Newsweek, 5/10/93	Cover- "Bosnia: Clinton Gets Tough-At Last; Will Air Power Be Enough?"	Magazine: Clinton Administration- Foreign Policy	POTUS Study-WW	
Business Week, 2/22/93	Cover- "Jobs, Jobs, Jobs: The Economy is Growing, But Employment Lags Badly, Will Clinton Plan Help or Hurt"	Magazine: Clinton Administration- Economic Policy	POTUS Study-WW	
The American Prospect, Winter 1993		Magazine	POTUS Study-WW	
Vanity Fair, 3/93	Cover- "The New Guard: An Exclusive Portfolio of Clinton's Powerful Inner Circle" and "The President's Mr. Inside"	Magazine: Clinton Administration	POTUS Study-WW	
The New Yorker, 12/23 and 12/30/96		Magazine	POTUS Study-WW	

1361-DC-00000035

34

S 019399

New Orleans Magazine, 3/93	Cover- "Our Man at the White House—Louisianan James Carville Discusses Home, Politics, and Fame"	Magazine: James Carville	POTUS Study-WW	
Family Circle, 5/18/93	Cover- "Hillary and Her Mom on Cookies, Curfews, Confidence ... and Prayer"	Magazine: Hillary Clinton	POTUS Study-WW	
The New Yorker, 10/21 and 10/28/96	Politics Special Issue	Magazine: 1996 Election	POTUS Study-WW	
Time Extra: Fall 1996	Cover- "The Election of 1996"	Magazine: 1996 Election	POTUS Study-WW	
Time, 11/18/96	Cover- "Election Special"	Magazine: 1996 Election	POTUS Study-WW	
Newsweek, 11/18/96	Cover- "Clinton II: Special Election Issue"	Magazine: 1996 Election	POTUS Study-WW	
Time European Edition, 11/18/96	Cover- "How He Won"	Magazine: 1996 Election	POTUS Study-WW	
Bill Clinton For President	"A Plan for America's Future"	Presidential Campaigns: 1992 Campaign Plan	POTUS Study-WW	
Richard E. Feinberg	Summitry in the Americas: A Progress Report	World Politics: Economic Relations	POTUS Study-WW	
Samuel G. Freedman	The Inheritance: How Three Families Moved From Roosevelt to Reagan and Beyond.	U.S. Economic Conditions	POTUS Study-WW	

1361-DC-00000036

35

Lester C. Thurow	The Future of Capitalism: How Today's Economic Forces Shape Tomorrow's World	Economic Forecasting	POTUS Study-WW	
Kevin Phillips	Boiling Point: Democrats, Republicans, and the Decline of Middle-Class Prosperity	U.S. Economic Conditions	POTUS Study-WW	Inscribed by "Bud" and "Barbara"
Kevin Phillips	The Politics of Rich and Poor: Wealth and the American Electorate in the Reagan Aftermath	U.S. Economic Conditions	POTUS Study-WW	Inscribed by Ronnie Cripe (?)
Edited by Eric Liu	NEXT: Young American Writers on the New Generation	Generation X	POTUS Study-WW	
Robert D. Putnam	Making Democracy Work: Civic Traditions in Modern Italy	Italy	POTUS Study-WW	Inscribed by the Author 6/94
Stanley B. Greenberg	Middle Class Dreams: The Politics and Power of the New American Majority	U.S. Politics: Middle Class	POTUS Study-WW	Inscribed by the Author
David Fisher	Hard Evidence: How Detectives Inside the FBI's Science Crime Lab Have Helped Solve America's Toughest Cases	U.S. Crime Investigation	POTUS Study-WW	
Henry G. Cisneros	Interwoven Destinies: Cities and the Nation	U.S. Urban Policy	POTUS Study-WW	Inscribed by the Author 12/10/93
Peter F. Drucker	Post-Capitalist Society	World Economic History	POTUS Study-WW	Inscribed by the Author
Robert Kuttner	The End of Laissez-Faire: National Purpose and the Global Economy After the Cold War	U.S. Economic Policy	POTUS Study-WW	

36

1361-DC-00000037

648

John H. Makin and Norman J. Ornstein	Debt and Taxes: How Americans Got Into Its Budget Mess and What to Do About It	U.S. Fiscal Policy	POTUS Study-WW	Inscribed by N. Ornstein
Thomas Byrne Edsall and Mary D. Edsall	Chain Reaction: The Impact of Race, Rights, and Taxes on American Politics	U.S. Politics: Race, Taxes, Civil Rights	POTUS Study-WW	Inscribed by T. Edsall to Governor Clinton
Thomas Byrne Edsall	The New Politics of Inequality	U.S. Economic Policy	POTUS Study-WW	
William Julius Wilson	The Truly Disadvantaged: The Inner City, the Underclass, and Public Policy	U.S. Urban Policy	POTUS Study-WW	
Charles C. Moskos	A Call to Civic Service: National Service for Country and Community	National Service	POTUS Study-WW	Inscribed by the Author 11/88
Holly Stone	Upon the River: Poems Inspired by Rowing	Poetry	POTUS Study-WW	
David Shenk	Data Smog: Surviving the Information Glut	Information Age	POTUS Study-WW	
Rick Pitino	Success is a Choice: 10 Steps to Overachieving in Business and Life	Philosophy for Success	POTUS Study-WW	
Lester C. Thurow	The Zero Sum Solution: Building a World Class American Economy	U.S. Economic Policy	POTUS Study-WW	Inscribed by Bill Brown (?) 1/21/86
Herbert J. Gans	Middle American Individualism: The Future of Liberal Democracy	Political Participation and Individualism	POTUS Study-WW	

Terry Anderson	Den of Lions: Memoirs of Seven Years	Autobiography: Terry Anderson	POTUS Study-WW	Signed by Author and his wife, Madeleine
David Hallerstein	The Fifties	U.S. History: The 50s	POTUS Study-WW	Inscribed by the Author to BC and HRC 1/20/93
Edited by Mark Green	Changing America: Blueprints for the New Administration	Clinton Administration: Agencies	POTUS Study-WW	
John Chancellor	Peril and Promise: A Commentary on America	Political Commentary	POTUS Study-WW	Inscribed by A.O. Nelson of Boynton Beach, FL
William Greider	Who Will Tell the People: The Betrayal of American Democracy	Political Participation	POTUS Study-WW	
	Midwest, Northeast, South, and West Binders with state information and buttons from every state	Presidential Campaign: 1996	POTUS Study-WW	
Joseph A. Califano, Jr.	The Triumph and Tragedy of Lyndon Johnson	Biography: Lyndon Johnson	POTUS Study-WW	Inscribed by the Author
Sam Harris	Reclaiming Our Democracy:Healing the Break Between People and Government	U.S. Political System: Lobbying	POTUS Study-WW	Inscribed by the Author 11/8/93
Paul Kennedy	Preparing America for the 21st Century	21st Century	POTUS Study-WW	Bookplate from Bernard Rapoport
Lech Walesa	A Way of Hope: An Autobiography	Autobiography: Lech Walesa	POTUS Study-WW	Inscribed by the Author 3/6/96

Pam Parry	On Ground for Religious Liberty: Six Decades of the Baptist Joint Committee	Religious History	POTUS Study-WW	
Edited by Dr. Constantine C. Menges	Partnerships for Peace, Democracy, and Prosperity	World Politics	POTUS Study-WW	
William N. Eskridge, Jr.	The Case for Same-Sex Marriage From Sexual Liberty to Civilized Commitment	U.S. Domestic Policy: Homosexual Policy	POTUS Study-WW	
Gordon K. Durnil	The Making of a Conservative Environmentalist	U.S. Environmental Policy	POTUS Study-WW	
Michael Balone	Our Country: The Shaping of America from Roosevelt to Reagan	U.S. History	POTUS Study-WW	
Edited by Ralph Evans	Register of Rhodes Scholars 1903-95	Rhodes Scholars	POTUS Study-WW	
Edited by Daniel Halpern	Antaeus: The Final Issue	Literary Works	POTUS Study-WW	
Naomi H. Rosenblatt and Joshua Horwitz	Wrestling with Angels: What the First Family of Genesis Teach Us About Our Spiritual Identity, Sexuality and Personal Relations	Religion	POTUS Study-WW	
Avner Falk	A Psychoanalytic History of the Jews	Jewish History	POTUS Study-WW	
National Council on Disability	Equality of Opportunity: The Making of the Americans With Disabilities Act	U.S. Domestic Policy: Handicapped	POTUS Study-WW	Inscribed by Marca Bristo, Chairperson of Committee, 9/10/97

Herbert Block	Herblock: A Cartoonist's Life	Autobiography: Herbert Block	POTUS Study-WW	Inscribed by the Author
Lyndon Y. Jones	Great Expectations: America and the Baby Boom Generation	U.S. History: Baby Boom Generation	POTUS Study-WW	
Peggy Noonan	What I Saw at the Revolution: A Political Life in the Reagan Era	U.S. History: The 1980s	POTUS Study-WW	
Jack Kemp	An American Renaissance: A Strategy for the 1980s	U.S. Economic Policy	POTUS Study-WW	
Foreign Affairs	July/August 1997	Periodical: Foreign Affairs	POTUS Study-WW	
Daedalus	Fall 1995; Cover: "American Education: Still Separate"	Periodical: Education	POTUS Study-WW	
Foreign Affairs	May/June 1997	Periodical: Foreign Affairs	POTUS Study-WW	
Foreign Affairs	March/April 1997	Periodical: Foreign Affairs	POTUS Study-WW	
World Policy Journal	Fall 1995 Winter 1995/96	Periodical: World Politics	POTUS Study-WW	
Presidential Studies Quarterly	Summer 1996; "Reassessments of Presidents and First Ladies"	Periodical: Presidency	POTUS Study-WW	
Autumn Stevens	Wild Women in the White House	U.S. First Ladies	POTUS Study-WW	Inscribed to HRC from Anna Jean See

Watty Piper	The Little Engine that Could	Children's Book	POTUS Study-WW	Bookplate from Governor Zell Miller of GA
Bob Hope	Bob Hope's Dear Pres. I Wanna Tell Ya: A Presidential Jokebook	Presidents and Comedy	POTUS Study-WW	
Compiled by Donald L. Miller	From George to George: 200 Years of Presidential Quotations	Presidents: Quotes	POTUS Study-WW	Limited Edition; Inscribed from Dyonne, Rod, Matt, and Zack Holt 11/15/92
Keith W. Jennison	The Humorous Mr. Lincoln	Biography: Lincoln	POTUS Study-WW	
Edited by Bill Adler	The Kennedy Wit	Presidential Quotes: Kennedy	POTUS Study-WW	Inscribed by Michael E. 12/25/94
Abraham Lincoln	Abraham Lincoln Great Speeches	Presidential Speeches: Lincoln	POTUS Study-WW	Inscribed by Helena Willett 9/9/92
Edited by Louise Bachelder	Abraham Lincoln: Wisdom and Wit	Presidential Quotes : Lincoln	POTUS Study-WW	
Franklin Delano Roosevelt	The Wisdom and Wit of Franklin D. Roosevelt	Presidential Writings: FDR	POTUS Study-WW	
Paul F. Boller, Jr.	Presidential Anecdotes	Presidential History	POTUS Study-WW	Inscribed by Carlyn 9/2/91
Gerald Gardner	Who's in Charge Here	Presidential Humor	POTUS Study-WW	
	One Hundred and One Famous Poems	Poetry	POTUS Study-WW	Inscribed by Clayee Maxwell 3/25/92

S 019406

Jim McMullan	Hail to the Chief: The Presidents Speak	Presidential Quotes	POTUS Study-WW	
Albert Huschinana	The Rhetoric of Reaction: Perversity, Futility, Jeopardy	Philosophy	POTUS Study-WW	
Kenneth P. O'Donnell and David F. Powers with Joe McCarty	Johnny We Hardly Knew Ye	Biography: John F. Kennedy	POTUS Study-WW	
Edward Hallett Cain	What's History?	History	POTUS Study-WW	

S 019407

White House Lawyer Bruce Lindsey's Notes About Linda Tripp

THE WHITE HOUSE

Linda Tripp 703/

Drudge Rpt

What I was told

*No lawyer speaks
to me because
I won't lie & say
I know she is*

lying

*— harassment —
blatantly untrue
— made no bones
about what her
_____*

*at several office —
volunteering*

*Claimed to be a
close friend of BC*

*gregarious, nice
woman*

*volunteer — 3 times
a week — hated ___*

. Airstock — a little

*— asked if we could
use a vol.*

— we brought her over

THE WHITE HOUSE

Shortly before Bernie

Turned violent —
in her attempt

on going fluctuation —
Richmond defeat
Clinton song

Rehearsed speeches

Notes —

Everything was said
w/ one attempt

The day this episode
occurred — she was
was meet - this is
What he did to

"They were doing
it in study area

Don't believe that
she is stable

No words of
sexual harassment

She claims now it
is harassment

Prior to her husband
shooting himself —

dry pran

She was in pursuit

3 times a week

5

THE WHITE HOUSE

I think Isikoff
leaked it —

Calamitta —

Her lawyer —

Called West Wing —

She chose to bring
this out — now
she is unsure —

Not only will I
not confirm

You were a happy
ecstatic, joyful

Aggressively pursued

Marriage shaky —
asking for a divorce

Told her husband
supposedly — he was
going to leave —

I don't know what
happen — he's nowhere

Temptation —
candidacy call — for
BC —

880-DC-00000006

880-DC-00000007

HB 004750

HB 004751

THE WHITE HOUSE

Tom Swims —
Telling about his
home in Annapolis

Great nonsense
boat —

Gross distortion of
the fact —

narrowly qualified
& would be fine

Photographs

PHOTO REQUESTS

1. 14 June 1996 The President's Radio Address

We were the second to last family to speak with the President. In our family photo, my father and step-mother are to the President's right and my and I are to his left. We spoke with him for a few minutes before the posed photo and it was within those few minutes that Bob and the other photographer were clicking away. In particular, I would love to get a copy of the picture of my brother shaking the President's hand.

We all have dark brown hair. I was wearing a light pink suit and my brother was wearing a medium blue shirt and khaki pants. My father is tall and wears glasses, and my step-mom was wearing a black and white polka dot (or small floral) dress.

2. 18 August 1996 The President's 50th (the cocktail party before the show)

I was toward the middle/end of the rope line. I have brown straight hair and was wearing a red, raw silk, sleeveless dress.

3. 17 November 1995 (during the furlough)

Bob McNeely took a picture of me with the President in Mr. Panetta's outer office. I was wearing a red suit jacket with a black collar and black pants. Bob had misplaced the film or contact sheet for a long, long while! Billie Shaddix kept checking for me if it ever appeared in the book, as we thought it was stuck in Bob's office somewhere. Maybe it is there now?????

4. 30 January 1996 Pat Griffin's, former Assistant to the President for LA, retirement party in the COS's office

Sharon Farmer took a couple of group shots of the Leg Affs staff with the President. I was wearing a black suit standing in the back row.

V006-DC-00003735

V006-DC-00003737   HB 004652

OFFICIAL WHITE HOUSE PHOTOGRAPH 17 NOV 95 P034249-J5 DMi

V006-DC-00003738   HB 004653

OFFICIAL WHITE HOUSE PHOTOGRAPH 17 NOV 95 P034249-16 BM

V006-DC-00003739   HB 004654

OFFICIAL WHITE HOUSE PHOTOGRAPH 17 NOV 95 P034249-17 BM

OFFICIAL WHITE HOUSE PHOTOGRAPH 17 NOV 95 P03424₹ ₃₆ BM

OFFICIAL WHITE HOUSE PHOTOGRAPH 17 NOV 95 P034248-19 BM

OFFICIAL WHITE HOUSE PHOTOGRAPH 17 NOV 95 P034248-20 BM

OFFICIAL WHITE HOUSE PHOTOGRAPH 17 NOV 95 P034248-22 BM

V006-DC-00003744   HB 004659